HISTORY OF
THE SECOND WORLD WAR

UNITED KINGDOM CIVIL SERIES

Edited by Sir Keith Hancock

The authors of the Civil Histories have been given free access to official documents. They and the editor are alone responsible for the statements made and the views expressed.

FINANCIAL POLICY
1939-45

BY

R. S. SAYERS

Sir Ernest Cassel Professor of Economics,
University of London

LONDON: 1956

HER MAJESTY'S STATIONERY OFFICE

AND

LONGMANS, GREEN AND CO

First published 1956

Crown Copyright Reserved

HER MAJESTY'S STATIONERY OFFICE

London: York House, Kingsway, W.C.2 & 423 Oxford Street, W.1
Edinburgh: 13a Castle Street   Cardiff: 109 St. Mary Street
Manchester: 39 King Street   Bristol: Tower Lane
Birmingham: 2 Edmund Street   Belfast: 80 Chichester Street

LONGMANS, GREEN AND CO LTD
6 and 7 Clifford Street, London, W.1
Boston House, Strand Street, Cape Town
531 Little Collins Street, Melbourne

LONGMANS, GREEN AND CO INC
55 Fifth Avenue, New York, 3

LONGMANS, GREEN AND CO
20 Cranfield Road, Toronto, 16

ORIENT LONGMANS, LTD
Calcutta, Bombay, Madras
Delhi, Vijayawada, Dacca

Price £1 17s. 6d. net

Printed in Great Britain under the authority of H.M. Stationery Office
by A. Wheaton & Co. Ltd., Exeter, Devon

CONTENTS

APPENDICES

PREFACE

THIS BOOK is based largely on official papers, but it has been written from a viewpoint entirely outside the Civil Service. Although I was a temporary civil servant during the war and accepted permanent employment thereafter, my official contact with problems discussed in the book was only of the slightest and most marginal kind; in fact, owing to the pressure of other problems I knew scarcely more of what was going on in this field than any other taxpayer was able to gather from the Press. The invitation to write the book did not come until two or three years after my resignation, when my approach to the material could be strictly academic and was in fact that of an almost complete stranger.

I have enjoyed absolutely unlimited access to Treasury papers. The understanding from the beginning has been that I should see everything I asked to see. I have appreciated this freedom, but it has involved one disadvantage: that I have had to know what to ask for. This meant a slow start, for the Treasury filing system was not arranged for the benefit of historians, and during the war many important documents escaped the files and many important words were spoken without being written down. Nevertheless, having tracked certain events and problems from outside sources, and talked to a number of helpful officials, I have eventually been able—with splendid help from the Treasury Registry—to follow the handling of those problems which have seemed to me proper for inclusion in the book. I found very substantial guidance in a detailed chronicle, covering a large part of the field, prepared by Sir Ralph Hawtrey during and immediately after the war.

Having chosen the formation of policy as my subject, I could properly depend mainly upon the official papers—supplemented by the memories of surviving officials—though, as will be seen, I have also kept an eye on outside printed material. Concentration on the formation of policy has one important implication which I hope will be noticed particularly by readers outside this country: it bears especially on my account of financial relations with Allied countries, both inside and outside the Commonwealth. My concern being to show how policy was formed in London, I have deliberately viewed developments in other countries *as they were understood in Whitehall at the time.* In so far as I have also tried to assess British policy, I have of necessity asked myself continually whether London's contemporary interpretation was fair; but in reading my exposition of the formation of policy the reader is asked to remember that I am not attempting an objective international view of what was happening elsewhere, but am describing developments as they were seen by Whitehall at the time.

This book is in no sense an account of Treasury activity. As the central department of State the Treasury has important functions— notably general control of the Civil Service—that are connected only indirectly with financial policy; these general functions lie outside my scope. The Treasury's function as the grand co-ordinator of interdepartmental policy was sometimes highly relevant, as when it was co-ordinating the development of price control by a number of other Departments. An exhaustive study of the application of policy would certainly have included much of this kind; but I have confined myself to the basic developments of the broad issues. Again, the Treasury as the enforcer of economy in spending—'the saving of candle-ends'—has important links with the broad strategy of war finance, but I have left it almost untouched. Another volume in this series—Mr. Ashworth's *Contracts and Finance*—admirably covers some of its major aspects. The Bretton Woods discussions, though falling within this period, were primarily directed to post-war reconstruction and therefore lie outside my scope; they are mentioned incidentally, as on p. 462, where they bore directly on the problems of war finance. I have also—mainly because life is short and Treasury files are long—left aside a number of minor problems despite their close ties with other matters having a prominent place in the book. Among these problems are compensation (both for war damage and for requisitioned property), silver supplies, and domestic currency. I found it especially difficult to resist the temptation to pursue the fascinating monetary problems of military occupation, on which I have been privileged to read an unpublished paper by Mr. M. J. Babington Smith. (There are two relevant chapters in Lord Rennell's *British Military Administration of Occupied Territories in Africa*, but much work remains to be done for other areas.)

It has been no part of my purpose to provide accounts showing how the war was paid for, in any sense, and some readers may be surprised at the scarcity of figures in the text. This reflects, though in an exaggerated way, the comparatively small use made of statistics in the war-time Treasury, especially in the early days. (This subject is noticed at various points in the book, particularly on pp. 379–80). But it is also partly due to the unwillingness of the authorities to allow the publication of some of the critical figures. Readers with a taste for statistics will find some Tables—most of them put together in post-war years—in Appendices I and III. I warmly appreciate the generosity of my colleague, Professor R. G. D. Allen, who consented to the use, as Appendix III, of his paper on

Mutual Aid, and similarly the generosity of the Council of the Royal Statistical Society in allowing the paper to be reprinted from the Journal of their Society.[1]

Appendix II provides, as a supplement to Chapters II–IV, a systematic list of changes in taxation. It has been prepared in the Treasury with the help of the Revenue Departments.

I am, I believe, well aware of all the arguments against the writing of very recent history, and against the limited use of public records for this purpose. I have been conscious of only two limitations in writing this book. First, some important statistics have been excluded for reasons of public policy. Secondly, an extremely difficult problem has arisen in relation to the names of the Chancellor's advisers—permanent civil servants as well as those eminent 'temporaries' who had a special place in the war-time Treasury. The British tradition is that the names of civil servants must not be publicly attached to the advice they have given, and experience elsewhere has shown how wise this principle remains. On the other hand, as Professor E. A. G. Robinson has forcibly argued in reviewing the first book in this Series[2] it would be quite impracticable to attempt to conceal Keynes when writing of the formation of financial policy. Keynes refuses to be 'disembodied'. After five years of reading Treasury papers, I am bound to add that this is only less true of several other advisers: Lord Catto, Lord Norman, Sir Hubert Henderson, Sir Dennis Robertson, and certain permanent officials all had their own characteristic points of view and characteristic sparkles, and these characteristics counted for something in the formation of policy. To have entirely suppressed the names of permanent officials while naming the temporaries would have distorted the picture, in that the influence of the temporaries would have been greatly exaggerated. The difficulty has been met partly by some relaxation of the rule against naming permanent officials, particularly when they are identifiable as leading representatives (almost Ambassadors) in other countries. Even after this concession it has been necessary, if a true balance was to be maintained, to suppress some of the references to temporary advisers. I have had, as will be appreciated, extreme difficulty in limiting references to Keynes; he wrote more copiously than other advisers, and his memoranda contain more than their fair share of quotable passages. Great though his influence became, it never matched his brilliance on paper, and to have quoted all his relevant passages would have had the effect of grossly underestimating the influence of other minds. I cannot claim to have got the balance exactly right: the problem is insoluble and I have done the best I could after having it on my mind for several years.

---

[1] Vol. CIX, Part III, 1946
[2] *Economic Journal*, March 1950, p. 114

The plan of the book is simple. Chapter I is straight economic analysis, designed to enable the economist to collect his thoughts before plunging into the story which occupies the remainder of the book, and to enable the non-economist to understand the importance I have attached to the various problems. Then follow three chapters on the budgets, three on internal 'capital' policy, and the remaining eight on external finance. At the beginning of Chapters V, VI, VII, VIII, IX, X, XI, XII and XIV the story switches back to the beginning of the war, or some other early date; and this occurs also at the beginning of many sections within chapters. These departures from chronological order, essential for ease of exposition, cause the reader to lose sight of one very important fact: that all the problems discussed in this book were being handled by very much the same small handful of men all the time. The Chancellor's immediate advisers, especially those within the Treasury itself, would be dealing in any week with budget policy, lend-lease, financial relations with India and the Dominions, foreign exchange control, and a host of other questions. Inevitably the story as I have told it overlooks this link in men's minds; I have sought to mitigate this shortcoming by the Chart reproduced as Appendix V. This shows, with page references, what was happening simultaneously under the main headings.

A book of this kind could not have been prepared and written within six years had the author not received abundant help from others. First, I must acknowledge the generous attitude of the General Editor of this Series and of the permanent officials at the Treasury and Cabinet Office who took the responsibility of inviting me to write it. They allowed me to follow my own conception of the subject, and interfered neither with the broad plan nor with the detailed execution; they have been ready to help whenever, but only when, I have sought advice; and they have ensured that I did have absolutely unlimited access to the papers. Other officials in the Treasury and elsewhere have helped both by discussion and by guiding me to the papers; a few have made invaluable comments on early drafts. Sir Ralph Hawtrey allowed me to draw freely on his massive chronicle, prepared for official purposes— I have even used some of its phrases. Besides commenting on some early drafts, he read the whole book in draft and commented at length; even where I have not adopted his suggestions, his comments have been illuminating and have I believe helped me to expound my own point of view more effectively. The late Sir Henry Clay took a great interest in the early stages of the book, and commented on early drafts of Chapters II–VIII. Sir Dennis Robertson read the completed draft, to my great advantage. Sir Jeremy Raisman commented on my first draft of the Indian part of Chapter IX, and for the pages on the Middle East I had help from Mr. E. M. H. Lloyd. Parts of Chapter X were read, at an early stage, by Professor S. J. Butlin of the University of Sydney and Professor H. M. Robertson of Capetown, and I had Canadian help in final revision of Chapter XI. For Chapter VIII, I was saved much time by using Mr. F. D. Forgan's *The British Exchange Control System, 1939–47*, an outstandingly thorough thesis submitted in 1951 for the degree of M.Com. in the University of London. For Chapters XIII and XV I drew useful hints from the Special University Lectures on Anglo-American Financial Relations, given at London a few years ago by Mr. Paul Bareau.

Among the many civil servants who have helped me in the ordinary course of their duties I must single out Mr. F. H. Dewar of the Chief Registrar's Office at the Treasury; for over five years he has ferretted out the files for me. Miss Sylvia M. Knight (Mrs. Johnson) and Miss E. Margaret Mills (Mrs. Mason) did excellent work as my research assistants, for Chapters II–VII and VIII–XV respectively; they were quick to sense my interests, and both will find that some of their words have penetrated to the printed page. Miss M. Cumpston prepared the printer's copy, Miss Mills the Chart and Mrs. Johnson the Index. Mrs. Margaret Gowing has been mainly responsible for reading the proofs; her major contribution was at the earlier stage of reading the first draft of every chapter— her corrections and her advice led to the smoothing of countless rough edges.

The length of these acknowledgments—and many names have had to go unmentioned—will serve to emphasise that this book has emerged from a co-operative effect. Nevertheless, the conception of the book, its point of view, and almost all its phrasing, are mine, and when criticism comes, it must be criticism of the author and not of those who have so generously helped him.

R.S.S.

August 1955.

CHAPTER I

THE PROBLEMS OF WAR FINANCE

IT IS SOMETIMES SUPPOSED that the sole duty of finance in time of war is to keep out of the way, leaving unhindered the armed forces and those engaged in war production. If there were any truth in this, there would be no occasion for the present book. In fact, finance has immensely important tasks both internal and external. The central task in a war economy, the mobilisation of resources for the war effort and the maintenance of that effort, calls for help from the financial system internally both in promoting the transfer of resources from one use to another and in raising to the utmost the productivity of the mobilised resources. Externally the task of financial policy is to ensure that the goods and services that are needed and are available from abroad—or to be denied to the enemy—can be bought. Both internal and external financial policy have also to take some account of the post-war effects of war-time actions. It is impossible to take any financial action upon the immediate situation without changing, in however small a degree, the financial situation that is carried forward into the future. Indeed only redistribution by financial measures can make many immediate burdens tolerable. A successful financial policy serves, in short, to intensify the war effort of the nation, to add to the resources drawn from abroad, and to make the burdens more tolerable without unnecessary complication of the nation's post-war problems.

The mobilisation of resources for the war effort involves the transfer of a large proportion of the adult population away from its peacetime occupations and into the armed forces, into the munition factories and even into export and home industries where new labour is needed to replace the young people withdrawn for more active war service. Transfer of other resources—of factory and warehouse space, of land from agricultural use into airfields and other military use, and from one agricultural use to another more appropriate to war conditions—has also to be effected on a huge scale. The economic system's normal way of securing transfers of resources from one use to another is the pull of high prices, high profits and high wages, the push of low prices, low profits, and low wages, and the push of unemployment and the bankruptcy court. In time of war these forces are not forceful enough—hence the resort, in greater or less degree, to conscription, requisition and 'controls' which in these circumstances can have a moral appeal

I

lacked by the bludgeon of the market. Theoretically it is possible to envisage complete dependence on such compulsory powers without any inflation of money incomes. But a nation at war which completely avoided an inflation of prices and money incomes would be either a completely militarised nation, in which everyone performed his allotted task under the sanctions of military law, or it would be a half-hearted nation not exerting itself to the extent of its powers. The war as fought by Britain fitted neither of these descriptions. To the majority of the population military sanctions were not applicable, yet patriotism was not enough; the ordinary economic incentive of the pay-packet at the end of the week remained in use. And there was no half-heartedness about this war; slow at starting, Britain willed the all-out effort directly the quietness on the western front was shattered.

Where the broad economic policy is a mixture of physical controls and financial incentives and deterrents there is evident opportunity for financial measures to assist in the fundamental task. These measures can bear directly on the strength of monetary incentives; they can help the nation to avoid the wastes of industrial strife; they can serve the principle of 'fair-shares' so vital to the maintenance of morale. As in other fields of action, the degree of success achieved must depend upon the acceptance of each step by public opinion. Judicious choice of technical details can do much to minimise the policing of compulsory measures, but the most economical policing is that of a supporting public opinion. Those measures that command the most public support are therefore those that involve least diversion of resources from the war effort itself, and this is as true of financial controls and of taxes as it is of the rationing of food and clothing. Financial policy has, in the end, to accept limits dictated by public opinion. This does not absolve the nation's political leaders, or indeed its administrators, from the effort to stretch those limits; much can be done to persuade the public to accept and co-operate in extreme or novel measures. But too much cannot be expected in this way, for financial policy is never a strong candidate for the attention of the man-in-the-street, and in time of war it has spectacular rivals for the scanty newspaper space. Moreover, war is apt to throw up political leaders whose tastes run in other directions, and it would be miraculous to find in a national war leader the genius, and in his daily round the time, for exposition of stern financial measures. In fact Britain in 1939–45 did not have the advantage of such a miracle. She did however have the advantage that a great pamphleteer in political economy was still at the height of his powers, and there were many followers who were quick to grasp and to propagate the war-time lessons of Keynesian economics. Whatever is said of the direct interventions of Keynes in particular questions of economic policy, there can be no doubt at all that his hold upon the professional economists was from the first a major factor in leading public opinion to acceptance of a relatively strong financial policy. For all that, there were the ultimate limits beyond which the public could not be pushed. Among the many tasks of the politicians and their advisers, one of the most important was that of sensing just where those limits lay.

However courageous the leaders of opinion, however perspicacious their advisers, a democratic country at war cannot avoid inflation. The initial impetus to inflation may come, as it did in Britain in 1939, mainly from the upward jerk of costs reflecting disorganisation and particularly the rise in the costs of imports. This is a point that has to be watched—for, as we shall see, inflation always tends to run to excess and every cause has to be tackled. But it is not the most fundamental cause of war inflation. The really fundamental cause, the cause that operates from start to finish, is the Government's effort to absorb into employment every scrap of employable resources—both human and material—and to attract a very large part of these resources into the direct war effort, leaving far less than is normal to maintain the living conditions of the civil population. The effort to attract resources manifests itself in the swelling tide of Government expenditure. The Government may ease the process by appeals to patriotism and by compulsory measures but, as every administrator of labour controls knows, the pay-packet has to be there at the end of the week, and the pay-packet has to be reasonably fat.[1] This transfer of resources is not, in a long war, a once-for-all process. As the aspect of war changes, shifts in war production are needed, and each shift is eased by the use of ordinary economic incentives. If every ounce of the nation's resources is to be brought into action, and kept in action in the right places however much the right places change, there must be sufficient Government expenditure to maintain a steady pull on resources. That is the root of wartime inflation, and neither heroic taxation nor forced saving nor skilful borrowing can completely exorcise it.

If inflation were no more rapid and no more pervasive than was necessary to serve the purposes of economic mobilisation, financial policy would be comparatively simple. But inflation tends to be altogether more rapid than this; it tends to get out of hand and so to wreck the monetary basis of economic organisation. There are two reasons for this. First, as the nation's pay-packet is swollen, people attempt to spend more on goods and services,

---

[1] For military conscripts the pay-packet is sometimes miserably thin, but the Government has to incur rather high maintenance charges even for the rank and file.

so adding further to the total market demand for goods and services, already strained by the rising Government demands, and meeting supplies which may already be suffering interruption. Secondly, as prices rise, employees seek protection against the rising cost of living by demanding increased wages and salaries. Because employers in general are enjoying buoyant demand for their products, and because the war effort demands industrial peace, the employees are in a strong bargaining position and rising wages and salaries become the rule. These increases raise costs to employers, who pass on the higher costs in the shape of higher prices, which in turn prompt further demands for higher wages to meet the increased cost of living. This cumulative process is usually, and aptly, referred to as the inflationary spiral.

The disadvantages of this process, if it is allowed to continue unchecked, are well-known, and their crippling influence is doubly to be feared in time of war. The distributive evil—the squeezing of those left behind in the race of incomes against prices—has at first its attractive aspect, in that it is part of the process of squeezing consumption to release resources for war production; but in the more extreme phase it creates social problems that add to the frictions and discomforts that impede the war effort. The inevitable spectacle of inflated profits leads to complaints of profiteering which aggravate the industrial strife caused by the struggle of wage-earners to maintain their share of the cake. Bargaining power does not always coincide with relative urgencies for war production; consequently the industrial disputes sometimes distort the price structure and encourage a wrong distribution of resources. Worst of all, the inflationary spiral gathers speed, people cease to talk of the rising cost of living and begin to talk of the falling value of money. Once this stage is reached, two new and growing drains open to weaken the war effort. People lose the incentive to save, and their spending leads to inessential consumption; and people with a flair for trading divert their efforts from useful channels to take every possible advantage of price changes.

A nation at war strives to limit these disadvantages by the multiplication of controls. To those designed directly to promote the transfer of resources are added others whose immediate purpose is the repression of inflation. These financial controls have their costs, and can never be completely effective. Many controls are, in any event, needed for other purposes, and their multiplication with little relation to highly specific war requirements serves to irritate, even to bring the law into contempt. Resources are employed in administering the controls and in policing them. Although they can play an important part in restraining the inflationary spiral, their method is to repress inflation rather than to weaken its roots.

A state of repressed inflation can be tolerable as a short-term solution; if the war is long, the impossibility of repressing demand at every point becomes a serious source of distortion in the price structure and of diversion of effort from the central purpose of the nation.

The prime task of internal financial policy is not to make physical controls unnecessary, but to moderate their growth and to ease the strain upon them. It has, that is to say, to do more than any restrictive controls can do—it has to weaken the roots of inflation. By one means or another, purchasing power has to be absorbed by the Government to match the real resources it is absorbing for the unproductive purpose of war. The most powerful weapon for this absorption of purchasing power is taxation, for this implies a final removal of purchasing power, without any complication of the financial problems of subsequent years. This finality about taxation would make it the sole weapon appropriate to the task, if it did not carry incidental drawbacks affecting the war effort. Taxation can act as a deterrent; this can be exploited to deflect demand from particularly scarce resources, and even from consumption in general. So far, so good; unfortunately taxation can also, when it falls directly or indirectly on earnings, discourage effort and the movement of resources in the desired directions. With the urge of patriotism to counteract the disincentive, it is likely that a nation wholeheartedly at war does not include many people who are slack at their work because taxation is high; the greater damage is likely to arise more subtly, through unwillingness to exchange the familiar for the unfamiliar task, or to move from place to place—to impede, in short, the transfer of resources to the points where they would make the maximum contribution to the war effort. This is true of taxation in any form, direct or indirect, but it is more true of some forms than of others. The same can be said of the other disadvantages of taxation—the feelings of injustice between one person and another, and the cost of administration of the tax. From all these points of view—and they are not independent of each other—there are great differences between one tax and another, between one tax structure and another. The disadvantages of each tax grow faster than the weight of the tax, and a heavy tax burden must therefore be spread over a variety of taxes which all have to be considered not merely in comparison with each other but also in relation to the structure of taxation as a whole. It is a major task of financial policy to choose not just between one tax and another but between one structure of taxation and another. We shall see, in Chapters II and III, how the British Government imposed a rapidly growing burden of taxation during the first years of war, and then during the later years (Chapter IV) had to review the detailed structure so as to minimise the harmful repercussions this heavy burden was believed to be having upon the war effort.

The disadvantages of taxation rise steeply as the rates of taxation increase; disincentives increase, hard cases become harder, the wastes of evasive effort and policing become not merely bigger but, what is worse, more prominent. Because of this, no Government in a major war has ever felt able to rely upon taxation alone. To the extent that the absorption of purchasing power by taxation falls short of the absorption of real resources in the war effort, the Government spending-machine must in other ways be provided with purchasing power. The means adopted by the United Kingdom Government in 1939–45 are discussed mainly in Chapter VII. The particular devices employed affect the inflationary situation only indirectly; the choice between the good and the less good is a highly technical matter, calling for some skill and, as we shall see, for some judgment of later repercussions, but the choice does not have decisive effect on the immediate situation. By hook or by crook the Government must spend enough money to pay for the required real resources, and the effect of this spending—and its amount—will depend upon the readiness of the public to refrain from spending, whether for immediate consumption or for the construction of capital goods unrelated to the Government's purposes. There must, that is to say, be adequate saving and what cannot be done without inflation will ineluctably be enforced by inflation.

In a state of suppressed inflation restrictive controls, the queues and the shop shortages play their part in forcing savings. But much to be preferred, either to this involuntary saving or to the forced saving squeezed out of the laggard incomes in a state of open inflation, is voluntary saving which directly reduces demand without injustice. This underlines the case for checking inflation— a rapid inflation strikes at the incentives to voluntary saving, and a reduction of voluntary saving in turn speeds the inflation. Financial policy must therefore aim at the encouragement of saving. This bears on the level of taxation, on the choice of taxes and on the methods of Government borrowing. All taxes are apt to diminish saving by reducing the individual's power to save: this has to be accepted and it does not, of course, imply that the taxation is useless, for the personal economy enforced by taxation will in general exceed the voluntary saving which would otherwise have occurred.[1] Secondly, given the total taxation, the choice between one tax and another should be influenced (though not necessarily determined)

---

[1] This is a point critics of forced saving are apt to miss. cf. pp. 33–4.

by the relative strength of the two taxes as deterrents to saving.
Here again it is possible to find positive advantage in some taxes:
a heavy tax on a specific commodity or group of commodities,
such as a tax on alcoholic drinks, may strike at 'luxury' consumption which may, in war conditions, more readily be replaced by
saving than by the development of alternative wants. Considerations
such as these are highly relevant to a wartime Chancellor's problems; they are unfortunately not readily measurable, and judgment
on the chosen structure of taxation must therefore always remain
a matter of opinion.

To the extent that a Government has to pay out in the country
more money than it collects in taxation, it has in one way or another
to borrow money in the country itself.[1] The terms upon which it
borrows—the promises it gives in exchange for immediate disposal
of purchasing power—are important in relation to post-war
financial problems and to confidence, both at home and abroad,
in the stability of the country's financial structure and of its money.
Leaving these considerations aside for the moment, we may note
at this point the relevance of borrowing technique to the encouragement of voluntary saving. The immediate consideration is that
people should restrict their consumption, and it might appear
a matter of indifference whether the saver buys a long-term bond,
makes an interest-free loan or gift to the Government, or accumulates
cash in a money-box. The momentary effect is certainly the same, in
whatever form the saver chooses to hold his savings. But the next
day, the next month, or the next year—any time before the end
of the war—the saver's position will be different according to how
easy it is for him to spend his savings. If they take the form of cash
in the house, they will more readily be spent than if they take the
form of a Savings Certificate. Something of the same force affects
the joint-stock company or other corporate organisation—a balance
at the bank is more easily spent than reserves that are held in the
form of long-term Government bonds, even if there is no question
of loss on the latter. It is in the interest of a Government at war
that 'savings' should go into the less liquid forms simply because,
human nature being what it is, a little more trouble about spending
will make spending a little less likely within the war period. Illiquid
savings are, in short, relatively unlikely to be offset by dis-saving at a
slightly later date within the war period. It is therefore Government

---

[1] This is not strictly true of money it creates by the action of its own printing press.
Here the Government obtains, without giving in return any significant promise, the
real resources released by the saving of the man who is building up the number of notes
he carries in his pocket. Where money is created by the banks, the Government has to
borrow from the banks, giving some promises to the banks in return for the purchasing
power. In Britain the Government uses the printing press in the 'Issue Department'
of the Bank of England.

policy to maximise facilities for, and encourage by propaganda, the 'investment' of personal and corporate savings in those forms which are less readily encashed and spent. The importance of this, and the effort a Government should put into it, are perhaps apt to be exaggerated; that they have some importance is indisputable.[1]

The Government's borrowing technique must have regard not only to the avoidance of a high liquidity of the public's assets while the war lasts, but also to the post-war situation. The bonds or other claims handed to the war-time savers have to be honoured one day, and the Government must avoid unnecessary embarrassment of its peace-time successors by these liabilities. Even in this the Government—especially a British Government, with its care for sterling as the currency of the Sterling Area—will be influencing its capacity to wage war. For a careful borrowing technique, which promises to leave the authorities well in command of the financial situation after the war, will command the respect of other people and, strengthening their confidence in sterling, make them more willing to hold sterling through the war.

Narrowly war-time considerations thus coincide with the longer view. Clearly the really important point is to get lenders—corporate as well as personal—to hold their securities as tightly as possible. Broadly this means that the securities should have long rather than short lives—that they should mature into claims for spot cash only after periods as long as the lender can be induced to accept. But the requirements of the various lenders—their preferences in maturity dates—are widely varied, and so are the sums they can be expected to lend to the Government from time to time. The borrowing plans should meet these varied needs by offering a suitable variety of securities. The authorities should, that is to say, strive to match in the securities offered the varied preferences of investors. But they should at the same time try to push investors always into slightly less liquid securities than they would readily have taken: propaganda and lavish facilities have a part to play here. Special privileges which will appeal to particular groups of investors may also be used, though a far-sighted Treasury will be cautious of elaborating the frills, which may prove awkward precedents at a later date.

While every effort is made to induce individual investors to take up long-term securities, the feeding of Government bonds to institutional investors—particularly the banks—must take full account of their conventional preferences for certain proportions of short-dated paper. Securities the public will not hold on terms thought tolerable by the Government have to be taken up by the

---

[1] On the methods of borrowing, see Chapter VI below.

banks and other financial institutions. It is of course possible for a Government to force the banks to take up Government paper, and in the last resort or for marginal requirements this is actually done, but even in this case the Treasury must, for the sake of public confidence in the banking system, have regard to the normal preference of the banks for short-dated assets. Without recourse to the extremity of compelling the banks to buy Government paper, the authorities can induce financial institutions to take up large amounts by issuing the various classes of Government securities in such a way that the banks can preserve something like their normal distribution of assets. For example, the banks will take some medium and long-term bonds if they can at the same time add to their cash and other liquid assets—including in this last item the Treasury Bills. Additional Treasury Bills can be issued to the discount market, which can sell some to the banks and hold the remainder with the help of additional call money lent by the banks; but, in order to preserve the customary ratios of cash to total assets (and so to liabilities), the authorities must be prepared to issue more cash against Treasury Bills sold to the central bank. Care in adjusting the details of its borrowing operations to the conventions of the financial institutions will enable the Government to collect the necessary purchasing power with the minimum addition to the liquid claims held at the end of the war and the minimum resort to persuasion or outright compulsion. Clumsiness may sap confidence in the future value of the currency.

In these technical details of the conduct of Government borrowing, success is necessarily dependent upon the sureness of touch shown by the authorities. In Britain in 1914–18—or at least in the first two years of that war—the Treasury's technical competence had fallen sadly short of the situation's requirements. This is understandable enough, in the light of the almost complete novelty of the situation. In the Second World War there was no such excuse: the lessons of 1914–18 were fresh enough, and the authorities showed themselves alive to them. They had another advantage, in that the inter-war period, with its mammoth problems of debt management and its international currency upheavals, had itself been a period of continuous activity by the authorities in the money market, and a certain degree of technical agility had been developed. Nevertheless, the technique of raising money for the Government could never become purely mechanical: there always remained questions of more of one security and less of another, more dependence upon one channel and less upon another, where the choice had a bearing upon the manageability of the situation at a later date and perhaps upon confidence at home or abroad. There remained, that is to say, room for the exercise of judgment, and the soundness of that judgment must remain a matter of opinion.

There was one most important aspect of Government borrowing on which the experience of 1914–18 dominated policy. This was the question of the rate of interest. In the first war the nation had allowed the question to be decided, in the earlier years, by the fact that London remained an open financial centre, and the rising interest rates dictated by this circumstance were perhaps thought appropriate to a swelling Government demand for loans, while a higher reward for savers might encourage saving. As is explained in Chapter V, this policy proved unmanageable for a long war, and created embarrassment for the monetary authorities after the war as well as adding to the post-war budget difficulties. It was not a precedent to be followed. Moreover, memories of the way it worked out were so fresh that in 1939–40 repetition would have been followed by quicker and more resounding failure, and it was therefore necessary to make a different policy plain from the start.

The policy adopted and made plain to all in the first year of the Second World War was that which gave rise to the phrase 'The Three Per Cent. War'. It is the subject of Chapter V and is further discussed in Chapter VII. Broadly it meant that through the course of the war the structure of interest rates for Government borrowing was held at the low level to which people had become accustomed during the 'thirties. For long-term borrowing and small savings the rate was at or near the three per cent. of the phrase. The rates on shorter paper were equally frozen at the levels normal to the last years of peace (1 per cent. upwards), although these were extraordinarily low in relation to long-term rates. This policy implied the absence of a high-price inducement to savers, and correspondingly made other methods of persuasion more important. It also meant that the authorities were abjuring high interest rates in their traditional functions of making London a relatively attractive international centre for money, and of restraining the private use of resources for real capital construction. The former of these was practically irrelevant, thanks partly to general international circumstances and partly to the innovation of foreign exchange restrictions. The latter function—the restraint of investment of real resources in competition with the Government's war effort— was perhaps still of some practical importance. In so far as this function still mattered, the low rate had to be protected by the control, by administrative decisions, of non-Governmental borrowing.

Direct control of private borrowing—the 'Capital Issues Control'—is thus to be regarded as an integral part of 'The Three Per Cent. War' policy. Here again there were lessons to be learned from the laxer conditions of the earlier part of the first war. If the rate of interest was to be kept down, private borrowers must be choked off by Government decree. Unfortunately the problem is not as simple as this. The business of borrowing and of the sale of 'securities'—the work of the capital market—is one market, in the sense that there is no clear distinction between the sale of a security— or other act of raising capital—for the purpose of embarking on the construction of new capital goods and the sale of a security for the purely financial purpose of purchasing another security or of adding to the seller's balance at the bank. A control of bor- rowing, a capital issues control of the English type, has to insert some arbitrary distinction, a hard and fast line where the real world knows none, if it is to permit continuance of transactions in paper assets ('securities') and yet prevent or regulate the 'issue of new securities'. To adopt the extreme course of prohibiting all transactions in securities—including notably the work of the Stock Exchange—would bring intolerable disadvantages. The ordinary work of the capital market immensely facilitates the Government's own borrowing operations; it takes in its stride many financial adjustments between individuals, adjustments that have to be made and that would call for troublesome administrative action if the market machinery went completely out of action for the duration of the war. For the sake of quick revival of the private economy after the war, there is always something to be said for keeping the existing mechanism in working order. The capital issues control is therefore to be aimed at regulating new borrowing, while allowing the capital market to remain unhindered in its dealings in 'old' securities. We shall see in Chapter VI something of the administrative problems that arose in the British attempt in 1939–45 to ride these two horses at once.

Interference in the financial operations of borrowing is, because of the integral nature of the capital market, all too apt not only to run into these problems but also to be given an exaggerated value as a means of protecting the Government's position as a borrower in the market. Its more important business is, as we have seen, to check the demand for real resources which people might otherwise seek to embody in capital equipment or stocks of goods. If they cannot borrow, they cannot spend in competition with the Government: so the argument runs. But people who already have the necessary money in hand or can get it by selling old securities in the Stock Exchange, escape restraint by a capital issues control. Only more direct control of real resources—labour and materials, building and machinery—is effective in restraining capital development by people who already have financial resources, and in total war the Government of course must employ these direct controls.

It appears, then, that a capital issues control is likely to prove administratively awkward and perhaps to lead administrators into queer positions, and that it cannot be expected to serve its real purpose of restraining the employment of real resources for which the Government is a competitor. What justification remains for resort to a purely 'financial control' of this kind? In a democratic country at war, there are two answers to this question. First, as part of the structure of controls designed to check private employment of real resources, the control of capital issues can serve as a long-stop. The community does not want to direct great efforts to the policing of raw material and labour controls, and the addition of a financial control, although it cannot touch firms already well-financed, does help by leaving less strain to be taken by the physical controls. Secondly, when many elements in the financial markets are being asked to co-operate with official efforts, and when the Government relies substantially upon an atmosphere of restraint in private financial operations, it is important that the authorities should have some power to prevent open and large-scale exploitation of purely financial opportunities such as may be afforded by the issue of new securities. The system of informal co-operation behind the scenes is an economical way of getting things done; but it does depend in some degree upon trust that sharp-witted competitors are not meanwhile being allowed to pick up easy profits in activities that bring no help to the war effort. So a control of capital issues and of other private borrowing may have more justification than appears at first glance. How strong the justification is, how elaborate the control should be, how far it should be pressed—these are questions to which, in the light of this discussion, there can be no hard and fast answers. As elsewhere in financial policy, the decisions partly depend upon judgments of the state of opinion, and whether in 1939–45 the decisions were right or wrong must equally remain a matter of opinion.

The problems examined up to this point are essentially problems of war finance in that, although related to peace-time financial problems, they arise out of the war-time problem of squeezing the last ounce of war effort out of the economy. They arise out of the need to employ the nation's resources to the utmost, and to direct them as far as is possible to the war effort. There are other aspects of war finance more closely related to the normal peace-time preoccupations of a Chancellor of the Exchequer and his official advisers. There is, for instance, the duty at all times to ensure that public money is used with due care and economy in securing the goods and services for which Parliament has voted the money. Under war conditions this control over public expenditure becomes at once more difficult and more important. The difficulty arises from the great expansion of public expenditure, much of it in new directions, while trained watchdogs, far from being more numerous, are needed for urgent tasks more directly contributing to the war effort. The peace-time restraints—the need for 'Treasury authority' and the inquests by the auditors who report to the Public Accounts Committee—become irksome, especially to war-time officers (both in and out of uniform) unused to the procedure and properly eager to speed the war machine. But good housekeeping, while becoming more objectionable on these scores, unfortunately also becomes more important. For financial economy, properly speaking, is a way of enforcing economy in real resources. Financial policy in time of war has above all to help the Government to squeeze the utmost effort out of the nation's real resources. The detailed methods employed in the spending of Government money can also have an important bearing on the development of inflation. The Government is no insignificant buyer who must accept 'market prices'. It is an all-important buyer, often the sole buyer, of the resources for which it is contracting, and it can be more or less careful in its methods of pricing contracts for war supplies, of fixing piece-rates in ordnance factories, and all the rest. Generous or conventional pricing always has the attraction that it buys the maximum co-operation, but it buys at a price—encouragement of the inflationary spiral.[1] One of the problems of financial policy is therefore to reconcile these conflicting interests—on the one hand the pressure to relax the peace-time vigilance of Finance Departments, and on the other hand the widened significance of true economy in public spending. How the United Kingdom Government endeavoured to reconcile these conflicting objects is not treated in this volume, but has its own volume in this series;[2] its separate treatment should serve to emphasise the difficulty and importance of the problem, and not to obscure its integration with the central problems of financial policy.

Another matter in which the Chancellor's war-time problems are closely parallel to those of peace-time is the distribution of the burden. The war effort includes, of course, many efforts and sacrifices beyond the realms of political economy; with these, immense as they can be, this book is not concerned. The nation's capacity to wage war depends also upon what real resources it can draw from beyond its borders; with these we shall be concerned later in this chapter. Here we are concerned with the internal war

---

[1] cf. pp. 60–1 on the fixing of commissions and pp. 86–7 on the 'E.P.T. argument' frequently pleaded by contractors.

[2] W. Ashworth, *Contracts and Finance*, in this series. (H.M.S.O. 1953).

economy and with the ways in which the Chancellor influences the distribution of this, the economic burden of war.

One popular illusion must be dispelled at once. No financial manipulations, no shifting of the balance between taxation and borrowing, can shift the main burden away from the present and on to future generations. What shift there can be between present and future is determined not by the major decisions of the Chancellor of the Exchequer, but by the decisions about the actual use of real resources. The country's capital equipment can be depleted in greater or less degree. In a short war this can appreciably ease the current burden. But although in a long war the depletion of real capital can be absolutely greater, its proportional contribution must become progressively less. By and large, and still leaving out of account the external resources, the inescapable fact is that every generation must bear the burden of its own war.

The economic burden of war is—apart from the use of external resources and changes in the nation's capital stock—the difference between national income and consumption, and individuals are bearing the real burden when the value of their consumption falls short of their gross incomes. In so far as the Chancellor can impose this gap upon individuals, by his measures of taxation, he is determining the distribution of the real burden, and in doing this he will try to have regard to equity and other non-economic considerations. A tax-payer may temporarily evade part of the real burden by financing consumption by sale of a security or other asset. The effect upon his own position is that he has in future lower total assets, from which he might have drawn income in the future. The effect upon the national position is aggravation of the inflationary pressure, or more strictly a partial failure of taxation to absorb the surplus of purchasing power. A war-time Chancellor, bound to inflict heavy taxation which cannot always take account of consumers' fixed commitments, is certain to find some of his taxation 'running to waste' in this way. Equity may compel him nonetheless to impose this taxation.

That part of internal Government expenditure which is not covered by taxation must in one way or another be covered by borrowing, whether from individuals and corporate businesses or from the banking system. Yet it remains an immediate real burden upon the individuals who make up the nation. In fact all the efforts and sacrifices not matched by the abstinence enforced by taxation must be matched by voluntary saving in one form or another. What happens is that a person who saves, accumulates in one form or another claims which he believes will be of value in the future. The claims may be simply in the form of additional money balances (in which case the Government will be able to borrow, with the minimum of ill consequences, from the banking system), or they may be newly-issued Government bonds, or they may be assets sold by someone else who is dis-saving—i.e. is financing his share of taxation otherwise than by reducing consumption. For various reasons the Government will, as we have seen, want these claims to be as illiquid as possible; but for our present purpose the important point is that these claims do not represent any shift from present to future of the real burden. The appearance of the claims means simply that to some extent individuals have not suffered an uncompensated burden, but that they bear the present burden in return for a claim upon their compatriots' production in the future. Sooner or later these claims may become troublesome, especially in aggravating post-war taxation problems.[1] Their multiplication is therefore an evil which a Chancellor would wish to minimise. To his desire to check consumption the Chancellor adds this further reason for maximising taxation during the war. These are the considerations that constitute the case for heavy taxation during the war; they affect the distribution of the burden between individuals, who may between themselves, so to speak, swap burdens now for burdens in the future, but by no financial jugglery can the nation push the main part of its burden forward into the future.

The problems of the distribution of the economic burden of war are of obvious relevance to the problems of taxation and might therefore have been appropriately discussed at an earlier stage in this chapter; they have been placed here because of their close relationship to some of the most difficult problems of external finance, the subject to which we now turn.

In addition to the use of resources within the country—both the current efforts and the resources accumulated in the past—a nation can sometimes throw into its waging of war an important contribution drawn from other countries. Britain did this on a large scale in the first war, and she did it even more exhaustively in the second. The problems of external finance are those of ensuring that all those external resources, which other countries are willing to supply and which can be transported home or to the theatres of war, can be 'paid for' in some way satisfying to the supplier and tolerable to the purchasing country. The resources drawn from abroad can be paid for in three ways—by current exports, by relinquishing assets[2] accumulated in the past, and by running up debts for the future.

---

[1] The higher the rate of interest paid by the Government on its bonds, the greater will be the aggravation of post-war problems of taxation; this is part of the case for keeping rates of interest down in time of war.

[2] Including not only securities and material capital abroad but also gold or any other commodity internationally acceptable and not drawn from current production.

Current exports imply a current burden of production, and compete with war production and the maintenance of essential supplies and services at home. The forcing of current exports is therefore something done at great cost, and can be justified only if the things not otherwise obtainable from abroad are worth the resources absorbed in producing the exports.[1] The assessment of the position—the decision whether certain exports are or are not worth while—is not a matter of financial policy, but the position can obviously depend on relative prices which in turn depend upon the rates of exchange between currencies. In the circumstances in which Britain waged war in 1939–45, it paid her to cut the volume of her exports severely and to charge as high a price as she could for those remaining; this pointed to a relatively high value of the pound in terms of foreign currencies. The need to keep down the prices of imported goods, in the interest of stabilising prices and wages, pointed in the same direction. The decision on the rate of exchange was thus an important one; it was a matter of financial policy bearing directly on the capacity of Britain to wage war. It had its indirect effects too; for example, maintenance of the foreign exchange value of the pound was an important ingredient in maintaining foreign confidence in the future of sterling, and so in maintaining foreigners' willingness to hold sterling—their willingness, that is, to allow the United Kingdom to draw real resources in exchange for promises to pay in the future.

Beyond what can be financed by the sale of exports and the gifts of Allies and other friends, the nation has to pay for the goods and services it obtains from overseas by selling its foreign assets and getting into debt. The sale of some of its foreign assets, in the shape of internationally marketable securities, can be a comparatively simple operation. But war conditions may make markets unfavourable, and at best the appetite of markets is likely to be abnormally restricted. The operation, simple as it is, therefore needs careful handling if the most is to be made of the assets sacrificed. Many other foreign assets find no such ready market: this is true of participations in, and the complete ownership of, industrial and trading concerns in other countries, especially when the value of the business overseas depends upon close connection with a parent firm at home. It is usually better to incur new debts than to press the sale of assets in this class, but when new lenders are not forthcoming, the sacrifice of value may have to be faced. A

---

[1] A country on the road to victory may in addition feel justified in maintaining, on a 'token' scale, exports whose main purpose is to keep alive post-war markets. (cf. E. L. Hargreaves and M. M. Gowing, *Civil Industry and Trade*, in this series, H.M.S.O. 1952, pp. 184–200). After lend-lease began in 1941, the financial aspect of exports was often less important than their importance in meeting minimum needs of Empire and Allied countries.

problem of this kind, and in a most acute form, was faced by Britain in the Second World War, when American aid became in some degree conditional upon Britain's 'scraping the barrel' of her foreign assets. The 'Courtauld sale', as it was known, was a very expensive demonstration by the British Government. In a less extreme form the problem is always present: how far should the sale of foreign assets be pressed?[1]

For the reason just given, the possibility of incurring fresh debts has to be faced long before all foreign assets have been realised. Both the sale of foreign assets and new borrowing abroad have serious post-war implications: they involve a diminished power to draw imports in return for a given value of exports. The debts are incurred (or the assets sold) in order to buy from abroad goods and services to be added to the war effort. The immediate flow of resources is obtained, however, at the price of a diminished flow in future: there is a genuine postponement, for the nation, of some part of the real burden of the war. At this point, therefore, it becomes impossible for a Government to evade attention to post-war considerations. How far is a Government justified in mortgaging the future for the sake of the current war effort? In the circumstances that form the subject of this book, the answer to this question was dictated in no uncertain terms by the fact that Britain was fighting for her life; and the shadow of post-war burdens was never allowed to be a determining factor in the pace at which she ran into debt. But this insistence on the paramountcy of the immediate effort made it all the more important to do what little could be done to seek lenders who would not press for rapid or unregulated repayment after the war.

Though the British were acutely conscious of the post-war burdens they were laying upon themselves when they borrowed abroad, the path to post-war indebtedness was in one way deceptively easy for them. London's position as the centre of the Sterling Area (though a shrunken Area) made it possible for Britain to run into debt automatically—as she overspent in the Sterling Area, all that happened was that the sterling balances of the supplying countries ran up.[2] Even outside the Sterling Area, the reputation of sterling as an international currency made it possible for British negotiators to persuade supplying countries (notably the Argentine and Portugal) to hold sterling. Both inside and outside the Sterling

---

[1] The sale of foreign assets, normally owned not by the Government but by private individuals and corporations, also poses problems of compensation. These, like other problems of compensation (for requisitioned premises or commodity stocks, for war damage, and other losses), are not treated in this book. They involve considerations of equity primarily, but the Treasury has also to keep an eye upon inflationary effects.

[2] See Chapter IX on the genesis of the sterling balances and the problems to which they gave rise.

C

Area, however, extensive resort to this way of financing overseas supplies had to be watched and it gave rise to delicate problems. For the bigger the sterling balances, the more important it became for Britain to persuade the creditors not to press for early realisation, yet at the same time to avoid all suspicion that sterling was not perfectly good to hold. As this dilemma became more threatening, sterling—at least sterling paid to some countries—became almost as 'hard' as any other currency.

In the early days of the war the hardest currency of all—the currency expenditure of which had to be watched most narrowly— was the United States dollar. Early in 1941, when Britain had spent all her dollars and faced huge dollar commitments for further supplies, the position was transformed by the introduction of lend-lease. Yet this never covered all Britain's dollar requirements, and the Americans saw to it that no more dollars were forthcoming than were necessitated by genuinely austere standards. The enforcement of these standards inevitably became a major concern of the Treasury, which had to take the lead in the more fundamental negotiations on lend-lease—negotiations which continued through the whole remaining length of the war. Moreover, conditions were attached to lend-lease. The most famous of these were 'Article 7', committing the United Kingdom to the principle of non-discrimination in post-war trade, and the 'White Paper' restrictions on the export trade. And there were others which, though of less importance, occasioned much work for Treasury officials throughout the war. There was, for example, the condition that no profit should be made in the sale of goods obtained under lend-lease. And it was not long before lend-lease begot reciprocal aid, involving relatively simple questions at home but also delicate negotiations with the Dominions.

For reasons such as these, there was never a time when Britain could be careless in her expenditure of foreign currencies, and in some phases the scarcity was extremely acute. It was therefore necessary to maintain foreign exchange control to ensure that no foreign currency was wasted on unauthorised imports or used without most particular justification for capital export, whether originating with residents or non-residents. Because the whole Sterling Area was for this purpose a single monetary area, a position the British authorities had good cause to maintain, foreign exchange control was not a simple fence round the United Kingdom, but was a fence round the entire Sterling Area. The administration of this control was necessarily shared between the widely scattered Governments of the whole Area and, though London was not in a position to dictate to these Governments, it was necessary for the British authorities to do everything possible to guide the control into a common form. More troublesome than this technical assimilation of foreign exchange restrictions was the attempt to secure reasonably uniform standards of austerity in the limitation of imports. It was one thing to say that no Sterling Area country should allow its residents to draw foreign currency for unauthorised imports; it was quite another to ensure that the standards of import policy should be enforcing no more hardship in one country than in another. The normal pattern of consumption varied from country to country; identical restrictions would therefore be indefensible. Yet without such a simple rule, who was to reconcile an Englishman's view with an Australian view of Australian (or English) consumption?

In these delicate questions and in all the other problems of external finance—the problems of aid, of borrowing, of post-war commitments and all the rest—the United Kingdom was negotiating (and negotiating more or less continuously) with countries whose products were more or less important for the war effort and whose political interests varied enormously. The underlying political relations varied from those with Spain, just keeping at arm's length from the Axis Powers, to those with our closest Allies in the Commonwealth. There was thus no simple pattern, no rule of thumb upon which Britain's financial negotiators could base their attitudes, their arguments, their immediate objects. Whether in one case or another they did the best that could have been done for Britain is a question that cannot be answered save with omniscience of the underlying political relations and of the perpetual variations in Britain's bargaining strength.

These financial questions, not only about debits and credits but also about economy in imports and comparative consumption standards, arose very largely between friends, between Allies both inside and outside the Commonwealth. It was therefore inevitable that they should have been increasingly affected as ideas developed and as victory grew nearer, by two laudable but often conflicting principles: that there should be equality of sacrifice, and that there should be no war debts between Allies. Experience of the inter-war period had undermined faith in inter-Allied indebtedness. There had been many defaults, and still more thoughts that the whole structure of war debts was obstructing healthy international monetary relations and ought to be wiped out. It was only logical, after this, to argue that a new structure of inter-Allied debt should not be built in the Second World War, and this was certainly in American minds when President Roosevelt, sweeping 'Cash and Carry' aside, put lend-lease in its place.

There are of course great attractions about a system that leaves the slate clean at the end of the war, especially when it is contrasted with the opposite extreme, the purely 'commercial' system whereby inter-Allied war debts are allowed to grow automatically by full charging for war supplies by the countries that happen to be in the best position for providing them. But once there is a departure from straight commercial methods, all kinds of difficult questions arise as to the fair distribution, between nations, of the real burden of war. The no-war-debts principle carries the implication that the cost of war production should remain a real burden upon the country in which that production takes place, and this is fair only if every nation is exerting itself to the utmost, is living as abstemiously as possible, and finishes the war with no new advantage or disadvantage as compared with its Allies. The attempt of Britain and the United States to work in partnership as nearly as possible on a no-debts principle left questions outstanding on all these three points. Had the compulsion of economic and military mobilisation been pushed equally far in the two countries? Was consumption being equally restricted? And would the Americans compensate us in some way for the greater distortion with which British industry and Britain's export trade finished the war? To these three questions a fourth had to be added: would the Americans in some way recognise the special burden we had borne in the early part of the war, when we had held the fort without their help? The financial discussions between the two nations at the end of the war really started with these four questions, and it was quickly evident that there were no readily acceptable answers.

With some of Britain's other Allies something approaching the opposite system—that of chalking everything up on the post-war slate—prevailed. Events have shown how deceptively easy it was, and how it tended to give rise to bad feelings. The trouble about this method is that it does not, as many imagine, protect the supplying country from the real burden in time of war, but that it gives that country as compensation (in whole or in part) a claim upon the post-war production of the receiving country. Thus between Britain and India, the accrual of the sterling balances did nothing whatever to protect India from the very heavy burden of being a great supply base for the campaigns in the Middle and Far East.[1] What did happen was that India accumulated a claim to some real compensation after the war for her real burdens during the war. There was naturally a great deal of feeling in Britain that, as Britain herself was getting no post-war compensation for her war-time efforts, other countries' claims should at least be scaled down. But such adjustment of the post-war compensation could only have been discussed on the basis of some comparison of the

---

[1] See Chapter IX for full discussion of financial relations between the United Kingdom and India.

real efforts and sacrifices of Britons and Indians during the war. Even if political conditions had been propitious for such discussions, the theoretical difficulties of such comparisons would have been overwhelming. It was difficult enough, in all conscience, to compare the restriction of consumption in America with that in Britain; but how infinitely more difficult was a comparison between Britain and India where a peasant population lives in entirely different ways and on different commodities. And, to put an extreme point, how were the pains and penalties of the Bengal famine to be weighed against fire and blast in London's East End? There are of course no answers to such questions. But whenever questions arose of adjusting the share of expenditure or of debts already incurred, men groped after solutions to these deeper problems and, failing to find common ground, brought to the financial discussions a sense of frustration that made working agreements less easy to reach. In later days the nations of the North Atlantic Community, nations whose living standards are not so completely incomparable, have brought up again these problems of the equitable distribution of a common burden of defence. Yet even these nations, for all their documented estimates of national income, find that the problem involves far more than arithmetic.

In the sense that financial obstacles were never allowed to obstruct the war effort, British policy in the Second World War was undoubtedly successful. Pounds were always forthcoming for supplies and services at home, and from abroad everything that could be supplied and shipped but could not be obtained by gift was paid for either in other people's money or in pounds that carried a promise for the future. In this sense financial policy never failed, and for this reason most of those responsible for organising Britain's war effort were never forced to feel that financial policy was important. But, as it has been the purpose of this chapter to show, there are many other tests of success. Was the balance between taxation and inflation just right? Would a more courageous policy of taxation have so freed us from queues and ration cards that production would have been on balance greater? Was the burden reasonably distributed between individuals and classes? Would a different borrowing policy, leaving the end-of-the-war situation rather different, have been worth while? Could Allies, inside and outside the Commonwealth, have been persuaded to exert themselves as fully without so many strings being tied to Britain's post-war balance of trade? Such questions as these are relevant, and the answers cannot be wrapped into tidy packages for weighing in the scales of justice. In a word, it is impossible to pass judgment, and this book makes no attempt. Its purpose is simply to explain what was done and, as far as motives left evidence behind, to show why it was done.

CHAPTER II
BUDGET POLICY
I: THE PRE-KEYNESIAN PHASE
(i)
The First War Budget, September 1939

THE STORY of budget policy is a story of struggle against inflation. The experience of 1914–18 and the financial nightmares of post-war Europe were fresh in the memories of statesmen, civil servants and private citizens alike, and this alone would have ensured more heroic financial efforts than those of a generation earlier. From the first, this struggle was envisaged as a struggle to avoid a gap, in some sense, between Government expenditure on the one hand and, on the other hand, the sum of taxation and the funds which could be borrowed by normal methods.[1] From the first, also, the behaviour of wages and the state of the labour market were seen as linch-pins in the struggle. From both points of view Sir Kingsley Wood's budget of 1941 takes the centre of the picture. Before that date, Britain's financial governors, though acutely aware of the risks of inadequate taxation, were only groping towards some standard of adequacy—and leading public opinion in the right direction. Equally, before that date, the policy of stabilising prices and wages was only in a formative stage. In the budget of 1941, the size of the financial problem was thrown up in a new way: budget problems were reformulated and budget arithmetic, if not fundamentally new, at least had a revolutionary look. In the same budget the policy of stabilising prices and wages—towards which the Government had already made important moves—was propounded with a new assurance and given new substance. After that date, the remaining war-time budgets were primarily designed to consolidate ground already won, and to trim the rough edges from the new measures of the earlier days.

But although the final shape of war-time policy did not emerge until 1941, the broad ideas behind the new arithmetic of that year had been seeping into budget discussions from the very beginning of the war and even earlier. In contrast to the narrow views of public finance propounded by Chancellors and other Treasury spokesmen in the previous decade, Treasury thought upon the

---

[1] This is the 'inflationary gap' in the old approach to Government finance; for the modern formulation, see pp. 72-3.

approaching problems of war-time finance went to the root of the matter. The source of these pre-war discussions can be traced back to 1929, when the Committee of Imperial Defence called upon its Sub-Committee on Manpower to consider certain labour problems in the event of war. It was perhaps fortunate that this first approach to the problems of war finance came from this angle of the manpower interest in stable prices and wages. In the earlier war the Treasury had never completely discarded such narrow views on taxation as had led to the 'McKenna principle' of 1916,[1] and it is significant that there were still, in the 1932 Progress Report of this Sub-Committee of the Committee for Imperial Defence, vestiges of this principle. These traces of earlier ideas were however already in 1932 pushed aside in favour of the broad conclusion that banking and financial policy and the control of profits and wages are one and the same problem. Inflation was already seen as the result of insufficient financial restraint on the total demand for real resources. The question was taken further when, just before Munich, this 1932 Report was taken from its pigeon-hole and discussions on how to implement its intentions in the field of finance were seriously begun. Since these discussions had to cover the possibilities of borrowing as well as taxation, the Bank of England was brought in at an early stage. The Governor, keenly alive to the importance, to a belligerent Britain, of stable money and world confidence in sterling, took a leading part. A paper by one of his advisers shows how ideas were crystallising in the autumn of 1938. The enlargement of Government spending, he argued, must result in an increase in total incomes. This increase must be diverted by taxation and by Government borrowing, and this diversion must work as speedily as possible. He suggested as immediately practicable measures

(1) acceleration of collection of taxes

(2) high-pressure selling of Savings Certificates etc.

(3) control of distribution of profits.

He thought, too, that Treasury Bills should be funded frequently in order to minimise inflation—presumably because this would restrain the liquidity of the commercial banks. Lastly, there should be control of supplies by rationing in order to prevent scarcities from producing their normal effect of raising prices.

In the discussion leading up to the first budget of 1939 (the last

---

[1] The principle is that new taxation should be imposed in sufficient amount to cover interest and sinking fund charges on the loans necessary to cover the year's deficit. See H. of C. Deb., Vol. 81, Col. 1052, and E. V. Morgan, *Studies in British Financial Policy*, 1914-25, p. 92. It is perhaps unfair that this principle should have become named after Mr. McKenna, who evidently regarded it merely as setting an absolute minimum to taxation requirements. He himself imposed much sharper increases in taxation than this principle alone would have warranted.

pre-war budget), views such as these had found little place. The Chancellor, Sir John Simon, was indeed warned of the danger of inflation, but this was not thought a serious threat as there were still some two million workers unemployed, and a big increase in national income without a great rise of prices therefore seemed feasible. Pre-budget discussion consequently ran very much on normal lines, concerning itself with subjects such as revision of the entertainments duty and implementation of earlier promises about the medicine duties. But in September, when the outbreak of war precipitated a supplementary budget, the balance of discussion was altogether different. The budget problem was now seen as the necessity for very heavy taxation to curtail civilian demands and so release resources for war-use. The rapidity with which this view developed was partly due to the reinforcement of the permanent staff of the Treasury by such outstanding economists as Mr. H. D. Henderson[1] and Professor D. H. Robertson,[2] but it would be a mistake to suppose that they alone were responsible for the pressure on the Chancellor. The Governor of the Bank of England, whose forthright advice was usually given orally, now sent one of his rare memoranda to underline his fear of inflation. Failure to curtail civilian demand would, he argued, lead to inflation followed eventually by Depreciation (with a capital D). Among the Chancellor's ministerial colleagues the First Lord of the Admiralty was quick to stress the need for stern measures.

While there was general agreement on the desirability of increases in taxation sufficiently sharp to check consumption, there was some hesitation about the speed with which the increased rates of taxation should be applied. Unemployment was still high, and this waste of resources would be increased if private spending were curtailed more rapidly than Government spending could be increased. Indiscriminate abstention from private expenditure was obviously out of place. Mr. Churchill agreed 'everything should be eaten up prudently, even luxuries, so long as no more are created' but that so far as the alternative was unemployment of resources, it would be sensible to continue producing for private consumption. In retrospect this appears a dangerous doctrine, as the employment of labour might well involve the use of materials that were destined to become scarce and were vitally important for war production, for export, or even for essential consumption at a later stage during the war.[3] 'Everything', in fact, should not

---

[1] Later Sir Hubert Henderson.

[2] Later Sir Dennis Robertson.

[3] The stock position of certain imported materials became uncomfortable surprisingly quickly. Alterations of shipping routes and other circumstances forced a quick drop in the level of imports, and even before Christmas 1939 there was a succession of 'import crises'.

be eaten up. On the other hand, it would have been difficult at this stage to urge, or indeed to induce, accumulation of stock or production for stock, as there was a very general expectation of widespread losses by bombing.

Uncertainty about the effect of the expected early bombing entered the taxation question also, from the angle of ability to bear taxation. Mr. Henderson advocated delay, both to see how the unemployment figures moved and for definite indication 'as to the extent to which businesses in the principal cities are likely to be ruined by the war'. Professor Robertson thought that the argument about waste of resources would be largely met if it proved practicable 'to temper the wind to the lambs who are being shorn of income'.

In the event arguments for delay were overruled in favour of an early budget which would tell people where they stood.[1] Heavy taxation was going to be necessary very soon, hitting incomes of every size, and the sooner people realised this the better. In consideration not so much of the slow growth of Government expenditure as of the existing unemployment, the impact of the announced increases in taxation should be softened. The principal measure was therefore an increase in the standard rate of income tax from 5s. 6d. to 7s. od. in a transition to 7s. 6d. simultaneously announced for 1940. The 7s. od. rate was estimated to yield an increase of £70 millions in the current year. Besides foreshadowing the rise of the standard rate to 7s. 6d., the Chancellor announced the reduction of reliefs in September 1939. The rate for the first £135 of taxable income was fixed at 2s. 4d. (formerly 1s. 8d.), and in 1940 it was to go to 3s. 9d. on the first £165. Earned income allowances and personal and children's allowances were also to be reduced in 1940. Surtax rates were raised from 1s. 1·8d. to 1s. 3d. at the bottom of the range and from 9s. od. to 9s. 6d. at the top; the yield of this tax was thus to be increased by £5 millions in the current year. Rates of estate duty had been raised in April 1939 by one-tenth of the previous duty on all estates above £50,000; in the September budget this one-tenth increase was doubled, and the one-tenth increase (not doubled) was applied to estates between £10,000 and £50,000.

For the 'shorn lambs' who had suffered reduction of income as a result of the outbreak of war there was special relief; for administrative reasons the relief was made general to all who had suffered a 20 per cent. reduction of income under Schedules D and E, irrespective of the cause of reduction. In such cases the individual was entitled to substitute the current year's actual

---

[1] In spite of the decision now taken, it was possible for *The Times* as late as 25th July 1940, when criticising Sir Kingsley Wood's first budget, to say, 'It is high time to make an end of interim budgets with all their consequent unrest and uncertainty'.

(reduced) income for the previous year's income as the basis on
which he would be assessed. The justification of this extraordinary
measure was that by relieving cases of hardship it left the
Government more free to raise rates of direct taxation sharply
and without delay. For similar reasons the reductions in allowances
(children, marriage, etc.) at the bottom of the scale were to take
effect only from the beginning of the next financial year.

Immediate increases of indirect taxes were regarded as the
counterpart of those of direct taxes. An all-round contribution
towards the cost of the war implied measures touching the poorer
people, few of whom were as yet assessed to income tax. The quickest
way to levy a contribution from this class was by sharp increases
in indirect taxation. The major items in this part of the Chancellor's
programme were 1d. a pint more on beer (nearly 50 per cent.
increase of the existing duty), 2s. a pound on tobacco and 1d. a
pound on sugar. In order to preclude criticism that the poor man's
drink was being made more expensive while the rich man's drink
was left untouched, there were increases in the wines and spirits
duties roughly corresponding to the penny a pint on beer.[1]

Of the increases of indirect taxation, the penny a pound on sugar
was the most hotly contested.[2] The sum involved was £8½ millions
in the current year, £18 millions in a full year. Inside the Treasury
it had been put forward with a good deal of diffidence, but this
was mainly on the ground that it would have a disproportionate
effect on the cost-of-living index number, the significance of which
from the point of view of the speed of inflation was already keenly
appreciated. In the budget debates, leading speakers from all
parts of the House complained of it not on this count but on such
grounds as the hardship to old age pensioners and detrimental
effects on nutrition. Its place in a general absorption of purchasing
power among all sections of the community was not appreciated
in the House, and the political capital which Members sought to
make out of their opposition to it illustrates the extent to which
at this stage Parliamentary critics lagged behind official circles
in understanding the necessities of war-time financial policy.

The lag in Parliamentary opinion, as expressed in debates,
was far more general than this reference to the discussion on the

---

[1] The increase in the Customs duty on wine involved a technical breach of the Anglo-
French Trade Agreement of 1934. Hence (these being the days before Vichy) the
intention had to be communicated to the French Government immediately before the
budget was opened. It is noteworthy that, though the Chancellor had previously agreed
that the French Ambassador should be told that 'the object of the increase is revenue,
not the restriction of consumption', the final brief for the Foreign Secretary used the
argument that it was necessary to avoid the appearance of discrimination in favour of
the rich.

[2] e.g. Mr. Attlee's speech, H. of C. Deb., Vol. 351, Col. 1384.

sugar tax might be thought to imply.[1] Although there were the usual differences of view about the equitable distribution of the burden, there was universal agreement that sharp increases of taxation were desirable. But this support for higher taxation was not based on the need to release real resources with the minimum of inflation. Its virtue was thought to lie in the consequential minimising of the post-war debt burden.[2] This burden was in turn only imperfectly understood: despite all the discussion of the 1920's (crystallised in the Colwyn Report), people still thought of war-time borrowing as being a way of postponing the real burden, and they were now, in 1939, supporting higher taxation in order to minimise the burden imposed on posterity by a growing National Debt. Although it is possible that crude views of this kind formed part of the Chancellor's thought when he first approached his budget problem, the Treasury views generally were enlightened by the Colwyn Report, by subsequent expert discussions and by the promptings of the economists already in their midst. The time of a formal national income approach to the budget problem was not yet, but the Chancellor's budget speech reflected the Treasury's understanding of the need for immediate diversion of real resources. The reports of the budget debate suggest that public opinion was not yet ready for this, and that Mr. Keynes's propaganda (which began in November 1939) was highly necessary. Pending such a development, general support for higher taxation was useful, even if the justification was not as weighty as it might have been. It may well be that fuller understanding would have led to more rapid increases, but the arguments put forward by Mr. Henderson and Professor Robertson[3] in September 1939 make it possible to suppose that this first war budget was reasonably adequate.

The increases of taxation, both direct and indirect, referred to in the above paragraphs were thus regarded by expert opinion as the necessary absorption of purchasing power to compensate for the rising tide of Government expenditure, and by less expert opinion as the way of shouldering the burden which was the proper alternative to burdening posterity. The remainder of the budget was concerned with the quite different problem of 'taking the profit out of war'. Memories of war profiteering in 1914–19 were still vivid, and there was universal insistence that nothing of the

---

[1] At this early stage, Parliamentary opinion was probably not unfairly represented by what was said in debate and at question time. As the war progressed, the spoken word perhaps became less representative of opinion on economic matters. Those who best understood the problems were often busy elsewhere or, accepting the Government's policy, sat silent while critical remarks were made in less representative quarters.

[2] e.g. Mr. Samuel's speech, H. of C. Deb., Vol. 351, Col. 1444.

[3] p. 26 above.

kind should be allowed to happen again. A start had indeed already been made in this direction in time of peace. The armament profits duty, imposed by the Chamberlain Government in the summer of 1939, was intended to prevent the armament firms from retaining any unreasonable profit made out of rearmament. When compulsory military service was introduced in the spring of 1939, the state of opinion was such that the Government felt compelled to pledge itself to 'taking the profit out of war'.[1] If personal liberty was to be surrendered in favour of strengthening the armed forces, those who escaped should at least be prevented from enjoying material benefit from the war.[2] In pursuit of this aim, two methods were to be adopted in addition to the peace-time special taxation of the armament firms. First, an excess profits tax would be imposed immediately after the outbreak of war. Secondly, steps would be taken to make possible an assessment, for a capital levy at the end of the war, of all war-time increases in personal wealth.

The first method was at once adopted in the September budget, and was universally approved. As from 1st April 1939 (i.e. covering the last phase of war preparation as well as actual war-time) an excess profits tax was imposed, the rate of tax being 60 per cent. on any excess of the profits of a trade or business over a pre-war standard. The pre-war standard was to be, at the tax-payer's option, the profit in the calendar year 1935 or 1936, or an average of 1935 and 1937 or an average of 1936 and 1937; this repeated the details of the armament profits duty which was merged in the new tax. For new firms, and for additional capital employed since the standard year by old firms, the profit standard was to be 8 per cent. for companies and 10 per cent. for individuals and partnerships. Any trader who thought the standard so prescribed was unfair in his particular case could appeal to an independent Board of Referees for a higher standard. The national defence contribution (dating from 1937) was partly superseded, in that every business had to pay the excess profits tax or the national defence contribution, but not both.

The second method to be followed, in fulfilment of the Prime Minister's pledge, was the preparatory work in anticipation of a capital levy on war-time increases in personal wealth. In April the Prime Minister had told the House of Commons: 'I think it is possible that the subject could best be grappled with by a levy on war-time increases of wealth such as was examined by the Select Committee in 1920, but not at that time proceeded with. I want to say again to the House that we are studying this matter further

---

[1] Mr. Chamberlain's speech, H. of C. Deb., Vol. 346, Col. 1350.

[2] For further reference to anti-profiteering motives in financial policy cf. pp. 40, 46 and 59.

at the present time, so that we can work out a scheme which can without delay be put into operation if ever the occasion should arise'. The occasion had now arisen, and definite steps were looked for in the autumn budget. The Chancellor originally intended to announce the intention to call for a register from all individuals whose pre-war wealth exceeded £10,000 or £5,000; the necessary legislation would not form part of the Finance Bill but would be introduced separately 'as soon as circumstances permitted'. This suggestion of delay was the result of the discouragement which Ministers and their advisers had received from the 'further study' Mr. Chamberlain had mentioned in April: a Committee of Imperial Defence sub-committee had been impressed by the difficulties, especially those arising from uncertainties of values both during and at the end of a war and from the dispersion of individuals in the early stages of a war. The reality of these expected difficulties was now emphasised by the Inland Revenue, who added that the Department could not during the war examine the returns with a view to determining the true value of the property declared—the returns would simply have to lie in the pigeon-holes. The Chancellor was accordingly persuaded to use a temporising formula: 'A levy of this kind could not appropriately or usefully be attempted during the progress of the war—the Prime Minister indicated as much . . . . . Apart from that circumstance, if one looks at it practically, delays in calculation, which are very elaborate, delays in assessment, and delays in collection are inevitable under war conditions, and would make any project for a levy during the war impracticable. In war-time taxation of income is the practical and effective method of proceeding'.[1]

From the Labour benches there was in the budget debates much pressure in favour of an immediate capital levy. But Ministers had by this time been thoroughly alarmed by the administrative difficulties and the danger of extreme public irritation (for example, of property owners on military service far from home) and they refused to make any firm commitment even about a register of wealth. The Chancellor's announcement was received by the Labour Party with indifference, and in winding up the Second Reading debate the Chancellor merely paid lip service to the notion. 'I do think', he said, 'there is a very great deal of justice in the view that if you could devise a practical scheme of getting a contribution from war-time increases of wealth, it might very well be a most suitable addition to our fiscal armoury.'[2] This proved to be almost the last word on the subject: after 1939 the passage of time, the rising rates of current taxation (especially the 100 per

---

[1] H. of C. Deb.. Vol. 351. Col. 1378.
[2] H. of C. Deb., Vol. 351, Col. 1786.

cent. excess profits tax) and the increasing disorganisation of civilian life justified the thickening dust in this particular pigeon-hole, and the idea was referred to in the 1940 budget speech only to say that no action would be taken.[1]

This first war-time budget is of interest mainly in relation to the early trend of ideas on war financial policy. That it had to be followed by more radical developments is appreciated when the main figures of the budget are considered. Expenditure in the fiscal year ending 31st March 1940 was in September 1939 estimated at £1,933 millions, including the Vote of Credit and expenditure under the Defence Loans Acts. This estimate was necessarily unusually hazardous, though in the event it was not far out—actual expenditure was £116 millions less. Revenue, also more difficult than usual to estimate, was put at £995 millions, and the realised figure was £1,049 millions. A deficit of some £800 millions was grim enough for Treasury officials brought up under such Chancellors as Lord Snowden and Mr. Neville Chamberlain, but much worse was obviously to come. Expenditure on defence services amounted in the financial year 1939–40 to little more than £1,000 millions. When compared with the 1938–39 expenditure of £382 millions, these figures, covering the last five months of peace and seven of actual war, afford a sharp commentary on the slowness with which the war machine was gathering momentum. Though detailed figures were not available, the general scale of expenditure was known, and it was therefore to be expected that the financial prospects of 1940–41, when they came to be discussed, would invite the criticism that the Government was not spending rapidly enough. And if the level of Government expenditure was to be greatly increased, prospective taxation in 1940 (the 7s. 6d. income tax for example) would be patently insufficient to achieve the ends already faintly descried as those proper to war-time financial policy. At best it could be said that the Government had been quick to make a start in the right direction; but it was only a start. Whether the whole course could be run without some quite revolutionary development was a question Mr. Keynes was about to raise in the columns of *The Times*.

(ii)

'Voluntarism on Trial'

The second war budget was introduced by Sir John Simon on 23rd April 1940. This was only a fortnight after the German

---

[1] H. of C. Deb., Vol. 360, Cols. 67-8.

invasion of Norway and Denmark, and it was before the collapse of the British effort in Norway raised the storm that, bringing the change of Government coincidentally with the German invasion of Belgium and the Netherlands, marked both the national change of heart and the end of the 'phoney war'. All the discussions in which budget policy was formed had taken place during the 'phoney war' period, and even the main budget debate in the last week of April was unaffected by the impending cataclysm. In these circumstances it is perhaps surprising not that this budget marked so feeble a step towards a policy appropriate to total war, but that it attempted as much as it did. A nation lulled by the absence of bombing and by the exaggerated optimism about German shortages of raw material might well have supposed adequate the taxation which had shocked it in September 1939. That this was not allowed to happen was due to four circumstances.

First, *The Economist* had been agitating opinion in favour of a more vigorous war economic policy and had been drawing attention to the magnitude of Germany's war expenditure. This was an important argument, whether the war was going to be short or long. If it was going to be short, Germany's huge current expenditure indicated her superior preparedness, and heavy immediate blows might be expected. If, on the other hand, it was to be a long war, the superior economic resources of the Allies could make victory possible only if they were mobilised as fully as were Germany's not much smaller resources. *The Economist's* figures of German expenditure, when compared with the British, showed how much more fully Germany was mobilising for total war.[1] The argument led to the conclusion that a total Government expenditure of £3,000 millions (£2,340 millions for the war) was 'a miserably low minimum'—but this was about three times the then rate of revenue, and made the couple of hundred millions of war taxation announced in the autumn look pitifully inadequate. Much heavier taxation was implicit in figures anything like these. *The Economist's* articles made sufficient impression to induce the Treasury to put both its own experts and the Ministry of Economic Warfare on to enquiries into the soundness of *The Economist's* figures. The pundits emphasised the theoretical difficulties involved in the estimates, and *The Economist's* figures could not be accepted in detail, but it proved impossible to dispute the broad conclusion that Germany's war expenditure was running far above the British. Some comfort could be derived from the fact that these comparisons had not brought France and the Dominions into the scale. There remained as an example to the Chancellor of the Exchequer what an official

---

[1] No satisfactory figures have since emerged to show whether *The Economist's* 1940 figures for Germany were accurate.

called 'the really formidable fact that all the authorities seem to credit Germany with a present tax revenue of 28 milliards, say £1,750 millions'.

Secondly, there was Mr. Keynes's propaganda on 'How to Pay for the War'. This opened with a series of articles in *The Times* in November 1939, elaborated and revised when they reappeared in pamphlet form in the early spring of 1940.[1] This pamphlet will be discussed more fully in connection with the 1941 budget, on which its influence was more direct. Mr. Keynes's fundamental innovation was a 'national income arithmetic' approach to the budget problem; it was essentially a reformulation which, while not uncovering any terrors previously unrealised by the Treasury, gave fresh point and so helped to bring home the true nature of the war-time problems. He added up the total value, at current prices, of resources becoming available for all uses during the year, and then added together the total demands—personal consumption, irreducible investment and exports, and Government expenditure. Comparing the two sums, he showed that a merely moderate development of the war effort necessitated a very large cut in general consumption. This cut would be enforced somehow—to the extent that it was not enforced by taxation, rationing and shop queues, it would be enforced by inflation of prices, with eventual development of a spiral of rising prices and wages which would inevitably impair the spirit and efficiency of the nation. Mr. Keynes showed that the gap could not without an inflation be closed by voluntary savings, even on the most optimistic view, or by taxation of the rich, even of a most vigorous kind. His remedy was forced saving, in the shape of sharp increases in income tax on the mass of the people, part to be refundable at the end of the war.

Immediately it was all too plain that opinion was not ready for such drastic innovation. The correspondence in *The Times*, following the Keynes articles in November, showed how completely unacceptable were the positive proposals. 'My discomfort', said Mr. Keynes in replying to the correspondence, 'comes from the fact, now made obvious, that the general public are not in favour of any plan'. In official circles opposition was at least as strong as outside. Those experienced in the detailed administration of revenue laws knew how measures that were simple to expound could yet give rise to troublesome complaints of hardship and inequity when their detailed enforcement hit individuals. Sir Robert Kindersley, whose task of encouraging voluntary savings was of the first importance, complained that talk about the Keynes plan was

---

[1] London, Macmillan & Co., 1940.

D

causing a decline in the response to National Savings appeals.[1] The Inland Revenue saw substantial administrative difficulties. One senior official pointed to the risk that wage-earners would claim wage increases to compensate for the new taxation.[2] Other Treasury experts, fortified by the views of the Stamp Committee, pointed out snags Mr. Keynes had overlooked. In short, neither outside nor inside Government circles was opinion ready for forced saving. But an important advantage of the agitation was in fostering realisation of the magnitude of the problem and of the imperative necessity of some drastic action if an inflationary spiral was to be avoided. 'Perhaps the greatest service that Mr. Keynes has rendered', *The Economist* thought[3], 'has been to impel the so-called "leaders of opinion" to reveal the state of their ignorance on the central economic problem of the war'. So though the forced saving proposal was left high up on the shelves, people were more ready as a result of it to impose and to accept severe treatment along more traditional lines.

The third factor operating in this direction lay within the Treasury circle itself. Softness was alien to the civil servants in immediate contact with the Chancellor, alien to the Prime Minister and alien to the Chancellor himself. The whole Treasury tradition favoured the utmost dependence upon taxation. Deficit finance for some purposes had in the previous years acquired a certain vogue in academic circles, but the Treasury was untouched by this, and still regarded a deficit with all the horror that was necessary to excite the utmost efforts to reduce it. Mr. Neville Chamberlain as Chancellor of the Exchequer had shown himself equally attached to the Gladstonian tradition. That the present Chancellor himself favoured stern measures was evident from the very beginning of the pre-budget discussions. He spoke of new taxes—'on football pools and bicycles, for example'—and of anti-evasion measures for established taxes, and urged his advisers 'to get some of these things going *in good time*'. He called for immediate investigation of the Keynes plan and emphasised Mr. Keynes's argument that in the absence of some plan the economic problem would solve itself by violent inflation. As the discussions wore on, and one after another of his suggestions encountered objections, Sir John Simon became

---

[1] Letter to the Chancellor, 5th April 1940: 'I have no doubt that the discussion of the Keynes scheme is making the small man button up his pocket—and we have direct and definite news to this effect from our people in Glasgow, Manchester and Sheffield. . . None the less I think we shall gradually pick up again if no other stupidities occur.'

[2] In a minute of 16th March 1940 he informed the Chancellor that he had that day heard 'that two of the most influential of the Trade Union leaders have said that deductions from wages in pursuance of the plan would inevitably be followed by claims for equivalent and compensating advances of wages'.

[3] 2nd December 1939, p. 325.

increasingly impatient. When budget day was at hand, he minuted his advisers, 'The more I go over the lines of my proposed budget speech, the more conscious I am that I end in a bog. Details of taxation apart, the big question is—how does the Chancellor *propose to avoid inflation* against which he has preached so stridently? I very much fear that the answer is that he does not propose to avoid it at all, but merely to be absurdly optimistic in his estimates of what can be done by way of voluntary lending'.[1] He doubted the capacity of traditional methods to cope with the problem and suspected that a more original approach was necessary: '*video meliora proboque, deteriora sequor*',[2] he wrote on that same minute. If the traditional approach was to be followed, at least it must be done in the spirit of an all-out attack. To him this budget was to be—to use his own phrase—'voluntarism on trial'. We should not again be able to risk failure in these methods.

Fourthly, the Treasury, worried for months about how the borrowing could be successfully organised, saw its first major effort—the issue of March 1940—fail rather badly.[3] Yet this attempt to get £300 millions into the bag after six months of war was a mere trifle as compared with the sums that were going to be necessary. A fortnight later a senior official, referring to the criticisms of the 'low' level of our war expenditure, wrote 'if to please Layton and Amery we say our expenditure will rise rapidly to the German level, our borrowing programme instead of £1,400 millions would become £2,200 millions which is totally impossible and a staggering blow for our credit at home and abroad'. 'Impossible' was a word suggesting too modest a view of war-time financial powers; but its use indicates an attitude towards the borrowing programme that implied extreme efforts on the taxation side.[4]

These four factors—critical comparisons with Germany's war expenditure, Keynes's plan, the Gladstonian tradition in the Treasury, and the discouraging opening of the borrowing programme—combined to preserve the 1940 budget from the softening airs of the 'phoney war' days. The Chancellor's broad plan was based on the assumption that the further increases in direct taxation previously announced (e.g. the increase of income tax to 7s. 6d.) were as much as could be done on that side, and

---

[1] 14th April 1940.

[2] 'I see the right, and I approve it too,
  Condemn the wrong, and yet the wrong pursue.'

[3] cf. below, Chapter VII, pp. 198–200.

[4] This official was ready to face the implication. If, he wrote, the Governor of the Bank was right in his estimate of the yield of voluntary loans, 'our methods are all wrong and we ought to go in for much more full-blooded confiscation of private wealth'.

that he must impose considerable new burdens in indirect taxation.

The situation plainly called for both increases in old taxes and the introduction of new devices. Even looking at the problem from the traditional angle of raising more revenue, innovation was imperative. As Lord Stamp had said, all the first-rate expedients for taxation being already in operation the country was thrown back on second-rate expedients. But the problem was also being looked at from the point of view of direct checks to inflation. This consideration operated in two ways: the Chancellor wished to avoid increases of those taxes which, by their effect on the cost-of-living index, would constitute a spur to demands for wage and other income increases, and secondly he sought to check by heavy taxation the pressure of purchasing power which was both intensifying rationing problems and drawing resources towards the production of luxuries.

Approaching the problem in this way, the Chancellor decided to leave such items as sugar and tea alone, and to strike hard at those commodities which, while they had the great attraction of productiveness from the revenue point of view, would be less likely to enter into wage-bargaining. He accepted proposals for raising taxation on beer by about a penny a pint, on spirits by 1s. 9d. a bottle, and a doubling of the duty on matches. He doubled the originally-proposed 1½d. an ounce on tobacco, the 3d. an ounce representing 1½d. on a 7d. packet of ten cigarettes. The increase on spirits involved, once more, reference to the French under the Trade Agreement. They had been upset by the nature and manner of the September increase, and on this occasion the Treasury took the precaution of early consultation with the French Ministry of Finance. To avoid irritation in this direction the Chancellor rejected a proposal to increase the duty on silk, leaving it to be caught up in the new purchase tax discussed below. Allied to these Customs and Excise changes were sharp increases in Post Office charges, which were henceforth deliberately to include an element of taxation over and above commercial needs. The ordinary letter rate went up by 1d. (to 2½d. minimum), the postcard rate similarly (to 2d.), and the printed paper rate by ½d. Foreign letters (other than Forces or airmail) went up by ½d. Telephone charges were increased by 15 per cent, and telegrams by 3d. each. There was a small increase in the poundages on postal orders. The total yield of all these increases in indirect taxes and charges was estimated at £66½ millions in a full year—about £59 millions in the current year. Not a striking contribution to a deficit of £1,500 millions or so.

A new purchase tax should, it was intended, yield appreciably more than all these changes put together. The broad conception emerged from the discussions on price control and inflation in the autumn of 1939. For administrative reasons both rationing and direct control of prices would obviously have to be confined to a fairly narrow range of goods, and this would lead to diversion of an unduly swollen stream of purchasing power towards the uncontrolled goods. Given the impossibility of allowing more resources to be diverted to the production of these less necessary goods—indeed, the imperative need was to divert resources *away* from such objects—the impact of rising purchasing power would provoke queues and, where traders took advantage, rising prices and unduly high profits. Shop shortages would mean waste, and a public outcry against profiteering would threaten morale and efficiency. A joint Committee of the Revenue Departments[1] was therefore directed to review thoroughly the possibilities of absorbing by new taxation—of a sales or turnover kind—part of this dangerously swollen and diverted stream of purchasing power.

Back in the pigeon-holes of 1922 was a long memorandum on turnover and sales taxes, prepared by officials when Sir Robert Horne had been casting round for ways of easing the burden of direct taxation, and public interest had been roused in the turnover taxes travellers had found operating in the inflationist countries of post-war Europe. The essence of the plan then evolved (but rejected on grounds of its difficulties for business men and tax collectors, its regressiveness and its impact on cost of living figures) was that all producers and wholesalers were to be 'segregated from their fellows by a ring fence and that all retailers and consumers dwell outside that fence. Then so long as goods pass from one person to another inside the ring fence, they remain duty free, but so soon as any person inside the ring fence . . . . . sells and despatches goods to a person (normally a retailer but sometimes a consumer) outside the ring fence, he pays the tax and passes it on in the price'. This is of course the plan of the 'registered trader' that has become familiar as the collecting machinery of the purchase tax.[2] It was unlike Continental

---

[1] The 'Revenue Departments' referred to in these paragraphs are (1) the Board of Inland Revenue and (2) the Board of Customs and Excise. The 1939 Committee was a joint body of the two Boards. At first the Inland Revenue Department was regarded as the potential administrator of the tax, and its officials made important contributions to the discussions. Following an Inland Revenue submission to the Chancellor, 11th April 1940, responsibility was vested in Customs and Excise, as the task was essentially one of recognising the nature of articles and the true recording of their values.

[2] The 'registered trader' as eventually defined had a minimum turnover of £2,000 a year. Representations from traders' organisations caused this limit to be brought down (by S.R. & O. (1941) No. 1389) to £500, not to secure extra yield but to meet a claim for equity on behalf of traders whose goodwill was so important in the administration of the tax. In 1941 the Customs Board sought in vain for the Chancellor's agreement to the abolition of the £500 exemption. In 1945 a Treasury Order was actually made, abolishing the £500 exemption, but owing to Parliamentary opposition the Order (S.R. & O. (1945) No. 482) was withdrawn.

examples in that collection was effected from wholesalers not retailers. But there were many doubts expressed before it was adopted. The official experts naturally emphasised all the difficulties of administration that had been thoroughly explored eighteen years earlier. They also, by reviving a 1922 objection that the tax would be regressive, evoked a vigorous protest in the Treasury of 1940.[1] 'What is gained', it was asked, 'by pointing out that this type of taxation is regressive? Of course it is; that is what we want. We have carried taxation of the rich and the middle classes to a point where further increases are exceedingly difficult to make. It is essential for war purposes to prevent consumption increasing further, and if possible to reduce it below its present level. The classes whom we have taxed account perhaps for one-third of this consumption, and the remaining two-thirds is consumed by classes who are not affected or scarcely affected at all by our direct taxation. How in the name of wonder could one hope to find any solution in the form of taxation, if such taxation were not regressive?'

Other disadvantages emphasised by the official committee were more relevant. Long and contentious legislation would be necessary, the lines between exempt and taxable goods would be difficult to draw, novel responsibilities for accounting would be placed upon traders already plagued by ration forms and handicapped by loss of staff, and the Departments themselves were ill-provided with staff of the competence required for the teething troubles of a new tax. On the other hand, the Board of Trade was attracted by the encouragement to production for export that would result from taxation of the home consumer of a wide range of products, thus underlining one of the tremendous advantages the Treasury saw in such a tax. For it was not merely as a revenue producer to help the budget in a narrow sense, but as a potent stimulus to the release of resources from home consumption, that the tax was welcomed in circles keenly aware of the more fundamental problems of war finance. These attractions were of the first importance and, after all, objections of the kind brought forward by the Revenue Departments were likely to be valid against any other measure that could make an appreciable contribution to the solution of the Chancellor's problems.

Besides legislation, much preparatory work—the registration of wholesalers in particular—had to be openly undertaken, and forestalling purchases by retailers and final consumers were therefore a disadvantage to be borne. It was not a very grave disadvantage, since the main effect would be a rapid passage of stocks into

---

[1] The official committee was not alone in using this argument: as lately as 27th April 1940 *The Economist* criticised the proposed purchase tax on the ground of regressiveness.

consumers' hands—not in any way deplorable—rather than further production of the taxable range of goods. There was accordingly everything to be said for immediate announcement, and in the budget speech the Chancellor announced that there would at once be registration of traders and consultations with the trade organisations concerned to ensure the smoothest possible working of a purchase tax,[1] the rate and commencing date of which would be settled later. Raw materials for industry, foodstuffs, articles already subject to a heavy duty (such as tobacco and petrol), fuel, gas, electricity and water were mentioned as categories that would be exempt. By implication all other goods would be subject to the tax, and this would have the advantage of making unnecessary individual luxury taxes (e.g. on cosmetics) which though commanding wide support would each be administratively troublesome and in the end yield little revenue. No sum was at this stage announced as the intended yield of the purchase tax, but the Chancellor indicated that he intended it to yield 'a larger additional sum towards our revenue than appears likely to be drawn from any other immediately practicable form of tax'. Nor was any figure given to the Cabinet; the Chancellor's advisers were working on the basis that a yield of £100 millions was being sought, and that a rate of 25 per cent. on wholesale values might be appropriate to this yield. The tax eventually came into operation on 21st October[2] and the actual yield was £26 millions in 1940–41.

While there were to be these substantial changes in indirect taxation, amendments in the law on direct taxation were confined to the implementation of the new rates of income tax and the reduced allowances as announced in September 1939, an enabling clause to allow the Chancellor a year later to reduce the level at which incomes became subject to surtax, from £2,000 to £1,500,[3] and anti-evasion measures relating to the estate duty.

The budget speech was also the occasion of announcement that there would shortly be legislation limiting dividends and prohibiting the issue of bonus shares. This proposal had its roots in pre-war discussions of the financial and broad economic problems implicit in the acceleration of rearmament. The Committee on Economic Information, a body predominantly composed of outside economists, reported on 20th July 1939 making recommendations

---

[1] Throughout the pre-budget discussions the tax had retained its 1922 name of 'merchandise sales tax' but a last minute suggestion by Parliamentary Counsel led to the adoption of the name 'purchase tax'. The lawyers had 'found it difficult to bring the provisions as to the tax on goods coming from abroad into a scheme of taxation which would be based on sale because one would then appear to be taxing the foreigner'.

[2] After a three weeks' delay due to bombing.

[3] cf. below, p. 79.

'to relieve the pressure of demand on the capacity of the investment industries, to mitigate the rise in prices generally, and to avoid the deterioration in our balance of overseas payments, which may occur as a consequence of these events'. Among the proposals were measures, similar to those already operating in Germany, to limit dividends and to secure that undistributed profits should be as far as possible invested in government securities. Parallel restrictions might be imposed on salaries above a certain amount. These measures were urged as having 'a double virtue. On the one hand they tend to reduce the rise in prices which would otherwise follow from inflationary expenditure. On the other hand, they facilitate the Government's borrowing programme, both directly, by providing a supply of new resources for investment in Government securities, and indirectly, by reducing the attractiveness of other forms of investment. An additional merit is that they may have a psychological effect in dissuading Trade Unions from demanding wage increases'.

After war had broken out, the adoption of other measures interfering with unwanted investment weakened one of the grounds on which this proposal stood, but in other ways the case was greatly strengthened. Checks to inflationary pressure had before the war been desirable; now they were imperative necessities. Moreover, public opinion, sensitive about profits made out of rearmament, demanded the complete elimination of 'the profits of war'. There were continual demands for the 'conscription of wealth'[1] and, as the Government turned its face more deliberately away from a capital levy or preparations for a post-war levy, it became increasingly important to prevent the well-to-do from enjoying any war profits. At the same time, the difficulties the Government was encountering in its borrowing programme[2] underlined the attraction of diverting company profits away from shareholders and towards the support of the bond issues. Another advantage urged by the Treasury now made its appearance for the first time, and was destined to reappear in all future discussions about the excess profits tax: this was that a statutory limitation of dividends would promote the accumulation of capital reserves to mitigate the difficulties of transition from war to peace.

In the budget speech, as a kind of appendix to his remarks about reliance on voluntary savings, the Chancellor announced that there would be immediate legislation prohibiting the distribution by a public company of a greater dividend than was distributed in any one of three pre-war years, subject to a minimum permitted dividend of 4 per cent. There would be special

---

[1] e.g. H. of C. Deb., Vol. 360, Col. 113.
[2] cf. p. 35.

provisions for new companies, and for hard cases a general dispensing power to be exercised by the Treasury on the advice of the Capital Issues Committee. To make the plan watertight, the issue of bonus shares would be prohibited except where very special cause could be shown. The Bill was introduced a fortnight later and was given a second reading on 23rd May. By the latter date, however, the new Government had come into both office and power, and a few days later the decision to raise the excess profits tax to 100 per cent. was taken. The case for statutory limitation of dividends thus largely disappeared (though there remained the undesirability of increased distribution of the peace-time standard profits) and the Bill was dropped.[1]

Parliamentary discussion of this budget on the whole showed that, though Sir John Simon himself might be unhappy, the temper of opinion had been correctly judged. The independent Liberals and other private members expressed dissatisfaction with the level of the Government's spending but this had ceased, in war-time circumstances, to be in any important sense a departmental responsibility of the Chancellor. The official Labour view was strongly antagonistic to the Keynes plan of compulsory saving—in fact, in his private view that he might well soon have to turn to something of this kind, the Chancellor was definitely running ahead of all but a handful of private members.[2] The Labour leaders welcomed the income tax and surtax proposals, and were critical of even the slightest relaxation of the excess profits tax.[3] The increases in indirect taxation were generally welcomed, except for those in postal charges. The latter, it was said, would bring little revenue to compensate for the irritation of people in all classes, war-time circumstances having occasioned family correspondence on an altogether abnormal scale. The purchase tax was discussed only in a very preliminary way—neither the rate of duty nor the precise range of taxable goods having been settled. There was however widespread recognition of the fact that it must hit a wider range than just luxuries.

The Economist was extremely critical.[4] As could be anticipated from its earlier articles on the level of war expenditure, it regarded the budget total as altogether inadequate. Almost equally unsatisfactory was the fact that only 46 per cent. of this inadequate

---

[1] When the proposal was revived in the post-war years, it was never given specific statutory force.

[2] Supporters of Mr. Keynes included Mr. Lipson (H. of C. Deb., Vol. 360, Col. 117), Mr. Amery (ibid, Col. 254) and Mr. Price (ibid, Col. 474). Mr. Silkin and Mr. Bevan (ibid, Cols. 452 and 461) envisaged its appropriateness for a later stage.

[3] The Chancellor proposed to deal more kindly with firms who had been having a bad time in the period on which the standard profit was assessed.

[4] 27th April 1940, pp. 759-60.

total was to be raised by taxation. Of the individual taxation changes it thought the increases on beer, spirits and tobacco 'undoubtedly stiff, and the increases in postal rates penal'. Oddly enough, it criticised the purchase tax as 'unfair and regressive in its incidence'. How *The Economist* could reconcile this view with its general attitude that there must be heavy taxation of the mass of the people, it is impossible to imagine. This blind spot in an article otherwise all too logical in its criticisms perhaps helped to create the impression in the Treasury (a most unfortunate impression) that *The Economist* was a carping and unfriendly critic. Its disappointment in the rejection of the Keynes plan was qualified by its view that 'the weakness of the Keynes plan is that it was ever associated with borrowing'. What it did want was outright taxation on the scale requisite to reduce consumption. It concluded that the Chancellor had 'gravely misjudged the economic needs of the situation' and hoped that by the autumn, by a 'change of personnel or some other minor miracle, a breath of realism and courage will have blown through the windows of the Treasury'.

This was a little hard on the Chancellor, whose budget had been prepared almost entirely in the 'phoney war' days and yet, for the reasons discussed above, was not as soft a budget as people might have expected. The Chancellor personally had throughout favoured severity, and at the very end of the long period of preparation had been keenly aware of the risks that were being run. He knew that without a sharp twist of the inflationary spiral the necessary volume of voluntary savings might not be forthcoming—which is another way of saying that the inadequacy of the budget proposals, if such indeed was the case, would leave inflation to balance the accounts. After very thorough consideration and in spite of many qualms, Sir John Simon decided to take the risk, and he therefore very properly devoted a long passage in his speech to a comparison between forced loans and voluntary savings and to urging the possibility of securing as good a result from the latter as from the former, and he urged the nation to make the effort. 'Why should we suppose,' he said, 'that the willing exertions of our people, if properly roused and directed, will produce less result than if we attempted to apply a cast-iron formula and compel our people to lend?' In his concern to encourage war savings in every possible way, he was prepared to introduce legislation to remove small savings from the means test calculations in the administration of certain social security payments.[1] 'What we have to do is to foster and improve the conditions under which the flow of voluntary contributions to Government loans may be stimulated and inflation may be avoided.'

[1] H. of C. Deb., Vol. 360, Cols. 82-3.

The arguments used against compulsory measures of the Keynes type—arguments that were developed in the budget speech[1]— were in principle equally valid against the taxation burdens actually imposed by the Chancellor.[2] The practical problem was to get the right balance between compulsion and voluntary savings so as to secure the maximum compression of consumption. There is in the papers every indication that this was grasped by the Chancellor's advisers,[3] and that it was fully appreciated by the Chancellor himself there is no doubt at all. Why then, in spite of the comparative insulation of the pre-budget discussions from the debilitating airs of the 'phoney war', and in spite of official knowledge of the degree to which the war effort must be stepped up, did the Chancellor not take courage and impose more severe burdens?

The only possible answer is that in looking at individual tax proposals the Chancellor and his advisers, instead of attending to changes in the citizen's net flow of purchasing power, continued to regard the changes simply as increases in particular items in the citizen's outlay. The cost of sending a letter was raised from $1\frac{1}{2}$d. to $2\frac{1}{2}$d.—a rise of 67 per cent.—and for sending a postcard, 100 per cent.—penal increases, as even *The Economist* described them. Similarly, the income tax payable by a married man without children, earning £300 p.a., was raised from £5 in 1938–39 to £7 in 1939–40 and to £15 in 1940–41. These were, the Chancellor thought, 'striking' increases. And so they were, when regarded in the light of price increases—a 200 per cent. increase in the price the citizen pays for some of the services of the Government. This way of looking at taxation changes has persisted, and has helped to make possible very fierce treatment of the surtax payer.[4] But if it sometimes works in the direction of making tax increases look easier to a Chancellor, in the earlier stages of the war its effect was undoubtedly that of a most unfortunate brake on tax increases. Given the imperative necessity to reduce spending power, the appropriate way to judge the adequacy of tax increases—and the appropriate way to present them to the public—was surely to show the effect on the amount of income left to a citizen after payment of tax. If, to take the example quoted above, the case had been presented as a reduction of net income from £295 in 1938–39 to £285 in 1940–41, it would not only have looked a small change,

---

[1] e.g. 'Experience goes to show, in many cases, that the first effect of compulsion is to kill the voluntary method.'

[2] cf. *The Economist*, 27th April 1940, p. 760.

[3] The essential principle of 'national income budgeting' was already part of the Treasury atmosphere.

[4] The extreme example was in the 1941 budget, when the raising of the top rate from 18s. to 19s. 6d. in the £ implied a *quartering* of the amount retained by the taxpayer from his marginal income.

but it would have been presented in a proper light in relation to
the overriding problem of the diversion of purchasing power, and
its inadequacy as a contribution to the needs of the situation would
have been patent to all.

The traditional way of presenting an increase of taxation has of
course great attractions to the politician who is anxious to make
the change appear to be 'only a very little one', and it is entirely
appropriate to times when the pressure of Government expenditure
is not threatening inflation, for then the citizen is in fact being
asked for the price of the services he is enjoying. But Sir John
Simon was not approaching his task in the spirit of a vote-catching
politician, and it would have been more helpful had the method
of presentation—not only to the public but also to himself and to
his advisers—been appropriate to the struggle against war inflation.
Reliance on 'voluntarism' might then have been kept within
bounds more in keeping with the doubts that privately worried the
Chancellor when he looked over his speech on the eve of budget
day 1940.

(iii)

The Breath of Realism

In commenting at the end of April 1940 on the inadequacy of
Sir John Simon's budget, *The Economist* hoped that 'by the
autumn . . . . . . a breath of realism and courage will have blown
through the windows of the Treasury.' The change came much
sooner than the autumn. The shock of British defeats in Norway
provoked early in May the downfall of the Chamberlain Government and the formation of a Coalition Government under Mr.
Winston Churchill. Almost simultaneously, in that brilliant Whitsun
week-end, the invasion of Belgium and the Netherlands gave the
British people a further shock and rallied them to the support of
the new Government to a degree never enjoyed by its predecessor.
From that moment onwards the British people were committed
as never before to total war to the end—to an end, moreover,
that was now realised to be a long way ahead.

This critical change was soon manifest in financial policy.
Comprehensive action was taken within the next ten weeks and
was not of a kind to be reversed when the national mood relaxed
so that although, as Lord Stamp wrote to the new Chancellor
at the end of July, 'patriotism and peril are curiously transient
as complete substitutes for the old incentives', the changes made
in the fiscal scene in those ten weeks remained for the rest of the
war.

The new political structure, too, had its importance in financial policy. As Prime Minister, a man intensely interested in financial policy and identified with traditional methods of approach gave way to another ex-Chancellor of the Exchequer who, though sometimes (even before he was Chancellor) ready to write advice in 'budget season', was not deeply interested in financial matters, but was ready to tolerate novel approaches to the problem. As Chancellor of the Exchequer Sir John Simon was followed by Sir Kingsley Wood. Sir Kingsley Wood was a highly successful politician—the junior Minister who always knew just what the troublesome back-bencher could be persuaded to swallow—and therefore commanded the full confidence of his own party. Respect from a wider public had been earned by an unusually memorable spell as Postmaster-General, followed by success as Minister of Health and then at the Air Ministry. 'His capacity for hard work, for seeking and acting upon the best advice he could command, and for getting things done proved its worth in every undertaking to which he put his hand'.[1]

'For seeking and acting upon the best advice'. In the Treasury itself extraordinarily able advisers, both permanent and temporary, were continuously available, and the Governor of the Bank of England called in almost every evening. But one of the first steps taken by the new Chancellor was to take advice regularly from eminent outside authorities. He appointed a Consultative Council representative of industry and commerce, banking, the Co-operative movement and Trade Unions, with Mr. Henderson and Mr. Keynes as economists.[2] A little later Mr. Keynes was provided with a room in the Treasury, and thenceforward he advised from the inside rather than the outside. On the initiative of the Governor of the Bank, the Chancellor had already appointed Lord Catto to be his Financial Adviser,[3] and Mr. Keynes and Lord Catto in fact worked in very happy partnership and in the closest contact with the civil servants.[4] Besides this widening of the channels through

---

[1] *The Times*, leading article, 22nd September 1943.

[2] The terms of reference were 'the special problems which confront the Treasury as a consequence of war conditions'. A separate minute of 25th June 1940 stated that these arrangements were not intended to impair the special position of the Governor of the Bank of England 'as the Chancellor's confidential adviser on all financial questions or the close and confidential contact between the Bank of England and the Treasury. Nor is it intended to disclose to the Council the practical working of those relations or of the relations of the Bank with City authorities generally'.

[3] Lord Catto's position was regulated by the following minute of 25th June 1940: 'The intention is that on all major matters affecting financial questions the Financial Adviser will be kept acquainted with the business in hand and will be brought into the discussions thereon both with his colleagues in the Treasury and with the Chancellor. If it should so happen, his views will be made known to the Chancellor where they differ from the views of others.'

[4] For a long time Mr. Keynes and Lord Catto occupied adjacent rooms in the Treasury, and they were affectionately referred to as 'Doggo and Catto'.

which advice would constantly come to him, the new Chancellor had the advantage of the sharp change in the political climate. The political atmosphere in which he had to work made his task altogether easier than Sir John Simon's had been; and now that his advisers had taken the bit between their teeth, there was less need of courage than there had been in the earlier stages. Then, a Chancellor of great political courage might have done more to moderate the growth of inflationary pressures; now that a more confident Chancellor was in charge, his courage made less difference.

Another great change was the inclusion of leading members of the Labour Party in the Government. This had of course a general influence on financial policy in that the views of this Party were taken into account more thoroughly and more skilfully at the formative stage in policy.[1] The Party views themselves became those of leaders sharing reponsibility for Government, of men who felt it their duty both to guide and to be guided by organised labour. In particular the formation of the coalition meant the inclusion of Mr. Ernest Bevin, who wedded his responsibilities as Minister of the Crown to his power as the *de facto* leader of organised labour, with a success that made him one of the most important leaders of the war. To the Chancellor in his stabilisation policy the support of Ernest Bevin was critical; and without a stabilisation policy a tough budget policy (in the narrow sense) would have been a broken reed.

The full effect of all these changes was not felt until the normal budget season of 1941, but some immediate changes were inevitable. The first was the replacement of dividend limitation by the raising of the excess profits tax to 100 per cent., and the second was a supplementary budget introduced late in July 1940.

The decision to raise the excess profits tax was essentially a political decision, hastily taken in the heat of the new political climate. This does not mean that it was necessarily an undesirable development—though it does mean that there was room for second thoughts, and second thoughts there were, eventually fructifying in important modifications.[2] What it does mean is that the decision faithfully reflected the mood of the moment and that it accorded with the new distribution of political power. There had from the beginning of the war been a universal feeling against war profiteering, but the case for a 100 per cent. excess profits tax had always been countered by the incentive argument. When Labour leaders joined the Government the popular view was given more weight,

---

[1] Unfortunately the record of Parliamentary debates during the first nine months of the war justified *The Economist's* view (27th July 1940, p. 112): 'The leaders of the Labour Party have never shown any particular sense of realism in fiscal matters.'

[2] Notably in the 1941 Budget. See Chapter III.

while the incentive argument was weakened by the strengthening of patriotic incentives as the national mood changed. The 100 per cent. E.P.T. thus became inevitable, and little time was lost before this was accepted.

When the new Government took office, Sir John Simon's budget was less than three weeks old and the consequential legislation had not gone beyond the early stages. It was therefore possible to introduce substantial changes in taxation by tabling amendments of the Finance Bill in the normal course of its passage through the Commons in the subsequent weeks. But the E.P.T. change was not in fact introduced in quite this simple way. Its first appearance was incidental to a Bill designed to implement the popular will to total absorption in the war effort: by the Emergency Powers (Defence) Bill, introduced on 22nd May by the Lord Privy Seal (Mr. Attlee) and enacted on the same day, the emergency powers of the 1939 Act were extended to require persons to place themselves, their services and their property at His Majesty's disposal. In the second reading speech Mr. Attlee envisaged the control, immediately or subsequently, of a large number of industrial and other undertakings, which would in effect be working on Government account. So that there might be 'no profit out of the national emergency', these controlled undertakings would pay 100 per cent. excess profits tax.[1] As these undertakings would be under direct control, the authorities would, it might be supposed, be able to check the wastefulness that could be expected when 100 per cent. E.P.T. removed the normal incentive to efficiency.

In the next few days Ministers perceived that this was an intolerably uncomfortable halfway house and that the general principle had better be universally applied. There were three grounds for this extension. First, the application of one rate of tax to a firm before the date of control and another rate after would embarrass the administration of control.[2] Secondly, the frontiers of control would be by no means co-terminous with those of war production. Thirdly, Ministers decided to accept the principle that 'excess profits in business in war-time should be ruled out altogether, whether the business is engaged on war production or on any other kind of activity'. These were the reasons given by the Chancellor[3] when, a week after the Emergency Powers Bill had

---

[1] The War Cabinet decision on 100 per cent. E.P.T. in controlled undertakings was on the ground that if the State had disposal of the workers in certain undertakings, it must also have disposal of all the profits.

[2] In putting his case to the War Cabinet, the Chancellor had supported the Minister of Supply in the view 'that great practical difficulties will arise in properly and fairly selecting the undertakings to be declared controlled if this declaration carries with it a higher tax liability', but the point was not so explicitly made in the Parliamentary statement.

[3] H. of C. Deb., Vol. 361, Cols. 564-5.

gone through, he spoke on the second reading of the Finance Bill and announced the generalisation of 100 per cent. E.P.T. to all trades and businesses with effect from 1st April 1940.

The prolonged discussions among the Chancellor's advisers on the implication of this decision and ways in which it might be modified, belong to the budget of 1941,[1] though they were already running strongly before Sir Kingsley Wood introduced his supplementary budget on 23rd July 1940.

When this supplementary budget was presented to the House of Commons, the primary reason given was that the events of the spring and early summer had led to great acceleration of war expenditure which increased the deficit to a point where it would certainly generate inflation to a dangerous degree. In April Sir John Simon had taken as a provisional estimate of expenditure £2,667 millions, including the round figure of £2,000 millions for war expenditure, and had introduced tax increases sufficient to limit the deficit to £1,433 millions. Since that date war expenditure had already increased from £40 millions a week to £57 millions a week, and it was expected to increase further. Sir Kingsley Wood therefore suggested £2,800 millions instead of £2,000 millions as a figure for war expenditure during the financial year, the deficit consequently becoming £2,200 millions. New taxation, both direct and indirect, was proposed to bring this deficit within less dangerous limits.

In fact the genesis of the budget in Ministerial discussions had been quite different from this, although there is reason to believe that as the discussions proceeded a lively sense of the economic implications of mounting war expenditure came to dominate the scene. The decision to introduce a supplementary budget in July was actually taken as a result of stresses within the Coalition Government, stresses occasioned by the Labour Party's reaction to the purchase tax announcement made in Sir John Simon's April budget speech. Then in Opposition, the Labour leaders had, in faithful reflection of the unrealistic attitude of the public towards the problems of war finance, criticised the purchase tax as regressive. The Chancellor at first believed that he could, in private discussion with his new Labour colleagues, secure a withdrawal from this position by concessions in favour of children's clothing, boots and shoes etc. Such concessions need not cost more than some £10 millions—a yield of the order of £100 millions might still be expected. By the beginning of July, however, the Chancellor had discovered his mistake, and the Labour Party had committed itself to wholehearted opposition to the tax.[2] To

---

[1] See pp. 85–90.

[2] There was a persistent newspaper campaign against the tax.

withdraw the proposal was unthinkable—by their unanimous rejection of this easy course, without any discussion, the Chancellor and
his advisers showed their appreciation of the dire need to do something to halt inflationary finance. The alternative chosen was to
make the purchase tax but one item among a number of stiff
increases of taxation, especially of the direct taxes that were accepted
as more reasonably assessed on ability to pay.

The tentative plans for increasing income tax by 6d. and reducing
some allowances were therefore thrust aside as inadequate, and it
was settled that the standard rate should go up at once by a full
shilling, from 7s. 6d. to 8s. 6d. The reduced rate chargeable on
the first £165 of taxable income was raised from 3s. 9d. to 5s. The
concession in respect of life assurance premiums was in effect
reduced by being pegged no longer to the current rates of tax but
to those of 1939–40.[1] With the increased amount of income tax
falling to be paid by wage-earners and small salary-earners, it was
recognised that personal liability to pay in half-yearly instalments
had ceased to be universally appropriate, and the Chancellor
announced that deduction from salaries and wages by employers
was to be compulsory.[2] Surtax on the first slice of income above
£2,000 was increased from 1s. 3d. to 2s. and the peak rate of 9s. 6d.
was to apply to incomes above £20,000 instead of £30,000. The
changes in the scale now made would add £8 millions in the current
year's yield, and £11 millions in a full year. Income tax and surtax
together now reached a peak rate of 18s. on income above £20,000,
as against the immediate pre-war peak of 14s. 6d. on income
above £50,000. A further 10 per cent. estate duty was imposed
on estates above £10,000, to yield £6 millions in a full year.
Including the April increases and the E.P.T. increase announced
in May, direct taxation was increased by over £200 millions
a year. This was the counterweight by which the Chancellor
sought to make further increases in indirect taxation, particularly
the new purchase tax, acceptable to the masses and to the
Parliamentary Labour Party.

The increases in indirect taxation were to be on the broadest
possible front, in accordance with the Treasury view that the time
had come to supplement the existing body of taxation by burdens

---

[1] The stabilisation of the income tax rate at 7s. 6d. related only to the income of
the life assurance funds, for any much higher rate might in some cases weigh too heavily
on such income. The gain to the revenue from the restriction of life assurance relief
to the person assured roughly compensated for the loss arising to the revenue from
stabilising the rate on the income of the funds at 7s. 6d.

[2] This is not to be confused with the P.A.Y.E. scheme, announced in September 1943,
of which it was merely the pale forerunner. *The Economist* welcomed the innovation
'not only for its immediate effect in facilitating the collection of the tax, but as an
improvement in machinery that prepares the way for that generalisation of income
tax into a universal direct tax which has been frequently advocated in these columns'.
(27th July 1940, p. 112).

E

on the great mass of small incomes. The Chancellor originally had it in mind to impose a number of novel taxes—on bicycles, expensive restaurant meals, football pools, and lotteries—which either had the attraction of hitting at luxury expenditure or would collect something from a large number of people.[1] Under the weight of broadsides from the Revenue Departments, generally using the well-worn arguments[2] but effectively reinforcing them with the plea of shortage of trained staff, these proposals for new frills[3] in the structure of taxation soon fell by the wayside, and the Chancellor decided to proceed on the basis that, leaving aside tea and sugar as 'cost of living items', he should proceed by way of further increases in the established taxes and rely upon the new purchase tax to catch most other items that were worth catching. He refused to be deterred by warnings that the beer and tobacco tax increases already imposed might be causing a large fall in consumption, and put a further 1d. a pint on beer and 1½d. an ounce on tobacco.[4] The wine duties were increased by 2s. a gallon on light wines and 4s. a gallon on heavy wines, bringing the totals up to 8s. and 16s. respectively.[5] The entertainments duty was increased, to yield an additional £4 millions in a full year.

In introducing details of his purchase tax scheme, the Chancellor was careful to present them to the general public as 'his revised proposals for a tax on personal expenditure'. This phrase was used in the summary for the news broadcast, and was an admirable reflection of the paragraph in the actual budget speech, which was carefully phrased to bring out three points—the need for a new source of revenue, the importance of restraining civilian consumption, and the fact that 'certain fundamental changes' had been made in the original proposals, by which differences might be composed without impairing the main objects. All food and drink would be exempt, as would services, fuel, gas, electricity, water, and certain goods (such as petrol and tobacco) already subject to high rates of duty. Children's clothing and boots and shoes, expensive medicines and surgical appliances, would also be exempt. The basic rate of tax was to be 33⅓ per cent. on the wholesale value, on luxuries and other articles, purchase of which could reasonably be avoided or at least postponed; and a rate of 16⅔ per

---

[1] There was also a proposal to tax coal at the rate of 2s. a ton but this was dropped at an early stage, apparently on 'cost of living' grounds.

[2] e.g. difficult administrative problems and small yield. 'Are oysters and white wine a meal?' was a question that caught the Chancellor's eye.

[3] 'Window-dressing taxes' was the apt description normally used by officials.

[4] He was amply justified by the event.

[5] The French Trade Agreement could now be disregarded; but the Dominions were expected to complain, and explanations to Portugal were thought advisable.

cent. was applied to 'more necessary articles requiring more frequent replacement such as clothing, boots and shoes, medicines and drugs other than those completely exempted, and such articles as domestic earthenware, domestic hollow-ware and domestic glassware and brooms and brushes. Newspapers and books would also be charged with the lower rate of duty'.[1] The tax could not be imposed at once, but would have to await completion of the register of wholesalers.[2] Because of this and of the forestalling that was inevitable, the yield in the current year would be only £40 millions, but a full year should produce £110 millions.[3]

Parliamentary comment on the budget concentrated largely on the new tax. In spite of the Chancellor's revisions, there remained much hostility.[4] The attack was developed on four lines: alleged infringement of the authority of the House of Commons, general objection to the tax as an attack on the poorer classes, objection to the inclusion of particular commodities, and pleas for relief of particular classes of purchasers.[5]

The Chancellor had from the beginning been in some difficulty about procedure, difficulty that was inherent in the necessity of touching the mass of miscellaneous consumption and yet collecting some money at the earliest possible moment. The resulting plan was attacked[6] on the ground that never before had the House been asked to give approval to what could only be the broad outlines of a tax which covered such a multitude of different objects. In the past, it was argued, the House had always been asked to give approval to specific rates of tax on specific objects, and though the Chancellor had indicated his classification of commodities in general terms, he had of course not been able to produce the complex schedules that eventually became all too familiar to the administrators of the tax. The Chancellor could not give way on

---

[1] Summary for news broadcast. Correspondence in *The Times* and pressure in Parliament, objecting to a 'tax on knowledge', led to the exemption of newspapers and books. cf. footnote 4 on p. 52.

[2] Eventually there was further delay on account of the disorganisation caused by the heavy bombing that began later in the summer.

[3] In his 1941 budget, the Chancellor estimated the yield of the tax in its first full year at only £70 millions, the reduction below the July 1940 estimate reflecting principally the extent to which the 'limitation of supplies' was becoming operative.

[4] The Chancellor was still encountering hostility even nearer home: antagonism in the business world found important expression in the Board of Trade.

[5] The Central Price Committee (Board of Trade) voiced another line of criticism unstressed in Parliamentary debates, though often referred to outside: as the tax implied higher prices, it had an inflationary aspect and was in this respect inconsistent with the aims embodied in the Prices of Goods Act under which the Committee operated, of restricting price rises. Later remissions (on which see pp. 128-9 below) conceded something to this view. (cf. *Civil Industry and Trade, op. cit.*, p. 85).

[6] e.g. by Mr. Pethick-Lawrence (H. of C. Deb., Vol. 363, Col. 909). It is astonishing that a constitutional argument of this kind should have been seriously raised only a few weeks after the sweeping Emergency Powers legislation of May 1940.

the main issue consistently with maintaining his position on his major objects, but in the second reading debate he conceded that the rates of tax should be alterable only by substantive legislation and not merely by Treasury Order.[1]

Secondly, the tax was attacked because it threatened to bear heavily on the poorer classes. The design of limiting consumption, it was argued, would be achieved by the well-to-do who would avoid luxury expenditure, leaving the Chancellor's second purpose— the raising of revenue—to be achieved largely at the expense of the poorer people. One speaker thought the Government might well lose as much through demands for increased wages, occasioned by the price effects of the tax, as it gained by revenue collected by it from the wage-earners. The Chancellor had deliberately exempted large groups of goods entering into the cost-of-living index, but it was alleged that some 12 per cent. of the index goods were in fact still included. Altogether the force of this attack, which included at least one influential speaker,[2] is impressive evidence of the distance that had yet to be travelled before the general views of the Chancellor and his advisers commanded universal acceptance. Equally, the partial resistance of the Government to the index number argument shows how far the stabilisation policy had yet to go.[3]

Thirdly, there were objections to the inclusion of particular commodities or pleas for the application of a lower rate of tax, generally on the ground of necessity or because reduction of consumption would lead to unemployment. Hollow-ware, bedding, industrial clothing and dress material were among the items cited. The Chancellor generally stood firm, knowing that hasty concessions might create awkward precedents eventually threatening the whole basis of the tax. But he gave way on clogs, rather as an item that had been overlooked when he exempted miners' protective boots. There was also agitation from quite different quarters for the exemption of books and newspapers, and here the Chancellor gave way on the ground that he did not wish to impose a tax on knowledge and culture or to hinder the dissemination of vital information in time of war.[4]

Lastly, there was pressure for the relief of particular classes of purchasers. Voluntary hospitals, other charitable organisations, and municipalities were put forward as groups which might be

---

[1] H. of C. Deb., Vol. 364, Col. 71.

[2] Mr. Glenvil Hall (*Ibid.* Vol. 364, Col. 1062).

[3] The Official Committee of 1939-40 had just mentioned a possible effect, through the cost-of-living index number, on wage-rates, but the point at this stage went unstressed and there is no evidence that it figured seriously in the pre-budget discussions.

[4] H. of C. Deb., Vol. 364, Col. 749. The organised agitation against the taxation of books and newspapers had provoked a scathing minute from the Customs House.

allowed to enjoy relief. These requests were rejected not merely on the ground of administrative complication, but also because it was shown that their expenditure on taxable goods was a relatively small part of their total expenditure.[1]

Other budget points raised in the House referred to the 100 per cent. excess profits tax, the problems of which were in fact being considered by the Chancellor's advisers throughout this period and were taken into account when the tax was amended in 1941.[2] There were pleas for the exemption of the 'living theatre' from the increases in the entertainments tax. The other tax increases were taken very quietly—there were even isolated suggestions that the tax increases had not gone far enough, and that compulsory saving should be introduced. But taking into account the arguments about the purchase tax it is difficult to say that the House of Commons yet faced the financial implications of the war: certainly the articulate quarters of the House were still a long way behind the Chancellor and his advisers. Throughout the debate there were many references to 'equality of sacrifice' for the war effort and to the desirability of precluding personal advantage, but positive and practical suggestions for determining equality of sacrifice and for achieving it were notably lacking.

To argue that opinion in the country was dragging along far behind that of Whitehall does not dispose of the argument that the Chancellor could and should have been much fiercer in his imposition of new burdens. A budget as nearly conventional as was this supplementary budget of July 1940 did not strike the imagination and evoke a widespread realisation that financial sacrifices must be on an altogether new scale, to match the altered complexion of the war effort.[3] The case was put to the Chancellor by Lord Catto. The country had been roused, by the Dunkirk evacuation and the collapse of France, to a sense of danger and the necessity for increased production. It was responding almost ferociously to the poster slogan 'Go to it!' 'Now', urged Lord Catto, 'comes the time to count the cost and provide for it before it is too late and we find that speed in one direction has brought ruin in another. Sacrifice and hardship there must be, in one way or another:[4] . . . . in my belief the country is ready for it: indeed

---

[1] H. of C. Deb., Vol. 364, Col. 1005.

[2] See pp. 87-90 below.

[3] cf. *The Times*, 25th July 1940. Commenting on the Chancellor's actual proposals, it complained of their 'wholly misplaced timidity, for the nation while impatient of waste, is ready to respond to bold and imaginative leadership in the field of finance as in every other field of the war'.

[4] Ministers were certainly open to criticism for failing to explain this point to the public. *The Economist* put it in a sentence in the course of its comments (27th July 1940, pp. 111-112) on the budget: 'Taxation does not impose sacrifice; it merely distributes equitably a volume of sacrifice that is determined by the prosecution of the war itself'.

the public are surprised that so far there has been only more prosperity, more employment and little sacrifice of any financial kind. The opportunity of your new budget should not be missed.' His own detailed plan was for a new flat rate tax (perhaps a shilling in the £) on all income of individuals, companies, corporations, etc., with a swingeing luxury tax 'to really "soak" people who in these times squander money'. An imaginative budget imposing burdens that matched the hour and was floated on a special publicity campaign would, Lord Catto urged, command popular support beyond anything that could be hoped for conventional proposals that 'cannot look like anything but the cold beef remains of yesterday's meal'.

It so happens that the detailed proposals Lord Catto put forward would have raised scarcely more additional revenue than the Chancellor's own proposals, especially when allowance was made for the concessions subsequently made by Lord Catto in modification of his original plan. Given this, and the fact that the Chancellor's actual budget did in the event command sufficient if grudging support, it may be argued that the Chancellor was right to turn down the Catto Plan, and to proceed with his own more humdrum proposals.[1] On the other hand, the spirit of the Catto proposals might well have been adopted for a budget to raise altogether more revenue than the increase of a mere £126 millions,[2] which was still leaving a gap of £2,100 millions between total revenue and the expenditure estimated at £3,500 millions.

The question therefore arises, whether this increase was adequate. The approach to the question of how much new revenue to raise was to some extent traditional—the Treasury estimated the deficit and then talked over with the Chancellor the possible tax changes with a view to getting as big a contribution towards the deficit as seemed politically possible. But even in the early days of the war there had been another approach—the Treasury had reckoned up the deficit, and then thought what was the maximum amount they could hope to collect by voluntary loans. The important cash relief enjoyed in the opening months as a result of gold losses during the summer of 1939 pointed the way to further development of national accounting—the adverse balance of international payments could be reckoned in as a contribution towards financing the deficit without generating inflationary pressure. One of the first lessons the new Chancellor had to learn—and one which he

---

[1] '. . . . its proposals were provisionally humdrum' said *The Times* leader on the following morning (24th July 1940).

[2] i.e. in the current year, £86 millions from increasing existing taxes plus £40 millions from the purchase tax. In a full year the increases would be worth £129 millions and the purchase tax £100 millions.

in his turn had to teach in Parliament—was this relevance of the balance of payments. He was therefore ready for Mr. Keynes's analysis, early in July 1940, of the size of the budget problem. Keynes's summary, for the year 1st July 1940—30th June 1941, was as follows:

	£ millions
Government expenditure	3,500
Sales of gold and foreign securities . . .	500
Increase of overseas balances in London . .	200
Receipts to certain Government funds . .	100
Depletion of private capital and stocks at home .	300
Accruals of taxation on the existing basis . .	1,500
Private savings by individuals and companies .	700
	3,300

The difference of £200 millions was the new tax revenue required, including the purchase tax. It might be increased, by expenditure in excess of £3,500 millions, or it might be diminished, by more rapid disbursements overseas. Keynes's provisional conclusion was, in his own words 'rather consoling', and he added as a postscript to his letter of 11th July, 'I do not believe that anything very dreadful would happen even if the amount of new taxes was somewhat less than the figure here suggested'.

Though this was not the first time the Treasury had seen an analysis of the budget problem in this form,[1] they had not readily at hand the facts for checking Mr. Keynes's figures. However, an examination was undertaken inside the Treasury[2] by Professor D. H. Robertson, who pointed out that Mr. Keynes depended on 'a series of estimates or guesses', plausible alternatives for which could be combined to give a resulting 'gap' (the amount of new taxation required) of £700 millions instead of £200 millions. This tickled Professor Robertson's academic taste as 'a pleasing illustration of how difficult it is to reach a convincing final figure by successive applications of the method of difference, when each successive item is open to doubt', but this was 'small consolation to those faced with the necessity for action', and evoked in the Treasury slightly acid reflections on Keynes's calculations, concluding, 'A doubt suggests itself whether his method of approach is as useful as might appear'. One senior Treasury official 'assumed

---

[1] The first part of the argument of 'How to Pay for the War' had revolved around such an analysis. The principal differences between the estimates given there and those Keynes now made were mainly due to '(1) a higher level of prices and national income, (2) a *much* higher foreign balance and (3) a considerably higher level of taxation'.

[2] Mr. Keynes had at this date become a member of the Consultative Council but was not yet settled inside the Treasury.

that the gap was of the character found by Mr. Robertson and not that found by Mr. Keynes'. There is no indication of any firm basis for this assumption: it was probably no more than the 'hunch' of a man who was familiar with the sort of figures Professor Robertson was using. It is easy to sympathise with Treasury doubts about the usefulness of this method of approach; at least it was important to recognise that a Keynesian budget would have to depend upon the solution of some highly intractable statistical problems. But it is also pertinent to ask why, if the 'inflationary gap' was thought to be of the order of £700 millions, proposals were not made for increases in taxation amounting to much more than £200 millions.

Which figure was nearer to the truth cannot be assessed by reference to the event, because the inflationary gap is necessarily closed by one means or another as we go along.[1] The figure, whether of £200 millions or £700 millions or something in between, has no counterpart in the subsequent statistics because it is simply a net measure of the extent to which the assumptions must be falsified by events. It is not even possible to argue from the actual course of inflation during the year to the inadequacy of taxation, for there are other pressures, to some extent independent of Government finance, making for inflation and these cannot be disentangled. What one can say is that during the twelve months or so after this supplementary budget of 1940, the value of the national product was rising much more rapidly than the numbers in employment; and that both the national product and prices were rising more rapidly than at any other period of the war except for 1939–40 when absorption of unemployment and the rise in import costs were special factors at work. There was even clearer evidence of inflation in the shop-shortages and queues, which were increasingly serious and were forcing the Government to consider major extensions of rationing. As regards the out-turn of Government finance, the deficit was mounting more rapidly than the Treasury expected: in the calendar years 1940 and 1941 it reached £2,115 millions and £2,822 millions respectively[2] and, while external disinvestment was relieving the strain by about £800 millions a year, reliance on the Floating Debt was very much greater than could be justified by reference to the external disinvestment alone: Ways and Means Advances increased by £111 millions, Treasury Deposit Receipts by £430 millions, and Treasury Bills by £784 millions.[3] These facts are not conclusive

---

[1] cf. above, p. 6, and below, pp. 58–9, and p. 72 *et seq.*

[2] *Statistical Digest of the War.* Table 185.

[3] Against these figures (which refer to the financial year 1940–41) must be set the decline of rather more than £100 millions in the total of Bank Advances. To some extent working capital was being financed by the Government (e.g. by progress payments on Government contracts) instead of by bank advances to private industry.

evidence, but they do all tend to support the view that the inflationary pressure in the economy was being appreciably aggravated in this period by the inadequacy of taxation, and comparison with other years suggests that the aggravation was probably greater in this period than at any other stage of the war. In short, the new taxation imposed by Sir Kingsley Wood in July 1940 was an altogether inadequate adjustment to the great acceleration of the war effort, and it might well have been better for the nation had he not left 'in reserve', as he put it in discussion with his advisers on 5th July, a further spectacular increase in the standard rate of income tax and greater tax liabilities for 'those near the foot of the income tax scale'.[1] Perhaps he sensed the dismay with which some of his Ministerial colleagues were going to greet the 10s. income tax in the following April.[2] At any rate, whatever the reasons for shirking the issue, 'the breath of realism' for which *The Economist* had hoped had resulted in little more than 'a few more turns of the old familiar screws'.[3]

---

[1] According to *The Economist* (27th July 1940, p. 126) a 10s. income tax 'was widely expected'.

[2] See below, p. 78 *et seq.*

[3] The last quotation is from the sharply critical leading article of *The Times* 25th July 1940, giving its second thoughts on the budget, under the title 'Shirking the Issue'.

CHAPTER III

BUDGET POLICY

II: THE 1941 BUDGET

(i)

The General Approach

SIR KINGSLEY WOOD's budget of 1941, introduced in the House of Commons on 7th April, was the fruit of longer and more exhaustive discussions in the Treasury than had preceded any other of the war budgets. Unlike its forerunners, it provided a systematic exposition of the fundamental problem of war finance and it included measures believed to be sufficient to cope with the problem. It was based on the conscious rejection of inflation as a solvent of Treasury difficulties. This rejection was due not merely to dislike of the social consequences of inflation, but also to the view that the conditions of wage-bargaining precluded all possibility that inflationary finance might force consumption downward and so extract from the community the essential volume of material resources.[1] The alternative adopted by Sir Kingsley Wood was to aim at the other extreme: cost of living subsidies were to be used in order to prevent, as far as possible, any 'cost inflation', and taxation (including forced saving) was to be pressed, ideally to the point of absorbing all excess purchasing power, so as to minimise the risk of a 'demand inflation'. This policy implied a new approach to the budget arithmetic. In the first place, allowance had to be made for the subsidies necessary to stabilise the cost of living and then, on the assumption that this would allow approximate stabilisation of gross incomes, the total pressure of money demand had to be estimated. Subtracting from this amount the estimated value (at ruling prices) of goods and services coming on the market, an 'inflationary gap' was arrived at. This gap represented the amount of excess demand that had to be siphoned off by new fiscal measures if the assumption of market equilibrium was not to be falsified by rising prices or intolerable queueing or

---

[1] As Mr. Keynes wrote: 'The traditional way out, which we adopted in 1917 . . . . is to let prices rise . . . . To-day we have cut ourselves off from this expedient because many groups of wages are linked to the cost of living so that they go up automatically when prices go up'.

regimentation.[1] The 1941 budget was different from the earlier budgets not only because it arrived in this novel way at the necessary amount of new taxation, but also because the Chancellor had the courage to impose new measures estimated to close the gap.

Besides this novelty of approach, which incidently implied the transformation of the budget speech into a comprehensive survey of the national economy, the 1941 budget was noteworthy for the acceptance of the principle that forced saving could make a net addition to the Government's resources and a net reduction of the inflationary pressure; and for an overhaul of the excess profits tax. On both these matters, as well as on the prior question of the formulation of the budget problem, discussions were already proceeding in the previous July when the supplementary budget was introduced. They began in fact as soon as the new régime—including not merely the new Chancellor but also his unusual advisers—was settled in authority. The 1941 budget, the cornerstone of Britain's internal financial policy, was the manifestation in the financial sphere of the national change of heart that marked the summer of 1940.

(ii)
Price Stabilisation

Though it was only in the budget of 1941 that Government policy on prices became an integral part of budget policy, there had been great anxiety about the movement of prices ever since the first days of the war. Then a combination of circumstances—the depreciation of the pound from about \$4.68 to \$4.03, the speculative rise in world prices, the rise in freights and the incidence of war risks insurance—had produced a sharp rise in the landed cost of imports, and there had also been small rises in internal costs, especially where A.R.P. costs were heavy. In order to secure a continued flow of essential goods into consumption, price increases sufficient to cover these cost increases had to be permitted. On the other hand, two important considerations pointed to restriction of price increases: public feeling against profiteering (a legacy from 1914–20) and the dangers of an inflationary spiral developing from 'cost of living' increases of wages. The first of these had been the main consideration dictating the Maximum Price Orders that were imposed in the earliest

---

[1] Mr. Keynes had convinced the Chancellor that increasing shop-shortages (the result of price control while demand continued to rise) must inevitably lead to comprehensive rationing.

days.[1] The second became impelling only as, in the course of the autumn, the rise in import costs penetrated to the cost of living, and particularly to the official index number of the cost of living. The question came to a head when the coal miners demanded wage increases to compensate for the rising cost of living, and responsibility for a decision was pushed by the coal owners on to the Government.[2] If there were to be no increases in the cost of living without compensating increases in wages, physical shortages would have to take the whole weight in enforcing the reduction in consumption—which was another way of saying that there could be no adequate development of the war effort.[3] But this was a matter not at all understood by the workers' leaders,[4] though the War Cabinet was advised that in the miners' present leaders it had 'a relatively reasonable set of men' to deal with. The major issue of industrial peace was therefore at stake and the War Cabinet decided that industrial peace must come first. A sufficient rise in the price of coal, allowing increased wages, was conceded, but the War Cabinet insisted that the 'cost of living' justification should be soft-pedalled and forgotten as soon as possible; and it decided also that early steps must be taken to educate the Trade Union movement in the compulsions of war economy.

Major forces were thus at work in both directions—tending to restrict and tending to encourage increases of prices. The authorities saw some small hope of reconciliation of this conflict in the treatment of overhead costs. All the weight of trade custom favoured the maintenance of fixed percentage margins at various stages of processing and distribution and, if these had been allowed to stand, the increases in importation costs would have been fully and rapidly reflected in the cost of living. Intermediaries naturally pressed for maintenance of their percentages, partly on the ground that they, too, had special war costs—for example, A.R.P. costs—and partly on the ground that higher absolute margins

---

[1] For control of food prices, see R. J. Hammond, *Food*: Vol. 1, *The Growth of Policy*, in this series (H.M.S.O. 1951) Chapter VII; and for control of prices of raw materials, J. Hurstfield, *The Control of Raw Materials*, in this series (H.M.S.O. 1953), Chapter XXIII; for the subsequent development of price control policy generally, see *Civil Industry and Trade*, *op. cit.*, pp. 77-86. For reasons discussed in the above passage, the Treasury always took the lead in determining price controls and co-ordinating them into a single policy.

[2] For a fuller account, see W. K. Hancock and M. M. Gowing, *British War Economy*, in this series (H.M.S.O. 1949), pp. 163-4.

[3] This fundamental point was clearly put to the Chancellor in a letter from Lord Stamp in November 1939 in which he emphasised that this was the first lesson for the masses to learn from Keynes's propaganda, though he regretted that Keynes had somewhat confused discussion by rushing into remedies.

[4] A letter from Mr. Ernest Bevin to Mr. Seebohm Rowntree in December 1939, forwarded to the Chancellor through Lord Stamp, showed this all too clearly: 'My time', wrote Mr. Bevin, 'has been taken up in trying to get wages commensurate with the cost of living. I am determined to try to keep them up to a proper level . . . . . . our people . . . . . will revolt against the depression of their standards'.

(fixed percentages of higher basic costs) were necessary to compensate for lower turnover. The official attitude to these claims was not altogether consistent. In some trades—particularly the food trades—the need to maintain the existing machinery of distribution was admitted as an overriding necessity and the claim for the customary percentage, or at least something very close to it, was allowed. More generally under the Prices of Goods Act traders were permitted to maintain their absolute level of profits in the face of reduced turnover. But in some important directions the Treasury argued, and the Departments argued to traders, that the reduction in turnover must be reflected in reduced costs of handling: even if some of the items could not be reduced, such frills as advertising and expensive systems of delivery must be completely eliminated. Some simplification of the machinery of distribution must release real resources for the war effort, and the trimming of percentage margins was the Treasury's way of inducing this release. This was a point little understood by traders or indeed by many of the administrators who had to negotiate with the traders. The Treasury's insistence on it often appeared as an argument over a few thousand pounds where millions were at stake on the whole business, and this tended to encourage the belief that the Treasury cared more for pence than for pounds. Actually the Treasury line on this matter derived from its anti-inflation policies, in which not merely millions of pounds but the viability of the whole war economy was at stake.

Another aspect of price policy on which the authorities were confused, more confused perhaps than on any other aspect, was its direct impact on the budgetary position. At this stage—and in the preparatory stage when some thought had been given to this matter—attention to the budget aspect meant attention to direct effects on Government receipts and Government outlay. Clearly, in so far as the Government was a buyer of goods and services, the budget strain was increased by rises in prices, and the Government had a direct interest in keeping prices down. On the other hand, the Government had become a trader, on a very large scale, in certain foods and raw materials, not all of which would go into absolutely essential final products. If in this trading it could make a profit, this would relieve the budget strain; at the very least, it must avoid losses, since these would impose additional strain upon the Chancellor in his search for the money to pay for the war. In the preparatory period concern over the strain upon the Treasury as paymaster had been a dominant view, and the general presumption was therefore established that the trading Departments must fix prices on the basis of full coverage of costs.

From the nature of the case, the Government-traded goods

were largely imported goods, the landed cost of which had risen sharply. The principal exceptions were home-produced foods, but here also costs were rising, as a result of Government measures to encourage home production. The cost-covering principle was therefore driving the Departments into steep increases for the goods they were selling, in uncomfortable contrast to the official policy of restraining increases in the prices charged by private traders.

Examination of some of the more extreme cases—notably timber and woodpulp—led to establishment of the rule that the war-time cost increases should be dampened by averaging the war-time costs with those at which stocks had been acquired in the preceding months. Where these stocks were still in private hands, special Treasury Charges Orders were made, imposing on the private stocks a levy the proceeds of which were used to moderate the rise in the price of Government stocks.[1] Thus the principle of cost-coverage was temporarily reconciled with the general policy of moderating the war-time rise in prices, a policy reinforced by growing realisation of the importance of holding the wage-line while the Trade Unions were being educated.

Unfortunately the inconsistencies between these various aims were sharpened as the weeks went by, and further consideration led to the emergence of a 'two-decker' price structure, in which cost of living items would be kept down as far as possible while less essential items would become much dearer. This suggestion found favour from two points of view. A senior Treasury official briefing the Chancellor on 3rd October 1939,[2] after referring to the 35 per cent. increase in the cost of Australian wool, wrote:

> The Government must sell wholesale at an increased price accordingly or else it will make immense losses. That would be an intolerable result having regard to the enormous burden already placed on us by the war. Government control schemes must show at least a modest profit. It is very true that we must have regard to the effect on the cost of living. But we shall not be able to keep down the price of goods which enter into the cost of living of the working classes unless we are free to raise prices substantially elsewhere. A policy of low flat rate prices for all the uses that can be made of a commodity is clearly wrong.[3]

The economists, while supporting this budgetary argument,

---

[1] Maximum Price Orders for goods entirely in private hands imposed similar principles. The 'Charges Orders', being in the nature of taxes, required confirmation by resolution of the House of Commons.

[2] The occasion was a Ministerial discussion on maximum wholesale prices of raw materials.

[3] It will be appreciated that wool prices entered appreciably into the clothing component of the cost-of-living index. That the official was nevertheless prepared at this point to propose a substantial increase in wool prices emphasises the length to which this school of thought was prepared to push the 'two-decker' price policy.

added that a policy of trying to keep down all prices indiscriminately was also undesirable from the broader point of view of the conservation of real resources. Higher prices for unessential commodities would tend to choke off demand and so to release resources for war production. To be effective for this purpose, price increases must be sharp and substantial: a series of smaller rises at frequent intervals would tend to stimulate buying, and would also be apt to convey the impression of a succession of failures.

This last argument had a broader application, and appreciation of its force helped to give a new direction to policy. The attempt to keep prices generally down as low as possible had important initial advantages from the wage-bargaining aspect and in allaying public fears of profiteering, but it could be no more than a temporary expedient. Government trading Departments were then given new instructions to avoid losses and 'in appropriate conditions' to aim at a substantial profit to assist in the conduct of the war. The intention at first was that these 'appropriate conditions' should be primarily the absence of appreciable connection with the working class cost of living, and though Departments did sometimes consider other conditions relevant,[1] the principal implication of this qualification was the introduction of the two-decker price structure. It is notable that at this date (late 1939) there was no suggestion of subsidising the lower price level; the position was that the higher price level should bring some budgetary relief. The prevailing theory—developed most clearly by Mr. Henderson—was that the economy would in effect be divided into two parts, the one closely controlled, with full rationing and low prices, the other relatively free, with more sharply rising prices but no assurance of maintenance of supply. It was not a long step from this to the stabilisation policy of 1941 and later years.

The first decision deliberately to subsidise food prices for the sake of wage stability was taken on 15th December 1939 by the Ministerial Committee on Economic Policy. The Ministry of Food had advised that rising costs indicated the need to raise the prices of bread and flour, meat, butter, cheese, milk and bacon, and that the increases would raise the Ministry of Labour's cost-of-living index number by 7.4 points (about $4\frac{1}{2}$ per cent.). In the absence of these increases, a trading loss at the rate of £60 millions a year would be incurred. The Treasury advised that it was strongly opposed to any permanent food subsidies such as the bread subsidy in the earlier war, but suggested that the price increases should be temporarily deferred (a period of six weeks was mentioned) in order to avoid prejudice to the discussions between Ministers

---

[1] e.g. It was thought advisable to minimise price increases of raw materials going mainly into Government contracts.

and the National Joint Advisory Council. The Committee concluded that 'the present policy of avoiding any appreciable increase to the consumer of the price of controlled foods should be maintained for a limited period, in order not to prejudice the discussions in regard to wages and prices proceeding through the National Joint Advisory Council, notwithstanding that this course would involve a loss to the Exchequer'.

The fact that Exchequer losses were being incurred for the sake of price stability was at first kept secret, but in January, on Treasury initiative, the matter was reviewed by the War Cabinet and the House of Commons was informed on 31st January 1940 of the broad (though not rigid) stabilisation of the prices of certain staple foodstuffs.[1] The War Cabinet also decided that some relief for the Exchequer should be obtained by monopoly profits on imports of unessential foodstuffs, that the outlook for fuel prices should be reviewed and that a standard clothing scheme should be investigated.

During the next few months this subsidy policy remained on a temporary basis, but discussion only served to show how dangerous its removal would be. By March 1940, it was believed that the Chancellor's talks with the Trade Union leaders were having some effect, but the possibility of a definite bargain seemed as remote as ever. If wage claims on cost of living grounds were forsworn, there would still be many other grounds—levelling-up, scarcity of skills, etc.—on which claims might reasonably be based, and in any case the Union leaders were not constitutionally able to bind their rank and file. A 'bargain' might in the event merely bind the Government, which would have to pay subsidies on an ever-increasing scale. The impossibility of any undertaking on the workers' side was from time to time mentioned as an argument against continuance of the subsidy, and Lord Stamp believed in April that the increasing tightness of the labour market so favoured the workers that the situation was past praying for. This was, of course, in the days of the 'phoney war', when there was still sufficient belief in a short war to enable all parties to cling to temporary positions. But with every month the labour leaders' understanding of the position was increasing: the Keynes propaganda on 'How to Pay for the War' was helping. Those officials most competent to judge the situation reported that the subsidies were helping more and more, in that the Union leaders were thereby given a cogent point to make to the rank and file. Ministers recognised this, and saw that there could be no revision of their January decision against pressing for a formal bargain.

---

[1] H. of C. Deb., Vol. 356, Cols. 1154-6. The War Cabinet decision referred to an experimental period of six months. This limit was not mentioned in the public announcement, though the Chancellor used the phrase, 'for a time at least'. It seems likely that officials did not seriously envisage any possibility of abandoning the policy.

In the summer of 1940, Ministerial support for the subsidies policy was reinforced by the accession of Labour leaders (especially Mr. Ernest Bevin) to office, and in August the War Cabinet resolved that 'the prices of essential foodstuffs should be kept down by subsidy in order to secure cheap food, to restrain a rise in the cost-of-living index figure and to prevent wages rising. The relative pressure on the Treasury from expenditure on food subsidies and from demands for increased wages and allowances shall be the subject of constant review'. Nevertheless, the pressure on the Treasury as paymaster was responsible for further rises in food prices, reflecting increased costs, in August and September, though by manipulating the incidence of subsidies on particular foods the effect on the index of these price rises was minimised.[1] The idea of standard cheap clothing was under discussion but was not materialising in time to prevent rising clothing prices as textile costs rose, and the new purchase tax threatened further rises.

The position in the latter part of 1940 was thus that Ministers, trusting in the effect of the policy in restraining wage demands, supported the subsidies strongly enough to allow the total sum to increase substantially,[2] but there was still enough fear of the burden on the Treasury to preclude any comprehensive or consistent stabilisation.[3] The policy was, however, gaining hold, and the pre-budget discussions necessarily forced some clarification, since the Chancellor would have in his budget to commit himself to provision of a certain sum. Acting in close consultation with Mr. Bevin, now Minister of Labour, Sir Kingsley Wood decided not merely to accept the subsidy policy but to make it an integral part of his budget plan. This was to be a 'stabilisation budget', and henceforward the subsidies were to be based on a clear and avowed principle, instead of a mere drifting from a temporising expedient. In his budget speech the Chancellor said outright that he had included in his estimated expenditure a margin to provide for important extensions, 'a considerably increased burden . . . in order to prevent or minimise the impact of increased costs, particularly of imports and of transport, on the prices of essential goods and services, apart from any increases in their prices rendered inevitable by further increases in wage rates'.

---

[1] cf. *Food, op. cit.*, Vol. 1, pp. 182-3.

[2] The rate of trading loss in the Ministry of Food rose from about £55 millions a year early in 1940 to about £100 millions a year early in 1941.

[3] Mr. Harrod has (in his *Life of John Maynard Keynes*, p. 493) referred to Keynes's inclusion of price stabilisation for a 'minimum standard' in his *How to Pay for the War* (especially pp. 33-34), but Mr. Harrod does more than justice to the Government in adding that 'the policy of subsidies was begun before Keynes published his views'. Only over the course of several months did the subsidy policy become finally entrenched as a permanent part of the Government's war-time economic policy.

He gave no undertaking to stabilise any particular price, but would 'endeavour to prevent any further rise of the cost of living index number, apart from minor seasonal changes, above the present range of 125–130 in terms of the pre-war level'. Steps had already been taken to cover increases in shipping freights, and measures for averting further increases in railway charges were under discussion. Fuel and light charges would also be covered by this policy, although electricity charges happened to be outside the official cost-of-living index. All this the Chancellor put forward in the hope of creating 'conditions which will enable the wages situation to be held about where it now is'.[1]

The stabilisation undertaking thus given by the Government was not the counterpart to any formal undertaking by the Trade Unions, but there was an understanding on the part of the Labour Party leaders in the Government that their influence would be exercised in favour of restraint. The Chancellor did specifically abstain from promising to prevent increases of prices 'rendered inevitable by further increases in wage-rates', though he wisely did not forecast his action should such increases become appreciable. In official discussions the possibility of considerable increase in the subsidies for this as well as other reasons was clearly foreseen.

The 'stabilisation range' of 25 to 30 per cent. above pre-war prices was subject to the qualification 'apart from minor seasonal changes', though in later years the Government thought it necessary to force all the seasonal movements into the range. It is notable that stabilising action was not to be narrowly confined to commodities included in the official index number, though its subsequent broadening to cover an appreciably wider range of goods was not implicit in anything the Chancellor said on this occasion.

The Parliamentary reception of this extraordinarily important announcement was not by any means enthusiastic. Mr. Pethick-Lawrence was mildly approving[2] but another prominent Labour speaker[3] thought it too late, and that its chances of success were already prejudiced by the purchase tax. Among the few other speakers who displayed interest, Sir George Schuster[4] urged that price stabilisation 'must be balanced by a complementary wages policy'. This idea that there should be some compulsory stabilisation of wages as a *quid pro quo* had been widely canvassed

---

[1] H. of C. Deb., Vol. 370, Cols. 1322-4.
[2] H. of C. Deb., Vol. 370, Col. 1442.
[3] Mr. Barnes, *ibid.*, Cols. 1362-3.
[4] *Ibid.*, Col. 1491.

outside Government circles in the preceding year, and in January 1941 the Editor of *The Times* had urged the Prime Minister to exercise, in the field of wage control, the compulsory powers already bestowed upon the Government.[1] The idea had been fully explored within official circles over a long period, but had been virtually abandoned as impracticable before the entry of the Labour leaders into the Government. After that event, the official view was that anything beyond what could be achieved by the informal (but weighty) influence of Mr. Bevin was not worth attempting.[2] By April 1941 this view had gained acceptance more widely, and *The Times* of 8th April, rather than Mr. Geoffrey Dawson and Sir George Schuster in their letters of 8th January and 8th April, represented informed opinion when it commented thus on 'A Stabilising Budget': 'For its most important single proposal is the Chancellor's promise to stabilise, by subsidy where necessary, the prices of all the essential goods entering into the cost of living and also the cost of essential services such as coal, gas and electricity. It is an extremely bold step to assume a liability of which the amount cannot be estimated; but the promise is essential if wages are to be stabilised; and it imposes a great moral obligation on all concerned to refrain from pressing for wage increases which would destroy the stability of our economic system thus engendered'.

The ultimate liability was, as *The Times* emphasised, beyond estimation. The Chancellor in fact allowed £200 millions for it on this occasion, and this figure was taken into the arithmetic on which the other budget proposals were based.[3]

(iii)

The Size and Arithmetic of the Problem

From the very beginning of the war, taxation policy had been based on the view that while the use of borrowed money as a supplement to taxation was not necessarily inflationary, deficit finance became inflationary if the borrowing exceeded some natural flow of voluntary saving. While the problem was formulated in these terms Chancellors could be expected to scrape round the

---

[1] This was in a private letter of 8th January 1941 in reply to a letter from the Prime Minister, asking for elucidation of the rather hurried leader that had just appeared in *The Times*.

[2] There were important discussions (ministerial as well as official) on wages policy at the end of 1941, but no change resulted. See *British War Economy, op. cit.*, pp. 338-9.

[3] The figure was not quoted in the budget speech, though it was used in preliminary drafting. It included the non-food as well as the food items. In the 1942 budget speech the Chancellor reported that £125 millions had actually been required.

barrel of the capital market and to impose such increases of taxation as appeared essential to fill any remaining gap between Government receipts and expenditure. Alternatively, the procedure in preparing the early war budgets may be described in these terms: the Chancellors imposed tax increases as sharp as they thought the public would stomach, and then hoped that the amounts they would have to squeeze out of the capital market would not exceed the supply of voluntary saving. The experts did however try to assess the volume of saving and so to encourage the Chancellors to aim at one figure rather than another in imposing new taxation.

The approach adopted by Sir Kingsley Wood in 1941 was a logical development and not a reversal of these earlier fumblings. The development was twofold: there was clarification of the theory of inflationary finance, and there was acceptance of a new statistical foundation for the gap that had to be closed by new taxation. The clarification of theory dates from Keynes's *Times* articles on 'How to Pay for the War' in the autumn of 1939: what was now achieved was its acceptance at the top level of the Treasury and by a Chancellor who was willing to base his budget speech frankly upon this new approach. Upon this theoretical foundation the actual budget arithmetic was based: on the assumption of a given national income, the amounts of voluntary saving and of revenue on the previous basis of taxation were estimated, and the remaining gap between total money demand and the value of goods and services becoming available was taken as the amount of new taxation to be imposed. Acceptance of the theory was more general than was confidence in the arithmetic. We have already seen how open to criticism were Mr. Keynes's first calculations for the Chancellor.[1] Although as the theory won acceptance efforts were made to secure more reliable data, there was still an uncomfortably large element of conjecture and Mr. Henderson among others remained sceptical of the arithmetic,[2] although he had been among the very first to see budgetary problems in the context of the balance of purchasing power against availability of real resources. The Chancellor did, in spite of this scepticism among his advisers, in the end accept the Keynesian arithmetic. His choice was probably dictated by a conviction that the situation was slipping out of control[3] and that the rather stern fiscal measures indicated by the calculated 'gap' were 'about right'. Even in later years, when the statistics had been greatly improved, those in authority never

[1] See pp. 55-6 above.

[2] Minute of 24th March 1941.

[3] cf. *The Economist*, 4th January 1941: 'One by one, the brakes are being taken off, and the 1941 problem is that of limiting inflation, not avoiding it'.

came to impute precision where in fact only rough and ready answers were available, and the exact burdens placed upon the taxpayers continued to be the outcome of the collective judgment of a handful of men depending in quite large measure upon common sense and the 'hunch' that eludes analysis. What was new in 1941 was the universal acceptance of the Keynesian formulation and the existence of Keynesian arithmetic as one weighty element—but only one element—in the emergence of the decisive 'hunches'.

This new approach to the dimensions of the budget problem brought out clearly the fact that the expenditure outside the United Kingdom being covered by the sale of assets, by the running-up of debts, or by mutual aid, was irrelevant to the immediate problem of domestic finance. The rapidly growing adverse balance on external account was automatically covered by depletion of international assets and by incurring new liabilities abroad, including among these new liabilities the vague obligations of the lend-lease arrangements as well as the more precise obligations involved in the accumulation of Sterling Area balances in London. The only theoretical qualification of this general rule was the domestic finance that had to be provided by the Exchange Equalisation Account when privately-owned international assets (such as American securities) were taken over for sale or mortgage abroad, but it was reasonable to assume that the private owners of these securities would treat the sterling compensation as a capital transaction, so that the money would through one channel or another come back to the Government without exerting any pressure in the markets for goods and services. This exclusion of the foreign balance from the budget problem did not imply any failure to consider with the utmost care the future commitments involved in overseas purchases, but merely that these grave considerations could be left out of account when current taxation policy was in question. The budget had in fact ceased to serve its peace-time purpose of providing finance for all Government activities and had become solely an engine for preserving, in the face of colossal defence expenditure at home, reasonable stability in the value of money and adequate incentives consistently with a distribution of the burden that people would accept as broadly just.

This exclusion of the adverse foreign balance, by eliminating the huge increase in overseas supplies now pouring in, made the dimensions of the budget problem look reasonably manageable.[1]

---

[1] In so far as the adverse international balance represented goods for which consumers had to pay (as distinct from supplies finally absorbed by the Government), the pressure of purchasing power was being absorbed and the broader budgetary problem of stabilisation was being lessened.

Writing in September 1940, Mr. Keynes set out the basic figures thus:

	1st year of War	*£ millions Current Rate*	*Hypothetical Prospective Rate*
Total expenditure out of Exchequer	2,600	3,500	4,200
Adverse foreign balance	400	800	1,200
Domestic expenditure	2,200	2,700	3,000
Accruing revenue on past and present basis	1,300	1,700	1,800
Balance to be met otherwise	900	1,000	1,200

This 'balance to be met otherwise' had in the first year of war, he thought, been covered by miscellaneous Government sources, £100 millions, and certain capital sources, £150–250 millions, leaving £550 millions—£650 millions as provided by voluntary savings (private and institutional). This volume of savings and yield of taxation had he believed been achieved with only a negligible amount of inflation.[1] He justified this view by reference to pre-war estimates that about £400 millions was saved out of £4,300 millions aggregate of personal and institutional incomes after deducting taxes. Since then, savings had been pushed up by more conservative dividend distributions by companies, and by war economies and war savings propaganda, as well as by the rise in total incomes. The current rate of new savings might be put at £650 millions. He could see no reason to expect increases in the sources other than savings, for covering the 'balance to be met otherwise', and it followed that 'a further £250 millions to £350 millions' would have to be raised either by taxes and compulsory saving or by additional spontaneous saving. How far could this last item be expected to increase without a further inflation of the total money incomes?

Analysing the total voluntary savings, Mr. Keynes considered that about half, say £300 millions, was institutional (company reserves etc.) and contractual (building societies' instalments and insurance premiums etc.), in which no appreciable increase could be expected. If the gap (£250 millions to £350 millions) was to be

---

[1] cf. *The Economist* 4th January 1941: 'The degree of inflation hitherto experienced has been amazingly small'.

filled by an increase in voluntary savings, the spontaneous private savings (i.e. excluding the institutional and contractual) would have to be virtually doubled. 'An increase of this magnitude is surely quite beyond the powers of War Savings propaganda'. Clearly Sir John Simon's 'voluntarism on trial' was going to fail now, even if it had been almost strong enough to bear the earlier strains.

To arrive at the figures for new taxation, it was not enough to subtract from the £250 millions to £350 millions whatever might be expected by way of increase in spontaneous savings, for further taxation (or compulsory saving) would have an adverse effect on spontaneous savings, though it need not greatly affect institutional and contractual saving. Mr. Keynes thought that savings might fall by £100 millions or even £150 millions as a result of collecting a further £300 millions by compulsory methods. War Savings propaganda was already doing its utmost and would be powerless to prevent a fall of this order of magnitude. Mr. Keynes therefore concluded that 'the dimension of the prospective budget problem is of the order of £400 millions'.

This was in September 1940, and at that date there were substantial elements of guesswork in Keynes's calculations. In the six months before Budget Day 1941 all these guesses were open to comment at the top level in the Treasury, and much effort was directed to providing a firmer basis. Particularly the newly-established Central Statistical Branch of the War Cabinet Offices made a systematic survey—the first such official survey—of national income data, and the fruits of their researches were published in the first National Income White Paper when the Chancellor eventually opened his budget. In February 1941 the main tables that were to appear in the White Paper were, in draft form, circulating in the Treasury, and it was in the light of the considerable detail available in these that the final view was formed of the amount of new taxation to be imposed. Net domestic expenditure by the Government was put at £3,700 millions, this figure having been shown to be consistent not only with Departmental estimates, and the current rate of expenditure, but also with the financial effects of the likely changes in employment—a cross-check that was rendered possible by the statistical analysis just becoming available in the War Cabinet Offices. Taxation on the existing basis was estimated at £1,636 millions, so that the amount to be found from other sources was now much larger than Mr. Keynes had guessed in September. The extra-budgetary receipts of Government Departments were increasing as premiums under the War Damage Act fell due, and as employment increased, and they could now be put at £250 millions. Unspent depreciation

allowances, sinking funds etc. were assessed with some confidence
at £300 millions, out of £440 millions gross. The reduction of
stocks—since it involved absorption of purchasing power without
creating further incomes—had in the earlier years been a great
source of easement, but as shops and warehouses emptied further
relief must inexorably dwindle. For a short time, however, there
might still be further squeezing of stocks, and £100 millions were
taken into the account under this head. Savings of local authorities
and institutions were put at £250 millions. The total of 'impersonal
savings' or 'accruals on capital account' could therefore be taken
as about £900 millions.[1] Personal savings had undoubtedly been
rising and the final budget estimates took the current level as
£700 millions, to cover both what Keynes had called the
'contractual' and the 'spontaneous' personal savings.

  Thus in the last weeks before the budget the basic statistics
took the shape:

	£ millions
Domestic expenditure	3,700
Revenue on current basis	1,636
Impersonal savings, including depreciation accruals etc.	900
Personal savings	700
Total 'finance'	3,236

leaving about £500 millions as 'the gap'. In September 1940
Mr. Keynes had guessed the figure as 'of the order of £400 millions',
and in the first weeks of 1941 figures of £350 millions to £450
millions were usually mentioned. At the last stage the figure of
£500 millions, calculated as above by Keynes, was finally accepted
even by those who distrusted the detailed components of the
Keynes calculations, and it was this figure of £500 millions that
was presented by Sir Kingsley Wood to his Ministerial colleagues
as the amount he had to find.

  This term 'the gap', or more fully 'the inflationary gap', to
which the figure of £500 millions was thus attached, became the
commonplace of budget discussions outside as well as inside the
Treasury. Just what this gap meant was not as widely understood.
In presenting his case to the War Cabinet, the Chancellor was
content to explain that if this excess were not taken up by increased
taxation, rationing, etc. the dangers of inflation would be greatly
aggravated. But inside the Treasury the economists had taken
great care fully to explain its significance, and the Chancellor

---

[1] i.e. £250 + 300 + 100 + 250 millions. 'Impersonal savings' were in these calculations net of such private investment as was then taking place.

himself was among those who learned that this gap was one that could not emerge in the event but would be closed automatically by an inflationary rise in the national income, pulling up revenue and savings, if deliberate action was not taken to close it by increasing taxation and savings without inflation of the national income.[1] It was by preaching this doctrine that Mr. Keynes secured in the Chancellor's mind the vital link between the stabilisation subsidies and the taxation proposals. A stable cost of living that would make wage increases unimportant and a taxation policy that removed excess purchasing power would remove the two sources of inflation. Failure to stabilise the cost of living would render the taxation proposals inadequate, and failure to absorb excess purchasing power would make it difficult to hold the cost of living down. The two sides of budget policy thus stood or fell together; the budget of 1941 was an integral whole, of which Sir Kingsley Wood later spoke, with justifiable pride, as 'my stabilisation budget'.

'Something in the neighbourhood of £500 millions' was, then, the figure which the Chancellor put to his colleagues and the country as the measure of the problem. How much of this would be covered by rising personal savings? Latest reports from the War Savings Movement were encouraging, and the full effect of personal commitments to save through deduction from the weekly pay packet was yet to be felt. Moreover, things in the shops were becoming fewer, and as people found shopping for inessential goods more difficult they might be expected to become more responsive to savings propaganda. The budget itself could be—and was—made the occasion for another spurt of savings propaganda. Altogether, the Chancellor decided to assume that personal savings would increase by some £200 to £300 millions. He decided therefore to aim at £250 millions in new taxation.

The immediate reactions in Parliament and the Press were by no means as understanding as the Chancellor might have expected. There were again complaints that the total of expenditure was too low,[2] complaints that were not entirely apposite in a budget debate. There were vague complaints about the estimates of savings—and welcome indications that the distinction between savings and the purchase of savings certificates was at last appreciated. Apart from a few Labour speakers[3], there was little appreciation of the Chancellor's general approach to the size of

---

[1] The inflation of the national income could be (and in the event was) slowed down by rationing, shop-shortages, etc., which caused people to save more than they intended.

[2] e.g. by Mr. Lipson and Mr. Clement Davies (H. of C. Deb., Vol. 370, Col. 1637 and Vol. 371, Col. 1623), and *The Economist* (12th April 1941, p. 477).

[3] Mr. Barnes (H. of C. Deb., Vol. 370, Col. 1362), Mr. Pethick-Lawrence (Col. 1439) and Mr. Wedgwood (Col. 1505).

the problem. The *Manchester Guardian*[1] strongly objected to the exclusion of overseas expenditure—the result was, it argued, 'a half-revealed budget'—and this complaint was also made in the Commons.[2]

The Economist,[3] however, welcomed unreservedly the Chancellor's attempt 'to arrive at the amount of new taxation to be imposed, not on the principle of "think of a number", but by working out the economic need for new taxes', and devoted a separate leading article to the National Income White Paper. *The Times*[4] took the same view: 'The Chancellor has made an honest attempt to evaluate the present inflationary "gap" between domestic expenditure and the receipts from taxation and genuine savings on the basis of the best statistical evidence of the elements in the national income; he has made that evidence available for all to see; and he has consciously imposed sufficient taxation to close the gap'.

This is a judgment that eventually commanded general understanding and acceptance, and the precedent created by Sir Kingsley Wood on this occasion was followed not only in the remaining war budgets, but also in those of the post-war years. The new budget approach had come to stay: meanwhile, it implied that the Chancellor had set himself the task of raising £250 millions of new taxation on top of the £1,636 millions expected from existing taxes.

(iv)

The New Taxation Proposals

In looking for the required £250 millions, the Chancellor from the first favoured a simple clear-cut burden. Taxes on 'frills' were possibilities that had been thoroughly explored both by his predecessor and by himself in his early months of office. The arguments in favour of concentration on direct taxation were conclusive. The purchase tax had only just settled into the house— though its chief administrator could already say, 'The present position of the purchase tax affords another example of the ironic silence which often follows upon a heated controversy'—and no reliance on commodity taxes could now disguise the compulsion

---

[1] 8th April 1941, article 'A Half-Revealed Budget', by the Financial Editor.

[2] Sir John Wardlaw Milne (H. of C. Deb., Vol. 371, Col. 1632) doubted whether it was right to assume that the sale of dollar securities had no inflationary effect (cf. p. 69 above).

[3] 12th April 1941, p. 475.

[4] 8th April 1941 (City Notes).

to tax directly and heavily the mass of the people. Moreover, there was the stabilisation aspect to consider. The purchase tax had added rather more than 3 points to the cost of living index number, and further measures with this effect would simply force additions to the subsidies bill which the Chancellor had now committed himself to footing as an integral part of his budget policy. There was much agitation outside the Treasury[1] in favour of a heavy tax on personal services, as a form of inessential consumption that eluded earlier taxation. Detailed examination showed however that a services tax comprehensive enough to raise important revenue would have to cover many services that were obviously essential to at least a large proportion of their consumers—housing and transport services, heating, water, hotels, restaurants, etc. If an attempt were to be made at discrimination between the inessential stay in a hotel and the enforced night's lodging of a weary war worker, an army of officials and a deluge of hard cases would be inevitable, while the yield would be whittled down to a mere fraction of the sum that was being sought.

There was, in short, nothing for it but a sharp increase in direct taxation, and a Chancellor preparing a fundamentally honest budget was willing to take the plunge. The real question was of the precise shape of the new direct taxation. There were great attractions in some novelty, a special war tax supplementary to the established income tax and surtax. Two widely-canvassed suggestions were (1) a tax analogous to the excess profits tax, whereby war-time *increases* in incomes of workers should be partly creamed off, just as war-time increases in profits were creamed off by E.P.T.; and (2) a flat war tax on all incomes—something much simpler than income tax, and so named as to emphasise that it was the special contribution everyone was to make towards the cost of the war, a contribution that would automatically disappear at the end of the war. The former suggestion was pressed mainly on grounds of equity—as between profit-earners and wage-earners, and as between those earners who had and those who had not 'done well out of the war'. For the second it was urged that by linking a universal and simple burden to the necessities of the war effort, the taxation would be more acceptable and (more controversially) would not have such grave disincentive effects as would a comparable increase in income tax.

The proposal of an excess earnings tax, which had been supported by *The Economist* at the time of the previous budget,[2] had at an

---

[1] *The Economist* especially favoured this suggestion. (e.g. leading article, 22nd February 1941).

[2] See e.g. 13th January 1940, p. 46, and 31st August 1940 p. 278; and leading article of 22nd February 1941, when it was coupled with a family allowance scheme.

early date aroused interest in high Treasury quarters and was examined and elaborated by Lord Stamp in September 1940. The plan was for a percentage charge on all excesses of earned income amounting to more than 20 per cent. over earnings assessed for a standard year, which might be the tax year 1938–39 or the previous year at the tax-payer's option. The tax was to be confined to earned income as distinct from total income partly in order to avoid discouragement of savings, but also because of the administrative difficulty of ascertaining total income not only for the current year but also for past years.[1] Such a tax had at first sight great attraction from the point of view of prevention of war-time enrichment, but upon examination it soon became clear that without infinite elaboration of exemption clauses this equitable consideration would be illusory. Unemployment, sickness or other misfortune might make the standard year's income altogether unreasonable as a basis for assessment—the man who had escaped such misfortune would escape taxation that fell upon his unlucky neighbour. Increased work and special effort would cease to meet their reward. Moreover, as individuals grow older and more experienced they can expect increased earnings in peace-time and their family responsibilities and other commitments are often deliberately related to this rising scale. To meet these objections on the score of equity would place an impossible burden on the Inland Revenue staff and at the same time necessitate very heavy rates of tax on those who failed to make a case for exemption: hard cases thus becoming doubly hard.

The excess earnings tax therefore fell early by the wayside. The various suggestions for a flat-rate war tax on all earnings had a much longer run. They were supported by Mr. Keynes and, to the very last ditch, by Lord Catto, and the Chancellor himself was greatly attracted. A shilling in the pound from everybody was a simple conception, leaving everyone knowing at a glance what his liability would be. The fact that it would hit—and hit quickly—the very numerous recipients of small incomes, especially young people without family responsibilities, was thought a great advantage. But here again little reflection was necessary before the virtue of simplicity was perceived to be a will o' the wisp. Pensioners and the unemployed would have to be exempt, and there would be great pressure to concede an exemption limit of perhaps £3 or £4 a week. Then there would be very many cases of small wage-earners with large family responsibilities, on whom the tax could be represented as being an intolerable burden. Yet

---

[1] The Inland Revenue knows the total income only of those taxpayers liable to surtax and of those who suffer deduction at source more than their total incomes require them to bear.

to introduce a relatively high exemption limit or to allow for family responsibilites would destroy the main attractions. The further the principle of equitable distribution of the burden was pressed, the nearer would the tax be to a duplication of the income tax, with the added disadvantage of duplication of work for the Inland Revenue Department.

These reflections on these novel suggestions thus served to underline the recurring theme of the Inland Revenue Department that the taxation of income ought to be carried out by one tax which measured for every income the ability to pay and prescribed what the contribution to the Exchequer should be. Income tax (coupled with surtax) was the only tax on individuals that purported to fit its burden to the shoulder that had to bear it, and the weight of this tax 'ought to be such as to exhaust the taxable capacity of the income and it is contrary to the very concept of the tax to regard the residue remaining after payment of the tax as having a taxable capacity that warrants the imposition of a new tax'. This argument, though strictly valid if the entire weight of a tax is being imposed for the first time, loses much of its force when applied to additions to a recurrent taxation burden to which the tax-payer has more or less adjusted himself. Mr. Keynes never tired of pointing out—especially with reference to the surtax-payer—that capacity to stand sharp increases in taxation is better indicated by income net of previous taxation than by gross income,[1] but his frequent impatience with the Inland Revenue Department's memoranda perhaps reduced the effectiveness of his presentation. The Revenue Department's argument was not met directly on its own ground and therefore lingered on in many minds, especially those to whom Keynes was still suspect.

Finally, the Chancellor was convinced that, when he came to present his proposals to the country, a war surcharge would inevitably sound 'like a rehash of income tax'. He was impressed, too, by the practical difficulties of imposing yet more work on the Inland Revenue Department, and by the fact that a new tax would not yield any substantial sum in the first year. The new taxation must be as simple as possible to administer, and as simple as possible to explain, consistently with a speedy and substantial yield. On these grounds the Chancellor decided in February that he must get the money by increasing income tax. The standard rate should

---

[1] In stating Keynes's position I am not implying any condemnation of the more usual view that total gross income is the fairest basis for taxation. I would merely emphasise that Keynes's argument was never related to a long-standing level of taxation but to sharp increases in taxation, and I would urge that in this short period context the Keynesian argument has a force that it would not have under more normal circumstances.

rise from 8s. 6d. to 10s. in the £, and the reduced rate (applicable
to the first £165 of taxable income) from 5s. to 7s. 6d. in the £.
The earned income allowance was to be reduced from one-sixth
to one-tenth, subject to a maximum allowance of £200. The married
allowance was to go down from £170 to £140, and the single from
£100 to £80, the exemption limit (total income) going down
consequently from £120 to £89.[1] These changes would, it was
anticipated, yield £150 millions in the first year (1941–2) and
£255 millions in a full year.[2] Their fierceness was to be moderated
by treatment of part as forced savings (discussed below). The
proposals would bring some 3¼ million new taxpayers into the
income tax net for the first time.[3]

Sir Kingsley Wood mentioned his intentions to the Prime
Minister on the 18th February, and encountered shocked
opposition.

> 'I cannot believe', wrote Mr. Churchill the next day, 'that
> an Income Tax of that rate would be compatible with National
> thrift or enterprise. Taken with the Super-tax it amounts to
> almost complete confiscation of the higher rates of income. If
> such a proceeding were capable of finding the money for the war,
> there would be justification. As in fact however it can only find
> a trifle and is avowedly adopted in order to placate other
> elements in public opinion, this cannot be pleaded. If you
> suppose you can collect at these high rates without waste or
> great diminution of effort, without striking a deadly blow at
> good housekeeping and good management in every form, you
> are greatly mistaken. People will be indifferent to whether they
> earn an income or not, and will live on their capital, as many
> are doing now, with the result that death duties will suffer . . .
> The fact that the Income Tax was raised to the enormous figure
> of 8s. 6d. at such an early stage is a complete justification for
> not making a further increase now. . .'

These views were destined to find expression from several speakers
in the budget debate,[4] but they were not held by all Mr. Churchill's

---

[1] The details stated here are from the proposals under discussion in February 1941.
Before the Chancellor introduced his budget, certain modifications were made, notably:
    (a) The reduced rate (applicable to the first £165 of taxable income) was raised
        to 6s. 6d., *not* to 7s. 6d.
    (b) The maximum earned income allowance was £150, *not* £200.
    (c) Although it would have been in accordance with the general reductions in the
        personal allowances to reduce the exemption limit to about £89, the
        Chancellor fixed an exemption limit at £110 in order to assist those with
        very small incomes.

[2] The fiscal proposals (as preceding note) were estimated to yield £252 millions
in a full year.

[3] In his budget speech (the proposals having been modified) the Chancellor spoke of
'over two million new taxpayers'. In the event there were about four millions.

[4] e.g. Sir F. Sanderson, H. of C. Deb., Vol. 371, Col. 1650, Mr. Hammersley, Vol. 372,
Col. 529. Even Labour speakers (Vol. 373, Col. 535) used the arguments against taxes
on overtime earnings.

colleagues. A junior Minister, though strongly disliking one particular part of the Chancellor's proposals, pleaded for austerity: regarded as weapons to beat Hitler, even the fiercest taxes would be endured. Which of these two was more nearly right in estimating the temper of the people is difficult to judge long after the event. The Treasury was not then using the social survey technique, though it did make use of the important and illuminating survey directed by Mr. Charles Madge under the auspices of the National Institute of Economic and Social Research.[1] Though primarily concerned with slightly different questions, this survey did reveal a quite considerable understanding of the broad economic compulsions of the war and an almost universal acceptance of burdens thought necessary by the nation's leaders. A large proportion of the population at that time had its thoughts dominated by other matters: would all the family get home safely at the end of the day, would it be a quiet night, where could shelter be found, how could the food be made to provide enough palatable meals for the week? In these circumstances people probably did not really worry over a few shillings a week more or less in taxation, and if their political leaders had the courage to tell them new financial burdens were necessary, they would probably be accepted with little more grumbling than is the Englishman's traditional right against any Government.

Whatever be the judgment on the central issue, Mr. Churchill was certainly unfair to Sir Kingsley Wood in some of his suggestions. Though £255 millions was only 'a trifle' as a contribution to the total cost of the war, it was on one reckoning about the whole sum necessary in order to achieve stabilisation. And the imputation of deference to Left-wing elements was unjust to a Chancellor who was making substantial concessions on the excess profits tax,[2] who was declining to take advantage of Sir John Simon's preparatory steps for dropping the surtax level to £1,500,[3] and who was anticipating and intending to resist demands for further 'taxing the dead'.

---

[1] Duplicated reports of this survey were circulated from time to time by the National Institute and found their way into the Treasury. Articles were published in *The Economic Journal*, *The Times* and elsewhere, and the results were eventually brought together in *War-Time Pattern of Saving and Spending*, Occasional Paper No. IV of the National Institute of Economic and Social Research (Cambridge University Press 1943).

[2] See below, pp. 85-90.

[3] This decision was based on two grounds: (1) the fact that the people between £1,500 and £2,000 were in any case to pay much more now that the standard rate of income tax was to be 10s. instead of Sir John Simon's 7s. 6d. and (2) that the change would add 50 per cent. to the number of surtax-payers to be individually assessed by a large and highly trained staff. (Except for surtax-payers and a few small income tax-payers, the Inland Revenue Department does not link unearned incomes with the earned incomes of the same individuals. It has much of the information for doing so, but the work would be pointless wherever the unearned income was fully taxed at source, and the tax-payer neither poor enough to claim relief nor rich enough to incur liability for surtax).

The final stages of the argument are hidden, but by some means or other the Prime Minister and his War Cabinet were converted. Perhaps it was because the Chancellor presented his budget to his colleagues, as to the country, as a 'stabilisation budget' that he prevailed. At any rate, his line was that by the subsidies and by adequate taxation he was going to hold the line against inflation, and that inflation would provide no alternative to the burdens he was distributing but rather an aggravation of them.

(v)

The Post-War Credits

The most novel measure included in the 1941 budget was the treatment of part of the increased income tax as a 'withholding tax'[1]—a tax to be repaid after the end of the war. The original proposal on which this measure was based was made by Keynes in his *Times* articles in November 1939, elaborated in the pamphlet *How to Pay for the War* early in 1940. Keynes saw in forced saving the one chance for war-workers ever to enjoy the increased consumption that should be the reward of their increased efforts. It was physically impossible for the community as a whole to consume during the war the equivalent of their increased effort; the effort was to pay for the war and could not also supply increased consumption. The only alternatives were for individuals to forego the equivalent consumption altogether, or to postpone it. To allow inflation was to choose the former alternative. The latter alternative—postponement of consumption—was the way of voluntary saving, but the additional saving would have to come largely from the poorer classes and 'would require a change in their habits of expenditure for which there is no evidence'.[2] The way out was enforcement of saving on the necessary scale, by making a proportion of each man's earnings take the form of deferred pay. This deferred pay might be deposited with an institution—a Friendly Society, a Trade Union, or the Post Office Savings Bank—of the individual's choice. These institutions would of course invest the funds in Government securities of some kind.

Keynes put this scheme forward as a solution for the problem

---

[1] The term 'withholding tax' is used here as it was used at the time; it should perhaps be emphasised that there was no confusion with the 'withholding taxes' of certain other countries, where the reference is to undistributed profits.

[2] The above passage is based on pp. 29-30 of the pamphlet. Without implying any criticism of the main argument, it may be pointed out that Keynes had no evidence either way on the savings habits of the poor; nor indeed had anyone else until the Madge Survey (see p. 79) which produced some surprising results.

of the moment,[1] but the more he reflected upon it the more he fell in love with it as an engine of social reform. The rights to deferred consumption after the war—'another name for the National Debt'—would be widely distributed amongst all those who were foregoing immediate consumption, 'instead of being mainly concentrated, as they were last time, in the hands of the capitalist class'. He saw the working man as receiving, as part of his pay-packet, a claim on his Friendly Society or Trade Union.' Thus there would be an encouragement to the working-man's own institutions to take charge of his resources for him, and, if desired, a considerable degree of discretion could be allowed to such bodies as to the conditions in which these resources could be released to the individual to meet his personal emergencies', such as illness or unemployment, or for payment of death duties.

In the post-war period the nation would derive great benefit from the existence of these claims. The best time for release would be at the onset of the post-war slump, when there would be capacity to produce in excess of current demand. 'Thus the system of deferment will be twice blessed . . . It is only sensible to put off private expenditure from the date when it cannot be used to increase consumption to the date when it will bring into employment resources which otherwise would run to waste'. The working-man would then be able to enjoy the fruits of his previous efforts and avoid the misery of present unemployment. Until such occasion for general release for deferred pay arrived, discretionary releases to meet individual emergencies would allow these forced savings to give that same personal security that is afforded by savings voluntarily accumulated. Altogether, the social gains in security and material enrichment for the broad masses of the people made the scheme doubly dear to Keynes.[2]

The plan made an immediate impression. It was almost universally accepted by academic economists,[3] Mr. Montagu Norman thought Mr Keynes the one man who had really got hold of the basic problems,[4] and the then Chancellor (Sir John Simon) was at least interested. But among the Chancellor's official advisers

---

[1] It should be emphasised that the deferred pay proposal was linked with schemes for family allowances and a minimum ration standard at fixed prices, and that Keynes regarded each of these proposals as part of a single comprehensive plan.

[2] The Inland Revenue Department was always somewhat impatient of Keynes's claims of incidental social advantage: e.g. 'In the Board's view none of these factors is of such paramount importance as the raising of revenue in a manner which is equitable and practicable. These factors do not, in the Board's judgment, warrant the abandonment of well-established principles of taxation for ones which are unsound and which involve enormous administrative difficulties'.

[3] cf. F. A. Hayek's review of Keynes's *How to pay for the War*, in *The Economic Journal*, 1940, p. 322.

[4] So the late Sir Henry Clay told the author.

G

opposition was at first very strong[1] and, as we have seen, Sir John Simon regretfully decided in the spring of 1940 to give 'voluntarism' a last trial. But the idea of deferred pay had bitten deeply enough to remain in the forefront of discussion inside the small circle which framed budget proposals. It gained support from the rising influence of Mr. Keynes inside as well as outside the Treasury. Like other radical proposals, it became more acceptable when the political climate changed in the summer of 1940. Most of all, perhaps, it gained from the use made of the social survey technique. The Chancellor's advisers in the pre-Keynes days of early 1940 had been most critical on the grounds that voluntary saving would decline as compulsory saving rose, and that wage-earners, failing to understand the position, would claim compensatory increases in wages. The important survey directed by Mr. Charles Madge under the auspices of the National Institute greatly diminished this pessimism in the Treasury, and provided an altogether firmer foundation for policy. It brought out clearly the fact that increased incomes were largely concentrated in the working classes, so underlining the arguments of Mr. Henderson and others that the middle classes were being gravely burdened by the increases in taxation that had already taken place. The survey also revealed the basis of the greatly increased voluntary savings of the workers. Finally, it showed that though most people would have preferred restriction of consumption by comprehensive rationing, many actually preferred forced savings, while the alternative of rising prices was generally rejected. Comprehensive rationing was not at any stage considered practicable,[2] and the immediate choice was considered by the Treasury (now thoroughly alive to the basic problems) to lie between inflation and compulsory contributions— whether by straight tax or by deferred pay. From the point of view of the financial policy-makers the Madge Survey provided support for forced savings as a plan that would command widespread acceptance among the working classes. The detailed investigation of savings habits confirmed the expectation that forced savings would be partly offset by a decline in voluntary savings, but it encouraged the belief that the net contribution would be substantial.

By the beginning of 1941 the principle of forced saving—a withholding tax it was generally called at this stage[3]—was more or less accepted by the Chancellor, and the Inland Revenue

---

[1] cf. Chapter II, pp. 33-5.

[2] It was seriously considered in the Board of Trade discussions between officials and economists when the proposals that emerged as clothes rationing were first tabled (*Civil Industry and Trade, op. cit.*, Chapter XIV).

[3] See footnote on p. 80.

Department was persuaded to admit that in some simple form it would be administratively practicable. The Department specified that it must take the shape of a deferred credit 'confined to an increase in the reduced rate (of income tax), or to reduction of the earned income and personal allowances'. This restriction was dictated by the Revenue Department's ignorance of the total income of any but surtax-payers,[1] a limiting factor that influenced other decisions[2] and was of great importance when trained staff was short. If so governed, the amount to be credited to each tax-payer could be ascertained by the Revenue Department with comparatively little trouble, though often only after some delay.

The Revenue Department objected strongly to Mr. Keynes's suggestion that the tax-payer might be allowed repayment on any one of eight events (including death, marriage, birth of a child, sickness, call-up for military service, evacuation) on the ground that no list of hardships would be administratively practicable. Once the general principle of repayment were admitted, 'all sorts of cases of hardship would be advanced and in the end the position would be that some general criterion of hardship administered by some local tribunal, that would be fairly certain to take a sympathetic view, would be the only condition'.

The Revenue Department was also responsible for the later rejection of the idea that the deferred pay might be credited to Post Office Savings Accounts or through other established institutions. Here the governing consideration was the prevention of fraud, and a new instrument—which became the 'Post-War Credit Certificate'—had to be devised, over which the Revenue Department would have complete and simple control.[3]

The final shape of the proposals was thus moulded by administrative considerations in the first weeks of 1941, and the Chancellor proceeded to put the plan to his colleagues. Strong objections were expressed to the new-fangled notion of 'repayable taxes . . . a contradiction in terms and repugnant to the intellect'. Were not Hitler's coercive measures the only precedent, and would not this be a gift to Goebbel's propaganda? The Chancellor replied that he was not aware that Hitler had done anything comparable, and that the analogy was rather with the proposed E.P.T. repayment concession then being widely

---

[1] Apart from the relatively few suffering taxation at source beyond the sums justified by their total incomes. In arguments on these matters, the Inland Revenue Department ignored these, presumably because they were relatively unimportant.

[2] See e.g. p. 79.

[3] Even if the Inland Revenue Department had not taken this view, the opposition of both the Post Office and the National Savings Movement to any confusion of compulsory savings with voluntary savings would probably have prevented any use of the Post Office Savings Bank.

canvassed. He went on: 'We must withdraw purchasing power *now*, and we must do it by serious inroads upon the normal income tax graduations and allowances—inroads which I should not feel to be justified if they were not accompanied by the arrangement for post-war repayments. In other words, without that arrangement we cannot deal adequately with the danger of inflation'.

When the Chancellor announced his plan—which underwent no further change—to the House of Commons, he justified it in much the same terms. He was reluctant to make 'any permanent inroad upon the existing level of the income tax allowances', but was looking at the problem not 'to raise revenue for the sake of revenue, but to make a considerable cut in purchasing power during the war'. The extra tax paid by any individual by reason of the reduction in the personal allowances and earned income allowance would 'be offset after the war by a credit which will then be given in his favour in the Post Office Savings Bank'.[1] The individual would thus, while complying with vital war-time necessities, 'find himself provided with an additional fund of post-war savings for himself and his dependents'. The amount involved would be about £125 millions a year—half the increase in the yield of income tax.

The arguments used showed plainly that Sir Kingsley Wood had been attracted by the essential elements in Mr. Keynes's original suggestion: the emphasis on this part of the new taxation as a purely war-time expedient (no 'permanent inroad' upon the existing allowances), the vital withholding of purchasing power from the mass of the people, and the fund of post-war savings diffused among the people. The form—particularly the link with income tax allowances—was not quite what Mr. Keynes had sketched, but this adaptation to meet the administrative requirements of the overstrained Revenue Department did not alter the essential basis of the plan, though it did perhaps help to set narrow limits to the sums involved. These sums were in the end so much smaller than Mr. Keynes had originally envisaged that it is hardly fair to describe Sir Kingsley Wood's innovation as an implementation of the Keynes plan. For, as Mr. Harrod has pointed out,[2] the deferred pay scheme was, for Keynes, to be the centre piece of war finance. Keynes had mentioned £550 millions a year as the sum to be so raised, whereas Sir Kingsley Wood aimed at £125 millions and in the event the annual average during the war years was £121 millions.[3] Moreover, Keynes's figure of £550 millions 'was geared to an increase in Government expenditure of only £1,950

---

[1] H. of C. Deb., Vol. 370, Cols. 1330-1.
[2] *The Life of John Maynard Keynes*, p. 494.
[3] If 1945-6 is included, the average becomes £160 millions.

millions. Our effort exceeded expectations, and, to achieve his desired effect, the amount taken in deferred pay would have had to be stepped up beyond his initial figure'.

At any rate when it is taken by itself, the post-war credits scheme was certainly, as Mr. Harrod concludes, only an interesting experiment that played a minor part in the whole situation. Post-war views of it have been affected by the failure of this scheme to play any spectacular part in post-war events. The post-war slump, at the onset of which these credits might have been released, did not come, and the steady fall in the value of money has reduced their real value in relation both to current earning power and to important assets such as houses. If, ignoring their post-war aspect, we go back to the war-time situation, it may well be that Sir Kingsley Wood was right in his judgment that the post-war credits scheme made more acceptable the level of taxation that was necessary if unmanageable inflation was to be avoided. Again we have to admit, with Mr. Harrod,[1] that the waste and inefficiencies of shortages and queues, which the original Keynes plan was designed to avoid, remained with us to the end. But the nation did manage to get through without major catastrophe; the war economy did in the event prove tolerable and successful. To this result Sir Kingsley Wood's 1941 budget—'my stabilisation budget'— certainly made an important contribution. To the Chancellor himself the budget proposals stood as an integral whole, and as one part of this whole the forced savings plan had its justification.

(vi)
The Excess Profits Tax

At the very beginning of the war Sir John Simon had introduced an excess profits tax both as a revenue-collector and as a device for preventing war-time enrichment of employers, and after the upheaval of May 1940 this had become a 100 per cent. tax. The detailed plan in 1939 had been as suggested by the Inland Revenue Department, a Department which, much as it disliked E.P.T., heaved a sigh of relief at a change which involved the disappearance of the armaments profits duty of 1939.[2] When the rate of tax was raised to 100 per cent., the administratively simple course of applying this to all firms was adopted, after a week's flirtation with the proposal that the 100 per cent. rate

---

[1] *op. cit.*, p. 494.

[2] The armaments profits duty involved distinguishing between profits arising from armaments business and those from other business—not a congenial task even for the most leisurely times.

should apply only to firms working directly for the Government.[1]
The adoption of this 100 per cent. rate, a step hastily taken for
political reasons, gave altogether new force to objections that had
been raised to the tax from the beginning, and gave a new urgency
to the search for practicable means of meeting these objections
consistently with maintenance of the main principles of the tax.

These objections were thoroughly reviewed by the Stamp Survey
in a memorandum dated 30th July 1940, which was not a
plea for immediate action but a note of warning and a plea for
systematic investigation of the effects of the tax on production.
It argued that the 100 per cent. rate had removed all incentive to
enterprise and economy in production, that it removed the
employers' interest as a check on wage demands, and that it gravely
aggravated the inequities as between firms, particularly those which
had and those which had not done well in the basic years. These
arguments were of particular force in new and expanding businesses,
where also the availability of profits as a source of capital expansion
was of most importance. The danger was, in fact, not so much
that of 'glaring cases of a refusal to undertake work of national
importance that is clearly within a manufacturer's capacity. The
danger is more subtle; it is likely to take such forms as a gradual
decline of zeal, and energy and enterprise. . . '

Lord Stamp's memorandum was doing no more than elaborating
and emphasising fears that had been expressed by permanent
officials ever since the tax was first proposed at the beginning of
the war. Expert opinion generally was strongly against it; indeed
Mr. Keynes opened a forceful memorandum of 21st October
1940 with the sentence: 'I know no responsible person who
does not think that the present version of 100 per cent. E.P.T.
is an injudicious, and inefficient, and a seriously unjust measure,
leading to a wasteful use of resources in circumstances where
we can least afford it, which hampers our war effort and will
hamper it increasingly as time goes on'. This unanimity of
responsible opinion does not, of course, mean that the politicians
were mistaken in the imposition; the objections raised to it were
very great indeed, but their main force related to a prolonged war.
The immediate output was most directly affected by the workers'
efforts and by managers in whom the habits of striving for bigger
output and of manœuvring for future strength were deeply
ingrained, while immediate needs of capital development for war
purposes were covered by Government aid of one kind or another.
Given the strong demand for 'taking the profit out of the war'
in the most obvious way, 100 per cent. E.P.T. could help in the

---

[1] For details, see pp. 47-8.

immediate need, although it would hinder in the longer run.[1] In May 1940 it was the immediate need for output and mass support that was paramount—if Britain did not avert defeat in 1940, there would be no long war to reveal the harm done by the tax. The almost instinctive dash into the 100 per cent. E.P.T. was surely right.

Once taken, there could be no direct going back upon the decision. Nevertheless, as time went on (and Britain survived) something might be done to mitigate the insidious effects of the tax. As Mr. Keynes put it, 'it would be a pity to accept the view that under a democratic system of Government uninstructed opinion must necessarily prevail, not merely on the principle but even to the point of preventing advisable amendments in detail'. The 100 per cent. rate, which was in a sense the root of the trouble, had aggravated the injustices between firms in addition to removing the direct profit incentive. If, therefore, the 100 per cent. rate was to be maintained in principle, at least some concessions should be made to reduce injustice and to increase incentives.

The Chancellor's advisers all felt so strongly in this matter that in fact both alternatives—a reduction in the rate and amendments in the structure—were exhaustively discussed in the winter of 1940-41. In its issue of 2nd November 1940 *The Economist* had given support to a suggestion[2] that, instead of an outright reduction of the rate, part of the tax—perhaps 20 per cent.—should be repayable after the war. This idea was at once thought more attractive than other repayment suggestions,[3] and it was soon part of the agreed proposals put before the Chancellor. As any repayment would be subject eventually to income tax, it was thought that 20 per cent. was the minimum allowance that could be expected to have any incentive effect, though some advisers favoured a rather greater relief. Those most closely in touch with business circles pressed the argument that, as industrialists were even then closely concerned with their post-war positions and were always tending to manœuvre for post-war strength, the 20 per cent. (less income tax) to be received after the war would operate very effectively as an incentive.

As regards amendments in the structure, improved allowance for increased capital and for the capital of new businesses, the

---

[1] Later the importance attached by workers to the 100 per cent. E.P.T. appears to have dwindled, especially where they thought the 'cost plus' contracts system was (by facilitating the concealment of profits in alleged costs) enabling the employers to escape the intended effect of 'taking the profit out of the war'. But even then it would have been difficult for Labour leaders to swallow a naked reduction in the rate.

[2] From Mr. Albert Good, Chairman of Clifford Motor Components.

[3] These generally related to the contingency of post-war losses.

grant of an allowance in respect of increased borrowed capital, and certain allowances in respect of operation of war installations were considered. There was also an approach to the problems of companies working wasting assets such as tin and copper mines.

Once these broad proposals had been evolved, their urgency was considered sufficient for the Chancellor to put them to the War Cabinet long before the usual budget season. On 14th January 1941, the War Cabinet decided that amendment of the tax must await the budget which, however, the War Cabinet hoped would be earlier than usual; and that the 20 per cent. repayment plan was to be favourably considered, provided that the repayment should be tied in some way to reconstruction and reconditioning of industry after the war. It was also agreed that there should be concessions by way of adjustment of standards and other 'structural changes' such as the Chancellor's advisers had been discussing. By this time the 20 per cent. repayment scheme had been widely canvassed in business circles, and it was clear when the War Cabinet took its decision that the business world would accept it as the next best thing to an outright reduction of the rate. It remained simply to work out details.

The major problem of detail proved to be the conditions to be attached to repayment after the war. The Inland Revenue Department at once pointed out that it would be quite impossible for itself as tax collector, and probably impossible for any Government Department, 'to sit in judgment on industry and pick and choose' the recipients deserving of repayment. Any attempt 'would be certain to collapse in actual practice'. Mr. Ernest Bevin, however, insisted that his support—which meant on an issue of this kind the assent of organised labour—depended upon the maintenance of some conditional clauses, and the Treasury was thereupon inclined to go back to other reliefs (such as deficiency payments), to the exclusion of the 20 per cent. post-war repayment plan. The matter had, however, really gone too far for steps to be entirely retraced. The 20 per cent. repayment plan had by now been so widely discussed and found broadly acceptable that any substitute (other than outright reduction, which was politically out of court) would have substantially lessened the business world's sense of relief. Moreover, reflection showed that the difficulties Mr. Bevin's conditions were likely to place in the way of the 20 per cent. repayment might also be put in the way of any scheme for making repayments to firms incurring losses in the immediate post-war period. The Chancellor eventually decided to hold to the 20 per cent. repayment plan, coupling it with conditions not now specified but to be determined after the war. When announcing this in his budget speech, he said that the repayment would be 'subject to such conditions as Parliament may then determine', but the passage which followed reflected closely the particular proposals that had been urged upon him by his Ministerial colleagues:

> 'The conditions I have in mind', he said, 'would be somewhat as follows: The ban upon bonus shares would be continued, and any necessary steps would be taken to prevent the money from being dissipated in dividends, and generally it must be assumed that the money would require to be expended for suitable purposes, among which I may mention the replacement of obsolete or unsatisfactory machinery by up-to-date machinery; the scrapping or adaptation to new uses of redundant installations; the extension of the export market; and, in the case of farmers, the improvement of the fertility of the land, and the promotion of good business'.

As they heard this list colleagues on the Front Bench must one by one have felt, 'This is for me'; but the civil servants must have come away with foreboding of many headaches.

The other principal changes in this tax were announced as those made necessary to remove anomalies and hard cases which, though tolerable in a 60 per cent. tax, had become indefensible at 100 per cent. First, borrowed money was not to be deducted in computing capital, and interest on borrowed money was not to be deducted in computing profits.[1] The effect was to leave a trader, who increased the capital employed in his business by borrowing, with the excess of the statutory percentage (8 or 10 per cent.) on the borrowed money over the interest paid. Secondly, some special allowance was to be made for 'wasting assets'; this was a matter that had particularly troubled the Ministry of Supply in its dealings with mineral producers, whose mines were being exploited at a greatly enhanced rate.

Public discussion showed that the Chancellor's plans for this tax were broadly acceptable. In the budget debate one Labour M.P. spoke[2] against the 20 per cent. refund, and at the Committee stage there was a good deal of protest that it represented an undue reward to capital, but the general welcome given was not confined to one part of the House. This applied also to the structural changes, though it was also emphasised that the concession on wasting assets was too restrictive to avoid hard cases.[3] When the Chancellor talked to his Consultative Council,[4] he was told that

---

[1] Except in minimum standard cases.

[2] H. of C. Deb., Vol. 371, Col. 1378.

[3] H. of C. Deb., Vol. 372, Col. 594. The Chancellor's reply was that the war supply efforts of gravel pits and quarries were not in general so great as those of the metal producers. This was not an adequate answer.

[4] On 21st April 1941.

the concession of 20 per cent. repayment was regarded by the business world as the most that could be expected, though there was some disappointment at the warning that the repayments would be subject to income tax at the time of repayment. Business men were then, however, sufficiently optimistic about post-war income tax not to be unduly worried by this qualification of the 20 per cent. refund. Altogether the Chancellor could feel that he had steered a comfortable course between those who cried out against the iniquity and fool-hardiness of the 100 per cent., and those who demanded that there should be no uncovenanted concessions to the capitalists. The really ticklish problem set by the political necesssities—the formulation of conditions qualifying for repayment—was pushed into the future.

(vii)
The Budget as a Whole

Such criticism as there was of this 1941 budget was mostly related to particular proposals in it—some people criticised the increases in income tax, some the forced savings plan, some the niggardliness and others the generosity of the E.P.T. concessions, and so on. Comments of this kind were in one way doing great injustice to Sir Kingsley Wood, in that to him the various proposals formed one consistent whole. The primary aim was avoidance of inflation. On this the twofold attack was launched: the cost of living subsidies were to remove—or at least reduce—the threat of cost inflation, and the increased taxation was to remove the threat of demand inflation. While increasing direct taxation sharply, the Chancellor made his inroads into the allowances only temporary, by the post-war credit proposals, so achieving his main object of absorbing purchasing power without prejudice to the equity of the established structure of taxation. Parallel to this temporary absorption of purchasing power from the mass of small taxpayers was the temporary absorption of purchasing power in the revised excess profits tax. Just as post-war income tax credits were to provide nest-eggs for the working-man, so was the 20 per cent. E.P.T. refund to provide a nest-egg for post-war reconstruction of industry, thus providing a powerful incentive for the industrialist who was by this stage becoming anxious about his ability to make a quick start in the post-war race. The budget was primarily to prevent inflation, to do this with equity, and to hold out brighter hopes for strength and comfort after the war. Into this whole, every one of the budget proposals fitted. The various proposals had origins in many different quarters, but by the time they were fashioned into a budget speech, Sir Kingsley Wood was able to see them and propound them as a single consistent plan.

If this view is to be qualified at all—and comparison with Keynes's earlier comprehensive plans does encourage qualification—it is in relation to the straightforward shape of the increases in direct taxation. The budget would have been more presentable as a consistent plan if, parallel to the tax on increased profits, there had been a general tax on increased incomes, part of which might have been similarly treated as a 'withholding tax'. As we have seen, the idea of such a tax on increased incomes did attract much attention, not only on the ground that the increases in income would be little missed but also because the alternative of taxing everyone bore hardly—indeed, many thought, savagely—on those whose money incomes had failed to increase at all. The case for such a tax was pressed hard, but was wrecked on forceful objections from the Inland Revenue Department that the task of income assessment would have been unmanageable. If this administrative difficulty could have been overcome, the delay in yield would have remained as a substantial disadvantage. The tax might also have had very serious repercussions in the labour market, where economic incentives remained important and could have been weakened only at the expense of enforcing much tighter controls and some deterioration in industrial relations. Nevertheless, Mr. Keynes and Lord Catto were by no means alone in regretting the disappearance of this runner from the Budget Stakes.

Alternatively the budget as a whole could be attacked on a much broader front. Mr. Kalecki, in an article in the *Oxford Bulletin of Statistics*,[1] an article showing little appreciation of the great advances made by Sir Kingsley Wood, took the line not that any part of the financial policy was wrong, but that the basic problem was too big to be solved by financial measures, or at least too big to be solved by equitable financial measures. The case was based on a very brief discussion of the 'inflationary gap', in which the Chancellor's estimates were characterised as rather optimistic. The obvious running down of stocks of consumption goods was adduced as evidence of the Government's failure to prevent inflation. Mr. Kalecki evidently also considered the taxation proposals unfairly burdensome on the low and medium income groups, and concluded 'the only fair and efficient way to stop the inflationary tendencies is some type of comprehensive rationing which should be organised before stocks fall to a dangerously low level'.

---

[1] Vol. 3, No. 6 (26th April 1941), reprinted in *Studies in War Economics* (Blackwell, 1947) p. 86, *et seq.*

The idea of minimising the task of financial policy by severe and elaborate regimentation of the economy had been in the minds of the experts from the beginning of the war, and there was quite serious thought of it from time to time in 1940 and 1941. But in general it was decisively rejected,[1] partly in distaste for the methods of a totalitarian enemy, partly on the ground of administrative impossibility, but also in the belief that the British people would be more whole-hearted in their war effort if such extreme reversal of established ways could be avoided. On this basis the task of internal financial policy was primarily to hold the inflationary pressures back sufficiently for economic organisation to be manageable, leaving rationing devices to be introduced *ad hoc* wherever the pressure threatened really important points. Before 1941 there was not always courage, perhaps not always understanding, to face the magnitude of this task; but in the 1941 budget a logical and systematic attempt was made to grapple with it.

In the event, was the attempt adequate? As Mr. Harrod says,[2] shop shortages and queues remained with us; indeed they became worse. Mr. Kalecki, reviewing the position after a year,[3] found many symptoms of an inflationary situation. There had been 'a violent increase of prices in the uncontrolled sector both in food and in household goods' and dangerous inroads into the stocks of 'unessential' goods, including 'household goods, the supply of which may be very important if the bombing of this country is renewed'. In spite, too, of the invaluable support which Sir Kingsley Wood received from his Labour colleagues, the increase in wages went on. The following table[4] shows the estimated percentage increase in weekly wage-rates since September 1939:

1939	.	.	December	4
1940	.	.	June	12–13
1940	.	.	December	16
1941	.	.	March	19–20
1941	.	.	June	22
1941	.	.	September	23
1941	.	.	December	26–27
1942	.	.	March	28
1942	.	.	June	31

The check in the summer of 1941—immediately following the budget—was not complete, and thereafter the rise was once more

---

[1] cf. *Civil Industry and Trade op. cit.*, Chapter XIV.

[2] *op. cit.*, p. 494.

[3] *Oxford Bulletin of Statistics*, Vol. 4, No. 6 (25th April 1942) reprinted in *Studies in War Economics*, pp. 88-91.

[4] *Ministry of Labour Gazette*, August 1946, p. 231.

uncomfortably rapid.[1] But it must be remembered that this was a time when the labour surplus of the early days had disappeared, and actual scarcity was becoming more and more acute. Given the state of the market, Sir Kingsley Wood and Mr. Bevin may claim to have made the rise in wage-rates much less steep than it would have been in the absence of a definite stabilisation policy.

When Sir Kingsley Wood himself looked back, in his budget speech of 1942,[2] he claimed that 'during the last year we have definitely held our own against the onset of inflation. The enemy is still at our gates. Our vigilance must not be relaxed for a moment, but we can at least claim that as yet he has not established a bridgehead across our financial defences'. The broad claim made in these metaphorical terms had some justice. Nobody—not even Mr. Keynes—evolving the arithmetic on which the budget proposals of 1941 were eventually based, can have supposed that any exact balance, any refined adjustment, was being made. Nor, given the specialisation of resources with its implication of local bottlenecks and shortages, can it ever be made. What was attempted was a broad attack on the mainsprings of inflation, using financial policy as the main battery but knowing that direct 'physical controls' could be used to stop particular gaps. In such an attempt, success or failure is necessarily a matter of degree, and it must remain a matter of opinion whether the difficulties and distresses of the home economy in 1941–42 were within the limits that foresight would have tolerated. But at least Britain's leaders did have a financial policy.

---

[1] On 27th June 1942 *The Economist* (leading article, 'Wages Policy', p. 885) summarised the immediate result of the 1941 policy: 'There was some check to wage increases. For the moment, wage claims became less insistent; tribunals were held back from being generous in their awards; wage negotiations tended to be long drawn-out, which in itself was a delaying factor'. But it suspected that this successful phase might be closing: the 'remarkable claim' just entered by the engineers 'should be regarded as a sign that the test may still be to come'.

[2] H. of C. Deb., Vol. 379, Col. 113.

CHAPTER IV

BUDGET POLICY

III: THE PERIOD OF CONSOLIDATION, 1942-45

(i)

The General Principles of the Later Budgets

THE FOUR BUDGETS of 1942, 1943, 1944 and 1945 covered more than half the length of the war, but their total contribution to the development of policy was relatively small. The central principles of budget policy remained as they had been established in Sir Kingsley Wood's stabilisation budget of 1941, and his remaining two budgets and Sir John Anderson's two did little more than consolidate the ground and polish the rough edges.

This was true not only of the substance but also of the form. The traditional budget speech before 1941 had consisted of a detailed review of the past year's Government revenue and expenditure, estimates for the new year, and proposals for remission and imposition of taxation. In 1941 Sir Kingsley Wood had dispensed with most of the detailed review of the past financial year, and had substituted 'a more general survey of the financial and economic front'. A year later, he opened by declaring his intention of following his own precedent. In 1944 Sir John Anderson revived in a limited form the opening review of the past year, but the substantial innovation of the broad economic review as the preliminary to new proposals, was retained and has become permanent.[1] Similarly, just as the figures of Government finance had traditionally been filled out in detail by the simultaneous issue of a White Paper—a course that continued to be followed—so was the statistical background of the Chancellor's broad survey of the national economy reinforced in 1941 by the first White Paper on Sources of War-time Finance, and this was repeated—with improvements—in 1942 and subsequent years.

---

[1] *The Economist* described Sir John Anderson's speech on this occasion as 'the classical example of the new-style budget'. His procedure seemed 'natural, so complete has been the acceptance of the revolution in the nature of the Treasury's stewardship that Sir Kingsley Wood and his advisers accomplished in the past three years'. (29th April 1944, p. 557).

In substance, the 1941 budget had been first and foremost a stabilisation budget, and all the remaining war budgets likewise took stabilisation as their central principle. This was manifest in the 'national income' approach to the arithmetic of the budget. The Chancellor still took pride in the extent to which taxation was meeting total expenditure—it was above 50 per cent. throughout this period—but he decided the amount of new taxation required by reference not to Government accounts alone but to the estimates of the threatened inflationary gap between total money demand and the prospective supply of goods at current prices. The stabilisation principle of course governed the amount of the subsidies. When these tended to grow not only because overseas supply prices were rising but also because wage-rates were rising, Sir John Anderson in 1944 altered his course slightly, but even then a new level of the cost-of-living index governed the subsidies. Similarly, the stabilisation principle entered into the choice of objects for additional taxation or for relief from taxation. Subject always to the overriding necessity of raising the required amount somehow or other, the Government chose to avoid increases on and to give relief to items that entered into the cost-of-living index. In these three ways—by determining the level of the subsidies, the sum of required taxation, and the choice of taxes—the stabilisation policy was responsible for the general shape of each budget. If the changes dictated by it were relatively few, this was not because stabilisation was unimportant but because earlier achievement was so substantial.

Although stabilisation became in 1941 and thereafter remained the dominant principle in budget policy, every Chancellor from beginning to end had of course also to pay great attention to equity, the first of Adam Smith's four canons of taxation. There had been early pressure from the Left for a 'soak-the-rich' policy, and this had ensured the rise in surtax and death duties, in the highest ranges, to almost confiscatory levels. Then the necessity had come to impose appreciable direct burdens on the broad mass of the people, and the most productive range in direct taxation was that including the lower middle classes and the more highly paid wage-earners—taxpayers numbering millions, each one of whom could afford an appreciable contribution. As easy revenue-collectors hitting less necessary spending, the taxes on wines, spirits, beer and tobacco had also been increased steeply enough to affect the distribution of the whole burden of taxation. In considering each of these changes, and particularly the detailed changes in the income tax and surtax structure, successive Chancellors had thought carefully about relative burdens on different classes, and public opinion expressed in the House of Commons in early budget debates had a good deal to say about this aspect. It was all tackled somewhat crudely, but after 1941 there was undoubtedly a general feeling that more or less the right result had been obtained. This satisfaction found some justification in, and was undoubtedly crystallised and encouraged by, an authoritative report published in October 1942. This was *The Burden of British Taxation*, a report by Professor G. Findlay Shirras and Mr. L. Rostas, sponsored by the National Institute of Economic and Social Research,[1] and its competence and importance were immediately recognised.[2] Among the principal conclusions of this study, it was shown that war-time tax changes had eliminated the former light treatment of the middle incomes, and that the tax structure was now 'noticeably progressive from incomes of £250 per annum upwards and especially on incomes of £1,000 per annum upwards', though below £250 per annum the burden remained regressive.[3] *The Economist* commented: 'Whatever else may be its defects [i.e. of the structure of taxation], substantial equity has been achieved. This is not the least of the social triumphs of the war; and it is one that should be retained when the war is over'.[4] The acceptance, at least from this date, of the broad equity of the structure of taxation was one of the basic facts underlying budget policy in the remaining years. In the later budget debates, silence was eloquent on what had formerly been the theme of many speeches.

The main structure and principles being thus determined, the Chancellor and his advisers devoted much energy to smoothing the rough edges of the edifice which had after all been hastily built. Some of the notable changes were designed in the interests of efficiency in tax collection. The pre-eminent example was the elaboration of the system of deducting wage-earners' income tax at source, culminating in the P.A.Y.E. system; but there were other examples as well. Secondly efforts were made to eliminate hard cases: minor injustice is bound to arise when there are great innovations in taxation, however thoughtful the experts have been. The later war budgets afforded opportunities to express second thoughts on matters of detail and to remedy minor injustices revealed by experience, and the opportunities were taken.

A third element that crept into budget discussion in these later years—though without immediate spectacular effect—was the growth of opinion favouring 'the Welfare State'. The obvious

---

[1] The book was published for the Institute by the Cambridge University Press.

[2] See e.g. leading article: 'The Burden of Taxation' in *The Economist*, 24th October 1942.

[3] *The Burden of British Taxation*, p. 36.

[4] 24th October 1942, p. 505. Even the detailed review, by Shirras and Rostas, of individual taxes brought out no glaring inequities, though the Treasury may have noted for future reference that the burden of entertainment duty was summarised as negligible (p. 37).

tendency was for the growth of war expenditure to impede the advance of 'social' policy, on grounds of economy, and improvement in the position of old age pensioners, under discussion in 1939, had foundered in precisely this way. But as the war went on and the burden of taxation became much weightier, the economists refused to accept this as barring all development of social policy. War-time dislocations of family life were setting social services in a new light: instead of luxuries to be put aside until easier times, they were becoming imperatively necessary to the maintenance of morale.[1] These circumstances created a host of new problems for Government Departments touching the daily life of the people, and pressure coming upon the Treasury from these Departments impelled a change in Treasury opinion. It also happened that among the Chancellor's war-time advisers there were powerful advocates of the view that more attention should be given, in financial policy, to 'social' needs. This strand of thought was expressed mainly by Mr. Keynes and Mr. Henderson. We have already seen how the former[2] saw in his deferred income scheme the chance of spreading the ownership of financial assets throughout the working classes, the germ of a social revolution of the kind that appealed most to him. As soon as the 1941 budget had established Keynes's prime object of financial stability, he formulated for 1942 suggestions for a budget which 'should be of a different character, fit to be described as a *Social Policy Budget*, and should primarily aim at adjusting various social anomalies which have been developed out of the war situation and also out of the previous budget itself'. The aim was the limited one of remedying social anomalies recently created not of remedying social injustices of old standing; and this was in the main the spirit also of Mr. Henderson's suggestions. There should be some tax relief, for example, for married women at work, because the higher rates of taxation had accentuated the injustice of their position and were perhaps acting as an undesirable deterrent to work. But there should also be family allowances, and in urging such a plan Mr. Henderson especially used arguments that were of equal force in peace-time, though the pressure of war-time taxation on the family man was the occasion of its urgency. Room was to be made for concessions of this kind by new or additional luxury taxation. For the most part the actual suggestions of Mr. Keynes and Mr. Henderson met strong opposition from the Inland Revenue Department on the ground that 'the purpose of the

---

[1] See generally R. M. Titmuss, *Problems of Social Policy*, in this series (H.M.S.O. 1950) and S. M. Ferguson and H. Fitzgerald, *Studies in the Social Services*, in this series (H.M.S.O. 1954), Chapter 1.

[2] See p. 81 above.

H

income tax is not the redistribution of income'. In the face of this opposition the Chancellors fought shy of the more far-reaching and more detailed proposals of this kind. Nevertheless, recognising that there was a growing feeling in favour of advances in social policy,[1] the Chancellors did shape some of their tax concessions with these considerations in mind, and Sir John Anderson authorised the preparation of a family allowances plan for implementation immediately after the war.[2]

These considerations of social welfare were thus linked with the fourth important factor influencing this series of budgets: preparation for post-war reconstruction. This last influence was of course not new in 1942. Britain was never reduced to the extremities of national peril in which alone it is permissible for financial policy to forget the post-war prospect. In the capital operations throughout the war the post-war consideration was always one of the two paramount influences;[3] but even in his taxation policy no Chancellor ever forgot the implications for post-war days. We have seen how already in the 1941 budget the excess profits tax concessions were made in terms giving prominence to post-war needs. From 1942 onwards these considerations of post-war reconstruction became rapidly more prominent, until in 1944 and 1945 the Chancellor's eye could never be off them for one moment. In retrospect the post-war considerations appear to have had extraordinary prominence at surprisingly early dates. This was due mainly to the fact that public opinion almost always greatly under-estimated the length of the war, and once the perils of 1940 and the invasion threats of 1940–41 were left behind, the end of the war generally appeared to be just round the corner, and the thought of manœuvring for post-war position came easily to the front of the mind. But it was not entirely the state of public opinion that gave weight to the post-war considerations. There was also the fact that, having coped with the overriding need for financial stability by imposing swingeing taxation, it would in any case have been proper for the Treasury to have second thoughts about the burden, and to consider how it might be adjusted for the sake of other objects—whether of social policy or of post-war industrial efficiency—as far as this could be done without endangering the war-time stability.

---

[1] How strong this feeling had become was shown by the political storm following the cool Government speeches in the Parliamentary debates in February 1943 on the Beveridge Report on Social Security (*The Economist*, article 'The Parting of the Ways', 20th February 1943).

[2] Preparation had commenced in 1943 and Ministers were sometimes envisaging the commencement of allowances *during* the war. The scheme eventually reached the Statute Book in June 1945 and payments began in August 1946.

[3] The other was war-time inflationary pressure.

(ii)
Pay-As-You-Earn

In the sphere of efficiency in taxation the outstanding innovation in the later war years was 'P.A.Y.E.' This was not an item in any of the budget speeches, but was the subject of a special announcement in the House of Commons on the 22nd September 1943, the announcement being made by the Financial Secretary to the Treasury in the gap between Sir Kingsley Wood's death on the 21st and Sir John Anderson's appointment to the Chancellorship on the 24th. It was a revolution in the technique of tax collection, occasioned by the extension of important income tax burdens right through the wage-earning masses, but delayed until the prospects of end-of-the-war adjustments began to worry the Treasury.

Until 1940 the problem of collecting income tax from weekly wage-earners had not been of great moment. Only a minority of wage-earners were liable to tax, and the amounts they had to pay were relatively small. When, during the first war, the weekly wage-earners were first touched by the income tax, the Inland Revenue authorities had proposed a plan for deduction at source, but Trade Union hostility had prevented the adoption of any such scheme. After the crisis budget of 1931 a further effort was made to help the small tax-payer to meet the bill. Under the scheme then adopted, public authorities and business concerns were permitted to collect tax from their employees by monthly deductions. Industrial employees assessed half-yearly were allowed to pay in effect weekly by purchase of stamps, and under the 1933 arrangements these also could be covered by deduction at source. The scheme depended on the initiative of employers, and at the beginning of the second war only 65 local authorities and 44 commercial concerns were operating the scheme. In addition, all civil servants and railwaymen had for some time been covered by similar schemes.

The prospect of increased taxation of wage-earners held out by Sir John Simon's first war-time budget (September 1939) led at once to suggestions that there should be some extension of facilities for spreading tax payments. A suggestion that the weekly stamps system should be extended and popularised was quickly discountenanced by the Inland Revenue Department, which had had experience of the trouble and cost this system involved when even as little as £650,000 a year was collected by it.[1] But this

---

[1] The difficulties included (1) 'at the end of the stamping period we often find that the tax-payer has not stamped his card and that all the trouble of collection has to commence anew', and (2) 'the stamps had to carry a title to repayment'.

Department was very much alive to the fact that the practicability of taxing the wage-earner on a much wider scale depended on some improvement in the procedure of payment. 'Any attempt', the Treasury was told, 'to deal with the "£5 to £12 per week man" through the income tax is only possible by the adoption of deduction at the source and giving the Revenue powers to make compulsory a scheme of deduction on lines similar to that laid down in the voluntary scheme'. This view was put even more strongly two months later, when the Chancellor was told that a compulsory scheme was necessitated by 'the fact that employees cannot pay their tax and the Revenue will not be able to collect it unless payment is spread over the year'. The new Chancellor therefore in his supplementary budget of July 1940 announced that deduction of income tax by employers would be compulsory, monthly payments suffering monthly deduction and weekly payments suffering weekly deduction. This system would apply to all salaries and wages—to those paid to the director or manager as well as to the clerk or the manual wage-earner. There was to be no change in either the method or the basis of assessment. In no case was the employer called upon to compute tax liability nor was any employee called upon to disclose his personal circumstances to his employer. And the liability continued to be assessed not on current earnings but on those of a previous period.[1]

This compulsory system was brought into operation for tax liabilities arising from income in the year 1940–41—i.e. for payments falling due in the financial year 1941–42. So important was this early start deemed that the Chancellor deferred projected changes in certain income tax allowances, rather than prejudice the collection scheme by forcing fresh complications upon the Inland Revenue Department. With this help, the Department coped with the change successfully. Deductions from wages started fairly punctually over the whole country. In the following year, however, with the continued expansion in the number of wage-earners liable to tax, difficulties increased, and there was some delay in starting the deduction due in January 1942. Once this awkward period was passed, the scheme ran smoothly enough.[2] But the delay, by increasing the amounts to be collected in the remaining months to June 1942, gave rise to criticism of the plan and to some demand that tax payments should be more closely related to current earnings. More fundamental criticism came from those whose deductions were affected by fluctuations in income. In industries in which summer earnings, for example, were appreciably

---

[1] For manual wage-earners the assessment was on the previous half-year ending 5th October and 5th April; for others the previous year ending 5th April.

[2] See Cmd. 6348 (1942) pp. 4-5.

higher than winter earnings, the adjustment of taxes some months in arrear brought the heavy deductions due to summer earnings into the lean winter months: tax deductions thus exaggerated the seasonal fall in income. Effects of this kind were bound up with the fact that, though compulsory deductions were spread over the six months or year in proportion to income payments, the assessment continued to be based on an earlier period and not on current earnings. While wages and small salaries generally were rising, the difficulties created by this time-lag were limited to relatively few cases, mainly those where seasonal fluctuations were marked. Consequently the Treasury and the Inland Revenue Department were able to stand firmly against any change in the basis of assessment. At the time of the 1942 budget, in the face of reiterated demands from the Press,[1] a White Paper, *The Taxation of Weekly Wage Earners*,[2] not only explained the existing arrangements but also put up a 'formidable barrage' (in the words of *The Economist*)[3] 'against any plan for deducting taxes on a current earnings basis'. The reasons given principally related to the complexity of the allowances: any scheme of this kind would, it was said, involve over-deduction in a very high proportion of cases followed by repayment at the end of the year, and this would create hardship and make computations even more elaborate and unintelligible than they were already.[4] This White Paper was, in short, an example of stonewalling, though when changing circumstances made scoring urgent the Inland Revenue Department soon showed that it had enterprising batsmen.

What did stir the Government to action was its increasing attention to problems of adjustment at the end of the war. As early as February 1942 *The Economist* had pointed to the danger of lagged-collection when incomes should fall at the end of the war,[5] but basic problems of this kind were not referred to in the White Paper issued a few weeks later. *The Economist* made the point incidentally to its advocacy of a radical change in the structure of the income tax, and official circles were unsympathetic to such revolutions in time of war. It was not until 1943, when Trade Unions as well as official circles had looked seriously at end-of-the-war problems, that the authorities were frightened into the realisation that, whatever was thought of the tax structure generally, the negative attitude of the 1942 White Paper would

---

[1] See e.g. *The Times* article of 13th April 1942.

[2] Cmd. 6348.

[3] 13th March 1943 (leading article 'Collection of Income Tax', pp. 331-2).

[4] The Chancellor gave a summary of the main points in his budget speech, 14th April 1942. (H. of C. Deb., Vol. 379, Cols. 117-20). In the Finance Bill debates (e.g. Vol. 380, Col. 994) he was pressed to reconsider the possibilities.

[5] 7th February 1942, pp. 176-7.

not do. In his budget speech on 12th April 1943 Sir Kingsley Wood said that his advisers were closely examining the problem and that 'a current earnings basis will not be ruled out of their deliberations',[1] and there was renewed pressure, both inside[2] and outside[3] the House, for speedy action. By September 1943, when the course of bomber production was already presaging the decline in munitions production, the matter had become so urgent to the Government as an employer that the Ministry of Aircraft Production had to be restrained from premature disclosure of the plan just adopted by Ministers.

The basis of the plan actually announced on 22nd September 1943 was first set out in an Inland Revenue Department memorandum of 28th June 1943. Most of the Chancellor's advisers at once hailed it as a very ingenious plan, though a few detailed changes were suggested. Lord Catto was alone in protesting that, though the plan solved the problem, it did so in such a complicated way that the cure was almost as bad as the disease. Criticism on this ground was very carefully considered in the ensuing weeks, but it lost much of its force when people realised that the plan was not really as complicated as it looked, and that the Inland Revenue Department's efforts to explain everything in detail had perhaps had the perverse effect of accenting the apparent complexity. The political passage of the plan was moreover helped by the readiness and ability with which the Department examined and either accepted or rejected suggested amendments. On 19th July the Chancellor was able to put a scheme, and the main issues it involved, to a meeting of the Ministers most directly affected. On 29th July 1943 the War Cabinet took note, and the Chancellor was free to go ahead with confidential consultations with employers' and workers' organisations. Opinion among these had meanwhile been moving, for the same reason as Government opinion had moved. On 29th July—the day of the War Cabinet decision—the Trades Union Congress had officially expressed to the Chancellor their 'very keen desire' to see a system of this kind 'introduced at the earliest possible moment', and when informed of the scheme they welcomed it as 'very fair and extremely practical'.

The employers also, as soon as they were brought into consultation, expressed the view that some such system was highly desirable. As a fellow taxpayer, the employer was anxious to see that the employee paid his share, and that he did so in such

---

[1] H. of C. Deb., Vol. 388, Col. 946.
[2] e.g. Finance Bill debates, 21st April and 7th July 1943.
[3] e.g. *The Times* City Notes, 12th April, leading articles 13th and 16th April 1943.

a convenient way that wage-incentives suffered the minimum disturbance. Public opinion generally had become much more interested, partly because both Canada and the United States had found ways of achieving the primary aim of switching to a current earnings basis.[1] Altogether, opinion was ready for the change and there was on all sides the goodwill and determination necessary to overcome difficulties of detail and to make the scheme a practical success.

In transforming P.A.Y.E. from a mere idea into a practical plan to be implemented by legislation and to be grafted, in the middle of a war, on to the running system, four major questions had to be decided. One of these, the question whether the assessment period should be brought right up to the deduction period or should stop just short of it, arose purely in an attempt to concede something to critics who complained of the pressure upon the wages-clerks of employers. The employers' representatives made much of the additional work—the task of calculating the P.A.Y.E. deduction from the pay-packet—to be accomplished in the 'lying-time' between the end of the pay-week and the time of pay-out. If, for example, the week's wages were made up to Thursday night for payment on Friday afternoon, the P.A.Y.E. calculations would be just one more burden to be carried by the wages-clerks during Friday morning's rush. In anticipation of this objection Keynes suggested that the deduction of tax should be made with one week's time-lag, so allowing a whole week in which to enter on the pay-sheet the amount of tax to be deducted. This suggestion was rejected as a substantial abandonment of the full principle of pay-as-you-earn, and because it would impose much additional work and irritation on the employer, even though there would be some alleviation of the burden at the wages-clerk's rush-hour. The former was a point of real importance, for any fluctuation of wages would produce problems of high liability in low-wage weeks—problems that it was the whole purpose of P.A.Y.E. to eliminate. Solution was rather to be found in increasing the lying-time between the end of the wage-week and the time of payment, and experience had shown that Trade Unions could be helpful in accepting such changes.[2] The Organisation and Methods Division at the Treasury was called in to assist with simplification of the operations to be performed by the wages-clerk, and to advise on their burdensomeness. It was shown that, in relation to the elaborate calculations of piece-wages and various conventional supplements and deductions, the work now to be

---

[1] *The Economist*, 11th September 1943, pp. 357-8.

[2] Experience with Liverpool dockers in 1940 was cited by the Inland Revenue.

added was very small. The difficulty was in fact greatly overrated at first, partly because full explanation of the plan was inevitably a lengthy business, unconsciously encouraging people to suppose that the plan's operation itself must be very complicated, and partly because employers were at this time feeling the shortage of clerical staff so acutely that they were quick to pounce upon any additional clerical burden the authorities sought to impose. The right thing to do was clearly to stick to the full principle of P.A.Y.E.—that is, to bring the assessment period right up to the deduction period—and to prove to people how simple the operation in fact could be. This course was taken, and the Chancellor was able in his budget speech of April 1944 to report that the new system had, with the co-operation of workpeople, employers and Government staffs, been successfully launched.[1]

The other issues on which the authorities had to make up their minds included the very important question of the scope of the scheme—which taxpayers should be included, which excluded? In the early official discussions the problem of 'forgiveness'— cancellation of overlapping liability—and the related problem of post-war credits were thought the more fundamental, and from this angle a narrow application of the scheme, to cover wage-earners only, was designed. Lord Keynes[2] however put the matter in an altogether different light, showing that the problem of forgiveness was really a problem of equity between classes of taxpayers. This provided a theoretical justification for the widest possible scheme, so that though in September the scheme was announced as applying to wage-earners only, Sir Kingsley Wood had already been half-converted and his successor soon broadened the scheme to cover all Schedule E taxpayers.

This problem of 'forgiveness' was at first looked at from a narrow tax-collector's point of view. The scheme was to come into operation on 6th April 1944, from which date earners would suffer deduction week by week or month by month in respect of their currently accruing liability on the income of the tax-year April 1944–April 1945. Under the previous system of collection in respect of liability accrued in the preceding period, these taxpayers would by the 5th April 1944 have paid, if manual workers, only two months of 1943–44 tax, and if others, only five months. It would clearly be impracticable to attempt collection of the remaining 1943–44 liability simultaneously with full collections under the new scheme. Deductions under the old basis must stop immediately the new scheme came into operation; the remaining 1943–44 liability— whether ten-twelfths or seven-twelfths—would have to be forgiven,

---

[1] H. of C. Deb., Vol. 399, Col. 655, 25th April 1944.

[2] Mr. Keynes became Lord Keynes in 1942.

and the Revenue on the face of it appeared to be a heavy loser. This loss would not manifest itself in any gap in accruing collections—indeed, since incomes had been rising, collections should increase rather more speedily. The Revenue's loss would be the employee's immediate relief when his earnings fell, when rates of tax fell, or when he died or left employment.

Even looked at in this narrow way, the element of forgiveness was largely illusory. For it was widely recognised that it would be impossible to collect tax on war earnings after earnings fell (this was indeed the argument that had clinched the case for P.A.Y.E.); if rates of tax were reduced, it would be impossible to make the worker continue for many months to pay at the high war-time rates; and the Inland Revenue knew from experience that when a wage-earner died or became unemployed the arrears of tax due from him nearly always had to be written off. In substance therefore, as far as concerned wage-earners to whom these last generalisations were applicable, most of what was to be forgiven would be uncollectable in any event. If taxpayers receiving substantial salaries were included, this argument would have less force: the escape from ultimate liability might be substantial. For this reason the plan was for long discussed—and the Bill reached its third reading before this was finally revised—on the basis of restriction to wage-earners and very small salary-earners. When the difficulties of excluding some or all of the salaried workers were appreciated, there was talk of 'limiting' the amount of tax forgiven—i.e. calling for some 1943-44 tax payment on top of the 1944-45 deductions.

The true nature of the forgiveness problem was referred to by Lord Keynes in his first comments to the Chancellor. The Revenue's real loss, he explained, was that 'the Chancellor, when he comes to reduce taxation, will not get the advantage he otherwise would in the yield of the tax through the time-lag[1] in its taking effect'. Finding it necessary to raise a certain sum of money by taxation, the Chancellor would therefore have to reduce the rates of taxation more slowly than he would under the old system. Taxpayers who had not benefited from P.A.Y.E. 'forgiveness', equally with those who had so benefited, would suffer from this delay in tax reductions. The practical effect of forgiveness would thus be a shifting of the burden from those included in to those excluded from P.A.Y.E.—just as the practical effect of default, under the old system, by wage-earners falling out of employment was not to leave the Exchequer short of money but to increase the burdens on other taxpayers. Lord Keynes suggested that on

---

[1] i.e. between assessment and collection on the old basis.

this view of forgiveness the scheme should be spread as widely as possible.[1]

This argument that the forgiveness problem indicated a widening rather than a narrowing of the scope of the scheme did not win the day at once, but it evidently made some impression. Other arguments in favour of a wide scope emerged as the implications of the plan were more fully examined. To exclude salaried nurses and schoolteachers with £150 a year while including skilled wage-earners receiving up to £700 or £800 a year could scarcely be defended: the case for P.A.Y.E. was above all a case for facilitating collection from the poorer people. Once any salaried people were brought in, any line of division between the higher and the lower ranks would create difficulties: how, for example, should a taxpayer be treated when he moved across the borderline?[2] Serious anomalies would, in particular, arise on demobilisation of the Forces. Because of the anomalies that would arise in one way or another, special and elaborate provisions would be necesssary, whereas Ministers and civil servants alike were determined to make the scheme as simple as possible. So, by the time the plans came to be divulged to the employers' and workers' organisations, the Chancellor was already sufficiently uncertain to wish to avoid discussion of the principle of limitation to wage-earners.

Linked with the forgiveness question was that relating to post-war credits. Since taxpayers coming under the scheme would pay only a small part of the tax due in respect of earnings in the financial year 1943–44, they could not reasonably expect post-war credits for that year equal to the full amounts prescribed by the 1941 budget,[3] but they should receive post-war credits only to the extent that the tax actually paid for that year—i.e. two-twelfths or five-twelfths of liability on the old assessment—exceeded the hypothetical tax for the *whole* year on the basis of pre-1941 allowances. The amount of tax 'forgiven' for 1943–44 would thus be, to quite a large extent,[4] offset by reduced Exchequer liability on post-war credits. This proposal was accepted and did not create any difficulty at any stage.

---

[1] An American view of the forgiveness problem has strong commonsense appeal: 'The Treasury would get the same income right up to the end of the world. Come the Day of Judgment it would take an awful loss, but on the Day of Judgment the Treasury is going to have so much else to answer for that it won't ever think about taxes'. (Quoted in *The Economist*, 13th March 1943, p. 332). Two earlier Chancellors (Mr. Lowe and Mr. Churchill) had made similar remarks about the Day of Judgment when they advanced certain due dates for income tax.

[2] 'Forgiveness' might in such cases open the door to collusion by employer and employee in tax-dodging.

[3] See above, pp. 78 and 84.

[4] When the scheme went before Ministers, this proportion was put at 'about one-half'.

Once the technique of the plan had been accepted as a solution of the urgent problem of getting wage-earners' deductions on to a current earnings' basis, preparatory action could go forward on the basis that weekly wage-earners at least would have to be covered. Preliminary soundings of employers' and workers' organisations proceeded on this basis and, these having gone satisfactorily, Parliamentary acceptance had to be sought without delay in order to enable the Inland Revenue Department to tackle the heavy task of preparing the tables and instructions for employers. So although by September there was much support in Ministerial and official circles for the widest possible scope, the first announcement in the House of Commons, on 22nd September 1943,[1] was of 'a new system for the taxation of weekly wage-earners . . . to confer on the wage-earner all the benefits of a pay-as-you-earn basis by regulating the weekly deduction of tax so as to keep in step both with the weekly earnings and the liability for the whole year'; and the accompanying White Paper set out the details of the scheme on this restricted basis.

The first supplementary question[2] expressed the 'great satisfaction' of wage-earners. The second[3] jumped to the desirability of equity as between these and other classes of tax-payers, and another enquired about the position of black-coated workers. These immediate Parliamentary reactions were an accurate foretaste of the whole course of Parliamentary discussions. There was no doubt at all about the welcome given to the central principle of P.A.Y.E., and the ingenuity that had produced it was frequently praised. On the other hand, there was from the outset much dissatisfaction with the proposal to limit its benefits to a particular class of income-earners. Because of the need to revoke by legislation the taxpayers' liabilities that had to be 'forgiven', the whole forgiveness problem received much attention. Though this problem appears to have been only imperfectly understood in these discussions, its existence served to secure strong support for extension of the scheme to all earners. More cogently it was argued that the attractions of P.A.Y.E. had universal appeal, and that it was unfair to refuse to salary-earners the convenience that was to be granted to the wage-earners.

The pleas for extension were at first resisted by the Chancellor (now Sir John Anderson). Though admitting the case in the abstract,[4] he argued that there was not for a wider scope

---

[1] H. of C. Deb., Vol. 392, Col. 210.

[2] Mr. Kirkwood.

[3] Sir H. Williams.

[4] 'If income tax were being started afresh as a new tax, I have no doubt that the new system would be applied universally to employment' (H. of C. Deb., Vol. 392, Col. 1101).

the imperative necessity that dictated application to wage-earners, and that he must pay attention to the cost—the element of 'forgiveness' that was no mere shadow for people from whom arrears *could* be collected after the war.[1] So Keynes's reformulation of the forgiveness problem, though it had had its effect in opening minds to a wider scope, was forgotten, and the ghost of the Revenue's loss continued in the Parliamentary debates to bedevil the efforts of those pressing for universalisation of P.A.Y.E. But even at this stage the Chancellor said outright that his mind was 'not closed', and the force of opinion led him to concede the inclusion, at first of those earning salaries up to £600 a year and then, on the third reading of the Bill,[2] of all Schedule E taxpayers.

The system as actually introduced on 6th April 1944 thus applied to all earners of income, at every level of wage or salary. The fact that this comprehensiveness was established in response to very definite public demand, expressed in the full discussions in the autumn of 1943, helped to give the scheme a good start.[3] The lapse of time between the first announcement and the institution of the scheme, necessary because of the heavy preparatory work in the Inland Revenue Department, was a blessing in that it gave the general public time to grasp the essential features. The Government's plans had had a good Press,[4] and special efforts were made by the Ministry of Labour and the Supply Departments to ensure wide understanding by workers. The Inland Revenue Department showed itself accommodatingly flexible in its detailed administration of the scheme,[5] and issued a booklet spelling everything out in simple language.[6] Some adjustments were made in the detailed arrangements for wage payments but, thanks to careful

---

[1] *Ibid:* 'I could not, in the crisis of a great war, when so much uncertainty enshrouds our financial future, lightly forego a claim to many millions of pounds—a claim which is in every respect legitimate and reasonable'.

[2] Though the Chancellor announced the final extension on the third reading of the original Bill (the Wage Earners' Income Tax Bill which became the Income Tax (Employment) Act of 1943) the extension to salary-earners above £600 a year was made by separate legislation, the Income Tax (Offices and Employments) Act of 1944. The decision to legislate separately for the higher-paid salaried workers was due to the Chancellor's view that anomalies requiring special legislative treatment would be substantial for these taxpayers, and that more time for thought should therefore be taken.

[3] In the course of legislation the Government (under pressure that should have been unnecessary) decided to remove inequities affecting temporary civil servants (see *The Economist*, 30th October and 6th November 1943). The Chancellor's eventual concession of the claims of justice on such counts as this helped to consolidate the public's welcome to the plan as a whole.

[4] e.g. *The Times*, leading article, 'Taxing without Tears', 23rd September 1943, and *The Economist*, 25th September 1943.

[5] e.g. after discussions with employers' and workers' organisations, employers were given the option of working on a modified plan whereby adjustments are made, bringing the cumulative deduction to the correct figure, every third or fourth week instead of every week.

[6] *Pay As You Earn*, H.M.S.O. 1944, Price 3d.

handling and the P.A.Y.E. propaganda, these did not prove serious irritants in industrial relations.

The establishment of P.A.Y.E. in the middle of the war was, as the Chancellor of the Exchequer claimed,[1] 'no mean feat'. About 16 million people came within the scope of the scheme, three-quarters of these being in the event liable to tax. About a million employers were concerned, and the amount collected in the first year was about £540 millions. From manual wage-earners alone £250 millions were collected, as compared with £200 millions in the last year of the old system. Looking back after the first year, Sir John Anderson claimed 'remarkable success'; his predecessor had been 'amply justified in taking the bold course'. 'At all events', he added, 'there can be no doubt that Pay-as-you-earn is a boon to the employee who has to live on a weekly or monthly budget and I believe it has been generally welcomed by him as such'.[2]

Meanwhile those concerned with framing the budget of 1945 were already beginning to realise that the tremendous gain in flexibility for the taxpayer had been won at the price of a new rigidity for the taxplanners. It has been remarked above that the time needed by the Inland Revenue for preparatory work in the winter of 1943–44 had been a blessing in that it afforded opportunity for public discussion and digestion. Some of this preparatory work—on the tax tables for employers, for instance— would have to be repeated every year, and the details of these tables depended upon the rates of tax and allowances. If these were to be altered in any budget, the Inland Revenue Department required long notice. The period was originally mentioned as six months, and it was suggested that changes might be announced in one budget to come into operation only in the *following* financial year—i.e. almost a year later. This appalled the Treasury. It would 'always have been regarded as very inconvenient, and indeed to be avoided at all costs. Today the argument is even stronger because it is said that changes in the rate of taxation ought from time to time to be introduced and made effective with the least possible delay for reasons connected with full employment'. The Treasury suggested that the solution might be found by continuing deductions, after a budget, on the basis of the old tables, followed by adjustments when new tables could be brought out; and the Treasury pressed for drastic abbreviation of the period for bringing out such new tables. Eventually ways and means were found for such an abbreviation and in the post-war years changes became operative about three months after budget

---

[1] H. of C. Deb., Vol. 399, Col. 655.

[2] *Ibid.*, Vol. 410, Col. 700.

announcements—a delay that does not in general imply an intolerable amount of adjustment.

This rigidity cramping a Chancellor's speed of action—a limitation that has been reduced to tolerable shape—is however only a comparatively minor manifestation of the fundamental rigidity imposed on the tax structure by the new system. The ingenious arrangements devised by the Inland Revenue Department in 1943 admirably served their immediate purpose in war conditions when the main structure of taxation was set firmly for the duration of the war. Minor difficulties have arisen (and have been overcome) when in post-war years Chancellors have wished to change rates of tax or the allowances. But if a Chancellor were to seek to change the entire structure of the income tax—to abolish the standard rate or to revolutionise the allowances for example—the P.A.Y.E. machine would be thrown far too completely out of gear to enable it to pick up in a mere three or four months. A Chancellor wishing drastically to reform the income tax might on this account be faced by the dilemma of a substantial gap in revenue receipts and wholesale tax holidays ('forgiveness' of a more substantial kind than that of 1944) or very substantial temporary departure from the current earnings' basis, provoking loud complainings in our streets. The recent (1955) Report of the Royal Commission on Taxation makes it unlikely that this problem will become a practical one in the foreseeable future, but a Chancellor bent on drastic reform may one day have to pay a heavy penalty in order to escape from the framework riveted on him by his predecessors who so boldly and wisely introduced P.A.Y.E.

This was scarcely the intention of Sir Kingsley Wood. In his confidential talk with employers' representatives[1] he explained two compelling reasons for his proposals; one was the prospect of falling earnings at the end of the war, the other was that 'it seemed most important that the present conditions under which the wage-earners as a whole were making a contribution to the affairs of the State through direct taxation, should be maintained',[2] and the collection from wage-earners should therefore be put on an efficient and non-irritant basis. Had it not been for these reasons, he would have been tempted to postpone any such drastic change until after the war, evidently on the general ground that war-time was not the time for reform. Schemes for radical reform of the structure of the income tax, such as those constantly propounded

---

[1] 17th September 1943.

[2] Had he foreseen the weight of Exchequer needs in post-war years, he would surely have felt even more strongly on this account.

by *The Economist* outside[1] and by Lord Catto inside the Treasury, never had a chance of acceptance during the war, on precisely the ground that permanent arrangements ought to have cooler and more leisurely consideration than could be expected in war-time. The P.A.Y.E. plan was thought to be the minimum innovation for presenting the first post-war Chancellor with an efficient running machine. The reflection that this minimum innovation was going to prejudice more fundamental reform would almost certainly have distressed the two Chancellors who had for once pleased nearly everybody, and would also have liked to please their successors. *The Economist*, harking back to its theme that the method of assessment should be revolutionised, commented 'a great chance has been lost'.[2] This appeared a little harsh at the time. That the chance was being crabbed for all time was not realised until long afterwards.

(iii)

Minor Adjustments of the Income Tax

With the rise in income tax rates to their peak in 1941—or rather to a plateau continuing to the end of the war—the disincentive effects became a matter for serious concern. To the extent that the high level of taxation did check the efforts of the people,[3] the arithmetic of the stabilisation policy was falsified and war production was harmed both directly and indirectly. In a broad way this risk had to be accepted, with the hope that patriotic and other motives would keep it within bounds, but it was a substantial factor in guiding Chancellors away from direct taxation and towards taxation of luxuries when they were compelled in 1942 and 1943 to find some extra revenue.[4] In two particular matters, however, there was over a long period a running fire of criticism of the disincentive effects of income tax. These related to overtime earnings and the earnings of married women.

The intensification of the war effort quickly raised the importance of overtime earnings, especially from the summer of 1940 onwards. The care and elaboration with which the income tax had been made an instrument of quite steeply progressive taxation, even in its lower ranges, caused the impact of the tax on

---

[1] e.g. 7th February 1942, pp. 176-7.

[2] 25th September 1943, pp. 422-23.

[3] There was some evidence, for example, that absenteeism in the coal mines was encouraged by the incidence of income tax. (Parliamentary Secretary, Ministry of Fuel and Power, H. of C. Deb., Vol. 409, Col. 1685).

[4] On the further taxation of luxuries, see Sections (v) and (vi) of this chapter.

marginal earnings—which was the light in which the worker naturally regarded overtime pay—to be very severe indeed, even for the less skilled workers who had in pre-war days been scarcely touched by this tax. Employers and the Ministry of Labour, the parties most directly interested in the supply of labour, therefore took up with the Treasury the possibility of some special treatment of overtime earnings and there were frequent representations in the Commons.[1] The objections from the Revenue angle were very strong: there were, for example, the administrative impossibility of policing the distinction between ordinary time and overtime, the ill-feeling created when some workers felt that others were successfully cheating the tax-collector, and the substantial revenue (and purchasing power) involved if any worth-while concession were made. The case failed.

The earnings of married women were similarly affected by the steeply progressive nature of the tax because, partly for distributional reasons, the incomes of husband and wife were assessed as a single income. Earnings of the wife were therefore regarded in nearly all homes as marginal income to be considered in relation to the extra taxation attracted. If the addition to net income was to have any importance at all in promoting the mobilisation of women—and everyone admitted that this must be so—the income tax arrangements must not absorb a very large part of the wages earned by wives. Moreover—and this was a practical point during these years—there must not be even the appearance or the suspicion that income tax would largely absorb the earnings of the married women. Unfortunately for war-time Chancellors, the experience and discussions of the recent past, when the professional woman at work had been heavily penalised[2] and the tax collector had indeed offered a premium on 'living in sin',[3] tended to magnify the problem in the public mind. It had become a common misconception that the joint assessment of husband and wife necessarily resulted in a greater tax burden than separate assessment:[4] in fact this was, after the 1941 budget, true only when the wife was not earning or was earning a substantial income. If she was earning a sum less than £168 a year, separate assessment would have been more burdensome.[5] But it was little

---

[1] The question was most frequently raised in relation to shipbuilding and engineering, e.g. H. of C. Deb., Vol. 374, Col. 1243, 14th October 1941, and Vol. 376, Cols. 1827-8. For other references, see Vol. 377, Col. 580, Vol. 390, Col. 1933 and Vol. 410, Col. 24.

[2] cf. *The Economist*, 2nd March 1940, pp. 373-4.

[3] H. of C. Deb., Vol. 342, Col. 2668.

[4] See, e.g. H. of C. Deb., Vol. 346, Col. 516.

[5] An additional allowance of £45 was given to a wife with earned income and this together with the £140 married allowance exceeded two single allowances of £80 each. The position was often explained in the House of Commons, e.g. in H. of C. Deb., Vol. 393, Col. 44.

use for Chancellors to reiterate this. The law was not easily understood by couples neither of whom had been used to paying income tax at all, and the extra tax due to the wife's addition to the joint income was naturally regarded as coming wholly off the wife's income so that 'it wasn't worth going out to work at all'.[1] As a concession to stimulate the movement of married women into employment, the Chancellor in his 1942 budget accepted a proposal, originating in the Trades Union Congress, that the married women's earned income allowance should be raised from £45 maximum to £80 maximum.[2] At most income levels that mattered for the attraction of married women into war production, husband and wife would henceforth be treated more favourably than if they were single persons. The concession was expected to cost the Exchequer £25 millions in a full year.[3]

Another concession having some bearing on the mobilisation of labour for war production, though also having other roots, was the allowance for travelling expenses incurred through a war-time change in circumstances. The traditional Inland Revenue view was that the cost of travelling between residence and place of employment was not a deductible expense in the assessment of income, and any reversal of this principle would have been most unwelcome, not only on account of the revenue lost but also for the administrative difficulties of keeping control over the many opportunities for abuse. But in war-time there was a very strong case for some relief. Many people had to incur much higher costs of travelling to work, not because they chose to live among green fields far away from factory smoke but because evacuation policy or actual bombing had forced them away; their ability to bear taxation was thus reduced. At the same time, the Government was anxious to move people into different employment, and there was some injustice in paying always for the soldier's travelling while the ordnance factory worker had to pay his bus fares out of taxed income. All these arguments would have been thought too trivial had not the marginal rates of taxation risen to penal levels. There had been some Parliamentary agitation of the question ever since the beginning of the war,[4] and the sharp increases of 1940 and 1941 magnified into practical issues hardships and disincentives that could earlier be dismissed by the *de mimimis* precept.

[1] For examples of Parliamentary representations, see H. of C. Deb., Vol. 370, Col. 1164; Vol. 374, Cols. 498-9, *Ibid.*, Cols. 2014-6; Vol. 390, Cols. 1535-45.

[2] The former allowance had been nine-tenths of the wife's earned income up to a maximum of £45; now it was to be nine-tenths up to a maximum of £80.

[3] H. of C. Deb., Vol. 379, Cols. 121-2. One M.P. attacked it as an unnecessary sop that the country could ill afford (*ibid.*, Col. 1789).

[4] e.g. H. of C. Deb., Vol. 351, Cols. 1050-1 (21st September 1939); Vol. 367, Col. 1152 (18th December 1940) and Vol. 371, Cols. 147 and 174 (23rd April 1941).

I

Any concession to meet this claim had, on administrative grounds, to be very simple and to be limited to a flat sum applicable to a group of incomes already identified in other ways. When, therefore, representations in the 1941 budget debates[1] induced the Chancellor to make some allowance,[2] it was limited to the manual wage-earners who were subject to six-monthly assessment, and they were allowed to deduct up to £5 in each half-year on account of additional travelling expenses due to war conditions.[3] Limitation to manual workers was defended on the grounds of (a) minimisation of cost, (b) the more intimate relation of manual workers' activities to the war effort, and (c) the fact that manual workers were more accustomed than, say, clerks and typists, to living near their work.[4] Even this simple scheme was at once criticised as inequitable and inadequate, so that Sir Kingsley Wood, having tried to find a manageable way of meeting an oft-reiterated claim, was stung into opening a speech with the words: 'I should like to remark first how little gratitude there is in this world'.[5]

Criticism on the ground of injustice as between manual workers and others did not cease with the budget debates. The Inland Revenue received a number of letters, and in December pressure within the Trade Union movement led to a formal request from the Trades Union Congress that the concession should be extended to those non-manual and salaried workpeople whose income did not exceed £420. The Chancellor was disposed to leave the matter over as one on which concession could be framed in the light of Finance Bill debates, but administrative considerations overrode Sir Kingsley Wood's Parliamentary inclinations and he made the announcement in the budget speech itself.[6] He gave no reasons and his action provoked no comment in the budget debates.

In the following year (1943) Sir Kingsley Wood turned his attention to another grievance that was an old story of minor hardship now aggravated by the higher rates of taxation. This arose from the restricted scope of the housekeeper allowance and the small amount of the dependent relative allowance. There was no question of incentives here; it was solely a question of equity. The two allowances had to be considered together. Narrow

---

[1] H. of C. Deb., Vol. 371, Cols. 196-7 and 201.

[2] H. of C. Deb., Vol. 372, Col. 1235 *et seq.* The Chancellor gave his reason as 'I think it will assist our war effort'.

[3] Section 23 Finance Act 1941. A Ministry of Labour suggestion that the allowance should cover expenses in excess of 3s. a week was rejected in favour of the simplest possible scheme.

[4] H. of C. Deb., Vol. 372, Cols. 1243-4.

[5] H. of C. Deb., Vol. 372, Col. 1240.

[6] H. of C. Deb., Vol. 379, Col. 115.

definition of the housekeeper allowance had always created hard
cases, but distinctions had to be drawn somewhere and, as the
Royal Commission on Income Tax had pointed out in 1920, there
were always so many variations in domestic circumstances that
it was 'not possible in any scheme to adjust taxation so closely
as to take into consideration the purely personal circumstances
of each taxpayer'.[1] Year after year anomalies were attacked and
hard cases cited, but successive Chancellors had taken their stand
on this general principle adumbrated in 1920. In the 1941 budget
debates there was a particularly strong attack on the narrowness
of these allowances,[2] but the Financial Secretary pleaded that,
difficult as it was to build up a satisfactory code in peace-time, it
was 'harder still to embark upon any patchwork of changes and
reliefs in war-time'.[3] But the weight that higher rates of taxation
had given to the plea could not be thus easily escaped, and the
Chancellor himself conceded, later in the debate,[4] a promise to
look into the question. This promise was redeemed in 1943 when,
accepting the arguments adduced in the previous year, the
Chancellor announced—and explained at some length—in his
budget speech[5] the broadening of the housekeeper allowance
and the raising of the dependent relative allowance from £25 to
£50, the latter being the amount of the housekeeper allowance.

The same ise in taxation rates that had necessitated new
concessions to cover hard cases equally called for a review of the
discrimination hitherto enjoyed, in income tax administration,
by the farmers. Largely because of their inadequate trading accounts,
farmers had been taxed under Schedule B on the basis of
the assessed annual value of the land they farmed: taxable profits,
it was assumed, could be guessed sufficiently by looking at the
rental value. In 1914 the basis used was one-third of the annual
value; this had been raised in 1915 to the annual value and in 1918,
when farmers were faring well, to twice the annual value; in 1922
the agricultural depression occasioned reduction to the annual
value, at which level it remained. A farmer who could prove
lower profits had the option of assessment on actual profits.

The privilege had always been open to attack as unfair,
especially by market gardeners who did not enjoy such treatment.[6]
The Inland Revenue Department, a little surprisingly, viewed

---

1 Paragraphs 237 and 271 of Report (Cmd. 615 of 1920).

2 See especially H. of C. Deb., Vol. 379, Cols. 1831-42.

3 *Ibid.*, Col. 1840.

4 *Ibid.*, Col. 1843.

5 H. of C. Deb., Vol. 388, Cols. 956-9.

6 The market gardeners' complaints had in previous years been considered by Mr.
Neville Chamberlain and Sir John Simon.

the privilege as unnecessary; they were so used to coping with the rudimentary accounts of shopkeepers and other small traders that they believed themselves capable of assessing the farmers' actual profits, and the Royal Commission on Income Tax in 1920 had recommended that the farmers be gradually assimilated to other traders.[1] With war-time developments a review became appropriate: the higher rates of tax made the injustices more substantial and the amount of revenue eluding the Exchequer also of more account. The matter was brought to a head when generous guaranteed prices were fixed for the 1940 crops: the Ministry of Agriculture believed these prices necessary in order to stimulate production on the poorer soils, but foresaw resulting high profits—perhaps very high profits—from the better lands.[2] Anticipating that the spectacle of these high profits would provoke criticism and might politically jeopardise the guaranteed prices scheme which was at the core of the home food production programme, the Minister of Agriculture proposed that at any rate the larger farms should be transferred to a Schedule D (i.e. actual profits) basis. The case was reinforced by strong comments within and without official circles: an eminent agricultural economist, for example, represented that unless the farmers were driven by the tax inspector they would never keep the accounts which alone could provide a serious basis for a scheme of guaranteed prices. The proposed change in the basis of assessment was accepted in principle by Ministers when in June 1940 they agreed to certain increases in the guaranteed prices, details of the change being left for further discussion on the understanding that the necessary legislative changes would be included in the Finance Act of 1941.

In discussion it emerged that the Minister of Agriculture wanted only to catch the really big farmers: to charge the smaller, or even medium-sized farmers on a profits basis would result in decreased production. This was a time when chances could not be taken about home food production, and the Chancellor allowed the disincentive argument about the smaller farmers to prevail. In the budget of 1941, accordingly, he announced that individual farmers whose lands exceeded £300 in annual value would in future be assessed under Schedule D, like traders generally, by reference to their actual profits.[3] Suspicion that, even so, many farmers were escaping very lightly, and that invidious comparisons might be made with their own employees,

---

[1] Paragraph 452 of *Report* (Cmd. 615 of 1920).

[2] See K. A. H. Murray, *Agriculture*, in this series (H.M.S.O. 1955).

[3] H. of C. Deb., Vol. 370, Cols. 1315-6. He said that the annual values 'often fall very far short of their actual profits'.

encouraged the authorities to watch the position very closely.

From the enquiries made thereafter, the generalisation emerged that the rate of profit averaged three times the annual value. In this light the Chancellor in 1942 went much further: the area of charge on profits was extended by reducing the £300 to £100. Only the small farmer was left to pay tax on annual value, and in his case the tax would henceforth be charged on three times the annual value, subject still to the proviso that he could be assessed on actual profits if these were less.[1]

By these minor adjustments in allowances—for married women in employment, for housekeepers and dependent relatives, and for travelling expenses—and by changing the basis of assessment for farmers, the income tax machine was in effect re-geared to fit the higher rates of tax. In making these changes, Chancellors were very careful not to bring into question any general principles affecting a substantial part of the revenue, and though considerations of both equity and incentive received important attention, they were allowed to undermine neither the yield of the tax nor its broad distribution between classes. In the closing weeks of the war Mr. Bevin, then Minister of Labour, brought forward proposals which did raise these broader issues. The context was a belief that as the war with Germany came to an end a substantial reduction of revenue would be acceptable to the Chancellor, and Mr. Bevin sought to stake as first claim the case for the very small income taxpayer. Precisely what were his proposals does not emerge in the papers: they were apparently made when Mr. Bevin called on the Chancellor in the second week of January 1945. It seems, however, that the starting point was a proposal that the exemption limit should be raised from £110, on the ground that this infringed upon the subsistence level. The principle that the exemption limit was intended to cover subsistence had never been explicitly admitted, though it might well be argued that it was always tacitly assumed, at any rate from the date when war necessities obliged the Chancellor to press taxation up to the hilt. But if it were admitted, the allowance for married couples—£140— must equally come under review, and even that did not provide a logical stopping-place. Ought the children's allowances also to be reviewed in the light of the rise in living costs? And what of the housekeeper allowance? The more the problem was looked at, the less defensible did any simple but piecemeal treatment appear. On the other hand, a complex revision needed more leisurely

---

[1] H. of C. Deb., Vol. 379, Cols. 116 and 117. The change necessitated review of certain agricultural valuation problems, which had apparently been partly responsible for the fears of the agricultural Ministers when they resisted for the smaller farmer the proposed change in 1941.

political examination and—a more immediately decisive consideration—more time for the printers to cope with adjustments
in the P.A.Y.E. machine.[1] Clearly an attempt to deal with these
important questions would have been untimely in the budget of
April 1945, introduced before even the German war was finished
and when a further long period of war against Japan was generally
assumed as inevitable. Even if the Chancellor had made proposals
to meet Mr. Bevin's suggestions, they could only have been made
in a preliminary way and would certainly have been dropped
when the Caretaker Government revised the Finance Bill. As it
was, Sir John Anderson, in his budget speech,[2] gave as his opinion
that justice could only be done after a comprehensive review for
which the time was not yet ripe.

(iv)
The Excess Profits Tax

In the 1941 budget the Chancellor had accepted the view that the
100 per cent. excess profits tax, dictated not solely by fiscal
considerations, had come to stay. He had sought, on that occasion,
to modify the disincentive effects of the 100 per cent. rate by making
one-fifth of the tax refundable at the end of the war. Even with
this modification, the height of the tax and its war-time permanence
made it desirable to avoid hard cases as far as possible. Certain
concessions had therefore been made: by allowance of borrowed
capital as part of the capital employed in the business; and by
special provision for wasting assets in oil and metal concerns. In
the ensuing years the Government's general attitude remained
the same; the 100 per cent. rate remained, subject to the refundable
20 per cent., and further efforts were made to relieve the hard
cases created by the ferocity of the general principle. In the course
of time the concessions to meet hard cases opened new loopholes
for evasion, and the steps taken to close these loopholes further
complicated the legal framework of E.P.T. But although for these
reasons the Inland Revenue came to administer a more and more
involved code, the essence of E.P.T. was not changed after 1941.

After the arrangements made in 1941—after some political
bargaining—about the 20 per cent. refund, the Chancellor was
obliged sooner or later to attempt to give some precision to the
conditions to be attached to repayment. The Finance Act of 1941

---

[1] H.M. Stationery Office wrote to the Inland Revenue in February 1945: 'For the
first time in history we have reached a position in this country where the limit of printing
capacity is itself a factor in policy'.

[2] H. of C. Deb., Vol. 410, Cols. 721-2.

had provided[1] that 20 per cent. 'shall, if such conditions as Parliament may hereafter determine are satisfied, be repaid at such date as Parliament may hereafter determine'. The vagueness of this provision had given rise to much criticism; no firm could base thereon any useful estimate of its future resources. Consequently much of the incentive effect, which was the whole point of the concession, had been lost. It would therefore be sensible to face the problem sooner rather than later; in fact, the sooner the better. The Chancellor's advisers, attempting to frame conditions that would have to be translated into statutory terms, advised that very serious difficulties would beset the Parliamentary draughtsmen, and that even when their task was done, quite intolerable difficulties would beset an executive charged with 'using the conditions' as a lever for securing a 'brave new world'. They therefore advised that the repayment should be made unconditionally at a time to be determined by Parliament. This simple course was, however, politically impracticable: the Minister of Labour continued to insist upon the exclusion of immediate benefit for shareholders. In the 1942 budget speech the Chancellor announced that this post-war credit would accrue to the firm by 'statutory right, subject only to its not being used for dividends or for the issue of bonus shares'.[2] The effective observance of these conditions was left for attention when the time should come. Two years later, when the harmful effects of the remaining element of uncertainty had been pressed upon Sir John Anderson, he stood firmly upon the formula adopted by his predecessor in 1942.[3]

The excess profit entirely creamed off by this 100 per cent. tax was the excess of actual profit over a 'standard', this standard being fixed by reference to experience in certain pre-war years, by a percentage on capital or, for small firms, as a flat sum for each working partner. Inevitably the Chancellor was under constant pressure to raise these standards. In his 1942 and 1943 budgets, Sir Kingsley Wood took the view that broadly the settlement of 1941 should stand. The provisions then made for concerns with low profit standards allowed, in the great majority of cases, the adoption of the alternative standard of six per cent. on capital employed—which now included borrowed capital. The provisions for personal standards were already 'far more generous than in the last war'.[4] In 1943 again he made no change. The budgets of 1944

---

[1] Section 28.

[2] H. of C. Deb., Vol. 379, Col. 125. *The Economist* noted this as one of the particular grounds of satisfaction with the budget speech (18th April 1942, p. 528).

[3] H. of C. Deb., Vol. 399, Col. 669.

[4] H. of C. Deb., Vol. 379, Col. 124.

and 1945, however, were more affected by the Government's rising interest in industry's post-war reconstruction and progress, and in both these years Sir John Anderson recognised a special case for the small businesses. 'As the Excess Profits Tax continues from year to year,' he said,[1] 'it cannot but have a cramping effect on the growth of small and young enterprises, an effect quite disproportionate to the Revenue involved'. From 1st April 1944 all standards except 'profit standards' were increased by £1,000. Applying to all cases where the standard was a minimum standard, or the personal working proprietor standard, or a standard representing a percentage on capital employed in the business, this concession in effect exempted some 10,000 small firms from the tax, and gave some relief to 20,000 more.[2] In the following year a somewhat complex relief was granted to all small firms— including this time the 'profit standard' firms who had been excluded in 1944. For all those whose standard was under £12,000, the existing standard was increased by one-tenth of the amount by which the existing standard fell short of £12,000.[3] Among its effects was the raising of the exemption limit to £3,000 and of the personal standard for the single working proprietor from £2,500 to £3,450.[4]

Given the 'standard', a firm's liability depended upon its recognised profits. With the tax at 100 per cent. (less refund) a firm's incentive to exaggerate its costs, so reducing *pari passu* its excess profits, was extreme, and the Inland Revenue Department had necessarily to protect itself by rigid rules. These rules were especially open to attack where they operated harshly on firms whose assets were being depleted by war-time activity, and where the rules threatened to allow insufficiently for an end-of-the-war fall in the value of fixed or working capital. In 1941 relief had been given to firms engaged in mining metal or oil if their exploitation of mineral deposits had been accelerated in the interests of war production. When in 1942 the Chancellor called for a pre-budget

---

[1] H. of C. Deb., Vol. 410, Col. 702.

[2] This relief was subject to a qualification. In general, deficiencies of actual profit below the standard could be carried either backwards or forwards, as a debit against the excess profits of another period. (This provision had become known as 'the E.P.T. cushion'; see e.g. *The Economist*, 16th May 1942 referring to J. & P. Coats Ltd.). Deficiencies due to the new relief, on the other hand, could be carried only forwards. (H. of C. Deb., Vol. 399, Cols. 669-70).

[3] i.e. where the standard had been £4,000, it now became £4,800. (H. of C. Deb., Vol. 410, Cols. 702-3). The benefit was limited to those under the £12,000 line, because the 1944 concession referred to above had also in effect been so limited. In both years, that is to say, the Chancellor deliberately confined the relief to small firms.

[4] This E.P.T. relief was one of the few items of Sir John Anderson's 1945 budget to be retained in the revised Finance Bill eventually presented by the Caretaker Government. Sir John Anderson claimed that this item had been 'generally welcomed' and that the desirability of avoiding uncertainty made it a special case. (H. of C. Deb., Vol. 411, Cols. 567-8).

report on the major criticisms of E.P.T., some attention was given to representations that the sand and gravel industry should be included in this 'wasting assets' concession. In this as in so many other cases the experts had to remember that nature does not make a jump,[1] and that for taxation purposes a hard line of distinction had to be drawn somewhere. Looking at the sand and gravel industry, they agreed that it was comparatively easy to transfer machinery from one gravel pit to another, and that there were almost unlimited sites for new gravel pits. The line therefore, they advised, should still exclude this industry from the concession enjoyed by certain metal and oil industries.[2] The representations therefore failed in 1942 and 1943, although disappointment was expressed in the budget debates both for this and other industries.[3] As the years dragged on the case grew stronger because, although the Revenue might still be right in urging that there was still plenty of gravel left in England, the producers were having to resort to less and less favourable sites. In his 1943 budget Sir John Anderson admitted the claim 'for certain minerals, such as sand and gravel' and at the same time elaborated the basis laid down in 1941 for metals and oil.[4]

Continuance of the war also meant continuance and intensification of the pressure to take a more generous line in other allowances to be set against profits. After the 1942 debates the Chancellor arranged for expert consultations between the Revenue Department, the principal industrial and commercial bodies and the accountancy profession, and these discussions were coloured by the growing interest, inside as well as outside official circles, in post-war reconstruction. It was in the light of these discussions that the Chancellor in his 1943 budget speech announced certain concessions, in principle if not always immediately in detail. The cost of repairs falling due but not undertaken until the end of the war, costs of restoring peace-time factory lay-out and the loss of value of equipment not scrapped but less appropriate for peace-time purposes, were among the subjects on which the Chancellor gave directions for more generous treatment, and the Inland Revenue came to satisfactory working arrangements with the tax-paying

---

[1] *Natura non facit saltum* was the motto inscribed on the title page of Marshall's *Principles of Economics*, which had dominated English economic thought for half a century up to 1936.

[2] The Indian E.P.T. regulations followed those of the United Kingdom and mica was excluded from the 'wasting assets concession'; but when the United Kingdom Government found that this exclusion was deterring the Indian producers from the expansion critically required for United Kingdom war production, the United Kingdom Government successfully pressed for extension by the Government of India.

[3] See, e.g. H. of C. Deb., Vol. 375, Cols. 225, 1306.

[4] The elaboration allowed relief 'where normal management practice . . . . has been departed from in order to accelerate production for the war, but in such a way that working costs after the war will be increased'. (H. of C. Deb., Vol. 388, Col. 962).

businesses. A parallel subject also referred to was the treatment of losses in the event of a fall in the value of stocks after the war—a subject in which memories of 1920–21 evoked keen interest. On this the Chancellor referred to the provision that had been made in the Finance Act of 1921, and agreed that similar provision might have to be made again. Consideration would, however, be deferred until the end of the war, when it could be undertaken in the light of conditions then prevailing.[1]

These concessions of one kind and another opened new loopholes for evasion and made old loopholes more profitable. The lapse of time, too, was operating against the Revenue. It was therefore necessary to complicate further the laws governing E.P.T. in endeavours to stop some of these loopholes. Among the most common evasions were those arising from abuse of the special provisions for working proprietors of small firms. The 1941 Finance Act had provided[2] that tax could still be recovered if evasion from liability had been 'the main purpose' of a change in the organisation of a firm. When the Chancellor on that occasion conceded that the phrase should be 'the main purpose' and not 'one of the purposes,' he warned the House that experience might force him to return to the charge,[3] and by 1944 it was deemed necessary to return to the first proposal. The House still disliked so sweeping a phrase as 'one of the purposes', and eventually it was limited to two specific classes of evasive transactions, namely those involving transfer of shares or changes in the persons carrying on the business.[4] The Revenue estimated that this would strengthen their hands in dealing with 1,700 cases then under consideration, to which 40 or 50 new cases were being added every week.

Usually these steps against evasion allowed horses who had already bolted to stay outside the stable door, or at least to enjoy a little grazing before they were brought back. Exceptionally the Chancellor thought the circumstances so scandalous that he resorted to retrospective legislation. In 1942–43 the Chancellor's attention was drawn[5] to transactions in shares in a whisky company whereby profits on the sale of whisky were ostensibly diverted, after payment of extravagant commission, to 'men of straw', often alleged to be living abroad, from whom the Revenue was unable to force collection. Clause 23 of the Finance Act, 1943 enabled the Revenue to recover jointly and severally from all those who had benefited from the transactions whether in shares or whisky. The case for resort

---

[1] H. of C. Deb., Vol. 388, Cols. 959-61.

[2] Clause 35.

[3] H. of C. Deb., Vol. 372, Col. 1279.

[4] H. of C. Deb., Vol. 401, Col. 740.

[5] e.g. by Sir George Broadbridge in H. of C. Deb., Vol. 383, Col. 2259 (10th November 1942).

to that objectionable step, retrospective legislation, looked pretty strong in this instance, but even this case led the Chancellor into a long dispute with a prominent shareholder who strongly protested that he, and many other shareholders too, had no idea of the purpose of the transaction.[1] The Chancellor stuck to his guns; those who had benefited had to pay, whether they had understood what it was all about or not. But the complications of the case probably encouraged the Chancellor in his wariness of this extreme anti-evasion tactic.

The controversy just referred to was a mere fraction of the barrage of representations—by private letters, by deputations, and in the Press—for this, that and the other modification of E.P.T. By the time the tax had been running two or three years, however, the Revenue and Treasury experts were well versed in every one of the arguments adduced and could point out with justice that most of the complaints were at bottom complaints about the rate or general principles of the tax, or at least that the hard cases were inescapably bound up with the basic framework of the tax. This basic framework the Chancellors would not touch as long as the war continued[2], and their attitude commanded very widespread support. *The Times* in 1942[3] deplored the arguments used against the tax—arguments that grossly misrepresented the part that manufacturers were playing in the war effort. But, as Lord Stamp had urged in the early days,[4] what evil there was in the tax was apt to be cumulative: the adage that an old tax is a good tax has no universal validity. Partly for such reasons as this, when the end of the war came this tax was singled out by the Chancellor's advisers for particular attack.

In the early months of 1945 this attack developed along two lines. There was first a desire to strengthen business incentives, now that patriotic motives could be expected to weaken, by reducing the rate of tax or at least by giving more substance to the promises of partial refund. Secondly there was an attack, led by Lord Keynes, on the principles of stock valuation which, in a period of rising prices, implied depletion of industrial capital by both E.P.T. and income tax.

The question of the post-war refund had always been complicated by the conditions that were to be attached to repayment, even after these conditions had been restricted in 1942.[5] One view was

---

1 Mention of the case reached *The Financial Times* of 30th June 1943.

2 See, e.g. H. of C. Deb., Vol. 399, Col. 668 (25th April 1944).

3 Leading article, 'Finance and War', 14th April 1942.

4 cf. above p. 86.

5 See above p. 119.

that business men were still so suspicious of the conditions that the incentive advantage of the post-war credit was negligible; on this assumption a reduction of the rate to 80 per cent., coupled with abolition of further post-war credits, would provide an incentive without costing the Exchequer anything over a period of a few years. On the other hand, if the prospect of a 20 per cent. credit was already giving substantially the same incentive as equivalent immediate tax relief would have, a reduction of the rate to 80 per cent. with no further credits, would provide no new incentive, though it would provide industry immediately with some funds and the Exchequer with less (but no less over a few years). There was no real evidence on which to choose between these alternative assumptions and therefore, if the Chancellor was to make sure that he gave additional incentives to business, he would have to reduce the rate of tax below 80 per cent. A tentative proposal to go down to 70 per cent. was therefore considered. To go as far as this, however, would be a major step and on distributional grounds could be considered only as part of a much wider reduction of taxation. Such general reduction the Chancellor was not prepared to contemplate: 'partly because it would be highly dangerous that there should be any greater pressure of purchasing power on the market before there can be any corresponding increase of supplies; and partly because any major reductions in taxation must await a comprehensive review of the probable level of normal post-war expenditure and of our taxation as a whole in relation to it'. For the moment, therefore, the rate was to remain at 100 per cent., subject to the 20 per cent. post-war credit.

Secondly, there was the problem of stock valuation. On this, Lord Keynes circulated a proof of an article 'Commodity Stock Values and E.P.T.', which subsequently appeared in *The Economic Journal*.[1] This gave an analysis of the effect of the current method of valuation upon E.P.T. assessments, and described alternative methods of valuation which might be claimed to produce a more equitable and realistic result. Very broadly, the problem arose because tax-accounting on the historical cost basis, in a period of rising prices with E.P.T at 100 per cent., caused the rise in the value of working stocks to be confiscated as an excess profit, leaving the firm to find elsewhere the funds wherewith to replace, to the extent that prices had risen, its working stocks.[2] Continuance on

---

[1] The article was by Mr. K. Lacey, and it appeared in the April 1945 issue of the *Journal* (pp. 2-16).

[2] 'If prices rise during the E.P.T. period from p_1 to p_2, if the quantity of stock is q_1, and if the whole of the stock is deemed to have been turned over in the last period, so that p_2 has been paid for all end stocks, the firm will have paid in E.P.T. $q_1(p_2-p_1)$, and it will have to borrow this sum or find it from other resources in order to hold its old volume of stocks q_1 at the new price p_2'.

these lines produced complaints from business men of a shortage of working capital, and if we wanted to remain a free enterprise country, we must not kill the goose. Lord Keynes proposed that stock valuation should take into account movements in the volume of stock but not movements of price. Both the United States and France had enacted arrangements of this kind, and Keynes was ready with a number of variants that might be considered forthwith, in order to get away at once from the current system.

The Inland Revenue Department objected that any substantial departure from the current rules was impracticable, and claimed fortification by the professional accountants and by the Federation of British Industries and the Associated Chambers of Commerce. Against such opposition there was no hope of immediate change, but Lord Keynes pressed the point that whatever happened about E.P.T. the probable height of income tax made the assessment of costs a matter of permanent importance. Departmental advisers thereupon recommended that the issues raised by Lord Keynes 'required leisurely examination', and that in the first place the Treasury should think out some simple concession to meet the early problem of a post-war fall in stock values. The Chancellor should avoid reference to the subject in his budget speech, but if pressed in debate he should refer to his undertaking given in the 1943 budget. This course was followed.[1] The anticipated fall in values did not come; on the other hand a continued rise in values aggravated the problem in the post-war years, and it was eventually referred to the Millard Tucker Committee which by no means disposed of it.[2]

The approach of the end of the war made urgent a clarification of the conditions and timing of the 20 per cent. repayment. In 1942 Parliament had laid down that these conditions should relate to 'the distribution, application or capitalisation of profits for the benefit of shareholders whether by the payment of dividends, by the issue of bonus shares or debentures, or by any other means whatsoever'.[3] The political essence of it was that the repayments were to put British industry on an efficient footing after the war, and not to fatten the 'capitalist' shareholders. A quick look at the administrative problem was not at all a happy experience for the experts. How was the use of the funds by private enterprise, aimed at making that enterprise more efficient, to avoid credit to the owners of the business? The Treasury said that the policing of this

---

[1] The Chancellor did, however, refer obliquely to the problem, but reminded the House of its alleviation by the 20 per cent. post-war credit (H. of C. Deb., Vol. 410, Col. 702).

[2] See *Report of the Committee on the Taxation of Business Profits* (Cmd. 8189); and L. T. Little, 'Historical Costs or Present Values?' in *The Economic Journal*, December 1952.

[3] Finance Act 1942, Section 37, amending Finance Act 1941, Section 28 (1).

was an E.P.T. task and therefore should fall upon the Inland Revenue Department; the Revenue said its duty was the collect-tion of taxes, not the policing of industrial investment; and all agreed that this would be an impossible task for anyone. So when 24th April came round the Chancellor was silent on this matter also: the war in Europe still continued, and E.P.T. refunds were left among the problems for the post-war world.

Thus for a variety of reasons Sir John Anderson in his last budget had relatively little to say about E.P.T. The reasons for the 100 per cent. rate still held good; it remained softened by the promise—on conditions still disappointingly vague for the business men and uncomfortably specific for the civil servants—of a 20 per cent. post-war refund; and the reliefs for the small business were carried further along the lines set a year earlier.[1] Six months later—war had meanwhile finished not only with Germany but also with Japan—the new Chancellor, Mr. Dalton, cut the rate to 60 per cent. as from 1st January 1946 and announced that the 20 per cent. repayments would be begun. With these changes, the tax would be retained for the present though the Chancellor recognised its increasingly unsatisfactory nature as its life lengthened.

(v)
The Attack on Luxury Spending
I: The Purchase Tax

As originally conceived in 1940, the purchase tax was to be a simple tax with the twofold purpose of raising revenue and restraining consumption. These two objects were of course logical alternatives: to the extent that consumption was checked, revenue would not be forthcoming, but the Chancellor's position was that either objective would help, and he in fact expected that he would get some of each.[2] Under the pressure of public opinion the original simplicity had given way to the extent that, instead of a single rate of tax applicable to all but specified commodities there were two rates of tax, one double the other, applied to two lists of specified commodities. In 1942 this pre-natal transformation was carried a stage further, in that a third rate of tax ($66\frac{2}{3}$ per cent.) was applied to a narrow range of luxury goods, while the undertaking was given that Utility clothing, when it appeared, would be free from tax.

This increasing complexity of the tax was unwelcome to the

---

[1] See pp. 119-20.
[2] cf. above pp. 36-7.

administrators, who still favoured the simplicity of the original conception. Though the broad objective of economic stabilisation was recognised to imply the use of taxation as a restraint upon the absorption of productive resources, all the instincts of the revenue experts made them discourage the Chancellor's wanderings from the narrow path of 'taxation for revenue only'. They knew that increasing complexity of legislation meant increasing complexity of the machinery of levy and enforcement. They knew that further discrimination between commodities would bring further trade organisations to the Chancellor's doorstep: though every such deputation accepted the tax in principle, every one could question the justice of distinctions between one trade and another. And the revenue experts sensed the inevitability of niggling Parliamentary discussions once such distinctions were introduced.

So when at the end of 1941 Mr. Keynes proposed, as part of his plan of a 'social policy budget' some elaboration of the purchase tax and particularly the raising of the $33\frac{1}{3}$ per cent. rate to 50 per cent. subject to more exemptions, he encountered strong opposition. The Customs' advice was that any enumeration of goods to be taxed as luxuries would be contentious. It was 'really impossible', advised a very high official, to carry out any further sub-division of taxable articles as between luxuries and necessities: any such attempt would lead to Parliamentary pressure for reductions and reclassification which would eat substantially into the revenue. In view of the general line developed in the pre-budget discussions, that this 1942 budget must attack the avenues of luxury spending in which excessive purchasing power was still manifest, Mr. Keynes's proposals—and variants of them—for a more discriminating purchase tax continued to be seriously discussed, but in the end this method of attack on luxuries was dropped, except for the higher purchase tax now applied to certain goods.[1] Discrimination in the other direction did however appear. The President of the Board of Trade informed the Chancellor of the progress of his plans for Utility clothing and footwear, and pointed out that the prospect of tax-exempt clothing would encourage postponement of purchases and so ease the problem of honouring the coupon in the earlier rationing period. Remission would assist in the stabilisation of the cost-of-living index number.[2] The difficulties of keeping this index down were much under discussion at the time, and exemption from purchase tax would enable traders to put Utility clothing and footwear on the market at prices that would offset other factors

[1] cf. p. 126.

[2] The Board of Trade also believed that their price control problems for the Utility clothing would be simplified by tax exemption.

likely to lead to a further rise in the index. The Chancellor accepted this plea, in the broad interest of his stabilisation policy and as an encouragement to the Utility plans which were of far-reaching importance in the development of the war economy.[1] It was not perceived at the time that the exemption of these specially-branded goods would facilitate later resort to a stiffer purchase tax as a weapon against luxury expenditure.

At this time (April 1942) the only goods in question were the Utility clothing just coming on the market, and the Utility boots and shoes planned for later in that year.[2] The Board of Trade approach to the Treasury had related specifically to these goods, and there was no general understanding that the grant of exemption for them implied that similar relief would be allowed for any further range of articles that might be brought under the Utility arrangements. The question arose in an important form in October 1942, when the Board of Trade adopted a Utility scheme for essential articles of furniture to be sold only under permit to the bombed-out, the newly-married, and other special classes of purchasers. The prices at which such furniture would have been sold inclusive of tax represented a very large increase over pre-war prices, and the President of the Board of Trade urged strongly that exemption should again be allowed. This proposal presented considerable difficulty from the Revenue standpoint: acceptance would create a precedent opening a wide door. The case was however very exceptional: the output of furniture would be so small that it could not be available to the public generally but only to persons in exceptional need, and this need was not of a kind that the Chancellor would wish to tax. After receiving conflicting advice, the Chancellor conceded the case, on the condition—accepted by the President of the Board of Trade—that there should be no further pressure from that quarter for further remissions 'on other household goods, or any other articles now subject to tax'.

In November 1942 representations from the Board of Trade in favour of black-out cloth, provoked the Chancellor to reiterate his warning that he was not disposed to exempt further classes of goods. With the approach of the budget season, however, there were renewed agitations in several quarters—including the Treasury itself. The most powerful argument in favour of general exemption of Utility goods was the stabilisation argument, an argument that now always found ready spokesmen in the Treasury and which was in this context receiving strong support from the Central Price Regulation Committee.[3] There was also the

[1] H. of C. Deb., Vol. 379, Cols. 132-3.

[2] Utility footwear was exempt as from 1st June 1942 and Utility clothing as from 3rd August 1942.

[3] cf. footnote 5 on p. 51.

commonsense argument that the exemption of Utility clothing
left taxation of Utility handkerchiefs looking a little odd. Lastly,
the Labour Party was continuing to attack the tax on distributive
grounds, and in March Mr. Pethick-Lawrence and others made
representations which led the Chancellor to take soundings among
his Ministerial colleagues. The variety of quite strong arguments
impressed him and he gave way. In his budget speech[1] he
announced extension of Utility exemptions to certain kinds of
domestic textiles, soft furnishings and haberdashery (Utility black-
out cloth, towels, handkerchiefs, bed-linen and mattresses, etc.).[2] In
making the announcement, however, the Chancellor was careful
to base himself on the grounds cited in the previous budget—the
encouragement of economical production and the necessity of
keeping down the cost of living. The fact that he had now, for the
first time, extended exemptions to unrationed goods, was glossed
over; and when Labour spokesmen invited a commitment to the
principle that price-controlled goods more generally should be
exempt, the Chancellor refused to be drawn.[3]

The effect of these further concessions on the yield of the purchase
tax was offset by the simultaneous increase of the rate applicable
to certain luxury goods, from $66\frac{2}{3}$ per cent. to 100 per cent. This
was part of the Chancellor's attack on luxury spending—in so far
as people insisted on continuing to buy luxuries, they should
contribute more handsomely to the Chancellor's needs. The goods
affected were those enumerated in the seventh schedule of the
1942 Finance Act, and included such items as ornaments, jewellery,
silk dresses, and fur coats.[4]

After these developments in favour of Utility goods and against
luxuries, the purchase tax remained substantially unchanged
through the remainder of the war. Experience in some directions
justified the experts' fears. By March 1944 the Commissioners of
Customs and Excise were seriously exercised by evasion of the tax
and by the encouragement it was giving to black-market activities,
and the Chancellor, much though he disliked heavy penalites
for what might sometimes be little more than technical offences,
agreed to the introduction of sterner clauses.[5] The different
scales of the tax, its weight and the concessions, in the Utility
exemptions, in favour of necessities had led to multitudinous
applications for exemption of small items, and the Treasury dealt

---

[1] H. of C. Deb., Vol. 388, Cols. 955-6.

[2] Proposals to exempt, on simlar grounds, certain pottery and hardware were
dropped owing to administrative difficulties.

[3] H. of C. Deb., Vol. 379, Col. 1250. 'Price controlled goods' was of course a very
wide category indeed.

[4] H. of C. Deb., Vol. 388, Col. 973.

[5] The statutory changes were made by Clauses 16 and 17 of the Finance Act 1944.

K

with this correspondence on no less than eighty-five special files, many of them covering a number of items. Most of these special cases were very small classes of goods that could properly be included in narrow definitions of 'necessity' but had administratively been bunched with a variety of other less necessary goods. In one other instance the action taken has special interest as illustrating the influence in late 1944 of post-war economic interests. This was the introduction of a reduced rate of tax on Utility fur garments. Since the 1943 budget fur garments generally had been liable to the maximum rate of tax (100 per cent.), fur coats being typical luxury articles. But in 1944 the Board of Trade was greatly exercised by concern for the fur trade, whose organisation was threatened by this heavy taxation and by the disfavour into which ostentatious spending had fallen. The trade claimed that its chance of making a quick start in the post-war export trade was thereby prejudiced and the Board of Trade, seeking means whereby a special relief from tax might be administered, devised a scheme for the production, mainly from sheepskin and rabbitskin, of 'Utility furs'.[1] The case for tax relief could not be assimilated to that for Utility clothing, though it was relevant that these Utility furs would be to some extent in competition with Utility garments. The main point was that without some tax relief there was little chance of success in the design of preserving the trade for post-war service. The Chancellor accepted this case, but, whereas other Utility goods were totally exempt, the relief took the form of reduction of tax from 100 per cent. to $16\frac{2}{3}$ per cent. Refusal of complete exemption was influenced by knowledge that the Board of Trade contemplated extending the Utility scheme to goods of higher ranges of price and quality, and the Treasury wished to avoid creating a presumption that all Utility articles would necessarily be free from tax.

As the end of the war approached, the Department undertook a thorough review of the purchase tax. Despite the furore that had greeted its inception, the tax was by this time an accepted fact of life and, even in circles optimistic about post-war tax relief, there was a disposition to forget that it had been tolerated only as a war-time measure.[2] In official circles there was strong attachment to it as an efficient and convenient method of raising an appreciable sum, and a diversity of interest in its possibilities as a weapon of economic policy. In addition to proposals from the

---

[1] This Utility scheme was devised only when it appeared that a tax concession could not be quickly obtained without it. The Board of Trade reconciled themselves to use of the term 'Utility' in relation to a luxury by arguing that it would help overcome traders' suspicion that Utility goods were 'cheap and nasty', and would prepare the way for more ambitious plans for extension of the Utility schemes.

[2] e.g. H. of C. Deb., Vol. 410, Col. 1033.

Ministries of Fuel and Works, there were weighty views in the Economic Section of the War Cabinet Offices and in the Board of Trade. The Economic Section wanted increased or at least continued high rates of tax in order to restrain expenditure by the public. Increased rates would help by taxing those who still continued to purchase; still more, perhaps, high rates would encourage people to postpone buying in the hope that at some later date the tax would have been reduced. The Board of Trade, on the other hand, wanted to develop economical production of essential articles, and to encourage this extended 'Utility' plan they suggested that essential articles of approved type sold under strict price regulation should be either exempt from tax or taxed at very low rates while other types ('luxury' types) should remain taxable at appreciably higher rates. The revenue experts looked upon both these policies with disfavour: they foresaw danger if the tax was to be complicated by non-revenue objectives. Eventually the Chancellor's advisers recommended that no change should be made in the 1945 budget. 'The tax', they said, 'is a delicate instrument, which could probably never have been set in being except in time of war. If it is to be retained permanently—and there are many grounds in favour of this—it needs to be handled meanwhile with care. Any sharp raising of the rates, even if otherwise practical politics in the near future, would appear to be a hazardous Parliamentary proposition. In its present graduated form it is capable of exercising a considerable restraint upon home consumption, especially of non-essentials, and our present recommendation is that, until necessity otherwise requires, it should be left just as it is'. So the Chancellor left it alone—he did not even mention purchase tax in his budget speech— and the first post-war Government found itself free to make up its own mind as to the future of this outstanding innovation in the tax structure.

(vi)

The Attack on Luxury Spending

II: Liquor, Tobacco, and Entertainments

Though Mr. Keynes would have liked to see the 1942 budget presented to the public as a 'social policy budget',[1] by the time the famous red box was ready to go across to the House, the note had changed to an attack upon luxury spending. In 1943 similarly, Sir Hubert Henderson opened the pre-budget discussions with his

---

[1] cf. above, p. 97.

plea for family allowances, but the headlines that caught the eye on budget night were once more dominated by penal increases in the taxation of luxuries. This does not imply the exclusion of other motives—all the elements referred to in the first section of this chapter were present on both occasions. Much of this was, however, now taken for granted, and much else was matter for quiet deliberation and minor legislative change. What had to be shouted from the housetops, in the Government's view, was that those people who felt able to continue spending freely on non-essentials must take the load of such additional taxation as was dictated by the stabilisation policy. Their luxury spending absorbed valuable resources and so aggravated the strain of the war effort. The Government did not want to create a nation of Dismal Jimmies by prohibiting such consumption: the Prime Minister did not for a moment forget the vital part of morale on the home front. But it did judge that, given that more money had to be collected from somewhere, the people who indulged in those things should contribute heavily and in proportion to their indulgence.

At the beginning of 1942 this principle, regarded in the light of market conditions, gave a clear lead. Apart from the purchase tax changes discussed above,[1] the obvious course was to impose steep increases in the existing taxes on tobacco, beer, and entertainments. In tobacco, the supply position called for a reduction of consumption by at least 15 per cent., and rationing was an administrative horror to be put off as long as possible. The demand for beer was competing awkwardly with food requirements, while shortages in many public houses were causing resentment. For entertainments the case was not quite so clear, though cinemas were enjoying a boom in many parts of the country. At the same time examination showed that administrative awkwardness would be great, and cash yield small, from the novel luxury taxes—on first-class railway tickets and restaurant bills, for example—proposed from a variety of quarters. Sir Kingsley Wood was also reminded of the saying that 'the Chancellor cannot merely carry around a pannier of trifles',[2] and he accepted the view that he must concentrate on sharp increases in existing taxes.

The attack was therefore narrowed to 10s. 0d. a pound on tobacco,[3] a doubling of the entertainments duty, and 2d. a pint on beer, the last carrying with it £2 a proof gallon on spirits[4] and

---

[1] pp. 126-9.

[2] The saying is attributed to Sir Winston Churchill when himself Chancellor of the Exchequer (1925-29).

[3] Equivalent to 3d. extra for a packet of 10 cigarettes.

[4] Equivalent to 4s. 8d. on a bottle of whisky.

a shilling or two a bottle on wine,[1] justice demanding that the rich man's drink should share with beer any increase in the burden of taxation. Though Ministers, the House of Commons and outside opinion[2] accepted the broad policy of attacking luxury spending, two items in the list caused much trouble, either in pre-budget discussions or in the Parliamentary debates. These were tobacco and entertainments. From the tobacco tax the Treasury itself proposed relief for the Services, and there was extreme pressure in the Commons for relief for old age pensioners. On entertainments, the possibility of some relief for 'the living theatre' caused headaches for the Chancellor both before and after budget day.

The trouble about tobacco for the Services began with a Treasury attempt to forestall demands for higher pay to compensate for the increased taxation. The increases in indirect taxation in 1940 had been directly responsible for such a demand, and as the result of pressure in the Commons and elsewhere the Chancellor had conceded an additional 6d. a day for all men in the Forces. Compensatory action of this kind was, from the point of view of the stabilisation policy, anathema since, far from checking inflation, it ensured that the taxation measures themselves should immediately inflate incomes.[3] The Treasury accordingly sought in 1942 to preclude a development of this kind, by excusing Service personnel from the full effect of the rise in the tobacco tax. The specific proposal was that the soldier should be given a free packet of ten cigarettes a week. In effect this meant that the soldier would be enabled to buy 40 cigarettes a week at the pre-budget price. As a way of achieving this end consistently with efficiency in revenue control and administration, this was to be secured by giving him the first ten cigarettes free, but this gave the proposal an appearance that provoked an uproar when it became known to the War Office. The Secretary of State complained to the Prime Minister that a gift of ten cigarettes a week would be regarded as 'either derisory or insulting', and that, rather than resort to a concession so trivial that it would fail in its object, the Army should be expected to fall into line with the rest of the community and give it a lead in tightening its belt. The question went to the War Cabinet on 10th April and to a further special meeting of Ministers the next day. The solution then hammered out was that Service

---

[1] The duties on Empire wines were doubled and the same absolute amounts were added to those on foreign wines. This implied about a shilling a bottle on light and two shillings a bottle on heavy wines.

[2] e.g. *The Economist*, 11th and 18th April 1942.

[3] There is of course always some risk of this kind when taxation is increased (or subsidies decreased) but the risk was exceptionally great in this sphere because (as the 1940 experience had shown) extreme political pressure could develop in favour of the Forces.

personnel at all home Stations should continue to be able to purchase cigarettes through N.A.A.F.I. at pre-budget prices,[1] and the budget speech included a promise to this effect.[2] The absence of argument in Parliamentary and public discussion, and the continuance of the plan when the tobacco tax was further increased the following year,[3] indicate that the solution was generally acceptable.

The Treasury recognised that such a discriminatory concession would excite demands for similar concessions to other sections— civil defence workers particularly—but advised the Chancellor to stand firm. In the event pressure came in the Commons in favour of old age pensioners. Throughout the war the public conscience was apparently uneasy about this section—it will be recalled that improvement in old age pensions had been a late pre-war development jettisoned when war came—and the increases in indirect taxation must have pressed hard upon them. In terms of Hansard, the House took nine columns[4] of debate to vent its feelings on grandfather's tobacco bill, but the Chancellor remained adamant.

In reviewing the entertainments duty, the simple course of doubling the scales throughout was first considered. Both cinemas and theatres were experiencing rising costs, but appearances suggested that the demand would stand these as well as a doubling of taxation. A cinema seat priced at 1s. 6d., including 4d. duty, would in future cost 1s. 10d. including 8d. duty, plus whatever increased cost the proprietors thought it necessary to pass on. The 7d. and cheaper seats would be unaffected. In the theatre the seat now priced at 10s. 6d. including 1s. 8d. tax, would have to bear 3s. 4d. tax. One effect of this simple doubling would be a doubling, in terms of shillings and pence, of the preference for 'the living theatre' initiated by Mr. Neville Chamberlain in 1935. Consideration of the stalls in West End theatres raised doubts about this. The Chancellor was regarding this part of his budget as an attack on luxury spending, and here was a proposal to increase a preference in favour of 'the most expensive seats in the most luxurious city in the country'. The Chancellor's advisers suggested therefore that the duty on theatre seats should be increased by the same absolute amounts as for cinema seats. The amount of money involved was trivial:[5] what was at stake

---

[1] The N.A.A.F.I. conditions involved restriction to about 40 or 50 cigarettes per person per week. Ministers discussed the possibility of a parallel concession on beer but decided that it was unnecessary.

[2] H. of C. Deb., Vol. 379, Col. 136.

[3] See below, p. 137.

[4] H. of C. Deb., Vol. 379, Cols. 646-656; see also on the position of old age pensioners more generally, Vol. 379, Col. 1305.

[5] 90 per cent. of the duty was then collected from the cinemas.

was the attack on luxuries. But the living theatre had powerful advocates in many quarters,[1] and by the time the budget proposals were through the War Cabinet, the increased absolute preference was restored. Subject to minor modifications in the light of Parliamentary debate and discussions with the theatre managers, this was how the matter was settled in 1942. The strength of feeling on the subject was to be manifest again in the following year.

When the budget season came round a year later, a review of the 1942 changes in indirect taxation showed that these increases, sharp as they had appeared at first, had not led to the anticipated abstention from consumption. Part of the trouble was of course that under the pressure of increasing war production the national income was still rising. A stabilisation policy that included maintenance of the traditional machinery of collective bargaining could not, under the extreme pressure of 1942–43, have a 100 per cent. success. To say, as the Chancellor did to the pre-budget meeting of the War Cabinet, that the further rise in the cost of the war necessitated further taxation to yield £100 millions was no confession of previous failure. Nothing about this situation indicated unwisdom in the 1942 increases in indirect taxation; everything pointed to the desirability of further twists in the same screws.

The only reason for hesitation was the possibility of repercussions on the wages situation. This kind of consideration had led, in 1942, to the tobacco concession for the Forces, and the Customs experts now suggested that if further substantial increases were now imposed on tobacco, spirits, beer and entertainments, it was 'by no means impossible that (despite the fact that only tobacco enters into the cost of living index) the increased burden would tend to stimulate application for wage increases'. The only course avoiding this particular risk would be a sharp change in income tax; but against this the same argument applied as in the previous year. P.A.Y.E. had not yet been introduced, so that quick effects were not obtainable; and the sum involved could be obtained only by a heavy attack on the lower ranges of income. Altogether, for the immediate purpose direct taxation appeared the less efficient instrument and at least as likely as indirect to have undesirable repercussions on incentives, industrial relations and even the wages situation itself.

The Chancellor therefore told the Prime Minister that he would again rely on the course he had taken a year previously: to aim at

[1] e.g. Keynes proposed that cinemas alone should bear the increase and in the Commons several members pressed for complete exemption of the theatre from the increases in the duty (e.g. H. of C. Deb., Vol. 379, Col. 662).

those (whatever the size of their incomes) who still had surplus incomes to devote to expenditure which could if necessary be avoided or curtailed. Suggested 'frill taxes'—this time on railway fares and newspapers[1]—were once more rejected, and besides changes in the purchase tax,[2] the estabished staples were lined up for shock treatment. On tobacco there was to be a further 6s. od. a pound—2d. more on the packet of ten cigarettes previously sold for a shilling.[3] On beer there would be another 1d., bringing the price of a pint of average strength up from 11d. to a shilling. These two increases alone would provide three-quarters of the required increase. Spirits could bear an additional £1 per proof gallon, equal to 2s. 4d. on whisky which had been selling at 23s. od. a bottle. Equity dictated corresponding increases on wines, though the extra revenue would be trivial. The entertainments duty was to yield £42 millions against £32 millions on the existing scale, the precise alterations to be settled in consultation with the trade.[4]

Press comment on the budget was devoted mainly to criticism of the continued absence of a P.A.Y.E. scheme for income tax;[5] what little comment there was on the changes in indirect taxation expressed unqualified approval.[6] Within Government circles and in Parliament, however, important arguments of a year ago were revived. In tobacco, the Chancellor proposed to allow the N.A.A.F.I. sales to continue at pre-1942 prices and this was accepted without comment;[7] but over tobacco for old-age pensioners and taxation of the living theatre, the Chancellor ran into heavy seas.

The agitation in favour of 'the pensioner's pipe' could point to some analogy with the N.A.A.F.I. concession, and could find sentimental support in many quarters. There was, however, no analogy from the administrative angle. Whereas N.A.A.F.I. supplies went in bulk from the warehouses, odd ounces and half ounces sold over the counter to old age pensioners could be relieved only by the distribution of coupons which would have a definite cash value to the retailers and would become readily negotiable instruments. It would not be possible to discriminate between

---

[1] Parliamentary suggestions in the budget debates also included advertising and bicycles (H. of C. Deb., Vol. 388, Cols. 1295 and 1323).

[2] See pp. 127-30 above.

[3] This proved to be the last war-time increase in the tobacco tax, but right up to the end of the war the supply position continued to constitute a special argument for yet further taxation. Early in 1945 the Board of Trade asked, on supply grounds, for a further 2d. on the packet. The Customs anticipated a public outcry if tobacco alone suffered and on supply, not revenue, grounds. The proposal was thereupon dropped.

[4] This was the summary as put to the War Cabinet. cf. H. of C. Deb., Vol. 388, Cols. 970-973.

[5] See p. 101 above.

[6] e.g. *The Times*, leading article, 13th April 1943 and *The Economist*, 17th April 1943.

[7] It involved a cost of £16 millions instead of £10 millions on the 1942 basis.

smokers and non-smokers, and the latter were a high proportion of the total. The coupons would therefore be freely traded at fixed prices, and would be indistinguishable from a cash increase in the old age pension. This was a different question which Ministers were not willing to open.[1] The Chancellor therefore repeated his 1942 rejection of the claim for 'the pensioner's pipe'.[2]

The proposal that the living theatre was to share in the additional £10 millions of entertainments duty was at once opposed by the Prime Minister, who enquired what money was involved. To exempt the theatres from any increase would cost about £750,000 but, the Chancellor argued, 'It is not the money. It is necessary for me to do this in order that I may follow the general line of the budget (and previous ones) to reduce spending power . . . . . . The difficulty is in making the distinction when everyone knows the theatres are packed. I am sure it will not hurt the theatres at all'. The Chancellor had also to bear in mind the fact that the cinemas had already been told that the same general principles were to be applied to cinemas and theatres. Eventually 'a more modest series of increases' was proposed for the theatres, the wrath of the cinemas being turned aside by the absence of any increase for seats priced at one shilling (gross) or less.[3]

This widening discrimination in favour of the living theatre inevitably prompted demands for further concessions. If actors and actresses, why not footballers and cricketers? Were the latter not equally living players on a stage? The cry came from *The Evening Standard*[4] and was taken up in the House of Commons.[5] On behalf of the footballers, it was urged that they had suffered war-time falls in attendances and numerous other difficulties. But they were unable to evoke the same interest as the theatres, and the Chancellor decided that he could not excuse the menfolk when attending football matches whilst collecting the increased duty from their wives and daughters at the cinemas.

The tenderness exhibited towards the living theatre was probably also responsible for the agitation in some quarters in favour of relaxing the conditions governing the complete exemption enjoyed by 'cultural' entertainments. The war had seen important developments in the provision of cultural entertainments, primarily under the impetus of the Council for Encouragement of Music

---

[1] Reports from the Assistance Board encouraged the view that there had been no such deterioration in the position of the old-age pensioners as would compel a rise in the rate of pension.

[2] H. of C. Deb., Vol. 388, Cols. 1747-51.

[3] H. of C. Deb., Vol. 388, Cols. 972-3. The concession for cheap seats applied equally to theatres and cinemas, but it was significant only for the latter.

[4] 13th April, 1943.

[5] H. of C. Deb., Vol. 388, Cols. 1756 and 1759 and Vol. 390, Cols. 229-33.

and the Arts (later the Arts Council) but not all its entertainments succeeded in qualifying under the exemption clause dating from 1916.[1] This question was, however, not one of great popular interest, nor of financial moment, and it was best left over to be considered at leisure.[2] It was not until Sir John Anderson's 1945 budget that the authorities were ready to legislate, and even then the relevant clause was one of those dropped when the Caretaker Government thought it appropriate to emasculate the Finance Bill.[3]

(vii)

Looking Forward

In the middle of his 1943 budget speech Sir Kingsley Wood paused to state the objectives of his financial policy.[4] 'First', he said, 'we have sought to assist the war effort by ensuring that war production suffers no hindrances from unsound economic conditions. Secondly, we have endeavoured to do this in such a way that our people, united in the firm will to work and produce to the utmost, may be secure in the knowledge that their standard of living will not be filched away by rising prices. Thirdly, we have sought so to order our economy now that the inevitable consequences of the war will prejudice as little as possible our financial and economic ability to engage ourselves in those progressive developments which we all desire to achieve and upon which we are already engaged'. As the war drew towards its close—and to Englishmen it appeared to be in this stage for a very long time—it was inevitable that the third of Sir Kingsley Wood's objectives should receive increasing attention. The Treasury was importantly concerned in the various foreshadowings of the post-war world—employment policy and Bretton Woods were the major items—which fall outside the scope of this book. There were also, however, certain changes in the detailed structure of taxation which, though inspired mainly by reconstruction objectives, were the subjects of immediate decision and have some relation to other war-time adjustments prompted by the steep rise in rates of taxation. Two rather special examples

---

[1] Section 1(5)(d) of the Finance (New Duties) Act, 1916. The conditions were that the society providing the entertainment was not conducted for profit, and that the entertainment itself was partly for educational purposes. For examples of exempt entertainments, see H. of C. Deb., Vol. 390, Col. 1021.

[2] cf. H. of C. Deb., Vol. 389, Col. 972.

[3] Sir John Anderson's proposals (which followed advice from a committee appointed in the autumn of 1943) were stated in his budget speech (H. of C. Deb., Vol. 410, Col. 698). Clause 7 of the first Finance Bill was among the dropped clauses.

[4] H. of C. Deb., Vol. 388, Cols. 954-5.

were motor taxation[1] and the duties on hydrocarbon oils.[2] Of more general application were the income tax reliefs for re-equipment and for research expenditure, and the relief from 'double taxation' of income accruing abroad.

Consideration of research expenditure began with agitations in industrial circles about the comparative lack of interest alleged to be shown by British industry in scientific research. As in the first war, so in the second, it was frequently said that Britain, though in the forefront in fundamental research, was slower than her competitors in the further steps of applying scientific discovery to actual industrial production.[3] In his 1943 budget speech the Chancellor had announced an enquiry into certain aspects of taxation of industrial profits,[4] and questions of allowance of research expenditure were raised before the Inland Revenue Committee then established. At the same time Sir Kenneth Lee and Sir Harold Hartley had enlisted the help of bankers through Mr. Montagu Norman, whose keen interest in the reconstruction of British industry had already shown itself in many ways during the inter-war years. The result was the circularisation through the branch banks and the Federation of British Industries of some 50,000 copies of a pamphlet written by Sir Harold Hartley. This was designed to make British industry more 'research-minded'. It provoked many comments to the effect that more would be spent on research if a more generous attitude were adopted by the Inland Revenue. The Revenue view was that existing legislation did 'not appear to have operated in practice to exclude much expenditure': 'the root of the trouble is not so much the taxation treatment as the absence in industry of the right attitude of mind towards research'. This was of course no answer to the argument that more research-mindedness was desirable, and that special taxation concessions would help to inculcate this state of mind; and it was not allowed to hinder pursuit of the subject. The growth of Parliamentary interest was signalised in a debate on the civil estimates in April 1944,[5] and a week later Sir John Anderson

---

[1] Sir John Anderson in his 1944 budget invited representations (H. of C. Deb., Vol. 399, Col. 657) and announced a new basis (cubic capacity of cylinders) in his 1945 budget (*ibid.*, Vol. 410, Cols. 698-9); this was dropped from the Finance Bill of the Caretaker Government but adopted in Mr. Dalton's budget in October 1945 (*ibid.*, Vol. 414, Cols. 1888-90).

[2] The problem of hydrocarbon oils was stated, and enquiry announced, in the 1944 budget (H. of C. Deb. Vol. 399, Cols. 680-1); that of 1945 provided for exemption of those oils used for chemical synthesis (*ibid.*, Vol. 410, Col. 697); but this also was dropped, to be implemented eventually in the October budget (*ibid.*, Vol. 414, Col. 1887).

[3] Russia was cited as taking much more interest than Britain in research (H. of C. Deb., Vol. 389, Col. 1073).

[4] H. of C. Deb., Vol. 388, Cols. 961-2.

[5] H. of C. Deb., Vol. 399, Cols. 216-311.

dealt with it in his budget speech.[1] *The Times* commented that on this subject 'he spoke with evident conviction and authority',[2] and this is underlined by his notes on the Departmental papers. His statement that 'current' expenditure (salaries and wages, materials etc.) on a research project would be allowed as a deduction from current profits reflected no change in the position; what was new was the provision that research expenditure of a capital character—on laboratory buildings, plant and machinery—would be allowed over a period of five years, and any payment made to a central research body or a university body would also now be deductible in the year of payment. The change was, in short, the substitution of a clear and comprehensive relief for a piecemeal treatment that business men had perhaps regarded as too niggardly to be interesting; and there was some propaganda value in the prominence given by the Chancellor to the whole question.

At the same time the Chancellor announced his decisions about another question on which he had received repeated representations in Parliament and directly from business organisations. Under previous legislation the cost of plant and machinery was normally written-off throughout its life by an annual wear-and-tear allowance and by an obsolescence allowance, the latter being given when the plant and machinery were replaced, to cover any part of the original cost, less scrap value, not already written-off. In future, said the Chancellor, the obsolescence allowance would be given whether a particular piece of machinery were replaced or not. Further, the wear-and-tear allowance would commence with an allowance of 20 per cent. of cost, so that industry would receive in the first year a substantial contribution towards the cost of new plant—though there would be offsets at the latter end of the plant's life. The allowance for buildings, hitherto restricted to 'mills and factories', was extended to all industrial buildings, and was to be at the rate of 2 per cent. per annum, with an initial allowance of 10 per cent. These various concessions were for purposes of post-war reconstruction, and were accordingly to operate only from 'an appointed day';[3] but the Chancellor was careful to emphasise that any war-time research expenditure not otherwise covered would rank for relief at the end of the war.[4]

Sir John Anderson regarded in the same light—'as a second main step in the same direction' of helping reconstruction—the relief from double taxation which he announced in his 1945 budget

---

[1] *Ibid.*, Cols. 677-80.
[2] Leading article, 26th April 1944.
[3] The date was eventually, by the Finance Act (No. 2) of 1945, fixed as 6th April 1946.
[4] H. of C. Deb., Vol. 400, Col. 2010.

speech.[1] For some time officials of the United Kingdom and United States Governments had been at work on this problem, a problem that arose from the principle that taxation is levied both in the country of origin of the income and in the country of residence of the taxpayer. By the beginning of 1945 these talks had progressed far enough for report to the War Cabinet and at budget time the Chancellor announced the conclusion of a treaty between the two countries. The promised relief was comprehensive—it covered all income liable to tax in both countries, including shipping and air transport profits, interest and royalties. The United Kingdom Government regarded this as a first step—negotiations with the Dominions and other countries were soon in progress—towards eliminating 'in a regulated fashion' all double charges, the cost being for equitable distribution between the two Governments. If these principles, now accepted by the United States and United Kingdom Governments, could be universally applied, the total help and encouragement to our export trades and particularly to the 'invisible exports' would be substantial.[2]

All these measures, announced by Sir John Anderson in his two budgets of 1944 and 1945, for adjusting the income tax were designed to give private enterprise in industry and trade 'a fair chance' to get off on the right foot at the end of the war. Apart from scattered growls about discriminating favours,[3] the Chancellor's broad approach on these matters was generally welcomed.[4] *The Times*, entitling its budget leader 'Looking Forward',[5] thought these measures 'extremely important in themselves,' but noted that they were 'even more important as a practical demonstration of the completeness of the revolution in the conception of the budget as an instrument of broad economic policy'. This was a far cry from 'the saving of candle-ends' once thought the proper function of the Treasury;[6] yet the beginning of it all lay in the wholesale burning of candles which was now becoming accepted as one of the facts of English Government. For every one of these streamlining measures applied by Sir John Anderson to the structure of the income tax had raised its head originally because of the altogether novel height of the rates of taxation. Already in his 1944 speech

---

[1] H. of C. Deb., Vol. 410, Cols. 703-7.

[2] H. of C. Deb., Vol. 410, Cols. 703-707. The relevant clauses were dropped when the Finance Bill was revised, but were eventually incorporated in the Finance Act (No. 2) of 1945. (See H. of C. Deb., Vol. 415, Cols. 439 and 493-6).

[3] See e.g. *The Economist*, 29th April 1944 and H. of C. Deb., Vol. 401, Col. 954.

[4] e.g. H. of C. Deb., Vol. 399, Cols. 801, 812-14 and 1027.

[5] 26th April 1944.

[6] The phrase was quoted by Sir Edward Bridges, in his Stamp Memorial Lecture (1950) on *Treasury Control* (p. 6), from Sir Algernon West, *Recollections: 1832 to 1886*, Vol. II, p. 82.

Sir John Anderson had warned the country against exaggerated hopes of an early lightening of the war-time tax burden. Many financial problems—some arising from the development of social policy—would remain, and by pre-war standards the burden of taxation would 'have to remain high for some considerable time to come'.[1] A year later he stated his conviction that taxation could not, 'and should not, be continued without material relaxation',[2] but he was unable at that date to offer even an instalment. It is against this setting as much as against any disposition to take a broader view of Treasury responsibilities that these adjustments of the income tax machine have to be regarded. When taxation continued year after year at such high rates, anomalies and hard cases had to be examined more carefully and more sympathetically than ever before. But if high levels of taxation were to be a permanent feature of the post-war world, minor adjustments of the 1944–45 variety would not be enough. Lord Keynes in 1944 alleged that there were already signs of widespread repercussions on business conduct.[3] If, with freedom from war-time restraints, these ill effects were to grow, it would be seen that the war-time Chancellors had bequeathed to their successors not only a new breadth of vision, but also a taxation structure that called for major reconstruction rather than the streamlining efforts of the last war-time budgets.

---

[1] H. of C. Deb., Vol. 399, Col. 670.

[2] H. of C. Deb., Vol. 410, Col. 723.

[3] 'The fact', he wrote in a paper for the Chancellor, 'that direct taxation has now passed the point which can be justified on merits is effecting a change in the psychology of the taxpayer, which, if it is not soon reversed, may become permanent. Everyone nowadays is concerned in re-arranging his affairs so as to attract as little taxation as possible, and this, as a general universally excused phenomenon, is something new in this country'.

CHAPTER V

THE RATE OF INTEREST

(i)

The Contrast with 1914—18

O N ONE critical question of financial policy—the rate of interest —the basic decision was taken at the beginning of the war and was not substantially altered at any stage. The decision was taken without formal discussion among Ministers; the informal discussions left little trace in the papers and evidently did not occasion any systematic discussions on the official level. Evidently 'a view' emerged easily, for no-one thought it worth-while either to direct the collection of papers in a special file or even to collect his own papers in a single folder. This state of affairs partly reflects the fact that the critical decisions were taken by a handful of men who were not addicted to much paper work,[1] but it is also some indication of the unanimity and strength with which the policy of a 'Three Per Cent. War'[2] was accepted.

Nevertheless, there is sufficient trace in the papers for it to be possible, with substantial help from the memories of a few who took part in, or were close to, the discussions, to analyse the reasons on which the decision was based. Among these reasons the most powerful—and therefore the most taken for granted—was the belief that Government borrowing had been ill-managed in the 1914–18 war, and the determination that the experience of those years should not be repeated. The confidence of this determination was based on the experience of cheap money during the 'thirties, when the monetary authorities had achieved a technical mastery not previously paralleled, and by the belief that in the Second World War circumstances would from the beginning make possible a policy which the men of 1914 had not been able to contemplate. Lastly, some influence must be ascribed to academic thought on the rate of interest as a weapon of policy: academic

---

[1] The Governor of the Bank (Mr. Montagu Norman) took the lead in this matter, generally by informal discussion with the Prime Minister (Mr. Neville Chamberlain) or the Chancellor of the Exchequer (Sir John Simon). Neither Mr. Keynes nor any other outside economist was consulted after the pre-war discussion referred to below (pp. 153-6).

[2] The phrase was the title of an excellent leading article in *The Economist*, 20th January 1940.

opinion had during 1939 been afforded opportunity for expression, if not a hearing, in exalted circles and, perhaps with more effect, it had over a longer period been penetrating Governmental circles in its usual unnoticed way.

The root of the contrast between interest rate policies in the two wars lies in the fact that in the first war the authorities continued to think of London as an open financial centre conducting its business broadly as usual, whilst in the second war London's international weakness was perceived from the outset and had to be protected by both internal and external controls. That London should remain an open centre in 1914 was an assumption that reflected the universal blindness to the calamity into which Britain had been dragged. But there was more positive justification than this, for in the international liquidity crises at the outbreak of war London's foreign exchange market had broken down not because of a flight of funds from London but under extraordinary pressure to remit funds to London. After the crisis had passed, the strength of London remained for many months: the pound stood high in terms of other currencies and the authorities, who had taken extraordinary steps to ensure ample liquidity in the domestic banking system, reacted in a normal way by allowing interest rates in London to remain at rather low levels. The Government was therefore able, without taking any special precautions—or indeed showing any technical skill—to borrow the comparatively small sums it then required on reasonably cheap terms. The great financial centre could stand and deliver without turning a hair.[1]

By the summer of 1915 a number of changes were beginning to show themselves, and in the course of the next eighteen months these completely undermined London's position. Government expenditure soon outstripped all expectations, and to it was added substantial finance for the war efforts of the Dominions and foreign allies. In the absence of any compensatory constriction of private demands, inflation gathered speed, wholesale prices rising in 1916 to almost double the pre-war level. The balance of payments soon felt the strain of this inflation: the war was far from world-wide and Britain was taking a heavy share in financing it. The foreign exchange value of the pound, unprotected by a fence of exchange controls, sank and the authorities, besides taking special steps such as the mobilisation and pledging of certain foreign securities, took the orthodox step of raising rates in the London money market. The measures taken in the second half of 1915 proved insufficient, and in the exchange crisis in the summer of 1916 Bank Rate was raised to 6 per cent. and the Treasury Bill rate to $5\frac{1}{2}$ per cent.

---

[1] On financial policy in the 1914-18 war, see E. V. Morgan, *Studies in British Financial Policy, 1914-25* (London 1952), particularly Chapters IV-VII.

It is notable that these measures were employed with the twofold intention of encouraging foreign balances to remain in London, and of checking the rise in domestic prices. When, early in 1917, interest rates declined in New York, Bank Rate was reduced to 5½ and then to 5 per cent.: quite clearly, the exposure of London to international markets in short money was the dominant factor in the determination of rates in London. In these circumstances the Government had to accept worse and worse terms in its efforts to place long-term and medium-term bonds with investors at home.[1] The peak was reached at the beginning of 1917, when some £2,000 millions of 5 per cent. War Loan 1929–47 were issued (less than half for cash) at 95.

This gigantic issue, to yield over 5 per cent. for a minimum of 12 years, was the last of the longer-term issues. In the remaining 22 months of the war the Government was unwilling to try again at high rates of interest, and it confined its issues to shorter paper. For this paper it was able to secure rather better terms than had ruled in the winter of 1916–17. Rates tended downwards partly, as we have noted, because money became cheaper in New York. There was another reason, reflecting the movement towards total warfare and foreshadowing the ways of British policy in the Second World War. The extension of control in the economy generally had diminished the usefulness of high interest rates as a check on domestic prices, and the foreign exchange situation was being protected in some measure by discriminatory rates for domestic and 'foreign' deposits at the banks, and by various interferences with the movement of funds abroad.[2] The fact that interest rates fell in New York helped not only directly but also by making discrimination between home and foreign money a feasible policy: there was always some doubt how well it worked,[3] and if New York rates had been high, the discriminatory gap could hardly have been made wide enough to leave rates reasonably low for Government borrowing.

Policy developed on these lines during 1917 and 1918, though it was hardly possible at that stage of the war to push these tendencies to their logical conclusion. Perhaps the authorities did not fully exploit the power they derived from the substantial

---

[1] It was thought necessary, for the sake of Government credit, to give holders of the earlier issues valuable options to convert into the later issues (cf. the 1939-45 handling of a similar problem, p. 202 *et seq.* below). Professor Morgan considers that the terms offered by the Government were sometimes unnecessarily generous (*op. cit.*, pp. 106 *et seq.*), and he notes the technical ineptitude which did not make matters any better (p. 110).

[2] cf. Morgan, *op. cit.*, p. 196.

[3] cf. the attitude of the 'Cunliffe Committee', paragraph 19 (reprinted in T. E. G. Gregory, *British Banking Statutes and Reports*, Vol. II, pp. 345-346).

L

mobilisation of the economy.[1] But they did not have the advantage
of a protective fence of foreign exchange regulations, and this
handicap sufficiently explains their inability to shake off the last
vestiges of traditional techniques. And when the men of 1939
looked back, they were naturally impressed by the comparative freedom they could exploit in internal policy by reason
of the restrictions they were having to put upon external
transactions.

They were in fact going to start from where their fathers had
left off in 1918. They were determined not to get themselves into
the position of having to pay higher and higher rates of interest,
if only because the market as well as the authorities themselves
would be remembering 1914-18. They believed that the
fundamental position of the Government as a borrower contrasted
with that of 1915-16, because international capital movements
would be prevented by exchange control and perhaps also because
a controlled economy at home would deaden the inflationary
stimulus of low interest rates at home. They were aware that
steady pursuit—to be successful, it had to be unflinching pursuit—
of a cheap money policy would call at times for very careful handling,
for a technical competence, indeed, which would itself be in sharp
contrast to the unhappy bunglings of 1914-16. It was in this last
respect—the confidence in technical mastery—that the Treasury
and Bank of England were undoubtedly influenced, though perhaps
unconsciously, by their success in enforcing a cheap money policy in
the years since 1932. If the 'thirties had gone differently, memories
of 1914-18 would still have driven the Government to the policy
of a 'Three Per Cent. War', but in the actual event the confident
technique employed by the authorities owed much to their
experiences since 1932, and it is relevant to consider briefly those
experiences.

(ii)

The Technique of Cheap Money, 1932–39

The outbreak of war found Britain still—happily for the Treasury—
in the long spell of cheap money. The policy of cheap money had
been evolved under the pressure of events at the beginning of the
decade, and in principle it had been maintained ever since, although
in practice it had been subject to some qualification in the latter

---

[1] cf. Morgan *op. cit.* p. 196.

half of the decade. After the collapse of the 1929 boom the Bank of England, to some extent in concert with other central banks, had adopted a cheap money policy partly as the classical reaction to the relaxation of strain upon the supply of money, and partly as a deliberate effort to reverse the world-wide slump. This cheap money policy was interrupted by the international liquidity crisis of 1931. The Bank then imposed very dear money (Bank Rate stood at 6 per cent. for five months) and this policy was continued—indeed reinforced by open market operations—in the face of the influx of funds into London in the first months of 1932. Not until all the foreign credits obtained in the crisis months of August and September 1931 had been paid off (as was announced on 9th March and 5th April, 1932) did the Bank of England relax the pressure. Thereafter the continued influx of funds, supporting some improvement in the current balance of payments, was allowed to exert its full effect in increasing the supply of money, and very soon the Bank was reinforcing this by its own open market operations. The phase of grooming the market for the great War Loan conversion had begun. Bank Rate was on 30th June 1932 brought down to 2 per cent., where it remained uninterruptedly until 24th August 1939.

The confidence crisis of 1931 having been overcome, it was natural enough that the Government should be eager to deal with this National Debt problem which had been overhanging markets—and Whitehall—for years. The big War Loan conversion was successful, and with that out of the way the authorities had to consider what level of interest rates was appropriate to the wider needs of the economy.[1] The departure from the gold standard had not rendered rates in other centres entirely irrelevant, but it had left the British authorities with a wider margin of freedom than they had latterly enjoyed. What use should be made of this freedom? Favour for cheap money as an anti-depression device quickly reasserted itself, and at the Ottawa Conference in July-August 1932 the United Kingdom delegation gave full support to cheap money for the purpose of stimulating a rise of international prices, which just then was being stressed as the first object in the efforts to get the world out of the depression. Thereafter British Ministers persistently spoke of cheap money as one of the Government's main methods of encouraging the revival of trade. Even after 1936, when recovery had gone a long way and unemployment was structural and seasonal rather than cyclical, Government spokesmen

---

[1] On this first phase of post-gold standard policy, see E. Nevin 'The Origins of Cheap Money, 1931-2' in *Economica*, February 1953.

maintained support for cheap money as a stimulant to trade and industry.[1]

The technical arrangements whereby this policy was implemented developed considerably during the period.[2] Between the end of 1932 and the end of 1937 a dominant influence was the influx of funds from abroad, neutralised, as far as the foreign exchange market was concerned, by Exchange Equalisation Account absorption of gold and corresponding sale to the market of Treasury Bills held by the Account. This release of Treasury Bills was the counterpart in the monetary system of the bank deposits created in favour of the owners of the foreign exchange sold to the authorities. Had these accretions to 'London funds' been held in Treasury Bills, not bank deposits, and had the Government allowed the Treasury Bills outstanding to grow correspondingly, there would have been no disturbance of the monetary system. Neither of these two assumptions was realised. To some extent overseas holders of funds did add to their holdings of Treasury Bills; but this aggravated the 'famine' of Treasury Bills created by continuing conversion operations of the Treasury, which appears to have been worried by the growth of the volume of Treasury Bills. This concern dates back to 1919–20, when the authorities had been embarrassed by a swollen floating debt at a moment when a speculative boom and the foreign exchange situation were both held to justify severe credit restriction. At that time (as in 1951) the ability of the authorities to force a restriction of bank advances was impaired by the high liquidity of the commercial banks, and the freedom with which the latter could obtain more cash consistently with continued holding of sufficient[3] money market assets. In 1919–20 the danger was that the banks would simply allow Treasury Bills to run off, so forcing the Bank of England to create additional cash by Ways and Means Advances to enable the Treasury to pay off the Treasury Bills. Alarm at this situation long outlived the appropriate moment, and dominated Treasury debt policy throughout the deflationary years when it was completely inappropriate.[4] The Colwyn Committee did not adequately expose the situation, and under its influence antagonism towards a large floating debt continued to be Treasury doctrine throughout the

---

[1] See, e.g. H. of C. Deb., Vol. 297, Col. 2214; Vol. 332, Col. 2109 and (as lately as June 1939), Vol. 348, Col. 1109.

[2] The subject of these paragraphs has been discussed by D. S. Lees, 'The Technique of Monetary Insulation, December 1932 to December 1937' in *Economica*, November 1953, and 'Public Departments and Cheap Money, 1932-38', in *Economica*, February 1955, and by W. Manning Dacey, *British Banking Mechanism, passim*, among others.

[3] 'sufficient' was perhaps not related to a very rigid '30 per cent. liquid assets' rule, but to a rather vaguer rigidity approximating to this.

[4] See E. V. Morgan, *op. cit.*, Chapter V.

'thirties.[1] Consequently the Treasury was always inclined to push forward with the funding of the debt whenever interest rates were relatively low, even though Treasury Bill rates might be lower still. The immediate result was at times a 'bill famine' in the London market,[2] the extreme effects being felt in 1934 when cut-throat competition between banks and discount houses forced the Treasury Bill rate down to about a third of one per cent. At this point banks and discount houses got together[3] and came to a working agrement whereby the discount market was saved from starvation, and the Treasury Bill rate was effectively given a floor of just over ten shillings per cent.

As the supply of commercial bills failed to return to anything like its former level, and Treasury debt policy kept the market generally short of Treasury Bills, the underlying tendency throughout the following years was for the Treasury Bill rate to bump along this floor without substantial open market operations by the Bank of England. When purely temporary disturbances (apart from the half-yearly window-dressings by the banks) threatened sharp movements of the rate, the Bank of England was increasingly ready to step in to prevent the rate from rising.[4] In general, the Treasury Bill supply situation and the desire of the banks to maintain something like a 30 per cent. 'liquid assets ratio'[5] were sufficiently powerful forces to render sustained Bank of England intervention unnecessary, and both the authorities and the market became accustomed to a Treasury Bill rate that was both low and extremely steady. The force of habit of these years was transformed into deliberate policy after the war broke out.

---

[1] The Colwyn Committee, largely at the instigation of Lord Bradbury, favoured contraction of the floating debt (*Report*, Cmd. 2800 (1927), paragraph 102), but the Committee did also consider that, in the process of contraction, regard should be paid to the needs of the money market. It is possible to suppose that this qualification would have been stronger had the disastrous shrinkage of commercial bills been foreseen, instead of an expansion hoped for (paragraph 104). In favouring reduction of the floating debt, the Committee was influenced partly by the desirability of starting from a low point in the event of a future war (paragraph 101), and this consideration was perhaps in the Treasury's mind increasingly as the clouds of the 'thirties gathered. Alternatively, the antipathy to floating debt was so ingrained that the authorities just reduced Treasury Bills whenever they saw the chance.

[2] This 'bill famine' was of course only partly due to the reduction in Treasury Bills; the shrinkage of international trade in the great slump had already greatly reduced the volume of commercial bills on the market.

[3] It is believed that the authorities either encouraged or actually got the banks together.

[4] In April 1939 when an international alarm excited a liquidity scramble, the Bank allowed the market rate to rise quite sharply; but this was quite exceptional. The peak rate for 3-months' bills was 1⅜. *The Times*, 11th May 1939 ('The Money Scare in Retrospect').

[5] The mention of '30 per cent.' should not be interpreted in a rigid arithmetical way; the important fact—one that is now generally accepted—was that the banks preferred to hold liquid assets in something like this ratio to deposits.

The success with which the short-term rates were stabilised at very low levels was generally regarded by the authorities as all they should do—perhaps all they could do—towards keeping long-term rates down. There had been exceptional action in the spring of 1932, when official intervention combined with the return of confidence to bring the Consols yield down from $4\frac{1}{2}$ per cent. in February to less than 4 per cent. in June. Then came the War Loan conversion operation, when all conceivable weapons— including patriotic propaganda and open market operations— were brought into play to get the market firmly established on a $3\frac{1}{2}$ per cent. basis. Thereafter the authorities, despite their public assertion of a continuing cheap money policy, generally left the long-term securities market alone. Looking back, they regarded their intervention in 1932 as something altogether exceptional, dictated in part by the magnitude of the conversion operation and in part by the imperative need to combat the slump which was then at its worst. In 1932 also the authorities had felt that they were operating on the same side as 'market forces'—they were hastening the downward trend of interest rates, not combating the market trend. Through the remaining years of peace, when the trend had turned upward, the avowed cheap money policy would have necessitated intervention against the market trend, if there was to be intervention at all. The Bank of England view was that to combat the market trend was to court failure, and it appears that the Government at no time asked the Bank to try to alter the trend.

To this general policy of non-intervention there was one class of exceptions, of some importance in its lessons for war-time operations. The authorities prepared the market for the successive conversion operations. There was, as the years went by, widespread belief that the authorities were using the 'Departmental funds' (the insurance funds, the savings bank funds etc.) to support these operations. In fact most of the transactions were kept inside the Issue Department of the Bank of England, where the Government securities held as 'backing' for the Fiduciary Note Issue formed a useful *masse de manœuvre*. The technique was twofold. The Issue Department would buy in the market maturing stock and convert, thereafter peddling the converted stock out in the market slowly enough to avoid swamping the market. Alternatively the Issue Department could support the new issues of stock for cash by applying, so in effect underwriting the issue though without an underwriter's commission and without its support involving public admission of under-subscription of the issue. On the rising market of the early years, these operations brought profits to the Issue Department; after 1935 losses grew, a contingency for which the

Currency and Bank Notes Act of 1928 had not provided. It was when Mr. Oscar Hobson spotted the consequent oddities in published Government accounts[1] that the underwriting activities of the Issue Department became generally known.[2]

Underwriting operations of this kind for Government bond issues have since become common form, and their value in preserving an orderly market is generally admitted. They have particular value when a large part of a maturing stock has passed into the hands of financial institutions and others who want a short-dated security, while it is desired to give the conversion issue a life too long to appeal to such holders. The British financial structure has during the present century been developing in such a way as to make this contingency a common one, even the normal one. But in the 'thirties it was—at any rate on the scale then practised—a novel one, and the revelations of 1938 excited much comment. It is of the essence of such operations that they should be conducted in secrecy, although their existence could be known, and the publicity of 1938, especially when comment by the Comptroller and Auditor-General seemed likely, frightened the Treasury into wondering whether the borrowing policy ought not to be modified. Extreme fears proved unjustified; the absence, noted above, of provision for covering losses on these operations was remedied by a clause[3] in the Currency and Bank Notes Act of 1939; with the outbreak of war the financial journalists became short of space; and everyone came to accept the official operations as part of the natural order of things.

Official policy between the end of 1932 and the outbreak of war may thus be described as one of cheap money in principle, aided by bill market conditions which kept the three months' Treasury Bill rate close to one-half of one per cent., but no interference with the long-term market beyond the underwriting operations. What happened to the long-term market under this régime was that the yield on old Consols kept close to $3\frac{1}{2}$ per cent. through 1933, dragged slowly downward in 1934 to its minimum of $2\frac{3}{4}$ per cent. early in 1935, tended to rise slightly in 1935, was stable through 1936 (a shade under 3) then rose in two steps early in 1937, and before Munich. Through the first nine months of 1939 it was jerked upwards by the successive stages in the crisis, to a maximum just above 4. The steps in the curve were entirely due to the international political developments, but after each collapse of markets the

---

[1] See *The News Chronicle*, 1st September, and *The Economist*, 3rd September 1938.

[2] cf. the Chancellor of the Exchequer's speech on the second reading of the Currency and Bank Notes Bill of 1939, H. of C. Deb., Vol. 343, Col. 675.

[3] Clause 2(3).

recovery did not take quotations back to their pre-crisis level. The authorities were thus acquiescing in an upward trend of long-term interest rates in apparent contradiction to the cheap money policy which the Chancellor as lately as June 1939 saw no need to change.[1] This rising trend of long-term rates of interest was apparently in official circles ascribed to two factors: the international political developments which had so obviously pushed them up sharply from time to time, and the higher level of economic activity. Despite ministerial pronouncements, there was an official view that as economic activity was increasing, it would perhaps be right to allow interest rates to be dragged out of their abnormally low levels.[2] Apparently it was not realised—until the circumstances had changed[3]—that the rising trend in interest rates was being encouraged by the operations of the commercial banks, who were faced by a rising demand for advances but were uncomfortably short of money market assets and were therefore selling securities. When Mr. Boothby mentioned[4] the relevance of 'premature funding operations'—which were largely responsible for the shortage of money market assets—the Chancellor refused to be drawn.

In summary, the Government's interest rate policy must be described as one in which, after the initial push of 1932, no overt action was taken to prevent the rising tendency of long-term rates, while the stability of very low rates on short paper was rejoiced in. The whole tendency was to decry the capacity of the authorities to alter the trends; the underwriting devices were regarded essentially as smoothing operations and as such they were highly valued. If, in contrast to the earlier war, long-term as well as short-term rates were to be held down, reliance would have to be placed upon restrictions of alternative employments for capital. Given such a change in the fundamental circumstances which were apt to pull long-term rates about, the authorities could now face a war with the confidence that at least they knew more about the technical management of debt than their fathers had shown in 1914–16.

---

[1] H. of C. Deb., Vol. 348, Col. 1109.

[2] In this sentence I am not attempting to pass judgment on the soundness of this view, nor on the 'abnormality' of interest rates, but merely to describe the official attitude. There had been, in the early months of 1938, a significant effort to ease the market when trade temporarily took a downward turn. Although the Bank did not go so far as to increase the Clearing Banks' assets, as in some quarters it was being urged to do, it did by offsetting operations prevent the usual seasonal decline in bank cash.

[3] In dealing with a Parliamentary Question in May, 1939, the Treasury showed awareness of the bankers' 30 per cent. liquidity rule, but (owing to a mistaken view of events taken by *The Midland Bank Review*) the Chancellor and his critics did not come to grips with the problem, and from that time onwards the growth of the deficit kept the market well supplied with bills.

[4] H. of C. Deb., Vol. 348, Col. 1108.

(iii)

Academic Opinion on the Rate of Interest

While memories of the first war, a better understanding of the fundamental factors and a growing mastery of technique were moving officials towards the view that they should, could and would manage things differently on the next occasion, academic opinion was crystallising in favour of a firm policy of low interest rates. There was during the 'thirties a marked swing in economic thought against the view that the rate of interest is an important means of influencing the volume of economic activity.[1] The relevance of this to war-time problems was that if by foreign exchange control the rate of interest was anyway to be deprived of its influence on the external situation, admission of its futility as a check upon internal inflation removed the last justification for rising rates in time of war, in which case there was everything to be said for the utmost effort to keep rates down in order to minimise the continuing burden upon the Exchequer. Views from academic sources always penetrate Whitehall sooner or later, but on this occasion exceptional opportunity arose out of an expert review of the economic problems posed by the expanding defence expenditure during the first half of 1939. The Economic Advisory Council had ceased to meet years before this, but there had been since 1931 a standing committee of this Council, charged with the preparation of periodical reports on the economic situation. Lord Stamp was Chairman of this Committee, the other members being (in 1939) Messrs. G. D. H. Cole, H. D. Henderson and J. M. Keynes, Sir Alfred Lewis, Professor D. H. Robertson and Sir Arthur Salter, with Sir Frederick Leith-Ross and Sir Frederick Phillips as official members. Under date 20th July 1939, this Committee submitted a report on 'Defence Expenditure and the economic and financial problems connected therewith'. This report is believed to have been circulated to the Cabinet, though apparently it was never formally discussed there. It was certainly seen by the Prime Minister. Whether it had much direct influence is doubtful; it is worthy of notice here principally because it set out arguments which were certainly heard by people who had to make up their minds on this issue, and must at least have found some comfort in the abundance of support for the direction their views were taking.[2]

The Committee saw the problem of the defence effort as one that was reaching a stage where it could scarcely be distinguished

---

[1] This change in economic thought is discussed in *Oxford Studies in the Price Mechanism* (ed. T. Wilson and P. W. S. Andrews, Oxford, 1951), pp. 1-16.

[2] The Governor of the Bank of England had already made up his mind.

from mobilisation for war, and most of its arguments were readily applicable to the circumstances of actual war-time. Basically it regarded the problem as one of increasing the total national effort and securing for the use of the Government and of the export trade (vital for financing defence supplies from overseas) the greatest possible share of the effort so increased. The programme was, briefly, the control of investment, the limitation of dividends, the stimulation of exports, and various other measures bearing on the pre-war and war-time balance of payments problems. The need to control investment pointed directly to the rate of interest. 'The classical remedy for the situation', the Committee said 'would be an increase in interest rates,' but it saw three objections to reliance on this remedy:

'(i) A substantial part of the demand for investment goods is financed not by borrowing, but through the undistributed profits of industry and through depreciation funds. These funds would scarcely be deflected by the offer of higher interest rates from the purchase of investment goods to the purchase of e.g. Government securities.

(ii) The investment industries where demand is most influenced by changes in interest rates are the building and constructional trades. Curtailment of demand at these points would release only a negligible capacity for export.

(iii) The Government is itself the greatest borrower in the market to day, and would have to bear substantially increased charges if it raised interest rates against itself.'

Having rejected the 'classical remedy' of dearer money, the Committee indicated that the main task of diverting the national effort would have to be borne by 'rationing on the physical plane', but it was thought that some financial restrictions might be useful: 'The kind of measures which we have in mind are the discriminative control of new issues and other sources of new capital, and a moderate rationing of bank credit.'

Earlier drafts, produced by the officials, had not been quite as definite in rejection of the use of the interest rate weapon. As far as can now be traced, the main responsibility for the position eventually taken lies with Keynes.[1] His main interest in

---

[1] Mr. Harrod has suggested (*The Dollar*, London, 1953, pp. 73-4) that on the major question Keynes had direct influence in Britain, but only indirect influence in the United States. In fact, his only direct influence in Britain was in this special contribution to this Committee's report; he had no position in the Treasury when the critical decisions were taken, and his views on this particular question were not placed privately (as far as can be traced) before either Ministers or officials. His indirect influence, both through policy during the preceding years and the swing in economic thought mentioned above, was of course immense.

amending the early drafts was to stress the immediate need to mobilise our productive resources, but he did also protest against two tentative suggestions of a dear money policy: 'Does the Committee believe,' he asked, 'that it would do good rather than harm to depreciate war loan 5 or 10 per cent. or raise the return on Treasury Bills to 1 per cent.? I should have said that such measures would be of absolutely negligible value from the point of view of restrictions, and yet would completely destroy the Government loan programme, and cost the taxpayer in the long run hundreds of millions of pounds.'[1] In the light of this, we may assume that Keynes was satisfied with the line eventually taken by the Committee that dear money could do little to help restrict the demand on real resources, and that it would make the Government's borrowing policy certainly more expensive, and perhaps more difficult.

The report was submitted to the Prime Minister on 21st July 1939, and in the few remaining weeks of peace Mr. Chamberlain's study must have suffered an avalanche of papers on a multitude of subjects. But it is known that he habitually read such papers, and the Chancellor of the Exchequer apparently read his copy. It may therefore be presumed that these Ministers did receive as the considered advice of the experts, outside and inside, this rejection of the interest rate weapon on the two grounds that it could not substantially help the mobilisation of the production effort and that it would be a nuisance from the point of view of Government borrowing.[2]

The only serious qualification to this academic advice came from Professor D. H. Robertson (a member of the Committee) almost simultaneously, in his capacity as member of the Committee on Control of Savings and Investment (generally known as the Phillips Committee). In a memorandum primarily concerned with the problem not of war itself but of the preparatory period, Professor Robertson stressed the danger of confusing the two causes of rising interest rates—the 'hope cause' and the 'fear cause.'[3] Gilt-edged prices might fall 'for either of two precisely opposite reasons: (a) because they are in too much of a funk to

---

[1] The only other recorded comment on this point came from Mr. Cole, who thought that 'generally interest rates ought to be kept *fairly* low'.

[2] It must not be supposed that pronouncements of such a body as this Committee automatically swayed Ministerial opinion. As lately as June 1939 a senior official of the Treasury had minuted, in this context: 'The Economic Advisory Council has not had any practical influence on the policy of H.M. Government and the Bank of England'.

[3] For a published exposition not exclusively related to this historical episode, see Professor Robertson's article, 'What has happened to the Rate of Interest' in *Utility and All That*, pp. 86 *et seq.*

buy anything at all; (b) because they are so full of beans that they are more attracted by the idea of buying equities, commodities, industrial plant. It is for the former reason that interest rates move up at times of political uncertainty, for the latter that they normally tend to rise during industrial booms. *Prima facie* the protection of the gilt-edged market requires, in the face of (a) an expansionist, and the face of (b) a repressive policy . . . . The extreme difficulty of framing ahead a programme either of pre-war or of war finance seems to me to lie in anticipating which of these two opposite threats to the gilt-edged market is likely during any phase to be the more serious. *Prima facie* one would be inclined to say that mood (a) is the product of pre-war, mood (b) of actual war-time mentality . . . . . . Mood (b) is of course more likely to be a danger if price inflation is allowed to develop in the early stages of the programme. This is an argument so far as it goes for the early imposition or at all events preparation of controls in the capital market, even though at the moment mood (a) may still seem to be predominant there. . . . . . .' Throughout his argument he stressed the importance of adjusting the policy to the diagnosis, and it is quite clear that he would have supported high interest rates only if hopes of war profits were outrunning fears of war-time disturbance, and that he regarded direct controls as, in some circumstances, appropriate substitutes for a high rate of interest. If the expected war was to be extremely uncomfortable and elaborate controls were intended, Professor Robertson was as strongly as the others in favour of low interest rates. Here, at any rate, was a clear lead for any doubters in Governmental circles.

(iv)

The Rise in Bank Rate, August 1939

There was thus no doubt about what general policy should be followed in the event of war—war of the kind that was envisaged. But in August 1939 war—particularly war in a matter of days— was not regarded by the British Government as a certainty, and it was by no means clear that the obvious war-time policy was appropriate to the extreme phase of 'near-war' conditions.[1] Nor was there any clear view of the immediate steps to be taken. The Treasury had no coherent theory of any relation between short

---

[1] Ministers had however publicly taken the line that the rising pressure of defence requirements had not demanded any modification of the peace-time cheap money policy (e.g. Chancellor of the Exchequer, 13th June 1939, in H. of C. Deb., Vol. 348, Col. 1109).

and long rates[1]: the latter would of course have to be kept in order once we were settled at war, but were meanwhile apt to waywardness and independence of short rates. As for short-term rates, they were primarily a matter for the Bank of England; neither 'Bank-Rate' nor 'interest rate' was mentioned in the Treasury War Book. It was in fact left to the Governor of the Bank of England to initiate action, Bank Rate being raised from two to four per cent. on 24th August. It is believed that the Governor acted with the concurrence of the Prime Minister as well as the Chancellor of the Exchequer, but the latter privately confessed six weeks later that he could never understand why the action was taken. In accordance with tradition, no public explanation was given. Markets, lacking any guidance, were merely encouraged to believe a little more strongly in the risk of higher interest rates, and Consols continued their fall, moving from $63\frac{1}{2}$ on the 23rd to $62\frac{7}{8}$ on the 25th. The London Clearing Bankers were kept equally in the dark, and were prompted by this incident to suggest that it would be helpful if the policy underlying any particular change or movement affecting the banking community could be made known to them.

It was not to be wondered at that the bankers and the journalists were puzzled. The inter-war period had seen prolonged academic and public discussion of the *modus operandi* of Bank Rate, in which the broad lines laid down by the Cunliffe Committee in 1918[2] had been greatly elaborated and given varying shades of emphasis, but had not been contradicted. The basic tenets were that Bank Rate had a quick effect on the international short-term capital position and a slower effect on internal prices, capital development and the levels of output and employment. Regarded from this point of view, the doubling of Bank Rate in August 1939 was certainly puzzling. The international capital position could not conceivably be affected by any change in interest rates in in London: the pound's value in terms of dollars was hurtling downward, and foreign balances were being withdrawn as rapidly as possible. Indeed, the official view was that this withdrawal of foreign balances was inevitable and that only Mrs. Partington would try to check it, whilst any flight of domestic funds would

---

[1] In briefing the Chancellor for his reply to the budget debate, an official pointed out that the experience of the 'thirties had shown that the yield on long bonds had varied greatly while Bank Rate was stable, and on the basis of this advice the Chancellor eventually said : 'Therefore it must be obvious that there are factors of enormous importance at work on long-term interest rates which are not concerned with Bank Rate.' Similarly in March 1938, the same official had advised: '. . . But in reality easy credit is *not* aimed at producing cheap long money but at producing prosperous trade and business. In other words it is quite as likely to injure trustee securities (by subjecting them to competition from industrial stocks) as to help them.'

[2] See First Interim Report, paragraph 5, reprinted in Gregory, *British Banking Statutes and Reports*, pp. 336-337.

have to be prevented by unofficial action of the banks, by appeals to patriotism, and very soon by exchange restrictions. As to the internal economic situation, this, it was assumed, would be governed at once by Government orders of one kind and another, and it was also assumed that private capital development would suffer immediate hindrance from uncertainties as to supplies of manpower and materials and indeed from the paralysing fears of wholesale air attacks. Even the purchase and sale of commodity stocks, in so far as they were not directly controlled by the Government, would be subject to hopes and fears completely insensitive to a two per cent. change in interest rates. What was there left for Bank Rate to do, except to make the Government's own short-term borrowing more expensive?

Outside criticism along these lines was given voice in the budget debate at the end of September.[1] The authorities appeared, said the critics, to be underestimating their power, and to imagine that the Treasury in competition with private borrowers must bid up the price of funds in order to supply itself. The Chancellor's reply[2] (the only record we have of the reasons for the Bank Rate change) referred to the world slump as the justification for the Ottawa cheap money policy, and went on: 'The situation which faced us [at the end of August] when the Bank Rate was raised for the time being from 2 to 4 per cent., was not that of a world slump or anything of that sort, but a situation in which the clouds were gathering, and we felt obliged to allow the sterling-dollar exchange to go free . . . . and, instead of encouraging conditions which might lead to an upward bound in prices, it was necessary to demonstrate at once that we intended to keep a firm grip of the situation'. Recollections at the Bank of England suggest that these phrases were at least very close to those Mr. Montagu Norman would have used had he been pressed to public defence of the Bank's action. The doubling of Bank Rate was a storm signal; it was to show the world (including our own business men) that there was going to be no looseness about our war finance, no avoidable inflation.[3] It was to warn the speculators off, and to encourage a general drawing in of horns, pending the imposition as rapidly as possible of the various physical controls and other financial controls that would render the higher Bank Rate unnecessary. Logically, Bank Rate was brought down once more as the new

---

[1] e.g. by Messrs. Pethick-Lawrence, P. C. Loftus, and R. Boothby. (H. of C. Deb., Vol. 351, Cols. 1532, 1426 and 1704). In its issue of 2nd September, *The Economist* (which had itself commented in approving terms the previous week) spoke of the 'bitterness' of some of the outside comment.

[2] H. of C. Deb., Vol. 351, Col. 1604.

[3] The argument bears a close relationship to that put forward by Professor Robertson (see above pp. 155-6).

controls were inaugurated[1] and the sharp increases of taxation were announced.

This is the best defence that can be made of the doubling of Bank Rate, and it must be confessed that the arguments had much force only if a relatively long preparatory period was in view. The few weeks in fact covered by the higher rate were weeks of extreme uncertainty, when the courses taken by individuals and corporations both home and foreign were unlikely to be influenced by a change in interest rates. It may be suggested that the action was a demonstration that inflation was not to be allowed to get out of hand in this war—but the ten per cent. rate in August 1914 had been followed by a highly inflationary war. On the other hand, the disadvantages were great, both immediately and at longer range. The gross cost of the floating debt was raised by some £2½ millions in the autumn of 1939.[2] What was more serious was that markets were confirmed in their expectation that long-term interest rates would remain much above the low levels of the mid-'thirties. The yield on Consols was only just under four per cent. at the minimum prices which became effective at the end of August. At the end of September *The Economist* reviewed the prospect,[3] and envisaged a rise in interest rates 'no more catastrophic in the present war than in the last', starting, it was fortunately true, from a slightly lower rate in 1939 than in 1914. This was all in contradiction to the advice given by the experts, in the report referred to above, in July 1939; and until some weeks had passed, there was no sign that the authorities had anything less than a 'Four Per Cent. War' in mind.

(v)

The Three Per Cent. War

In fact opinion both inside and outside official circles was rapidly crystallising the idea of 'A Three Per Cent. War'. The clearest outside statement of the case was perhaps that given by *The Economist* in an article bearing that title, in its issue of 20th January 1940. It was there argued that savings for war finance would have to be

---

[1] Negotiations with the Clearing Banks for discriminating control of bank advances were put in train in the fourth week of September. The Governor of the Bank made it clear that without this step he was unwilling to bring Bank Rate down (and the Treasury official view was the same). The consequent reduction to three per cent. on 28th September was not as sharp as the Chancellor hoped, but he was advised that 'it would be quite impossible to go lower for the moment'.

[2] There were various Parliamentary Questions about this, but they failed to elicit either a figure or a defence.

[3] Article, 'Investment and War-Prospect', 30th September 1939.

steeply increased, that this could be brought about only by resort to exhortation and such extreme measures as compulsory savings, and that the rate of interest was too feeble a weapon to bring about the increased saving and unnecessary to secure its distribution between Government and other uses. The classical work of the rate of interest—to stimulate savings and to secure the best distribution of them between different uses—must be performed by more direct, more brutal methods. There was accordingly no reason 'why the rate of interest should not be pushed below its present level, rather than raised above it'.

The writer proceeded to give a definite plan of campaign. The yield on perpetual stocks, he pointed out, was virtually down to $3\frac{1}{2}$ per cent. (it had been up to 4 in the autumn), and 'a comparatively small continued exertion would bring it still lower'. The existing 3 per cent. Defence Loan (14–18 years) was within $1\frac{1}{2}$ points of par. It should therefore soon be possible to issue a 3 per cent. loan, possibly at a small discount, with a life of 15 to 20 years. 'This shows the way to Government loan policy'. The next four sentences gave a clear view of the course that events were destined to take: 'If the first war loan were a security of this character, two advantages would be secured. The first would be to fix in the public mind the notion that 3 per cent. is a reasonable rate for the Government to pay. And secondly, by keeping the life of the issue short, it would still be possible to keep up the pressure on the gilt-edged market, and as the long-term rate of interest fell, the life of subsequent issues could be gradually lengthened, until it might eventually be possible to offer really long-term securities on a 3 per cent. basis'.

Official opinion had meanwhile been travelling the same road; indeed, in the idea of exploitation of the Government's protected position as borrower, official ideas had reached much greater refinements than those suggested by any of the journals. The principal reason for the failure of policy to emerge during the autumn of 1939 was that the heavy withdrawals of foreign funds in July and August had placed hundreds of millions of sterling in Treasury hands, in exchange for the gold released by the Exchange Equalisation Account. This put the Treasury in funds to an extent far more than sufficient to cover the slow growth of war expenditure, and through the first weeks of war the floating debt was actually smaller than it had been at that season in previous years. The respite thus given was known from the outset to be temporary—the Treasury was living on a 'capital item' and it was known that, even in the absence of heavy raiding, the deficit must rise as the war effort gathered momentum. But it was an invaluable respite, in that it allowed the authorities to watch markets emerge from the depression that had been rather ill-advisedly encouraged by the temporary rise in Bank Rate, and it also gave them time to think very carefully over their borrowing policy. When the compulsions of 1940 arrived, the Treasury policy in its main essentials was ready, and there was no plunge into hasty improvisations such as so often cramp the style of subsequent developments.

In the formation of this policy there were three outstanding elements. First, the Government was determined to act as a discriminating monopolist, breaking the market up into its various sectors and treating with each sector separately.[1] In this way it could hope for better average terms than if it operated as a competitive borrower bidding the market price up to the level required by the marginal lender, though in its monopolistic manipulation of markets it was prepared to concede something to notions of 'fairness' as between one party and another. Secondly, it was determined that, on whatever rate of interest basis the borrowing programme was opened, there should be no winding stair towards higher and higher rates as the war progressed.[2] The disastrously expensive mistakes on borrowing policy in the earlier war must not be repeated. Thirdly, the 'central rate' for the major operations should be 3 per cent. This choice of 3 per cent. was based on the very strong view that public opinion expected 'a really low rate of interest', and the Governor's opinion that 3 was, if not the most desirable rate (he once said he would have preferred $3\frac{1}{2}$), at any rate the 'rock bottom rate' which could be successfully imposed on the markets. The Chancellor and the Prime Minister both took the line that 'politically it would be exceedingly difficult to justify a rate of interest above 3 per cent.', and a 'Three Per Cent. War' it was destined from that point (26th October 1939) to be.

In fixing upon 3 per cent. as the key rate, it appears that the authorities were influenced indirectly if not directly by the fact that people had during the cheap money 'thirties become used to that kind of return on capital. The small saver was paid $2\frac{1}{2}$ per cent. in the Post Office Savings Bank, and £2 18s. 4d. per cent. on National Savings Certificates. A quick decision had to be taken about the latter rate, in order to get the National Savings Movement into action. It was desirable to give the encouragement, for propaganda purposes, of a slight rise, but to raise the rate

---

[1] This was the attitude of a senior official from the very beginning of the war, and he found ready support in the Governor of the Bank. The possibilities were discussed in a general way in the Report of the Committee on Control of Savings and Investment ('The Phillips Committee'), 11th August 1939, which however stressed the delicacy of any legislative action.

[2] 'He (The Governor of the Bank) said once we had started on the 3 per cent. basis we must make up our minds never to depart from it and he was disposed to advocate that from the outset we should say definitely that throughout the war no better terms would be offered than those in the first loan.'

appreciably would be at once interpreted as a sign that the war
was going to cause a higher and a rising level of interest rates
generally, which would be quite unthinkable. The new certificates
were therefore announced to yield £3 3s. 5d. per cent. free of tax,
while bonds yielding £3 2s. 7d. (subject to tax) were made available
up to £1,000 for each holder. These steps having been taken, it
was politically undesirable to offer a higher rate to the large lender
than the rates available on small savings, so that the maximum
of about 3 per cent. for small savings became also the maximum
for large loans.[1] On the other hand, to force rates much below
3 per cent. would create difficulties for many of the great financial
institutions, who had become used to something like this level
and whose financial structure was in some measure based on the
assumption that rates would not go appreciably lower. Most
obviously this was true of the insurance companies, whose premium
rates were broadly based on this assumption. On the other hand it
was realised that some financial institutions—notably the banks—
could get along on much less than this, at any rate as their total
resources increased. Bearing in mind the possibility of discrimination,
the borrowing policy came to revolve round 3 per cent. as the
basic rate, the Treasury at the same time reserving to itself the
right to squeeze money out of particular classes of institutions
at lower rates.

Public announcement of the basis of the Government's policy
was made by the Chancellor in March 1940 after the first large
issue (for £300 millions) had been made. The relative failure of
the issue was covered by a large absorption into the Issue
Department of the Bank of England, there was Ministerial assertion
of the over-subscription of the loan, and the moral of success of a
3 per cent. loan was pointed: 'The purport of my answer was to
establish as far as I can the principle that 3 per cent. is a proper
rate which we ought to hold, and to discourage any idea that the
Government will be willing to contemplate more favourable
terms hereafter. If it turns out that I can get money cheaper, so
much the better.'[2] Eleven months later the three per cent. rule
received statutory recognition when the rate on Ways and Means
borrowing was limited to three per cent. by the Consolidated
Fund (No. 1) Act.[3] For the remainder of the war, the three per
cent. rule had statutory sanction.

---

[1] The 'small savings' rates were not properly comparable with those paid to large
lenders, but for political purposes the superficial appearance was important.

[2] H. of C. Deb., Vol. 358, Cols. 1649-50 (18th March 1940). In his 1941 budget
speech, Sir Kingsley Wood was more explicit: 'We have no intention of borrowing
on worse terms as the war proceeds; we shall hope to improve on them' (H. of C. Deb.,
Vol. 370, Col. 1298).

[3] H. of C. Deb., Vol. 368, Col. 1386. For *The Economist* comment, see p. 250 in the
issue of 22nd February 1941.

CHAPTER VI

CAPITAL ISSUES CONTROL

(i)

The Establishment and Purposes of the Capital Issues Committee

CONTROL over private capital operations was from the very beginning an integral part of the Government's financial policy. Those experts who had immediately before the war regarded the basic problem as that of freeing resources for the war effort approached the question of control of capital issues via the problem of reducing the amount of capital construction. Such, for example, was the approach of the Committee on Economic Information,[1] which in July 1939 recommended:

> the rationing of the investment expenditure which firms and individuals in this country are permitted to incur, with a view to maintaining the capacity in the investment industries available for defence production and for exports.

On this view the more important instruments of control might well be those on the acquisition or use of materials, rather than any financial controls. Indeed Keynes went so far as to argue that control of the new issue market would be of such slight effect as to be not worth imposing during the preparatory period: 'It is no good handling the matter via the new issue market, which comes in at much too late a stage'. This doubt about capital issues control was valid enough against any expectations of quick results, but on a longer view and in time of actual war there was something to be said for employing a financial control which would remove from the business man any expectation that he could finance an undesirable expansion, even if by one means or another he could lay his hands on the labour and materials with which to get it in train. A financial control, too, had the attraction of administrative simplicity, and the Committee thought that 'by excluding at source a number of projects of doubtful economic necessity', the difficulty of direct control (i.e. rationing of material resources) might be reduced by 'the discriminative control of new issues and other sources of new capital, and a moderate rationing of bank credit'.

---

[1] cf. pp. 153-4.

The desirability of some such control was more strongly urged by those who were approaching the problem from the slightly different angle of the channelling of private savings into the finance of the Government deficit, and in the event the control did tend to concentrate on technical protection of the market for Government bonds. This was the approach of the Committee on Control of Savings and Investment (the 'Phillips Committee') which reported in August 1939. This Committee made the specific proposal that the peace-time Foreign Transactions Advisory Committee, the Chairman of which was Lord Kennet and the chief function of which was to advise on new issues that might weaken the foreign exchange value of sterling, should extend its work to cover 'domestic and imperial' as well as 'foreign' issues. 'The chief consideration on which the Committee judges applications at present, support of the sterling exchange, will stand for foreign issues; for domestic issues the prior needs of rearmament finance should be the decisive consideration and issues permitted only if they can be related to rearmament.' This was specifically for the pre-war preparatory period, but the recommendations were applicable *a fortiori* to the actual war period, and the Treasury War Book included detailed plans for the transformation of Lord Kennet's Committee.

On 25th August 1939 Lord Kennet returned to London on being advised by the Treasury that swift action on these lines might become necessary, and his Committee met on 1st September to be advised of, and to advise upon, its impending transformation. The legal control that it was to administer was enacted on 3rd September as Number 6 of the Defence (Finance) Regulations[1] and an Exemption Order[2] of the same date. A press notice was issued on the following day (Monday the 4th) notifying the imposition of the control, the transformation of Lord Kennet's Committee, and the broad principles upon which the various classes of issues would be considered.

The Committee, henceforth known as the Capital Issues Committee, was appointed by a Treasury Minute of 12th September. The members were, besides Lord Kennet, Mr. B. G. Catterns (Deputy Governor of the Bank of England), Sir Austin Harris (Deputy Chairman, Lloyds Bank), Mr. Thomas Frazer (an insurance manager), Mr. A. A. Jamieson (of Robert Fleming & Co.), Lt. Col. J. B. Neilson (Vice-Chairman of Baldwin's Ltd.) and Mr. R. F. Wilkinson (Deputy Chairman of the Stock Exchange). Its terms of reference were 'to consider and advise upon applications made to the Treasury for consent to the issue of capital, to the

---

[1] S.R. & O. (1939), No. 1067.
[2] S.R. & O. (1939), No. 1007.

public offer of securities for sale or to the renewal or postponement of the maturity date of securities, in accordance with the provisions of Regulation 6 of the Defence (Finance) Regulations, 1939'. On the same date the Treasury sent Lord Kennet a memorandum for the guidance of the Committee. This somewhat elaborated the information already given in the press notice, gave the Committee clear instruction as to consultations with the Bank of England and the Board of Trade and other Government Departments, and instructed the Committee to provide the Treasury with monthly statistics.

The memorandum of guidance dealt with possible issues in four main classes. (1) Issues for renewal, whether of short-term instruments or of maturing long-term obligations, were to be allowed only to the extent that the applicant was not in a position to meet the maturities from funds already available and not required to finance business of national importance. (2) Domestic issues for new money were to be allowed for (i) production or services directly attributable to Defence (including Civil Defence); (ii) similar production or services for Empire Governments, Allied Governments or potential Allied Governments[1]; (iii) the maintenance of food supplies and other essential services (e.g. transport); and (iv) to assist the export trade where there was a definite chance of increasing exports to neutral countries with free currencies. (3) On Empire and Foreign Issues the Committee was given no guidance; all cases were to be referred to the Treasury directly. (4) The applications of local authorities to issue stock or bonds should be referred to the Ministry of Health, and those to issue bills or promissory notes should be referred to the Bank of England.

The instruction to refer these short issues of local authorities to the Bank of England was intended to support Bank of England efforts to keep the money market well under its own control, and the criterion by which applications would be considered would evidently be technical market conditions. On longer term local government borrowing, the Ministry of Health and the corresponding Scottish Department were made the effective sieves, and they at once indicated by circular to the local authorities the criteria by which applications would be judged. Broadly, permission would be given only for war requirements or to meet pressing public needs. Works already in progress were to be postponed or slowed down wherever possible.

Experience during the first few weeks brought to light a few unforeseen difficulties, and these necessitated amending Orders

---

[1] Readers of Professor Medlicott's Volume I of *The Economic Blockade*, in this series (H.M.S.O. 1951), will recall that these first months of war were a period of extreme tenderness towards neutrals.

on 26th September and 23rd November 1939. The first[1] met the complaints of banks that their business was hampered by the requirement of Treasury consent for issues of securities by way of collateral for bank advances in the ordinary course of business. Such issues were now exempted, provided that there was no expectation that repayment would be provided for wholly or partly by the issue or transfer of securities. Another teething trouble arose in relation to mortgages, and the treatment of this matter manifests the emphasis already given to the capital issues control as a technical protector of the gilt-edged market. The intention had been to exclude all mortgages, on the ground of their supposedly local character, but doubts arose both as to the wisdom of this course and as to whether the Regulations had in law implemented the intention. The Committee advised that municipal mortgages had become a serious element in the market for British Government and home Corporation bonds: 'They are no longer local issues as, for some time past, organisations have sprung up in every market and Stock Exchange of importance, which specialise in placing municipal mortgages among investors as an alternative to British Government and municipal securities'.[2] Then the lawyers advised that in fact mortgages were covered by the Regulation. The position was cleared by the enactment of a new Regulation (No. 6(5))[3]—specifically including mortgages. On the same date, by Capital Issues Exemption (No. 3) Order[4] the list of exemptions was generally overhauled, the most important change being the raising of the limit for small issues from £5,000 to £10,000, this limit being applicable to mortgages as well as all other securities.[5]

After these teething troubles had been dealt with, the broad legal framework of the control was not substantially changed through the remainder of the war, though possible amendments of the regulations were frequently being suggested, and on one occasion at least[6] were rejected only because the times were thought unpropitious for a proposal for extension of control. This discordance between stability of the legal framework and continual agitation

---

[1] S. R. & O. (1939), No. 1291.

[2] Memorandum by the Deputy Chairman of the Stock Exchange, 19th September 1939.

[3] S.R. & O. (1939), No. 1620 of 23rd November.

[4] S.R. & O. (1939), No. 1621.

[5] During 1940 there were difficulties about successive small issues totalling more than £10,000, and the Regulations were further amended by S.R. & O. (1940), No. 2187 of 27th December, and S.R. & O. (1941), No. 648 of 9th May, the final effect being that successive issues need not be aggregated for this purpose, except for those in the previous twelve months exempt *merely* on the ground of being below the £10,000 limit.

[6] December 1943.

for its amendment was paralleled by a similar contrast in the actual operation of the control. While the Committee was comparatively inactive and its small staff was not heavily engaged in a succession of difficult cases, and a large number of cases went very smoothly, there was a minority of cases in which irritation and misunderstanding were serious and received much publicity. The explanation of these paradoxical contrasts lies in the confusion of purposes regarded as proper to the control. Public opinion accepted as its principal object the check on the use of real resources for inessential purposes. But, as Mr. Keynes had foreseen,[1] the capital issues control was of little use for this, and the Treasury and the Bank of England turned it to quite different service as an instrument in the business of 'grooming the market' in gilt-edged securities. The control became one whose critical decisions were not whether an issue might be permitted, but what should be the terms of issue.

Though perhaps of some use as a long-stop, the control was not of major importance in its ostensible purposes of controlling the use of real resources. The operative decisions to employ real resources in capital construction are no doubt sometimes affected by doubts as to the marketability of related securities but, on the whole, the issue of securities comes too late in the process for it to be a suitable point at which to apply control, and the check on the use of real resources has therefore to be enforced by other conditions (including both deliberate controls and the accidental unavailability of labour and materials). The success of these prior checks leaves little relevant for a control of capital issues to do. The Kennet Committee therefore found itself chiefly occupied by a few oddities. The views of relevant Government Departments were generally ascertained, and these of course took account of any related use of labour, materials and factory space. These and other consultations normally preceded consideration by the Committee itself. The business in actual Committee was usually not at all difficult and there appears at this stage to have been little reference to questions of the diversion of real resources, though when foreign exchange questions were touched, the Committee applied the same kind of scrutiny as had been customary during its previous incarnation as the Foreign Transactions Advisory Committee.

Most of the questions that did prove difficult and gave rise to prolonged exchanges between Lord Kennet, the Treasury and the Bank of England arose from official perception of the alternative use to which this control could be put. The issue of securities is primarily a mattter of transfer of title to existing resources, and by interfering with the course of such transfers the authorities

---

[1] cf. p. 163.

were able—or at least believed themselves able—to influence
the marketability of the new Government bond issues required
to finance the budget deficit. This emerged very clearly in connection
with conversions and issues of bonds of local government bodies
and of Dominion Governments, with restrictions on the issue of
bonus shares, and with 'placings' of securities. The Committee
did not consider, except indirectly and by implication, the use of
real resources. The need for restricting private real investment
was always of course a background element, but the direct
impact of the Committee's work was on the functioning of the
market in paper titles.

(ii)

The Regulation of Trustee Issues

Involvement in the prolonged arguments about the conversion
and new-money issues for local authorities arose directly from the
Treasury's fears about its borrowing programme in the winter of
1939–40. Ever since the War Loan conversion of 1932 an informal
control of issues of trustee stocks had been exercised by the Bank
of England with a view to their orderly marketing, and the powers
now in the hands of the Treasury enabled it, in consultation with the
Ministry of Health and other Departments and the Bank of England,
to enforce queueing by borrowers, queueing at a door that opened
only when the Bank of England thought the market could absorb
securities without damage to the desired price structure for the
central Government's own securities.

Optional maturities in 1940 for local authority loans raised at
6 per cent. in 1920 were the first to be dealt with in this way: as
they were running at 6 per cent., whereas the current market basis
indicated the possibility of conversion to something like $3\frac{1}{2}$, the
margin of prospective saving in interest was enough to make even
the slackest municipal treasurer smack his lips. The Treasury
was at this time very worried about its own borrowing programme,
and local authorities were at once reminded that under Regulation
6 they could not undertake conversion operations without Treasury
consent given after reference to the Capital Issues Committee, and
they were informed that until further notice no such consent would
be given. Local authorities were of course free to redeem bonds out
of their own cash resources, but they were not allowed to issue any
new securities. The fact that a conversion issue, even if not
fully subscribed, does not involve a net absorption of cash from the
investing public was regarded as irrelevant. There could be no
shadow of competition with the forthcoming War Loan issue.

By the end of March the failure of the first War Loan issue had underlined the Treasury's caution. Meanwhile inspection had revealed a substantial list of securities, repayment (and therefore conversion) of which was optional in 1940. Besides £40 millions for local authorities, there were £50 millions of maturities for the Dominions. After consultation with the Bank, the Treasury instructed the Capital Issues Committee that access to the market would be allowed, so far as sums over £250,000 were concerned, only for non-trustee issues for new money. Even these would have to come to the market in an orderly queue checked by the Government broker (i.e. in effect by the Bank of England). The preference given to non-trustee issues—issues by companies and other bodies not susceptible to direct Government decision—and to 'new-money' issues as opposed to conversion issues is paradoxical, if one remembers only the control-of-real-resources aspect of the capital issues control. For the bodies denied access to the market were just those whose activities were already subject to Government decision (of one kind or another), and who were not seeking new money wherewith to obtain disposal of real resources. True, the other, non-trustee, borrowers requiring new money, had to apply to the Committee, and could get through the hoop only by proving national interest in the object of their capital expenditure; but comparison of this procedure with the complete frustration of trustee borrowers desiring to convert old high-interest securities serves to emphasise how far already the capital issues control had been turned from its ostensible purpose to the alternative of grooming the market in favour of the War Loan issues.

This remarkable standstill was held throughout 1940, through most of which successive shocks of war news prevented securities markets from developing any real strength. In the second half of the year the Consols yield fell from about $3\frac{1}{2}$ to $3\frac{1}{4}$ per cent., but the improvement was shaky until well into the autumn. Meanwhile the queue lengthened, not only on local authority account but also for the Dominions. Australia alone soon had £45 millions of old high-interest stocks in the queue. Borough Treasurers and Dominion Governments were becoming restive, and their complaints were being taken up in the Press. There was severe comment, for example, in *The Financial Times* of 3rd February 1941. 'The Government's attitude is even more difficult to understand', this newspaper wrote, 'when it is remembered that it pays a good deal of the interest to local authorities in connection with the high rate of housing loans. . . . . . With more authorities coming on to the list of those affected it is possible that increased pressure will be brought to bear upon the Government in an endeavour to secure the removal of the embargo'. The authorities were in fact already moving. At the beginning of the year the Bank of England had advised that the technical position of the gilt-edged market was strong, and that impending events—notably Treasury disbursements for requisitioned Indian, United States, and Canadian securities, as well as the pressure of accumulation in the statutory insurance funds—would tend to strengthen the market further in the coming months. The time was ripe for letting some of the queue come on the market. There could be no general opening of the capital market, and the spectacle of local authorities publicly competing with His Majesty's Government in the market might provoke complaints from the War Savings Movement. Still, a gingerly start might be made in a quiet way. The question was, by what precise procedure could a reasonable amount be worked off without undesirable repercussions.

A source had to be found for any money required for entirely new securities—by this date about £20 millions had been agreed in principle for local authorities—and to cover any unconverted portion of any maturing securities for which conversion was offered. Sources suggested included the Local Loans Fund and the Vote of Credit. The Local Loans Fund was fed by the issue of Local Loans Stock, but this could be taken up privately by Government funds. There was, it will be remarked, no net relief of demand upon the capital market for the financing of all public activities taken together, but the authorities greatly preferred a single central Government demand of say £x + 30 millions to the appearance of separate demands up to £30 millions in competition with a central Government demand of £x millions. The difficulty about the use of the Local Loans Fund was that legislation was required to enable the Fund to lend to any local authority for any purpose other than new capital developments. The requirements now in question were partly the repayment of old debts running at high interest rates, and partly revenue shortages. The Chancellor objected to use of Parliamentary time for a purely technical matter, and the Treasury also feared that the attendant publicity might encourage local authorities generally to clamour for finance by the central Government of their capital requirements at the more favourable rates now prevailing. Such a claim would involve broad long-term issues on which the Treasury would not wish to be stampeded by purely temporary war-time exigencies.

Alternatively resort might be made to the Vote of Credit—i.e. the general funds voted by Parliament for the prosecution of the war. The Treasury directly controlled the use of these funds and could therefore hold the borrowing local authorities on a tighter rein than they would perhaps feel if the Public Works Loan Board was syphoning out money through the Local Loans Fund.

While these discussions were proceeding, the problem was rapidly growing under pressure from the Australian Government for dealing with some £45 millions of its maturities. Eventually a decision was taken to proceed with conversion operations, to cover both the Australian maturities and those of local authorities. The local authorities requiring new money would however have to wait, financing themselves by bank borrowing meanwhile. The conversion plan became a twofold one: unsubscribed conversion stock would be taken up (a) by the Treasury, using Vote of Credit funds, for Australia, and (b) by the Local Loans Fund for local authorities. The latter operation was to be covered by a Public Works Loan Bill, to be enacted as soon as possible. Nineteen conversion offers for the local authority securities, all of which had borne interest above 4 per cent., were made simultaneously on 1st May 1941, the stock offered being in every case 3½ per cent. stock redeemable 1960–70. The unconverted stocks taken by the Local Loans Fund totalled £1,304,460, after the debtor corporations had been pressed to make available any surplus balances they themselves held.

The Australian operation was complicated by the existence of a £13 millions loan falling finally due on 1st October 1941. It was felt that, though the Vote of Credit might be used to assist in a conversion operation which was discretionary, its use in meeting a non-postponable obligation might be open to the inference that Australia was unable to pay her debts. Accordingly a separate operation was undertaken to dispose of this particular security, the Australian Government undertaking to pay off any dissenting holders from its own sterling balance. Having got this out of the way in April, the authorities proceeded to announce at the end of May 1941, a larger operation, analogous to that for the local authorities, covering the optionally redeemable stocks bearing above 4 per cent. There were three such stocks, totalling £30 millions, and they were replaced by 3½ per cent. stock, 1961–66 issued at 99. New stock representing the unconverted portion was handed to the Bank of England against advances made from the Vote of Credit, totalling £6,345,762, the advances being gradually repaid by unloading the stock on the market in the course of the next two or three years.

The habit once acquired was followed throughout the war. Local authorities were carefully regimented and their conversion operations were kept waiting, in some cases for many months.[1]

---

[1] In the later years the position was reviewed in the light of post-war reconstruction plans, and the policy, implemented in the Local Authorities Loans Act of 1945, of restricting all local authorities' borrowing to the Local Loans Fund was then adopted. This was however designed to provide for the quite different post-war circumstances and must not be confused with the war-time expedients by which the market in Government bonds was buttressed.

Australian maturities were more troublesome, especially when in 1941–42 Japanese advances so shook Australian credit that the Treasury thought no better rate than 5 or 6 per cent. could be expected on a market issue. In 1942 the market for Australians greatly improved, but, even so, the British authorities were not willing to test the market severely. Rather than this, the Australians were allowed to offer a 3½ per cent. basis for the £16½ millions maturing on 1st January 1943, and the Treasury as underwriter drew nearly half this sum from the Vote of Credit. The advances were repaid by proceeds of sale of stock by October 1943.

Other classes of securities were scrutinised from just the same point of view. During 1941, for example, conversion issues for optional maturities of public utility companies were held up and eventually allowed only where the old rate of interest was above 4 per cent. The total involved in 36 issues was little more than £2½ millions, and it must be supposed that the dissented portion of these could scarcely have been more than a fraction of a million. Even such chicken-feed as this could not be allowed to go to the market unhindered: it was safer to 'avoid divided allegiance on the part of the investing public'.

In all these transactions there is no trace of the control as a conscious check on the use of real resources. The outward emphasis was always upon the grooming of the market for gilt-edged securities. It was perfectly clear that encroachment of any competing issues on the resources available to meet Government borrowing could not be avoided by making conversion issues wait, nor could it be avoided by letting the Government itself provide any money required. The sole purpose was to avoid the danger that an unsuccessful flotation would have a damaging effect on the psychology of the market, and would cause the market to turn its views in the direction of higher rates of interest.

The policy found its justification in the delicacy of the 'Three Per Cent. War' policy. If the three per cent. standard was to be maintained, market confidence must be maintained with a high degree of consistency. If market confidence had once been badly shaken by an appreciable period—say a month or so—of prices below the appropriate level, people would have believed that three per cent. had gone for the remainder of the war and that interest rates would go higher and higher until the end of the war. Once this happened, memories of what had happened 'last time' would have become the dominant element in the market. When people believe that the long-term rate is going to rise to say six per cent. within two or three years, they sell their securities at once in an effort to avoid the implied depreciation of capital values, and this pressure to sell forces the rate of interest up at once. The rise in interest rates, once started, would therefore have been much more rapid than it had been in 1914–18, and the immediate budgetary weight of the debt service would have been substantially increased.

Against allowing any such demoralisation of the market, there were other weighty objections as well as the immediate burden on the budget. It would serve little purpose as a sieve for capital projects—other conditions must anyway be relied upon to provide this check; and once this is admitted, it is implicit that there is no 'equilibrium' level at which the rise in the interest rate can be expected to stop. It was impossible, that is to say, to foresee any certain end to a rise in interest rates, once the market began to slide, save the doubtful brake that market opinion might apply when the historical maximum of 1919–20 was reached. Secondly, a high rate of interest during the war would probably mean a very high rate at the end of the war, which might be highly undesirable for British industry as well as a great nuisance from the point of view of the Treasury as a debtor.

All this constituted a powerful case for doctoring the market sufficiently to maintain the three per cent. basis without faltering, provided that there was no better way of achieving the same object. It may well be urged, however, that the Bank of England could, by direct operations in the stock market, have supported the market whenever it sagged, and that measures of this kind would have made possible the floating of all possible conversion issues without any manipulation of the issue machinery itself. Indeed, the spectacle of a long succession of conversions from four and five per cent. stocks to $3\frac{1}{2}$ for municipalities and Dominions might well have reinforced market confidence in the viability of the three per cent. régime. Why was this simpler measure not adopted?

The choice of policy was probably influenced in some measure by certain traditions that had become firmly established during the inter-war period. The Bank of England had become well accustomed to open market operations in Treasury Bills but, perhaps partly because of the ease of these operations, it was strongly opposed to operations, in the ordinary course of events, in longer term securities. In the very exceptional circumstances of early 1930 and early 1932 it had engaged in such operations, but on these occasions it had engaged on the same side as the weight of market opinion—i.e. its action had been to hasten and accentuate a market trend already incipient. Intervention against the market trend—which is what the Bank might have thought war-time action involved—is a very different kettle of fish; and central bankers who had grown up oppressed by the colossal size of the National Debt felt that if they once embarked on such operations they might have to go on and on, buying more and more securities thrown on the market by incredulous sellers. It is one thing to steady, by waving the hat of the Government broker, the slide in a momentarily demoralised market. It is quite another to try to stem an avalanche set in motion by a war to which no early end can be foreseen. The British authorities thought that, if they made such an attempt, the consequent inflation of the floating debt (since floating debt must replace the bonds unloaded by the investing public) would have immediate adverse effects on confidence, aggravating the situation with which they were trying to cope, and that it would also make post-war control of the credit situation much more difficult.

The authorities had also to consider possible reactions from the big 'institutional investors' who formed the backbone of the market. Early in the war the Governor of the Bank of England, by arrangement with the Chancellor of the Exchequer, had secured from these insurance companies, building societies and other investing bodies undertakings that they would invest all their available funds in Government bonds. To protect in some measure investments made under this pressure, by enforcing 'orderly marketing', was one thing; to protect it by unlimited purchases— that might be terminated on a change of policy, with disastrous effects on security prices—would have been quite another. In war-time conditions the Bank could hardly have expected to keep heavy supporting operations secret from the big institutional investors, and the possibility of their dislike of artificiality in market conditions had to be reckoned with. On the whole, the more cautious policy would be more acceptable to the market, and was therefore more readily adopted by authorities who had from the first chosen to rely greatly on voluntary co-operation.

It is possible to suppose that comparatively small interventions from time to time would have prevented the emergence of a consistent market view that interest rates were bound to rise. As long as there is no firm and consistent market view, the authorities are in a strong position. On the other hand, known pegging of the market by official dealings at times offers the attraction of a one-way option (as when a pegged currency seems likely to be devalued). The authorities were never, it appears, sufficiently confident of their hold on the market to run risks of this kind. The more cautious policy was followed, confining Bank of England interventions to minor operations at critical moments of preparation for new Government issues. Abjuring any outright pegging of the prices of long-term bonds, the authorities preferred to rely on the less direct method that had in a small way become a habit during the nineteen-thirties, but was now destined to become a cornerstone of capital market policy. This was the enforcement of orderly queueing of trustee issues coupled with the use of Government funds for underwriting conversion issues. By arrangement with the Capital Issues Committee, all borrowers of over £100,000 were instructed 'to approach the Government broker with a view to the settlement of details (e.g. of date of issue) with the Bank of England'.[1]

Against this plan borrowers could scarcely grumble. After all, it only meant that they had to pay rather higher interest rates for a little longer than appeared necessary; and if the authorities had not enforced this queueing, the borrowers might not have been able to get money at any reasonable rates at all. The imposition of a small temporary charge on particular borrowers was therefore a trifling burden they might reasonably be expected to shoulder in the interest of maintenance of the three per cent. standard, which benefited not only the Government but also all other borrowers once the latter did get into the market.

If the matter had ever been seriously disputed, it seems that the authorities would have defended their action on these lines. In fact it was not seriously disputed, though there were critical references from time to time in the financial press. The line taken by the authorities was part and parcel of the cheap money policy, and this broad policy was not one to excite hostility in Parliament or among a wider public. This tacit acceptance helped to make the policy successful and to justify it.

(iii)

The Restriction of Bonus Issues

The action of the Chancellor of the Exchequer in using the capital issues control to restrict the issue of bonus shares can be justified on much the same lines, although the implied threat to the stability of the gilt-edged market was altogether more trivial and it is very doubtful whether this part of the control was worth the irritation and bother it occasioned.[2]

Bonus issues, made for capitalising profits or reserves, were controlled from the outset, but at first very little restriction was applied to them. In the first four months of the war there were 111 applications, involving some £12 millions, and of these only

---

[1] Capital Issues Committee, Memoranda on Principles and Procedure, p. 16.

[2] Resort to this measure was undoubtedly encouraged by the prejudice in the Labour movement against bonus issues, and as early as January 1940 the Treasury and Ministry of Labour were discussing its usefulness as a move to conciliate the Trade Unions when wage claims were rejected.

one was rejected. In justification of this permission to create a batch of marketable shares, the theorist's argument adduced was that the greater number of shares available should be offset, on a fair market view, by a proportionately lower price for each share. But the experts suspected that this was perhaps not always the whole story,[1] and thought it would be safer to assume objectionable any operation that added to the number of securities in the market. How far this should be carried was under discussion when in April 1940 the Chancellor announced in his budget speech[2] the plan to limit all dividends. In view of the popular prejudice against bonus shares 'as a means of putting money into people's pockets surreptitiously', the Government decided to couple with dividend limitation a prohibition of bonus issues, subject to special exceptions. Such exceptions might occur 'where two companies amalgamated, and something had to be done to adjust the position'. To close a loophole the Capital Issues Committee was also instructed 'that any issues of capital, the offer of which is to be made to existing shareholders in a company, should be made only on terms which do not involve any element of bonus'. This implied that the Committee would have to estimate the fair market value of any shares on offer, a task of some difficulty that had to be undertaken not for the sake of controlling the use of real resources, but solely in support of the political object of effective limitation of dividends.

A few weeks later, on the raising of the excess profits tax to 100 per cent., the Bill for limitation of dividends was dropped.[3] The Chancellor, however, appealed to companies to conform to the limitation voluntarily. If a company could issue bonus shares, it could, though limiting its dividend to the former rate, inconspicuously disregard the Chancellor's appeal, and it was therefore thought right to maintain the ban on bonus issues. No doubt this decision was reached easily enough in the light of the discussions that had been in progress before dividend limitation was proposed. The ban thus confirmed remained in force for the rest of the war. It provided continual worry for the Capital Issues Committee and occasional heart-searchings in the Treasury. One official commented in 1941 that the ban was 'a great nuisance. Many a sensible arrangement to divide accumulated profits without draining the business of cash, when, e.g. a partner has died and a general re-arrangement is necessary, has been frustrated by the ban. In that, of course, we may have been wrong,

---

[1] For a thorough analysis of the effects of bonus issues, see the article by M. Rix, 'The Value of Bonus Issues', in *Economica*, February 1952, pp. 44-58.

[2] cf. pp. 39-41.

[3] See pp. 41 and 46 *et seq.*

since we have discretion to lift the ban in altogether exceptional circumstances. But lots of such cases are never put up of course, and those which reach us have received rigorous treatment just because we felt the justification of the ban was so slender that once we admitted "hard cases" we should not know where to draw the line'. This judgment reveals the trained administrator's normal attitude in operating a control which he believes unreasonable, and it constitutes a strong case against this particular control. Nevertheless, the authorities continued their practice almost unmodified.[1] The Treasury policy remained that any addition to the face value (irrespective of the true value) of the stocks and shares available to the market was likely to diminish the total fund available for subscription to Government loans, and must therefore in general be restricted to special 'national interest' cases. At the beginning of 1945 one of the Chancellor's advisers protested: 'Why we persist in this rule I have not the foggiest idea. Might it not be given up? Is it not a hang-over from the pre-100 per cent. E.P.T. days, when various rather ineffective psychological alternatives were being proposed by the Chancellor to keep criticism quiet?' There was, and could be, no answer to such questions, and the Capital Issues Committee expressed the opinion that 'the present restrictions on bonus issues have no material effect in promoting the purposes of the control, either by increasing the funds available for investment in Government securities or by diminishing the value of competing securities'. As post-war reconstruction came into view, there were further relaxations, but no general scrapping. Only the political flavour the measure had had since April 1940 and the stress laid by the Treasury on the minutiae of market control could have made possible such a long life for such a petty and irritating control.

(iv)

The Regulation of 'Placing'

The regulation of Stock Exchange 'placings', another matter that gave rise to much trouble, had a sounder basis, in that it was concerned with a major loophole in the control of new issues. Given that the capital control was to be a control of changes of ownership—which is what the general conditions and the official predilection for grooming the market had pushed it into being—it was only reasonable that all substantial avenues through which companies might obtain new money should be subject to effective

---

[1] There was a slight extension of the 'entirely exceptional grounds' in May 1942.

N

supervision. The legal position established by the control was that a public issue of securities was subject to Treasury consent. But if a large block of existing securities previously tightly held (e.g. by a family) was 'placed' on the Stock Exchange and a market made in them, the Regulation 6 did not touch the operation. Even the public advertisement, required by the rules of the Stock Exchange before permission to deal is granted, did not constitute a public offer for sale and therefore did not render the transaction subject to the control. The Treasury, however, insisted that the marketing of a holding previously dormant had just the same effect on the market as the issue of a corresponding volume of new securities, and early in 1942 consideration was given to the possibility of amending the Regulation so as to obstruct these transactions. A little thought soon showed that it would be quite impossible to draft a satisfactory legal instrument for blocking all such transactions while leaving free the main part of the market in old securities. The Treasury policy had in fact no logical stopping point short of restriction of all changes of ownership of securities of all kinds.

Consultations between the Bank of England and the authorities of the Stock Exchange led however to a *via media* which satisfied immediate Treasury requirements and postponed any facing of the logical implications of the policy. In May 1942, by exchange of letters, an agreement was recorded between the Treasury on the one hand and the London Stock Exchange and the Council of Associated Stock Exchanges on the other.[1] The Stock Exchange made permission to deal conditional on Treasury consent, on the understanding that this arrangement could be disclosed to the applicants. Privately it was agreed that for the present applications need not be referred to the Treasury if they were below £100,000, unless special features suggested to the Stock Exchange authorities the desirability of an official opinion.[2] It was not, of course, to be taken for granted that permission to deal would automatically follow Treasury consent: the Stock Exchange would continue to apply its own tests.

It was not long before a wagon was driven through the hole left in this extension of control. A finance company, which had already distinguished itself in finding ways round control, proceeded to market securities beyond the writ of the Stock Exchange,

---

[1] The House of Commons was informed on 21st May 1942 (H. of C. Deb., Vol. 380, Col. 357).

[2] The £100,000 limit, which was not published lest companies be tempted to avoid control by keeping their issues just below it, applied to the nominal value of the securities, but the Stock Exchange was asked to consult the Treasury if the market value considerably exceeded £100,000.

developing an outside market by circularising its numerous clientele with offers of shares, and advertising in the financial press. The Stock Exchange became restive at the way circumvention of the extra-statutory control was leading to diversion from the Stock Exchange of business it regarded as its legitimate preserve, and irritation and murmurings increased through 1943. Not merely was the control being avoided; in the event, the public was also being deprived of the benefit of safeguards the Stock Exchange had so carefully built up in the light of experience. It was in the public interest that companies should conform to the conditions imposed by the Stock Exchange itself, and that a Stock Exchange quotation should supply the public with an effective measure of the value of any security. Now the market outside the range of Stock Exchange machinery, with none of the latter's protection of the public, was getting the business, because it was free from the unofficial control which bound the normal channels. In some cases the Treasury had given consent for a proportion only of a block of shares to be sold. Such half-measures had created additional technical difficulties in the Stock Exchange, and outside dealers had been able to take advantage.

After rejection of a Stock Exchange suggestion that the loophole might be stopped by bringing into operation the Prevention of Fraud (Investment) Act of 1939—which, as its title implies, was a quite inappropriate measure—the authorities decided to try stopping it by negotiation with the banks, the insurance companies, the investment trust companies, the accepting houses and 'finance and issuing houses'. The Stock Exchange pressed for the employment of jobbers in the placing of approved securities but this was too much like opening the market—precisely what the Treasury desired to avoid. Eventually it was agreed that brokers acting for issuers might place securities with jobbers on the understanding that they would be disposed of only to institutions on an approved list. Once again there was no statutory Regulation, but a memorandum of agreement, to stand for six months from June 1944, was accepted by the institutions concerned.[1] They pledged themselves not to take unquoted securities, except where the raising of money by a vendor was approved by the Capital Issues Committee, and they undertook not to sell the securities at a discount within six months of acquisition. This arrangement was usually referred to as the 'Grey Market Agreement'. The

---

[1] 19th June 1944. The arrangement was continued in response to a request which the Chancellor made in answering a Question in the House on 20th February 1945 (H. of C. Deb., Vol. 408, Col. 625-6). In his answer the Chancellor added the condition that after the six months' holding period, permission to deal would still need Treasury approval.

authorities also adopted a practice whereby the 'placing' of securities—or the underwriting of a 'rights' issue to existing shareholders—was in the main limited to institutional investors. These could be expected to be firm holders, and they were required to give undertakings that any allotment would not be sold below the issue price for a period of six months. Under this practice it was customary to allow a small proportion of any issue or underwriting to be placed with the jobbers in the particular market concerned, primarily with a view to providing the necessary shares to 'make a market' when dealings opened.

In these developments of their control the authorities were exposing themselves to difficulties which, though not arising in the general run of cases, could lead to misunderstandings and hard words in the exceptional instance. At the end of 1944 an unexpected combination of circumstances came along to excite an uproar in the City and one of the most unpleasant outbursts of feeling that any Government Department suffered during this part of the war. Arrangements were made for the placing of two million £1 Preference Shares in the General Electric Company, which secured the permission of the Capital Issues Committee to raise the money in order to repay a five-year loan from a large insurance company (the Prudential). The issue was placed privately through Morgan Grenfell and Company for a commission of one and a half per cent. £150,000 of the shares were allotted to three firms of jobbers in order that they might make a market when permission to deal had been given. Certain approved financial institutions (parties to the Grey Market Agreement) took the shares at par on the usual understanding that they would not sell at a discount within six months. What went wrong was that owing to difficulties which the General Electric Company experienced in making the arrangements—they had perfectly legitimately gone to Morgan Grenfell's without official advice after other negotiations had broken down—a month elapsed between official approval of the conditions of issue (including the price) and the conclusion of the transaction with public announcement, and it so happened that during this month news about the German counter-offensive in the Ardennes caused Stock Exchange prices to rise.[1] The houses that had secured the shares had therefore received very good value for their money; and though of course bound not to sell at a discount, they were free to sell at once and take a quick and substantial profit. The borrowers appeared to have received worse terms than necessary, the rank and file of the

---

[1] It should perhaps be emphasized that none of the parties had acted in any improper or incompetent way, and that if there had not been this unfortunate lapse of one month, no bad feeling would have been occasioned.

Stock Exchange saw the chance of profit confined to the favoured few, and existing General Electric Company shareholders thought they should have had first option. The fury of the City found expression in the Stock Exchange New Issues Sub-Committee. This body had been expected by its officials to give permission to deal, and indeed it had usually run true to form so that consultations between the Treasury, the Capital Issues Committee, the Bank and the Stock Exchange officials had normally meant that permission to deal followed automatically on Treasury permission.[1] On this occasion the less influential members revolted, and the Sub-Committee refused permission to deal.[2] The financial journalists took it up, charges of official favouritism and interested advice were bandied about, and even inside the Treasury some hard words were used.

The Treasury officials had no difficulty in refuting the allegations of scandalous action and explaining how the opportunity for profit had unwittingly arisen. But this did not dispose of the whole matter: it was essential to take all possible steps to preclude a repetition of the circumstances, and to secure more satisfactory contact between the Treasury and the members of the Stock Exchange whose dissatisfaction was largely responsible for the bitterness with which charges were being thrown at the authorities. The immediate remedy was found in elaborating the undertaking given by certain allottees of securities, to preclude not only sales at a discount but also sales at a profit within six months; after this period permission to deal would still need Treasury approval on advice from the Capital Issues Committee. This did not entirely satisfy the critics, who pointed out that the lucky ones could still get their handsome rake-off, only after waiting six months. But the authorities considered that institutional investors would take up securities to hold for a minimum of six months only if they were in fact intending to be firm holders: speculators would not be prepared to hold for such a period. As regards liaison with the Stock Exchange, some attempt was made to improve relations, but the position remained confused and dissatisfaction in considerable measure continued.

After these events Lord Keynes, who had interested himself particularly in the case, urged the Treasury in very strong terms to reconsider the control root and branch. He had always been sceptical of its usefulness, and the lessons of recent experience and

---

[1] The Stock Exchange permission had to come last, because it was customary to announce the fact on the following day.

[2] The main Committee confirmed the Sub-Committee's decision and, according to *The Economist*, this decision had 'the warmest support in almost every quarter of the City' (6th January 1945, p. 23).

the prospect of an early end of the war combined to make him positively hostile.

> 'It is a fallacy', he said, 'to suppose that it assists in the smallest degree the control of the gilt-edged market and the rate of interest . . . . . Practically all the attack [upon the Committee] has been directed to what should be a very secondary aspect, namely the conditions in which approved new issues and existing securities should be allowed to change hands. Most outsiders (myself included) believe that official policy on this aspect is partly fallacious, partly unnecessary and partly of a minor order of importance . . . . . In the first place, it is clear that, rightly or wrongly, this part of the policy fails to carry general conviction, with the result that it injures the prestige and authority of the primary aspect of control, the prestige and authority of which it will be more important to maintain (in much more difficult circumstances than now exist) during the transitional period. Moreover, being fundamentally based (as I believe) on a fallacy, it is extremely difficult to be consistent in practice . . . . . In the second place, an attempt to control in detail the conditions in which securities change hands inevitably causes the authorities, if not in fact certainly in appearance, to get mixed up in all sorts of City matters from which they had much better keep aloof. . . . Far transcending in importance either of the above considerations is the fact that the time will soon arrive when the existing officially-favoured technique for the distribution of approved new issues will be utterly unable to handle the situation.'

These comments on the existing arrangements reached and disturbed the Chancellor, but the very fact to which Lord Keynes's last point referred, namely the imminence of the transition period, gave the Treasury a sufficient reason for refraining from any drastic overhaul at the moment. There were minor attempts to patch over the continuing loopholes in the system, but on the main issues decision was postponed. The Chancellor even went so far, when announcing minor changes to the House of Commons,[1] as to imply that his review of the working of control had had broadly satisfactory results. He emphasised, however, that he was 'dealing only with the present situation. The transition from war to peace will, of course, involve the opening of the market to a larger flow of issues by borrowers other than the Government. It will still be necessary to regulate that flow in an orderly manner; but modifications of our present policy and procedure will be required, and these are under consideration . . . . '

---

[1] H. of C. Deb., Vol. 408, Cols. 625-6 (20th February 1945).

The Chancellor's qualified satisfaction had the justification that in the great majority of cases the control had in fact worked smoothly and had commanded a reasonable degree of respect among the established institutions and people in the City. The space given in the above paragraphs to a particularly awkward case is no indication of its relative importance in the entire history of the control; as with all controls, it is the few cases at the margin that attract special attention at the time, and the necessary reference to this case here has entailed adequate explanation of the circumstances. That this control, broadly accepted by the affected parties, could give rise to a storm of this kind was due to the basic weakness that it rested on the theory that changes in ownership of securities needed careful watching, and to the fact that there was no logical stopping point short of the completely impracticable regulation of all transactions in securities.

Despite the fundamental difficulty, the bad odour that hung about this outburst in the last year might have been escaped had some effort been made to explain the Treasury's theory and to convert critics, who were not all interested parties.

'On the really critical question', wrote *The Economist*,[1] 'of why the Treasury should think it necessary to dictate the means of raising money—once the permission to raise it has been granted—there is still not an atom of official guidance'. This secretiveness was in keeping with the pre-war desire to cloak the action of the authorities in grooming the market for new bond issues[2] when it was believed that publicity would render the customary devices ineffective. But secrecy about principles in 1944–45, when the actual operations were more or less visible to all and sundry, was a very different matter. Failure to defend the principles made the Treasury an easy target for those who were charging it, not with corrupt discrimination in the grant of valuable privileges, but with taking exclusive advice from interested parties.

A reasoned defence would certainly have staved off the strongest attacks; but it could not have been entirely convincing. In view of the lack not only of visible boundaries but also of logical boundaries, this control of changes of ownership could be justified only on the two assumptions that protection of the 'three per cent. basis' was desirable and that this particular device was a vital part of the defence of the three per cent. line. It has been argued in the preceding chapter that the three per cent. decision was a right decision, but the second assumption is open to the objection that open market operations by the Bank of England could have

---

[1] 13th January 1945, p. 55. A further note, in the issue of 3rd March 1945 (pp. 288-9), complained that the principles of policy still remained unexplained.

[2] cf. p. 151.

protected the Government bond market sufficiently from any strains occasioned by the relatively small issues that were unobjectionable on more fundamental grounds. In peace-time the authorities had probably been right to insist on orderly marketing of competing trustee securities, and to refrain in general from open market operations in the long-term market; but in a long war, instead of extending and developing their peace-time methods, the alternative technique would probably have been at least as effective.[1] The reasons for not employing this alternative technique have already been discussed.[2] It is only fair to say that the methods actually used were accepted by most parties, and that the control was therefore broadly workable. But the alternative would have avoided the bad odour in which the Treasury and the Bank of England found themselves (a little unluckily) in the last year.

(v)
The Control of Bank Advances

From the very beginning the Treasury had foreseen the necessity of supporting the statutory control of new issues by a control of bank advances, in so far as these could be used instead of funds raised in 'the capital market', for the purchase of real resources for capital purposes. Steps were taken in the first month of the war to implement the intention. The banks themselves were quick to complain that they were being left without advice about the policy of the authorities, and this complaint led to acceptance, by both sides, of the Governor of the Bank of England as the natural channel of contact. In the view of the Governor himself—and this view was accepted by the Treasury—the banks must at once be called upon to restrict their advances to 'national interest' cases, and a reduction of Bank Rate from its 'crisis level' of four per cent. must await the acceptance by the banks of an obligation to act in accordance with these non-statutory instructions. The discussion was entirely against the background of capital issues control in the interest of conservation of real resources, and indeed it so continued throughout, the later emphasis on use of the control to influence the terms of permitted issue finding no place in these discussions with the banks.

On 26th September 1939 the Chancellor accordingly sent to the Governor a letter pointing out that the restrictions of

---

[1] The experience of 1946-47 cannot be cited in contradiction of this statement, since the fundamental conditions governing the investment demand for funds were again in large measure those normal to peace-time.

[2] p. 173 *et seq.*

capital issues could be frustrated 'if finance were made available by means of banking accommodation in amounts or for purposes which would conflict with this policy and which might result in an unnecessary expansion of credits, contribute to any general rise in prices, or cause a diversion of resources towards non-essential needs'. The Chancellor went on to ask the banks to undertake prompt restriction of advances, except those needed to cover the direct needs of defence production, the export trade, coal-mining and agriculture. The banks replied[1] 'we think we realise what is in the mind of the Chancellor of the Exchequer and what his wishes are', but they hesitated about the list of exemptions given in the Chancellor's letter. There appears to have been some impression that the items mentioned were given merely by way of example, and that there must be other objects to which special consideration ought to be given. It was not, from the Treasury's point of view, an entirely satisfactory letter, and efforts were made through the Governor of the Bank to get the matter more firmly settled. It was suggested by the Treasury (where differences between the banks were suspected) that the banks might submit to the Treasury drafts of their circular instructions to branch managers. Perhaps owing to the attitude of the Governor of the Bank, this suggestion came to nothing. Eventually however the Governor was able to produce a formal letter from the bankers, at the conclusion of which they undertook to 'take steps to ensure that their advance control departments will loyally observe the general policy which is embodied in the fourth paragraph of the letter of the Chancellor of the Exchequer dated 26th September'.

Relying on this co-operation by the banks, the Treasury, in exercise of its powers under the Defence Regulations, gave general exemption to advances made in the normal course of banking business. Logically the Treasury's guidance to the banks should have precisely followed the principles applied by the Capital Issues Committee. This was not clearly brought out in the correspondence of September 1939, but the link was established quite soon afterwards, and it was broadly observed throughout the war. Precise interpretation was left to the banks, who could of course refer to the authorities for guidance. A Treasury note five years later recorded that there had been only two cases in which a bank[2] had asked the Treasury directly for its opinion on a particular advance. It was, however, quite common for the Capital Issues Committee to be approached by a bank customer for leave to borrow from the bank, because the bank had been in some doubt whether the advance would be in accordance with national

---

[1] 5th October 1939.

[2] The same bank, one of the smaller banks, in both cases.

policy and had therefore stipulated that the applicant should get Treasury consent. The impression remains—especially in the light of post-war experience—that this control was always rather vague and haphazard. The Treasury could not have run a detailed control of this kind from Whitehall, and had to leave the business substantially to the banks. The looseness that resulted—not that it was of great moment—was perhaps enhanced by the way in which the Treasury and the banks kept at arm's length from each other: either the banks resented attempts by the Governor of the Bank to dragoon them into the adoption of a clear-cut non-statutory control or, more probably, the Governor feared the possibility of such a reaction and therefore abstained from any attempt at clarification. No attempt was ever made to take a check on the operation of the control, nor did anyone in authority ever suggest such a check.

As the war took shape, the rather unsatisfactory position of this control of bank advances probably did not matter much to anybody. The bankers understood clearly enough what extreme cases they should bar; and before very long the controls and shortages of materials and labour were making financial controls largely superfluous. The critics' argument about the late hour at which capital issues control would touch transactions[1] applied in some measure even to bank advances. At any rate, without public discussion being stirred by any sense of severity in this control, bank advances fell away by about 20 per cent. during the first two years of war and continued to fall thereafter.

Far from feeling any need to intensify pressure on the banks to restrict credit further, the Government found itself in the position of asking the banks to be a little more generous in certain fields. Right at the beginning of the war, the Ministry of Agriculture expressed fears that the general ploughing-up campaign might be hindered by lack of capital. This was in the early days of confusion over credit policy, and it was thought that a general restriction of bank advances would cause agricultural merchants to cut down the credit they normally gave to farmers, even if the banks were not themselves cutting the farmers short. The Governor of the Bank of England was therefore asked to approach the banks with a letter which, being mainly a catalogue of the various Government guarantees to the farmers, emphasized that this class of borrower was no longer the bad risk it had been. The Treasury also had to see that work on defence contracts was never held up by lack of funds. For the most part this was ensured by the system of progress payments on these contracts, but the increasing importance of sub-contracting led to special appeals to the banks.

[1] See p. 163.

A quite exceptional step in this field was taken in May 1940. The immediate occasion was the spurt in production that followed the change of Government—and change of heart—in May 1940. The weekly wage bill jumped, inevitably ahead of the jump in Government contract payments, and special steps had to be taken to see that firms were supplied with enough cash to pay the weekly wage-bills on Friday, 31st May 1940. In dealing with this situation, the authorities had very much in mind the possibility that invasion or other disruption of communications might in the near future occasion serious local shortages of cash. Consultations with the banks were therefore followed by secret instructions that the banks must recognize that the production of vital war supplies was a primary consideration, 'and that bankers must be prepared to depart, in a greater or less degree, from their traditional methods of prudence, in regard to the grant of advance accommodation or of increases in advance accommodation'. Also 'the arrangement made last Thursday for the payment by local branch banks of all wage requirements, of all producers working directly or indirectly on Government account, without reference to the state of their banking accounts or the safety of the needed bank accommodation, must be continued over the next few weeks, and this arrangement should be exceptionally extended where *vitally* necessary to cover such cash payments as are required to be made for the immediate supply of material'.

Under war conditions these positive encouragements to the banks to lend were more important than any injunctions *not* to lend. The control of bank advances had had its root in the desire to control the disposition of real resources, and as the material mobilisation developed this objective tended to slip into the background while the capital issues control became primarily an auxiliary in the Government's effort to doctor the securities market. In this effort the control of bank advances had no part to play, and the easy and shadowy rein on which it was run was as good as the occasion demanded.

CHAPTER VII

THE INTERNAL BORROWING PROGRAMME

(i)

The Mobilisation of Small Savings

THE NATIONAL SAVINGS MOVEMENT, of which Sir Robert (later Lord) Kindersley was the chief representative, was a direct legacy from the 1914–18 war. It had never gone out of action, but had merely substituted in its title the word 'National' for the word 'War' when the latter became inappropriate. The original issue of War Savings Certificates had been followed without a break by five successive issues on sale from April 1922 until November 1939. The 'Movement' had been in continuous existence as a voluntary organisation, altering the emphasis in its propaganda very little. To some extent it regarded its business as the encouragement of thrift, though with the change from war to peace thrift was enjoined less as a patriotic duty and more as personal prudence. Its main stress however was on the facilities for the small saver: the purchase of National Savings Certificates was portrayed as more advantageous, more sensible than the stuffing of notes into the mattress. This emphasis on the facilities for investment was one of the main features carried over from peace-time into the Movement's propaganda in the second war.

The peace-time structure of the Movement consisted of a National Savings Committee, covering England and Wales, with Scottish and Ulster Savings Committees covering Scotland and Northern Ireland respectively. Under these central committees, the voluntary Savings workers were organised in some 1,200 local committees and in 'Saving Groups' covering particular factories, offices, schools and so on.[1] The enlargement of Government borrowing for defence was made the occasion for strengthening the organisation in 1939, and shortly before the outbreak of war

---

[1] The Savings campaigns in Scotland and Northern Ireland were closely co-ordinated with those in England. But constitutionally they were directed by their own Committees, under Lord Alness and Lord Justice Andrews respectively. The small savings securities in Scotland were the same as in England. Northern Ireland had its own certificate issued by its own Ministry of Finance which lent the proceeds to the United Kingdom Exchequer.

an appeal was issued to all Savings Committees asking them to make preliminary plans for an autumn campaign enlisting support in financing the defence programme. This step ensured the readiness of the Movement for the war savings campaign that was actually launched on 22nd November 1939. In these months and subsequently, the local committees were partially reorganised while the smaller units—Street Groups, Works Groups and so on—increased enormously in number[1] and especially in activity. Later (from 1941 onwards) 'Savings Centres' were established in most of the larger Committee areas. These were offices in which much of the organising work of the local committees was centred, and which at the same time relieved pressure on the Post Office, hard-pressed by the increasing volume of war-time business.

The appeal that might be made when the autumn campaign opened had already been considered by a small Committee established by Treasury Minute on 22nd June 1939 and presided over by Sir Robert Kindersley. This Committee looked at the problem of mobilising small savings for the Government in its peace-time context. It therefore had regard primarily to the competitive attraction of the National Savings Certificate as compared with the Building Societies and other facilities open to the small investor,[2] the importance of saving in total as a competitor of consumption in total being relegated to a secondary place. Against this background the Committee had, before the outbreak of war, recommended a new issue of certificates bearing a rather higher— i.e. more competitive—rate of interest, and a Savings Bond which would allow the small investor to invest rather larger amounts without suffering the risk, normal in other Government securities, of capital depreciation in the event of premature encashment.

Within the first fortnight of the war the Committee was called together again to consider how far its recommendations ought to be modified in the light of the new circumstances. The tone was at once set by the Chairman, who by a reference to the new level of Bank Rate indicated a desire for upward revision of the proposed interest rates in order to attract even more small savings into an Exchequer that would be even more needy—an interesting sidelight on the effect of Bank Rate in creating expectations of higher interest rates. This view was resisted by the Treasury representatives, who insisted that there must be no appreciable break from the interest rates previously thought adequate, and confined their suggestions to some adaptation in the period of the certificate to

---

[1] There were nearly 300,000 Groups in 1943.

[2] The terms of reference were 'to consider methods by which a greater volume of small savings might be attracted to the Exchequer'.

make it more attractive to young people.[1] There was no indication whatever of any need to change the theme of propaganda towards reduction of spending on current consumption.

Continuing therefore on the basis of competing for the small investor's savings, the Committee recommended an autumn campaign which should open with the launching of a new National Savings Certificate and a Defence Bond. Taking the Treasury's point about the period of the certificate, the terms were settled at 15s. purchase price, rising to 17s. 6d. after 5 years (£3 2s. 7d. per cent. interest) and to £1 0s. 6d. after 10 years (£3 3s. 5d. per cent.)—a rise of about ¼ per cent. as compared with the previous issue of 10-year certificates. These certificates continued to have their great attraction of freedom from liability to income tax, and because of this privilege the maximum holding continued to be 500 units, taking the new and all previous issues together. To meet the needs of small investors who could go beyond this amount but who would not risk capital depreciation, the new Defence Bond was offered as a serious competitor with the Building Society Deposit. These bonds were called 3 per cent. Defence Bonds, and were repayable at 101 after seven years, or at par at any earlier date after six months' notice had been given by the holder.[2] If held to maturity they yielded £3 2s. 7d. gross. As the Treasury did not want to face the risk of large repayment demands by large holders, and the issue was avowedly to meet the needs of the small man, individual holdings were limited to £1,000. The interest was of course subject to taxation, but to make the bonds more attractive to small income recipients the tax was not deducted at source.

Once Bank Rate had come down and the expectation that rates would soon be settled at a much higher level had been dissipated, there was much to be said in favour of immediate opening of the small savings campaign. The intention had originally been to open it simultaneously with the issue of the first big war loan but, as the weeks went by and the arguments for postponement of the loan issue until after Christmas strengthened, the decision was taken that the small savings campaign should not wait on the other move. The mechanical preparations—printing of new certificates

---

[1] The Treasury view was that the original (1916) certificates had been successful partly because of their five years' life (15s. 6d. purchase price, value £1 after five years), five years being a period short enough to attract the interest of young people, who were not so interested in the ten-year certificates which afterwards became usual. This was probably a sound point, though there is no indication that the Treasury arrived at it in any scientific way.

[2] The Postmaster-General had discretion to dispense with the notice in cases of private emergency, subject to a deduction equal to six months' interest. The 1 per cent. premium on repayment at maturity was recommended by Sir Robert Kindersley as an important selling point.

and propaganda material—needed only about a month, and it was therefore possible to open the campaign on the 20th November 1939.

In the leadership of the Movement and in the rank and file up and down the country, there was enough enthusiasm to make the campaign then opened a continuous one lasting right through the war, though there were of course variations in its intensity. But before it could develop its full force an important obstacle had to be overcome in working-class opinion. The National Savings Movement had wisely approached both employers' and workers' organisations for their co-operation and had met an unqualified response on the employers' side, a response generally given material form in the facilities given for the collection of weekly savings in factories and other work places. The General Council of the Trades Union Congress expressed anxiety to help, but considered it necessary first to obtain assurances on two specific points. One point was met by a definite assurance from the employers' organisation that the savings of workpeople would not be used as an argument against applications for wage advances. The second matter raised by the General Council of the Trades Union Congress became a matter of high political importance. This was the relevance of war-time savings to the means test imposed upon applicants for unemployment assistance and other forms of relief. On the one hand the trade union leaders called upon the Government to ignore war-time savings when needs were being assessed, and in this they were supported by Sir Robert Kindersley, who considered the lack of assurance on this point a major obstacle in the way of working-class support for the Savings Movement. On the other hand the civil servants pointed to the administrative impossibility of distinguishing between a man's war-time savings and assets previously owned, and to the probability of extensive switching if holdings of National Savings Certificates alone became the subject of particular exemption. The entire controversy was coloured throughout—and it lasted some months—by the knowledge on both sides that anything touching the means test was political dynamite. The trade union leaders realised that they were playing a useful pawn while the officials, terrified by the threat of having to draft legislation on a fantastically difficult administrative problem, emphasised these difficulties and urged, perhaps wrongly, that the people liable to be involved in the means test would in any event not save much.[1]

The question was considered by the Ministerial Committee on Economic Policy on 30th January 1940 who, impressed by Treasury

---

[1] The Madge Survey (see p. 79 above) was to reveal the surprising extent to which saving is done by just this class.

arguments, deferred any decision pending further trade union demonstration of interest. The latter was however quickly forthcoming, as the Minister of Labour found that the question was drawn, even if as a red herring, firmly across the trail of the National Joint Advisory Council discussions on the problem of wage restraint, discussions of the first importance in the formative period of stabilisation policy.[1] Direct discussion with the Chancellor underlined the critical position to which trade unionists had, consciously or unconsciously, raised the matter, and Sir John Simon came to the conclusion that failure to announce a concession quickly would have widely damaging effects on the relations between the Government and the working classes. He therefore decided, in the face of discomforting advice from his Departmental officials, to make an announcement in his budget speech on 23rd April. He promised[2] legislation, the general effect of which should be 'to withdraw from the calculation of means for purposes of unemployment assistance the new money lent to the nation during the war up to a total of £375'.[3] It will be appreciated that an amount 'lent to the nation' would be more readily identifiable than an amount saved.

With these firm undertakings from the employers and the Chancellor in their pockets, Sir Walter Citrine and his colleagues issued a declaration urging all who were able to save to do so to the utmost of their ability, and to lend their savings to the State.

In the organisation of facilities for small savings the Savings Movement certainly performed a most valuable service. The arrangements made for weekly deduction from the pay packet are widely believed to have made a substantial difference to the amount really saved by workers in war and other factories, where overtime and other earnings were rising. The collections through street and school savings groups also helped to tap those family incomes which had risen more than family commitments. The actual degree of success of these and other parts of the organisation cannot be measured for, quite apart from some transference of wealth by the small people, the 'savings' figures recorded always suffered in greater or less degree from inflation by the inclusion of larger operations that had little to do with 'saving' in any important sense. It does seem probable, however, that the organisation of these facilities and the quiet efforts of the rank and file of voluntary workers in the Savings Movements helped more

---

[1] See pp. 63-4 above.

[2] H. of C. Deb., Vol. 360, Cols. 82-3.

[3] The pledge was implemented after the Bill had had a rough passage, by the War Savings (Determination of Needs) Act in August 1940. It referred to supplementary old age pensions and blind persons' allowances, as well as unemployment assistance.

than all the propaganda that told us to take the money out of the old stocking.

Into this propaganda and publicity great effort went. During the next five years, every conceivable medium was employed. Press advertisements were supplemented by generous editorial and news space, while the B.B.C. broadcast talks by Cabinet Ministers and other prominent personalities, and from February 1941 carried a 'Weekly Savings News' following the 6 o'clock news bulletin on Sundays. Some forty films and trailers for exhibition in cinemas were added to the library of 16mm. films circulated for private exhibitions organised by local savings committees. Leaflets and posters were distributed by the million. Special drives, with great local activity, were organised in National Savings Week (June 1940), War Weapons Weeks (September–October 1941), Warship Weeks (Winter 1941–42), Wings for Victory Weeks (March–July 1943) and 'Salute the Soldier Weeks' (March–July 1944).

The propaganda had a twofold theme—that saving was a patriotic virtue, and that the war was helped by the lending of money to the State. Thanks to the pre-war tradition of the Movement, to the strong views of its leader and perhaps to some lack of understanding of the problems of war finance, the emphasis in the early years was heavily on the virtue of lending money to the State through the recognisable channels of Savings Certificates, the Post Office Savings Bank, Defence Bonds, and the like.[1] A film, for example, was devoted to the action of a boy in finding coins in a forgotten money box and using them for the purchase of Savings Certificates. 'Little Albert' was thus, the film purported to tell the public, helping the war effort, although in truth he had merely, by abstaining from spending the coins on useful real resources, abstained from hindering the war effort. Propaganda of this kind irritated those who understood the problems, without guiding the uninitiated to the central importance of releasing real resources for war production.

Such propaganda as this rightly provoked criticism in *The Economist*. 'The mere swelling of figures,' it wrote on 10th August 1940, 'by the exchange of idle bank deposits or free company reserves does nothing to assist the war effort, or to reduce the risk of inflation.' This comment roused strong feelings in Treasury circles, and the Chancellor thought seriously of complaining to the newspaper's proprietors. Later in the war Treasury officials themselves came round to *The Economist's* views. Outside

---

[1] The 'Squander-Bug' advertisements, much the most impressive propaganda to stress the act of saving rather than the facilities, did not appear until January 1943.

O

criticism became louder when the figures of 'total subscriptions' in local savings weeks were swollen by insurance companies and other financial institutions whose subscriptions in hundreds of thousands or even millions of pounds[1] completely swamped the man in the street's efforts, rendering the attainment of fantastic 'targets' almost automatic but removing them from all contact with the real savings efforts of the masses. Even the figures of the sale of certificates of different denominations supported the criticism that switching of assets was the main source of the 'savings' totals.[2] Publicity of this kind carried to excess could and perhaps did have a boomerang effect. 'All the drum-beating of War Weapons and other similar weeks,' wrote Mr. Oscar Hobson in *The News Chronicle*,[3] 'and the almost automatic attainment of these huge target figures has if anything a discouraging effect on the regular saver. When the little man, who by dint of much stinting and scraping has been putting his 10s. in savings, hears of the Midland Bank or the Prudential putting down a cool £10 millions on the savings counter, it is more likely that he will be inclined to minimise the value of his own seemingly puny effort and wonder whether by some magic the banks and the insurance companies cannot do quite painlessly the task which costs him so much in the sacrifice of little luxuries.'

The Treasury became increasingly sensitive to these criticisms, but apart from mild suggestions when opportunity occurred—and particularly forthright exhortation in the annual budget speeches— the Departmental officials felt unable to press the leaders of the Savings Movement to change the whole emphasis of the campaign. Pressure would have involved a change in the leadership of the Movement, a change that would certainly have lost valuable goodwill and might have taken some of the heart out of the Movement. It had been necessary, too, to launch the war-time campaign with propaganda that would be readily understood by the voluntary workers of whom the Movement was composed; and at the beginning only the peace-time arguments were readily grasped. The Treasury officials therefore consoled themselves with the belief (perhaps not wholly justified) that no harm was done and that a little good was coming of it all. For,

---

[1] These large subscriptions by financial institutions went, of course, into the larger bonds and not into the 'small savings' with which this section is concerned. Figures for 'local weeks' did however frequently include these larger items and criticism provoked the Treasury to enquire of the Prudential Assurance Company what sums it had subscribed, up to May 1944, to local savings weeks (war weapons weeks etc.). The reply is the justification of the phrase used here.

[2] Of the £1 issue sold 11th January 1943 to 21st November 1944, 76·1 per cent. of the £51·4 millions total was in certificates of 50 units each.

[3] 15th January 1943.

they argued, the more people got used to the idea that it was foolish to hold money in large blocks of notes and that it was both sensible and patriotic to put it into Savings Certificates, the more people would in fact put their savings into these less liquid forms from which withdrawals for expenditure on consumption were less easy and therefore less likely. Moreover, the later phases of the campaign, including the spectacular and somewhat expensive 'Wings for Victory' and other 'Weeks', had their uses in sustaining civilian morale and ought therefore to be judged in a wider context than the stimulation of saving which was their ostensible purpose. Altogether it is permissible to wish that the propaganda had been less crudely fashioned after the peace-time model and that it had clung more closely to the texts of successive budget speeches, but on balance perhaps it did not matter very much.

As the years went by, the limits on individual holdings of these Savings Certificates and Defence Bonds, limits imposed as a corollary of their special position in relation to income tax, became a wider and wider check on further accumulation. Just how widespread the check was operating is a matter on which no direct evidence was collected. Enquiry did show that by mid-1942 some 750,000 holders—5 per cent. of the total—had reached the maximum holding; of these, 40 per cent. had taken the whole in one block and could therefore hardly be described as small people whose weekly savings were likely to be checked by the ceiling. These figures were however held to create some presumption in favour of Lord Kindersley's reiterated requests for raising the limit. On the other hand, a simple raising of the limit would represent a gift of extraordinary income tax concessions to the 300,000 or so who had been rich enough to buy 500 units on a single occasion—in effect, a big increase in the rate of interest available to them. Now Lord Kindersley was continually urging upon the Treasury the desirability of raising the rates of interest on Savings Certificates, but the Treasury, intent on pressing rates of interest generally downward rather than upward,[1] consistently refused any concession on this point. When, therefore, it was felt that the prolongation of the war and the figures produced did justify some qualification of the maximum holdings rule, this was coupled with a sharp reduction in the rate of interest paid on the holdings beyond the former maximum. A new issue, called the One Pound Issue, was announced in October 1942, and was put on sale in January 1943. Of this new issue the holder might acquire 250 units of £1 each, in addition to the unchanged limit of 500 units of all previous

---

[1] In July 1941 the Treasury seriously considered reducing the yield on Savings Certificates and Defence Bonds; only after strong resistance from the National Savings Committee was the proposal dropped.

issues. The £1 unit rose in value to £1 3s. after 10 years, this representing a yield of £1 8s. 2d. per annum, free of tax, in contrast to the £3 3s. 5d. on the former issue (which continued to be on sale to all who had not reached their 500 units limit). This low yield could not be attractive except to the surtax-payer, so that the Treasury was conceding no more to Lord Kindersley than some extension of the convenience and freedom from depreciation which were the principal attractions of the Savings Certificate to the small man.[1] This was the only change in Savings Certificates made between the opening of the war-time campaign in November 1939 and the end of the war.

Lord Kindersley and his Committee from time to time opened the same questions—the rate of interest and the maximum holding—in relation to the Defence Bonds, the big brothers of the Savings Certificates. Towards these, since the savers affected were necessarily rather wealthier people, the Treasury was even less tender, and as opinion strengthened in favour of reducing interest rates, there were proposals to make the bonds less attractive. From time to time administrative necessities made a new issue desirable: registers checking the total holding of each individual became cumbersome with successive small purchases, and the number of dividends to be paid on the half-yearly dates became unwieldy. New issues enabled the Post Office to begin new registers and to fix new dividend dates for further purchases—which however were still subject to the one limit for all issues taken together. On the first occasion of a change, in the summer of 1941, the Treasury tide was flowing strongly in favour of some turn of the screw against the investor: it was at this time that it was considered all-important to demonstrate to the investor that interest rates were going lower rather than higher. The National Savings Committee successfully resisted a proposal that there should be some actual reduction in the rate of interest offered, but the life of the Bond—the period through which it had to be held for automatic repayment with the one per cent. premium—was lengthened from seven to ten years.[2] These new Bonds, the second issue of 3 per cent. Defence Bonds, were put on sale on 1st September 1941, the maximum holding of these and Bonds of the first issue, taken together, remaining at £1,000. When administrative needs dictated a change of issue just a year later, the terms remained precisely the same. The third issue remained on sale from 1st September 1942 until 5th May 1945, the Post Office struggling on with cumbersome registers in the hope that the European war would end and a

---

[1] See *The Economist*, 24th October 1942, p. 518.

[2] The original suggestion that the life should be lengthened by one year only was rejected as too ridiculously a mere gesture.

fourth issue would not—at least on a war-time basis—be necessary. In the spring of 1945, the position became intolerable, and a fourth issue began just before V-E Day. Lapse of time had made an increase of the £1,000 limit appropriate, to encourage continuance of savings by those who had reached the limit, and a lift to £1,500 was agreed by the Treasury. At the last minute the National Savings Committee advised deferment of this change, in order to use it as a highly necessary fillip to a peace-time issue (the 'Freedom Bond'), and eventually the fourth issue of 3 per cent. Defence Bonds carried terms in this and all other respects precisely the same as those of the second and third issues.

The Treasury attitude on the terms of these successive issues of Savings Certificates and Defence Bonds, in the face of continual pressure from the leaders of the Savings Movement, was fundamentally that these issues to the small investor must conform reasonably closely with the remainder of the borrowing programme. Never could there be a breath of suspicion that interest rates might rise—the presumption must always be that any change would be in the opposite direction. Subject to this overriding consideration, the Treasury was willing to go as far as possible to meet the suggestions of the National Savings Committee. In measuring the results of its work, the Movement never produced really convincing figures, but the cumulative evidence overwhelmingly justified the Treasury's confidence in the important part the Movement was playing in the mobilisation and probably in the encouragement of small savings. The Treasury therefore always gave it strong support—but always within the framework of the general principles of its borrowing programme.

(ii)

The Bond Issues

Throughout its borrowing programme the Treasury remembered a central doctrine of the Phillips Committee which had reviewed possibilities just before the war:[1] this was the doctrine that the Treasury would get the best terms if it split its security offerings to suit the peculiarities of the various broad sectors of the capital market. The separate mobilisation of small savings was, of course, one special application of this principle, while further application was apparent in the differentiation between the National Savings Certificates and the Defence Bonds. The extreme manifestation of this policy was the arrangement by which the banks were called

---

[1] See above, p. 252.

upon to lend stated sums to the Government on special non-negotiable instruments called Treasury Deposit Receipts. These 'T.D.R.'s' are discussed in the concluding section of this chapter. In the general run of bond issues, the subject of the present section, the policy showed itself not in any pressure upon particular institutions, but in the care with which successive issues were designed to meet the varying needs and views of particular investing groups. By this diversification of issues the Treasury sought to attract the maximum response to interest rates squeezed as far as possible below the political ceiling of about 3 per cent.

Even the first bond issue, though only a relatively small conversion operation, was treated more or less in this way. This was in mid-January 1940, when the Treasury offered conversion of £353 millions of 4½ per cent. Conversion Loan 1940–44, into a 2 per cent. stock dated 1943–45. Of the maturing stock, public Departments held over £70 millions and a very large proportion of the remainder was held by banks and other financial institutions. For these institutions a short stock was obviously appropriate as a replacement of the maturing stock, and the 2 per cent. rate chosen for a three-to-five years' stock fitted pretty closely[1] into the pattern of rates as it had emerged after the return of Bank Rate to its 2 per cent. level. There was some surprise that cash subscriptions were not invited; but the Treasury was still well provided with sterling purchased from foreigners in the 1939 flight from sterling, and regarded the present operation as almost purely a money market affair with which its first major public appeal was not to be confused.

When that public appeal for cash did come, in March, it was found that the Treasury was attempting to spread its net very widely, and in this way this War Loan issue of March 1940 was untypical. It was also untypical in not being a tap issue. The Treasury invited subscriptions, on 12th March, for £300 millions of 3 per cent. War Loans 1955–59, and the lists were closed on the following day. It was intended as, and was interpreted as, a rough and ready general purpose issue, suitable for financial institutions, the general run of business firms and the substantial private investors alike. The authorities looked upon it as an effort to secure the necessary money by substantially conventional steps—no special effort was made to cater for one section of the market rather than another, and no undue pressure was exercised to persuade institutions to subscribe. At the same time, the issue had been held back until, under the influence of the reversion of Bank Rate to 2 per cent., the airing of views on a 'Three Per Cent. War', the absence of competing issues and the accumulation of institutional

---

[1] *The Economist* described the terms as 'not generous' (20th January 1940, p. 109).

and company savings, markets had sufficiently improved to allow a 3 per cent. loan of this moderately long date to have a good chance of success.[1] An effort was made to encourage the gilt-edged market by simultaneous announcement of the raising of Stock Exchange minimum prices from the low levels fixed late in August 1939. The Bank of England took extraordinary steps to 'groom the market' immediately before the issue, and the Governor had already let the insurance companies and other City concerns know that they were expected to support the Government issues to the exclusion of the wider range of securities in which they normally dealt.

The amount of the issue had been the subject of anxious discussion for months. The Treasury expected to need to borrow something of the order of £1,200 to £1,500 millions during the ensuing twelve months,[2] and the immediate question was, how large might be the first bite. The Bank's advice was against a single very large issue, on the ground that a single big maturity might come round at an inconvenient time. This argument appealed to the Treasury. Notwithstanding the success of the 1932 operation, which had been helped rather than hindered by its gigantic proportions, the Treasury still felt that the £2,000 millions block issued in the first war was a nightmare not to be repeated: perhaps it felt it had been lucky in 1932, and that repetition of such favourable circumstances could not be relied upon. So, although the Treasury thought the exigencies of war might force the issue of rather large blocks later, for the time being the principle of a succession of small bites was accepted. The Governor proposed £200 millions as the most that could be hoped for in public subscriptions, but this looked an absurdly small sum—enough to cover the needs of eight or ten weeks at most. An issue so small in relation to known requirements might, it was anticipated, be interpreted as a sign of weakness, of timidity in grappling with the problems of non-inflationary finance. The sum was therefore fixed not at £200 but at £300 millions.

The event amply justified the Governor's prognostications. Appearances were thought important enough to justify a statement in the House of Commons, by the Chancellor, that the issue had been over-subscribed.[3] This was true in the sense that total applications exceeded the amount offered, but a substantial

---

[1] Also relevant to the holding back of the first War Loan issue was the fact that expenditure did not really get under way until early 1940.

[2] This was probably an over-estimate, on the basis of the then expenditure prospects.

[3] H. of C. Deb., Vol. 358, Col. 1652. The phrase used was simply 'has been over-subscribed'. An air of verisimilitude was added by the conventional statement, in reply to a supplementary question, that 'the larger applicants have been allotted about 80 per cent. of their applications'. Presumably these 'larger applicants' were the Issue Department and other 'Departments'.

proportion came from public Departments; private subscriptions certainly fell short of the amount hoped for. The peddling of these public holdings proved a very slow process.

After this serious though unconfessed failure the authorities had to think again. The notion of a close succession of general-purpose issues to provide an average of fifty to a hundred millions a month would have been ludicrous, and the rapid worsening of the war in the early summer made this all the more obvious. It became necessary to resort to less conventional methods, in pursuance of the principle of getting loans from various parts of the market separately. The immediate needs were covered by adoption of the Bank of England plan for special direct loans from the commercial banks—the Treasury Deposit Receipts plan discussed below. These 'T.D.R.'s' were introduced with a good deal of reluctance and were in some quarters at first regarded as a purely temporary expedient. It was not until some time later that their place in the permanent plan of campaign was perceived. Meanwhile the cash so obtained did enable the Treasury to avoid precipitate action in other directions. Perhaps it also helped to give the Treasury courage to take risks in setting the terms of the next operation.

A little courage at this moment was in the event of great importance, for in the discussions now proceeding the main elements of the borrowing programme for the remainder of the war emerged. The first idea was to open subscription lists for a week or two only, a system appealing most to the big financial institutions. This was rejected partly because the time (Dunkirk and the collapse of France) was unpropitious for big commitments by institutions which anyway did not appear to be glutted with investible funds. The failure of the March issue might be ascribed to its rather long term, but it might also have been due to the adoption of the conventional plan of opening and closing subscription lists quickly. An attempt was now to be made to attract not so much the big institutions, but rather the general run of business firms and private investors not desiring a fixed investment, but wanting to have their money available at or soon after the end of the war. Particularly the Treasury was seeking the accumulating depreciation funds and undistributed profits now unspendable but intended for industrial re-equipment after the war. This was a steady flow, and the tap method of issue was best suited to attract it.

The great risk of a tap issue was that it might freeze the market in previous issues. When the war loan had been issued in March, minimum prices for gilt-edged had, by arrangement with the Stock Exchange Committee, been lifted close to the ruling market prices: this was all part of the campaign to consolidate the three per cent. line. When in the summer the adverse war news sent prices down a little, they knocked against the minima and stocks became more or less unsaleable.[1] Had this freezing of the market become at all general, the implications for Government bond issues would have been very serious indeed. Investors, who are obliged occasionally to raise relatively small amounts for personal emergencies, would have ceased to buy the new securities the Government was attempting to issue. This situation, brought about essentially because minimum prices had been fixed at uncomfortably high levels, provoked considerable agitation against the continuance of minimum prices. There were also suggestions that the authorities should themselves be prepared to keep a market going. Fortunately the war news ceased to get any worse, the nation gathered new courage, and the Governor of the Bank inspired some buying by the institutional investors: this combination of events gave sufficient resilience to the market, and the danger of a general freeze-up passed away. The shock did however serve to underline to the authorities in what a difficult position the Treasury would find itself if the market in old gilt-edged securities were to be frozen. Now if a tap issue was to attract an important part of the market, and offer terms as attractive as those of earlier issues, investors would buy the new issue from the tap in order to avoid brokerage and other market buying costs. Ordinarily the market in old securities can adjust itself and keep alive by a sufficient fall of prices to compensate for the buying costs, and this is what had happened during the first war, when indeed successive issues offered better and better terms to investors and so depressed further and further the prices of previous issues. On the later occasion this course was ruled out by the general interest rate policy, and particularly by the high and rigid minimum prices adopted in pursuance of that policy.

The authorities were indeed in a serious quandary. By putting bonds on tap and so attracting this continuous flow of company and private savings the authorities might run on the rocks of minimum prices, destroy the investors' confidence in marketability and so dry up the flow completely. Alternatively they might reduce minimum prices; but this would be interpreted as a retreat from the three per cent. line, just as that line had been reinforced by raising minimum prices in March. In assessing the seriousness of the dilemma in which the authorities found themselves, it is essential to remember that any course other than the attraction from the public of sufficient funds to cover expenditure was at this time regarded as perilously inflationary. Technically it would have been possible to allow security markets to freeze at the minimum prices, and to absorb indirectly accumulating idle bank deposits

---

[1] The degree of actual freezing was slight. See *The Economist*, 22nd June 1940.

by an unlimited extension of the Treasury Deposit Receipts. Against such a course the Treasury and the Bank of England alike instinctively recoiled. Though their fears were exaggerated, in that an accumulation of idle deposits does not itself constitute inflation, their instinct was soundly rooted in the inflationary risks that overhang a market in which liquidity has become altogether abnormal. They had also, in this and other contexts, to remember that appearances interpreted by people abroad as symptoms of inflation would indirectly damage the war effort, especially by making overseas holders less willing to add to their sterling balances. Given the very proper assumption that, as far as was consistent with meeting the overriding immediate needs, post-war liabilities and post-war dangers should be minimised, the authorities were surely right in casting round for some way of 'mobilising' the flow of savings—which was their phrase for curtailing the liquidity continuously created by the rising tide of war expenditure.

It was against this theoretical background that the Treasury sought a way of establishing a tap issue of bonds, adapted to the company and large private investors, a course which would not freeze the market in earlier issues for as long as the tap remained open. The solution was found in the plan, firmly established from this time onwards, of worsening slightly the terms offered to the investor. Each time this was done, it was an act of faith on the part of the authorities, and it could hardly have been attempted had not the ground been well prepared by the Chancellor's statements after the March issue and again on later occasions,[1] that interest rates were going to go down rather than up. Success on each occasion increased the chance of success the next time. On this first important occasion, in the fixing of the terms for the tap issue of War Bonds in June 1940, the Treasury actually wavered: the market conditions indicated rather more than $2\frac{1}{2}$ per cent. for a 6–8 years' bond of the kind contemplated,[2] and there was a Treasury suggestion that anything below $2\frac{3}{4}$ per cent. would run too great a risk of failure. The Governor of the Bank, fearful that the competition of the new issue would freeze the earlier issues at their minimum prices, pressed strongly for $2\frac{1}{2}$ per cent. His arguments found support in a Chancellor who was ready to make a bold bid in a venture that could exploit the patriotic tide then running at its utmost strength ('This was their finest hour'). The decision was taken to shorten slightly the life of the bond—it

---

[1] cf. the occasional references in *The Economist* to Government statements that 'the present rate of interest was not sacrosanct' (e.g. *The Economist*, 22nd June 1940).

[2] On 14th June $2\frac{1}{2}$ per cent. National Defence Bonds 1944-48 were quoted to yield £2 15s. 4d., and $2\frac{1}{2}$ per cent. Conversion Loan 1944-49, £2 18s. 5d.

became the '1945–47' issue—and to stick to the $2\frac{1}{2}$ per cent. proposed by the Governor. The very extremity of the nation's position, the Chancellor thought, was their opportunity. Patriotism could be enlisted for immediate support, to give the issue a good send-off despite its niggardly terms. If the war then went badly, the Government would have to resort to altogether more drastic measures in finance as elsewhere, and nobody would then care whether the June issue had been at $2\frac{1}{2}$ or $2\frac{3}{4}$. On the other hand, if the hour of extreme peril passed, the relief would be such that investment markets would be ready enough to believe that $2\frac{1}{2}$ per cent. was a fair price. Either way, $2\frac{1}{2}$ per cent. was defensible; so $2\frac{1}{2}$ it should be. Perhaps financial policy might with advantage have been infused more frequently by this cynicism.

In the third week of June 1940 the project took final shape on these lines—a tap issue of 1945–47 bonds, bearing $2\frac{1}{2}$ per cent. The bonds were to be called, not 'War Loan' as first proposed, but National War Bonds, because 'War Bonds' was a name that had proved very popular in the first war, particularly among the two classes of investors at which the Treasury was particularly aiming. The Chancellor decided that he would portray it as a patriotic loan, drawing an analogy between the offers of personal service then being so freely made and the lending of money.[1] Official preparations were put in train without delay: on the 22nd *The Economist* was able to report official support in the gilt-edged market, the normal harbinger nowadays of a new issue.[2] At the request of the authorities, the British Bankers' Association announced that banks would henceforth not pay interest in excess of one per cent. on any bank deposits.[3] On Monday 24th June the prospectus appeared, and the tap was opened on the 25th. It remained open until the end of 1940. Press comment was favourable, and it was generally believed that, with general closure of other outlets for investible funds, the bonds would prove popular not only with the company and private investors for whom they were particularly designed, but also with the big financial institutions.[4]

In the event the response was disappointing, except from institutional buyers. Once the collapse of the equities market had

---

[1] The dribble of free-of-interest loans offered to (and accepted by) the Treasury became at this time a stream of appreciable proportions. These patriotic loans varied in size from £50 to £200,000, and by 31st March 1940 they totalled £376,000. In June 1940 an appeal by the Chancellor (H. of C. Deb., Vol. 365, Cols. 27-8) for more of these evoked £3,350,000 in cash in a single week, and promises of £1,000,000 more. In the first half of 1941 these loans were still arriving at the rate of over a million pounds a month; after 1941 some were absorbed in the Tax Reserve Certificates (on which see below, p. 210 *et seq.*), though a considerable amount remained as free-of-interest loans throughout the war.

[2] *The Economist*, 22nd June 1940, p. 1080.

[3] *Ibid.*, 6th July 1940.

[4] See, e.g. *The Economist*, 29th June 1940, p. 1113.

been steadied by new official advice to the insurance companies,[1] security markets brightened all round—paradoxically the removal of a restriction which had been intended to protect the gilt-edged market helped more than hindered this market. The yield on Consols fell during the third quarter of the year by 0·16 per cent., and War Loan $3\frac{1}{2}$ at $101\frac{13}{16}$ reached its highest point since Munich. During this period sales of the new War Bonds were quite considerable, but they were larely sales to the banks, helped perhaps by a temporary swelling of the cash base.[2] This was not the way to extinguish out of public subscriptions to the new War Bonds, the Treasury Deposit Receipts initiated in the summer, before the 'inflationary effect' of this bank finance had time to develop. The National Savings Committee was called upon to help, and in the course of August a major propaganda campaign was developed. Local 'War Bond Committees' were established—three of these in the City of London under the Lord Mayor—and *The Economist* carried full-page advertisements headed 'A Message to Leaders of Business and Finance'.[3]

The meagreness of response among the wider public was a great disappointment to the authorities, and might easily, following upon the failure of the March War Loan, have caused them to lose their heads. Persistence of the ideas, common in official circles through 1939 and most of 1940, that choice of the channels through which money should be obtained was a matter of the first importance and that 'bank finance' was almost immediately and peculiarly inflationary, might have driven the Treasury to panic steps and particularly to an irrevocable plunge into higher interest rates. That this major disaster did not occur was due partly to the firmness with which the 'Three Per Cent. War' decision had eventually been taken. More important than this, however, in giving to the authorities the nerve to persist in their borrowing principles was the increasing influence of Keynes and other economists, both in discussions directly bearing on the borrowing programme and more generally in their illumination of the fundamental causes of war inflation. Though the Treasury, properly mindful of implications for the post-war situation, never became careless of the choice of channels for the mobilisation of finance, the battlefield on which inflation was to be fought was henceforth to be the budget and the even wider ground of Government economic policy in its entirety. This change of ground found its principal manifestation, of course, in the new spirit that infused budget policy in 1941; but

---

[1] *The Economist*, 29th June 1940, p. 1117.

[2] *The Economist*, 10th and 17th August, 14th and 29th September and 19th October 1940.

[3] e.g. 17th August 1940, p. 221.

it was also of considerable moment in toughening the Treasury nerve in its borrowing operations at this critical phase in the autumn of 1940.

This important change did not emerge in any single memorandum or recorded discussion. A symptom of it was the Chancellor's announcement in November[1] that there would be no ceiling to the issue of Treasury Deposit Receipts: the idea that these were a merely temporary expedient, slightly disreputable and to be wiped off the slate as quickly as possible, was dead and buried. In unpublished papers the Treasury's attitude is clearly apparent in the discussions during the autumn, leading up to the issue at Christmas 1940 of two new tap loans, the $2\frac{1}{2}$ per cent. National War Bonds 1946–48 and the 3 per cent. Savings Bonds 1955–65. These discussions turned on the application of principles and not on the principles themselves. The principles, that were to govern the major borrowing operations for the remainder of the war, had by this time won such general acceptance that they were not themselves in the forefront of discussion, on this or on any later occasions.

First among these principles was the three per cent. rule. On the Savings Certificates and Defence Bonds, holdings of which were narrowly restricted, the rates paid were a trifle above 3 per cent., but with these exceptions no borrowing was to be undertaken at a higher rate. The 'three per cent.' itself, which was frequently alluded to, was the rate at which the Government expected to borrow for a moderately long term, and it was consistent with a yield on 'irredeemables' of $3\frac{1}{4}$ to $3\frac{1}{2}$ per cent.—terms on which no borrowing was undertaken. To the 3 per cent. rate for moderately long maturities there was attached a structure of rates for shorter periods, ranging down to about 1 per cent. on 3 months' Treasury Bills. In the latter half of the war there was much discussion of the possibility of shifting this entire structure down by about $\frac{1}{2}$ per cent., and in the earlier part there were from time to time suggestions— particularly by a few members of the House of Commons[2]—in favour of reduction of those particular rates which were in a sense private to groups of banks or other financial institutions. Apart from these agitations, the only notable modification of the structure was the very slight downward pressure on it. This was a course chosen by the authorities in the first place because it gave substance to their threats that interest rates might go down, threats that were designed to scotch expectations that the experience of the

---

[1] H. of C. Deb., Vol. 365, Col. 1830.

[2] e.g. H. of C. Deb., Vol. 365, Col. 29 (referring to Treasury Bills) and Col. 1830 (referring to Treasury Deposit Receipts).

earlier war would be repeated. It became a doubly attractive course when tap issues were initiated and it became necessary to avert the freezing of earlier issues at the minimum prices which were then close on the market's heels. Partly because the desired change in yield on each successive occasion was very small, and partly because par issues were thought simpler and more popular, the shading of rates of interest on successive issues generally took the form of a gradual lengthening of the life attached to a given yield. Thus the first $2\frac{1}{2}$ per cent. National War Bonds had a life of 5 to 7 years, while the last war-time issue[1] had a life of 9 to 11 years. Similarly with the 3 per cent. issues. The main difference between the first two—the War Loan issued in March 1940 and the Savings Bond on tap from January 1941 till April 1942—was that on the second the bondholder lost the remote chance of benefiting from higher rates after 1959. In the remaining issues, the pattern was more standardised, and the turning of the screw against the bondholder became quite plain in the regular pushing backward of the maturity period—from 1955–65 to 1960–70 and then to 1965–75.

In deciding the precise maturity dates for bonds of the various issues, the authorities endeavoured to distribute maturities reasonably evenly over the post-war years. The £2,000 millions of the 5 per cent. War Loan of the first war was always considered a precedent to be avoided at almost any cost. Throughout the nineteen-twenties this huge block of maturing debt had hung like a cloud over Treasury debt policy, and though in the event of 1932 its very size had contributed to the success of the conversion operation, the Treasury never forgot the discomfort it had so long caused. For this reason each issue was restricted in size, the tap being turned off and a new issue, with a new maturity, being sooner or later[2] brought forward in its place. £1,000 millions appears to have been regarded as the limit, though only the 1960–70 Savings Bonds and the 1965–75 Savings Bonds, at £1,010 millions and £1,057 millions respectively, were allowed to reach it. These were relatively distant maturities, and the Treasury option to redeem was spread over ten years for each, a total period of fifteen years covering the two issues. For other issues, particularly the shorter-dated issues, the tap was turned off well before this point was reached. The first War Bond issue, 1945–47, for example, was stopped at £444 millions. Its successor, 1946–48, went to £493

---

[1] Opened 13th June 1945.

[2] Occasionally, when the market's absorptive capacity appeared to be dwindling away, there was a gap between one series and the next. For example, National War Bonds were 'given a rest' between August and October 1941.

millions. The 1949–51, 1951–53 and 1952–54 issues went to £714, £522 and £810 millions respectively.[1] The first Savings Bond issue, with the relatively near maturity period 1955–65, rose to £713 millions before the tap was turned off. In this way, and by spacing the maturity dates in relation not only to each other but also to those of pre-war issues, the Treasury succeeded in spreading a total of some £5,700 millions of new Government maturities over the post-war years in such a way as to satisfy market preferences without leaving itself exposed to a very large maturity in any particular year that might prove peculiarly unpropitious. This desire to spread the maturities well over the post-war years provided an additional argument in favour of a gradual lengthening of the life of bonds of a given rate of interest (whether $2\frac{1}{2}$ or 3), as long as the preference for issues at par was maintained.[2] Indeed at least one Treasury official wrote that the gradual lengthening of periods was, for the Treasury, largely a matter of convenience of maturity dates. Certainly both the Treasury and the Bank of England attached high importance to the spacing of maturities, and throughout the war it remained a governing consideration in the borrowing technique.[3]

As has already been indicated, the Treasury from the first sought to minimise the interest burden created by its borrowing, by dealing separately with the various parts of the market. Thus small savers on the one hand and banks on the other were parcelled off, the one in 1939 and the other in mid-1940, and given terms peculiar to themselves. After the failure of the general-purpose War Loan in March 1940, the authorities settled down to the habit of catering separately on the one hand for the large private investor and the institutional saver, (for which groups the rather long Savings Bonds were designed) and on the other hand for the business firms and other temporary savers who were looking simply for a war-time use for accumulating funds intended for spending in the immediate post-war period (for whom the National War Bonds

---

[1] The 1951-53 bonds were restricted to a smaller amount because their final maturity date (1st March 1953) coincided with the final maturity date of an earlier issue—the 3 per cent. Conversion Loan, 1948-53.

[2] Issues at a discount were avoided partly because the authorities had come to fear that the discount might (quite irrationally) be regarded as a reflection on the Government's credit, and partly because the implied offer of capital appreciation free of tax for the rich investor would provoke embarrassing criticism. Keynes thought this latter 'a newfangled objection' having 'no real justification'.

[3] Given the large volume of debt to be thus spaced, the technique implied providing the post-war banking system with a close succession of maturities. The authorities, sensitive as they had been since Cunliffe Committee days to the embarrassment of central banking control by a large floating debt, must have been worried about implications for post-war central bankers, of this succession of maturities now being created. There is no trace of this concern in Treasury papers; doubtless officials took it for granted as a necessary evil.

were designed).[1] This broad grouping remained to the end; but
as Keynes became more interested in the internal borrowing
programme—from 1941 onwards—there were continued suggestions
of more subtle catering for the preferences and expectations of
particular groups of investors. One element of this was Keynes's
belief that many institutions and firms were beginning to want
post-war liquidity in order to take advantage of higher interest
rates at that time, and that this development ought to be met by
the issue of very short bonds at low rates of interest. He believed
that as the war approached its end, the 2½ per cent. War Bonds had
become rather too long to be attractive to this group. In the process
of discussion this argument gradually merged into a more general
argument about the future course of interest rates. The general
expectation in the stock markets was that interest rates would rise
after the war. *The Economist*[2] pointed out that capital issues control
would certainly continue, but as long as people believed that
controls would be loosened at all, expectation of higher rates was
quite rational. Growth of this expectation found its market expression
in a hardening of 'shorts' relatively to 'longs'. Given the official
determination that the 'longs' could not be allowed to fall
appreciably in price, this relative hardening of the 'shorts' meant
that the Treasury should be able to get plenty of money on
favourable terms by offering a very short date. Its policy of
lengthening the life of the 2½ per cent. War Bonds had taken these
securities outside the range of the investors now wanting to speculate
on rising rates immediately after the war, and for these the issue
of a short-dated 2 per cent. bond would be attractive. On
similar grounds it was urged that the Treasury should keep an
early repayment option in the terms of Savings Bonds.

Against these suggestions the Bank of England objected that the
implied maturity date was undesirable. Inside the Treasury others
objected that a bond of so short a life would attract the banks,
who would convert Treasury Deposit Receipts (then carrying
1⅛ per cent.) into the 2 per cent. bond, so that the Treasury would
be paying more to the banks, even though it might save ½ per cent.
on the money of some non-banking investors. More fundamentally,
the proposals failed to carry conviction because they were based on
an expectation of very low interest rates after the war, whereas most
of the Chancellor's advisers thought it might be difficult even to hold
the war-time levels beyond the end of the war, and that it would
certainly be unwise to speculate on rates going down at all. This

---

[1] This consideration was, in the latter part of the war, becoming a serious impediment
to the lengthening of life of the 2½ per cent. War Bonds, and was partly responsible for
the issue in November 1944 of the 1¾ per cent. Exchequer Bonds.

[2] 13th June 1943.

difference of view on the post-war prospect entered into many aspects of the borrowing policy. The majority view on post-war interest rates carried the logical implication that bond maturities ought to be well spread, even if this meant paying a higher average rate of interest.

For a long time—through 1942 and 1943 and well into 1944— the latter view prevailed, although the slackening sales of $2\frac{1}{2}$ per cent. War Bonds provided further argument against it. In November 1944 there was at last a move in the other direction, when a five-year bond bearing $1\frac{3}{4}$ per cent. was issued on tap. The name 'Exchequer Bonds', as well as the departure from the $2\frac{1}{2}$ per cent. rate, tended to make this issue appear as a major change of technique. To some extent this was intentional: the demand for War Bonds had dwindled away, and some innovation was necessary in order to 'awake' the 'industrial money' which was described as having 'gone to sleep'. But the arguments put forward in the discussions preceding the issue showed no real break with the past. Once again there was the inspection of the list of maturities the Government would have to face in the post-war years, and one of the main considerations shaping this particular issue was that 'we have kept the date of 1950 in reserve for some years, and the time is approaching when we must use it or discard it entirely'. 1950 was a date that ought to attract 'the industrial money' which now found the War Bonds too long. 1950 it was therefore to be, and a five-years' bond indicated a rate between $1\frac{3}{4}$ and 2 per cent. The authorities did not want to appear to squeeze the market and invite failure, and this pointed to 2 per cent. On the other hand, there was the old argument in favour of pruning rather than raising the rate a trifle: the argument that the market must never be allowed to think that interest rates were turning upward. Given that the existing market level was about $1\frac{7}{8}$ and that $1\frac{7}{8}$ involved an inconvenient fraction, and an issue at a discount or a premium was ruled out,[1] the brave choice seemed to be $1\frac{3}{4}$ per cent. A further argument in favour of this rather than 2 per cent. was that a five-years' bond would certainly attract a good deal from the banks, and that the difference between $1\frac{3}{4}$ and the $1\frac{1}{8}$ paid on T.D.R.'s was more defensible than the difference between 2 and $1\frac{1}{8}$. On balance, $1\frac{3}{4}$ appeared to be the better course, but the risk of failure was regarded as substantial. There was to be no confession of failure: never must the market suppose that the situation was getting out of hand. Accordingly, the market

---

[1] The Treasury was advised that both market and other investors would dislike a premium issue, 'since on paper the premium represented a certain capital loss'. For non-market investors, the taxation implications were an important objection. For the objection to an issue at a discount, see p. 207, footnote 2 above.

P

was from the first informed that this tap would be open only for a comparatively short time, and no definite sum was aimed at.

In the event, this issue was a comparative failure. When the tap had been open six months, about £250 millions had been attracted, but of this over two-thirds had come from the Issue Department of the Bank of England. On 12th June 1945—i.e. after another month—the tap was closed, the total issue then being £327 millions. A new issue of 2½ per cent. War Bonds, which had been 'rested' during the seven months, was then put on tap. The failure of the 1¾ per cent. Exchequer Bonds can hardly be adduced as conclusive evidence of market preferences. In November 1944 the end of the war appeared certain in a matter of months or even weeks, and the fact that investors then declined to lock up money for five years cannot be used as evidence that investors would not in 1942 or even 1943 have shown a keen appetite for say a four-years' bond. The case turns rather on whether the post-war probabilities were such as to justify the Treasury in grasping the immediate relief implied in lower interest rates on several hundred millions of debt. This immediate gain was clear enough, but there was the risk that thousands of millions maturing in early post-war years might have to be funded at rates of 3 per cent. or more. The actual course of events since the war shows that this was no idle fear, even when allowance is made for the fall in the purchasing power of money which has diminished the budgetary weight of every pound required for service of the debt.

(iii)

Tax Reserve Certificates

The Tax Reserve Certificates first issued at the end of 1941 were designed to meet a quite specific demand, to tap a quite specific source of funds, and in this respect they were like other classes of securities issued to suit the preferences of particular investing groups. But they were unique in that the idea—and even some of the details—came from American experience. While in the United States in the summer of 1941 (before the United States had entered the war) Mr. Keynes was impressed by the United States Treasury's plan, announced by Secretary Morgenthau on 3rd July 1941, for the issue of special Treasury Notes acceptable, with interest, in payment of taxes, or repayable in cash without interest. The plan was warmly received by the public and by business in the United States, and Mr. Keynes believed that a similar plan would meet a real need in Britain, and that it would improve the appearance of our financial position.

The essence of the plan was to take advantage of the ordinary practice of prudent businesses and individuals in putting aside provision for tax liabilities accrued but uncollected. Income tax and excess profits tax payable by business accrued on the average from nine to eighteen months before payment to the Inland Revenue Department was due. In peace-time many firms took advantage of this time-lag to make provision appreciably later than the profits to which each slice of tax strictly related, so in effect enlarging the capital employed in the business; but with high and changing taxes based on fluctuating profits, this procedure was liable to lead to financial embarrassment, and in the war years it had become sound accounting practice to reserve accruing tax out of the accruing profits to which it strictly related.

The accumulating taxes were then held by the firms in the shape of bank deposits until the payment to the Inland Revenue was due. In the earlier war many of the larger firms had invested the sums in Treasury Bills, but very low rates of discount ruling in the second war, the higher taxation of the discount, and a change in Inland Revenue practice,[1] combined to make purchase of Treasury Bills by ordinary business just not worth the trouble—a trouble recurring every three months as the Bills matured. The 'tax anticipation' sums now held in bank deposits had, through the increase in taxation, become very substantial, and were seriously distorting the total figures of bank deposits. On the basis of the current rates of accrual and collection of income tax, surtax and E.P.T., Mr. Keynes believed that the distortion amounted to hundreds—certainly two or three, probably four hundreds—of millions, rising to a very high peak immediately before the heavy revenue collections in the March quarter.

This distortion of the statistics of bank deposits had its alarming aspect. There was already, Keynes believed, 'a disposition abroad due to various causes to exaggerate the strength of the existing inflationary tendency. It is, therefore, of real importance to exclude misleading accretions from the published figures'. Of course the Treasury already secured use of these funds, by borrowing from the banks on Treasury Deposit Receipts, on which only $1\frac{1}{8}$ per cent. gross[2] was paid. But opinion fastened on the figure for T.D.R.'s as well as on the figure for bank deposits, as signals of inflation, and an operation which collected the tax reserves would enable T.D.R.'s to be reduced *pari passu* with the collection of bank deposits from businesses and individuals. If Mr. Keynes's estimate was

---

[1] In the first war a firm's holding of Treasury Bills had been treated, for E.P.D., as capital employed in the business; in the second war Treasury Bills were not so treated for E.P.T.

[2] It is impossible to quote a net rate, as the gross interest went to enlarge the banks' gross earnings, only the net earnings being taxable.

right, perhaps £400 millions could simultaneously be knocked off the totals of bank deposits and outstanding T.D.R.'s without any inconvenience to anybody. This would seem to be a piece of window-dressing well worth while, even if the Treasury had to pay a little more net interest on the tax anticipation notes than the net cost of the T.D.R.'s.

Because of the repercussions on our prestige and our power to borrow abroad, window-dressing of this kind had a real value. Moreover, the plan was not merely one of window-dressing. There was some substance in the foreigner's reading of the figures. Though probably not to an important extent, the reduction in liquidity would cause these tax reserves to be more tightly held. It is human nature to spend most readily when the actual cash is in the pocket, and even a slight reduction of liquidity, such as the substitution of tax anticipation notes for bank deposits, would have some effect in reducing the disposition to spend. Slight though this check on spending would be, it would be operating in the right direction.

These arguments found a keen supporter in Lord Kindersley, who had previously reported, without making any impression, that he had received many letters asking for a security of just this kind. Much as he disliked 'fancy finance', he disliked the growth of the Government debt to the banks even more, and he believed that inflationary appearances had their dangers at home as well as abroad. A combined Keynes-Kindersley front on a matter of Government borrowing was as formidable as it was unusual. The Treasury was receptive, and serious examination of the project was undertaken as a matter of urgency.

The proposal had to be considered in the light of the long-standing arrangement for prepayment of Schedule D income tax. Prepayment of Schedule D income tax had been allowed by statute ever since Peel's Property Tax Act of 1842—that is to say, throughout the continuous history of the income tax. The rate of discount allowed, fixed in 1842 at 4 per cent., was reduced to 2½ per cent. in 1889, and there it had since remained. The Royal Commission on Income Tax, 1920, had described the provision as illogical and, remarking that prepayments were in fact trivial, recommended abolition. The Commission suggested that the possibility of more comprehensive 'Income Tax Redemption Certificates' should be examined, but the suggestion was not pursued, apparently because the Treasury expected that the rate of discount allowed would have to be higher than that ruling on Treasury Bills. The question now, in 1941, confronting the Treasury was whether to generalise the ancient Schedule D provision (on cheaper terms than the 2½ per cent. free of tax) or to adopt a Tax Anticipation Note of the American pattern, or to do nothing at all about it.

There was actually decided inclination towards this last course. In favour of doing nothing was the fact that, even after Ministerial exhortations in support of early payment of taxes and with the powerful incentive of $2\frac{1}{2}$ per cent. discount free of tax, the use made of the Schedule D arrangement was relatively small: some £60 millions in 1940–41.[1] Anticipation of tax payments on any considerable scale would necessarily be offset by a corresponding shortfall of revenue in a subsequent financial year when the system was abolished or lost its popularity. Lastly, there was some feeling against it on the part of the financial purists in that the 'window-dressing' element in the project was recognised. The experts foresaw elaborate arrangements, tiresome to the hard-pressed Inland Revenue Department, and they expected the interest charges to exceed what the alternative T.D.R.'s would cost; were these disadvantages worth enduring for the sake of a window-dressing operation? That grounds such as these should have occasioned hesitation in the Treasury reveals the distance travelled by the permanent officials since the early days of 1939–40. At that time the particular source of funds for the Treasury was considered a matter of vital concern, bearing very directly on the growth of inflation. There was then, in the Treasury's eyes, all the difference in the world between the safe orthodox course of borrowing from the public and the inflationary course of borrowing from the banks, and T.D.R.'s had been created only with a certain reluctance and with an eye on the dislocation that invasion or serious bombing might occasion in the financial system. Now, in the autumn of 1941, officials were ready to ask, why bother to attract this purely temporary money from the public, when it could be borrowed simply and cheaply from the banks with whom the public were depositing it?.[2]

There were answers to these objections. The amount attracted by the Schedule D arrangement was little indication of what might be attracted by a scheme collecting money further ahead of tax dates and covering a wider range of taxes—especially if it received publicity such as had not been accorded to the Schedule D scheme. The argument that there would be a corresponding

---

[1] The Inland Revenue Department thought it unlikely that, in the absence of some new scheme, this amount would be maintained.

[2] The movement of Treasury opinion on this matter at a slightly later stage may be judged from papers arising from Lord Kindersley's desire, in the autumn of 1942, to circularise bank branch managers asking them to incite their customers to invest their 'idle' deposits in Government securities. A National Savings advertisement at the same time provoked *The Financial Times* (9th November 1942) to protest that bank deposits were not 'idle money'. An Assistant Secretary wrote in comment : '. . . . we admit the charge of false doctrine, but the Treasury passed that feature of the advertisement with its eyes open. . . . It is, we think, desirable, though the Bank of England are not so keen on the point as we are, that deposits should be funded rather than invested by the Banks at six months' call as T.D.R's.'

shortfall of revenue in a later year was exposed as a purely technical difficulty of Treasury accounting: otherwise the position would not differ from that of any other temporary borrowing. The reluctance to indulge in window-dressing was overcome partly by showing that it was not mere window-dressing: every reduction in the liquidity of the public's assets operates as a check, however slight, upon spending. Finally it was urged that, since public opinion both abroad and at home was still in the stage of 1939–40 Treasury opinion, even mere window-dressing was advantageous.

So the choice remained between generalising a discount scheme and copying the American Tax Anticipation Notes. Three weighty objections to the discount scheme soon settled this issue. First a discount plan could be conveniently applied only to taxes already assessed and notified by the Inland Revenue. This would limit the period covered, in most cases, to a few months, whereas the gap between 'accrual' and due date ranged up to eighteen months and even longer. As firms were most willing to invest the money outstanding longest, a discount system limited to a short period would fail to meet a considerable part of the demand. Moreover, it would operate unfairly in that a firm's opportunity for participation would depend upon the accident of the date at which the Inland Revenue Department got round to dealing with a particular file, and this unfairness would militate against the popularity of the scheme. Secondly, the Inland Revenue Department pointed out that a discount scheme would involve calculation and deduction of the discount by this Department's collectors at the time of payment. This would be a troublesome business, of a kind not usually undertaken by the collectors, who were by now in any case both hard-pressed and suffering some decline in efficiency by dilution of labour.[1] On the other hand, tax anticipation notes could be issued through the banks, like any other bonds, and could bear on their faces (or reverses) a table showing their value at various dates: values at which they would be acceptable in lieu of cash by the Inland Revenue collectors. Thirdly, a generalisation of the Schedule D arrangement would imply the dilemma of continuing the unthinkably high rate of $2\frac{1}{2}$ per cent. free of tax or underlining the reduction of the rate of discount, not a course that would commend itself to those charged with publicising the innovation.

In the face of these arguments, the case for notes on the American pattern was clear. Other important questions were their length

---

[1] The Inland Revenue Department pointed out that the Schedule D arrangement was itself troublesome in this way and that 'if it were resorted to by all Schedule D taxpayers big and small, the practical difficulties in administering it would be serious'.

of life, their validity for tax payment or encashment, the rate of interest and whether this should be tax-free. Since the notes were designed to cover the gap between the accrual of profit or other income and the payment of the corresponding tax, a maximum life of two years was appropriate. As to interest, having regard to the maximum life of two years (and a minimum of two months imposed largely to avoid very 'hot' money), to the bank deposit rate of 1 per cent. (taxable), the T.D.R. rate of $1\frac{1}{8}$ per cent. and the Schedule D discount rate of $2\frac{1}{2}$ per cent. (tax-free), the rate chosen was 1 per cent. tax-free. There was some objection to its being tax-free, the Treasury having set its face for many years against tax-free interest payments as being unfairly generous to surtax-payers and inconsistent with the spirit of progressive taxation. But it was clear that to deduct tax at source would destroy that simplicity of the tax-notes scheme which made it tolerable to the Inland Revenue Department, and that the alternative of calling upon taxpayers to include these small sums in their succeeding tax returns would constitute an irritant considerably handicapping the whole scheme. Moreover, if 1 per cent. were subject to tax, there would be so little left to many of the surtax-payers for whom the scheme was largely designed, that they could hardly be expected to participate. If there was to be a scheme at all, it seemed that it would have to allow interest tax-free. In the end this was agreed, partly because it was felt that the surtax-payer had already been hit so heavily that a small concession in this matter—a concession that to the taxpayer would rather be regarded as the absence of an irritant—was after some hesitation swallowed by Ministers.[1]

The decision that the interest should be tax-free had a bearing on two other questions: whether these notes should be accepted in payment of death duties, and whether they should bear interest in the event of encashment. It was at first proposed that they should be valid for payment of death duties, though the Americans had excluded this from their scheme. But this was thought an unnecessary concession to the wealthy. If the notes were to be made acceptable in payment of death duties, it would have been logical to give them a much longer life than the two years proposed. Like other parts of the Government's borrowing programme, this scheme was aimed at a particular section of the supply of funds— in this case, money set aside between accrual and payment of taxes payable at regular dates by firms and persons. In general, money is not temporarily so earmarked for prospective payment of death duties; such provision as there is more usually takes the

---

[1] Legislation was necessary to free the interest from taxation: the point was covered in the Finance Act, 1942 (5 and 6 Geo. 6 ch. 21), cl. 29(1) and cl. 38.

form of assurance premiums, and these were netted by the Treasury in other parts of the borrowing programme. In allowing interest to be tax-free, the Treasury was making a serious concession which would attract from other Government securities large investment funds, if the validity of the notes were not narrowly restricted. It was therefore settled that they should be valid for the payment of income tax,[1] surtax, national defence contribution, excess profits tax, land tax and contributions under Part I of the War Damage Act 1941, provided the payments fell due not more than two years after the purchase of the notes.[2] The same consideration led to the decision that they should not be negotiable, and that they should not be redeemable in cash except on penalty of complete loss of interest. The purchaser of one of the new notes was to be made to feel that his position remained virtually as liquid as if he had held the balance at the bank, but if he wished to exercise his right to draw cash, he was to be allowed no advantage in interest. Thus he was denied all incentive to take up notes beyond his accruing tax liability. There should be no loop-hole for general temporary investment at one per cent. tax-free.

The provision for encashment without interest did incidentally make the new notes a convenient means of making interest-free loans to the Exchequer: without any special correspondence with the Treasury, the notes could be purchased and then the capital could be reclaimed at any time after the initial two months.

Having settled the major questions of life, validity and interest-rate, and given the notes the name 'Tax Reserve Certificates' the Treasury framed the details with considerable care. In particular, certificates were to be issued for units as small as £25, and larger units were to be divisible when tendered in payment of taxes. The Chancellor announced their impending issue just before Christmas 1941,[3] and when the details were published a week later,[4] *The Economist*[5] commented that the new security seemed 'well designed for its purpose'. The Treasury was not always so careful of detail, and to people who wanted to hold the certificates

---

[1] Schedule E tax was excepted, mainly because much of it was already collected through employers.

[2] As from March 1944, certificates were accepted in payment of taxes due within five years of purchase, but interest was paid for not more than two years. This and various administrative details mainly relating to the assessment of E.P.T. were set out in a revised prospectus issued in July 1944.

[3] H. of C. Deb., Vol. 376, Col. 1853, 16th December 1941.

[4] The prospectus was issued by the Bank of England on 22nd December 1941, applications being receivable on and after the 23rd.

[5] 27th December 1941, p. 794.

for the full two years the Treasury took a harsh attitude on a petty question, thereby incurring some unnecessary ill-will.[1]

The issue was clearly a success. There were three or four thousand purchases a month, the average amount applied for being rather over £10,000. Encashments during the first year were quite small, and their use in payment of taxes lagged sufficiently behind the purchase dates to cause rapid accumulation of large sums. The total outstanding passed £66 millions in a month, and it reached £300 millions in July 1942. It continued to increase and reached a maximum of £788 millions at the beginning of 1945. As was to be expected, there was a considerable seasonal movement, the seasonal peak being generally reached at the end of each year. The statistical result thus far surpassed the £400 millions Mr. Keynes had thought possible, a figure thought unduly optimistic when the Treasury first looked at the plan.

Success measured in these statistical terms has of course only a very limited meaning. The sums swept up by the Treasury were limited, as precisely as was possible by the main features of the scheme, to funds that taxpayers regarded as earmarked for accrued tax liabilities, and to the extent that the money could otherwise have been held in bank deposits, the statistics merely mean that some hundreds of millions were knocked off deposits on the one side and T.D.R.'s on the other side of the banks' balance sheets. If this was all that happened, no difference was made to the fundamental financial problem of easing the inflationary pressure, and the half-heartedness of the welcome given by the Press[2] was

---

[1] In accordance with the essential features of the scheme, certificates ceased to bear interest after the tax payment, for which they were tendered, fell due. Thus if tendered in payment of income tax instalments falling due on 1st January, no interest was earned after that date. But because 1st January was throughout the war a Bank Holiday, the Bank of England refused to issue any certificates on this date. Those issued on 31st December 1941 could not be tendered for taxes due on 1st January 1944, the interval exceeding two years; those issued on 2nd January 1942 could be so tendered, but then earned interest only for the 23 completed months. The Treasury received many letters from irate taxpayers, who considered that they had been defrauded of one month's interest. The Treasury's objection was that concession would be followed by the same claim 'for any firms for whom the date six months after the end of their accounting period for E.P.T. fell two years from a day which was a Sunday or an ordinary Bank Holiday'. A question was asked in the House, but the Chancellor refused any concession (H. of C. Deb., Vol. 386, Col. 86, 19th January 1943). His successor, however, announced on 30th March 1944 (H. of C. Deb., Vol. 398, Cols. 1569-71) that certificates could henceforth be held up to five years, interest being payable for a maximum of two years; thus this particular grievance disappeared. The change was accompanied by a back-dating concession in certain cases.

[2] e.g. *The Economist*, 20th December 1941, '. . . . the new issue will bring very little contribution to the closing of whatever inflationary gap may still persist. . . . This, however, is not to suggest that the new securities will not play a useful role in Government finance and in the improved control of the banking situation. . . . The new bonds must therefore be regarded as an interesting technical equilibrating device, and not as a new contribution to the solution of the fundamental financial position'. cf. *Sunday Times*, 21st December 1941. More considered criticism, by Mr. W. T. C. King (quoted in *The Economist*, 7th November 1942, p. 579) had substance but ignored the effect on opinion overseas.

justified. But the amount of window-dressing was substantial enough to stand a chance of bringing the real advantages its advocates claimed. And the slight qualification of the liquidity of £300 to £700 millions may well have checked spending in amounts no Chancellor could ignore.

(iv)

The Residual Borrowing: Treasury Bills, Ways and Means Advances and Treasury Deposit Receipts

In the inter-war period the methods of meeting residual needs of the Treasury were two, the sale of Treasury Bills and borrowing on Ways and Means at the Bank of England. Restriction of Ways and Means Advances to the incalculable residue of fluctuation within the week was a matter of policy.[1] These advances, because they implied equal addition to the cash basis of the banking system, were regarded as a peculiarly inflationary method of finance,[2] and after the end of the first war it had been a prime object of the Treasury to eliminate the war-time growth in them. The Treasury sought to provide its residual needs—those remaining after revenue and bond operations—by issuing each week the appropriate amount of Treasury Bills and when, as in 1920, it worried about the difficulty of placing all the Treasury Bills on offer, its worry reflected its reluctance to resort substantially to Ways and Means Advances at the Bank of England. These views continued to prevail when the second war came, and though in certain difficult phases of 1940 there was substantial resort to these advances not followed by early repayment, the general presumption was that the money must be found in other ways.

In the early stages there was only one other way, and that was expansion of the outstanding volume of Treasury Bills. At the beginning of the war there were £1,100 millions[3] of these three months' bills outstanding, and the rate of discount on them had been pulled up to 3¾ per cent. when Bank Rate was raised to

---

[1] cf. *Report of the Committee on National Debt and Taxation* ('Colwyn Report') Cmd. 2800 of 1927, paragraph 96.

[2] During the first war the authorities had partially countered the effect of these Advances upon bank cash by taking 'Special Deposits' (not closely analogous to Treasury Deposit Receipts) from the banks, on which see E. V. Morgan, *op. cit.*, p. 177 *et seq.*

[3] £411 millions of these had been issued by tender to the market and £707 millions through the tap—that is, by direct sales to certain special lenders.

4 per cent. late in August 1939. The total outstanding included the very large holdings of the Exchange Equalisation Account, and the flight of foreign funds from London, especially during the summer of 1939, had brought into this Account hundreds of millions of sterling which had been used for adding to the Account's holding of Treasury Bills. The Exchange Equalisation Account was handing out its gold to those selling their London balances, and the Account was in effect channelling these balances of sterling into the coffers of the Treasury by its operations in Treasury Bills. In fact, the Government was able to meet the first rush of its war expenditure by using the sterling thus acquired from overseas holders, who took gold in exchange. For the first six months of the war the Treasury was thus relieved of immediate pressure to choose between borrowing from the public and borrowing from the banking system.

This adventitious source of money was soon dried up by the advent of exchange control, and in the early months of 1940 the choice between less comfortable means of finance had to be faced. The heavy revenue collections of the first quarter of 1940 were soon gone, the first War Loan issue in March 1940 was a dismal failure, and then the successive shocks of the war news in the spring and early summer hindered the raising of money by unloading on the market the substantial unsold portion of the War Loan.

For the moment the Treasury felt able to look to increased sale of Treasury Bills without putting any strain upon the banking system and the discount market: there had been some 'slack' in the system remaining from the lean phases in the 'thirties, and this slack had been increased by the declining trend in bank advances. The weekly tender issue of Treasury Bills had been raised from the level of £50–55 millions at which it had been held until mid-November, to £65 millions until mid-January. In the big revenue weeks it was reduced only to £50 millions and was back at £65 millions in May, as compared with £30 millions a year previously.

This expansion in the Treasury Bills outstanding could not go much further without substantially changing the banking situation. As early as December 1939 the Governor of the Bank was thinking of the steps that should be taken when this point was reached,[1] and in the second week of May he handed to the Treasury a detailed plan that had just been worked out in the Bank. By mid-June the Chancellor had accepted a slightly amended plan, and the

---

[1] The late Sir Henry Clay had the following note in his diary for December 1st 1939: 'The Governor said the only way to borrow was to borrow back from the banks on six months' notice all their surplus money—put it back on Public Deposits just as quickly as it got on Bankers'—then issue Funding Loans as and when possible.'

banks had been brought into consultation. The first Treasury Deposit Receipts were issued at the beginning of July 1940.[1]

Had it not been for the need to prepare against possible invasion or other dislocation of the financial mechanism, the case for the innovation would not have been strong. The money could quite conveniently have been collected by sale of more Treasury Bills, the banks being if necessary told to hold these in sufficient amounts to avoid strain on the discount houses, which by custom (since 1934) alone bought them directly from the Government. Alternatively, the custom could have been modified to allow special direct purchases of Treasury Bills by the banks, and direct transactions of this kind would have been feasible in the contingency against which some provision was now desirable. Once, however, special direct transactions between the banks and the Treasury were admitted, there was much to be said for using a new name to which new terms would be appropriate, leaving the established mechanism of the discount market to deal with a manageable volume of the usual Treasury Bills. Some direct arrangements with the banks were clearly called for, if the customary ratios of the discount market were to be preserved; and these direct arrangements could with advantage take the form of transactions in a security slightly different from the usual Treasury Bill. The introduction of a new medium for the truly 'residual' borrowing would also allow the utmost flexibility in meeting the Exchequer's needs, without such abrupt changes in the volume of Treasury Bills as might have strained the conventional market. The introduction of the Treasury Deposit Receipt was thus a conservative rather than a revolutionary measure. The authorities concocted the T.D.R. scheme because they preferred not to disturb the customary relationship and the customary 'ratios' of the peace-time system.

Given the desirability of some new security, to be issued to the banks in return for sums called by the Treasury, what should be its nature and terms? The argument for preserving the customary ratios was essentially that the risk of inflationary lending by the banks would be enhanced by increasing their liquidity. The argument, which is identical with that against financing by direct borrowing at the central bank, had not a great deal of force, but it was at this time (1940) still thought of some account, and rightly so. The new security should therefore be rather less liquid than the Treasury Bills which the banks included in their 'liquid assets', though obviously also liquid enough to induce the banks to accept the scheme without any substantial protest. The economic experts

---

[1] The Chancellor informed the House of Commons on 4th July 1940, H. of C. Deb., Vol. 362, Col. 1033.

in the Treasury advised that the T.D.R.'s as proposed by the Bank of England were not so clearly less liquid than Treasury Bills as to bring any advantage in the fight against inflation. The event, however, rather justified the Bank's scheme, in that the bankers did during the war find the T.D.R.'s sufficiently liquid to make them feel perfectly comfortable and accept the scheme without protest, while on the other hand they definitely regarded the T.D.R. as less liquid than the Treasury Bill, never liked it, and after the war (when the T.D.R.'s liquidity was significantly reduced[1]) became increasingly keen to be rid of it. It is a duty of the central bank to estimate and advise upon the commercial bankers' reaction to Government action, and on this subtle if unimportant question the Bank of England judged the bankers' reaction with precision.

The differentiation from the Treasury Bill was partly obtained by giving the T.D.R. a six months' life as against the Treasury Bill's three months. Also, whereas the Treasury Bill is a freely negotiable instrument (though by long tradition the banks do not in fact ever sell their bills, except to the Bank of England on the latter's initiative), the T.D.R. was made non-negotiable. It was thus a simple loan extracted from a bank for a period of six months. On the other hand, the T.D.R. could, to cover emergency needs,[2] be repaid at the Bank of England subject to discount at the penal Bank Rate of 2 per cent.; and it could be repaid in full when the bank, either on its own account or for a customer, was paying for a newly-issued Government bond[3] or for a Tax Reserve Certificate.

The rate of interest thought appropriate to these terms was $1\frac{1}{8}$ per cent. The first suggestion was for $1\frac{1}{4}$ per cent., but the Chancellor was already under pressure in the House of Commons to reduce the Treasury Bill rate, then a shade over one per cent., and severe criticism was to be expected if the banks were given appreciably more for these new loans, so obviously similar to Treasury Bills. Here again, the object was to differentiate T.D.R.'s from Treasury Bills, but by the smallest possible margin. So $1\frac{1}{8}$ per

---

[1] The T.D.R. could be tendered as cash by a bank in payment for bonds bought for itself or its customers; during the war bonds were on tap and this privilege therefore gave the T.D.R. a high degree of liquidity, whereas after the war the infrequency of bond issues made the privilege comparatively insignificant.

[2] It is not clear that the banks who were called upon to hold T.D.R.'s understood the limitation to emergency needs. On an occasion when a small amount was presented for repayment under this clause, there was no emergency and the authorities at first declined to repay. On further representation they relented and repaid the small sum in question. It was referred to in the answer to a Parliamentary Question on 20th July 1943. H. of C. Deb., Vol. 391, Col. 708.

[3] This provision had its origin in the intention of the authorities to regard the T.D.R.'s as stop-gap instruments to be absorbed into funding loans from time to time.

cent. was fixed, and 'in the light of prevailing conditions', as promised to the bankers, at $1\frac{1}{8}$ per cent. it remained until after the war. The scheme could be represented as one for transferring to the Treasury deposits lying in the banks at 1 per cent. interest: the bankers' margin of $\frac{1}{8}$ per cent. looked very moderate.

The scheme was confined to the London Clearing Banks and the Scottish Banks, with the addition of the central banks directly operating in the London market—namely, the Commonwealth Bank of Australia and the National Bank of Egypt. These banks were notified, through the Bank of England, every Friday of the amount to be borrowed by the Treasury during the succeeding week, and the sharing of this total sum between the banks was arranged outside the Treasury.

Both in the official discussions while the scheme was coming to birth and in public discussions after the announcement, reference was frequently made to the apparently similar borrowing on 'Special Deposit' from the banks in the first war. On that occasion the Bank of England had acted as principal, relending the money to the Treasury on Ways and Means. There was, however, a much more important difference, in that in the first war the Special Deposits were designed not to meet residual Government requirements but to protect from the pressure of surplus funds a high rate of discount in the London money market, this high rate then being judged desirable in order to hold foreign funds in London. In the second war there was no question of inducing, by high interest rates, foreigners to keep money in London, and the need for 'Special Deposits' to absorb surplus banking funds therefore did not arise. What did arise was the protection not of a high but of a *low* rate of interest. To prevent the rate of interest from rising, the Treasury had to have some residual means of raising money without causing upward pressure on interest rates. The needs were met by calling upon the banks to take up T.D.R's.

We have seen that one of the motives behind the T.D.R. plan was the desire to prevent abnormal liquidity from developing in the banking system. But it was also necessary, as the figures grew, to protect the banks from undesirable illiquidity. The banks still wanted to maintain their customary cash ratios, and additional cash had therefore to be provided whenever the net T.D.R. borrowing[1] by the Treasury exceeded the decline in the public's demand for bank advances.[2] The banks found the additional cash through their usual channels: they reduced their purchases

---

[1] The *net* borrowing in any week was the week's call on new T.D.R.'s less repayments on maturity and encashments on subscription for new bonds.

[2] These were the major variables: the above discussion abstracts from variations in the other items, these variations being mainly seasonal.

of bills from the discount houses. The latter were then forced to rely upon help from the Bank of England. Since the authorities wished to avoid any disturbances in the short rate of interest, the discount houses were in fact always helped by 'the special buyer' (the Bank of England's operator) at the ruling rate of 1 per cent. The T.D.R. system, as a plan to provide the residual requirements of the Government without forcing interest rates up, thus did not—it could not—eliminate residual resort to creation of cash at the central bank. The willingness of the banks to take six months' paper at 1⅛ per cent. was dependent on a tacit understanding that the authorities would in practice always meet any consequential cash needs of the banks without allowing money market rates to rise. The Bank of England's back door, to which the discount houses could resort on much cheaper terms than the formal Bank Rate chargeable at the front door, had to become a guaranteed ever-open door, with an automatic machine which would turn Treasury Bills into cash at the fixed discount rate of 1 per cent.

The banks needed to draw cash not only to enlarge their own cash reserves, but also to enable them to meet the rising cash requirements of the public. As prices and incomes rose, the public required more notes (and coin). These expanding cash requirements of course operated as a minor drag on inflation, in that people had to save—to spend less than they were receiving—in order to secure the bigger holdings of cash. As people failed to pay back into the banks as much cash as they were drawing out, the banks themselves had to replenish their tills by drawing on their own balances at the Bank of England, replenishing these balances in turn by forcing the Bank of England to take more Treasury Bills through its broker. Thus the expanding cash needs of the public, as well as the expanding cash reserve needs of the banks, added to the volume of Treasury Bills held by the Bank of England. The 'customary ratios' that were to be preserved as far as possible necessarily excluded central bank figures.

The upshot of all this procedure, in terms of figures, was that in the period 2nd September 1939 to 25th August 1945 the Treasury borrowed, in net amounts

£2,186 millions on Treasury Deposit Receipts
£2,087 „ „ Treasury Bills
£770 „ „ Bank-notes (Fiduciary Issue)

a total of about £5,000 millions out of £14,800 millions borrowed at home through all channels. Was this inflationary finance? On one count clearly not at all: the level of Government expenditure determined the amount of borrowing, and not vice versa. Was the public more spend-thrift because the supply of money and financial assets was thus expanded? The banks were in any case asked not to lend unnecessarily, and the structure of their assets was so influenced by the Treasury's arrangement as to minimise the risk that they would in fact lend unnecessarily. This elaboration of the Government's borrowing policy thus more or less stopped a leak which was probably never a serious threat, at any rate after the 'phoney war' had come to an end. It can be argued that the elaboration was a work of supererogation, and that a cruder technique of meeting the residual requirements would have been equally innocent of adding to the immediate inflationary pressure. But it can hardly be argued that the Treasury did not do its utmost, when borrowing what was not raised by taxation, to avoid 'inflationary finance'.

So much for the situation at the moment. But it is the business of the Treasury in war-time to think also of the post-war days. In its bond issues, for example, the Treasury very properly strove to avoid heavy bunching of maturities in particular post-war years, and may have sacrificed something in immediate interest charges in order to secure a reasonable spread of maturities. Similarly in financing its residual requirements, the Treasury had a duty to take into account the post-war liquidity position created by its war-time actions. The experience of 1919–20 was a warning to the Treasury of the danger of high liquidity in the banking system at a time of brisk demand for advances to private trade. From this point of view the preservation of 'the customary ratios' in the financial structure was of high importance. Even in war conditions the authorities felt that the effects of an increase in the volume of Treasury Bills could not be so easily controlled as those of the T.D.R. issue, and the degree of control was much increased after the war when the privilege of encashment on purchase of new bonds became insignificant. It is true that in the post-war event the authorities in some degree compromised their control by virtually guaranteeing an inexhaustible fount of cash at the Treasury Bill rate of $\frac{1}{2}$ per cent., but their power to call upon the banks to take up more and more T.D.R.'s could have been a useful sanction had the banks inflated more rapidly than the authorities could tolerate.[1] However slight the risk of unnecessary bank advances in time of war, the threat of inflationary bank advances after the war had undoubted substance. The usefulness of the T.D.R. as a potential weapon for controlling such bank inflation depended upon the distinction drawn in the bankers' minds between the liquidity of the Treasury Bill and that of the T.D.R., and the creation of this distinction justified the authorities in their introduction of the new instrument as an alternative to exclusive

---

[1] The funding operation of November 1951 was similar to this kind of check.

reliance upon the Treasury Bill for their residual requirements. Post-war as well as war-time needs pointed to the desirability of elaborating the Government's borrowing arrangements; and the T.D.R. was just different enough from the Treasury Bill to count as a worthwhile elaboration.

Q

CHAPTER VIII

THE INTRODUCTION OF EXCHANGE CONTROL

(i)

Pre-war views on Control

THE NEED, to economise in foreign currencies was something that had to be taken for granted throughout the war. Even on the most optimistic assumptions about the possibility of borrowing abroad, this held good, since an unfavourable turn of the war might dry up a stream of foreign loans at a critical juncture, and in any event post-war overseas indebtedness was an evil to be shouldered only in the clear interest of the immediate war effort. Pre-war inspection of the problem, when legislation in the United States[1] had ruled out all probability of substantial American credits, encouraged planning on the assumption that there could not be appreciable borrowing. This legislation also adversely affected the use that might be made of Britain's overseas assets,[2] and although these would certainly have to be drawn upon, neither their availability nor any conceivable level of exports could make foreign currencies so abundant as to render their expenditure unimportant to the authorities.

It was by arguments such as these that the Treasury, the Bank of England and Ministers were forced—reluctantly—to accept the inevitability of some form of foreign exchange control. Recognition of the requirements of total war would have short-circuited these arguments; yet even as the war did become total, the conservation of foreign exchange was justified more by particular circumstances than as an implication of total mobilisation. In 'the phoney war' period the problem was seen as one of making our foreign currencies last through a three-years' war. Then through the last seven months of 1940, every dollar was

---

[1] The Johnson Act passed on 13th April 1934 prohibited 'financial transactions with any foreign government in default on its obligations to the United States'. By a ruling of the United States Attorney-General a token payment was held to be equivalent to a default.

[2] The Treasury was advised that according to an unofficial opinion of the United States Attorney-General the Johnson and Neutrality Acts ruled out loans by private United States citizens, though not by the United States Government against dollar securities requisitioned by His Majesty's Government and put up as collateral.

226

thrown into the struggle as quickly as possible, and the knowledge that the barrel was rapidly emptying dictated a tighter control of the disposal of all foreign currencies. When lend-lease became effective in 1941 and for the remainder of the war, the position justified no easement: there were always doubts about the adequacy of lend-lease cover for our North American requirements, strict economy in the use of foreign purchasing power was an essential part of the justification of our need for American help, and there was also the need to accumulate foreign exchange reserves against our growing post-war liabilities to holders of sterling. The reasons for economy thus remained compelling from start to finish, and the source of variations in the form of foreign exchange control is therefore not to be found here. The course of events was dictated not so much by changing need as by growing realisation of that need, and especially by the facility and confidence that lengthening experience gave to administration. Not that that administration ever became bureaucratic in spirit—on the contrary, it was characterised throughout by the reluctance that was a drag on pre-war preparation, and gave the control in its first six months a looseness that was sharply criticised.[1]

The liberal spirit in which the problem of foreign exchange control was approached was undoubtedly in part an instinctive reaction against the methods known to be employed by Germany. Developments there under Dr. Schacht had put an entirely new complexion on the possibilities of war-time exchange policy. During the war of 1914–18 only the most rudimentary control had existed in any country,[2] and not much more could be said of efforts made during the currency disorganisations of Continental Europe in the early post-war years. The substantial history of foreign exchange control begins in 1931.[3] In the London discussions that led up to the Standstill Agreement, the American delegation opened the way by suggesting that the Germans must have a tight foreign exchange control. The Germans took up the suggestion and in the succeeding years—particularly when rearmament placed new strains on the German balance of payments—under the presiding

---

[1] e.g. *The Economist*, 9th December 1939, and T. Balogh in *The Economic Journal*, 1940, pp. 1-26.

[2] 'Complete control was so much against the spirit of the age that I doubt if it occurred to any of us that it was possible' wrote Mr. Keynes in September 1939.

[3] The Government feared a disastrous collapse of the pound when the gold standard was suspended on 21st September 1931. The Treasury consequently made an Order (S.R. & O. (1931) No. 991) on 22nd September 1931 (under Section 1 (3) of the Gold Standard (Amendment) Act) prohibiting purchases of foreign exchange or transfer of funds for the acquisition of foreign exchange except for (1) normal trading requirements, (2) pre-existing contracts, (3) reasonable travelling or personal purposes. No control organisation was established, responsibility for observance of the regulations being left with the banks and the customers themselves. In the event there was no panic and, as soon as the pound was stronger, the Order was revoked (3rd March 1932).

genius of Dr. Schacht they developed an enormously elaborate and effective control over all foreign transactions. The essence of this German system was the complete supersession of market operators (all exchange being supplied and requisitioned by the official operator) and absolutely comprehensive licensing of imports. The control was commonly said to employ 30,000 people, and the regulations after five years occupied some eight immense volumes.

A system of this kind, though the more distasteful to Englishmen from its association with the Nazi régime, had the virtue that it did the job thoroughly, allowing the authorities to impose without qualification their ideas about economy in foreign exchange resources. But even had the British authorities found it more palatable, there were substantial objections making the German system inappropriate as a precedent for the United Kingdom. These all derived from the position of sterling as an international currency. In official discussions and in the form given to the control, the problems appear as twofold: those arising from the existence of the Sterling Area, and those arising from the use of sterling by other countries. This is logically a distinction only of degree, since the pre-control Sterling Area was merely the area in which sterling circulated most easily.[1] The pre-war planners were, of course, right to draw the distinction in analysing the problem, since it was of the first importance for administrative purposes, and it was inevitable that the necessities of control should impose a sharp legal distinction where hitherto there had been an almost imperceptible economic shading.

Sterling's international position had to be taken into account not merely because it imposed administrative complication but also, and more fundamentally, because it was a war-time asset of considerable value. Treasury officials, arguing in pre-war days against elaborate exchange control, were over-stating the case when they claimed that control would so interfere with the export trade as to reduce the country's foreign exchange income, but there were other arguments with more substance. Briefly, these arguments claimed that as an international banker London could to some extent live on credit. The sinews of war could be toughened at the expense of overseas owners of sterling balances, even though formal loans to belligerents were out of fashion.

Sterling balances were held—with varying degrees of tightness—on account of banks and trading firms whose principal place of business was elsewhere. At the one extreme were the balances of central banks—for example, the Commonwealth Bank of

---

[1] The vagueness of this definition has its reflection in the difficulty of saying precisely what countries were included in the pre-1939 Sterling Area.

Australia—whose London balances were not merely working balances, but also the depositing country's principal international reserve. At the other extreme was the 'hot' money held by individuals domiciled in countries that could not be expected to come readily to a monetary understanding with Britain, and could by no stretch of the imagination be counted in the Sterling Area. Those funds at the former of the two extremes could be expected to remain in London and perhaps to increase as the war proceeded; those at the other extreme could be expected to leave at some fairly early stage in the proceedings, and to do so with such certainty that no step taken by the British authorities could influence their withdrawal.[1] But between these two extremes lay a wide range of other balances, and the willingness of owners of these balances to leave them in London, and perhaps to increase them, was susceptible to influence in a number of ways. It was on the nature of this susceptibility of the holders of mobile-but-not-'hot' sterling balances that, in official circles, the pre-war debate on foreign exchange control turned.

Financial policy in war can never be considered wholly in relation to the war period, and it would not have been surprising if arguments as to the post-war value of London's reputation as an international banker had weighed in the balance at this time. In fact the need—for post-war as well as war-time reasons—for conservation of our foreign exchange resources was felt so strongly as to force the controversy about control entirely within the narrower frame of the war-time effect on sterling balances. The question was indeed at one critical phase argued in the even narrower frame of the £300 millions of 'neutral' balances estimated to be held in London before the Munich crisis, but references to the prestige of sterling generally indicate that the officials had in mind also the attitude of a much wider range of holders and potential holders of sterling.

On the question of how to deal with these mobile balances, two extreme views were possible. On the one hand, there was the 'good banker' argument that the banker who always stands ready to pay cash never has to face a run and may even attract additional deposits. This argument tuned well with the dislike of German methods and the fear of bureaucracy. 'Is not freedom', wrote one official, 'our greatest asset?' At the other extreme was the

---

[1] The political situation during the spring and summer of 1938 gave a foretaste of what was likely to happen. Some £150 millions of gold was withdrawn from London between 1st April and 30th September. The settling of the Munich crisis brought no reversal of this trend, with the result that the Exchange Equalisation Account had to be replenished by a transfer from the Bank of England of £350 millions worth of gold (at the current market price) on 6th December 1938 to provide 'the maximum possible sum for the present and future defence of the pound'.

answer developed by Germany during the pre-war years, particularly in her trade with south-eastern Europe. This was the complete control of foreign exchange transactions, the bilateral organisation of foreign trade and the accumulation of balances against Germany in the bilateral clearings. Regimentation could, the Germans had shown, enable a country to live on its neighbours. In the pre-war discussions the extreme claims for freedom were pressed strongly in the Treasury. The really 'hot' money would, it was agreed, go quickly as war alarms rose in pitch; and this liability was covered by the gold reserves which we must be prepared to use for this purpose. Domestic holders of sterling would listen to patriotic appeals; the 1931 experience had been encouraging and, though some slightly closer control would probably be desirable, the Englishman was not likely to abuse the freedom the Treasury would like to see maintained. A Schachtian army of foreign exchange controllers must be avoided except in the very last resort.[1] Lastly, if by appropriate import and export policies we took care of the balance of trade, the foreign exchange position would largely take care of itself.[2] All these arguments were used in support of the 'good banker policy' of attracting rather than regimenting the overseas holder of sterling. '. . . . . What we think', concluded the Treasury, 'is above all to be avoided is for the Treasury and the Bank of England to display publicly their own lack of faith in sterling at the very commencement of war'.

The Bank of England, though greatly attracted by the policy of freedom to which Treasury arguments pointed, thought the risks too great. It was more sensitive to the magnitude of London's short-term debtor position, and believed that the initial shock, without evidence of official determination in the handling of it, might do irretrievable harm. 'Bitter experience has made people exchange-minded, and they would take alarm if, in an emergency, nothing were done to protect sterling and conserve the country's reserves'. In such circumstances the volatile portion of the sterling balances would prove far larger than the £300 millions of neutral money the Treasury had in mind—even British nationals might be infected by panic developments. Gold reserves would be insufficient to stem this tide, even if they proved to be fully available for this purpose. The rate of exchange would therefore

---

[1] The main arguments the Treasury put forward against a German-type exchange control system were (1) the high degree of state interference and control of every branch of economic life inevitably involved, and (2) the large number of officials needed to work the system.

[2] This point was reiterated at many stages, both inside and outside official circles. See e.g., *The Times*, 11th April 1940, in commenting on the 'Dollar-Invoicing' Order: '. . . apart from all technical measures, far the best way to maintain the exchange value of sterling is to increase the volume of British exports.'

fall catastrophically, with irretrievable damage to London's position as an international banker and therefore damage to the war effort.

In urging this case, the Bank was undoubtedly inspired by a more realistic appraisal both of Continental financial opinion and of the nature of the struggle that was impending. An institution headed by Mr. Montagu Norman could not readily have brought itself to argue against the Treasury's desire to preserve sterling as an international currency; but its superior channels of intelligence—deriving partly from Mr. Norman's cultivation of central bank contacts and partly from the technical necessities of recent foreign exchange policy[1]—led its experts to believe that action would have to be taken very soon, and that it would have to be drastic. Germany was believed to be basing her plans on the assumption that Britain would again try to maintain a free economy, and would therefore be vulnerable to various forms of economic pressure, including floods of counterfeit sterling notes.[2] The only answer to such a threat was a tight foreign exchange control, and from 1937 onwards the Bank had this in blueprint.

Neither the Treasury departmentally nor Ministers were ready for anything of this kind, and the Bank therefore proposed a compromise solution: a control, informal and decentralised, but holding the sterling balances tightly at first, afterwards gradually relaxing. We should not 'impound' these balances, but enable their withdrawal to take place in an orderly way. The Bank believed this field to be entirely appropriate for application of its philosophy of no regimentation but orderly markets. This compromise did not prove at all acceptable. The Bank's notion of gradual relaxation was suspected to be a mirage; the necessity for rapid elaboration of the control was thought more likely. But as tension heightened in the summer of 1938, sterling was under severe strain, and Britain's gold reserves began to look much less adequate. The dangers of freedom—dangers the Bank had stressed—began to look more substantial. It was in these circumstances that, at the end of July 1938, the Chancellor of the Exchequer decided

---

[1] Another relevant aspect of Mr. Montagu Norman's work had been the recruiting of a body of young men who were given time to think—in striking contrast to the Treasury, where the administrative grade, for all its high ability, remained in numbers starved by the economy measures of the early 'thirties.

[2] Reports, eventually backed by actual forged notes as evidence, came from varied sources during 1939 and 1940, and again later. There was more than one plan: the Germans at one time had the idea of unloading notes from aircraft over Britain, but chief reliance seems to have been placed on the flooding of neutral markets with sterling. These stories led the Bank to include in its preparations an entirely new note issue, and close control of travellers' pocket money was eventually insisted upon. The import of bank notes was narrowly restricted from August 1940 by Regulation 2B (S.R. & O. (1940) No. 1514); export had been restricted from the beginning, by the original Regulation 3.

that, though he favoured the freer course advocated by his advisers in the Treasury, some preparatory steps should be taken in case 'a full exchange control' should after all prove necessary upon the outbreak of war. Regulations were to be drafted imposing both the minimum control that would in any case be necessary, and the blocking of non-resident balances that was in dispute. The question whether the entire code or only the minimum should be adopted was to be left in abeyance.

(ii)

The Institution of Control, August–September 1939

The regulations in draft when the final crisis broke upon the Government in August 1939 had taken as their starting point the short-lived control of 1931–32, though, in order to avoid both legal difficulties[1] and paralysing doubts, the onus of decision as to the legality of a transaction was now placed firmly upon the banks who were to operate as agents for the Treasury. The primary control, from which exemptions were to be allowed, was a prohibition of transactions 'for receiving a payment or acquiring property' abroad. Exemptions were allowed, upon certification by the Treasury or its agents (the authorised banks), in favour of (1) normal business requirements, (2) pre-war contracts and (3) reasonable travelling or other personal expenses; beyond these particular exemptions, the Treasury was to have a general power to make exemptions[2]—a residual power under which the Sterling Area was to receive its first legal recognition. As an administrative safeguard, the Treasury was given a monopoly of transactions in gold and foreign currencies, and certain banks were to be its authorised agents in these transactions. Other regulations required residents to sell to the Treasury any gold or specified currencies—the list of these latter being the beginning of the 'hard currencies' list. Residents were to be forbidden to sell securities likely to be marketable outside the United Kingdom, and they were to be compelled to register these with the Treasury; and the Treasury was to have some power to requisition such securities. All these powers were considered the minimum legal framework, but in the summer of 1939 it was hoped that exemptions

---

[1] The 1931 Order had forbidden purchase of foreign exchange except for certain purposes. The banks were exhorted to take certain precautions, but the customer was the legally-responsible party. Consideration in 1938–39 showed that it would be intolerable to ask the banks to dishonour cheques without giving them the protection of some legal status in the control.

[2] Under the 1931 Order the Treasury had had no power at all to grant exemptions.

would be wide and that most business would continue in the normal channels and unhindered save by a minimum of form-filling.

The disputed question of the foreign balances was covered by the inclusion, in Draft Regulations of 25th August 1939, of a paragraph numbered 2A, the effect of which was to block, subject to exemption by the Treasury, all sterling accounts standing in favour of foreign Governments, bodies incorporated under the law of any country outside the United Kingdom, and persons not British subjects or British protected persons.[1] At one stage in the pre-war discussions the intention emerged to negotiate with the more important countries reciprocal payment arrangements which would provide conditions for the withdrawal of these balances.[2] Exemptions appropriate to such agreements would be issued by the Treasury, leaving subject to the block only those 'non-residents' whose Governments had not made agreements with the United Kingdom. Negotiations with the French in fact proceeded some way,[3] but the last days of August arrived before negotiations had even been opened with the United States or any other Government. The imposition of this Regulation would therefore have appeared as a blunt act of repudiation by London, an act which it was feared might excite retaliatory action by the United States and perhaps others. In short, the Government was caught with its mind not made up to the desperate plunge of complete blocking of non-resident sterling, and with preparatory steps towards a compromise arrangement—a negotiated composition with London's creditors—scarcely started. At the last minute the disputed Paragraph 2A was dropped; 'non-residents' were left free to draw on their sterling balances. After all this blowing hot and cold, it is not surprising that when, on 27th August, the Draft Regulations had to go forward for signature, a senior official thought it necessary to warn his assistant, 'Mr. X will no doubt make sure that the right copy of the Regulations goes forward to the Council'.

The structure of the control was at once developed by the notification of the hard currencies list and by the legal establishment of the Sterling Area. Regulation 5 authorised the Treasury to

---

[1] The odd inconsistencies in this definition of 'non-resident sterling' can be ascribed to the Treasury's preference for the simplest legal categories until officials had had time to think out both the legal and economic problems more thoroughly. The paragraph does not appear in the draft of 9th August.

[2] The Bank of England had already envisaged the desirability of bilateral payments arrangements with each of a number of countries.

[3] A provisional agreement had been reached between the two central banks whereby French-owned sterling balances would be paid to a special account of the Bank of France at the Bank of England (and British-owned franc balances to a similar account at the Bank of France) and the central bank would pay out francs (or sterling as the case might be).

designate currencies to be offered for sale to it, and on 4th September the following currencies were designated by a Gazette notice:

> United States dollars
> Argentine pesos
> Swedish kronor
> Swiss francs
> French francs
> Belgian francs
> Dutch guilders
> Canadian dollars

These currencies were selected as being vital either for the procurement of supplies in the countries themselves, or for procuring in foreign exchange markets elsewhere the means of payment for supplies from other countries. Currencies fulfilling neither of these conditions—currencies, that is to say, that were in plentiful supply and were not dependably saleable against scarce currencies—were excluded from the list, and became known as 'soft currencies'.

In evolving the list of specified or 'hard' currencies, pre-war discussions had taken account of the probable war-time requirements of the whole Sterling Area, and had assumed that bilateral trading, already prominent in the pre-war world, would become much more the rule. There had been little variation from the earliest drafts: Norwegian kroner had been dropped out, and French francs had been added when it was realised that the intended close economic alliance would not remove the need for careful husbanding of francs. The very important question of the position of Canada had been settled some months earlier, by Canada's own decision conveyed in correspondence between the Bank of Canada and the Bank of England. The Canadians, while anxious to be helpful—an intention later expressed in substantial loans—declared their inability to stand inside the Sterling Area fence. Canada's economy was closely geared to that of her great neighbour, whose currency was obviously going to be scarce for everybody. While believing that they could police Canadian capital movements across the frontier, the Canadian authorities said that they would be quite unable to prevent movements of United Kingdom capital seeking refuge in the United States *via* Canada.[1] There were also political difficulties in the way of a step that might imply some loss of independence. Canada, therefore, alone in the Commonwealth, stood outside the intended war-time Sterling Area; and by the same criteria as had been relevant to other currencies, it was held that the Canadian dollar would be a hard currency. The list of

---

[1] This was an argument of great importance to the United Kingdom authorities, who in the event had trouble enough in checking such movements via Australia and South Africa.

currencies designated under Regulation 5 was thus fitted to the anterior determination of the boundaries of the Sterling Area.

By sweeping up all supplies of the designated currencies, the Treasury made itself at once responsible for the supply of them for all approved purposes, and buying and selling prices had to be fixed. The United States dollar prices were fixed, at first at $4.06 and $4.02 to the £, and shortly afterwards at $4.03½ and $4.02½; and those of all the other currencies were fixed by multiplying these basic rates by the cross-rates prevailing in the foreign exchange markets of the world.[1] From this point onwards disposable[2] currencies designated under this Regulation 5 could be obtained in the United Kingdom only from the Exchange Equalisation Account through an authorised bank, and all transactions were at the fixed rates.

Given the wide use of sterling in international transactions, restriction merely of the acquisition and holding of other currencies would have left a very large hole in the control. Regulation 3 therefore controlled sterling as well as foreign currency payments to non-residents, subject to the Treasury's power to authorise transactions arising in the normal course of trade, pre-control contracts, or reasonable travel. The opening phrase of this Regulation also gave the Treasury a general power of exemption, and by the Currency Restrictions Exemption Order of 3rd September (S.R. & O. (1939) No. 1168), the Treasury allowed sterling payments without formality to persons, corporations and governments within certain territories. In this way the Sterling Area became a legal entity, an area inside which payment in sterling was unrestricted. This freedom of payment inside the Area could be allowed only on the understanding that all countries in the Area would impose exchange restrictions substantially parallel to those enforced by the United Kingdom. The central banks of the Dominions had at an early stage been in touch with the Bank of England on this matter, and during the summer of 1939 satisfactory assurances were received from their Governments. With the Colonies matters were not as far forward, but their general position was established on the eve of war, so that the first Exemptions Order could take in the entire Commonwealth (including the neutral Eire), except Canada, Newfoundland and Hong Kong.[3] The ring fence obstructing payments was thus to

---

[1] On the general question of the foreign exchange value of the pound, see below, pp. 238-9 and Section (vi) of Chapter XIV.

[2] Designated currencies could be obtained by traders and others engaged in permitted transactions, but the currencies so obtained had to be sold to the Exchange Equalisation Account.

[3] There were inevitably some delays, and the initial confusion took some weeks to clear.

run not round the United Kingdom alone, but round the entire Sterling Area. When, besides Commonwealth countries, there was question of including Egypt inside the Area, the Bank of England received assurance from the Governor of the National Bank of Egypt that he was reasonably confident of the adequacy of the exchange control then established in Egypt.[1] Similarly Iraq was admitted because the currency board system[2] operative there was believed to exclude, in practice, an exchange market; but when evidence accumulated that Iraq's failure to institute exchange control had allowed it to become a gap in the Sterling Area's ring fence, the country was excluded from the Area[3] until exchange control was instituted there a few months later.[4]

The administration of the control was extremely simple. The principle was adopted that imports not prohibited by law could be paid for either in foreign currency or sterling merely on proof of the genuineness of the transaction. The trader had simply to complete Form E, for payment in foreign currency, or Form E1, for payment in sterling. It was for the Customs Officers to see that nothing was imported contrary to the law, and for the Treasury in consultation with other Departments to see that the law did not allow any imports the country could not afford. The duties imposed upon the banks were thus restricted to the absolute minimum, and the Treasury and Bank of England always successfully resisted both suggestions of more onerous duties for the banks, and suggestions of a 'control organisation' whose business it would be to say what imports could be afforded. Administration of the Regulations was greatly helped by the full support they enjoyed throughout the war from public opinion, and by the willingness of the banks to undertake all the routine work. There were inevitably some awkward problems, but public acceptance of the control eased the task of the authorities in overcoming the difficulties.

(iii)

The Transition to Tighter Control, March–July 1940

The broad principles of the control established at the outbreak of war were simple enough, but their application involved many day-to-day decisions on awkward marginal cases. The distinction

---

[1] The Egyptian Control was established by decree of 25th September 1939. The Treasury Order of 28th September added Egypt, the Sudan and Iraq to the Sterling Area. These countries had in the pre-war period always held all their reserves in London.

[2] Comparable to the currency boards in various British Colonies.

[3] S.R. & O. (1941) No. 632 of 5th May 1941.

[4] S.R. & O. (1941) No. 1890 of 28th November 1941.

between the 'resident' who may not transfer sterling to the account of the 'non-resident' without a declaration, and the 'non-resident', who could transfer sterling freely both to resident and to non-resident accounts, was relatively simple in terms of persons but more elusive in terms of corporations, especially those whose business was clearly spread across frontiers. The term 'foreign account' was well understood by bankers, but the lawyers found it inadmissible to a legal instrument, and for some months the Treasury and Bank of England struggled along without any satisfactory legal basis for the distinction they were applying between the prohibited and the permitted transfers of sterling. The provisions restricting operations in securities also proved troublesome: even the term 'security' itself was unsatisfactory. A reasonable check could be kept on the transfer of inscribed stocks and shares on company registers, but bearer shares or bonds lent themselves readily to evasive transactions, and many securities of the former kinds could be converted into bearer form. Difficulty was experienced also in establishing satisfactory Customs procedure. The Customs had been empowered, by a Regulation of 21st September 1939,[1] to require a declaration stating the sum to be received or expected to be received for any goods exported. To devise a form that would minimise evasion (e.g. by under-valuing the goods) without vexing traders was a task that bothered officials for months after the inauguration of the control.

By amending Regulations and by enlisting the co-operation of the banks, the Capital Issues Committee and other bodies, many of these difficulties were reduced to manageable proportions during the first six months or so. Meanwhile it had become clearer every day that the control could only be very partial as long as non-resident sterling was freely disposable and exports could be invoiced in sterling. As long as sterling was useful to foreigners for the purpose of purchasing British exports, non-resident sterling could find a good market. To the extent that this was happening, exports were 'unrequited' in the sense that they were adding nothing to Britain's capacity to make purchases abroad: they simply served to reduce indebtedness to non-residents—to reduce, that is to say, the sterling balances. Britain wanted to finance imports in part by running the sterling balances up; what was now happening was that currently-accruing sterling and sterling balances were being run down by their use in payment for current exports. To stop this drain on our resources, either non-resident sterling must be blocked or the invoicing of exports in sterling must be stopped; and to be effective the change, whichever it was, needed to be made throughout the Sterling Area.

---

[1] S.R. & O. (1939) No. 1251, published on 30th September.

There is no doubt that the original intention of the Treasury had been to see that all exports were invoiced in foreign currencies which would be sold to the Control in accordance with the first Regulations, and it seems probable that the Treasury was unaware of the extent to which this form of invoicing would upset customary trade practices. Once the magnitude of the leak was appreciated, the Treasury view swung at once in favour of blocking non-resident sterling. This was out of tenderness for the export trade. Pre-war discussions had consistently emphasised the importance of maintaining the export trade on the highest possible level in order to pay for supplies from abroad. The fact that exports were for the moment in part 'unrequited' was not a conclusive reason for rashly introducing hindrances to traders. Novel methods of invoicing and the complications of foreign exchange transactions might be irritating, and there were universal fears that even comparatively mild measures would discourage exporters— particularly the small people up and down the country who knew nothing of foreign exchange. It would be idle to force collection of foreign exchange from exporters if exports were killed in the process.[1]

Proposals were therefore formulated for blocking non-resident sterling held before 3rd September, and requiring that the proceeds of sale of securities should be credited only to the blocked accounts. Income items—interest, dividends, etc.,—would continue to be freely transferable (at official exchange rates) but the remnant of pre-war balances and all securities would be blocked. The disadvantages were, however, substantial. It would be necessary to block the balances of Empire as well as foreign holders, until the Empire countries had introduced effective blocking. More fundamentally, a step of this kind would be our first act of repudiation, and the victims would be those very foreigners who had hitherto of their own free will continued to hold sterling. Rather than resort to this step, the authorities should, it was argued, be prepared to see a trickle of foreign balances leave London at the free exchange rates which at that time were close to official rates. If the trickle should swell to a flood, the authorities would have to face the possibility of a major movement in free rates and adopt altogether more drastic measures. Until that flood came, better to leave sterling unblocked and go gently with exporters.

Nevertheless the flood might come, especially if there were an adverse turn in news of the war, and this fear gave point to concern about 'the free rate'. To those to whom the international reputation

---

[1] For the first phase of promotion of exports, see *Civil Industry and Trade, op. cit.*, Chapter III.

of sterling was dear, the free rate was a standing insult. There was always, even in the grimmest days, some care for the post-war prestige of sterling as an international currency, and some struggle to maintain its war-time value untarnished was worth-while on this account alone. But there were also more immediate, more pressing, reasons for maintaining the foreign exchange value of sterling. If its post-war prestige was worth a struggle, its war-time prestige was infinitely more so, since the willingness of other countries to hold sterling balances enlarged the sources from which supplies could be continuously drawn. Moreover, the rate of exchange bore directly on the value received in return for British exports: in so far as British producers were pricing these on the basis of sterling costs at home, a higher foreign exchange value of the pound implied a higher foreign exchange value for British exports. When, in the autumn of 1939, the free rate threatened to assume importance in determining the foreign exchange value of British exports, thought was turned—virtually for the only time during the war—to the question whether it would pay Britain to adopt a lower or higher value than the $4.03 that had been settled, rather by market conditions than by considered °choice, at the beginning of September. The experts leaned rather towards a higher than a lower value, mainly on the grounds that exports were likely to become determined by the limits of home capacity rather than by their competitive power in world markets, and that inflation would more easily be held at bay if imports were cheap in terms of sterling. These views were not urged strongly enough to persuade the authorities to take the unexpected step of actually raising the dollar value of sterling, but they did serve to reinforce the reasons of prestige that were valid against any measures of depreciation.[1]

For these reasons it became, in the succeeding months, a cardinal point of policy not only to maintain the official rate unchanged but to make that official rate the normal, indeed if possible the only, effective rate, and to squeeze out of existence the free rate which might otherwise undermine the official rate. The inspiration of British policy in this phase thus had a twofold aspect—to bring the proceeds of exports into the hands of the authorities, and to enforce the official rate of exchange on the widest range of transactions. In pursuit of these objects two lines of attack were employed, in the main simultaneously, although their results so worked out as to give the appearance that they were two successive phases rather than simultaneous developments. The one was the enforcement of 'dollar-invoicing', the other was the negotiation of 'Payments Agreements'. The former provided directly for an

---

[1] For further discussions of this general question, see section (vi) of chapter XIV, below.

effective official rate of exchange and for collection of the foreign exchange proceeds of the exports affected. The latter also provided for the canalising of certain trade—in this case trade with certain countries—through channels in which the official rate alone was operative, and for ensuring that, in so far as Britain was able to export, she received immediate value for her efforts.

These two technical devices appear as successive phases partly because there was some reluctance in high quarters to swallow the triumph of bilateralism so clearly implicit in the Payments Agreements. But the appearance is mainly due to the fact that Payments Agreements took time to negotiate—negotiators in this novel and delicate business were rare animals, and it was not wise to push the opposite parties too fast—while on the other hand the technique of dollar-invoicing required only action which, although it had to be concerted with the whole Sterling Area, was essentially unilateral imposition of new foreign exchange regulations. In the following paragraphs the order of appearance is followed, the development of dollar-invoicing being first discussed and then that of Payments Agreements. But it is necessary throughout to remember that there were from the first officials who believed that the Payments Agreement technique was the proper and inevitable major solution for the basic problems, and that they and others were working on these lines behind the scenes even while open action was confined to dollar-invoicing. As will presently appear, the development of dollar-invoicing no sooner made itself felt than it produced conditions that focussed attention on the other line of attack, rendering it at once more acceptable and more urgent.

For the moment, however, the obvious line of development was in the direction of securing that exports should yield useful currencies which existing regulations would bring into the official net. The exporter was still at this time thought of as a little man who must not be frightened by unnecessary new forms; he must be treated gently. Officials sought a minimum modification of export procedure, and thought first in terms of 'persuasion and encouragement'.[1] The Federation of British Industries, the Association of Chambers of Commerce and other interested parties were called into consultation. These bodies simply underlined the arguments that had already been used against compulsory dollar-invoicing; it was thought that even compulsory declarations by exporters[2] might be disadvantageous in that their existence

---

[1] In pre-war discussions a proposal to make a Regulation compelling invoicing in foreign currency had been dropped as impracticable.

[2] The declaration envisaged would have stated whether payment was due in sterling or foreign currency, and was designed to enforce the Regulation that all specified currencies should be sold to the Control.

would encourage more, not less, exporters to invoice in sterling. Then, at the end of the year, official discussions swung to a new footing, with the suggestion that a few important and administratively manageable exports should be brought under a dollar-invoicing system. 'Important Empire exports such as jute, rubber, tin, whisky and furs' were those first in view. It appears that furs were included primarily because their export was suspected as a device of residents wishing to get their capital out of the United Kingdom;[1] the others were named as 'easily recognisable commodities which were good dollar-earners'.[2] Some risk of driving the commodity markets away from London was deliberately taken. But the authorities were trying to make the new system reasonably tolerable, and traders in tin and rubber were sounded at an early stage.

This limited scheme avoided nearly all the difficulties of a comprehensive dollar-invoicing regulation, and was quickly accepted as the next step. The Treasury accepted the criticism that it would not be a completely watertight control; it would bring hard currency from the bulk of certain exports, with as little administrative interference as possible, and this was sufficient. The original idea that it might be worked on an entirely voluntary basis was dropped because India and the Colonies judged that they would have to legislate for their commodities (tin, rubber and jute), and they could hardly be expected to legislate without parallel action in the United Kingdom. This necessity for legislation made the period of preparation rather longer than had been expected, but all was ready at the beginning of March 1940, and the Order[3] was published on 7th March. It came into force on the 25th, the breathing space allowing reasonable time for shipment of pre-Order contracts. The Order provided that all exports of tin, rubber, jute, whisky and furs, to the American Continent (excluding Canada and the Argentine[4]), Dutch territories, Switzerland and Belgium, were to be invoiced in United States dollars, Dutch or Netherlands East Indies guilders, or Swiss or Belgian francs.

Discussions with the Birmingham Jewellers' Association had

---

[1] As was to be expected, fur was the item that caused difficulties of definition in the administration of the Order.

[2] Linen, pottery, diamonds, cotton goods and woollen goods were also considered. Diamonds were ruled out by a Customs objection that they were 'uncontrollable as an export commodity'; there was subsequently a short-lived experiment with them (see p. 242). The other items were rejected on other administrative grounds; the essence of this first export-invoicing scheme was that it should be simple and easy to run.

[3] S.R. & O. (1940) No. 291.

[4] Canada, Argentine and Sweden were 'hard currency' countries, but by agreements between their central banks and the Bank of England, all sterling paid by their importers (for Sterling Area exports) had to be obtained through the central banks at the official rates.

R

already opened the prospect, duly fulfilled, that the plan might by voluntary arrangements be extended to other trades. Besides the Birmingham jewellers, certain diamond firms (covering virtually all the trade) made definite arrangements. In this case, however, the voluntary control broke down because diamonds could be bought in South Africa for free sterling and the Union Government was politically unable to enforce restriction. As a special case, the voluntary control was replaced by statutory control on 9th May, 1940,[1] the co-operation of the Diamond Trading Corporation ensuring that this strict British control would not be upset by free trading in South Africa.[2]

Discussions thereafter proceeded on the basis of extension of the list of commodities, and of Treasury freedom to specify by destination any other exports and to prescribe any method of payment for a specified destination. This freedom of action was desired in connection with negotiations for payments agreements with various countries: the existence of a payments agreement with a country allowed sterling invoicing, provided that the sterling was obtained in accordance with the payments agreement, and countries with whom the Bank of England was trying to negotiate were apt to have views on dollar-invoicing. The web was further tangled by the necessity at every stage to carry the agreement of any Sterling Area countries particularly affected by a commodity under discussion. India and Australia could be counted upon without question, New Zealand was expected to fall into line, and there were hopes about South Africa. Iraq was not important enough, in terms of quantity of trade, to worry about; but when cotton came up for discussion, how could Egypt be ignored?

The Treasury took its wider statutory powers on 9th June 1940: S.R. & O. (1940) No. 894 was particular in relating to exports to the United States, Switzerland and Sweden, but S.R. & O. (1940) No. 892 was general, giving the Treasury power to prescribe both the destinations to which it was to apply and the method of payment to be required in each case. S.R. & O. (1940) No. 894 in effect extended the range of 'dollar-invoicing' commodities, by adding to the original list all other goods exported to the countries now specified. S.R. & O. (1940) No. 892 allowed further extension as and when the Treasury became ready for it—a readiness that came with the various payments agreements, of which that with Sweden was a forerunner.[3]

---

[1] S.R. & O. (1940) No. 689.

[2] The Corporation undertook that if dollar-invoicing were made compulsory in the United Kingdom, they would themselves impose sales conditions in South Africa that would make it useless for purchasers to buy there.

[3] On the Swedish and other payments agreements, see pp. 443 *et seq.*

Meanwhile the original Order[1] was having substantial effect on the market for free sterling, an effect more or less expected but creating a major complication in the further development of control. At one blow a substantial part of the demand for free sterling was removed, and its market value fell for the first time substantially below the official rate. Although the authorities secured the proceeds of a much greater proportion of exports than before, and in this sense made the free market less important, their very success made the remaining free market a more worrying problem that it had ever been before. The market having been narrowed also became more jumpy, and sharp movements in a rate now far below the official rate attracted much more attention not only from speculators but also from public opinion in many countries.[2] Moreover, the wider gap between the two rates made the practice of invoicing in sterling, now denied to the specified commodities (rubber, tin etc.) a privilege of some value, whose removal by wider enforcement of dollar-invoicing would be a matter of some moment to leading British export trades. The authorities therefore became more anxious to hasten the process of strangling the free market, while simultaneously they encountered new resistance against their efforts to do so.

The reaction to the first dollar-invoicing Order was that of a market already shrinking. From the very beginning the supply of sterling had been dwindling, for three reasons. The 'hot' money had largely gone, so that each new turn of opinion against sterling brought less of it to the market.[3] The loopholes in Sterling Area controls—particularly in the Colonies—were being tightened up. Most of all, permitted British transfers of sterling to non-resident account were being more and more restricted. From 3rd September such transfers had required completion of Form E.1, but at first this was a mere declaration. Only from the end of November was documentary evidence required (parallel to applications for foreign currency). On 8th January 1940 a list of bankers authorised to approve Forms E.1 was published, together with a list of transactions for which transfers could be authorised, the procedure becoming virtually identical with that for foreign currency transactions. In the face of this narrowing supply, the demand had been elastic enough to give the market a fair measure of stability. As any non-resident having to pay sterling—whether for Sterling Area exports or anything else—was at perfect liberty to acquire the

---

[1] S.R. & O. (1940) No. 291.

[2] *The Economist*, 6th April 1940. Press comment on the Order itself had been generally favourable (*The Times*, 11th April 1940; *Financial News*, 28th March 1940, was less friendly).

[3] According to the Stamp Survey the market was fed 'on a substantial scale' by the sale by foreigners of the proceeds of sales of securities.

sterling in the free market, there were always plenty of buyers whenever rates were just sufficiently below official rates to make the trouble of resorting to the free market worth while. Under these conditions rates had settled, after an erratic start, within a range of about $3.90 to $3.97 to the pound.[1]

That the partial dollar-invoicing Regulation of March 1940 would, by cutting the demand for free sterling, cause a fall in the free sterling rate was foreseen by the authorities. It was impossible to forecast whether this would be substantial and whether it would occur in a dramatic way. At least one expert was inclined to think that it would come rather slowly, and it was suggested that steadiness might be encouraged by a Parliamentary statement by the Chancellor, to the effect that the fall in the free rate was a testimony to the increasing efficiency of the exchange control. In the event the fall was spectacular. From about $3.90 just before the publication of the Order, the rate fell to a minimum of $3.44 on 27th March, and although there was some recovery thereafter, it seldom rose above $3.55. The authorities believed that the sharpness of this fall was due partly to fears, among foreign holders of sterling and sterling securities, that the new Regulation was the first step towards a tight control that would make withdrawal from London virtually impossible. This view strengthened the case for a Ministerial pronouncement, and indicated the desirability of something rather more general than had been suggested a month earlier.

Accordingly the Chancellor circulated a statement to the House of Commons on 9th April.[2] He first made the point that the fall in free sterling was 'the incidental result of tightening up the exchange control'. He stated his policy as requiring that the bulk of transactions should come through the Control at the official rates,[3] and said that already the proportion of transactions going through the free market was 'a very small one'[4]—too small to be of importance for the cost of living. Perhaps there was in the statement so far a trace of whistling to keep up courage; but it went on to

---

[1] *The Economist*, leading articles, 'The Free Market in Sterling', 24th February and 2nd March 1940. Keynes, writing on 16th March 1940 to R. F. Kahn, pointed out that these high rates were 'symptomatic of the large amount [of export proceeds] we must have been losing'. (Quoted in *Life of John Maynard Keynes, op. cit.*, p. 495).

[2] H. of C. Deb., Vol. 359, Cols. 461-3

[3] This carried the implication that other important exports, not yet specified, would soon be included in the dollar-invoicing plan. It therefore created uncertainty in these trades, an uncertainty that was evident in the succeeding weeks both at home and in the Dominions.

[4] *The Economist*. A leading article of 2nd March 1940, 'The Free Market in Sterling', estimated that the business in free sterling might be about between 5-10 per cent. of total exchange business in sterling, private and official.

give positive encouragement to the foreigner to continue to hold sterling. The Chancellor rejected, for example, the suggestion that the authorities might intervene in support of sterling in the free market, and he did this in terms that were rightly interpreted as implying that there had been no such support.[1] He explained at length that, in view of sterling's position as an international currency, the Government had chosen not to freeze non-resident balances and securities, and that 'it would not be to our advantage' to block them now. He concluded that 'sterling . . . . is good to hold; and I believe that this opinion is spreading in neutral countries. The best way of ensuring that it will continue to spread is to maintain, for ourselves and others, so far as we can, the essential liberties which, in the financial and every other field, are traditional in this country'.

This important statement of policy may have helped to steady the market but it had no chance to do more: on 9th April 1940, the very day the statement was circulated, the 'phoney war' came to its abrupt end and the succession of shocks in the war news began. Through the next few weeks the free rate was more often under than over $3.50, and during May it was to go almost to $3.00.[2] This was, as the Stamp Survey put it, 'disconcerting'. That it looked bad was itself important,[3] in that Britain was wanting to run up sterling indebtedness only less rapidly that she was having to exhaust her dollar supplies. But it also produced some 'anomalous and most disadvantageous consequences'. Although the five 'specified commodities' formed the bulk of the Sterling Area's exports to the United States, most of the Area's exports to other markets could still be invoiced in sterling, and the foreign importers could now get the sterling in the free market at a discount not of 2 or 3 per cent. but of 20 per cent. below the official rate. Free sterling therefore became the principal accounting medium for the sale of Sterling Area exports, other than the five specified commodities and that other valuable item, gold. Suggestion that a 'free' commodity might be added to the five already specified became a matter of some moment to the Sterling Area exporters; it was in effect a threat that either its dollar price would be raised

---

[1] cf. *The Economist*, 13th April 1940, p. 692.

[2] The market had become extremely sensitive to war news, and the invasion of the Low Countries sent the rate to its minimum of $3.02. The average rate in succeeding weeks was about $3.20, though movements continued to be erratic, especially in the latter part of June.

[3] The French authorities, who had in December reluctantly accepted the official rate as the basis for all Anglo-French transactions, were seriously perturbed. M. Reynaud wrote on 28th May 1940 to Mr. Churchill to the effect that Britain's exchange control policy, with the concomitant fall in free sterling, was prejudicing the continuance of Anglo-French financial co-operation.

or its sterling proceeds would be reduced by some 20 per cent.[1] The exchange control was, for the first time, meting out arbitrarily differential treatment to different sections of Empire producers.[2]

There was disadvantage also from the point of view of the terms of trade. In effect two exchange rates were established, one for imports and a limited range of exports, and the other—some 20 per cent. lower—for the general run of exports. This was a reverse application of the principle which more usually inspires discriminating exchange rates, implying as it did the exchange of a comparatively large volume of exports for a comparatively small volume of imports. It was at this juncture that the whole question of the optimum level of the official rate came under discussion, and the upshot was to strengthen the case for moving at once from this uncomfortable and unsatisfactory half-way house between comprehensive hard-currency-invoicing and the earlier complete freedom.

Of possible routes by which the Treasury might move away from this half-way house, some had already been ruled out by the Chancellor's recent statement. He had decided against official support of the free rate, which alone would have been consistent with the early policy of maintaining sterling as an international currency while preventing the flight of British capital. To destroy the free market—more precisely, to limit it to a black market—by blocking non-resident balances, was another course explicitly ruled out by the Chancellor. To enforce comprehensive hard-currency-invoicing would, by removing virtually the whole lawful demand for free sterling, send the free rate down even further, and make it even more vulnerable than it had been in recent weeks. Such weakness could not be invited by restrictive action so soon after the Chancellor had described sterling as 'good to hold'; and in any case a system of this kind would inevitably create difficulties for the export trade in some of its markets. The only course open was, as the technical experts had long foreseen, to hurry the development of the virtual 'bilateralisation of sterling' by payments agreements and other steps which would dry up the supply of free sterling. This involved virtual abandonment of sterling's position as an international currency; on the other hand it did eliminate the spectacle of a low and fluctuating New York quotation, which besides undermining sterling's reputation had occasioned some wasteful marketing of exports; and it rendered unnecessary the

---

[1] At the beginning of April there were complaints from Manchester that 'the export trade in textiles is being considerably hampered by uncertainty as to the possibility of export control being imposed on the lines now in operation for whisky etc.'

[2] The Australian regulations compelled wheat exporters to invoice in dollars, and when the gap between free and official rates widened these exporters complained of the freedom allowed to many British exporters.

damaging step of formal blockage of sterling balances. In the long run, therefore, sterling's international reputation was well served by this war-time abandonment of its multilateral currency.

The bilateral arrangements now to be developed had as their main object the stoppage of accruals to free sterling from current trade, but if the market was really to be starved out of existence it was necessary also to prevent its being fed from the sales of sterling securities by non-residents. This important step was taken by S.R. & O. (1940) No. 708 on 12th May 1940[1]; thereafter the pool of free sterling could be fed only from payments (permitted by Form E.1 procedure) for current imports, visible and invisible, and through leaks in the exchange control in any part of the Sterling Area. The latter were by now very small; free sterling could be substantially eliminated by restricting, in some way, the use that could be made of sterling accruing to non-residents under the Form E.1 procedure.

Technical arrangements between central banks had at a very early stage moved in this direction: the Swedish Payments Agreement of December 1939 and the temporary Agreement with the Argentine of October 1939, were on lines which, when generalised, would prevent free sterling from arising from current trade. The procedure introduced in the Swedish Agreement involved the creation of 'Special Accounts' in London and Stockholm, into which all payments had to be made. Imports from Sweden to England, for example, might be paid for either in Swedish kronor (obtainable only from the Control) or by sterling paid into the Riksbank's 'Special Account' at the Bank of England. The use of this Special Account sterling was regulated by the Agreement between the two central banks: the essential point for our present purpose was that it could not get into the free market, though it could be used to pay for Swedish imports from any part of the Sterling Area. The arrangements with the Argentine, though broadly the same, depended for their precise form upon the existence of an exchange control already established in the Argentine. There was also the important difference that under this Agreement only one currency— sterling—was used, and this form, since it allowed the United Kingdom to receive but not to give credit, came to be preferred by the United Kingdom negotiators.

In May, June and July Treasury and Bank of England officials worked hard to make this procedure cover as large a part of the

---

[1] These measures introduced a new Regulation 3A and amended Regulation 3 (Export of Gold, Currency and Securities) by omitting securities, thus divorcing securities from gold and currency: their main result was that all sales of securities by non-residents were subject to licence. A further Order (S.R. & O. (1940) No. 1732) of 27th September 1940 closed certain loopholes, particularly those relating to bearer securities, by banning the import into the United Kingdom of sterling bearer securities.

world as possible. Powers were taken in June[1], whereby the system might be imposed upon any country by United Kingdom Regulations. The Treasury was careful to retain these powers but did not use them[2], and it seems unlikely that they could ever have been effective.[3] It was altogether more satisfactory to secure the co-operation of the central bank in the other country, and this could be enlisted by offering reasonably attractive facilities for the use of Special Account Sterling. Payments Agreements were in this way negotiated with Argentina, Roumania and Brazil by mid-July 1940, when new Regulations[4] came into force, and with the Portuguese Empire, Hungary, Greece, Peru, Uruguay, Bolivia, Chile, Turkey, Spain and Paraguay by the end of the year. A rather different plan was applied, as we shall see, to the United States and Switzerland. Meanwhile several other countries had been over-run by the Germans, and the countries that were neither part of the Sterling Area, nor covered by the new plan were comparatively unimportant in war-time trade. The sources of free sterling were virtually stopped.[5]

To the United States and Switzerland the approach had to be rather different because their currencies were, and were clearly going to continue to be, the scarcest. Neither political nor trading considerations allowed any pressure of any kind to be applied, and inter-governmental arrangements were unlikely to be appropriate. On the other hand, relations between bankers of the three countries˙ were good, and among the powerful New York bankers particularly there was a disposition to help which could not at that time have found expression in any inter-governmental negotiations. The British authorities had, moreover, a *quid pro quo* to offer to the New York bankers. Given recognition by the British that an adverse balance of payments with the United States itself would in any event have to be covered by drafts on Britain's gold and dollar balances, and given the desire of the British authorities to universalise the official rate of exchange to the exclusion of all free rates, it was not difficult to say that all *new* accruals of sterling

---

[1] See footnote 1 on p. 250.

[2] A threat to exercise this power was at one time considered, when difficulties were encountered in negotiating a payments agreement with Japan.

[3] Without co-operation from the other monetary authority, the United Kingdom Treasury could not have forced their official exchange rates on another country, nor had they any means of policing a prohibition of the use of free sterling in payment for invisible exports.

[4] See footnote 1 on p. 250.

[5] On 26th October 1940 *The Economist* reported that the New York market for sterling 'must gradually dwindle into oblivion'. The rate, in a very narrow market, had already practically closed up with the official rate. For further reports see *The Economist*, 26th April 1941, 30th January 1943, and 5th February 1943.

to American (or Swiss) account would be convertible into gold, dollars or Swiss francs, at the official rates, on demand. The American and Swiss bankers, with this promise of full convertibility at official rates in their pockets, were willing to accept the mechanism of the *Registered Account*, in particular undertaking not to buy free sterling ('old sterling') from their residents. All permitted sterling payments to United States or Swiss residents had henceforth to be credited to Registered Accounts, and from these Accounts the Americans and Swiss could pay anything due by them in the Sterling Area. Old sterling could still be used for anything except purchase of Sterling Area goods, but further amounts would not accrue to such accounts, and they would not be convertible into gold or dollars or Swiss francs through the Control.

The Registered Account was therefore substantially the same as the Special Account, except in one important respect: a balance in a Registered Account was fully convertible at the official rate, whereas balances on Special Accounts were only partially convertible, the exact arrangements being part of the payments agreement negotiated with the country concerned. The Registered Account was, on the other hand, precisely the same as the Special Account in that the sterling balances in these accounts were not, as sterling, transferable to the residents of any third countries. International transactions in sterling had, as far as the Registered and Special Account systems extended, become strictly bilateral.[1]

These various arrangements necessitated a series of new Orders, made in June and July 1940. These, besides much redrafting and clarification of earlier Regulations, prohibited:

(a) the crediting of sterling to the free ('old sterling') accounts of residents in the United States or Switzerland; or of countries with which Special Account agreements had been made;

(b) the crediting of sterling by non-residents in the Sterling Area to the accounts of residents in Canada, Newfoundland and the French, Belgian and Dutch possessions.[2]

Treasury Orders had also been made providing that exports to the United States, Switzerland and Sweden might be paid for only in their respective currencies or Registered or Special Account sterling; and that exports to other Special Account countries

---

[1] An early and tentative request that one country's sterling balance might be transferred to a third country was cold-shouldered, and it was not until a much later stage that the idea of transferable sterling was taken up. (See below, Chapter XIV, esp. pp. 457-8.)

[2] There were exceptions to both (a) and (b) in favour of pre-Order exchange contracts and of transfers between the free accounts of residents in the same country.

might be paid for only in Special Account sterling of the country concerned.[1]

The publication of the new Orders in July 1940 was greeted by *The Economist*,[2] which had continually complained of the looseness of the exchange control, as 'the arrival in this country and the Sterling Area as a whole of really effective control of the exchange market. There may still be minor adjustments to the new system of clearing agreements, and other countries may be brought within their scope. But the essential outlines of the system are now finally drawn'. The strict bilateralism imposed would, *The Economist* continued, seem to 'involve the temporary dethronement of sterling from its position as an international currency', though this might not be the end of the matter: 'it bears within itself the seeds of a multilateral clearing system which will fit well into our present system of international trade'. The event was to prove this too rosy a view: fifteen years later, after ten years of peace, 'the seeds of a multilateral clearing system' have not yet emerged from their chequered germination. On the more immediate administrative problems, too, *The Economist* was underestimating the agenda: Treasury and Bank of England officials had before them unending negotiation of further payments agreements and re-negotiation of those already in force. But the opening comment, that 'the essential outlines of the system'—a system of strict bilateralism—were now finally drawn, has stood the test of time. In the summer of 1940

---

[1] S.R. & O. (1940) No. 892 of 7th June 1940 provided for (i) an amended Regulation 5B applying to goods of any class and description (instead of to a limited list as in the Regulation of 7th March instituting doller-invoicing) and gave the Treasury power to prescribe not only the destination to which it was to apply but the manner of payment to be required; (ii) a new Regulation 3C prohibiting payments or transactions equivalent to payments to residents in any territory specified by Treasury Order. The old Regulation 3(1) (ab) provided for such a prohibition to apply to residents outside the Sterling Area, but with the qualification that transactions necessary for the reasonable requirements of trade and business carried on in the United Kingdom, existing contracts, and reasonable travelling or personal expenses should be exempt. Under the new Regulations it became possible to prohibit payments to residents in a specified territory even for these purposes and the Treasury was thus empowered to make conditions for all current payments to such territories. It was by administrative action that the actual detailed conditions governing payments to a Special (or a Registered) Account were laid down, by Bank of England Notices to Banks and Bankers; (iii) giving the Treasury power, failing agreement, to apply the Special Account system to any country unilaterally.

S.R. & O. (1940) No. 1254 of 17th July 1940, redrafted and clarified the June amendments and earlier Regulations without any alteration in effect. The most significant change was the introduction of a new Regulation 3C which dropped the specific directions concerning payments to Special Accounts in the case of countries with which payments agreements had been concluded, but inserted in paragraph (1) a general restriction upon sterling payments in favour of persons resident outside the Sterling Area, subject to exemptions granted by Treasury Order. The Regulations had needed clarifying and simplifying to avoid, as one person put it, 'such inconveniences as the making of an Order excepting a particular class of transactions from an exemption from the restriction imposed by a Regulation as modified by the amendment'.

[2] 20th July 1940, Notes 'Exchange Control at Last' and 'The Problem of Bilateralism'. The absence of any Parliamentary discussion may well be accounted for by the extremity of the country's military situation.

the view that sterling must remain a free currency was finally put aside as a peace-time luxury, and the control at last became strict enough to prevent any appreciable leakage of the proceeds of exports. From this point onwards Treasury and Bank of England officials ceased to argue about the kind of exchange control that was appropriate, and concentrated their efforts in the long struggle to make the most of what bargaining power was left to them by the compelling needs of the Supply Departments.

CHAPTER IX
THE GENESIS OF THE STERLING BALANCES:
INDIA AND THE MIDDLE EAST

(i)
Financial Relations with India

WITHIN the Sterling Area proper, the finance of supplies from India created the problems that were the most complex from political points of view as well as the largest in terms of figures. India being a pure Sterling Area country, the mechanism for financing trade between India and the United Kingdom was completely automatic: all transactions were in sterling, and the monetary authorities of India had contemplated no limit to their holdings of sterling. In the past there had been periods when India's sterling balances were in danger of exhaustion, but they had always been saved in the last resort by Indian borrowing in London. Circumstances of the war created the opposite position: a chronic excess of payments by the United Kingdom for supplies and services caused India's sterling balances to accumulate throughout the war period, and indeed to accumulate with a rapidity that became alarming.

The rate at which India's sterling balances rose depended mainly upon three factors. The first of these, the Allied expenditure on defence and war supplies, consisted at first of an agreed United Kingdom share of defence expenditure incurred in India, but later there was also large American expenditure.[1] The second factor was the rapidity of the Indian inflation which, in so far as it involved rising Indian export prices and rising costs of military supplies, swelled India's sterling receipts. Thirdly there was the turn of the real trade balance in favour of India, especially as United Kingdom export capacity declined. An important factor on the other side of the account was the repatriation of India's sterling debt.

The sharing of defence expenditure between India and the United Kingdom had been the subject of special arrangement in

---

[1] Allied expenditure included several strange items, such as rupee expenditure in Iraq and Iran, and a rupee loan to China, which came to an important total.

the summer of 1939, following acceptance of the Chatfield Modernisation Programme for the strengthening of India's defences.[1] Under this plan the United Kingdom was to shoulder the initial capital expenditure, and was to increase its former annual contribution ('the Garran contribution') so as to enable India herself to bear the increased maintenance expenditure resulting from the Chatfield Modernisation Programme. Immediately after the outbreak of war—a war not yet on India's doorstep—this financial plan was reviewed, and a new settlement was accepted in an exchange of letters between the Chancellor of the Exchequer and the Secretary of State for India in February 1940.[2] The effect of this second settlement—which held for the remainder of the war—was that the United Kingdom defrayed:

(1) the cost of the Chatfield measures for the reorganisation of the Indian Army;

(2) the war-time increase (due to rising prices, rates of pay etc.) of such external defence troops as were in existence pre-war but were subsequently sent abroad;[3]

(3) the whole of the cost of forces additional to Indian peacetime establishment which India raised in war-time for services abroad, after they were actually sent abroad;

and (4) the cost of military stores supplied by India for all British Forces in the Middle East.

This, like various other arrangements within the Commonwealth, meant that British war expenditure was by no means confined to equipping the combatant strength of the United Kingdom alone. Nevertheless, India was bearing a large and increasing burden. Item (3), for example, left India to pay for enormous numbers— eventually between two and three millions—of soldiers while they were being trained and awaiting transfer overseas. India also supplied considerable stores—small arms and clothing among them—for these troops. In spite of this heavy burden on India itself, the financial settlement provided for the United Kingdom to spend substantial amounts even in the fleeting rearmament period, and as the war progressed, the United Kingdom share ran into hundreds of millions a year.[4]

Two critical developments of the war caused the sums to mount at a pace quite unthought of when these terms were settled. First

---

[1] On 'the Chatfield Measures', see H. Duncan Hall and C. C. Wrigley, *Studies of Overseas Supply* in this series (H.M.S.O. 1956), Chapter IX.

[2] The second settlement was announced in Parliament, 29th February 1940 (H. of C. Deb., Vol. 357, Cols. 2255–6).

[3] India did in 1940 make a once-for-all payment towards these 'extra costs'.

[4] On the importance of India as a source of military supplies throughout the war, see *Studies of Overseas Supply, op. cit.*, Chapter IX.

there was the decision, in 1940, to make India an arsenal for the Near and Middle Eastern Command. Second, there was the entry of Japan into the war and the rapid spread of her Forces towards India. The effect on the expenditure figures was that at first India's defence expenditure merely doubled, while the United Kingdom contribution shot up from the £40 millions of 1939 to £145 millions in 1941–42. As the number of troops kept and largely equipped in India mounted, however, India's contribution rose more rapidly, so that in 1941–42 the shares were £230 millions paid by the United Kingdom and £200 millions by India, and in the next two years India's share at £297 millions and £343 millions actually exceeded the United Kingdom share at £283 millions and £330 millions. Opinions in United Kingdom Government circles were undoubtedly coloured, for the whole of the war, by the earlier phase when the United Kingdom had been financing two-thirds of the total cost.

Opinion on the whole question of the sterling balances was also affected by the prevalent belief that defence and other United Kingdom expenditure in India was inadequately controlled, and that Indian prices were exorbitant.[1] Eventually these suspicions led to two thorough enquiries from the British side—by the Select Committee on National Expenditure[2], and by an official Committee appointed by the Ministerial Committee on Indian Financial Questions. Both committees explained in their reports how all the defence expenditure was subject to the normal tight control by finance officers of the Government of India, and to enquiry by the Public Accounts Committee of the Indian legislature. The official Committee made particular enquiry into the adequacy of measures that had been taken to strengthen finance and costing staffs as the total of expenditure grew, and it went to some trouble to compare the cost of certain stores in India and in Britain. Its conclusion was that 'the evidence available does not, in our view, sustain a general conclusion that His Majesty's Government has not had value for money'. The Select Committee reviewed the same field, and considered also the prices paid by United Kingdom Departments for food and raw materials. These prices were in general subject to some measure of control by the Government

---

[1] This argument was, for example, used by Keynes in representing the United Kingdom's case to the United States Treasury : 'If Treasury control over expenditure had continued, unquestionably many economies would have been made. But these economies would not have been possible without setting up a machinery of control which would have impeded the prosecution of the war. . . . The principles of good housekeeping do not apply when you are fighting for your lives over three continents far from home. We threw good housekeeping to the winds. . . .' Keynes's impressive phrases no doubt had some justification in relation to field operations, especially in the Middle East, but they bear no relation to the facts of purchases of military stores etc., by the Government of India for joint United Kingdom Indian account.

[2] Fourth Report of the Session 1944-45: *British Expenditure in India.*

of India, though they were not held down as tightly as were the prices of direct defence materials. In the latter field, the Committee noted particularly the prices negotiated for steel, a very large item in the total expenditure. In 1944 the Government was getting steel for defence contracts at only 27 per cent. above pre-war rates.[1] Their broad conclusion was that 'taking all the circumstances into consideration, fair prices have on the whole been secured for war stores and for food bought by this country'.[2]

It will be remarked that this judgment leaves exported raw materials unmentioned; it also takes 'all the circumstances into consideration'. These circumstances included the progress of inflation in India, which substantially affected the value put on India's exports of raw materials, and also pulled upwards the cost of military stores, although the Government of India did everything possible to put on the brake.[3]

As compared with inflation in the Middle East, inflation in India was a comparatively mild disease, but it was more marked than in the United Kingdom.[4] The administrative difficulties of control were infinitely greater in India than in the United Kingdom, although only at one stage did the situation threaten to get out of hand. The official index of wholesale prices (all commodities) rose by only about 20 per cent. in the first two years of war,[5] but in the third and fourth years soared to 245 (August 1939 = 100). This index, covering a wide range of commodities over a continental area, concealed in its averaging relatively low prices for the price-controlled military supplies, but at the other extreme there were many important price rises far steeper than the index suggests. This was notably the case in the summer of 1943, when the Bengal famine gave a sharp twist to the price spiral and the cost of supplies frequently reached five or six times the pre-war level.[6] The note circulation increased by over 300 per cent. in the same period.

---

[1] Report of Select Committee, paragraph 43. cf. W. S. Churchill, *The Second World War*, Vol. IV, p. 181: 'Contracts were fixed in India at extravagant rates. . . . Without sufficient scrutiny or account we were being charged nearly a million pounds a day for defending India from the miseries of invasion . . . .'

[2] Report, paragraph 47.

[3] H. Duncan Hall and C. C. Wrigley (*op cit.*, p. 490) suggest that the real extravagance may have been in the plan of creating ' large and costly new capacity' instead of concentrating on 'small-scale improvement and reorganisation of existing facilities.'

[4] The index of Indian export prices overtook that of United Kingdom export prices only in 1943, and even then the difference was not great. There are, however, pitfalls in the use of these indices when the composition of trade is disturbed, and the precise figures bear little weight.

[5] As lately as November 1940 Keynes described the Indian situation as showing 'not the slightest sign of inflation'.

[6] In this phase the authorities found it almost impossible to draw to the market the 'surpluses' of 55 million cultivators. These, having no customary outlets for purchasing power, ate up their surplus produce whilst the towns starved. cf. Famine Enquiry Commission, *Report on Bengal*, and C. B. A. Behrens: *Merchant Shipping and the Demands of War* (in this series, H.M.S.O. 1955) Chapter XVI.

This inflationary situation developed all the usual unsettling features—queues, strikes, speculation, commodity hoarding etc.— and a serious risk of civil disorder.[1] It therefore became, in its own right, a subject of concern in the War Cabinet at home; though not now concerned with all these wider aspects, we must note the inflation as one of the factors which, despite all the efforts at control, did drag upward the cost of military supplies and so was partly responsible for the rapid rise in the sterling balances.[2] Inflation helped, too, to breed economic and political friction in the atmosphere in which Anglo-Indian financial problems had to be discussed.

The third factor fostering the growth of the sterling balances was the difficulty India was experiencing in drawing supplies from the outside world. This was to some extent a general difficulty, resulting from the shipping stringency, the closure of enemy sources of supply, and so on.[3] But after the summer of 1940, this general tendency was aggravated by the absorption of British industrial capacity in direct war production, to the virtual exclusion of export trade except along a few very special lines. United Kingdom exports to India fell from £34 millions in 1938 to £18 millions in 1943. As compared with the rise in military expenditure, this looks a small item, but when allowance is made for the rise in India's national income, the deprivation over the war period as a whole was substantial. This deprivation had its counterpart in the accumulation of India's post-war purchasing power. In India as elsewhere the United Kingdom was, by reducing its current shipments of goods, financing its overseas supplies to a greater and greater extent by piling up post-war claims against herself. Post-war exports would have to pay not only for post-war imports and for war-time military expenditure, but also for a large part of the more normal imports of the war years.

By one important series of operations the United Kingdom Treasury and the Government of India were able to moderate the rise of the sterling balances, at the expense of reducing the United Kingdom's future invisible income. The repatriation of India's sterling debt, carried through in 1941, 1942 and early 1943 was, as *The Economist* remarked,[4] an 'extraordinary transformation' of India from a

---

[1] For the effect of inflation on war production, see *Studies of Overseas Supply, op. cit.,* pp. 472-5.

[2] Equally, in the post-war period the rise in United Kingdom prices has eased the real burden on the United Kingdom of these sterling balances.

[3] On the shortage of shipping to India—particularly the repercussions of the shipping requirements of the North African campaign—see *Merchant Shipping and the Demand of War, op. cit.,* Chapter XVI.

[4] Article, 'India's War Gains', 6th March 1943, pp. 302-3.

debtor to a creditor country. Before the war India had a sterling debt amounting to about £360 millions, including railway stocks and annuities. By using some of her sterling balances to buy these securities, India could extinguish her contractual liabilities to United Kingdom bondholders and annuitants—a course attractive to Indian nationalist opinion, and calculated to defer demands for converting the sterling balances into gold.

During the summer and early autumn of 1940 the Government of India was effecting this repatriation by making purchases in the ordinary way on the London Stock Exchange,[1] but after the Battle of Britain the sellers' market in securities disappeared, and it proved impossible to tempt further substantial holdings on to the market without forcing prices up unduly. Unless extraordinary measures were to be employed, the only alternative was for the Government of India to exercise its right to call the £72 millions of 3½ per cent. bonds at one year's notice. This issue was however at a substantial discount, and Indian opinion might well have complained at paying 100 for paper whose market price had only just risen to 97. So at the beginning of 1941 the Government of India sought the co-operation of the United Kingdom Government in a twofold operation involving the exercise of Treasury emergency powers.

In August 1939 the Treasury had taken power[2] to requisition from British residents any securities 'likely to be marketable outside the United Kingdom', for the purpose of strengthening the financial position. This power had been exercised during 1940 in the vesting of United States and Canadian securities, in order to provide dollars. In January 1941 India asked the Treasury to requisition from the 36,000 holders some £60 millions of sterling bonds; the U.K. Treasury paying the holders at current market prices and then reselling the bonds to the Reserve Bank. In effect, £60 millions of India's sterling balances would be distributed among the 36,000 United Kingdom residents, who would surrender their contractual rights to interest and capital repayment over the years. The operation clearly suited both parties—the U.K. Treasury and the Government of India—and it was speedily carried out.[3] Whether it suited also the 36,000 investors was another matter, on which the financial press had something to say.[4] There was much talk of 'breach of contract'

---

[1] Some £17 millions were involved.

[2] S.R. & O. (1939) No. 950, of 25th August 1939.

[3] The vesting Orders were S.R. & O. (1941) Nos. 141 and 142.

[4] *The Daily Telegraph* (17th February 1941) was slightly critical, the *Stock Exchange Gazette* (22nd February 1941) and *The Financial News* (24th October 1941) more sharply so.

S

and of repercussions on the investor's faith in the word of the British Government. There was little point in such argument at this stage. The borrower (India) had not broken faith; it was the United Kingdom Treasury that, for financing war needs, had exercised the compulsory powers assumed without complaint at the outbreak of war. The powers had previously been exercised in relation to United States and Canadian securities, when the urgency of dollar needs had been accepted as a sufficient reason for expropriating holders of those securities. The difference between the Treasury's dollar needs and the rupee requirements was not such as to justify special favours to holders of Indian bonds.

When, a year later, the second vesting operation was undertaken, some care was taken to avert repetition of these grumblings, and the operation in the event went off quietly enough.[1] It included about £8½ millions of a 2½ per cent. loan and £64 millions of 3 per cents. At the same time the Government of India gave notice of repayment of the 3½ per cent. bonds referred to above. These were now almost at par, so that one of the earlier objections had disappeared; there was also the advantage that compulsory acquisition of other Indian stocks would be more palatable to British investors now that India was doing all she could in redeeming a callable stock. The only remarkable feature of this second episode is that the U.K. Treasury hesitated about it, as it had over the earlier operation, on the ground that India ought to hold large balances of sterling free, against a post-war reversal of the situation. In the light of later development it is almost incredible that the Treasury was still afraid that India might finish the war with insufficient sterling.[2]

Further operations in 1942 and early 1943, when fears about the post-war balances had been completely reversed, covered certain railway stocks and annuities, bringing the total of vested securities above £185 millions. Meanwhile the Indian authorities had been quietly taking opportunities to make small purchases in the market, and these added over £31 millions to the £17 millions purchased in 1940. With the £72 millions of 3½ per cents. redeemed in accordance with contract, the total amount of debt repatriated was well over £300 millions.[3]

---

[1] S.R. & O. (1941) Nos. 2072 and 2073. For comment see *The Economist*, 3rd January 1942.

[2] There were exceptions to this view. The Bank of England in October 1939 envisaged the probability that India would accumulate large sterling balances, and proposed 'to consider positive action to keep these balances within manageable limits'.

[3] In his 1944 budget speech in the Indian Legislature, Sir Jeremy Raisman mentioned a total of £350 millions. This included, besides the items mentioned above, certain other purchases of railway securities, and a payment of 'Chatfield debt.'

In spite of these huge operations the sterling balances soared. From a pre-war figure of about £40 millions, they rose through the rest of the war as follows:

Mid–1942	£295 millions
End–1942	£441 "
End–1943	£709 "
End–1944	£1,006 "
Mid–1945	£1,138 "
End–1945	£1,321 "

From the immediate point of view of finding some means of payment for war supplies, it was convenient enough for Britain that the automatic mechanism of the Sterling Area provided for these enormous amounts. Certainly this was in attractive contrast to the insistence of most other countries—including the United States before lend-lease—upon partial or complete payment in harder money than sterling.[1] But war-time financial policy has to look to post-war days, and the accumulation of India's sterling balances was an accumulation of rights to draw on Britain's real resources after the war. War-time sterling balances implied, that is to say, 'unrequited' exports in post-war years.[2] While the figures mounted, preliminary prospecting of Britain's post-war balance of payments was revealing the threat of those chronic difficulties that have since become all too real. Earlier suggestions that Britain should rejoice in the growth of India's post-war buying power now gave way to fears that post-war demands on Britain's export capacity would be excessive. The growth of India's sterling balances was henceforth to be a subject of increasing concern not only among officials but in the War Cabinet itself.

This thought of the post-war trading position of the United Kingdom, though perhaps the most insistent thought underlying all discussions of the Indian payments problem, was by no means the only consideration. The spectacle of rising claims in London was not one that Indian political opinion found attractive. At best it was a sign and measure of the real burden, in resources and manpower, borne by a poor country in a war that an important section of Indian opinion did not unreservedly support. At worst it was a debt that Britain might in part repudiate when she found her post-war difficulties unmanageable. The swelling sterling balances therefore became an irritant in Anglo-Indian relations, at a time when irritants were unusually dangerous.

---

[1] Representatives of the Government of India were able to point out, with justice, that the United Kingdom was not enjoying the same facility of supply from any other major country, whether outside or inside the Commonwealth.

[2] cf. *The Economist*, 6th March 1943: 'The counterpart to the locomotives and machine tools exported to India after the war will not be a current import of tea and jute: it will be the sterling handed over to the Indian Government during the war years. . . .'

This irritation of Indian opinion had of course a bearing on the Indian supply situation, and there were times when the British authorities in India advised that Indian efforts to expand the flow of war supplies would not indefinitely respond to a reward in I.O.U's. There were, too, some specific demands for reduction of the sterling balances: in 1942 the demand for gold for India, and reduction of the sterling balances, became a political cry causing anxiety for the Government of India.

The whole question was continually under discussion, year after year, and many remedies were suggested at one time or another. At first the tendency was to regard the problem from a rather narrow budgetary point of view, and to ask the Government of India to take a bigger share of the actual expenditure. The desire to avoid a post-war structure of inter-Allied indebtedness— 'the principle of no war debts between United Nations'—was another early influence, though it was neither fully discussed nor its implications fully appreciated.[1] As time went on and inflation became a serious source of strain within India, more thought was given to remedies that would moderate the inflationary tendencies. But through every phase after 1942 the underlying thought was the need to avoid unmanageably large sterling balances after the war.

The first remedy explored was a revision of the 'Financial Settlement' governing the sharing of defence expenditure between the two Governments. In 1940 and 1941 there were attempts on the Departmental level to get India to make a larger contribution. These discussions never looked promising: the most that India would concede was a trifling addition to the particular items of expenditure within India, amounting to less than a million pounds a year. As the figures shot upward, the Treasury became impatient with this tinkering, and early in 1942 discussions moved on to a higher plane, preparatory to Ministerial action.[2] The entry of Japan into the war and her rapid advance towards India was obviously going to enlarge further the joint burden, and might also be supposed—at least from London's viewpoint—to have so altered the political angles as to make India more willing to bear an altogether more substantial share. That the burden falling on India was in fact going to become very heavy indeed was not always appreciated in London, and it was thought right that the 1940 financial settlement should be so revised as to shift a weightier share on to India's budget. There were two possible approaches to this—to find a sufficient amount of special claims where there

---

[1] cf. pp. 19-21 above and p. 272 below.

[2] Both the Chancellor's war-time advisers, Lord Keynes and Lord Catto, had special authority in discussion of Indian financial questions, and both took a prominent part in advising Ministers on this matter throughout the remainder of the war.

were exceptional reasons for asking India to shoulder the burden, or to apply some rule of rough justice such as equal division of the total.[1] A third course, an explanation to India that the present allocation was to be regarded as provisional and subject to eventual adjustment in the light of the whole position at the end of the war, was rejected as going too far and too fast; and the use of language having implications of this kind, suggested by the Prime Minister himself, was avoided. It was desperately necessary to avoid giving any handle, in India or elsewhere, to those who alleged that we meant after the war to repudiate our obligations.

Official advice from India threw cold water on any suggestion of a general re-opening of the settlement. The reasons that seemed so convincing in London cut no ice in India. India was a poor country, already bearing a heavy load;[2] any open discussion in Indian Governmental circles would lead to a hardening of opinion against the British, and the co-operation of Indian industralists and business men, on which war production depended, would be forfeited.[3] The Government of India advised privately that on specific items it might be possible to add to India's contribution about £27 millions a year, plus a non-recurrent amount of £29 millions, but that this adjustment would involve abandonment by the United Kingdom of the major claim for revision of the whole basis of the financial settlement. The Treasury was reluctant to grasp the one bird at the price of forever abjuring the hypothetical birds that remained in the bush, and eventually in October 1942 the United Kingdom Government briefly informed the Viceroy that the question was dropped for the time being, the Chancellor retaining the right to raise it again on some future occasion.[4]

---

[1] At this date India's share was already about 40 per cent.; without any ensuing revision of the financial settlement, the Indian share eventually came to exceed that of the United Kingdom.

[2] It was not always perceived that the war-time real burden on India was unaffected by the extent to which a post-war claim was registered against the United Kingdom. This current real burden included not only direct war production, but also the internal adjustment (as in the gigantic growth in cloth production: *Civil Industry and Trade*, *op. cit.*, pp. 188 and 201) to the disturbance of international trade. Not all the current burdens attracted postponed compensation: the growth in India's absolute share of defence expenditure was an immediate real burden on India, without any prospective post-war compensation.

[3] British officials in India, advising London, were in the position of trustees, and the co-operation they received from Indian Ministers depended considerably upon their rejection of anything that might be represented as exploitation of India. British officials and Indian Ministers were watched with suspicion by important sections of Indian opinion, and a false step on this issue might easily have made the position of co-operating Indians impossible. These circumstances have not always been taken into account in London comment. (For comparatively mild comment, see *The Economist* 6th March 1943, p. 302; for quite unfair comment, see W. S. Churchill, *op. cit.*, Vol. IV, p. 181).

[4] The decision probably cost Britain a hundred millions in post-war sterling debt.

Secondly there were suggestions that at least the apparent growth in the sterling balances should be moderated by the segregation of part of the accruing balances for certain capital purposes. One such purpose was the funding of the Government of India's liabilities for pensions to United Kingdom residents. Army pensions had been mentioned in the discussions of possible redistribution of defence expenditure, and the idea was, in the more general discussions, extended to cover pensions to United Kingdom residents in general. In return for an appropriate capital sum paid by the Government of India to the United Kingdom Treasury (reducing the sterling balances), the Treasury would agree to make available over a long period of years sterling amounts estimated as covering the Government of India's sterling pensionary outgoings. Through the greater part of 1943, the proposal was under discussion in more or less precise terms. One precise form was that in return for about £150 millions, the United Kingdom Exchequer should pay an annuity of £6 millions for 25 years, gradually diminishing thereafter till it vanished after 75 years.[1] It was thus a funding, not a reduction of indebtedness; nor was there any transfer of liability for expenditure. So limited an attack on the sterling balances could hardly excite much enthusiasm, but it had some attractions—a funded debt always is in a sense less burdensome than a floating debt, and the United Kingdom Government would have felt free from the contingent moral liability to assure the pensions of personnel recruited by the Secretary of State in London. On the other hand, terms such as those under discussion might seriously prejudice the rate of interest question in further adjustments of sterling indebtedness. The 3 per cent. basis, taken as reflecting current Treasury borrowing terms for the 'weighted average period' of the annuities, was quite inconsistent with the ideas of post-war settlement that Lord Keynes, under the inspiration of Rooseveltian and Churchillian largeness, was now propagating in Treasury circles. After the Ministerial discussions on the general question of a settlement with India, these objections and doubts prevailed, and the idea of any immediate funding of the pensions was dropped.[2]

Another funding plan was that for a segregation of part of the balances as a 'Reconstruction Fund', to be drawn upon in regular amounts over the post-war years, for the purpose of financing imports of capital goods and equipment. This plan originated in the India Office early in 1942; there was correspondence

---

[1] The scheme was described in general terms in Sir Jeremy Raisman's budget speech, 1943-44, paragraph 48.

[2] When the operation was eventually performed, after the war, the terms were less favourable to the United Kingdom.

with the Government of India in the summer, and by the end of the year, there was sufficient support for it to become a serious item in Treasury discussions for an Anglo-Indian settlement. At this stage it was suggested that this Reconstruction Fund might amount to £200 millions, drawn at a rate not exceeding £20 millions per annum. According to authoritative private advice from India, the Indian business world was 'very keen on this', though the Indians might insist on awkward conditions.[1] Those who were hesitant about the post-war usefulness of sterling balances might yet put their trust completely in a specially-labelled fund of sterling, about which specific commitments had been made. But here again, as with the pensions funding proposals, attraction for the United Kingdom depended upon what was settled about the rate of interest, and whether a Reconstruction Fund could be used as a counter in a much wider settlement. As 1943 went on, the Chancellor's advisers increasingly insisted that no rate of interest would be appropriate to funded war debts, but this was not practical politics in India. After the War Cabinet had abandoned the idea of an immediate general settlement on India's balances, this Reconstruction Fund proposal, like the pensions proposal, was dropped. Had it materialised on the scale suggested in these 1942–43 discussions, the Reconstruction Fund might conceivably have operated to restrict India's post-war demands, as compared with those the United Kingdom actually had to meet in the early post-war years.

Although it did not prove possible to agree on the establishment of a large fund of segregated sterling on these lines, the idea had bitten deeply into Indian ambitions, and when, late in 1943, India was asked to extend reciprocal aid to raw materials and food,[2] the idea of a Reconstruction Fund was at once revived. Reciprocal aid meant for India rupee expenditure uncompensated by further accrual of sterling balances, since the displaced dollar receipts would have been sold by India to the central pool in London, in exchange for sterling credited by the Bank of England to the Reserve Bank. Equally it meant for the Sterling Area dollar pool some sacrifice of accrual of dollars. In the interest of harmonious relations with the United States on lend-lease questions, the United Kingdom, which was already providing reciprocal aid on her own account, pressed other parts of the Commonwealth to make parallel arrangements. There was no logical connection linking a measure of this kind, the direct effect of which was to reduce the Sterling Area's dollar reserves, with the earmarking of dollars for India;

---

[1] The project was referred to in some detail in Sir Jeremy Raisman's budget speech, 1943-44, paragraph 49.

[2] India was already providing certain military supplies under reciprocal aid.

but this was what India proposed, and she proposed it as a help in reconciling Indian opinion to the real burden of providing reciprocal aid. The proposal was not now that some of India's sterling balances should be earmarked for special convertibility privileges after the war, but that India should actually receive and herself hold dollars, to an amount related in some way to India's continuing dollar earnings (i.e. the proceeds of her exports to the United States and her services to Americans in India, in so far as these remained outside reciprocal aid).

This proposal was strongly opposed by the Bank of England, which rightly saw in it offence against a cardinal principle of the Sterling Area—namely, that the dollar reserves of the entire Area were pooled. Any exception to this principle 'would be the beginning of the end of the Sterling Area. If we once give way on this principle we see no grounds on which we shall be able to resist similar pressure from other members of the Area. . . .' This was not only a sound argument; it was one of the first importance. The end of the war was not even in sight, and disintegration of the Sterling Area would have been a major disaster to Britain during the war, quite apart from post-war considerations. Nevertheless, the political value of grasping India's somewhat unexpected willingness to play on reciprocal aid was deemed sufficient cause for taking the risk. The Treasury decided that the risk of the precedent was perhaps not as high as it looked at first sight: the political aspects could be explained to the Dominions, and firmness could be shown elsewhere. In short, a concession that could not have been contemplated in peace-time could be risked in time of war, and war-time relations with the United States and with India herself made the risk a justifiable one.

Eventually therefore the principle was conceded. On a formula which in fact allowed £20 millions in 1944 and the same in 1945, India was allowed a privileged position. The form of centralised dollar reserves was maintained: India continued to sell all her dollars to the Exchange Equalisation Account in London, receiving sterling balances at the Bank of England as before, but in the Exchange Equalisation Account the two sums of $20 millions were 'earmarked' for India. India received, that is to say, a guarantee of unhindered convertibility, for expenditure in the United States after the war, of sterling into dollars to the total of $40 millions. Having conceded the principle for 1944, the Treasury was not inclined to press arguments about the amount appropriate in 1945, but thereafter the earmarking ceased as reciprocal aid had ceased.[1]

---

[1] Again, there was no logical connection with reciprocal aid, but as the extension of reciprocal aid had been the occasion of the concession to India, its termination provided the appropriate occasion for getting rid of an arrangement which the British authorities could only afford to regard as a war-time measure.

In the event, India's dollar requirements after the war far exceeded this earmarked sum, and its existence made no difference to what India was allowed to draw from the pool. The Reconstruction Fund survived merely as a slightly irritating complication of the machinery, but it had served a political purpose of some importance back in 1943-44.

In addition to the Pensions and Reconstruction Fund proposals, in which the funding operation would attach repayment to specific post-war Indian requirements, there was one general funding proposal. This was late in 1943, when the idea of a redistribution of expenditure had just been abandoned. The suggestion was that the United Kingdom Treasury should issue in India 'a joint Anglo-Indian loan of a large amount'—perhaps £150 millions as a beginning. Both interest and eventual repayment would be either in rupees or in sterling, at the option of the holder. It was suggested that the currency option would be attractive to Indians who were sceptical about the future of sterling, and that this attraction should be enhanced by attaching a Government of India guarantee to the rupee liabilities. There would be some advantage in an operation of this kind for the Indian authorities. They were having considerable success in their absorption of purchasing power by successive issues of bonds, but always had room for further issues if fresh attractions could be offered to investors. But if it was to have these peculiar attractions, the operation would necessitate special legislation in the United Kingdom, and officials here were uncomfortable about parading an altogether novel dependence of British credit on the guarantee of the Government of India. There was not, in short, a sufficient balance of advantage to induce the United Kingdom to embark on a mere funding operation, and the proposal came to nothing.

In one way some part of India's sterling balances was becoming immobilised by that very progress of inflation which was so enlarging the balances. Under the statutes of the Reserve Bank of India[1], the increase of the circulation of notes necessitated a substantial proportionate increase in the sterling assets held by the Reserve Bank itself. The enlargement of the Reserve Bank's unused power to issue notes provided no relief for the United Kingdom, and, in the same way, a purely war-time increase in the required sterling reserves would still leave the burden of post-war realisation hanging over the United Kingdom's balance of payments. But in so far as the Indian note circulation was permanently enlarged by the surge of the Indian price-and-income structure, and in so far as sterling

[1] Reserve Bank of India Act, 1934, Section 33.

was required as legal reserve against this increased circulation, the United Kingdom's sterling debt to India was virtually funded on whatever basis might be settled with the Reserve Bank. In the early days, when inflation in India was slight and expectations of a post-war relapse of prices were still extreme, there was little trust in this quasi-automatic relief for the United Kingdom. When the extensions of the war and the intensification of India's effort altered the face of these things, officials came to realise that the amount of sterling balances permanently absorbed in this sentry-duty at the Reserve Bank might cover a substantial proportion of the total.

The reality of this relief depended, however, on the assumption that India would not modify her statutory requirements. This assumption was dangerously optimistic: though India would, as a member of the Sterling Area,[1] always need some sterling reserve, it would be idle to argue that this requirement had risen eightfold since pre-war days. Even if India were willing to hold such a swollen international reserve, she might insist on holding more of it in gold and less in sterling. In anticipation of such developments, attention was given to the possibility of freezing, in some way or other, a substantial part of the sterling reserve. As an inducement India might, it was suggested, be provided with some gold forthwith. A much larger sum would be tied up in Treasury Bills redeemable only after the gold had been used—an occasion which might be supposed to arise only if India were in dire straits, or after a period of several years. To make this 'tied' sterling reserve more palatable to Indian opinion, it might carry an exchange guarantee protecting its rupee (though not gold) value. Figures mentioned at first were £50 millions of gold and £100 millions of Treasury Bills. By the end of 1943 all the magnitudes in the problem had risen, and the United Kingdom Treasury was also, for reasons mentioned below, more willing to part with gold; the figures talked of at this stage were therefore much higher—£100 millions of gold and £250 millions of Treasury Bills.[2] Like other proposals, this was regarded as a possible item in a general settlement, and when the idea of such a settlement was dropped, this particular proposal was dropped with it.

The shrinkage of Britain's exports to India was, as we have seen,

---

[1] In addition to the 'earmarking' of dollars referred to above, there were some inconclusive discussions in 1943 about the possibility of India's retaining her dollar accruals, but this was apparently envisaged as only a war-time arrangement without prejudice to post-war re-establishment of the Sterling Area.

[2] Earlier it was proposed that the Treasury Bills should carry the current rate of interest on Treasury Bills in London, but during 1943 opinion against post-war interest payments hardened, and the fixed low rate of ½ per cent. was suggested.

a factor in the growth of the sterling balances, and it was natural enough for the Chancellor's advisers to urge that exports to India should be increased. After some early vicissitudes, however, the Treasury came to accept the almost complete diversion of resources from the export industries.[1] There were nevertheless some efforts to stimulate the movement of goods into India, goods for which India would pay in sterling, when these goods would have other important effects. In 1943 inflation became rapid in India, and even more so in the Middle East, and the Treasury was seriously considering whether there should be some diversion from war production to the production of consumer goods for export to these particular markets. No such drastic steps were taken, but these considerations did tend to check further squeezing of the export industries. There were also special efforts occasioned by special circumstances: notably there was the effort to avert famine by securing and (an important addition) shipping Australian wheat. These precious cargoes had the incidental but useful effect of absorbing some of India's sterling: they also checked inflation, both by absorbing purchasing power and by bringing speculators' hoards on to the markets. Most vital of all, they fed the starving Bengalees, whose dire state had become a special threat to the contribution an orderly India could make to the war effort.

Parallel in some ways to the relief that might be afforded by special exports of goods to India was the relief that might be expected from the shipment of gold for sale to private buyers in India. Gold, like goods, could be sold for abnormally high prices, and the sale would serve to absorb some of the inflated purchasing power. The sale price could be far above the official United Kingdom price, so that the post-war sterling balances might be reduced by say two pounds for every one pound of reduction in the United Kingdom's gold reserve. In the Middle East, the United Kingdom authorities agreed as early as December 1942, to sales of gold at market prices. India, however, was regarded as a more delicate case. The Bank of England feared that Indian taste for gold might be whetted by relatively small sales, and that the eventual demands in a market of 400 million people might well make unthinkable inroads into the central reserve of the Sterling Area.[2] The Bank was uncomfortable on other scores also: premium sales of gold were a tacit recognition of depreciation of sterling, and there might be (as indeed there were) embarrassments in our relations

---

[1] For export policy generally, see *Civil Industry and Trade, op. cit., passim.*

[2] The Bank was also sceptical of the possible advantages: they thought the sales would have 'as much effect on the Indian market as a pea-shooter would have on an elephant.' *The Economist* was supporting the Bank's fears as lately as 15th January 1944 (Business Note, 'The Gold Cure').

with the great gold-mining Dominion. The Reserve Bank of India had similar qualms, and on its advice the Government of India at first totally opposed the suggestion. The sharp inflationary turn of events in 1942–43, however, greatly strengthened the case for every anti-inflationary plan. The new situation had created new arguments for moderate sales. As gold was a normal store of wealth for the Indian peasant, the inflation had involved an extreme rise in the price of gold, a phenomenon that implied some threat to confidence in the paper currency. Sales that would moderate the rise could therefore be regarded as underpinning confidence in the rupee. Moreover, availability of gold for hoarding purposes should tend to lessen the hoarding of commodities; by bringing supplies of foodstuffs on the market, the gold sales would put a brake on the inflation of commodity prices.

These possible effects of gold sales were to some extent alternatives: to the extent that confidence in the currency was increased, the demand for gold hoards would be weakened. But whatever particular reactions the gold sales provoked, it did appear that the result would be desirable from the point of view both of the Government of India in keeping the situation in hand, and of the United Kingdom Treasury in keeping down the bill: always provided, of course, that India's demand was not whetted to the point of insatiability. There was also at this stage the important argument, on the United Kingdom side, that a reduction in the United Kingdom gold reserve, coupled with equal reduction in United Kingdom liabilities to India, would improve our bargaining position with the American authorities, who were inclined to ignore the growth of the sterling balances but to cut lend-lease whenever London's gold reserve grew.[1]

In June 1943, when the situation was becoming desperate, the Indian and United Kingdom authorities decided that the balance of advantage justified a trial for the plan, and they embarked upon sales at an initial rate of 750,000 ounces a quarter.[2] Selling began on 18th August 1943, and the price eased immediately. Apart from a flurry in October 1943, the general effect was to steady the market price of gold, at a level nearly double the official United Kingdom price.

Meanwhile the United States Government had decided to join in. While American supplies to India were in general on a lend-lease basis, only certain raw materials were supplied by India for the

---

[1] The case had been urged in some detail by Lord Keynes on 11th May 1943. At one stage the Americans appeared unwilling to let London's gold reserve rise above £250 millions; even in 1945 they were still regarding £500 millions as adequate. cf. Chapter XIII, Section (vi) and Chapter XV.

[2] The decision to sell gold covered also the Middle East: see below, pp. 280, et seq.

United States on a reciprocal aid basis.[1] For other Indian goods and services the United States paid cash, and as India enlarged her work as a supply base for the Far Eastern war, American cash disbursements in India were on a rising scale. To provide for their estimated continuing needs, the Americans decided that 250,000 ounces of gold a quarter should be sold for their account in addition to the 750,000 sold on United Kingdom account. In December the United Kingdom share was increased to 2,250,000 ounces a quarter, and from April 1944 there were also some sales on South African account.[2] In order to secure the widest distribution of gold among the mass of the people, small bars were made available in 1944, for sale in up-country centres. Prices were above £15 an ounce in the spring of 1944, but were later approximately stabilised a little lower. By the middle of 1944 proceeds on all accounts amounted to £67 millions.

Some £56 millions of this total was for United Kingdom account, and this implied an equal reduction of sterling balances. On the assumption that the post-war price of gold would be about £8. 8s. an ounce, the reduction in the United Kingdom's gold reserve necessary to secure this relief was less than £33 millions. If hypothetical American reactions are also allowed for, the loss of gold reserves was even smaller. Nevertheless, the policy was by this time being called in question. Concern over actual loss of gold continued to nag the Bank of England, and the approaching end of the war, with all that implied for Anglo-American financial relations, weakened the earlier argument that the cost to London's reserves would be compensated by easier lend-lease conditions. The Government of India, however, had now completely escaped from its original fears and was shocked at the suggestion that the gold sales should be suspended: it was 'the most substantial piece of assistance which His Majesty's Government have so far been able to give the Government of India in connection with their economic stabilisation policy'. The Government of India had made great efforts and feared that the co-operation of Indians, in its internal measures against inflation, would be jeopardised if this important help from Britain were withdrawn. For the moment this view was allowed to prevail, even to the extent of calling in Royal Air Force aid when shipping facilities for the gold fell short.

---

[1] The cost, however, of reciprocal aid provided by India was, under the Anglo-Indian financial settlement, largely met by the United Kingdom—that is, added to the sterling balances.

[2] The United Kingdom was obtaining newly-mined gold from South Africa at a price corresponding roughly to $4.03 to the pound sterling. Sales by the United Kingdom in India at nearly double this price naturally caused some embarrassment in discussions with South Africa. South Africa pressed participation in the 'profits' of sales in India, and the sales referred to above were the result of some concession to this viewpoint. cf. pp. 316-8 below.

The balance of argument was shifting, however, and in July 1944 the United Kingdom reasons for not selling gold prevailed over the Government of India's reasons for continuing sales.[1] The situation in India itself was changing—the cost of living had fallen a little—and the suspension of United Kingdom sales, involving reduction of total shipments by three-quarters, was not followed by any alarming developments. Already in the autumn of 1944 the Treasury was pressing its new view-point to the extent of asking the Americans also to suspend gold sales in India.[2] For some months the United Kingdom Treasury—perhaps to appease the Government of India—stood by while American rupee requirements were met by the sale of gold. As the 'Stage II' discussions took shape and the German war approached its end, however, the United Kingdom developed a strong preference for supplying the rupees required by the Americans, so fortifying London's gold reserve, although this procedure involved adding to the sterling balances as payment to India for the rupees. But in the end it was American over-estimate of rupee requirements that brought their gold sales in India to an abrupt stop in April 1945.

So ended, as far as India was concerned, an experiment that may be claimed as one of the most successful in war finance. It had kept down the sterling balances by £77 millions at the expense to the United Kingdom's gold reserve of £44 millions at most— perhaps a good deal less. Substantial evidence of its success lies in the conversion of the Government of India, at first sceptical, to the view that by these 'salutary means' the United Kingdom Government had secured 'the double benefit . . . . . . that the rise of sterling balances is restrained . . . . . while the check on inflationary tendencies keeps down, with similar results, the cost of materials and services provided by India'. It is true that when the gold sales began, the end of the Bengal famine was a powerful factor relieving the inflationary pressure. The internal financial measures taken by the Government of India were also beginning to bear fruit about the same time. It is thus impossible to ascribe to the gold sales the full credit for the substantial easing of the situation in the last two years of war, but they may well, coming at a time

---

[1] United Kingdom sales were not definitely stopped, but the authorities fixed a minimum price which effectively suspended sales as long as there was no new upsurge of commodity prices.

[2] It will be appreciated that the 'normal' way of financing United States expenditure in India was for the United States Treasury to buy sterling (an addition to London's gold reserves) and to pay that sterling to the Reserve Bank of India (an addition to India's sterling balances) in exchange for the required rupees. The short-circuit of acquiring rupees by sales of American gold to Indian peasants avoided addition to the sterling balances, but also avoided the counterpart addition to London's gold reserve. Through one phase of Anglo-American financial relations this counterpart was nugatory; but now it had become of great moment.

when other factors were favourable, have made just the difference between success and failure in a many-sided assault.[1]

This important success stood alone in the attempts to limit the growth of India's net claims on London. As we have seen in earlier paragraphs, all other specific measures for limiting the accrual of Britain's liabilities were one after another put off in the earlier years in favour of 'a general settlement' with India, and when in 1943 the general settlement came to be examined, nothing politically practicable was found. At Bretton Woods the problem was raised, but the inclination of United Kingdom advisers to leave it for Anglo-Indian discussion prevailed. A little later, the Chancellor told his colleagues that he thought it 'necessary to wait until there has been a more decisive turn in the Eastern War before approaching the Government of India. We shall then be speaking to India with the authority of a Power which is proving itself victorious in her defence, and we may expect that the Indian respect for success will recognise the significance of such a fact'. So from Bretton Woods onwards the problem haunted all the British experts—and Indians, too. In February 1945 a Treasury official advised the Chancellor: 'We have two external financial problems after V.E. Day: the deficit on current account for the first two or three years, which is urgent, and the disposal of the sterling balances'. This latter problem—essentially the Indian problem—thus passed out as an unsolved problem of war finance to become one of the major post-war problems of international finance.

To say that this problem was put back and put back is to confess a partial failure in financial policy. In total war, financial relations between Allies, like financial arrangements within a state, have primarily to ensure that no financial obstacle impedes the flow of war supplies. So far, Anglo-Indian financial relations were completely successful, perhaps even more so than those between Britain and any other of her Allies. But financial policy has to do more than this. It has to see to it that the final incidence of the real burden is more satisfactorily distributed between nations (as between individuals within a nation) than is the immediate burden. Sir Winston Churchill has recently written, in Volume IV of *The Second World War*[2] that 'No great portion of the world was so effectively protected from the horrors and perils of the World War as were the peoples of Hindustan. They were carried through the struggle on the shoulders of our small Island'. This scarcely squares with the facts. The immediate real burden of

---

[1] It is conceivable that if the commencement of gold sales, instead of chiming in with other favourable factors, had coincided with the dangerous conjuncture earlier in 1943, the early fears of the Bank of England and the Government of India would have been justified.

[2] p. 181.

British, as of Indian, expenditure within India fell exclusively upon India. No financial wizardry could protect the peoples of Hindustan from this burden. What finance could do was to reach forward into the post-war structure of claims so as to compensate part of the immediate real burden by post-war claims. In the context of Anglo-Indian financial relations, this means that India could be compensated in part by Britain's incurring post-war obligations in the shape of the sterling balances. Two students of the great contribution India made towards the Commonwealth's military supplies have concluded that 'For India, not very much less than for the conquered areas of Asia, the immediate impact of war was economically disastrous, though the sterling balances offered hopes for the future'.[1]

During the war, the thoughts of many turned to a principle that there should be no monetary debts between Allies after the war. This principle carries as its corollary the principle that the real burdens of war should finally rest just where they first fall. The latter principle is one which Britain has thought it unreasonable to accept in her discussions with the United States, and it is a principle that has been rejected in recent thinking about the distribution of the burdens of defence in the North Atlantic community. It is a principle that Britain could never have seriously pressed against India, even if the political circumstances of Anglo-Indian relations had permitted it. There could be no doubt that Britain must acknowledge some post-war claims as partial compensation of the real burden borne by India during the war. The question was, how much and on what terms?

During the war the Government of India was content to allow the answer to be determined by the 1940 financial settlement. Britain, on the other hand, constantly thought of re-opening this settlement in order to reduce her post-war liabilities. In the event she put off the awkward negotiations until after the war. But meanwhile in British circles there was no doubt that she was being altogether too generous to India. This was true of the Chancellor's advisers both official and temporary. It was true also of Press commentators, as typified by *The Economist's* remark in 1943[2] that 'it will surely go down in the Imperial record that Britain gave twice and gave quickly'. Above all it was true of the Prime Minister himself, whose second thoughts are no different. Indian opinion, on the other hand—and this is true of those who co-operated unreservedly in the war effort—believed that India was not merely pulling her weight, but was also paying her fair share of the ultimate bill. That this gap persisted between the views held in the most

---

[1] *Studies of Overseas Supply, op. cit.*, p. 493.
[2] 6th March, p. 303.

responsible quarters in the two countries is due to a combination of circumstances. Firstly, in the first two years the 1939 financial settlement as revised in 1940 did place the greater part of the financial burden on Britain and, although India's expenditure soon equalled and eventually overtook that of Britain, feelings excited by the earlier unbalance never caught up with the changed facts of the later years. Secondly, the very ease with which Britain could spend money in India—an invaluable facility—perhaps unconsciously fostered a suspicion that financial control was too slack, and the suspicion remained to rankle long after the contrary fact had been exposed by Parliamentary enquiry in Britain. Thirdly, when opinions in London were crystallising, the unfortunate coincidence of a monsoon failure and the loss of Burmese rice after the Japanese had overrun that country gave a sharp twist to Indian inflation, and produced the impression that the Indian authorities had let the situation get out of hand. In fact, the Indian budget had in 1942 undergone the same kind of transformation as the British budget underwent in 1941, and by adding fierce taxation to a successful borrowing programme, the Government of India had held inflation in check despite the heavy odds of 1942 and 1943.

These misunderstandings were never entirely removed, and while they lasted there was no real meeting-ground for British and Indian views. The British, always thinking in terms of a larger revision, let slip the opportunities there were for minor adjustment, and the 1940 financial agreement remained, until after the war, the last word on how the financial burden should be spread.

(ii)
The Middle East

The group of countries which became known as the Middle East— Egypt, the Sudan, Palestine, Transjordan, Syria and Lebanon, Saudi Arabia, Iraq and Persia—presented problems closely similar to those which characterised Anglo-Indian financial relations. All except Persia and Saudi Arabia were, for at least part of the war, in the Sterling Area;[1] Egypt and Palestine, where most was spent, were in the Area throughout. The large share borne by Britain in Allied military and political expenditure in these countries, coupled with the inability of Britain and other parts of the Sterling

---

[1] Iraq left the Sterling Area for a few months in 1941: on this and on Egypt and the Sudan, see p. 236. Syria and the Lebanon were effective units in the Sterling Area only from 1941 until 1944.

T

Area to enlarge their supplies to these countries, raised their sterling balances to heights threatening to Britain's post-war balance of payments. At the same time, this heavy expenditure and scarcity of imports caused rapid inflation, which further aggravated the post-war liabilities that Britain was piling against herself. Normal checks on the inflationary process could not, for one reason or another, be exercised even to the extent to which they were exercised in India. On the other hand, just as the Bengal famine gave the inflationary spiral a savage twist in 1943, so had inflation in the Middle East been sharply accentuated by the widespread failure of cereal crops in 1941. To cope with the problems thrown up by all these circumstances, the British made a notable contribution by their policy of selling gold at market prices about double those fixed in London and Washington. This experiment—an experiment in which, as we have seen, India shared—was generally acknowledged to have been successful in dampening inflation in the latter part of the war, and it certainly helped to keep the end-of-the-war level of the sterling balances significantly lower than it might have been. The political atmosphere in which these financial problems had to be tackled was rather different from that of India, where the British authorities enjoyed the open co-operation of important sections of the community. The peoples and Governments in the Middle East were largely not interested in the war. But important military campaigns were fought either actually within their territories or on their very doorsteps, and their peoples inevitably regarded the shortages and rising prices as being the responsibility of the British and other foreigners who were engaged in these campaigns. Whatever other views the British themselves may have held, it was essential throughout to remember that in the Middle East they were treating with sovereign peoples to whom material inducements would be more persuasive than any fine words.

Egypt was the country where the figures were biggest; it was also that in which the problems began to show in the earlier phases of the war. Although Italy did not enter the war until 10th June 1940, the strategic importance of the Suez Canal and the likelihood that Italy would eventually join Germany necessitated from the outset important provision for the defence of Egypt. There was already a peace-time British garrison, and steps were taken in the preparatory period to strengthen this force. Then in the autumn of 1939, when British military plans envisaged an army of fifty-five divisions, twelve divisions were on paper allocated to the Middle East; most of these were to be in Egypt itself. These plans were slow to materialise: by September 1940 only six of these twelve divisions had actually arrived. But thereafter the force was built up more quickly, and it was always an expensive one. By the end of 1941 the British forces[1] in Egypt were spending some £50 millions a year. In a country whose pre-war national income has been estimated at £200 millions a year,[2] this spending by the British forces represented a colossal extraction of real resources; it might be compared in peace-time terms with the disturbance that would be created if Britain suddenly doubled her expenditure on gross investment.

The market impact of this expenditure was not evenly diffused over the whole economy, but was concentrated largely in the towns and the relatively small regions where the British forces were stationed. Elsewhere the economic impact of the war could be—and sometimes was—in sharp contrast, and while British expenditure was already exercising an inflationary influence in Egypt, the British Government felt obliged to take special action to protect the mass of the peasantry from a threat of falling prices. This meant support of the cotton market, and this apparently contradictory action was accepted by the Treasury under pressure from the Foreign Office for reasons, we may say, of economic warfare. Egypt was a sovereign state and in 1939 she was (and she remained) non-belligerent. Our armed footing in the territory of such a country depended upon the existence of a friendly Government. In 1939 Egyptian Ministers were well disposed towards Britain, but British representatives advised that the continued power of these Ministers depended upon keeping the mass of the peasants reasonably satisfied. These peasants depended largely upon the cotton crop, and Germany and contiguous neutrals were normal destinations for an important proportion of this crop; these destinations we could and did strangle easily and therefore strangled fairly quickly.[3] At that stage Britain did not want on supply grounds to take more Egyptian cotton, but the political case was considered overriding and as early as 19th October 1939 the Foreign Under-Secretary announced that His Majesty's Government recognized the vital importance to Egypt of the

---

[1] These included not only the Army divisions but also Royal Air Force squadrons; and Alexandria was a major base for the Royal Navy.

[2] In Chapter 20 of his *Food and Inflation in the Middle East, 1940-45* (Stanford University Press ; Geoffrey Cumberlege, Oxford University Press), Mr. E. M. H. Lloyd has estimated, on the basis of estimates by Matmoud A. Anis published by the United Nations, that the proportion of military expenditure to the total amount of goods and services may have been about 20 per cent. in the three years 1941 to 1943 and between 8 and 12 per cent. in 1940, 1944 and 1945.

[3] One of the grievances of the Egyptians was that because we could, we did cut Egyptian shipments more than American shipments. Other primary producers equally could have made a claim on this basis; this was an element in some of the bulk purchases by the Ministries of Supply and Food. Egypt was able to press the case strongly simply because her territory was a uniquely important military base.

cotton crop, and was considering what action it could take to assist in the crop's orderly disposal.[1]

In the event the crop of 1939 passed off reasonably well. The published British support policy was given precision in an unpublished undertaking to make support purchases at the prices ruling on 15th November 1939.[2] But, thanks to market intervention by the Egyptian Government itself, the market stayed well above this level, and no actual support purchases were made.[3] Then came the entry of Italy into the war, implying further sharp curtailment of Egyptian cotton exports,[4] and implying also a sharpening desire on the part of Britain to keep Egypt sweet. Discussions already in progress were speeded up and their result was announced in August 1940.[5] The British Government established a Cotton Buying Commission, on which the Egyptian Government was represented, to purchase all 1940 cotton offered to it at fixed prices somewhat above those of November 1939. The United Kingdom would bear any net loss but would share equally with Egypt any net profit. There was not, at this stage, any Egyptian undertaking to limit production, though the desirability of this had been discussed on the British side.

The Times thought the price a good, perhaps a generous, one that had been received with 'relief' in Egypt.[6] *The Economist* reported that Egypt had 'been rescued from one of the worst crises in her history'.[7] The G.O.C., Egypt, is reported to have said that the agreement was worth at least three brigades to him.

This military valuation was often quoted in the following months, when the handling of the 1941 crop had to be considered. But by this time the inflationary developments were so evidently getting the upper hand that there could be no automatic repetition of the 1940 arrangements. Egypt must be told that we could not carry every baby indefinitely, that the fellah must be doing pretty well out of military expenditure in Egypt, and that the Egyptians should take serious steps to help themselves. Eventually the United Kingdom agreed to a joint Anglo-Egyptian Purchasing Commission to buy at the same prices as in the previous season,

---

[1] H. of C. Deb., Vol. 352, Col. 1082.

[2] Support purchases were to be limited to the amount Germany had been taking pre-war.

[3] There were some normal supply purchases made by the normal United Kingdom private buyers.

[4] An article in *The Times*, 29th July 1940, stated that the Egyptian farmers were facing ruin: 'The most serious problem with which Egypt is faced at the moment is not that of the war, but of how to dispose of the coming cotton crop together with 1,500,000 kantars left over from the last crop.'

[5] H. of C. Deb., Vol. 364, Cols. 216-7.

[6] 8th August 1940.

[7] 5th October 1940, 'The Anglo-Egyptian Cotton Deal'.

purchases to be limited to 8 million kantars against 9 million of the 1940 crop. Further restriction of acreage would in the 1942 season reduce production to 5 million kantars. An important change as compared with 1940 was that the Egyptian Government would pay half the total cost, though this was qualified both by temporary British help in finance and by unequal arrangements about the disposal of any profits. In later seasons the whole economic position was dominated by inflation and food scarcities, and the British authorities were able to avoid any further commitments for protecting the cotton producers from the burden of falling markets.

The transformation of the economic climate came in the early months of 1941. Before the end of 1940 the price indices had moved very little above their pre-war levels, the inflationary impact of military expenditure scarcely balancing the deflationary markets for Egypt's exports. But military expenditure had now gathered momentum,[1] imports of goods for civilian consumption had dwindled, and then in the spring of 1941 it became clear that the wheat crop was going to be disastrously short. As so often happens, it was dire shortage of food for the towns that set the inflation rocket off. The weather that had created this food shortage was common to the Middle East countries and, instead of trying to support a collapsing economy, the Allied authorities found themselves in Egypt, as everywhere else in the Middle East, trying to organise food supplies in conditions of rampant inflation.

The food difficulties, though in their extreme form created by the harvest failures of 1941,[2] were aggravated and hardened by the shortage of imports and plethora of money. Grain producers in the countryside found that money was easily earned, but of use neither for the purchase of imported consumer goods nor for loading themselves and their wives with the sovereigns and other gold ornaments which were their conventional stores of wealth. The alternative was to hoard their grain and feed more to livestock, so creating shortage for the towns, a shortage that became acute enough to have political implications when drought took a hand in 1941.

Military developments in the summer of 1941 and in 1942 served only to intensify the inflationary pressures. In June 1941 there were heavy bombardments of Alexandria, and the subsequent exodus of population affected production and disorganised the

---

[1] Military expenditure in Egypt in 1941 was £55 millions. During the first six months of 1942 it totalled £41 millions. For the Middle East as a whole, the figures were nearly double these.

[2] Cereal crops in the Middle East failed generally. In place of the normal export surplus there was a deficiency estimated at 800,000 tons, of which 500,000 tons were wheat.

distribution of consumption goods.[1] Allied military expenditure soared as the critical campaigns of 1942 were prepared. In the summer of 1941 General Catroux's campaign won Syria for the Allies—and served to feed the inflation there.[2] Immediately after that, Persia, sharing the same problems of food shortages and import-starvation, was brought into the fold—and subjected to the pressure of Allied military expenditure.

These developments, common to an area now immensely enlarged by military and political success, suited small sections of the populations admirably, and their Governments enjoyed unusual freedom from budget deficits and international payment difficulties. The food-producing peasants, too, could at least live comfortably off the land, even if the lack of consumer goods were irksome. But for the masses, especially in the towns and other trading centres, the prevailing conditions spelled misery and resentment.[3] These were the people who were being touched by the real burden of the war. They were also people who could be politically dangerous—and their countries straddled the springboards for southern offensives against Hitler's Europe and enclosed within their borders vital sources of oil.

These economic problems called, therefore, for action no less vital than the earlier anti-deflation action that had been worth three brigades to General Wavell. The common phenomena to be attacked were soaring prices, scarce food, import-starvation and floods of paper money. The paths of financial prudence seemed to point to action by the Governments of the countries themselves: would not higher taxes and mammoth bond issues absorb the excess purchasing power which was making everything worse and worse? There were times when Allied financial pundits tried to point this moral. Not surprisingly, ears charmed by the news of unwontedly full treasuries were deaf to such entreaties. Why should Ministers incur the odium of new taxes, or bother themselves with bond issues, to help belligerents? Why, again, should they try to control prices when they had been so relieved to see the prices of primary commodities rise?

In short, little was going to be done unless the Allies themselves undertook an economic offensive against the economic evils which

---

[1] *The Economist*, 8th November 1941.

[2] It was in Syria that the first signs of inflation had appeared. In the second half of that year Allied military expenditure totalled £7.3 millions. The inflationary trend is reflected in the increase in the note issue which rose as follows:

December, 1939	.	47.9	millions Syrian pounds		
December, 1940	.	81.0	,,	,,	,,
June, 1941	.	100.0	,,	,,	,,
December, 1941	.	105.6	,,	,,	,,

[3] cf. *The Economist*, 26th September 1942, 'Inflation in Egypt'.

their own activities had largely created. Anything that helped to close the balance of payments gap would help; steps that relieved particular shortages would obviously help most. For example, while Allied military expenditure had come to exceed the value of Egypt's exports, the quantity of imports into the Middle East countries had shrunk to one-fifth of its pre-war level.[1] There could be no slackening of military expenditure; could the value of those one million tons of imports be raised by raising their prices, or could the volume be increased?

The Chancellor's advisers, worrying over the rising sterling balances and seeking some brake upon Middle East inflation, often thought of the desirability of raising the prices charged. It was a case that had equity as well as economy on its side: why should we, paying fantastic prices for some of the supplies we bought in Egypt, sell our precious British exports to the Egyptians at prices little above 1939 levels? Against this strong case the Treasury always felt nagging doubts about the repercussions on the inflationary situation at home.[2] The sterling prices of British exports were low directly through measures of price control, indirectly through the substantial success of the anti-inflation policy in total. Sharp increases now in export prices, whether to all or only to certain destinations, would create awkward problems of price control, and might well suck resources towards export production and excite competitive bidding for labour and materials. When lend-lease supplies to the Middle East came into the picture, this reluctance to juggle with the price situation was reinforced by the rigid American rules against anything that could conceivably be represented as profiteering in lend-lease goods. So the idea never came to fruition, though the general question of the under-pricing of British exports was a factor in the decision in 1943 to remove much of the subsidy element from shipping freights. It was a question, too, which remained in Treasury minds to the end, and cropped up in many directions.

What the Middle East countries would themselves have liked most was of course an expansion in the volume of imports. They were well aware of the disadvantages of their inflationary conditions and regarded themselves as earning a claim to more imported goods, which they would have liked to exercise without delay. There were two insuperable difficulties in the way: the limits of foreign—particularly British—export capacity and—especially after the closure of the Mediterranean in 1940—of shipping capacity.

---

[1] One million tons in 1942 against five millions pre-war.

[2] cf. the statement of the United Kingdom Treasury representative at the Middle East Financial Conference (Cairo, April 1944) commenting on the excellent analysis by Professor Leduc, the French financial adviser to the Syrian and Lebanese *Interêts Communs*. (E. M. H. Lloyd, *op. cit.*, Chapter 21).

There could be no substantial alleviation in this direction: on the contrary, the shipping situation continued for some time to deteriorate. But as the import famine was affecting the food situation, which became especially difficult in 1941, the British authorities had to ensure that the best use was made of such shipping as could be spared for this trade. Accordingly, when the Middle East Supply Centre was established in Cairo in April 1941, it was made responsible for marshalling essential import programmes for all the Middle East countries, and for co-ordinating the procurement of goods from Britain, from the United States and from other sources in the free world. When lend-lease was extended to Middle East destinations, the programming of such demands upon the United States became an important part of the Supply Centre's work. The supposed marginal eligibility of many of these lend-lease demands led, indeed, to great American activity and interest in the Supply Centre.[1]

This work of assuring the really essential import requirements of the Middle East, important as it was in preventing bad from going to worse, did not and could not dissipate the difficulties occasioned by the gap in the balance of payments, the inflation of purchasing power and prices, and the unwillingness of the food producers to bring their produce to market. Nor—to look at the other side of the medal—could they stop the growth of Britain's post-war liabilities. As early rejoicing in mounting sterling balances gave way to fear that these might imply uncomfortably large demands on Britain's post-war capacity, the financial authorities at home became more receptive to novel proposals.[2] Special shipments of wheat in 1941 had constituted a serious strain on the shipping situation, yet they appeared, to observers in the Middle East, to be a drop in the bucket.[3] Why not instead ship a commodity that would use the very minimum of shipping space, and exhaust just no productive capacity at all? Why not, in short, ship gold?

Oddly enough, it was the upheaval in Persia, a silver-rather than a gold-loving country, that first put the idea of gold sales on the map.[4] The occupation of Persia by British and Russian troops in the summer of 1941 and the establishment of a friendly Government

---

[1] For an account of the work of the Middle East Supply Centre, see E. M. H. Lloyd, *op. cit.*, Part II; also Guy Hunter, 'The Middle East Supply Centre', in Part II, Section X of *The Middle East in the War*, edited by G. Kirk (Survey of International Affairs 1939-46).

[2] The possibility of reducing Egypt's sterling balances by repatriation of Egypt's bonded debt in London—parallel to the Indian operation—was apparently looked at only to be rejected out of hand.

[3] In an abortive attempt to bring down the price of wheat in Syria in 1941, 80,000 tons of wheat were sold by the authorities. (E. M. H. Lloyd, *op. cit.*, Chapter 17).

[4] There had earlier been isolated suggestions—e.g. from the Economic Adviser to the G.H.Q., Middle East.

in Teheran were followed early in 1942 by a payments agreement to cover the important trade the Allies now expected to develop. This agreement gave Persia the right to demand gold at the official price (£8 8s. a fine ounce) to the amount of 40 per cent. of her sterling balance at the end of each half year. The Persians were not satisfied with this, and the agreement was amended to provide that the gold proportion should be raised to 60 per cent., this covering not only all future settlements but also that of June 1942 which had already passed. By the end of 1942 they had earned, under this amended arrangement, some £7 millions at the official price. But the gold was worth nearly double this in Persia, and the Treasury's representative on the spot pointed out the extravagance of selling gold to Persia on this scale without getting the market price for it. The actual gold released to Persia in respect of her 1942 sterling balance would, if sold at the market price, have just about cleared Britain's debt, instead of our being left some five millions in the red. On simple arithmetic alone—and there were of course other weighty arguments—there was here a strong case, and this was being urged from officials in Teheran throughout the summer and autumn when these first obligations under the payments agreements were accumulating.

The suggestion soon found a strong supporter in an economist who had been brought by Mr. Oliver Lyttelton to advise the Middle East Supply Centre in Cairo. At an Anti-inflation Conference held there in September 1942, a resolution advocated sales of gold in the open market on three grounds:[1]

(1) that a supply of gold in the form of coins and jewellery would be likely to absorb surplus purchasing power which would otherwise be invested in commodities;

(2) that the proceeds of sale of gold would provide some of the currency required for military expenditure and thus slow down the rate of expansion of the note issue; and

(3) that a fall in the price of gold in Middle East markets might have the effect of bringing down other prices in sympathy.

In the following months opinion in Allied official circles throughout the Middle East rapidly hardened in favour of this proposal.[2] The Allied, and in particular the British, authorities saw that the feeding of the towns of the Middle East was of high political and strategic importance, and they knew that locally-produced cereals must be the main provision. Experience in Persia and Syria had shown that the problem of inducing peasants and landowners to part with their grain in exchange for depreciating

---

[1] This sentence is taken from E. M. H. Lloyd, *op. cit.*, Chapter 22.

[2] This paragraph closely follows E. M. H. Lloyd *op. cit.*, Chapter 22.

paper money was a real one. Gold in the form of coin or jewellery was the traditional means of saving and of personal display. In good times when prices were high, producers bought necklaces of English sovereigns, bangles and other jewellery of solid gold to adorn their women—and in bad times the gold was sold as soon as the money-lender pressed. Realisation of the relevance of these facts to the 1942 situation was winning the day, and one telegram after another added to the case. Teheran reported a tendency for the prices of commodities to follow the price of gold, and pressed for experimental sales. In Syria, reputed to have the keenest appetite for gold,[1] political disturbances in November 1942 led to an exceptional demand, and the sovereign was changing hands at £4. In December 1942 action in Persia and Syria was pressed at a conference in London, and an experiment in the former country was in principle agreed.[2] During the early months of 1943 discussions went forward on the basis that, owing to geographical conditions and the closeness of market connections, any large-scale operations should be concerted, covering all the Middle East countries and preferably India as well.

As we have seen in discussing India, there was at first some opposition from the Government of India, opposition based on the fear, also being strongly expressed by the Bank of England, that freely available gold might create distrust of paper currency and so lead to demands for complete gold circulations. This fear was also expressed by certain Allied representatives in the Middle East countries. But by April 1943 India had come round, and support in London had been greatly strengthened by propagation of the argument that the Americans would further reduce lend-lease if London's gold reserves continued to increase.[3] In June 1943 the decision was finally taken to generalise the gold sales. While India was to be allowed 750,000 fine ounces a quarter, the Minister of State in Cairo was to be allowed 375,000 fine ounces for sale in the Middle East Supply Centre countries. Coins were provided at first, but as soon as possible tiny gold bars (of 5 tolas) were offered as being less likely to usurp the paper currency.[4]

The actual marketing of the gold called for considerable skill in estimating the appetite of buyers and particularly the reactions of

---

[1] Subsequent experience in actual sales rather supported this view. Syria had also been the first to experience sharp inflation.

[2] As Persia was not a member of the Sterling Area and as neither gold nor paper played an important part in her currency system, the Bank of England considered it a fairly safe place in which to experiment on a small scale.

[3] cf. p. 268 above.

[4] In Palestine and later in Iraq it was stipulated that with every five sovereigns at least one bar must be bought. The market soon became accustomed to these little bars, although sovereigns always commanded a substantial premium. (E. M. H. Lloyd, *op. cit.*, Chapter 22).

dealers to price changes. At the outset the general line was to bring down the price of gold because of its reactions on commodity prices generally and in order to avert a flight from the paper currency. Sales began therefore at falling prices. These, however, soon encouraged dealers to hold off in the expectation of further falls and the authorities, though achieving some of their objects, found themselves getting little contribution to the financing of military expenditure. To make the most of the limited supplies of gold available, it was necessary to watch both the price situation and the volume of sales very closely. When sales fell off unduly, a tonic could be applied by sharply reducing the price and then increasing it as sales began to recover.

Up to the end of 1943, nearly £9 millions, in local currencies, had been received from the sale of gold in all the Middle East Supply Centre countries—a figure which may be compared with £40 millions military expenditure and £23 millions increase in note circulation in the same period. Through the first half of 1944 the same policy was followed, bringing the total proceeds to £19 millions. Thereafter only very small amounts were made available, and the total for the whole period from the initiation of sales in June 1943 until the end of the war amounted to £22 millions. In addition, the United States authorities—using the British as their agents—sold gold in order to finance their local expenditure in Persia and Egypt, thereby depriving London of possible accession to gold reserves to a market value (nearly £5 millions) equal to the additional sterling balances also avoided.

In the spring of 1944 anxiety about the size and prospects of London's gold reserves forced a reconsideration of the policy. The usefulness of the gold sales in checking inflation and in securing the flow of food supplies, was strongly urged from Cairo and elsewhere, and this powerful argument was admitted by London. But the state of London's gold reserves—a matter originally providing support for the gold sales—had now changed sides in the argument, and after warnings in April and May the Chancellor on 17th July 1944 informed Lord Moyne in Cairo that United Kingdom sales of gold would have to stop.

The reluctance with which the Chancellor announced this decision was amply justified by the success attending this experiment. £22 millions is a sum that looks small against the £500 millions total of sterling balances of Middle East countries at the end of the war, but it must be remembered that the figure of £22 millions relates mainly to one year, while the £500 millions was the accumulation of six years. The £22 millions were obtained by selling gold officially valued at little more than half that sum; moreover, this loss to London's reserves may have had some effect on lend-lease generosity. Altogether, the £22 millions direct saving on sterling balances probably cost London very little.

Beyond this direct advantage there were other benefits defying all measurement. In Persia there were no discernible effects in lowering the prices of commodities, but there were impressive effects in property markets, tending to check further inflation. Similarly in Palestine, the effect was to check the rise rather than cause an actual fall in prices. Elsewhere commodity prices—especially the critical grain prices—were brought down as the price of gold fell, and a large share of the success of the cereals-collection campaign of 1943 in the Levant States was due to the availability of relatively cheap gold. This readiness of the peasant to part with grain in exchange for the gold—a perfectly normal phenomenon of Eastern prosperity—was immensely important. Even when the peasant had been ready to take paper money, he liked the paper money so little that he was ready to spend it at the first opportunity, whereas the gold round his wife's neck would be wrung from him only under the duress of depression. The brake which the gold sales put upon the inflation of the paper currency thus gave the situation some stability—it reduced the element of 'repressed inflation'.

No other measures were found to stem the flood carrying the sterling balances of the Middle East to unheard-of levels. It was generally believed in London that part of the trouble was the lack of any real control on military expenditure. As there was never any systematic enquiry into this, parallel to the double enquiry into expenditure in India, it is impossible to judge what truth there was in this supposition. The absence of any established local financial department, such as that provided by the Government of India, the geographical conditions and the proximity of the front line over a period of years necessitated some relaxation of normal measures of financial control. This relaxation was not so complete as to justify all the sweeping statements made about it in London, but local currency was certainly in very great demand for military purposes, and the monetary arrangements between London and these countries never impeded expenditure by the military authorities. In consequence, London was left at the end of the war facing the tremendous bill represented by over £500 millions of sterling balances held by these countries. Four-fifths of this total was for Egypt and the Sudan, the remainder mostly for Palestine. Without satisfactory monetary arrangements—and the traditions of the Sterling Area count among these—it would have been impossible to wring from the Middle East the real efforts and sacrifices represented by this appalling bill. The policy of the gold sales did something to moderate it, and with an earlier start might have done more. That it could have been smaller through more stringent control of expenditure is difficult to believe: as Lord Keynes put it, 'The principles of good housekeeping do not apply when you are fighting for your lives over three Continents far from home. We threw good housekeeping to the winds. But we saved ourselves, and helped to save the world'.

CHAPTER X

FINANCIAL RELATIONS WITH THE SOUTHERN DOMINIONS

(i)

The Common Ground

INDIA and the Middle Eastern countries proved to be the countries which accumulated massive sterling balances during the war, by the normal mechanism of international payments within the Sterling Area. Apart from these countries, the Sterling Area countries whose international accounts constituted major problems for the United Kingdom authorities were the three 'Southern Dominions'—Australia, New Zealand, and South Africa. These areas were alike in their constitutional status within the Commonwealth. They were completely self-governing nations, free to stay out of the war if they wished and entirely free to decide what contribution they would make, not only financially but in every other way. Negotiation with these Dominions meant negotiation with independent nations, though there was always confidence—varying in degree between the three Dominions—in their unity with Britain on the fundamental issues of international law and order. On this unity alone could the United Kingdom depend when it assumed that the Dominions would in the end always ensure that financial problems found a solution.

In addition to this uniformity of status within the Commonwealth there were other similarities between the three countries, giving a certain unity to the financial relations between the Southern Dominions on the one hand and the United Kingdom on the other. As self-governing Dominions they had come during the First World War to accept the broad principle that they financed their own armed forces used in any theatre of war. They were not, that is to say, just friendly nations who paid for the direct defence of their own territory and hired out a few divisions as mercenary supports of an allied country; on the contrary, they accepted the principle that the war was the Commonwealth's war into which they would, at their own expense, throw their forces wherever they were most needed. We shall see that in some phases South Africa was inclined to qualify this view, and that in all three cases the principle gave

286

rise to troublesome practical problems; but it was the starting-point common to all, and at bottom it remained throughout a valued principle.

The three countries were all members of the pre-war Sterling Area, in the sense that all their international transactions were conducted in terms of sterling, their banking systems had close ties with London, they held important reserves in sterling, and their currencies were generally (though not invariably) stable in terms of sterling. There was therefore, at least superficially, the same automatism in the payments arrangements between these countries and the United Kingdom—if United Kingdom purchases from them exceeded their own sterling expenditure, they took the difference as an addition to their balances of sterling in London, and correspondingly ran these balances down when their payments abroad were in excess. To the extent that the system was genuinely automatic, it did mean that the United Kingdom escaped both the threat to London's international reserves if its balance with these Dominions were adverse, and the trouble of bilateral payments agreements. But, as we shall see in the course of this chapter, things were never quite as easy as this. South Africa was in a unique position among Sterling Area countries, in that her principal export industry was gold-mining. She therefore always had the option of adding to her own gold reserves instead of earning 'surplus' sterling; she did in fact commonly exercise this option and to this extent stood outside the Sterling Area 'pool'. The pool's need for South African gold enforced negotiation more akin to payments negotiations outside than to automatic settlement inside the Sterling Area. Australia and New Zealand were neither in this position nor in the Indian position of accumulating uncomfortably large sterling balances; in general they tended to be uncomfortably short of sterling, and after 1930 the Australian public knew all too well that depression followed a shortage of sterling. Their prospective balance of payments positions were therefore closely watched—and allowed for when any financial matters were under discussion.

Arising from their historic connection with London's money, all three Dominions had large bonded debts which were in terms of sterling and were held mostly in the United Kingdom. We have seen how India took the chance afforded by the war to swallow up this sterling indebtedness. South Africa succeeded in parallel operations, though with her it was not a question of disgorging superfluous sterling but of disgorging superfluous gold, which was sorely needed by London but which South Africa was reluctant to release in return for sterling balances. New Zealand, already in balance of payments difficulties before the war and at no stage gorged with sterling, was in a position almost the reverse of the South African and Indian. Her constant anxiety was whether she would have enough sterling to meet maturities when conversion was uncertain; this anxiety and the paramount need to maintain her credit were factors that had always to be taken into account in relations between the United Kingdom and New Zealand Governments.

In one respect the three Dominions all received at the very beginning of the war a major support for their international payments positions. This was the United Kingdom wool purchase. It began primarily as a supply purchase from Australia; New Zealand was quickly brought in, partly for supply reasons, partly to give equality of treatment with Australia, partly with an eye to her precarious balance of payments. For both, the agreement covered the entire length of the war. Then South Africa sought and received some temporary support for her wool market, damaged by loss of enemy markets and believed to be of political importance to a Government not commanding the support of a large part of the electorate. In course of time, and for a mixture of reasons, the South African purchase was prolonged and assimilated to those in Australia and New Zealand. For the rest of the war, 'the wool purchase' was one of the important facts of life in relations between Britain and the Southern Dominions.

Although post-war experience was to put a different complexion on the deal, and although the terms of the agreement probably represented a fair deal for all parties, the wool purchase was at the time regarded by the United Kingdom Treasury as a very expensive item, and there was undoubtedly some feeling that Britain had thereby given the Dominions a handsome start, and that this generosity should have relieved any feelings that London had been stingy over pre-war rearmament. So London expected the Southern Dominions to emulate Britain's efforts in related directions—especially by economising in foreign exchange, which was threatening to be one of the bottlenecks to the war effort. The Dominions did in fact quickly accept the need for foreign exchange restrictions, comparable to those imposed in the United Kingdom, in order to complete the ring fence round the Sterling Area.[1] But these restrictions implied, it will be remembered, independent restriction of imports, since imports not prohibited by law had an automatic claim to foreign exchange. In the imposition of austere controls on imports, the Southern Dominions seemed to London to be deplorably slow. Perhaps it was that they were, in those early days, so remote from the theatre of war—or perhaps

---

[1] cf. p. 235.

it was, as Dominions representatives sometimes had to remind their opposite numbers in London, that their geographical conditions made British standards of austerity inapplicable. In some quarters there was also a well-intended if confused response to Britain's own export drive: imports of British goods were believed to be helping Britain's war effort. The United Kingdom authorities had themselves in the earliest phases stressed only the need to economise in hard currencies, and it was only as the shortages became acute in Britain itself that, after an inevitable time-lag, the Dominions fully realised that spending and importing as such were hindrances to the war effort. But whether or not there was a defensible explanation, their slowness in tightening their belts seemed to London a poor return for British underwriting of their wool producers. Eventually this ground for criticism disappeared, or at least contracted. First New Zealand,[1] then Australia and finally even South Africa took restrictive measures; comparisons are difficult, but it seems clear that in New Zealand and Australia the restriction of consumption was in the end very severe. The purpose and implications of economy in imports were not however always understood, and there was a phase in which the Dominions— particularly Australia—seemed to think of import cuts as a reason for the development of secondary industries. This was congenial to certain political quarters, following the pre-war trends, but it was inimical to the Commonwealth's war effort which demanded that consumption and not merely dollar imports should be cut. The lesson did in time get home; Australia was indeed the scene of tremendous industrial development during the latter part of the war, but this was geared to military supplies and the like,[2] not to the replacement of dollar consumption that a nation at war cannot afford.

Thus even those problems which looked, at first sight, the same for all three countries in practice worked out rather differently in each case. The timing of various phases varied too, from one Dominion to another. In other respects their differences were more fundamental, and the full development of their financial relations with Britain can be traced only by examining each case separately. Through the remainder of this chapter, therefore, the discussion is of one Dominion at a time, but the reader should throughout remember that the Dominions did have some starting points in common—above all, that their relationship with Britain was

---

[1] New Zealand had already imposed certain exchange restrictions and import controls in December 1938, when she was in balance of payments difficulties. The war-time measures were therefore, for this Dominion, merely a development of earlier measures.

[2] On Australia's development of war production, see *Studies in Overseas Supplies, op. cit.,* Chapter IX.

U

something they shared with each other. London had always, in treating with one Dominion, to remember that the others were likely to claim 'equality of treatment', whatever that meant.

(ii)

Australia

Australia is herself a Commonwealth, whose member States jealously retain substantial powers against the encroaching tendencies of the Federal Government. In the economic sphere the division of powers had been highly relevant to the development, during the inter-war period, of Governmental attempts to reduce the amplitude of cyclical fluctuations; particularly the Federal Government had encountered opposition in its efforts to restrain the sometimes extravagant capital projects of the States. These strained relations on matters of economic policy were much in evidence in the last two years of peace, when Australia was caught by falling export prices concurrently with an expansion of internal demand. This was a situation that had regularly recurred in the Australian economy, the only distinguishing feature of the 1937–39 episode being its relative mildness. The mildness arose on both sides of the account—the fall in export prices was not as catastrophic as it had been on some earlier occasions, and the internal expansion (originating in earlier prosperity) had been kept in bounds by some caution at the centre. Nevertheless, the strain was sufficient to bring Australia's London funds (her international reserve) below £35 millions—a mere three months' requirement for imports. The position was not, that is to say, really critical but uncomfortably tight.

Australia thus first encountered her war-time financial problems at a time when she was already experiencing some difficulty on the international side, a difficulty that did not appear so overwhelming as to make the States quick to acknowledge a restraining hand from Canberra. It was not clear, in the light of shipping uncertainties, how far Australia's export income could be maintained, while on the other side of the account she was quick to acknowledge her Commonwealth responsibilities by planning an overseas force which she would, according to the common rule, have to pay for out of her own resources. Australia was not in a mind to shirk her responsibilities, but it was obvious at the start that she was going to have to watch her purse pretty closely.

That the position would be no worse than this was quickly ensured by the purchase, by the United Kingdom Government, of the entire wool clip of Australia and New Zealand for the duration of the war and one wool year thereafter. This gigantic transaction was already under discussion when war broke out. It followed a valuable precedent of 1915–18, when supplies had been protected and prices held at a reasonable level by an inter-Governmental deal. Inspection of the supply prospect in 1939 provided a strong case for purchase by the United Kingdom: it seemed likely that five-sixths of the entire Australasian production would be required for the United Kingdom, and the demand of the outside world was expected to absorb easily the remaining one-sixth—and if the United Kingdom did not buy the lot, to raise prices steeply against the United Kingdom and all other buyers. Accordingly Britain raised no objection when the Australian Prime Minister prematurely announced that the deal had been agreed. The British negotiators believed that they had not committed themselves, but it was plainly good business on their part to accept Mr. Menzies' statement—and so the United Kingdom made a purchase that involved three or four hundred millions pounds sterling in the course of the war.[1] For year after year a formal agreement was spasmodically discussed, but the end of the war caught the draft still unsettled. In the British Commonwealth scraps of paper are not always necessary.

The absence of a formal agreement did not mean that the essential terms were left open. First there was the question of price. Australia looked back to 1936–37, when the average price realised had been over 13d. per lb.,[2] the highest since 1929. In 1938–39 the price had been down to about $8\frac{1}{4}$d: a fall that had, as we have seen, occasioned some strain in Australia's sterling position. There was never any doubt that Britain would have to pay rather more than this; the question was how much, and why? That the Australian farmers were reasonable in expecting an end to the period of unprofitable prices was accepted from the start. It was also accepted that the sale of the wool clip must not only keep the individual producers solvent, but must also provide a secure basis for Australia's general economic position. The wool price had a bearing, too, on the budgetary position and upon Australia's capacity to develop war production. For her part, Australia accepted the principle of no exploitation of the United Kingdom war needs, and was prepared to settle on 'a modest payment' for the work of producing the wool. The price was soon agreed at 10.75d. sterling per pound. Profits on wool sold outside the United Kingdom

---

[1] Quite apart from its importance to United Kingdom textile supplies, the transaction proved to be profitable from the point of view of ordinary accounting. It looked a colossal liability when it was assumed in those early days.

[2] This and all following figures are in English terms; for prices in Australian currency, add one-fifth.

were to be shared equally between the two Governments; any final net loss was for account of the United Kingdom alone. The detailed application of these basic terms left some room for argument, but in general the purchase ran smoothly enough, and through the early part of the war it was universally accepted as of mutual interest to the parties.

When, in the very first month of the war, the United Kingdom thus assured to Australia, in exchange for the assurance of wool supplies, strong support for the balance of payments throughout the war, the Treasury urged Ministers to couple that assurance with a hint to economise in imports from hard-currency countries. The wool deal would 'set a good deal of money afloat in Australia', and this should not be 'wasted on unnecessary imports from countries whose currencies are not attached to sterling'. It is notable that the hint was not to refer to imports generally, but only to those from outside the Sterling Area. In these early days the Board of Trade was still urging the importance of maintaining United Kingdom exports to the Sterling Area, partly because the Dominions might otherwise extend their secondary industries, with unfortunate effects after the war. But economy in hard-currency imports was urgent and no opportunity was lost of emphasising this to Australian Ministers. Before the end of 1939 negotiations about Australia's war expenditure in relation to her sterling balances[1] kept the whole question of import economy to the fore, though the United Kingdom negotiators were afraid that Australia might develop a bias against sterling imports. To persuade Australia that she could afford to meet sterling expenditure on her defence at the same time as she was urged to maintain her imports from the United Kingdom was a little difficult, and the dilemma was not clearly resolved until the developments of 1940 put a different complexion on United Kingdom export policy. The authorities in London could thenceforward urge upon Australia, without any awkward qualifications, the simple need for 'belt-tightening'. The time had come for Australia to follow the United Kingdom's example by diverting resources from activities which did not directly increase the Empire's strength for war production. Non-essential civilian consumption must be restricted, and the corresponding imports of non-essential goods restricted from all sources. Petrol, newsprint, and cotton and rayon goods were mentioned as particular examples where there was ample scope for economy. The principle of exchange control—and indeed of all other Commonwealth arrangements—was that Australia must settle her own internal arrangements; but little purpose was served by Britain's austerity if Australia was continuing to live well.

---

[1] See below, pp. 293-5.

The upheaval of 1940 did have its effects in Australia—the reality of the war carried a conviction it had previously lacked—but some considerable time necessarily elapsed before war-time austerity became the rule in Australia. At a distance London's policy on overseas trade had looked equivocal, to say the least, and it was some time before its simplification enabled Australians to see the position as London saw it. It was a long time, too, before the unemployment obsession, a legacy of the depression, could be left behind. War production necessarily took time to develop; why risk unemployment by stern economy before the war industries were ready to absorb the resources released by austerity? And so, through 1940 and much of 1941, Australians continued to live well[1]—to the irritation of observers from London, who were not always quick to appreciate that the luxury goods filling Australian shops resulted from Britain's earlier export drive. But in the course of 1941 real progress was made, and further import restrictions late in the year were coupled with a Government statement, highly valued by London, that 'it would be directly contrary to the present Government's policy if the war-time restrictions now being imposed . . . . . were to lead to a greater use of Australian manpower and resources in non-essential production'. Immediately after this, the entry of Japan into the war changed the atmosphere in Australia, and the ensuing eighteen months saw a remodelling of the continent's economic structure. This was genuine mobilisation for total war and Britain, never spotless in her own austerity, could make no further complaint about Australian extravagance.

The Treasury in London had been concerned at Australia's early laxity not only because of its implications for London's foreign exchange reserves, but also for the narrower Treasury reason that Australia was pleading difficulty in paying the bills incurred by and for her armed forces overseas. The general principle that as a self-governing Dominion she should meet these bills was never questioned by Australia. Unlike South Africa,[2] she did not at any stage differentiate between her own war in one theatre and other peoples' wars elsewhere; for Australia as for Britain the war was one war, the enemy one enemy to be fought wherever he cropped up. But while admitting the principle, Australia did plead certain practical difficulties precluding straightforward settlement of the account. Despite the wool deal, Australia felt unsure of her capacity to meet the drain on her London balances, and her continuing fears of internal economic crisis were brought into play. The

---

[1] Mr. Fadden's budget speech (26th September 1941) included the statement 'civilian consumption, except in a few directions, has not fallen below peace-time levels, but has rather increased'. See also *Australia in the War of 1939–1945, War Economy, 1939–1942* by S. J. Butlin.

[2] See below, pp. 308-9.

Commonwealth Government therefore asked the United Kingdom Government to advance enough of Australia's overseas war expenditure to enable her to maintain her London balances at a reasonably safe level, which Australia assessed at £50 millions. The proposal was accepted by the United Kingdom, on the basis that the advances should bear the same rate of interest as the United Kingdom Government was having to pay for similar borrowing internally.[1] For 1940 Australia estimated her total external war expenditure at £15 or £16 millions; the United Kingdom agreed to advance £12 millions, plus the Canadian dollars for Australia's share in the Air Training Scheme. The figure was settled without any acknowledgment by the United Kingdom that this was the proper proportion for United Kingdom advances in future years, or that £50 millions was the proper figure for Australia's sterling balances.

In fact Australia was able to sell rather more abroad than she had anticipated, and her London balances tended to rise. When, therefore, the 1941 Australian defence expenditure outside Australia looked like rising sharply—perhaps to £50 millions in 1941—it seemed to London that Australia's own share should become much bigger. Meanwhile Australian representatives had begun to argue about the detailed costing of her Forces overseas. It appears that accommodation for Australian Forces overseas had in the first war been paid for by the United Kingdom, and the Australians thought this a precedent that should be followed. The negotiations also threatened to get bogged down in arguments about the proportions of Australian personnel engaged in combat zones and in waiting to fight, arguments that were sometimes double-edged. Then in the early months of 1942, negotiations were further complicated by pressure from the United States of America for reciprocal aid from Australia, at least to cover certain supplies to her Forces in Australia. The United Kingdom Treasury took its stand on four principles: that each Dominion should provide the cost of its Forces, that this cost should not be subject to meticulous accounting but should be reckoned in a broad way, that reverse lend-lease (reciprocal aid) should cover part of Dominion services to the United States of America, and that nevertheless Australia's London balances should receive adequate protection. Eventually Australia accepted these principles, and made herself responsible for charges that were reckoned in a very rough way on the basis of 9 shillings per day per head of Australian Forces overseas, while the United Kingdom would maintain her advances on a sufficient scale to maintain Australian balances in London at £40 millions: the United Kingdom would no longer

---

[1] The rate was eventually fixed at 3 per cent.

charge any interest on either previous advances (the £12 millions) or any further advances necessary for this purpose. We may note in passing three points about the agreement: that matters were allowed to proceed through many months without any agreement, that the sums referred to were in round figures, all attempt at meticulous accounting being deemed out of place, and that now, in 1942, interest was deemed inappropriate on certain debts between fellow-members of the British Commonwealth.

It was a principle of financial policy that an agreement of this kind should not be allowed to influence the terms of a commodity transaction such as the wool agreement. Nevertheless, the fact that for the Southern Dominions the wool purchase was one stable factor in an unstable world did colour all succeeding discussions on this subject. In 1941 there was a suggestion, having regard to possible post-war surpluses, that the Dominions should be asked to share losses as well as profits. This was dropped partly because such a revision would have implied new rights as well as new liabilities for the Dominions, but also partly because of a half-heartedness due to United Kingdom feeling that the economies of these countries had to be underwritten in one way or another. This feeling was more prominent in 1942, when the Australians asked for a substantial rise in price for the wool. The increase was claimed on the ground of rising costs; but the post-war prospect was one of surplus. The supply reason for raising the price by the full 22½ per cent. asked for by the Australians therefore appeared purely ephemeral, and the Treasury was disposed to raise the price only on the logical condition that the Dominions should share in post-war losses. Considering the undertaking about London balances,[1] the immediate rise in price appeared a small sacrifice for the sake of Dominion acceptance of a share in post-war losses. Actually in May 1942 the two Governments settled on the basis of a 15 per cent. (not 22½ per cent.) rise in price and a promise by Australia that she would 'participate in a generous way' in the cost of any contribution towards post-war relief of territories overrun by the enemy. Subsequently an important question of interpretation arose: was the 'war', for whose period (plus one wool year) the wool was bought, the German war or the Japanese war? Here again the importance of underpinning the Australian economy was a major, though not the only, consideration, and London decided tacitly to accept the longer period as the basis. As the end of the war actually approached, discussion of the wool agreement became more and more wrapped up in the discussion

---

[1] The basic figure was, in the May 1942 discussions between the Chancellor of the Exchequer and the Australian Minister (Dr. Evatt), agreed by the United Kingdom authorities as £40 millions, not as the £50 millions which the Australians had urged since 1939.

of post-war commodity surpluses, and problems of war-time finance dropped into the background.

The claim for a higher price for wool was based on the rise of costs in Australia, and the Australian Ministers insisted that they had done everything possible to moderate the inflation of Australian costs. This point was also made when, half-way through the war, the Australian Government sought adjustment of its long-term contracts for the supply of dairy and other produce to the United Kingdom. In the interest of price stability within Australia—a policy similar in aim to that which inspired Sir Kingsley Wood's great budget of 1941—an elaborate system of subsidies had been developed. The Australians now pointed out that these subsidies had been subsidising not only the produce that went into local consumption, but also the important quantities exported to the United Kingdom under the war-time contracts. The United Kingdom could hardly have disputed the appropriateness of increased prices if the Australian Government had relied simply on prices to call forth the supplies wanted by the United Kingdom; why then should not the United Kingdom contribute to the subsidies which were in fact disguised price supplements paid to the farmers, especially having regard to the indirect benefit the United Kingdom received from the fact that the Australian economy was not being over-turned by a disorderly inflation? This might have been a troublesome and exceedingly complicated argument, if taken to its logical conclusion: the United Kingdom might, for example, have suggested that cost of living subsidies in Britain were keeping down the cost of maintaining Australian Service personnel in Britain. The suggested device of contribution to the subsidies was therefore not one to accept in principle, but as a rough and ready method of adjusting the prices paid to Australia, it appealed to commonsense and it would help the Australian Government in its price stabilisation policy. Accordingly, without awkwardly thrashing out all the implications of such an arrangement, the United Kingdom conceded an adjustment in the contracts for these foodstuffs. Annual payments—backdated into 1943—were arranged, one for canned meat and one for dairy products. These lump-sum contributions to Australian subsidies settled the food contracts for the remainder of the war.

The result of all these arrangements—economy of imports, the acceptance by Australia of full liability for her Forces overseas, the wool purchase and the rise in the wool price, and the adjusted food contracts—was that Australia's sterling position strengthened appreciably during the middle years of the war. In October 1943 the Commonwealth Government had been able to repay the £12 millions advanced by the United Kingdom in 1940, consistently with keeping well over £50 millions in hand. By the end of 1943 another influence was at work—heavy spending by American Forces in Australia—and Australia's London balance was up to £77 millions. This put a new light on Australia's capacity to deal with her pre-war bonded debt in London, and at the beginning of 1944 the Commonwealth Government felt able to redeem rather than convert £4.6 millions of stock then maturing.[1] About the same time, the Commonwealth Bank of Australia made a tentative approach to London on the possibility of converting a small proportion—perhaps £10 millions—of her sterling into gold. This naturally excited London's dislike of independent reserves within the Sterling Area, but there did happen to be at that moment an argument on the other side. The American attack on London's dollar balances was in full swing,[2] and there was something to be said for tucking away part of the Sterling Area's resources in ways like those suggested by the Australians. There was, too, a certain confidence that the Australian attitude to Sterling Area problems after the war would be co-operative, and on balance London decided that the Commonwealth Bank of Australia should be allowed to hold a private nest-egg of £10 millions in gold.[3]

This sum, which Australia took out of her London balances, still left these balances in a very healthy condition. Australia was in fact receiving far more by the expenditure of United States Forces than she was losing by the diminution of food exports imposed by the necessity of feeding those Forces in Australia. In the Australian fiscal years[4] 1941–42, 1942–43 and 1943–44, the net expenditure of the United States Forces in Australia was £9.5, £38.7 and £68.9 millions, while the exports other than wool were £88.2, £41.4 and £44.8 millions. The proceeds of the wool sales were at the same time benefiting from the adjustment of the price. In the year 1944–45 the net expenditure of United States Forces disappeared, but the non-wool exports picked up again; and the balance remained in Australia's favour. Her balances in London accordingly remained well over £100 millions, and at the end of 1945 they were still £125 millions, though there were some charges to be set against this total. After allowing for these and for all immediate contingencies, the figures had left far behind the £40 millions specified in London's early undertaking to protect a minimum balance. Looking back through post-war years, £125

---

[1] This was the only operation of 'debt repatriation' undertaken by Australia during the war.

[2] cf. below, Chapter XIII, Section (vi).

[3] The £10 millions were in terms of English pounds.

[4] 1st July to June 30th.

millions in 1945 may be judged not so very different from £50
millions in 1942; but this is not the comparison that was—or
could have been—made in London at the time. In the circumstances
of 1945 Australia's position appeared an enviable one, and it was
London's turn to plead that her own position needed protection.

(iii)
New Zealand

London has the habit of grouping closely together in its mind the
two quite separate Dominions of New Zealand and Australia—it
has even a geographical term combining them in a single word,
Australasia. This habit is perhaps too careless and display of it
certainly sometimes gives offence; nevertheless the two countries
have so much in common that London has some excuse. Their
populations, unlike those in any other part of the Commonwealth
overseas, are overwhelmingly British in origin, and this combines
with the absence of a dominant neighbour to keep their political
temper close to the traditions of the Mother Country. Their
dependence on the same small group of agricultural exports—
mainly the pastoral products wool, meat and dairy produce—gives
an underlying unity to their international economic relations.
Their dependence on the London capital market, and the close
links between their banking systems (themselves mutually entwined)
and the London money market, make Australia and New Zealand
dependable if independent members of the Sterling Area.

It was therefore inevitable that their financial relations with
Britain should be bound together at many points, and much of
the story as regards New Zealand has close parallels with, indeed
is part of, the story of Australia's relations with Britain, outlined
in the preceding section of this chapter. But there were differences,
differences arising partly from the variations incidental to the
behaviour of their independent political systems, partly also from
differences in political personalities. In some way that defies
definition, one gets the impression that the country geographically
most remote from Britain is closest to it in political feeling. In the
early days the determination of the country to make the utmost
effort, in a war unreservedly regarded as her own war, was just a
shade more evident in New Zealand than in Australia. On the
other hand, New Zealand had got herself into serious difficulties
in her balance of payments in the immediate pre-war period,
and from this weakened position it looked as though her power to
help might be gravely handicapped. With the best will in the

world she narrowly escaped being a financial burden in the first years of the war.

The root of the trouble was the policy of social amelioration pursued by the New Zealand Government which came into power in 1935, a programme New Zealand could scarcely afford in the good years 1936 and 1937 and could not afford at all in the world recession that dominated 1938 and affected 1939. Extensive public works were undertaken, social services expanded, a social security programme developed, wages raised and hours shortened. These measures were financed to an undue extent by borrowing, and the consequent expansion of spending power in the hands of the people stimulated imports beyond, in 1936, New Zealand's power to pay its way internationally. In the boom year of 1937 the high price of wool saw New Zealand through, but in 1938 the adverse balance of payments was six or seven million pounds sterling. Meanwhile there had been a substantial flight of funds from New Zealand, owing to the fear that the country's prodigality would sooner or later force a monetary crisis.[1] By the end of 1938 the net sterling balance of the Dominion had dwindled to about £5½ millions, and in order to protect the service of the external debt, the Dominion Government introduced a comprehensive restriction of imports exchange. The sharp cut in imports made during the succeeding months was not, however, matched by any curtailment of purchasing power internally; on the contrary, the Government continued to borrow heavily for public works and allowed the loss of revenue from import duties to weaken its budgetary position. There was no sign of the kind of radical adjustment in the economy that was necessary if New Zealand was to pay her way internationally.

This was not a position that could be commended to the London capital market, and the view of this market happened to be of acute interest to the Dominion. There was an important debt maturity to be met in London and, unless this could be converted into new loans, New Zealand's trivial London balance would not be there any longer to maintain even her restricted volume of imports. The Dominion's Minister of Finance came to London in the summer of 1939 and sought from Ministers and from the Bank of England their good offices in a conversion operation and a substantial amount of hard cash to be getting on with. His reception was not encouraging.

In one particular, however, he was on a good wicket. The

---

[1] There had earlier been speculation the other way, in the belief—fostered by some good years—that the New Zealand pound might be raised from £NZ125 = £100 sterling to its old parity; in 1936 these bulls abandoned hope and withdrew their money. Including both this exodus and that of New Zealanders' funds frightened by the Government's policy, a total of £NZ15 to 18 millions left the country in the three years 1936, 1937 and 1938.

Government of New Zealand had taken part in Commonwealth defence discussions, and London was looking to New Zealand to take part in strengthening Imperial defences. With the war clouds blackening as they were, there was no disposition to force New Zealand into a crippling economic crisis which would have detracted from the defence effort she was obviously determined to make. As compared with the credits that were going to potential Allies outside the family—Poland and Turkey—the sums Mr. Nash mentioned were not so very big. Under the lowering skies of July 1939 it was not difficult to come to terms. The New Zealand Government's undertaking to try to live within its means was put in writing, a short-term loan was issued and officially underwritten to cover the January maturity, and New Zealand received £5 millions for defence expenditure and export credits up to £4 millions.[1] These were exceptional measures, but they do illustrate the ways in which, under exceptional stress, London could come to the help of a country in the Sterling Area.

The discussions had naturally involved some comment on the volume of imports into New Zealand, still permitted under the system of control introduced several months earlier. This early London interest in New Zealand's scale of imports, coupled with London's undertaking to make advances for New Zealand's defence expenditure, set the tone of financial relations between the two countries and helped to bring certain questions to a head earlier with New Zealand than with other Southern Dominions. New Zealand from the beginning assumed full eventual liability for the expenditure of her Forces overseas—this was an expression of political affinity—and, with her rickety financial position bolstered by the arrangements of July 1939, she felt she could safely hold to this promise. It was clear that the overseas military expenditure would have to be advanced by the United Kingdom, and the United Kingdom naturally expected New Zealand to relieve the situation as much as possible by reducing her still prodigal scale of imports.

Meanwhile the New Zealand balance of payments had received important protection by the great wool purchase. Talks at the Ministry of Supply during the last few weeks of peace had included New Zealand as well as Australian representatives. The case was essentially a supply case, even stronger perhaps for the New Zealand product than for the Australian, since the crossbred wool produced in New Zealand is peculiarly useful for military clothing. The two Dominions had been jointly in the satisfactory arrangements of

---

[1] The undertaking was given by the New Zealand Prime Minister to the Governor of the Bank of England, 20th July 1939. The credits were announced in Parliament by the Dominions Secretary on 25th July. (H. of C. Deb., Vol. 350, Col. 1284.)

1914–18, and it was obvious from the outset that they should again be together in the new scheme. On the whole the pace in the negotiations was set by the Australians, but New Zealand had her say before prices were settled towards the end of the year.[1]

This meant security, for the duration of the war and one wool year thereafter, for New Zealand's export receipts to the annual amount of some £12 millions sterling, in addition to the food contracts being made with the Ministry of Food. The effect of the wool purchase in immediate strengthening of New Zealand's balance of payments was disproportionately great, since sterling was to be credited immediately the wool was appraised, whereas trade practice had been for payment to be received against shipping documents. This factor, and the considerable uncertainty about the rate of New Zealand's overseas defence expenditure, made it difficult to measure her immediate need for support. Accordingly when he met the New Zealand acting Prime Minister late in the year, the Chancellor of the Exchequer fell back on a general undertaking to protect New Zealand's sterling balance. The United Kingdom took over part of the cost of training New Zealand pilots in Canada, (though New Zealand accepted various liabilities under this scheme), but for sterling expenditure on defence New Zealand was to employ her own sterling balances in so far as these stood above the customary level. To the extent that this left some sterling defence expenditure uncovered, the United Kingdom would make advances, on which interest would be charged at whatever rate the United Kingdom Treasury found itself having to pay on newly-issued bonds.[2] The United Kingdom Government could not take over New Zealand's debts in the London market, but as these fell due all possible facilities for conversion would be offered. It would, of course, be up to New Zealand to economise in imports, especially from dollar countries.

The existence since 1938 of some control of imports made it relatively easy for New Zealand to implement this last item in her share of the bargain. As compared with the fiscal year 1938–39, imports in 1939–40 were down by 16 per cent. (in value), and of this fall rather more than half was in imports from non-sterling countries. This compared favourably with what had been achieved elsewhere, but the desperate situation in the summer of 1940 seemed to call for yet more economy. Particularly New Zealand was asked to face the consequences of the full employment of resources throughout the Commonwealth. If a bigger effort was to be made, there had to be actual diversion of resources within

[1] For the negotiations more generally, see above, pp. 290-2.

[2] The interpretation of this condition was naturally matter for considerable argument.

the Commonwealth. This implied for New Zealand further economy in sterling imports (which were straining the resources of other parts of the Commonwealth) and above all a stop to the higher expenditure on public works. This further effort was made much more reluctantly, and more spasmodically, than had been evident in the first round of economy. A year later United Kingdom officials were still complaining that New Zealand was clinging to a policy of guns *plus* butter, and comparisons of petrol rations were a prepetual irritant in the financial relations between the two countries. Nevertheless progress was made—sufficient progress in fact for New Zealand to become alarmed about the exhaustion of her capital equipment, a point she was soon pleading as a reason for being well supplied with sterling at the end of the war.

While London was inclined to remain critical of New Zealand's expenditure on imports, and of allegedly extravagant use of resources in the Dominion, New Zealand on her side was becoming restive about the failure of her export income to grow in proportion to the rising cost of the goods she needed from abroad. As early as December 1940 New Zealand producers were arguing that rising prices for British exports would justify higher prices for butter and cheese. This 'terms of trade argument', as it became known, became a persistent element in the New Zealand case. Its basis was a claim in equity for stable purchasing power for a given volume of New Zealand produce. The argument was never accepted in London. It was in the nature of war, at least in the first phases, to make industrial products scarce as compared with agricultural products, and therefore to depress the value of the latter in terms of the former. There were statistical traps about the calculation of adjustment, traps of which the New Zealanders did not appear to be aware.[1] More fundamentally there were, in the British view, two insuperable difficulties in this principle. First, there was nothing sacrosanct about the relative prices at a particular date, whether 1939 or any other, and no Government could attempt for long to stereotype relative prices in defiance of underlying market conditions. Second, though New Zealand sent most of her exports to the United Kingdom, United Kingdom exports went to many countries interested in many different products; the 'stable terms of trade' principle could be applied only by pushing world trade into a series of bilateral bargains, which would give completely

---

[1] In 1944 New Zealand was using the argument to suggest that she had been underpaid £100 millions for her exports; this was arrived at by multiplying New Zealand exports by the United Kingdom export price index and dividing it by the New Zealand export price index. It would be equally valid to reprice United Kingdom exports by assuming that United Kingdom prices had moved up no more than those of New Zealand products, and in this case the result was, not that New Zealand had been £100 millions underpaid, but that she had been overcharged £18 millions for United Kingdom goods.

unrelated values to any commodity that happened to figure in the trade of more than one country. It was, in short, quite unthinkable for British negotiators to accept the principle.

In conveying this refusal to the New Zealand Government, London was prepared to acknowledge some case in equity for raising the prices paid for New Zealand produce. It was undoubtedly true that the United Kingdom as a purchaser of New Zealand produce had benefited from the stabilisation subsidies whereby the prices of New Zealand produce had been kept down. The United Kingdom negotiators were very much aware that even this was a two-edged argument, since Britain also had its stabilisation subsidies which helped to keep down the prices of goods sent to New Zealand. The Dominion Government, however, persistently pressed its case on the 'terms of trade argument'; first mooted as early as 1940, it was a central element in the case made by the New Zealand Minister of Finance when he came to London early in 1944, and after he had failed to find acceptance for the doctrine, his Prime Minister (Mr. Fraser) came to London and hammered at it in June and July 1944. It was all too clear that without substantial concession there was going to be really bad feeling in New Zealand, and Mr. Fraser made it plain that in these circumstances there could be no settlement of the new long-term food contracts. Eventually a broad settlement was reached. The Chancellor felt bound to record his refusal to accept the 'terms of trade argument', but conceded a cash payment of £12 millions in respect of the past and £4 millions a year for the future, as a contribution towards New Zealand's stabilisation subsidies, and in lieu of price increases. Thus New Zealand took the cash and let the doctrine go. The United Kingdom Government regarded the payments as substantially justified without any dependence upon the unacceptable doctrine,[1] but there was sharp criticism in the Press. Even the *Manchester Guardian* saw fit to use the headline 'A Gift for New Zealand',[2] and the Chancellor felt obliged to make a further statement,[3] in which he underlined the stabilisation subsidies and added that New Zealand's contribution to the common war effort constituted 'a very serious problem for New Zealand'. This was of course true; but New Zealand had already enjoyed for two years the higher price of wool[4], and by this time it was apparent that her balance of payments was receiving help in other

---

[1] The Chancellor briefly announced the terms of the agreement in reply to a Question on 14th November 1944 (H. of C. Deb., Vol. 404, Cols. 1805-6).

[2] 15th November 1944.

[3] 27th November 1944. The statement was made to the Press as the House was not sitting.

[4] See above, p. 295, for the agreement between the United Kingdom, Australia and New Zealand, May 1942, advancing the price of wool by 15 per cent.

directions. New Zealand was undoubtedly facing serious problems; whether these problems were as grave as those facing the United Kingdom was another matter, on which no doubt the Chancellor did not wish to pronounce.

Officials in London watched New Zealand's balance of payments being strengthened by one change after another, and her sterling balance therefore running up. The discussions about the level of New Zealand's London balance—and these discussions continued on and off throughout the war—took place against this background, and British officials were therefore increasingly unable to justify special help. New Zealand, on the other hand, always remained mindful of the tight corner in which she found herself in 1939. Conscious also of war-time exhaustions—and every Government sees most clearly the exhaustions of its own economy—her Ministers were inclined to be cautious; they also argued as though the difficulties of 1939 might easily be repeated, and sought every protection against post-war strains.

In the spring of 1942, the Chancellor of the Exchequer had reaffirmed the United Kingdom's undertaking to safeguard New Zealand's sterling position during the war, and the opportunity was taken to free the British advances from interest, thus bringing these inter-Allied loans into line with others. The assurance remained in general terms, no specific figure being named for the minimum balance. At that time advances outstanding were less than £3 millions, earlier advances totalling £12 millions having been largely paid off; there were also some unpresented bills from the War Office and other United Kingdom Departments which ran into millions. London thought New Zealand's immediate prospect was so good that she would soon have paid off all these debts. But New Zealand was not at all satisfied that the Chancellor's general assurance met the situation created by the initiation of reciprocal aid. To the extent that New Zealand furnished supplies to United States Forces, her capacity to export to the United Kingdom would be weakened. Moreover, the United Kingdom would now be receiving from the United States lend-lease goods in replacement of goods ordinarily bought from New Zealand; and Canada's gift to the United Kingdom further complicated the position. Inter-Allied trade was shifting heavily on to a no-charge basis and New Zealand, while not suggesting that either her exports or her imports should be put on this basis (apart from the provisions of lend-lease and reciprocal aid), was inclined to ask now that any net debt running against her, after allowing a reasonable sterling balance, should be wiped out.

The United Kingdom, on the other hand, was not ready to discuss with New Zealand alone what should be done at the end of the war: the matter was clearly not one for piecemeal settlement, and there was no possibility of an all-round settlement during the war. Once again, therefore, when Mr. Nash visited London in the summer of 1942, the discussions were mainly concerned with the treatment of particular items during the war. New Zealand's obligation to keep her army in the field was reaffirmed and, in line with the rough-and-ready Australian settlement, a round sum of £400,000 a month was agreed as the appropriate charge to New Zealand. A sum of £6 millions odd was paid by New Zealand in final settlement of all old accounts for the initial equipment supplied long ago for the New Zealand Government. As for the level of the sterling balance, the Governments could still not agree on a figure. The Chancellor's advisers thought that Mr. Nash was seeking protection from every contingency, and was forgetting that Britain was more likely than New Zealand to be impoverished at the end of the war. The assurance therefore remained in general terms: after a reference to reciprocal aid, the wording ran, 'are ready to safeguard New Zealand as regards her sterling position during the war and for the duration of the war the United Kingdom Treasury will make any advance required to prevent the New Zealand balance being unduly depleted'.

Mr Nash was pressing on the procedure to be followed in dealing with New Zealand's heavy post-war maturities. In the end he was given a promise that the Treasury would 'co-operate in every possible way to assist your Government in successfully dealing with these loans'—a form of words which was thought in some quarters to be 'much too forthcoming'. It might well be taken to mean that the United Kingdom Treasury would have to underwrite a conversion issue.

After this 1942 settlement there was little further discussion. New Zealand's sterling position remained much stronger than her representatives had been ready to assume: shipments under the food contracts, for example, do not appear to have been affected by any diversion of supplies to American troops, and the latter spent considerable sums in New Zealand on items not covered by reciprocal aid. Through the first half of 1943 New Zealand paid more than £20 millions off the advances, and still held plenty of sterling. Thereafter she borrowed a little more, and in 1945 the advances account stood at £18 millions. There it was left for post-war discussion,[1] while New Zealand earned enough sterling to raise her London balance to £63 millions at mid-1945 and £81 millions at the end of the year. The United Kingdom Treasury and the Bank of England need not have worried over the formula used about helping New Zealand to deal with her maturities: on 31st

---

[1] The £18 millions were repaid in March 1946.

W

October 1945 the New Zealand Government was able to give notice of repayment of two sterling loans totalling over £23 millions. So New Zealand in effect finished the war with a bonded debt in London totalling £139 millions against £157 millions in 1939, while after repaying the £18 millions of 'defence advances', her London balances stood in the spring of 1946 at about £60 millions, against a shaky £7 millions seven years earlier.

This transformation of New Zealand's position, like the transformation of India's position, was of course part of the measure of her war effort. It reflected her success in producing essential commodities—mostly wool and foodstuffs—for the United Kingdom, and in denying imports to her own consumers. To the extent that this denial left her real resources exhausted, her strong financial position was illusory. But at least she was fortunate in emerging from the war with a smaller bonded debt and a cash balance that would amply cover reconstruction once the goods became available.

(iv)

South Africa

From many points of view the Union of South Africa was in a far stronger position to help Britain financially than was either Australia or New Zealand; yet financial relations with the Union were throughout the most difficult. This was at bottom due to the vitally different political situation in the Union. Australian politics have a bitterness Englishmen scarcely realise, and her Commonwealth Government always had to be looking over its shoulder at its election prospects. This sometimes led to a certain touchiness in financial negotiations, but there was not even a threat of anything worse. Australia's alternative Government might have different views about how the war effort should be conducted, perhaps even how great the effort should be; but the necessity of the war effort was never in question. In South Africa this basic unanimity was lacking. The Government led by General Smuts, like that of Great Britain, entered wholeheartedly into the war and at no stage was there any question of its drawing back; but that Government's majority was a narrow one, with scarcely any support among certain important sections of the population, and the Opposition leaders were openly against participation in the war. The neutrality policy was defeated partly on the ground that alliance with the rest of the Commonwealth would be to the economic advantage of South Africa. In all Britain's war-time dealings with South Africa, the Union Government's precarious position and its promise of economic advantage had to be accepted among the most important facts of life.

The contrast between the political position in South Africa and that prevailing in the other Dominions, in its effect upon financial discussions, emerged most strikingly in the grimmest days of military adversity. When news reached Australasia of calamities in Greece and Crete, involving heavy casualties in the Forces of the Dominions themselves, the immediate effect was to goad their civilian populations into new efforts and to dispose them to make new sacrifices. The news that brothers and sons were being killed and wounded intensified support—all-round support—for the common cause; the first intensity of this reaction might pass, but it had its value while it lasted, and there was some lasting stimulus. In South Africa reactions were quite different. The fall of Tobruk, to take an extreme example, brought experience of loss—either casualty or capture—into many a South African family. This was immediately exploited by the Opposition, which denounced the Government for sacrificing South African families to the interests of Britain. The loss of soldiers meant the loss of Government votes, and an early general election was due. 'With the Government and Opposition as evenly balanced as they are,' reported the United Kingdom High Commissioner, 'the loss of votes may mean the loss of several seats, and, as you know, it only requires a turnover in ten constituencies to result in the defeat of the Government and the formation of an administration pledged to make peace with the Axis'. This may have been an unduly alarmist appraisal—to others on the spot there were more encouraging symptoms[1]—but it was the advice upon which the financial authorities at home had to base their view of the Union Government's strength.

In this general situation it is not to be wondered at that the Union Government was always inclined to limit its commitments altogether more narrowly than did Britain's other partners in the Commonwealth. Most damaging was its attitude on the central pool of gold and dollars, the principle of which was never really accepted by South Africa. Another important aspect of South Africa's limitation of liability was its attitude on the question of overseas Forces. In the early part of the war the operations of South African Forces were confined to the campaigns in East Africa and Abyssinia, and the Union Government accepted financial responsibility for these contingents. There was continual discussion about the method by which the sum should be reckoned; actual payments, a rough capitation rate, and a 50–50 sharing of the total costs of the campaigns—each in turn was favoured as a

---

[1] There was strengthened recruiting and an intensified civilian war effort, and the Minister of Finance believed that the Government need have no electoral fears.

basis for settlement. But throughout these discussions South Africa accepted the basic principle common to all the Dominions, that it should pay for its own Forces in the field; the Union Government showed moreover a disposition to settle without haggling over detailed figures. So far, so good; the trouble came in 1942, when South African air squadrons were employed mainly in the Middle East. In addition to the two squadrons in East Africa (for which South Africa admitted full financial responsibility), 12 squadrons were operating in the Middle East; the Union Government offered to pay all personnel charges for these latter squadrons but looked to Britain for the cost of equipment with aircraft and subsequent maintenance. The money involved was £6 millions non-recurrent and subsequently £13 millions a year. The total of 14 squadrons did indeed represent *pro rata* a far greater Air Force contribution than any of the other Dominions had been able to make, but this should not have made any difference to South Africa's willingness to pay.

The question of financing these South African squadrons in Libya developed during 1942 into a general argument about South Africa's contribution, and all sorts of detailed matters were sooner or later dragged into it. The Union's Minister of Finance proved an obstinate bargainer. Under his lead the South African negotiators took the line that the extension of South Africa's commitments now proposed was beyond South Africa's financial capacity. But ability to pay was a doubtful criterion for the South African negotiators to raise; it implied comparison with Britain's own ability to pay, a comparison that could not be pressed in South Africa's interest. The United Kingdom negotiators regarded the South African case as fundamentally indefensible, in that it differentiated between the war in one theatre and the war in another. The British insisted that action in North Africa was in defence of the Union just as much as was action against the Italians in Abyssinia: the war was one war, the enemy one enemy to be attacked in every possible quarter. Similarly they were bound on the figures to insist that South Africa could pay, if only she had the will to pay. On the other hand, London was realistic enough to appreciate that the South African political position implied a serious limitation of willingness to pay. As this was at the bottom of the matter, the only sensible way of settling the argument was on a very round basis with General Smuts himself: the Chancellor of the Exchequer must put the case candidly to General Smuts, press him 'to go as far as he could', and in the end accept General Smuts's judgment of how far he could carry his country. As the argument dragged on through 1943, London officials came to accept this as the only end. Their hopes were realised when the

Chancellor met the South African leader on 9th November 1943. The agreement then reached bore little relation to the meticulous arguments that had filled the files with telegrams over a long period. The broad settlement now reached in London included certain arrangements about supplies of gold, to be referred to below.[1] As for military expenditure South Africa agreed to pay £35½ millions in respect of the past (in addition to certain sums previously paid), and £1 million a month for the future upkeep of South Africa's forces in North Africa. The latter sum was to be revised at any time if there should be a substantial increase or decrease of the number of South African troops involved. The cost of upkeep of the South African Forces in North Africa had been roughly estimated at £17½ millions a year, after allowing for lend-lease supplies, but this had been arbitrarily reduced to £12 millions 'to take into account South Africa's ability to pay'. The £35½ millions for the past was in final settlement of all claims, and Britain undertook to accept payment at dates convenient to South Africa.

South Africa's limited ability to pay, which was thus the ostensible reason for adding £5½ millions a year to Britain's own burden, was of course in one sense dependent upon the willingness of her people to finance Government outlays. More fundamentally it depended upon what was happening to South Africa's exports and imports. Her receipts from exports had in fact been substantially underpinned by another generous gesture by the United Kingdom. This was the wool purchase, eventually assimilated to the purchase of wool in Australia and New Zealand. In 1938 South Africa's wool exports had been worth £9 millions, about 30 per cent. of her total exports other than gold. Roughly one-fifth of the wool came to the United Kingdom, one-fifth to France and almost all the remainder to Germany or countries contiguous with it. At first the Union made no request for purchase of the whole clip; wool, though important to certain sections of the population, had not in South Africa the overwhelming importance it had in the economies of Australia and New Zealand. On supply grounds the United Kingdom Government would at this stage have been unable to justify action covering the whole clip. But some support was judged necessary, in order to show that the agreement with the other Dominions did not imply loss of United Kingdom interest in South Africa as a source of supply. To avert these fears and thereby to help the Smuts Government to carry the country into the war, the United Kingdom in effect agreed to insure South Africa against a collapse of the market following the cessation of German purchases. United Kingdom Government buyers would intervene as far as was necessary to prevent prices at the South African auctions from

---

[1] See pp. 318-9.

falling below a schedule calculated to correspond to the prices being paid to Australia. The arrangement was strictly limited to one season and to a maximum expenditure by the United Kingdom of £3,700,000, this being the value of German purchases in the previous year.

The amount actually spent by the United Kingdom during the 1939–40 season was only £1,300,000, about half of this being for parcels wanted on supply grounds, and the remainder for market support in accordance with the undertaking given in the autumn of 1939. South Africa had in fact done rather well; the Australasian deal with the United Kingdom had led the United States, Japan, France and Belgium to switch their purchases to South Africa. The changed complexion of the war in 1940, particularly the over-running of South Africa's European customers and the entry of Italy, made it questionable how far this favourable experience of the 1939–40 season could be repeated. In any case the behaviour of international markets in that season held a warning for Britain. Under the arrangements for Australian wool the United Kingdom shared profits on outside sales, but would bear any net loss arising— as it was feared—from post-war sales; under the South African arrangements, the United Kingdom had no share in profits but took a risk of loss. Moreover, it looked as though South African sales both during and after the war might be thrown on the market in competition with the Australian with damaging effects on Britain's profits and losses. On financial grounds alone, a continuance of the 1939–40 undertaking could hardly be contemplated. To decline to give any assistance was politically impossible: the Smuts Government could not stand such a blow at the wool-growers. Evidently the United Kingdom, unable to pull out or to stand still, would have to go in more deeply. Would it not be wise to put South African wool on the same basis as that of Australia and New Zealand?

That Britain should become more deeply involved in supporting rich wool-farmers within the Commonwealth was naturally repugnant to those charged with the care of Britain's financial position. There must, after all, be many Colonies, infinitely poorer than South Africa, whose markets had been equally hit, and Britain was in no position to compensate everybody who might have lost by the war. So when South Africa sought not merely a continuance of the 1939–40 undertaking, but a purchase of the whole clip, London refused. But the refusal was coupled with an offer to join with the Union Government, on a 50–50 basis, in purchase from the growers, for the duration of the war and one year thereafter. This was a generous offer, but the Union Government turned it down. Several reasons were given, the really operative one being that the Union

Government had given definite assurances inside and outside Parliament that the Union would receive at least as favourable treatment as Australia and New Zealand.[1] The latter were protected against losses and shared only in profits. The Union Government had therefore felt able to defend the 1939–40 arrangement, and would be prepared to continue it, but could not accept a new arrangement which would be obviously less favourable than that agreed with Australia and New Zealand.

The pressure succeeded. The role South Africa was being asked to play in the prosecution of the war was becoming increasingly important;[2] moreover she was at this stage being obliging in selling gold to the United Kingdom for sterling. London was not prepared to risk the fall of General Smuts, and Smuts needed a wool contract as good as that reached with the other Dominions. In August 1940 the Chancellor accepted the case. Later argument about details followed the same line. Once the principle of appeasement is accepted, the argument that it is not worth spoiling the ship for a ha'porth of tar is always successful. South Africa naturally shared in the 15 per cent. price increase negotiated with the other Dominions in 1942. The only ways in which she insisted upon different treatment concerned detailed matters of procedure, in which the Union Government felt unable to exercise powers to convenience the United Kingdom authorities.[3]

While the wool purchase was sustaining both the Union's export income and the prosperity of the individual producers, and while the Union's Minister of Finance was successfully pleading the country's inability to pay in full for the equipment and maintenance of its own Forces in the field, little hindrance was being put in the way of consumer spending on unnecessary imports. This was not altogether surprising given the confusion, associated with the 'Buy British' campaign, as to the needs of the situation; and General Smuts wanted to show the Opposition that the declaration of war had not hurt South Africa. Early in 1940 London began to complain: why was the Union doing nothing to check extravagant use of petrol? The reply was that supplies of petrol to the Union were not being endangered by any lack of tankers, which was the immediate reason for shortage in Britain, that rationing would

---

[1] It will be appreciated that the Australian and New Zealand agreements then looked, to many people, generous to the point of prodigality. The extent of benefit which Britain in the result derived from these agreements, largely because the war was long and was followed by prolonged international inflation, was not foreseen.

[2] For example, the safeguarding of the Cape route depended upon active co-operation, and Air Training Schools were being established in the Union.

[3] As the Union Government would not themselves buy the clip from the growers, the Ministry of Supply had to continue its buying organisation. Nor would the Union Government ever compel growers to sell their clip to the Ministry of Supply; they did, however, refuse export licences for all other destinations.

upset the farming population on whose marginal votes the Smuts Government depended, and that budget calculations would be upset if the petrol tax yielded two or three million pounds less. There were also difficulties with the American oil firms, who demanded regular acceptance of their tanker offerings. The most that could be extracted at that time was a Ministerial warning to the people of South Africa to the effect that there was not much petrol to spare for joy-riding.

A whole year later, when London's gold reserves ran out during the period preceding the initiation of lend-lease, another attempt was made to explain to the South African Government the nature of the Commonwealth's needs. All consumption that directly or indirectly created a demand for dollars, or reduced the supply of gold or dollars for the Sterling Area's central pool, was striking at a vital root of the whole Commonwealth's war production. Everywhere else this had been recognised, however inadequately, before the end of 1940, but whenever the financial experts suggested that South Africa should be asked to co-operate, they were told that there were insuperable political objections.[1] London's financial straits were by this time desperate, and a telegram did eventually go, emphasising that London needed more help from South African gold, and pointing a moral about unnecessary expenditure on imports. In reply, General Smuts expressed himself anxious to help and promised consultations, though he emphasised that it might be 'difficult politically to administer any drastic shocks to commercial and private consumers'. Reports during the next few weeks tended to emphasise how right the South African Prime Minister was in his estimate of the country's unreadiness for any severe restriction; but his intention of doing something about it received strong support from the Union's representatives in Washington. The latter had been learning that South Africa's ability to draw on lend-lease supplies—perhaps any supplies of certain goods from the United States—was likely to depend upon strict Governmental supervision at the very least.

It was this fright about supplies from the United States that finally shocked the Union Government into a measure of import control, which was announced at the beginning of August and came into operation on 1st September 1941. Restriction was at first practically confined to a short list of non-essentials from non-sterling countries, and even this evoked strong protest from the Opposition. The year 1942 did, however, see an appreciable reduction in the volume of imports: the shipping stringency and

---

[1] It is possible that these political difficulties in South Africa were sometimes exaggerated in London; but the impression that existed in London was the operative factor influencing London's financial policy.

difficulties in supply countries reinforced Union control measures, and the total from all sources fell from £135 millions in 1941 to £117 millions in 1942 and remained about this level through the remainder of the war. By comparison with what was being achieved elsewhere, this was not austerity. Extravagant living in South Africa continued to impress British observers and some in South Africa itself, but at least it was not such wanton extravagance as had prevailed through the first two years of the war.[1]

The connection between the beginning of import control and the question of supplies from the United States was symptomatic of the underlying interests of South Africa's financial relations throughout the remainder of the war, for upon American interest depended the equipment of her all-important gold-mining. The position of the mines has to be considered against the background of the gold reserve and the balance of payments. The balance was in fact running pretty strongly in South Africa's favour. The value of commodity exports was being sustained largely by the United Kingdom wool purchase, South Africa was moderating expenditure on imports, and the Union Government was haggling with some success about the bill for her Forces in the field. The strength of the Union's balance of payments showed itself in the gold position. While enjoying the Sterling Area privilege of access to the Area's central dollar pool, South Africa did not automatically make her gold production available to the pool. The position in the early part of the war was that South Africa merely sold the amount of gold necessary to meet her own needs for sterling. Consequently her favourable balance of payments did not show itself, as did that of India, in an accumulation of sterling balances standing in her favour, but in accumulation of gold in the South African Reserve Bank, to which the mines had sold their output since the London bullion market closed. Production steadily increased during the early part of the war and in the course of 1940 the South African Reserve Bank was able to add over three million ounces to its gold reserve. This gold continued to be valued, for balance-sheet purposes, at the pre-1931 price, so that the published 58 per cent. proportion of gold to Reserve Bank Liabilities implied a proportion of 116 per cent. at the current price of gold; the Reserve Bank statutes necessitated a minimum of 30 per cent.[2] An attempt was made in October 1940 to persuade the Reserve Bank to revalue its gold reserve and to release some £30 millions (at the current price) for

---

[1] A recent South African academic judgment is that 'the South African war-time exchange and trade controls were relatively mild'. (G. de Kock, *A History of the South African Reserve Bank* (Pretoria 1954), p. 241).

[2] (South African) Currency and Banking Act 1920/33, Sections 17 and 23. cf. de Kock, *op. cit.*, p. 262.

sale to the United Kingdom against sterling. The matter was carried to General Smuts personally, but although both he and his Minister of Finance were reported to be personally sympathetic, great political difficulties were alleged and nothing came of this effort.

As 1940 ended, the continuing growth of this hoard of gold in South Africa—a part of the Sterling Area—inevitably excited strong feelings in London. South Africa was accumulating gold not so much by any economy in imports, as by hesitating to pay the bill for her Forces in the field and by enjoying participation in the Commonwealth wool purchase. London suspected, too, that South Africa was a serious gap in the exchange control fence: there were persistent stories of a flight of capital to the United States through South Africa, some of it originating in the Union itself, but some in the United Kingdom or other parts of the Sterling Area. A clarification of the statistics disposed of the worst fears on this account, but the suspicion was never entirely scotched. At the time when London's gold reserves were running out and lend-lease was not yet operating, all these points added up to a serious cramping of the Commonwealth's war effort. The first months of 1941 therefore saw an all-round attempt by the United Kingdom Government to persuade the Union Government to alter its ways. We have seen how eventually some little impression was made on South Africa's expenditure on imports, and on the problem of military expenditure; on the exchange control leak South Africa pleaded not guilty. On gold, the Reserve Bank was asked to reverse its policy of not increasing its sterling balance; but London suggested that if South Africa, unlike India, was unwilling to hold more sterling, at least it should repatriate more of its sterling debt, since this would have the same effect of adding to the Sterling Area's central reserve of gold.

South Africa had in fact already been absorbing securities previously held in the United Kingdom, without any special action on the part of the British authorities. In 1940 the Union Government redeemed at maturity about £8 millions of bonds in the London market, and there had also been 'considerable repatriation of mining shares';[1] given the Reserve Bank's method of financing its net sterling requirements by sales of gold to the United Kingdom, this repatriation had added correspondingly to the gold available to the central pool. But if the process was to go much further, active co-operation by the United Kingdom authorities was required, so that South African stocks might be compulsorily acquired from United Kingdom residents. South

---

[1] *The Economist*, 18th October 1940.

Africa offered £31 millions of gold for sterling, on condition that
the sterling should be used for a vesting operation of this kind.[1]

This was the general position when late in May 1941 Lord
Harlech arrived in South Africa as United Kingdom High
Commissioner, fully briefed to take up all these matters as quickly
as possible. He was to try to persuade South Africa to sell all her
current gold production to the central pool, but, as a favourable
response was not seriously expected, he was to indicate London's
readiness to proceed with the vesting on the agreed basis. Lord
Harlech advised action without delay, and the Chancellor of the
Exchequer agreed on 7th June 1941 that the Vesting Order[2]
should be made forthwith. Both the official machine and public
opinion were by now familiar with the process; all went well and
four stocks, of nominal value £32.4 millions, were taken over at
the ruling market value of £33.9 millions. This provided some
immediate help to the central gold reserve, though nothing like
the amount South Africa could have provided. As a precedent
the value of the operation was limited, since only another £70
millions or so of South African securities were eligible for maturity
in the early future. The principle of relating amounts vested to
the surplus gold currently accruing in South Africa was open to
technical objections: market reactions might easily give rise to bad
feeling. Finally, from the long-term point of view, the British
authorities were always unhappy about these vesting operations,
by which the position of the United Kingdom as a great owner
of overseas capital was being signally terminated; there was at this
stage a real preference for running up sterling balances.

For reasons of this kind, London's policy in 1942 remained one
of trying to persuade South Africa to sell more of her gold for sterling
without any further vesting operation, and in this context American
views were beginning to have some relevance. The maintenance
of gold mining on a very high level was politically vital to the
Union Government, and it depended substantially upon United
States and United Kingdom provision of steel and equipment.
Congress and popular opinion in the United States were inclined
to assume that South African gold was British gold, and if the
United Kingdom confessed inability to persuade South Africa to
release it for use by the United Kingdom, difficulties might well
be made about American supplies of mining equipment.

But all these arguments were rather complicated and it seemed
doubtful whether they could profitably be impressed upon General

---

[1] For an account, based on Reserve Bank sources, of the repatriation operations,
see G. de Kock, *op. cit.*, pp. 253-4. de Kock states, on Reserve Bank authority, the
total war-time repatriations as amounting to £73,670,000. The repatriation operations
suited the Reserve Bank in the latter's attempts to restrain inflation. (de Kock, pp. 272-3).

[2] No. 5 of 1941 (S.R. and O. (1941) Nos. 1574 and 1575) made 10th October.

Smuts, who was the one fully sympathetic listener. Perhaps it would be wiser to concentrate on other issues, such as South Africa's contribution to military expenditure. When, however, the Chancellor saw General Smuts on 6th November 1942, Smuts was unexpectedly forthcoming on the gold issue; he sought 'one more repatriation of some £35 to £40 millions', but beyond that South Africa 'would collect sterling against gold pretty extensively'. The broad arrangements reached immediately thereafter provided for an immediate vesting operation, a United Kingdom option on £90 millions of gold in 1943, and all possible United Kingdom support in securing equipment for the gold mines; into the questions of military expenditure General Smuts would look further.

The agreed vesting operation went through quickly: after excluding three small issues which the South Africans wanted to include, Vesting Order No. 3 of 1942 was made on 18th December,[1] covering four issues. The nominal amount of stock repatriated was just over £38 millions, and the actual proceeds £40 millions. Final definition of the *quid pro quo*, in the shape of the option on gold, did not come so quickly. This was partly the fault of the United Kingdom side, who in the last weeks of 1942 had begun to be worried about the effect of mounting gold stocks upon the breadth of lend-lease.[2] An option, in the strict sense, really suited London best. On the other hand, it seemed likely that General Smuts had understood that the gold was really needed and needed quickly; if London now hesitated, he might cease to believe that London's need was a serious one. After wobbling on the question through most of 1943, London decided that a South African bird in the hand was worth as much as a highly theoretical American bird in the bush, though London asked that delivery of the gold should in part be delayed. By the end of 1943, in addition to gold sold by South Africa to meet her London requirements, the South African Reserve Bank had acquired about £20 millions sterling against the sale of gold to London. The United Kingdom used this gold to discharge liabilities to certain neutral countries, thus avoiding the appearance of adding to United Kingdom gold reserves. An option on a further substantial amount in 1944 was sought.

Meanwhile the situation had been complicated by the initiation of sales of gold in India and the Middle East at market prices—prices very substantially above those at which the United Kingdom was buying gold from South Africa. Why should South Africa

---

[1] S.R. and O. (1942) Nos. 2545 and 2546.

[2] London's change of front on the question of gold reserves (see Chapter XIII, Section (vi)) must have been extremely confusing to her friends elsewhere; the complexity of this particular phrase of relations with the Union Government cannot be understood except against the background of this chopping and changing of reserves policy.

not enjoy the gold premium? Was not Britain buying from South Africa at £8 8s. od. on ounce and selling the gold at £14 or so?

This was an awkward point. If taken to its logical conclusion, the situation might lead to South Africa's insistence on selling all her gold at 'market price', and the breakdown of the British effort to maintain the official gold value of the pound—with fearful repercussions on payments agreements with neutrals, on Anglo-Indian relations, and in many other directions. Opportunity was therefore taken, when the Union Secretary for Finance was in London, to explain carefully the limited nature and very special purpose of the gold sales. Stress was laid, both then and later, upon the British use of the rupees so obtained to meet military expenditure in the inflationary markets of India and the Middle East. When General Smuts met the Chancellor in November, the matter was further pursued and it was agreed that South Africa should sell gold in India (strictly in concert with the British sales there) to the extent that would cover her direct rupee requirements for Indian goods.[1] The Union Government undertook that it would not use the profit on the gold sales directly to cheapen the Indian commodities in South Africa. Arrangements were eventually settled in an exchange of telegrams in April 1944.

Although South Africa enjoyed the substantial profit that arose in these transactions, and persistently made the point that she was in equity entitled to do so, Union Ministers were a little uneasy. There was anxiety—evident in South African reactions to the White-Keynes international currency schemes—that the currency position of gold should be maintained, and General Smuts publicly spoke of fighting 'the black market' in gold.[2] Elsewhere more consistently hostile feelings prevailed. In India—where South Africa was unpopular for other reasons—an arrangement that looked like 'exploitation' was politically embarrassing. In London, where opinion on United Kingdom sales of gold in India had always been divided, South Africa's insistence on participation was viewed as a first example of the repercussions of these sales on the general position of sterling. When the Union Government proceeded, in June 1944, to suggest that its expenditure of £2 millions a year on South African troops in Egypt should be settled on the basis of the realised price of gold, it seemed as though another nail was being hammered into sterling's coffin. There was consequently great relief when a few weeks later the South African Prime Minister could be given notice of the impending cessation

---

[1] South Africa's normal practice was to pay sterling, or rupees bought for sterling in London, for imports from India. The departure from this practice made the whole business doubly repugnant to those who had the future of the Sterling Area much in mind.

[2] *The Economist*, 8th April 1944.

of United Kingdom sales of gold in India and the Middle East. As the arrangements were essentially for joint sales, and as it was anyway politically impossible for South Africa to act alone in India, this source of great embarrassment came to a natural end before the full repercussions had time to develop.

The arrangement for premium sales of gold in India did however serve during its short life to promote South African willingness to help London as much as possible on the major question of supplying gold to the central pool. This favourable disposition was also being helped by realisation of the importance of maintaining American interest in the activity of the South African mines. On the other hand, the amount of help South Africa could give was now somewhat reduced both by falling gold production and by her special treatment under the lend-lease and reciprocal aid arrangements. During 1942 the Union received about £11 millions' worth of supplies under lend-lease, but the United States Congressional elections in November led to a tightening, and the Americans questioned the need of a great gold producer for dollar aid. Eventually it was agreed between the Union and the United States that lend-lease and reciprocal aid should be confined practically to military items.[1] Although non-military supplies by the United States to South Africa were paid for in gold for the remainder of the war, American goodwill remained a pre-requisite for such supplies, and the Sharpstone Mission on mining equipment had shown how particular the Americans could be.[2] South Africa was recognised as the Sterling Area's major source of gold, she saw how important it was to herself that she should be so recognised, and she needed altogether less prompting than she had done in the earlier years.

It was in these circumstances that, in November 1943, General Smuts informed the Chancellor of the Exchequer of South Africa's willingness to supply in 1944 as much gold as possible. He estimated that only £80 millions would be available against the £90 millions promised (and substantially delivered) for 1943. The £80 millions would have to cover all South Africa's sterling requirements, but London hoped that it would imply a large increase in South Africa's holding of sterling. In the event, South Africa did deliver £80

[1] In July 1943 the United States asked for raw materials from the Commonwealth to be included in reciprocal aid; South Africa's reply was a suggestion that for her everything both ways should go on to a cash basis, but it was was not until April 1945 that this cash basis was substantially agreed.

[2] The United Kingdom consistently backed South African requests for the essential priorities for American equipment for the mines, and in 1942 an American Mission under Mr. Sharpstone visited South Africa to investigate the demands. Its somewhat critical report led to closer co-ordination and more systematic marshalling of demands from the mines.

millions of gold, but her sterling balance rose by only £7. 5 millions, to £28 millions. When the time came for discussing 1945, opinion in London had more or less settled to the view that the central gold reserves must be strengthened as certainly, if not as quickly, as possible. In the belief that this would raise the sterling balance to £45 or £50 millions, South Africa was asked for, and agreed to sell, £75 millions of gold in 1945, of which £50 millions were to be spread over the year and £25 millions were to be concentrated in the last three months of it. The upshot was that South Africa's balance in London rose to £33 millions at the half year and £72 millions at the end of 1945; the reserve of gold held in South Africa rose meanwhile at the rate of more than £3 millions a month, bringing it well over £200 millions at the end of the war.[1]

Even this tangled story of financial relations with South Africa appears more simple than the truth. For all the topics discussed in successive paragraphs above—the wool purchase, economy in imports, the allocation of military expenditure, the gold sales— were under discussion and had to be settled, not successively, but more or less simultaneously. The same group of men had to deal with the various problems, which were therefore approached in a common way and were sometimes linked together—more or less consciously—as bargaining counters are linked. Running through the early years there was the uneasiness of the Smuts Government,[2] an uneasiness that raised to first importance its endeavours to protect the Union's economic life—first most obviously in the wool negotiations, then in the glances over the shoulder at American equipment for the gold mines. The British on their side always recognised and allowed for the weakness of General Smuts's political position, and their overriding consideration was to avoid undermining the Smuts Government. Consistently with this, they had to extract what they could towards the military costs of the war. Above all, the British had to attract as much gold as they could from the South African mines; ideally to attract it as South Africa's contribution to the military costs, or next best against sterling in London. In the event they secured some £70 millions of gold against debt repatriation (which the British liked least), some £55 millions against the amounts paid by South Africa under the agreements about military supplies, and some £30 millions against sterling balances accumulated in London. South Africa

---

[1] In these figures the gold is valued at the official London price, although until 1946 it continued to appear in the South African Reserve Bank's Balance Sheet at the pre-1931 price. For a summary of the reasons for the Union's favourable war-time balance of payments, cf. G. de Kock, *op. cit.*, p. 251.

[2] This element was always much stressed in official discussions in London, even after General Smuts's success in the 1943 elections had removed all substantial danger of his fall.

did pretty well out of it. In the course of the war she had reduced her overseas debt by more than £70 millions, she had added £150 millions to her gold reserves and £30 millions to her London balances, and meanwhile had enjoyed a standard of living less restricted than almost anywhere else in the Commonwealth.

CHAPTER XI

CANADIAN DOLLARS

(i)

The Underlying Conflict in Financial Relations

EXPENDITURE in Canada created financial problems that had
no parallel in relations between Britain and other parts of the
Commonwealth. Some of these problems were actually more
akin to those of Anglo-American relations than to those within
the Commonwealth. Nevertheless, the setting against which the
Anglo-Canadian problems had to be tackled was always a
Commonwealth setting, implying a closeness of alliance that
always assured some tolerable financial settlement without
restriction in the flow of men and materials. Canada was an
independent nation and her action throughout was that of a
willing partner. The Dominion assumed from the outset the
principle that she paid the cost of her own Forces overseas as well
as at home and although, as elsewhere, the application of this
principle involved troublesome problems of detail, there was
never any question of differentiating between the various theatres
of war. The Canadian Government made it plain, from the start
to finish, that the war was for Canada, as for Britain, a single war.

This is not to say that the Dominion Government was entirely
free from political embarrassment on questions affecting her
contribution to the Allied war effort. The Mackenzie King
administration, in office since 1935, always faced a strong opposition, an opposition based partly on regional fears of central
usurpation of the powers of provincial Governments. In 1940 the
political situation was further complicated by the fall of France:
the French Canadians, a large minority dominating Quebec
Province, do not automatically identify themselves with metropolitan
France, but their sympathies were inevitably affected by the action
against the French fleet and other steps Britain had to take. The
political pendulum, too, was swinging after so many years of
Liberal Government, and the personal prestige of Mr. Mackenzie
King did not confer upon his Government anything approaching a
dictator's power. Canadian popular opinion was self-conscious:
the Prime Minister was regarded as a worthy war leader but his
every move was to be watched lest he give way to a too-motherly

321

Mother Country or to an overbearing Uncle Sam. This political embarrassment has always to be borne in mind in interpreting the hesitation of the Dominion Government in taking financial steps that were, in the last analysis, outstandingly large-minded. Especially it was relevant to the delays in the winter of 1944–45, when Mr. Mackenzie King's Government was weakened by changes in provincial Governments and by its failure to carry the country on the issue, just become urgent, of conscription for overseas service.

Not only in her political relations but also in some highly relevant economic relations with Britain, there were parallels between Canada and other members of the Commonwealth. Much of the country in area, and in political weight, is in the hands of primary producers who are heavily dependent on the British market: in 1939 this was true not only of the wheatlands in the Prairie Provinces, but also of British Columbia's fruit-farms and the mixed farming of the eastern provinces. Secondly, when Canada entered the Second World War the process of debt repatriation had scarcely begun; there were still very large British holdings of Canadian Government bonds and railway bonds, as well as mining and other stocks. The bonded debt was a debt in sterling, an important relic of London's heyday as the world's supplier of capital.

On the other hand, there were close links with her great neighbour to the south, links that sharply differentiated Canada from the other Dominions and were destined to bring Anglo-Canadian financial relations more and more closely into the orbit of Anglo-American relations. Across the frontier there was a large tourist traffic, in both directions. There was considerable integration of Canadian and American industrial and mining firms, implying a two-way traffic in business capital and, more embarrassing, of payments that could not be easily sorted into necessary current payments on the one hand and avoidable capital movements on the other. These conditions and the close links between the Canadian banks and the New York money market were important in determining that Canada should stand apart from the Sterling Area in the organisation of foreign exchange restrictions although the Dominion did have its own effective foreign exchange control. The closeness of her business ties with the United States would have made her too easy a channel for the flight of funds from the Sterling Area to the United States, and Canada itself might have been an attractive home for British funds. With these considerations in mind, London was ready to co-operate in the erection of a control fence excluding Canada from the Sterling Area.

But whether Canada stood outside or inside the Sterling Area, there was bound to be difficulty about the Dominion's need for U.S. dollars. Her pre-war economy was based on bilateral unbalance within a balanced 'North Atlantic Triangle'. Broadly speaking, Canada financed her excess purchases from the United States by an excess of exports to Britain, the latter being able to supply the required U.S. dollars from the surplus dollar earnings of the Sterling Area. From the outset it was clear that, however much the supply side of this equation might dwindle, the demand side—the Canadian need for U.S. dollars—was likely to persist if full use was to be made of Canada not only as a source of food and materials but also as an arsenal. In the interest of the Allied war effort Canada was to bend her economy more than ever to a flow of goods eastward across the Atlantic. This she could only do if she could depend upon some net flow of goods and services from the United States, a net flow that had to be paid for in gold or U.S. dollars. The natural expression of strain within the Canadian economy was a pressure to import more from the United States. The Canadian authorities could (and did) restrain internal inflation and so check demands for U.S. dollars, but there were limits to the compression that could be forced without weakening Canada as a supply base for the Allied effort.

A consequence of all this was that Canadian supplies to Britain had to be paid for partly in gold or U.S. dollars, though Canada did not press Britain to find more of these than were necessary to meet her own liabilities to the south. What was even more important—and this was what distinguished Canada from the Sterling Area countries—Canada's dependence upon the United States, certain to continue into the post-war world, made it dangerous for her to accept, as an unlimited residual payment, sterling which might not be readily convertible at a fixed rate into U.S. dollars. On the other hand, Britain was unwilling to incur straight dollar debts; this would be not only a dangerous form of indebtedness, but also an awkward precedent when talking to Sterling Area partners who would also have post-war requirements in the United States.

These conditions underlying financial relations between Canada and Britain may be summarised as three lines of conflict. First Britain sought from Canada supplies—eventually the utmost supplies—of men, munitions, materials and food, while Canada had to avoid over-burdening her economy to the point of disorganisation or the weakening of the will to war. Secondly, Britain had to minimise her payments in gold and U.S. dollars, while Canada had to insist upon sufficient to pay her debts to the United States. Thirdly, Britain, keeping an eye on post-war problems, had to watch both the amount and the form of any residuary indebtedness, and was reluctant to part with all her investment connections in Canada, while Canada had to be careful lest her generosity left her too weak an economic neighbour for the United States after the war.

To see the conditions in the form of these major sources of conflict is, it must be appreciated, to see only the difficult side of the problems. The other side may be summarised in the message sent, on 1st September 1939, by the Canadian Prime Minister to the United Kingdom Government. After referring to the complete unanimity of his Cabinet in support of the declaration of war, Mr. Mackenzie King spoke of a united Canada 'ready and willing to help Great Britain to the utmost of its power and resources', and invited London to send an immediate programme of participation and supplies. It was in this spirit that the conflicts were, in one way or another, resolved right through the war.

(ii)
The Sterling Overdraft, 1939–41

Pre-war inspection of Britain's war-time import programmes very quickly revealed the probability of difficulties with Canada. While much of Europe might be inaccessible, Canada stood at the end of a relatively short shipping haul. The inter-war period had seen great development of Canada's mineral resources, and of her processing capacity for a variety of materials of outstanding interest in war-time. In March 1939 United Kingdom requirements from Canada in the first year of a major war were estimated at £126 millions, and it was known that French requirements, which might involve some financial collaboration by Britain, were also likely to be substantial. The figure far exceeded British earnings in Canada, even before these began to suffer from compression of the export industries: it was quite clear that Britain must find from somewhere at least 100 million Canadian dollars[1] to see her through the first year. Though put in terms of war-time expenditure, the problem was already urgent. Plans for war supplies were having to be made beforehand, and the Air Ministry was having to contract with Canadian firms for the immediate erection of new capacity to cope with war-time production. Whether or not war actually came that year, some of this defence expenditure would have to be incurred without delay. Ways and means had to be explored at once, and in the knowledge that the outbreak of war would immediately multiply the bill. Unless dollars could be found, orders could be placed only on a narrowly restricted scale.

---

[1] In this chapter, all figures in dollars are in Canadian dollars, unless otherwise stated. Throughout the war, the official rates of exchange were 4·47 Canadian dollars= £1 and 1·10 Canadian dollars = 1 U.S. dollar.

Mr. Osborne, who had been the first Deputy-Governor of the Bank of Canada and was now back in the Bank of England, was at once sent to Canada to explore the ground on behalf of the Treasury and the Bank of England. He was to investigate the possibilities of an issue of short-term dollar bonds by the United Kingdom Government, and of repatriation of Canada's sterling debt, and he was to impress upon the Canadian authorities the disagreeable fact that unless special financial measures were adopted, it would be impossible for Britain to implement her intentions to make great purchases of Canadian food and raw materials. He was also to inform the Canadian authorities of the probable shape of the United Kingdom foreign exchange control in time of war. The mission had considerable importance in clearing the ground on the more technical matters, though the international position was changing too rapidly for anything definite to be settled. The major result was that the Dominion Government became fully aware of the fact that Britain would have to borrow if Canadian goods were to be purchased in the quantities that seemed both desirable and physically possible.

Mr. Osborne's mission also served to bring into closer touch with each other the Canadian and London officials—both civil servants and central bankers—who were to handle, through the succeeding years, the problems arising from this basic need to finance British purchases on the highest possible scales. In their early discussions several possibilities were put forward and sooner or later dropped. One of these non-starters was the issue of United Kingdom dollar bonds in Canada; this would have had the advantage of striking directly at the root of the difficulty, but as a pre-war measure it was open to the objection that United Kingdom dollar bonds would have appealed too strongly to investors in the United Kingdom itself, while in war-time such a striking reversal of London's traditional role would have been a gift to enemy propaganda in the world at large. The course that seemed to have most to recommend it on technical grounds was repatriation of Canada's sterling debt. British investment in Canada included some £340 millions of sterling securities which the experts thought suitable for repatriation. Theoretically these would most effectively be brought into play if the Dominion Government paid Canadian dollars for them (these dollars to be used for United Kingdom purchases of supplies), the Dominion Government financing the operation by issuing bonds in New York. London would thus get the wherewithal to pay Canadian farmers and manufacturers, while Canada would get the U.S. dollars to finance her anticipated surplus of imports from the United States. This would all be very fine, but the aftermath would be less welcome. For debt repatriation financed on these lines would weaken Canada's economic links with Britain, and strengthen those with the United States. Canada would become less interested in sterling, more interested in U.S. dollars; in effect, there would be cumulative aggravation of the very tendencies that made the Canadian dollar the hardest currency in the Commonwealth. Though this argument was not always developed explicitly, it is quite clear that it was present in Canadian as well as British minds, and that it was disagreeable to both. Nevertheless, the problem of financing British orders had to be tackled somehow, and as the weeks went by it became patent to all that debt repatriation in some measure would have to come into the picture.

The measure would, however, have to be much less than a first inspection had suggested, for it became plain, at a very early stage, that substantial refinancing in New York must be ruled out. The Neutrality Act stood in the way; feelers in New York brought unexpected discouragement, and when the Canadians revealed their repugnance, there was no point in further test of American reactions. The Dominion Government could therefore absorb no more of these securities than the savings that could be attracted within Canada itself: in terms of goods and services, if American lending did not finance a net flow of goods northward into Canada, the extent to which Canada could afford a net flow of goods to Britain was correspondingly restricted.[1]

Recent experience had suggested that Canadian appetite for Dominion Government bonds was in fact uncomfortably small. Conditions of war would of course put many competing borrowers out of the market; on the other hand, Canada's own war effort required finance. By no financial wizardry could the size of the cake be transformed, and the Canadian authorities were realistic enough to perceive from the start the fundamental limits set to supplying Britain in return simply for the repayment of old debts. The Canadian economy had to be expanded, and this involved increased imports from the United States.

Debt repatriation was therefore to be part of the story, but any notion that it could be on the spectacular scale necessary to make ends meet had been dispelled before the war actually broke out. There was in any case no point in forcing all the possible debt repatriation into a short period when plans were being made on the basis of a war running into years. Neither the British nor the Canadians really wanting to hurry the process, no more was settled in October 1939 than that a start should be made by repatriating

---

[1] The limit thus set applied to *all* debt repayment and new borrowing by Britain; in the event 'the sterling overdraft' was substantial and debt repatriation lower than underlying economic conditions would have allowed.

the $3\frac{1}{2}$ per cent. Dominion loan. This provided some £18 millions towards the needs of the first six months of the war, leaving open the question how far and how fast debt should be repatriated thereafter.[1]

This was not going to go very far, and the Dominion Government, now fully alive to the connection between United Kingdom purchases and their financial arrangements, showed some impatience with a London that appeared to be letting things drift.[2] Action was however precipitated by the energy of certain United Kingdom official purchasers in contracting for the output of Canadian metal concerns. Certain powerful Canadian concerns had been persuaded, by British negotiators apparently aware of dollar difficulties but lacking clear guidance on payment procedure, to accept part payment in blocked sterling. When this came to the knowledge of the Dominion authorities, they expressed dislike of such arrangements. The United Kingdom Treasury quickly accepted the view that piecemeal private arrangements of this kind would not increase the total credit available from Canada, and realised that friction would be created in Canada if some firms granted credit while others were unable to do so. The principle of centralising all credit arrangements was thereupon adopted, and it was settled that all future purchases made in Canada by United Kingdom Government Departments should be settled in dollars provided by the Bank of Canada in return for sterling paid to the account of the Bank of Canada at the Bank of England. The 'sterling overdraft'—the sterling debt incurred to the Bank of Canada—thus became the residual source of finance for United Kingdom purchases in Canada.[3] The 'overdraft limit', and the means (other than debt repatriation) by which it should be kept within this limit, were still unsettled. The telegram from Prime Minister to Prime Minister[4] did however include the clause: 'with a United Kingdom

---

[1] The first communications about this operation mention the sum of $137 millions, or roughly £30 millions, but the Canadian authorities had already accumulated a substantial Sinking Fund against it, and part of the loan was held outside the United Kingdom. The net relief to the United Kingdom's Canadian dollar position was estimated at £18 millions.

[2] The Canadians were 'straining at the leash to know what we want and how best they can help us' and were bewildered by the failure of London to send out an experienced Treasury man.

[3] This 'overdraft' was of course a sterling balance held by the Bank of Canada, and was in technical form precisely parallel to the sterling balances accumulated by India and other members of the Sterling Area. I have preferred to regard the Canadian balance as a United Kingdom overdraft, because additions to it were very nearly always subject to specific agreement by the Canadian authorities, whereas other 'sterling balances' accrued automatically, although their amounts were subject to discussion between the parties from time to time. The distinction is, it should be noted, one of degree only.

[4] The clause quoted appears to have slipped into the telegram without attracting much notice, but it was destined to attract more attention during 1941 (see below, p. 339).

Government exchange guarantee for such sterling, so that no loss can accrue to Canada when it eventually is converted into dollars'.

Before anything further could be settled, two matters were forced on London's attention by Canada's reasonable insistence that they were highly relevant to Canada's capacity to provide financial assistance. First, there was the alleged discrimination against Canadian producers of wheat and other foodstuffs. Second, there was the lack of co-ordination of British purchases. The wheat question flared up in October 1939. On Treasury instructions, arising from the scarcity of Canadian dollars, the Ministry of Food had bought no wheat in Canada, but had been buying heavily in neutral countries. This caused resentment in Canada, where it was believed that the Ministry of Food was holding off in order to squeeze the Canadian price down. The suspicion seemed to receive justification when, in October, shipping difficulties caused the Ministry of Food to swing round to Canada and then complain that payment of Canada's price would cause the British cost of living to rise. The Canadian price was indeed well above that ruling elsewhere; on the other hand, the Canadian wheat farmers felt the same as Australian sheep farmers—that pre-war prices had been uneconomically low, and that they should be paid a fair living in return for providing the British consumer through the war. The British method of centralised purchasing, dominated by powerful business men, also gave some colour to Canada's fear of monopsonistic exploitation. The British, for their part, were not inclined to put the case on a par with Australian wool, for it was already clear that the Canadian economy was going to have the stimulus of huge British demands for other products. A boom for their mining and manufacturing neighbours was not, however, a satisfying answer to the wheat-farmers, and the problem continued to rankle and disturb Anglo-Canadian relations throughout the autumn. Eventually supply considerations obliged Britain to go some way toward meeting the Canadian case. The atmosphere had meanwhile been helped by the news, in November, that in spite of exchange shortage and her own large crop, the United Kingdom would be buying Canadian apples; there was similarly satisfaction at purchases of poultry, honey and cheese.

The second matter tending to sap Canadian eagerness to help, was the lack of co-ordination of United Kingdom requirements and the abrupt way in which successive heavy demands were being presented without apparent consideration of the total impact upon Canada. This strain upon relations was really due to the different positions of the two Governments. The Dominion had expressed willingness to help to the utmost of her capacity and looked for very rapid presentation of a properly co-ordinated programme of United Kingdom requirements, which could be considered in relation both to Canadian real resources and to the provision of finance.[1] The United Kingdom administration, on the other hand, was in no state of readiness with comprehensive programmes; instead each Department, dreadfully undermanned, was scrambling to get something, however provisional, fixed about critical supplies from individual Canadian producers, and it was several weeks before the Treasury was able to formulate anything like a programme on which financial arrangements could be based. The United Kingdom High Commissioner in Canada, seeing many Departmental telegrams that came through his office and sensing the Canadian reaction, warned Whitehall that more care must be shown in the phrasing of British requests.

The Greenley Mission, whose primary task was to purchase supplies for the Service Departments, and the Riverdale Mission, which was to co-ordinate contracts with the aircraft industry and to discuss the proposals for training pilots, strove to eliminate the worst faults on the British side[2]. The attachment of Mr. Osborne as financial adviser to both these Missions facilitated the formulation of the total bill in Canadian dollars. A first attempt at this sum, made by the Treasury early in October, indicated a likely deficit in the United Kingdom's balance of payments with Canada during the first year of war, of between $330 and $400 millions. This allowed only £10 millions ($45 millions) for the Empire Air Training Scheme, which the Riverdale Mission was to discuss with the Dominion Government and representatives from Australia, New Zealand and South Africa. It was already threatening to be one of those 'immense and in some cases impossible demands' that were creating a sense of strain; certainly it became one before the business was settled at the end of November. The location in Canada of most of the advanced training of pilots from all the Dominions as well as the United Kingdom had obvious immense advantages, both technical and political,[3] but it did mean very heavy expenditure in dollars, part of this expenditure being in U.S. dollars for aircraft and instructors obtainable only (to make up sufficient numbers) in the United States. At each successive meeting the estimated cost rose further.

The rise in the total cost, implying a proportionate rise in each country's share, would have been bad enough for the United

---

[1] Mr. Mackenzie King's message of 1st September 1939 included a statement that 'he must present to Parliament some definite programme of participation including . . . . food, supplies, raw materials, munitions, aviation pilots . . . .'

[2] In November 1939 the Greenley Mission, now the 'British Supply Board in Canada and the United States', arranged to make its Canadian purchases through the Canadian War Supply Board recently established by the Dominion Government.

[3] These were all discussed with Dominion representatives in London on 23rd September 1939.

Kingdom Treasury, which was already failing to see how its gold and hard currency reserves could last more than two years. But as the financial implications of the scheme were further examined, far heavier blows fell. The Treasury realised that, while the cost would be primarily in Canadian dollars, the contributions of Australia, New Zealand and South Africa would be paid by them— probably even only chalked up on the slate—in sterling; the full dollar burden for all Sterling Area participants would inevitably fall on London's reserves. Worse than that—the Canadians made it clear that, in estimating the financial aid they could give Britain (figures of $200 to $400 millions had been mentioned), they had already reckoned on the most generous basis possible, and that Canada's own share of the cost of the Air Training Scheme would therefore have to be deducted from the aid available for the United Kingdom.[1] The United Kingdom Government had to make up its mind whether the scheme was important enough not only to take priority in Canada but also to displace other demands upon the central reserve, or to bring nearer the day when there would be no reserve left. The decision went in favour of the scheme: it was to be given priority over any other new plan of war production inside Canada, and the United Kingdom accepted the heavy strain on the gold and dollar reserves.[2]

Discussions were meanwhile going forward on the amount of credit Canada could allow to Britain—the size of the sterling overdraft—in the first year of war. At the end of October 1939 a report from Mr. Osborne in Ottawa indicated the broad approach of the Canadian authorities. The national income of Canada in 1938 was estimated at $3,500 millions. The current Governmental expenditure was at the annual rate of:

> $850 millions in the Federal budget,
> $300 millions, the net expenditure of the Provinces,
> $275 millions in Municipalities;

a total of $1,425 millions. If to this were added $400 millions for aid to the United Kingdom, Government expenditure would represent 52 per cent. of the national income; if only $200 millions

---

[1] It should not be supposed that the Canadian attitude flowed from any reluctance to co-operate as fully as possible. Their reservations were due rather to their conservative view of the limits to Dominion war finance: a view which had its parallel in Britain itself.

[2] The financial arrangements for the scheme, as settled in the winter of 1939-40, were extremely complex; the United Kingdom Treasury thought them inconsistent with the principles that should govern Commonwealth financial relations but felt unable to press its views at that stage. Later in the war, United Kingdom officials always thought of this as a card to produce at moments when some financial concession by Canada seemed appropriate and, as will be seen below (pp. 350-1 and 357), the Dominion did in 1943 and 1944 make substantial concessions relating to the cost of the Royal Canadian Air Force.

were allowed for the United Kingdom, the percentage would be 46. $200 to $400 millions appeared to be the range in the minds of Canadian Ministers, and on the basis of the above calculations they were evidently inclined to gravitate towards the lower figure. Even so, Canada's intended financial effort looked commendable in relation to parallel figures for the United Kingdom, and there were reasons for not expecting Canada's maximum effort to be proportionately as great as the United Kingdom's. 'A country with ten governments is less efficient—and there are, of course, the racial and sectional interests to be allowed when endeavouring to regiment it. The chief difference, however, is of course the fact that the war cannot be brought home to Canada as it is to England . . . . . ' This was tó be proved—in the long war—an unduly cautious view, but it was sound enough in relation to the immediate problem, and British experts did not contest it.

But they did have substantial reservations about Canada's calculations. There were many pitfalls in estimates of 'war effort' as percentages of national income, especially when one country's figures were compared with those of another. The art of estimating national incomes had made some progress since the early efforts of Bowley and Stamp, but the progress had been mainly in the realisation that insoluble problems abounded, and little progress had been made in filling the purely statistical gaps. Moreover, the Canadians were using for Canada figures of the 'slump' year 1938 and for Britain those of the 'boom' year 1937. They had allowed for a subsequent 15 per cent. increase in both national incomes— which United Kingdom experts thought much too low for Canada. The probable error in the calculations could be several times as great as the residual figure of possible assistance to the United Kingdom. There was, however, no point in shooting all the possible criticisms at the Canadians, for nothing constructive could come out of it—there were not in existence the figures to support an agreement, even if the experts could agree on precise interpretation of the figures. The Canadian approach could be—and was— accepted as an attempt in good faith to settle on a scientific basis the distribution of a common burden between two single-minded nations. It gave a foretaste of the international discussions that were to be prompted by another defence need more than a decade later.

Meanwhile the British were inclined to state their total needs and to welcome the substantial figures that appeared to be in Canadian minds, without quibbling about the calculations from which these figures had emerged. Mr. Graham Towers, Governor of the Bank of Canada, came to London late in November and joined the Canadian Minister of Mines and Resources (Mr. Crerar) in talks from which an agreement emerged. At this stage it looked as though London's deficit in its dealings with Canada was not going to be less than $300 millions but would not be beyond this order of magnitude. The Canadians spoke of $237 millions, but this, they insisted, must include the cost to Canada of the Air Training Scheme. The latter was expected to be $311 millions over three years, $46 millions of this relating to the first year, giving a net figure of $191 millions for aid to Britain. The Canadians finally agreed to bring up to about $200 millions the amount they made available either by repatriation of debt or by accumulation of sterling balances in London (the sterling overdraft, from Britain's point of view), while the United Kingdom undertook to use $45 millions in gold, and to make further gold payments to the extent that the total deficit exceeded $245 millions.

Canada's ability to stand by this arrangement, without both inflationary pressure and strain on the dollar exchange, depended upon the fulfilment of certain assumptions about the disposition of Canadians to spend on consumption and of Americans and Canadians to spend on each other's goods and services. In March 1940 there was cause for anxiety on both counts, and the anxiety was accentuated by the low level of Canada's gold reserve and by the temporary failure of the tourist traffic to earn U.S. dollars. The American tourist traffic had been reckoned an important source of finance for the imports Canada depended upon drawing from the United States of America, but it appeared now to be serving as a channel for the withdrawal of United States funds from Canada. This development had been greatly encouraged by the appearance of a wide discount in the New York quotation for the Canadian dollar, this in its turn being due partly to a pessimistic turn in views about the war and partly to Canada's own heavy expenditure in the United States of America.

With tenuous reserves and the prospect that Canadian expenditure in the United States must rise, the Dominion authorities could not pass off a temporary aggravation with a mere shrug of the shoulders. London feared that Canada's reaction would be to press for more gold and U.S. dollars in payment of Britain's needs. Strong views were expressed on this possibility: 'Must we really,' one writer asked, 'divert our American dollars to pay for the joy-rides of Canadian motorists?'[1] This was of course precisely parallel to the feeling that was being aroused in United Kingdom official circles over the continued high level of consumption in other parts of the Commonwealth,[2] and only a sharp restriction of Canadian

---

[1] Private reports reaching the United Kingdom Treasury supported the view that Canada was becoming steadily more prosperous and her standard of living (at least in some Provinces) was steadily creeping up.

[2] See Chapter X above, especially pp. 289, 292-3, 301-2, 311-3.

consumption could solve the problems. This was already appreciated in Canadian Government circles, where the Deputy Minister of Finance, for example, was expressing great interest in Keynes's proposals for compulsory savings in the United Kingdom. For the present, progress in Canada along this fundamental line was slow,[1] although eventually Canada was to make an impressive effort. The immediate strains were overcome partly by technical measures to tighten the exchange control and partly by stimulating American tourist traffic in Canada; certain steps were also taken to strengthen the resources of the Canadian Exchange Board with a view to more complete control of the market.[2]

As the second year of war approached, it became necessary to make some arrangement about the financing of the United Kingdom's continuing adverse balance. At this stage, the sharp turn the war had taken in the spring of 1940 affected the problem in two important directions. First, the defeat of France, the consequential assignment to Britain of French contracts in North America, and the huge additions to British needs revolutionised Britain's attitude on her central reserves: the strain on them became tremendous and, though they were now to be thrown into the struggle and not husbanded over another two years, every possible ounce of gold was needed for purchases in the United States and London grudged any further payment in gold to Canada. Secondly, the British were now accepting much more stringent consumption standards and a much more intensive effort, and they expected other peoples in the Commonwealth to move in the same direction. Any idea of paying gold to Canada in order to maintain 'joy-riding' in Canada was therefore out of order. Britain expected Canada to provide the maximum real contribution to the Commonwealth's effort consistently with avoidance of further drain on those central reserves which were now so quickly running out.

For our present purpose, the implication of all this was that the Sterling Area's adverse balance with Canada must be financed either by reduction of Canada's historical sterling debts or by increasing Canada's sterling balance (the sterling overdraft). There was some rather academic discussion, in London official circles, of the possibility of providing automatic adjustment of the position by bringing Canada inside the Sterling Area, which

---

[1] In April 1940, however, temporary civil servants were already suffering 5 per cent. deduction for compulsory saving.

[2] Although the tourist traffic was financed partly by an exchange leak, the authorities believed that a substantial part of additional traffic would benefit the official exchange position.

would have put her, for these purposes, in the same position as India. But there were many good reasons why Canada should not have accepted the suggestion if it had ever been put to her, and there would have been quite serious incidental disadvantages for the United Kingdom.[1] Anyway there would have been little point in such a proceeding, when the fundamental matter of restraining Canada's U.S. dollar requirements would still have had to be faced.

The position reached in June 1940, under the arrangement made (with Mr. Crerar and Mr. Towers) for the first year of war, was that after spending the dollars available from the first debt repatriation, the United Kingdom had paid both the agreed $45 millions in gold and a further $5 millions in gold, and the rest had been provided by Canada mainly against the piecemeal repatriation of securities. Since April 1940 the Canadian market had been open to the sale of Canadian securities owned by United Kingdom residents (and mobilised by the United Kingdom Treasury) and sales had in fact reached $300,000 to $400,000 a week. These market sales were not, however, thought capable of much further extension. London's dollar needs, on the other hand, were continuing at a very high level, although there had been some shortfall against estimates in the first nine months of the war.[2]

After the great upheaval of United Kingdom programmes in the early summer of 1940, the United Kingdom's adverse balance with Canada during the second year of war was estimated at over $600 millions.[3] The Canadians were ready to help as much as they could, but felt the position altogether too uncertain to enable them to make an adequate offer to cover as long a period as a year. Their own war expenditure was 'quite uncertain', and their prospective adverse balance with the United States was rising very steeply, owing to the large elements of American components in all objects of war expenditure in Canada. Eventually they agreed with Sir Frederick Phillips, when the latter went up to Ottawa from Washington in August 1940, that Canada should provide $150 millions by debt repatriation and sterling accumulation during the six months commencing 1st August 1940, leaving the subsequent six months for future discussion. Within the half-year, the United Kingdom would finance the next $100 millions by selling gold.

---

[1] Particularly, there would have been the extraordinary difficulty of preventing the flight of funds from the United Kingdom via Canada.

[2] In the end, the first year of war left Canada with an addition of £5·3 millions to her sterling balances.

[3] £140 millions.

By November the $150 millions had run out and Britain was in desperate financial straits. Owing to further orders for war supplies, the estimate of the adverse balance had jumped to $800 millions (from $600 millions). The Treasury had begun to reckon the gold reserve in terms of weeks—it seemed certain to run out before Christmas. The Presidential election in the United States had brightened the longer view, but there were alarming forecasts (they were all too well justified in the event) of the time that must elapse before financial aid would begin to flow from that source. Though London sent another £15 millions of gold, there was nothing for it but to go hat in hand to Canada, and on 11th November the Treasury cabled to Ottawa begging to be helped out by further purchases of sterling and repatriations 'or by temporary loan, at least for the next few months until U.S. intentions regarding financial assistance are known'.

London had, at this juncture, strong arguments up its sleeve. While the central reserve of the Sterling Area was all but exhausted and Britain had been running down her Canadian investments, it had become clear that, despite all the strains, the Canadians had managed to keep substantially intact not only their gold reserve but also their investments in the United States. Indeed, a recent statement by the Canadian Minister of Finance indicated that the maintenance of these assets was a matter of continuing policy. The Canadians had, moreover, only just taken belt-tightening measures that evoked a British comment: 'It seems to be a fairly good effort'.

There was also Mr. Mackenzie King's evident embarrassment at the hints about the French gold. There were in Canada two considerable hoards of French gold. The first, some £70 millions, was held for the Bank of England, which owed it to the Bank of France, and had been transferred to Ottawa at the latter's request; disposal of this depended upon United Kingdom administrative action under the Trading with the Enemy Act. The second, some £90 millions, was held by the Bank of Canada on behalf of the Bank of France; disposal of this depended upon administrative decision of the Dominion Government.[1] London, facing the virtual certainty of an empty cash-box, was under increasing United States pressure to scrape together all accessible hoards in the Empire and, as well, those of its Allies and its enemies. Awkwardly enough, France was neither clearly an Ally nor clearly an enemy. The

---

[1] There was also a balance of about £125 millions worth of U.S. dollars held on behalf of 'The State of France' in the Bank of Canada's account at the Federal Reserve Bank of New York; this was related to the French contracts in the United States, taken over by the United Kingdom, and it included £60 millions reimbursement by the United Kingdom of French advance payments on the contracts.

technical position under United Kingdom Trading with the Enemy legislation was, however, clear enough for British officials; they thought the moral position equally clear, and were prepared to lay hands on the £70 millions[1]. Naturally enough, they preferred to act in concert with the Canadians, and the Dominion Government was asked to take parallel action with the £90 millions. Canadian Ministers, though wanting to help, showed a good deal of reluctance. Since the fall of France, Ministers had felt unable to count on the former wholehearted support of the French Canadians of Quebec, and they feared that high-handed action with France's gold reserve might alienate these people. United Kingdom representatives acknowledged these political anxieties and, when successive approaches through the latter part of 1940 were met by evasive replies, they did not press the matter. Unwilling in such a matter to act independently of the Dominion, the United Kingdom authorities did not in the end even use the £70 millions that were at their own disposal.[2]

The Dominion Government, pledged to see Britain's programme through and never faltering in this intention, was thus failing to help along some of the obvious lines. If Canada wanted to maintain her international assets vis-à-vis the United States, if she was only just taking serious action to cut consumption, and if she felt too uncomfortable about laying hands on French gold, it was only reasonable that she should show herself willing in some other way. Canadian Ministers had not hitherto been adequately informed by London of the facts; when they were properly informed, they accepted the logic of the situation, and agreed on 13th December 1940 to sell Canadian dollars against sterling to the amount of $50 millions, to which was added on 16th January 1941 a further $25 millions. By the end of January all these dollars had been used. In the succeeding weeks, while Canadian Ministers hesitated[3] to commit themselves to an indefinite programme of assistance,

---

[1] The moral issue was faced in a 'Prime Minister to Prime Minister' message to Ottawa on 25th August. 'To allow gold to remain blocked instead of purchasing it for sterling would confer no benefit on the Bank of France but would seriously prejudice the war effort of the Empire. There is no future hope for the French nation except through the victory for which we are all fighting and our trusteeship for the future existence of a free France cannot be rated as less important than our trusteeship for the post-war financial interests of the Bank of France'. Account had nevertheless to be taken of the possibility that German propaganda would represent it as an act of robbery, and this certainly worried official circles; but the view prevailed that 'This is not a war to be fought with kid gloves'. Subsequently a question of expediency arose: whether seizure of the French gold would arouse anxiety in American suppliers as to the availability of the French balance in New York for payment on the French contracts. Eventually, however, American pressure was all on the side of seizure, and it was the Canadian scruples that prevented action.

[2] On the means whereby the 1941 crisis of exhausted reserves was overcome, see below, pp. 383-97.

[3] Their hesitation can be ascribed to the fact that the details of Britain's financial extremity had only just been brought to their notice.

further amounts of sterling were taken up by the Bank of Canada.[1] But the complexion of the whole problem was being, in these weeks, revolutionised by discussions on the American lend-lease plans, and when the Dominion committed itself, in March, to an indefinite sterling overdraft, it did so on conditions that were tied closely to the emerging pattern of the lend-lease world.

(iii)

Lend-Lease and the Billion Dollar Gift, 1941–42

During the winter of 1940–41 financial relations between Canada and the United Kingdom were affected by two events that made either repetition of the first year's arrangements or continuation of a policy of drift quite impossible. The two events were the exhaustion—complete exhaustion—of London's gold reserve, and the Roosevelt decision on the principle of lend-lease. London, previously reluctant to pay gold, now became quite incapable of paying, and for some little time the reconstitution of her reserves had a prior claim on the gold she could earn elsewhere. Even more importantly, if less obviously, London's attitude in its financial dealings with the Dominion was henceforward subject to pressure from the United States: at the least, United Kingdom representatives had constantly to glance over their shoulders to see how the Americans would take the situation. In their extreme form, American reactions could be a limiting factor. In March 1941, for example, news that London was expected to pay gold to Canada was seized upon in the United States by opponents of lend-lease 'to sustain the argument that the U.S. should not yet lend while a Dominion is insisting on payment in hard cash'. Less extreme instances were constantly appearing through the remainder of the war—the Canadian dollar problem became inextricably entangled with lend-lease and all the complications that implied.

The first news of lend-lease gave rise in Canada to fears that there might be an unwelcome diversion of United Kingdom orders from Canadian to American suppliers. Without waiting for any official expression of this anxiety, the United Kingdom Government hastened to assure the Dominion that no appreciable modification of the purchasing programme was contemplated. If for no other reason, the United Kingdom was bound to take this line by American

---

[1] The Bank of Canada was in these transactions acting as agent for the Dominion Government. Important sums were also being obtained for the United Kingdom by the sale in Canada of vested securities. These realisations, which had been negligible after the operations in the autumn of 1939, amounted to $58 millions in the third quarter of 1940, $50 millions in the fourth quarter, and $47 millions in the first quarter of 1941.

Y

insistence that before resorting to lend-lease Britain must make the most of the capacity of herself and her Allies. But the assurance given to Canada was necessarily conditional upon the extension of adequate financial aid by Canada. The need to get this question settled was just as urgent as ever. The 'adequacy' of financial aid had to be judged against requirements that were now on an altogether larger scale than during the first year of war. In that year the Sterling Area had, in the event, a deficit of about $360 millions; for the second year of war the gap was estimated at $1,100 millions. Towards this about $66 millions had been paid in gold, securities were being sold at the rate of $150 millions a year, and Canada had added about $250 millions to her sterling balance. Further gold payments out of the Sterling Area's production or earnings elsewhere could at most be small, and were anyway open to the objection referred to above. What was to be done about the other hundreds of millions?

When considering what should be their response to this need, the Dominion authorities did not return to comparisons of national incomes, but they were watching two narrower limiting factors, their budgetary position and their balance of payments with the United States. Whether the Dominion Government provided the United Kingdom with Canadian dollars in exchange for repatriated Canadian securities or for a sterling balance, the dollars had to be found by the Dominion Government either by taxation or by the sale of securities to the Canadian public. The ease with which the dollars could be squeezed out of the Canadian public depended upon their taxable capacity and their disposition to save. In the last resort, a clash between Canadian consumption levels and war production would be resolved by inflation, which raises the money yield of taxation and the money level of voluntary saving. But Canada wanted to avoid—or more realistically to minimise—the inflation, and Canadian Ministers sometimes felt that Canadian consumption levels were no more compressible than was the United Kingdom's demand for war supplies. After the belt-tightening measures taken in 1940–41, there was some inclination on the Canadian side to think no further compression necessary—the implication being that supplies for the United Kingdom were the residual element. London had strong views to the contrary: Canada should face some inflation and acknowledge the need for war supplies as the determining factor.

The Canadians' other source of anxiety was the U.S.–Canada exchange, and in this context everything depended upon what was arranged about lend-lease. The normal adverse balance that Canada had in her trade with the United States had been restricted by measures against non-essential imports, but the large munition orders placed in Canada by the United Kingdom involved additional imports of raw materials and components from the United States: the United States element was apparently about one-third of the total. At the same time, the expansion of Canadian income—as long as it was outstripping America's own expansion— raised the pressure to buy goods imported from the United States into Canada. Up to the end of 1940 the United Kingdom had in fact provided most of the gold to cover Canada's deficit with the United States; this had now to cease. Was Canada to encroach at last on her own international reserves, small as they were, or could the deficit be in some way covered by lend-lease?

Direct lend-lease for Canada was no answer. Though other countries could accept favours from the United States, Canada's contiguity made implications for national sovereignty a very serious consideration. And there were other difficulties of a more practical kind. The Americans would not provide lend-lease goods for Canada until the latter had (like Britain) stripped herself of all her more liquid international assets, and anyway Canada from the first showed a strong distaste for lend-lease. To shift British demands from Canada to the United States, with the effect of avoiding the Canadian deficit, had already been ruled out and would have been inconsistent with the aim of employing *both* Canadian and American capacity fully. On the other hand, it did not appear unreasonable to take on lend-lease for Britain such American components and materials as were sent into Canada for embodiment there in war supplies for Britain. Any arrangement of this kind would ease the budgetary as well as the exchange strain on Canada.

It was against this background that the Dominion Government decided late in March 1941 to continue the accumulation of sterling without any prescribed limit. On the understanding that there would be no diversion of orders to the United States, that there would be consultation on any further United Kingdom purchasing programmes, and that the questions of gold payments and lend-leasing of components should be considered at a later stage, the Dominion agreed to provide dollars indefinitely against repatriation of securities, to the extent that this proved reasonably practicable, and for the rest against accumulating sterling balances. In view of this last intention, Canada thought it appropriate to revive the exchange guarantee that had been mentioned in the Osborne negotiations in October 1939.[1] The Dominion Government's financial strategy was further unfolded in its April 1941 budget, which made substantial provision for United Kingdom needs, both directly and by further belt-tightening measures. It also

---

[1] For the exchange guarantee in October 1939, see above, p. 327.

slashed import duties to facilitate the earning of dollars by United Kingdom exporters. At this stage of United Kingdom industrial mobilisation, this tariff revision was too late to make much difference to the arithmetic, but the gesture added to goodwill.[1]

Almost immediately, the assumption that Canada's adverse balance with the United States might be covered by some arrangement under lend-lease appeared to be justified by the Hyde Park Agreement. This was the outcome of discussions in April 1941 between Mr. Mackenzie King and President Roosevelt. The joint communiqué issued to the Press on 20th April, and known as the 'Hyde Park Declaration', embodied three main points:

(a) that United States and Canadian production programmes should be integrated as far as possible;

(b) that the United Kingdom would obtain on lend-lease terms, and would transfer to Canada, such 'defence articles' as Canada required from the United States for the execution of United Kingdom orders in Canada;

(c) that the United States would increase her purchases from Canada, particularly of aluminium and merchant ships.

The second and third points would, it was assumed, sufficiently ease for Canada the strain of her adverse balance with the United States; the second meant that lend-lease facilities were going to be used as fully as was consistent with Canada's wish to avoid incurring lend-lease obligations on her own account.[2]

With this problem solved in principle, Canada's offer became a firm one. But it was not an unqualified offer of cash, and the conditions were for London to consider. There was some discussion in London on how far the repatriation of securities should be pushed,[3] and eventually the Dominion Government was asked to restrict this to Government or Government-guaranteed securities. There was anxiety lest the undertaking to consult about further purchases implied generous prices for Canadian farmers, from which no relief could be obtained by drawing instead on lend-lease food and materials. But London felt unable to express hesitations on this count—'Mr. Morgenthau has cleaned us out and leaves us unable to handle the question on level terms'.

---

[1] Special efforts were made to maintain United Kingdom exports to Canada throughout the war; in 1941 they reached about $170 millions, and in each of the remaining years a little over $100 millions.

[2] Owing largely to the difficulties inherent in lend-lease procedure, it was possible to handle only a few sizable items by this method. The Dominion continued to pay cash to the United States for the majority of the components—let alone the materials—obtained from the United States for inclusion in war supplies sent to Britain. The comparative failure of this arrangement was an important cause—overlooked by London—of Canada's continuing need for U.S. dollars.

[3] It was at this time that the United States Treasury was pressing the United Kingdom to strip itself of all marketable overseas assets, and was stretching the term 'marketable' to extreme lengths. (See below, pp. 388-9). At this stage the London authorities were still inclined to welcome the prospect of large post-war sterling balances. (cf. p. 258 above).

Most serious of all, there was the Canadian request for an exchange guarantee. Although London saw that it must accept— and did accept with a good grace—the broad lines of the Canadian offer, the United Kingdom Government was compelled to negotiate cautiously in this matter of the exchange guarantee. London regarded the undertaking given in October 1939 as having lapsed when Canada restricted her accumulation of sterling, but it was not unreasonable for Canada to regard it as once more appropriate now that she was again envisaging indefinite accumulation of sterling. And, quite apart from the question of any standing commitment, the proposal was reasonable in itself. Canada's peculiar dependence on trade and other connections with the United States made it prudent for her to safeguard the North American purchasing power of any international assets she was to possess, and fears that India and other holders of sterling balances might seek to follow a Canadian precedent could be answered by reference to this unique position of Canada. Nevertheless Britain, denuded of gold reserves and unlikely to rebuild more than a bare minimum reserve before the end of the war, could not afford to commit herself in gold or dollars whose commodity value could depend upon North American policies over which London might have no influence. How serious the conflict was depended upon guesses at the course of war-time and post-war prices in Britain and North America, a point that gave rise to some rather academic exercises on the British side. From these exercises nothing emerged to help the two sides in their attempts to find a formula that would reconcile the conflicting interests. Even resort to the word 'consultation' proved fruitless, the Canadians realising that 'consultation' over a change in dollar-sterling exchange rates 'could mean no more than previous notice and in view of the danger of leakages such notice would have to be very short'—a view that was to find justification when sterling was devalued in September 1949. Weeks passed by without any solution of the problem and eventually, with bigger thoughts in his mind, the Canadian Minister of Finance suggested 'postponement' of further discussion of an exchange guarantee. This was the end of the matter, to the great relief of the United Kingdom authorities.

Before the wider proposals emerged, the Canadian authorities asked for some development of the general undertaking about United Kingdom purchases from Canada. They now sought to add to the general undertakings that orders would not be diverted and that there should be full consultation on further United Kingdom purchasing plans, a more specific undertaking about the prices of foodstuffs. The request arose from the desire of Canadian Ministers to improve the lot of the farmers, partly on the ground that their position had worsened relatively to that of the industralists, partly on the budgetary ground that expensive subsidies (such as both Dominion and Provincial Governments were now paying) were inappropriate in face of the keen world demand for the products. The Canadian Ministers recognised that more generous prices would create fresh difficulties (if only financial) for the United Kingdom in its stabilisation policy, and from the first held out some expectation of a *quid pro quo* in the shape of a favourable settlement of the broader question of financial aid. Departmental negotiators on the United Kingdom side were naturally under constant Treasury pressure to keep purchasing prices down; they had always to consider the repercussions of a bargain with one country on its later negotiations with suppliers elsewhere. This attitude was, in the summer of 1941, still appearing in negotiations over bacon prices and other items, and the United Kingdom High Commissioner in Ottawa advised that there was 'a strong tendency in some official circles here to feel that Canada's generosity is insufficiently appreciated in the U.K. and is responded to by a policy of cheeseparing and hard bargaining on the part of the U.K. Government'. The Ministry of Food did, however, settle on higher prices for bacon, fish, apples and eggs at an early stage in these discussions, and the Canadians disclaimed any intention of including wheat in the general arrangement. The area of discussion was thus narrowed down to cheese, although an assurance in the general terms now sought might well commit the United Kingdom to higher prices for all products later. London had also to admit that the spirit of wheat negotiations would obviously be affected, at some cost to the United Kingdom, although wheat was specifically excluded from the general assurance now under discussion. All in all—allowing for the repercussions on prices paid elsewhere—the cost to the United Kingdom of giving the general assurance would be a matter of a few million pounds. Private advice indicated that if the United Kingdom appeared niggardly over this matter, Canadian Ministers would not dare to put before their people the very generous financial proposals they had in mind. Therefore, without awaiting these proposals, the United Kingdom Government decided to cast its bread upon the waters, and on 5th September 1941 the general assurance was given.

It was indeed 'many days' before the bread returned. The Dominion Cabinet found itself too occupied with internal matters[1] to deal speedily with the proposals for financial aid to the United

---

[1] The elaboration of its stabilisation policy was almost monopolising its attention at this time.

Kingdom. When the proposals did come, in the first days of 1942, the Chancellor of the Exchequer found that they were certainly generous, but that the Dominion was not yet ready to abandon 'the money sign'. There was also one really difficult hurdle for the United Kingdom to face, and almost the whole of January passed in hot-foot negotiation before agreement was reached.

The proposals were for (i) funding of the accumulated sterling balance, (ii) further repatriation of Canadian securities, and (iii) a gift of $1,000 millions (the 'billion dollar gift'). It was this third item that caught the imagination and reflected most accurately the spirit of co-operation that inspired the proceeding. The official communication described it as 'a free and unconditional gift, ... foodstuffs, raw materials and munitions of war up to a maximum of $1,000 millions. In other words, we would provide free the Canadian dollars necessary to meet from month to month the United Kingdom's deficit in her balance of payments with Canada to the extent that it would not be met by other Canadian dollars that would be available to the United Kingdom'.

The repatriation clause promised that 'Canada would repatriate remaining Canadian Government and Canadian National Railway securities now held by British investors, amounting to approximately $295 millions. The U.K. Government would take immediate steps to vest these securities at the prices now prevailing. Thus by process of repatriation, the Dominion Government would pay off at or before maturity all its own indebtedness to the United Kingdom and indebtedness of the Government-owned Railway held by British investors'.

It was anticipated that these further repatriations with the billion dollar gift would provide for United Kingdom requirements 'up to some time early in the year 1943'.

So far so good. The snag lay in the 'funding' proposal, which was placed first in the Canadian memorandum. Approximately the whole of Canada's sterling balance at 30th November 1941— $700 millions out of $728 millions—was to be converted into a Canadian dollar, loan interest free for the duration of the war and 'to be secured by the hypothecation of remaining Canadian securities held by British investors, which are payable in Canadian dollars'. (These were believed also to amount to about $700 millions). 'The U.K. would not be asked to take over ownership of the pledged securities from their present holders who would continue to receive in pounds sterling the interest and dividends of the pledged securities' and would be free to sell on condition that dollar proceeds would be applied to reduction of the loan. 'During the war period the U.K. would arrange to make payment on the principal of the loan in amounts equal to the annual earnings of the pledged securities. This loan would thus be reduced by annual payments estimated to be of the order of $40 million to $50 million'.

London's reaction can best be described by quoting Sir Richard Hopkins when he tackled the draft reply: 'This is a very ticklish business and the first thing to do is to get away from the formal phrases of diplomacy and to produce a rather undiplomatic and almost human document which will make it apparent (i) that we really are grateful (ii) that there really is a very big snag . . . . .'

The snag was the proposal that the United Kingdom should provide, for another Government within the Commonwealth, collateral security. It was true that the United Kingdom had recently, under special Parliamentary authority, given collateral security to the Reconstruction Finance Corporation (a United States semi-Government body) for a dollar loan,[1] but the United States was a foreign country (to which the United Kingdom was technically in default on previous loan obligations) and it was still a non-belligerent country. Moreover the Reconstruction Finance Corporation was a quasi-commercial body which always obtained the best possible security before granting loans. For one Commonwealth Government to give collateral to another was quite a different proposition, and one without precedent. It would be 'seriously damaging to the Commonwealth conception: it would certainly reflect seriously on our credit and would set a dangerous precedent both for ourselves and other Empire countries which may borrow either during or after the war'. The securities could be so pledged only by special Act of Parliament, which would inevitably draw attention to the proceeding. By this time it had become plain that both India and South Africa would have to be asked to hold large amounts of sterling for indefinite periods, and both of them would certainly ask for collateral if the Canadian proposal were accepted.

Enquiry soon showed that Canada regarded the collateral provision as an integral part of the plan, and that downright refusal by the United Kingdom would mean withdrawal of the 'billion dollar' offer, with a good deal of bad feeling in Canada. It was essential to reach some compromise and the first step in this direction was to ascertain the reasons that lay behind Canada's insistence. The Canadian Minister of Finance had in fact included this part of his proposals, United Kingdom representatives in Ottawa were informed, in order to side-track the demands that would otherwise be pressed in certain quarters that Canada should repatriate all British-owned Canadian securities. The latter view appeared to London to be uncomfortably close to the prevalent American

---

[1] See below, pp. 392-5.

view that Britain must strip herself of her overseas assets before receiving aid. This was an injustice to the Canadians, whose external obligations both to British and to other investors put their country in quite a different position from that of the United States. Further enquiry showed that, though Canadian Ministers felt it necessary to side-track demands originating in this attitude, they did not themselves think in terms of stripping Britain. Their underlying motive was rather a fear that the United Kingdom might at a later stage be constrained to sell or pledge Canadian dollar securities to the United States. This fear might be met by a 'negative pledge'—an undertaking not to sell or pledge the securities outside Canada without the consent of the Dominion Government. In effect the Canadians accepted this, but they reasonably coupled their acceptance with a requirement that if the United Kingdom should give collateral to any other part of the Empire, collateral should then also be given to Canada in respect of the $700 millions loan now under discussion. Canada also received the right to require the pledge of collateral security if the United Kingdom should, in respect of any other part of the Empire, extend repatriation of securities beyond the general sphere of Government and Government-guaranteed securities. The intention of this was to insist that if other Dominions adopted the policy of 'stripping Britain' (e.g. of South African gold-mining shares), Canada would feel free to revert to her requirement of collateral. London was reluctant to accept all these conditions, as certain practical difficulties were foreseen. But the price of failure in these negotiations was too high, and the Canadians obligingly promised not to exercise the call for collateral if the United Kingdom should vest small amounts of non-Governmental securities 'of a marginal character'.[1] The United Kingdom inserted in the agreement the statement: 'In this connection the United Kingdom Government desire to place on record that it is not their intention to agree with the Government of any part of the Empire to pledge securities as security for a loan.' With these qualifications, the plan was finally agreed and announced by Mr. Mackenzie King in the Canadian House of Commons on 27th January 1942.

As draft succeeded draft in this hectic month of negotiation, the Canadians had dropped their original clause about applying interest and dividends on the Canadian securities remaining in United Kingdom ownership (the securities that were proposed as collateral), to repayment of the $700 millions loan.[2] They had

---

[1] This was of practical importance, as there was a prospect that certain Indian Railway annuities would be bought out (they eventually were—see pp. 257-8 above) and there might elsewhere have been question of vesting provincial or municipal bonds.

[2] No doubt they perceived that the effect of such a clause would be to increase the rate at which the United Kingdom had to eat into the billion dollar gift.

also dropped, before ever presenting any proposals to the United Kingdom Government, any ideas they may originally have had of purchasing Canadian war factories from Britain or taking over additional items of Services' expenditure. The plan as it finally emerged was therefore simple—the funding into an interest-free loan of $700 millions outstanding, coupled with the much-qualified 'negative pledge' about the non-Governmental securities, the repatriation of the remaining 'Governmental' securities, and the billion dollar gift.[1] But with all its simplicity, it was magnificent in scale, and this was fully recognised both by the Prime Minister's announcement at Westminster[2] and by its reception in the British Press.[3] 'No more forceful reply', said *The Financial Times*, 'could have been made to earlier criticisms which sought to saddle the Dominion with a reputation for demanding cash on the barrel-head'.

The Canadian Press also regarded the settlement as generous, and it was natural enough for some to emphasise the burden implied for the Dominion. The *Toronto Daily Star*, for example, headlined an article, '120 days work each is gift to Britain. Means $87 from every living Canadian.' As the days went by, this calculating element loomed larger in Canadian comment and Ministers found it necessary to shift their ground a little. From claiming that the gift was a normal part of Canada's war effort, they shifted to protestations that the transaction represented an excellent business proposition for Canada in stimulating home industry and maintaining the goodwill of Britain as a post-war market. That defence of this kind was necessary appears to justify the Dominion Government in not having gone further: the Minister of Finance had pushed his colleagues and his country just as far as he could. Financial authorities in London were already moving towards a new conception of a pooled Commonwealth effort, in which the money-sign would be inappropriate, but Canadian second-thoughts about the billion-dollar gift showed all too clearly that Canada was not nearly ready for so revolutionary a change. However, the gift had the advantage that it made provision for a year or fifteen months: this would give plenty of time for the evolution of new ideas. So, at least, it was supposed; but the pace of war production had grown too hot for this, and within a few months both Ottawa and London could see that the billion dollars were going to run out long before the end of 1942.

---

[1] The terms were formally embodied in a letter from the Chancellor of the Exchequer to the Canadian Minister of Finance, 21st May 1942.

[2] H. of C. Deb., Vol. 377, Col. 615. The 'negative pledge' was not mentioned in the public statements.

[3] Issues of 28th January 1942.

(iv)
The Transition to Mutual Aid, 1942–43

By the early summer of 1942, when London was aware that the billion-dollar gift would be exhausted in the autumn, events as well as the broader movement of ideas were already pushing the Anglo-Canadian financial problem in the direction of reciprocal aid and away from the 'money-sign'. Three important currents are distinguishable in the tide that carried the Dominion Government from the settlement of January 1942 to the first Mutual Aid Act of May 1943. First there was a technical obscurity about the 1942 gift, consideration of which raised the question of aid to other members of the Commonwealth and so opened the possibility of an 'Empire-wide' plan of reciprocal aid. Secondly, opinion over a very wide front—and especially in Anglo-American relations—was moving away from the money sign and towards a general pooling of resources; this movement of ideas was associated with the establishment of the 'Combined Boards' for allocation of pooled resources. Thirdly, though everybody recognised that Canada would have to provide further assistance after the exhaustion of the gift, internal political developments made it virtually impossible for this further provision to take the same form and, something different having to be devised, it was natural enough for men to turn to the ideas of mutual aid that were very much in the air.

When the billion dollar gift was made, the reference was to 'the United Kingdom's deficit in her balance of payments with Canada' and there had been no reference to other parts of the Sterling Area. In fact the Area worked as a unit in requiring Canadian dollars, and as individual transactions passed through the various bank accounts, no distinction was made between those originating in United Kingdom requirements and those originating in, say, South Africa or Australia. Canadian supplies sent to other parts of the Sterling Area were, however, charged for by the United Kingdom in sterling (that is to say, any Canadian dollars they required were paid for by drafts on their sterling balances), and in the case of South Africa this might of course affect the amount of gold sold by South Africa to the central reserve in London.[1] It was thus possible—indeed natural, if the complications of financial relations between the United Kingdom and other Dominions were ignored—to represent London as taking materials from Canada as a gift and selling them to other parts of the Commonwealth in exchange for sterling balances or even for gold.

---

[1] cf. above, pp. 313-4.

This last possibility was particularly embarrassing, since Canada was still wanting gold for settling her accounts with the United States. The answer to these representations was that the Sterling Area (including the United Kingdom) did still have other sources (e.g. from repatriation of securities and from exports) of Canadian dollars, in addition to her drawings on the gift, and that the latter in fact fell short of the United Kingdom's own requirements for the 'foodstuffs, raw materials and munitions of war' that had been specified when the gift was offered.[1] Though correct, this answer was not altogether satisfying. The only really satisfying answer would be an extension of mutual aid throughout the Commonwealth.

As the American economy became fully mobilised, the first conception of lend-lease broadened out into the notion that the United Nations, engaged in a common struggle, were throwing all their resources into a common pool which must be allocated with singleness of purpose and without inhibitions arising from financial problems. In the course of 1942 the growing tightness that signalised the progress of mobilisation demanded some international machinery to allocate scarce resources. This trend did not pass unnoticed in Canada. By the weight and progress of her war effort and by the fact that she had already, by the billion dollar gift, stepped aside from the market-place, Canada had established a claim to participate in any international organisation, and there was strong feeling when the Combined Boards were established by Britain and the United States alone. The logic of the Canadian position was inescapable but the parallel, if weaker, claims of other partners had also to be considered, and a cumbrous multi-nation board would defeat its own object. The question dragged on, unhappily, for months through the latter part of 1942. By this time it had become clear that some system of mutual aid was the only method by which the Dominion Government could continue to finance a large-scale contribution, and the United States and the United Kingdom Governments acceded to the request for Canadian membership of the Combined Production and Resources Board, the one Board for which it was relatively easy to single out Canada for a seat as a third chief partner. This concession to Canadian views probably helped to crystallise Canadian opinion in favour of mutual aid.

The third circumstance favouring a switch to some form of mutual aid was the political difficulty Dominion Ministers had encountered in their defence of the billion dollar gift. We have seen[2]

---

[1] It was particularly expedient to impress upon Canada the help the United Kingdom was affording to Australia and New Zealand.

[2] p. 346 above.

how in its second thoughts the Canadian Press tended to emphasise the direct burden of this gift upon every Canadian citizen. As the months went by, there was no diminution of this criticism: 'The cleavage,' reported Ottawa in June, 'between the English and the French Canadians was greatly increased and the French were constantly embarrassing the Government with cracks about the gift.' Then in September the new Canadian income tax, deductible at source, was to take effect. This would entail adjustment of domestic budgets throughout the country and 'as the people become increasingly aware that (as they put it) 25 per cent. of their taxation is due to a gift to Britain and in excess of their own domestic war commitments, it is in my opinion,' a British expert advised from Ottawa, 'apparent that neither Parliament nor the people will again be gift-minded, at least before the end of 1942'. Obviously there would be advantage in dressing financial arrangements up in different clothes next time.

In all these circumstances much thinking had to be done on both sides of the Atlantic, and it was clearly best not to try to rush the Canadians into a new major settlement. No such settlement was really feasible while the Dominion Parliament was in recess: it was not due to meet until 27th January 1943 and it had been led to believe that the billion dollars would last beyond that date. The United Kingdom Treasury therefore decided that, while the movement of Canadian opinion on the broad issues should be encouraged in the hope of a satisfactory large-scale plan in 1943, palliatives must be found to tide over the period between the exhaustion of the gift (expected about November) and early 1943. By what ways and means could the United Kingdom pay her bills over a period of, say, three or four months?

There were four important possibilities. Gold (or U.S. dollars) was once more in hand, but it was still desperately scarce. On the other hand, Canada's continuing preoccupation with her adverse balance with the United States, and her difficulties over lend-lease, made gold very attractive to her, and a United Kingdom offer of a significant amount out of her scanty store would impress upon the Canadian authorities the lengths to which London was prepared to go. The second and third items were recalled from the disappointed expectations of September 1941, when the Dominion Minister of Finance had been thinking of taking on to Canada's bill two items Britain had hitherto financed—the Royal Canadian Air Force squadrons in the United Kingdom and other theatres of war, and certain munition plants in Canada. Fourthly, under standing financial arrangements United Kingdom Government Departments had constantly to present bills to the Dominion Government (e.g. the Service Departments, for supplies to Canadian military personnel in the United Kingdom) and these bills were usually far in arrears; by presenting them more promptly, dollars due in respect of, say, a year could be collected in two or three months.

A small amount could also be expected from the tail-end of repatriation of the Government and Government-guaranteed securities. In the financial year ended 31st March 1942 these had provided $405 millions. During the year 1942–43 (most of the period now under review) they yielded a further $114 millions.[1]

Payment of a small amount of gold would have a number of advantages. Canada had lately been rather less uncomfortable in her balance with the United States (partly through the operation of the Hyde Park Agreement, whereby components for supplies to Britain were covered by lend-lease, and partly through American investment) but there was acute anxiety about the future; a contribution from the United Kingdom would therefore please the Canadians. Secondly, it would strike at the root of the Canadian suspicion that we were taking a gift from Canada and selling some of it to South Africa for gold. Thirdly, it would show the South Africans that we wanted gold to use and not just to hoard. With the gift running out[2] and the Canadians evidently not quite ready to agree other interim arrangements, London decided to take the initiative, and paid 150 million U.S. dollars[3] to Canada. The Canadians in return promised to accumulate sterling to bridge the further gap while other measures were being considered.

On the cost of the Royal Canadian Air Force, there was a good deal of hesitation during the autumn of 1942. In recognition of the heavy burden Canada was shouldering in the Empire Air Training Scheme, the United Kingdom had, early in the war, made to Canada substantial concessions in qualification of the general principle that a Dominion pays for its own Forces.[4] The Royal Canadian Air Force squadrons overseas—there were by November 1941 25 of them—were financed by the United Kingdom, at a cost rising well above $200 millions a year. In addition (and this was a more normal arrangement) the United Kingdom was paying and equipping Royal Canadian Air Force personnel attached to the Royal Air Force in the United Kingdom, costing $44 millions

---

[1] A driblet continued to the very end: $72 millions in 1943–44 and $81 millions in 1944–45.

[2] It had been expected to run out late in October or early in November, but by more speedy collections of money due to the United Kingdom the end was delayed to 22nd December 1942.

[3] The United Kingdom offer was intended to be 150 million Canadian dollars; inadvertently it was described as in U.S. dollars, and the United Kingdom stood by this. The amount included £5 millions in gold which had already been sold to Canada.

[4] cf. p. 330, footnote 2.

a year. To take over these items would not be politically difficult for the Dominion Government—they were a well-recognised part of Canada's 'own' war effort—and the suggestion had been mooted much earlier. Eventually, partly with a view to keeping the mutual aid figures down, the Dominion Government decided to take over the cost of the squadrons—whose number was to rise to 35—and of the 'attached' personnel; this decision was communicated to London in January 1943 and became operative from 1st April 1943.

It was also politically easy for Canadian Ministers to help by taking over munition factories which had been built and provided with working capital at United Kingdom expense. In the early days of the war it had been necessary for the United Kingdom to take the initiative and pay the bills (at least in form). Now that Canada was self-consciously a leading partner in war production and was also looking forward to her industrial status in the post-war world, she was attracted by the idea of 'buying-out' the United Kingdom interest in these factories in her own land. The matter took a long time to settle only because the details needed careful thought and because Canadian legislation was necessary. From December 1942 onwards, if not before, it was plain that Canada meant to buy these. The definite intention was communicated to London in January, and in March a draft agreement was ready and Canada made an advance payment of $200 millions. Final settlement later in the year added $323 millions, making a total of $523 millions covering both the plant and working capital.[1]

The two 'capital' items—gold and the munition factories—together with some acceleration of payments by Canada provided some $700 millions in 1943. In addition, the transfer of financial responsibility for the Royal Canadian Air Force squadrons and personnel brought a continuing $240 millions a year from 1st April 1943. These measures, originally envisaged as covering a gap between October or November 1942 and the spring of 1943, eventually sufficed to cover the gap between the end of the billion dollars (December 1942) and the first drawings under mutual aid, which did not become available until September 1943. During almost the whole of this interim, however, the broad principle of the new system was already known: London was confidentially informed on 24th January of the Canadian Cabinet decision, and the Mutual Aid Act became law on 21st May 1943. The delay in

---

[1] The formal agreement for taking over plant was signed on 27th May 1943. The price named in this agreement was $206,359,705.99, but this was later amended to $206,963,965.85. The continued meticulousness of public accounting, despite the broadness of the successive financial settlements between the two countries, may be noted.

implementation was solely due to the complicated mechanics that had to be devised for implementing a principle that was as simple as it was far-reaching.

The new system was described by the Canadian Minister of Finance on 8th February 1943: ' . . . . . it is our national duty', he said, 'and our privilege to share our abundant supplies with the other United Nations, putting the excess of our supplies, over the requirements of our own Forces, into a pool to be allocated among those of our allies who can make best use of them in accordance with strategic needs.' An essential feature of the proposal was that when supplies were transferred to other United Nations, such supplies should be used in the effective prosecution of the war. To ensure this a Cabinet Committee was established, called 'The Canadian War Supplies Allocation Board', or more usually 'The Mutual Aid Board', whose duty it would be to purchase supplies and to transfer them to those nations requiring them in accordance with strategic need. The Board was to receive an appropriation of $1,000 millions, and the war supplies it was allowed to purchase for transfer were to include raw materials and foodstuffs as well as the more obvious war supplies.

When this announcement was made, the Canadians were committed to the figure of $1,000 millions, as the aid to be given to all the United Nations over a period, it was thought, of about one year. United Kingdom representatives had been warned of this, and on the basis of Sterling Area estimates had expressed the opinion that it would be insufficient, and had sought to persuade the Canadian Ministers to raise it to $1,250 millions. They refused, taking the view that $1,000 millions was 'the limit practicable at the present time'; if more were needed in the event, they would face the situation when it arose.

The mechanics of mutual aid proved exceedingly difficult to work out, and both Canadian and British officials were inventing and rejecting plans all through the spring and summer of 1943. The difficulty arose from the variety of principles the Canadians wanted their mutual aid system to satisfy. It was, in the first place, a grand gesture whereby Canada, striking out the dollar sign, would allocate the actual goods—tanks, aircraft, explosives, bacon, wheat, aluminium and all the rest—for the war effort. Secondly, it was a gesture in favour not of the United Kingdom alone, nor even of the Sterling Area alone, but in favour of all the United Nations—Russia, China, and the United States, as well as the Commonwealth group—and there was some notion of allocating according to 'need', 'deserts', or 'equity'. Thirdly, as a matter of history, the act sprang from the exchange problem between Canada and the Sterling Area: mutual aid was at bottom designed as the balancing item. Whatever paraphernalia were erected for the allocation of goods between individual countries had therefore to be reconcilable with the solution of the Sterling Area's Canadian-dollar problem. The benefits had to be distributed in such a way as to achieve this object, yet at the same time account had to be taken of equity—'or at all events of sentiment and of propensity to grumble'. The Canadians added a further complication when they disclosed that, because they wanted to bring into their allocation system more classes of goods than the Mutual Aid Fund could bear, they wanted the United Kingdom to pay into the Fund some of its dollar receipts from other sources.

Fortunately the Canadian Government had no wish to press to its logical conclusion each one of these irreconcilables, while United Kingdom representatives were accommodating as long as their primary object—the financing of the Sterling Area's deficit with Canada—was achieved. The views of other Governments had to be taken into account: some of these Governments reacted strongly against Canadian suggestions, as the Australian Government did when it heard that the Canadian Board was to deal directly with private parties in Australia. Administrative difficulties cropped up here, there, and everywhere. But, like the British, the Canadians were in the last resort not going to be pernickety, as long as there was some framework of Canadian control of the allocation of aid and as long as their arrangements did effectively syphon sufficient dollars into the Sterling Area's balance. The arrangements that emerged from all this were described by a United Kingdom Treasury official as 'an exceedingly complicated scheme'; all he could say in its defence was that it was 'the simplest scheme yet proposed in months of discussions and the one least likely to interfere with normal trading and banking procedure, while meeting the needs of the Canadians'. (He had implicitly recognised that it met the United Kingdom's needs.) The scheme was accepted by telegram of 24th August 1943 and came into operation a week later. The deficit that had accumulated since December 1942 was thereupon cleared by completion of the payments for munition factories and the other stop-gap expedients discussed above.

It would be tedious to detail the accounting arrangements at last evolved, even if it were possible to ascertain them. In fact it is not, since nobody on this side of the Atlantic ever understood exactly how and why the Canadians handled the day-by-day transactions. Out of all the ideas the Canadians originally sought to embody in mutual aid, the one retained as the essential operative principle vis-à-vis the United Kingdom was that mutual aid should be applied as the balancing item, to cover the current deficit of the Sterling Area with Canada, taking into account

z

munitions as well as non-munitions. All the Canadian dollar receipts of the Sterling Area were canalised through a system of accounts, and any available dollars over and above the Bank of England's minimum working balance, were placed at the disposal of the Canadian Mutual Aid Board, by whom they were applied to financing purchases of munitions, foodstuffs, etc., for the United Kingdom and other Sterling Area countries.[1] To the extent that these dollars, provided from the Sterling Area's usual sources of dollars, were insufficient to cover the accepted purchases of supplies for the Sterling Area, the Board drew on mutual aid funds (the $1,000 millions voted by the Canadian Parliament). Control of all the funds so canalised, whether accruing from the Sterling Area's dollar earnings or from the mutual aid appropriation, was wholly in the hands of the Mutual Aid Board. United Kingdom officials never learned clearly how the Mutual Aid Board operated in regard to specific contracts. It would be possible for one particular munitions contract to be financed wholly out of funds handed over by the United Kingdom and another, apparently similar, contract to be financed simultaneously out of mutual aid funds; and the same would apply to non-munitions contracts—for example for foodstuffs—placed through the mutual aid machinery. Some contracts may have been financed partly from one source and partly from the other.

This machinery ground into action during the autumn of 1943, and early in 1944 the 'Mutual Aid Master Agreement' between Canada and the United Kingdom was signed.[2] This Agreement included an undertaking by the United Kingdom (Article V) not to sell mutual aid goods to another Government or to persons in other countries, and a provision (Article IX) requiring the United Kingdom to return, if the Canadians should so desire, bomber equipment and aircraft; Canada also took an option of requiring the United Kingdom to transfer to Canadian Forces after the cessation of hostilities vehicles, aircraft, tanks and military equipment.[3] A very large part of the $1,000 millions appropriated for the first year was in fact devoted to covering the needs of the Sterling Area, and it proved sufficient beyond 31st March 1944 when the Dominion's financial year ended.

---

[1] The Canadians had agreed that it would be inconvenient to have all items of Sterling Area expenditure in Canada channelled into the Mutual Aid Board, and certain minor items were therefore met from the Bank of England's account before the 'available' surplus was handed over; but all the major supply items were covered by the Board.

[2] 11th February 1944.

[3] There were Mutual Aid Agreements also between Canada and other recipients (including Russia). The story as told in this chapter is of course only one side of the Canadian mutual aid story, being confined to the aspects directly touching United Kingdom arrangements.

(v)

Mutual Aid, Stage II, and Post War Prospects, 1944–45

When mutual aid was at last going full steam ahead, the United Kingdom authorities could hardly have been blamed if they had looked upon the Canadian dollar problem as solved for the remainder of the war. The attitude of non-financial Departments of the Dominion Government was certainly such as to encourage comfortable views of the kind; a surplus of steel production had developed and the United Kingdom was being urged to buy it beyond programme requirements, and there were also moves for new contracts at higher prices.[1] In fact the British did not relax their caution in commitments in Canada; nonetheless, they had a shock when the new mutual aid appropriation was announced at the end of March. The Sterling Area's 1944–45 deficit with Canada was then estimated at $1,475 millions; the appropriation amounted to a mere $800 millions, out of which Canada proposed to provide about $75 millions for U.N.R.R.A.[2] and $275 millions for Russia, China and France. Apparently Mr. Mackenzie King's Government, conscious of the rising tide of opposition in Quebec, expected difficulties there if too loose a rein was allowed to mutual aid. Actually, by the time the new appropriation bill was debated in the Canadian House of Commons, the Second Front had been opened, and opinion had swung decidedly in favour of the Government's policies; but it was then too late—Ministers were committed to the figure of $800 millions. They were sounded about the chance of a further appropriation, but replied that with the possibility of a Federal election[3] there was 'too much uncertainty for reasonable prediction'. London had therefore to face a net deficit, after allowing for mutual aid, of the order of $1,000 millions.

No minor measures could conceivably add up to a bridge for this gap, and it became necessary to contemplate a wholesale diversion of orders from Canada. United Kingdom Departments were instructed to prepare programmes on this basis, though not to commit themselves elsewhere pending discussion with the Canadians. Advantage was then taken of the favourable atmosphere of Bretton Woods—which the Dominion Minister of Finance and his Deputy visited late in June—to expose the intolerably weak position of the United Kingdom and the consequences for Canada of any drastic curtailment of aid. Britain's undertakings in

---

[1] Some weeks later, when London was anxiously searching for some relief from the prospective shortage of Canadian dollars, Canadian Departments were still trying to inveigle United Kingdom Departments into facing big new contracts.

[2] United Nations Relief and Rehabilitation Administration.

[3] The election was not in fact held until May-June 1945.

1941—the undertakings not to divert orders from Canada and (in effect) not to haggle over prices—depended upon the Dominion's willingness to underwrite the Sterling Area's dollar account; if this underwriting were now to break down, the United Kingdom would be morally free to—and would be compelled to—reorientate her purchasing programmes.

The day at Bretton Woods certainly promoted among Dominion Ministers and their officials a clearer understanding of the British position, and particularly prompted realisation that ahead there was a major problem in post-war Anglo-Canadian economic relations. But the discussions did not yield appreciable fruit for the immediate easement of the balance of payments. Canada merely confirmed her willingness to relieve the United Kingdom of some $200 millions of expenditure on the Canadian Forces (the Dominion was still far from paying the whole cost of her overseas Forces),[1] asked for some $250 millions in gold, and for the rest indicated willingness to accept sterling as the alternative to arranging a formal loan.

These terms, which were substantially those on which the Dominion Government had decided just before Bretton Woods, were most unwelcome to London. The demand for gold arose from Canada's termination, for reasons of her own, of the Hyde Park arrangement of 1941[2] whereby the United States had provided, as lend-lease to the United Kingdom, certain material sent to Canada for incorporation in war supplies destined for the United Kingdom.[3] The United Kingdom was now—after a wavering interval—again seeking to accumulate every ounce of gold against her huge post-war liabilities, and felt that in asking for gold the Canadians were striking at the post-war strength of sterling. Any kind of formal loan or 'book-credit' was anathema in London: it infringed the principle of 'no war debts between Allies,' a principle that London, now foreseeing the need for post-war loans, was particularly anxious to maintain. Moreover, if Britain began negotiating loans within the Commonwealth, the Americans might get similar ideas into their heads. Simple accumulation of sterling

---

[1] The items in question were (1) the equipment and maintenance of 14 further Royal Canadian Air Force squadrons and (2) increases in capitation rates for the Canadian Army, in recognition of their higher cost when campaigning in Europe. Canada still refused to meet the cost of operational training of the Royal Canadian Air Force in the United Kingdom.

[2] See above, p. 340.

[3] The decision to terminate the arrangement was taken when the Canadian Minister of Finance met the Secretary of the United States Treasury in April 1944. It had never worked satisfactorily for Canada: the lend-lease procurement procedures were inconvenient and in effect restricted aid to a few major items, and the Americans had been critical—the Canadians thought unreasonably—of Canada's reserves. Mr. Ilsley reported the change to the Canadian House of Commons on 21st April, 1944.

was free—or relatively free—from objections of this kind, but London was terrified by the prospect of big and free sterling balances in Canadian hands. It was one thing for a Sterling Area member to accumulate sterling, of which a substantial part might be tied up by the local regulations governing the note issue and by banking custom. It was quite another thing for Canada, without any tie of this kind, but with her insistent demand for U.S. dollars, to accumulate sterling. By mid-1944 London's 'sterling balances problem' looked quite big enough already, without adding to it in new and difficult directions.

After all that had gone before, it was impossible to believe that these arguments would not bring Mr. Mackenzie King's Government to a more helpful frame of mind. When the Bretton Woods Conference finished, Lord Keynes and Sir Wilfred Eady went up to Ottawa to exercise their persuasive arts. Their persuasion was reinforced by a new unity in Canadian Governmental circles. Hitherto the Ministry of Finance had played almost a lone hand in urging concessions to the United Kingdom in financial matters, and was constantly having to face the contention that 'Canada was being had for a sucker', while other Departments—Agriculture and Munitions and Supply—urged the United Kingdom to buy more freely, without appreciating the dependence of purchases upon financial arrangements. The tougher attitude displayed by United Kingdom purchasing Departments in the summer of 1944 (due partly to the Treasury's instruction to think about alternative sources, and partly to the declining curve of certain requirements) shook Canadian Departments into a new attitude more useful to the Minister of Finance. The soil was thus more congenial to the arguments expounded by the United Kingdom negotiators, and in mid-August Lord Keynes was able to telegraph from Ottawa new Canadian proposals that were accepted just before the mutual aid money ran out at the end of the month.[1] In effect, the Canadians acknowledged the necessity of filling the gap and accepted four major claims by the United Kingdom for payments by Canada. The claims were:

(a) higher capitation payments to correspond to the actual cost of Canada's army.

(b) payment for advance training in the United Kingdom of Royal Canadian Air Force personnel, to be back-dated to 1st April 1943.

(c) payment for reserve and transit stocks attributable to Canadian Forces.

(d) rebate of taxation on mutual aid contracts.

---

[1] The Chancellor of the Exchequer, telegraphing to the Canadian Minister of Finance on 28th August, accepted the proposals.

(a), (b) and (c) merited description as items that Canada ought to have been meeting anyway, and (d) as the refund of a charge that ought never to have been made. The Canadian Government was in this way able to go ahead without awaiting Parliamentary sanction—a useful point in August. The total sum involved was estimated at $655 millions, enough to cover the gap then estimated for the remainder of the financial year, with about $160 millions to spare. As a gesture to help the Canadians, the United Kingdom agreed to sell U.S. $80 millions (88 million Canadian dollars) to help Canada with her United States exchange position. It was agreed that if, as was estimated, the United Kingdom should have a surplus of Canadian dollars at the end of March, payments should be made to Canada on account of certain claims for the Air Training Scheme and for lend-lease adjustments.

'One major anxiety is removed for the time being': this was the Chancellor's breath of relief when he heard the news. The relief could not last long. This Canadian dollar gap had persisted right through the European war, and on a huge scale: notwithstanding the billion dollar gift and mutual aid, it had cost Britain some $1,600 millions in capital assets sold and new debts incurred, in addition to gold and U.S. dollars drawn from the Sterling Area's tenuous reserve. And although the latest adjustments had increased Canada's payments for her Forces overseas, the gap now threatened to widen. For Canada's actual fighting effort served to narrow the gap, while her supply of food and materials for Britain widened it. As the German war ended, Canada's fighting effort would be less, but supplies to Britain must go on. The gap thus widened would have to be filled by expedients which, as Canada had come to know them, would look more than ever like 'assistance to Britain' and less like Canada's contribution to a common effort. The difficulty of obtaining an *increased* mutual aid appropriation for 1945–46 (assumed to be part at least of Stage II) was acknowledged by London. Therefore when, in September-October 1944, the Treasury was looking forward to Stage II, entirely different accounting arrangements were put before the Canadian Government.

The plan—it became known as 'the pooling plan'—was simple enough. Canada would put her munitions production into the pool, without charge, while the United Kingdom would provide without charge all supplies and services (except pay) needed by Canadian Forces outside Canada. Mutual aid would be limited to food and ancillary services, and all other transactions would be settled in cash in the ordinary way. The amount of mutual aid to be voted would, by these arrangements, be greatly reduced—a political advantage in Canada. The Treasury represented that there were great advantages to both parties: 'These proposals represent a radical change in the basis of accounting between our two countries. But we believe that they follow the facts of partnership in a common enterprise much more realistically than our arrangements in the past; they avoid much inevitable arbitrary accounting; they should avoid the periodic crises in our financial relationships which have always in the past been resolved by an act of generosity by Canada but which we cannot ask always to be so resolved; they may be of a nature which may commend them to the Parliaments and public opinions of the two countries as a fair and realistic sharing of the physical and financial burden of the Japanese war.'

Canadian Ministers did not take kindly to this. They feared that it would be interpreted as a political device 'to cloak further aid to the United Kingdom'. Fearful as they had been originally for the reception of mutual aid, they had now become attached to it as 'the most straightforward and easily understood formula'. Lord Keynes went up to Ottawa, following his Stage II talks in Washington, in the autumn of 1944, but the Canadian Cabinet was involved in a prolonged political crisis[1] and it was impossible to bring matters to decision. Two facts did however emerge: that the amount of mutual aid was unlikely to be anything like sufficient, and—foreshadowing post-war economic relations—the Canadians were getting alarmed about the prospect of Sterling Area discrimination against Canadian as well as United States exports. When the Canadian Ministers did, in February 1945, once more bring their minds to bear on the problem of financial aid, it quickly became apparent to London that this question of post-war international trade policy had leapt to the forefront. The telegram announcing that mutual aid would be continued in the new financial year informed London that the object of this was to ensure that post-war commerce should not be burdened by the imposition of trade restrictions or otherwise prejudiced.[2] The United Kingdom would, the telegram pointed out, have good reason in the existence of the sterling balances to be as cautious in importing from sterling as from dollar countries; as Canada was continuing mutual aid, would it not be reasonable to avoid discrimination against Canada, even at the cost of some drain on reserves? A policy of discrimination would be 'unnecessary and inappropriate' and would 'make it increasingly difficult for the Canadian Government to maintain the provision of mutual aid'.

---

[1] The crisis arose from opposition to the sending of conscripts overseas. Hitherto Canada's overseas Forces had depended entirely on volunteers.

[2] The Canadian Prime Minister telegraphed to the United Kingdom Prime Minister to emphasise the high importance attached to these views on commercial policy.

This was a question that might easily have caused a major rift between Canada and Britain. Both countries were looking with some anxiety into the post-war world. Britain had become acutely conscious of her shortage of reserves, her huge sterling liabilities, and the imperative need to develop exports far beyond their pre-war level; to her, imports from Canada were going to need very careful scrutiny. Canada, on the other hand, had her great food production, largely dependent on the United Kingdom market, and her industrial capacity that was looking round for markets to replace the munitions demand. But although this fundamental conflict of interest was to underlie relations for many years, the two sides found it surprisingly easy in 1945 to keep on speaking terms. Fundamentally this was due to the relief experienced by the Canadians when they discovered how the land lay in British official circles. The Canadians had been misled, by contemporary discussion outside official circles, into supposing that Britain had become a doctrinaire bilateralist; they soon realised that the influential people were strongly attached to multilateral trade policies, and that the British were going to follow bilateral policies only to the extent to which they were forced into them. Canadian relief did not find expression in substantial concession of their demand for non-discrimination, but it made them more willing to understand the nature of London's hesitations and to welcome every gesture London could make. This friendly disposition on the Canadian side naturally had its effect on the British negotiators and very great efforts were made to satisfy Canadian requirements.

Apart from the scarcity of Canadian dollars, the major obstacle was the risk of setting an inconvenient precedent for Anglo-American economic relations. London, as the guardian of the central reserve, could not afford to let the Sterling Area drop discrimination against imports from the United States. Therefore, if a concession was to be made to Canada, a distinction must be drawn between the Canadian and American cases. One point of distinction was that Canada had, and the United States had not, approached the United Kingdom Government with positive proposals for 'a broad settlement of the Stage II problem'. Another distinction was that lend-lease, as compared with Canadian aid, was based on a less generous appraisal of Sterling Area needs.[1] Finally, there was the sum involved. By limiting 'non-discrimination' to essentials (strictly interpreted), it was possible to believe that the extra imports would cost less than $25 millions. In talking to the Americans, this might be regarded as a very small sum—the United

---

[1] The estimates of London's Canadian dollar requirements, from which this amount of Canadian financial assistance was fixed, included provision for the miscellaneous import needs of the Sterling Area; there was no similar provision in lend-lease.

Kingdom could afford the concession to Canada, to whom it would mean much, whereas $25 millions would be neither here nor there to the Americans. On this basis of application to 'essential goods only', agreement was thereupon reached. It represented a real concession by both sides, and resulted in the maintenance of a genuinely understanding attitude.

The Canadians did not, in return for this limited British advance to non-discrimination, explicitly promise to see London through by continuance of mutual aid, but the implication was there and it was observed. At the beginning of the new financial year the Dominion Government had obtained Parliamentary authority to spend $2,000 millions on war purposes, including mutual aid; this was intended to cover five months, the intention being to introduce a new budget including final provision after the forthcoming General Election.[1] After the Cambridge and London discussions in May, the United Kingdom Treasury was confident that the Dominion would in fact provide sufficient to see them through Stage II. And then Stage II came to its abrupt end in August, before the two billion appropriation was exhausted.

The Americans at once gave notice of the termination of lend-lease, and the Canadian Government thereupon decided likewise to terminate mutual aid. The date and the precise arrangements were left open until Lord Keynes arrived in Ottawa early in September, on his way to the Washington negotiations on the American loan.[2] The termination was dated at 2nd September; the Canadians agreed to assume all cancellation charges for their own account, and they agreed not to exercise their 'recapture' rights in respect of goods in transit or in United Kingdom hands. On all three counts these terms represented some concession by the Canadians, and the broad upshot was that, given the abruptness with which arrangements were terminated, the settlement was favourable to Britain both as compared with the termination of lend-lease and as compared with the conditions previously envisaged.

There were also for settlement various claims and counter-claims relating to the cost of the Canadian Forces in the United Kingdom and overseas. In contrast to the broad settlements on the major financial issues, and in contrast also to the simple accounting for Air Force charges, the United Kingdom War Office had throughout the war had constant trouble with the meticulous methods of Canadian departmental officials. It is therefore hardly to be wondered at that these accounts should still have been the subject of argument into 1946. The liability of the United Kingdom under the Empire Air Training Scheme had also in some way to

---

[1] The election was at the beginning of June.
[2] See p. 485.

be settled. This resulted quite clearly from the terms originally agreed. The United Kingdom Treasury thought of urging that, as matters had turned out differently from expectations, the contract should be revised and the United Kingdom liability abated; but this was quite a different matter from the haggling over detailed bills for Army supplies.

The interest-free loan—the 'funding' of January 1942[1]—was also due for review. Originally $700 millions, it had been reduced to about $540 millions by redemptions, as the proceeds of sale of Canadian securities by United Kingdom residents were applied. The 1942 agreement had provided that the loan should be free of interest during the war; both interest and repayment terms had now to be discussed. Adding this amount to the other items mentioned above, the United Kingdom Treasury estimated United Kingdom net liabilities to Canada at some $1,200 millions. The most immediate need was to convert this quite formidable liability into something that would leave the United Kingdom in a position to follow a reasonable trading policy.

Beyond these $1,200 millions under other headings, Canada never had any intention of constituting mutual aid as a claim against Britain and other nations. The three billions the Dominion had expended under this head, together with the billion dollar gift, represented a definitive contribution by an autonomous partner in the war effort. It was of course a contribution of first-rate importance, not least because of the implicit underwriting of the Sterling Area's dollar position; the four billions represented almost two-thirds of the Sterling Area's net war-time requirements of Canadian dollars. After the war was over, Canada's $1,200 millions of outstanding claims against London were substantially written-down. Nevertheless, Canada was able to emerge in an extraordinarily strong international position. Her pre-war sterling liabilities had been reduced to a mere fraction of their 1939 total, and her international reserves and her capital position vis-à-vis the United States were virtually untouched. For this comparative strength there was a price to be faced: Canada carried into the post-war period the fear that the contrast between her strength and Britain's weakness was striking at the roots of 'the Atlantic trade triangle' on which her primary producers depended for their markets. The new creditor nation still wanted to sell.

---

[1] See above, p. 346.

CHAPTER XII

UNITED STATES DOLLARS, 1939–40

(i)

The Sale of Securities

IN THE EARLY DAYS of the war financial relations between the United States and Britain were extremely simple, in that they scarcely existed. The United States Neutrality Act forbade lending to a belligerent, and the Johnson Act of 1934 prohibited transactions in the obligations of any country that had defaulted—as Britain had—on the war debts of 1917–20. At the outbreak of war there was no prospect of relaxation of the United States attitude; borrowing being thereby excluded, Britain had to meet all the dollar outgoings of the Sterling Area by using the gold and dollars in the Exchange Equalisation Account (including foreign exchange requisitioned from United Kingdom nationals at the outbreak of war) and by the sale of securities marketable in the United States. The former amounted to some £525 millions. The securities were subject to Treasury control by virtue of Defence (Finance) Regulation No. 1, and by S.R. and O (1939) No. 966 (26th August) the Treasury had called for their registration; the value of securities reasonably marketable in the United States was estimated at about $1,000 millions. In addition to these strictly financial limits, the possibilities of spending in the United States were at the outset further limited by the prohibition, under the Neutrality Act, of export of arms from there. Whatever hopes the British authorities might secretly harbour for help in the long run, they could in the first weeks obviously do little but accept a narrow limitation of spending in the United States. Apart, therefore, from some exploratory measures in the United States and some review of the programmes for purchase there of machine tools, raw materials and foodstuffs, the British authorities directed their main attention to Canada which, as part of the Commonwealth, could be expected to facilitate rather than obstruct supplies for Britain.

In November, however, the United States Congress amended the Neutrality Act with the effect of enabling Britain and her Allies to purchase war supplies provided that they paid cash and that they did not use American shipping. This 'Cash and Carry'

363

legislation, which continued to be the operative control until the lend-lease legislation of March 1941, allowed a wide extension of British orders.[1] Commitments were rapidly entered into for munitions and particularly aircraft and aircraft parts. A programme under which United States industry began to develop additional capacity, at Allied expense, for the implementation of Allied orders, was also put in hand without delay.

These measures greatly increased the immediate cash requirements, and the marketing of securities therefore became urgent. The shipment of gold across the Atlantic was a risky business and it was necessary, at any rate for a time, to put the main weight on sales of securities, although it was desirable to have some gold ready for times when the stock market might become unreceptive. There were reasons for fearing that markets would become unfavourable before long: a disappointing volume of Allied orders would be followed by bearish markets, and we might simultaneously encounter the competition of heavy French sales of securities. The Chancellor of the Exchequer, after consultation with the American Ambassador, therefore decided to send at once to New York a representative with detailed experience of American securities. Mr. Walter Whigham, of Messrs. Robert Fleming and Company and a Director of the Bank of England, was appointed and he sailed early in November 1939.[2] His task was to advise on the technical problems and to take any practical steps approved by the Treasury as a result of his advice; he would incidentally be the expert adviser of the United Kingdom Ambassador in Washington, who was in touch with the United States Treasury on this and related matters. Mr. Whigham and Mr. Gifford, who succeeded him, worked in very close touch with Messrs. Pierpoint Morgan, New York, whose co-operation made an important contribution to the efficiency of the British arrangements.

The main course to be followed was by no means self-evident. Although money had to be raised by selling securities, it was doubtful whether a vesting operation was desirable. Sales on private account were permitted conditionally upon surrender of the dollars to the Treasury, and such sales were in fact proceeding at a rate of nearly £2 millions a week. It was doubtful whether the market could absorb securities more rapidly than this, nor was there early prospect of net dollar requirements rising greatly above this level. The publicity attached to a vesting operation would signalise to the Americans our abandonment of hope for their good offices in some alternative means of raising the dollars. On the other

---

[1] cf. *British War Economy, op. cit.*, Chapter IV.

[2] Mr. Whigham took with him Mr. Carlyle Gifford, who took charge when, after Christmas, Mr. Whigham was unable to return to New York.

hand, any upset of the market would check private sales, nor could there be any assurance of their continuance even in favourable markets. The longer vesting was delayed, the bigger the operation would have to be, and the capacity of the New York market to withstand shocks might well decline—at best, 1940 would have the touchiness of a Presidential election year.

By the end of 1939 the balance had swung clearly in favour of immediate vesting. While prospective dollar requirements were rising, private sales of securities were falling off. The United Kingdom had had to ship appreciable amounts in gold, which did not at all please Mr. Morgenthau, Secretary of the United States Treasury, who still had occasional political trouble over gold purchase arrangements and made it quite clear that he preferred the sale of securities.[1] Mr. Morgenthau actually delayed the further development of British vesting operations, by a short-lived plan whereby the British, French and Canadians might jointly sell their securities to New York issuing houses, but by February this idea had been dropped and the way was clear for the first Vesting Order. By S.R. and O. No. 213 of 1940 (17th February), some £30 millions of United States securities were vested, and Mr. Gifford began to sell them almost immediately—by the end of April about $34 millions had been obtained by sales. Far from meeting any 'shock effect', Mr. Gifford sold so skilfully that the market was for some time unaware that sales had begun. In these conditions Wall Street quickly became accustomed to successive small vesting operations and a continuous stream of official United Kingdom sales.[2] The authorities were thereby encouraged to proceed with a series of moderately small vesting operations at short intervals, and the second Order,[3] covering about £26 millions, was made on 13th April 1940. This left some £130–140 millions of 'good class securities' registered but unvested,[4] but ideas had at this stage to be revised in the light of the market's collapse when April's bad news of the war was followed by worse in May.[5]

The market continued to be unfavourable throughout the summer. Given the policy of not selling below the vesting price, this meant a mere trickle of sales and Mr. Gifford advised that even at lower

---

[1] The implied threat, on the part of the United States, to refuse gold was so absurd that the British refused to take it seriously, but not much far-sightedness was needed to underline the desirability of keeping Mr. Morgenthau sweet.

[2] Private sales of unvested securities continued but proceeds were becoming relatively small.

[3] S.R. & O. (1940) No. 527.

[4] There were in addition unsold vested securities to the value of about £42 millions.

[5] Immediately after 25th May 1940, most of the securities in official hands in London were shipped to North America for safety.

prices little more could be sold until the Presidential election was
out of the way.[1] In these circumstances there was no further vesting,
except a tidying-up operation in November 1940.[2] Even the more
rapid sales of the last two months of the year would scarcely have
justified further vesting, had not the whole question become
overshadowed by the exhaustion of London's gold reserve and
the United States Administration's view that Britain must 'scrape
the barrel' before aid could be given.

(ii)

The Exhaustion of London's Reserves, 1940−41

The last months of 1940 saw a revolutionary change in Anglo-
American relations; that such a change must come was implicit
in the decision taken, in June 1940, that all London's dollars
and gold must be thrown into the struggle at once. Until that
time, the rate at which Britain entered into dollar commitments
had been influenced, though not determined, by the War Cabinet
ruling in September 1939 that preparations should be made on
the basis of a three years' war. This ruling, originating in the need
to resist a German 'peace offensive' when Poland was over-run,
had been given without reference to any financial considerations,
but it was taken seriously by Departments, the Treasury among
them. Calculations in the winter of 1939–40 indicated that London's
reserves would run out in little more than two years; in the light
of the three-years' rule, this was about as imprudent as the Treasury
felt it could afford to be. In fact it seems likely that Treasury officials
reconciled themselves to such prodigality only by private
expectations that sooner or later America would loosen the
purse-strings. German successes in Denmark and Norway in
April 1940 provoked an abrupt shortening of the time-scale, even
before the Low Countries were invaded or the Chamberlain
Government fell. On 4th May the Chiefs of Staff Committee made
detailed recommendations on the assumption that Germany was
seeking a decision in 1940, and that this would involve a major
offensive against Great Britain. Their final recommendation
inevitably was that 'financial considerations should not be allowed

---

[1] Over a long period the official sales averaged well under $1 million a week. In
the first two weeks after the election they jumped to $5.3 and $4 millions. The relatively
big figures realised in the concluding weeks of 1940 were made possible only by selling
outside the Stock Exchange.

[2] S.R. and O. (1940) No. 1979 (16th November) covered about £1 million of 'late
registrations' of securities already referred to in the first and second Vesting Orders.
The only later Vesting Orders were S.R. and O. (1941) Nos. 20 and 520 (11th January
and 19th April) covering respectively £20 millions and £26 millions.

to stand in the way'. A fortnight later the Stamp Survey, looking more thoroughly into the implications of the new shipping situation,[1] concluded that 'for the time being the importance of husbanding our exchange resources carefully has greatly diminished'. Before France fell, this had been formally adopted as Ministerial policy and the pace at which new dollar commitments were entered into depended exclusively on technical circumstances, among them competition with United States Service Departments for priority in the output of American industry. Almost immediately, commitments were increased overnight by some £125 millions when the French contracts were taken over.[2]

Commitments on this scale went far beyond the cash resources the United Kingdom Government had in sight, and the time for relying on secret hopes of American assistance had gone by. On 3rd July 1940 the British Ambassador at Washington, Lord Lothian, presented to the State Department a memorandum on the new economic situation.[3] After reviewing the imperative need to draw on altogether greater American production, fair warning was given: 'So long as gold and other foreign assets at their disposal permit, H.M. Government will, of course, continue to pay cash for essential armaments or supplies and foodstuffs. They feel however that they should in all frankness inform the United States Government that it will be utterly impossible for them to continue to do this for an indefinite period . . . . .' Sir Frederick Phillips visited Washington in July, his principal object being to inform Mr. Morgenthau of the financial entanglement and to explore with the United States Treasury means by which aid might be forthcoming. Arriving just after Dunkirk, he found that '95 per cent. of the population expected the Germans to win'; much as the Americans wanted us to win, there was a good deal of reluctance to put money into a supposedly sinking ship. But by the end of July defeatist views were weakening—in one sense at least, time was on Britain's side. But financial aid remained a difficult subject: although opinion in the Press and among informed Americans was that America would have to lend to Britain in the end, Sir Frederick Phillips had received 'no commitments or promises of any kind of credits, nor would this be possible before the election'.

Whether or not this had been explicitly stated, British policy was, through the three months that remained before the election, based

---

[1] 16th May 1940.

[2] For an account of this step, see H. Duncan Hall, *North American Supply*, in this series (H.M.S.O., 1955), Chapter V, Section iv.

[3] The Prime Minister had already, in his first personal message (as Prime Minister) on 15th May, said 'We shall go on paying dollars for as long as we can, but I should like to feel reasonably sure that when we can pay no more you will give us the stuff all the same'. (W. S. Churchill, *op. cit.*, Vol. II, p. 23).

on the assumption that financial aid of some kind would be quickly forthcoming thereafter. Sir Frederick Phillips had left the United States Administration under no illusions as to either the need or the expectation of 'massive financial help'. There had been no official American assurance, nor indeed could any assurance have been given that would be binding on an Administration of either party. None the less, the assumption that President Roosevelt meant to help, and could help effectively, was the only one upon which forward contracting had to proceed; the risk had to be taken. Although all forward commitments involved this risk, immediate cash requirements involved no immediate difficulty: there was enough cash in hand to last, it seemed, well into 1941. But a fresh round of arithmetic in August gave a more threatening result. There were two reasons for the acceleration of dollar payments. Much the weightier was of course the placing of colossal new contracts including, since the June stock-taking, the programme for 3,000 'planes a month. Secondly, it was noted during the spring and summer that American suppliers were insisting on more in the way of advance payments; this was partly due to lack of confidence in Britain's powers of resistance, but it also reflected doubts about her ability to pay all the bills she was running up.[1] Gigantic new contracts were therefore involving an immediate acceleration of the dollar drain, and it began to look as though the liquid reserves could not last much beyond Christmas. At the same time, now that actual exhaustion of the reserves was at hand, the full implications were more clearly realised. Our supply lines both within the Commonwealth (especially from India) and from neutrals depended upon the continued acceptability of sterling, and without any reserves at all London could hardly expect the world to continue to treat her as the banker. If 'the whole elaborate convention of London funds, special accounts and the rest' was not to 'crumble like a house of cards', London must always be known to have some gold in the cellar.[2]

Given that the Americans would take no definite steps until after the election, given the pace at which the dollars were running out, and given the risk of exposure of London's plight, Treasury officials had to exert themselves along four lines. First they had to enforce, more strictly than ever before, economy in commitments involving dollar expenditure before mid-1941, even if a chance had to be taken on the more remote period. Secondly, they had to look round for any hoards of gold that might be scraped into the

---

[1] The possible effect on United States suppliers had to be considered when disclosure of United Kingdom reserves was under discussion.

[2] The phrases quoted are taken from a memorandum by Professor D. H. Robertson.

central reserve to improve the look of things even if they involved no permanent relief. Thirdly, they had to press the liquidation of any assets marketable in the United States. Fourthly, they had to attend to American ideas so that the critical legislation should go through the machine as speedily as possible after the election.

American ideas were in fact such that attack along the first three lines provided also for the fourth. Throughout the summer the American Administration had been by no means backward in telling the British how they could get by until massive aid was forthcoming. In his conversations with the President and Mr. Morgenthau as early as July, Sir Frederick Phillips had been shown that Britain was expected to help herself by selling all her foreign assets, including South American securities and 'direct investments' in the United States. As the months went by this view hardened. Just before the election Lord Lothian reported categorically that to forestall criticism (in getting legislation through Congress) the Administration would require the United Kingdom to show that all available resources, including direct investments in the United States and United Kingdom investments in South America, were exhausted, and that the Administration was likely further to ask for a share in United Kingdom tin and rubber investments in Malaya. The negotiations that dragged through 1941 were to show, all too well, how accurate was the Ambassador's judgment.

The 'readily marketable' securities (vested and unvested) were reckoned in August 1940 as £200 millions, and they were down to £170 millions at the end of October. But 'readily marketable' was hardly an accurate description. The most easily saleable securities had been sold in the winter and spring, and the remainder included much that could only be peddled out very gradually in favourable markets. The events of the summer made markets decidedly unfavourable. The rump remainder consisted of securities that the Americans would assume could be turned into dollars, but that were doubtful starters if 'dollars' meant 'dollars in 1940'. Actually the British authorities managed to raise another £38 millions in dollars from these sales by March 1941, a total of nearly £70 millions in seven months.

The other assets, of which it was already clear that the United Kingdom was expected to strip itself, were altogether tougher propositions. Lord Catto, in preparation for Sir Frederick Phillips' November journey to Washington, analysed the 'direct British investments in the United States'. There were, he said, three classes:

(i) those securities capable of being sold with reasonable advantage to an American investor. Here the practical difficulty was to find quick buyers for the very miscellaneous items.

In some cases the parent company in the United Kingdom was under obligation to offer the investment first to American associates who already owned substantial portions of the subsidiary or associated company;

(ii) others which were either not profitable, or if profitable so dependent upon the present company in Britain as to make the American business incapable of separation without serious injury to the goodwill. It would be 'hopeless even to attempt the sale to American investors';

(iii) subsidiary and associated insurance companies owned in part or in whole by British insurance companies. This was an important class of concerns, comparatively small in capital and resources, but of great value as long as they enjoyed the backing of, and connection with, the parent insurance companies in Britain.

As regards tin and rubber investments in Malaya—a class that inevitably excited American attention after events of the inter-war period—Mr. Keynes commented that the properties were held by a multitude of small companies whose shares had never been popular with American investing institutions. It was unthinkable that they could be sold on the American market at prices bearing any reasonable relation to their intrinsic value. The alternative of selling directly to the United States Government would raise difficult political issues: Mr. Keynes's own view was that 'if the U.S. wished to take over the tin and rubber resources of the British Empire, they must be prepared to take over at the same time the responsibility for the territories in which they are situated'. Arguments of this kind did not, however, stand in the way of sales of investments in South America—but many of these did not at that time look worth much.

This preliminary inspection did not encourage the British authorities to jump into rapid action, but it was as well that Treasury spokesmen in Washington were henceforward well briefed in this matter, for it was to be a major bone of contention during succeeding months. As regards the collection of every conceivable hoard of gold, on the other hand, positive action was more rewarding and was quickly taken. It was clear that the Americans would expect the United Kingdom to use all the Allied gold upon which hands could be laid. There were £87 millions of Belgian gold, £23½ millions of Dutch, and £285 millions of French gold and dollars, to all of which the United Kingdom had some moral claim while it was fighting the battle of those countries. The United Kingdom was equally expected to get hold of Indian and South African gold reserves, there being scant understanding in the United States of the political standing of these members of the

Commonwealth. The difficulty about French gold and dollars has already been explained;[1] in the end Mr. Morgenthau understood sufficient of our difficulties to acquiesce in these hoards being left virtually unused.[2] The Belgians were finally persuaded to offer to lend part of their gold for the duration of the war,[3] and the most that could be hoped from the Dutch was that they would take the same line as Belgium. An offer to lend gold for the duration of the war was not, unfortunately, the same as an outright sale for sterling—a definitive obligation to provide the gold at the end of the war was worse, for the United Kingdom reserve position, than an addition to post-war sterling balances. But refugee Governments, liable to be held to account if they alienated the patrimony of their people, felt unable to go further. In its extremity early in 1941 the United Kingdom accepted, against post-war replacement, some £59 millions of the Belgian gold, with an option on most of the remainder, an option that was not in the event exercised. The Treasury was meanwhile trying to persuade the Dutch to come into the Sterling Area, which would have involved selling their gold for sterling. The Dutch, for reasons that never satisfactorily emerged,[4] preferred to retain their monetary independence, and wanted to hold on to their gold lest dollar receipts from Indonesian exports should collapse. They did eventually give a general promise that if the United Kingdom were in dire straits the gold would be lent, but the tightness that preceded lend-lease had then passed and the Dutch gold was in fact never used. It always remained a sore point with M. Gutt, the Belgian Minister of Finance, that the United Kingdom Government had not pressed the Dutch to 'equality of sacrifice'. The Norwegians, like the Dutch, clung to their gold—some £13 millions; on the other hand, the refugee Czech Government had readily parted with about £7½ millions.[5]

In all these negotiations for gold the United Kingdom authorities were only half-hearted wherever it was clear—as it nearly always was—that an immediate post-war replacement of the gold would be demanded. Britain was stripping herself and there was no prospect that she would embark on the post-war period with any gold to spare, nor indeed was there certainty that she would have

---

[1] pp. 335-6 above.

[2] Not entirely unused, for during critical days in January 1941 French gold in Canada was actually used by the British, being replaced by simultaneous earmarking in London.

[3] The negotiations had been initiated by the British in August 1940, and the Belgians did not agree until 4th March 1941. On this episode, see also pp. 383-4.

[4] Memories of 1931, when the depreciation of sterling involved heavy losses for Dutch bankers, may well have been at the bottom of it all.

[5] Negotiation for the Czech gold had originally been linked with British recognition of the Provisional Government of Czechoslovakia; it was taken over by the Custodian of Enemy Property in July 1940 and put by agreement at the disposal of the Bank of England, but was not actually used when London's reserves ran out in December 1940.

any gold at all. It was necessary to explain to the Americans that the assumption of any such post-war liabilities implied equivalent increase in the bare minimum of reserves required throughout, and these explanations were really the beginning of the long process of educating responsible Americans in Britain's need for some post-war assets. In the context of the collection of Allied gold at the end of 1940, the United States Administration appears to have accepted United Kingdom explanations. But the offer of some Belgian gold had to be accepted, despite the onerous condition, simply in order to provide cash for payments from day to day before lend-lease aid began to flow.

While the President and members of his Administration had made it perfectly clear that Britain had to exhaust her own resources as a prior condition of financial assistance, they were not at all clear as to the form that assistance should take. Sir Frederick Phillips had put out feelers during his July and November visits to Washington but there was no positive response. There was at no stage any weakening of America's unwillingness to make ordinary loans, and this unwillingness to lend was matched by British unwillingness to assume responsibility for post-war debts.[1] The simplest method would have been a 'Payments Agreement' whereby the United States Exchange Account (i.e. the United States Treasury) would hold sterling, as India and other Allies were doing, although of course even this method would leave a post-war problem of debt settlement. This idea was scarcely mentioned before it was silenced, for the phrase 'Payments Agreement'—or indeed anything akin to it—was anathema to Mr. Cordell Hull, President Roosevelt's Secretary of State.

In short, the position reached when Mr. Roosevelt was re-elected at the beginning of November 1940, was that the United States Administration and the weight of informed American opinion were ready to continue—and greatly to increase—physical supplies to Britain while all were casting round for some means of avoiding financial indebtedness of the conventional kind. An American lawyer with important connections on both sides of the Atlantic privately suggested that Britain might offer the United States 'various facilities the value of which could not be measured exactly in terms of money', and he thought that a transaction of this kind would require only amendment of the Neutrality Act, which would be a great deal easier than any interference with the Johnson Act.[2] Mr. Oliver Lyttelton[3] suggested that American supplies

---

[1] This method was so completely out of court that it went virtually unmentioned in the papers.

[2] The relevance of the Johnson Act was that under it loans to Britain, as a nation defaulting on the debts of the first World War, were prohibited.

[3] At this date President of the Board of Trade.

might be obtained against an undertaking to return them in kind, 'beginning say in five years' time'. The Chancellor was alive to the post-war strain that an undertaking of this kind would imply; but the Treasury had grasped the broad idea that Britain must get away from talking about loans and must substitute some other plan.

The plan came, almost at once, from the President himself in response to a long letter from the Prime Minister, which the latter has described as 'one of the most important I ever wrote'.[1] The letter was not an appeal for aid, but 'a statement of the minimum action necessary to achieve our common purpose'. It was largely concerned with naval matters, but there were important paragraphs referring concisely to the need of merchant shipping, aircraft manufacture and supplies for the army. In paragraph 17 he came to the financial consequences: 'The more rapid and abundant the flow of munitions and ships which you are able to send us, the sooner will our dollar credits be exhausted'.[2] Orders already placed or under negotiation many times exceeded the remaining exchange resources. 'The moment approaches when we shall no longer be able to pay cash for shipping and other supplies.' Sir Winston Churchill has himself told[3] how President Roosevelt, cruising in the Caribbean, brooded over this letter, and how the United States Treasury lawyers had pulled out of their lumber-room a Statute of 1892 which had given the Secretary for War discretion to 'lease' Army property 'for the public good'. The outcome was the famous Press Conference the President gave on 17th December 1940, the day after his return to Washington. He insisted that 'the best immediate defense of the U.S. is the success of Great Britain defending itself', he thrust aside all notions that wars depended on the availability of money, and so reached the heart of his proposal: 'Now, what I am trying to do is to eliminate the dollar sign'. United States factories turned out munitions; the United States Government would now buy all of them and those materials more useful in Britain's hands would be leased or sold, subject to mortgage, to Britain. Then came the well-known story of the fire in a neighbour's house and the loan of a garden hose.[4] This Press Conference was followed immediately after Christmas by the President's 'Fireside Chat' to the American people.[5] On this occasion no explicit reference was made to Britain's financial difficulties; the President's policy

---

[1] W. S. Churchill, *op. cit.*, Vol. II, p. 501. The letter (dated 8th December 1940) is there reproduced in full, pp. 494-501.

[2] The phrase 'dollar credits' might be taken to imply the use of dollars lent to the United Kingdom. Both the writer and the recipient of this letter of course well knew that there had been no such 'credits'; the word was used in the sense of 'balances'.

[3] *op. cit.*, Vol. II, pp. 501-503.

[4] E. Stettinius, *Lend-Lease—Weapon for Victory*, pp. 65-66.

[5] Broadcast of 29th December 1941, as reported in *Keesing's Contemporary Archives*.

was simply to provide the implements of war for others who would do the fighting, in order 'to keep war away from our country'. These two Presidential talks were immensely successful in clarifying America's political position; the fog created by isolationist arguments was dispersed.[1]

The main principle that was to govern the future flow of war supplies to Britain was thus settled for the remainder of the war. The material and equipment that were necessary for 'the defense of the United States', as the Lend-Lease Act put it, could be handed over to Britain if the President thought this the most efficient way of using them; goods so transferred were not to be paid for in money, but would be acknowledged by some 'consideration' to be negotiated. This was the essence of the plan proposed by the President to Congress immediately upon its assembly early in January. The Lend-Lease Bill became the Lend-Lease Act on 11th March 1941, and on 27th March Congress passed the first Appropriation of dollars to enable the Executive to implement the Act. It was necessarily some time before the machinery for operating the Act could be established, and the actual procurement and delivery of materials were therefore delayed into the early summer. Before August 1941 only the merest trickle of lend-lease supplies arrived in the United Kingdom; not until 1942 did the trickle become a flood.

To recount events in this summary fashion is to gloss over months of tribulation for Britain's financial administrators. London's reserves of gold and dollars were exhausted at the end of 1940; between that date and the time when the lend-lease trickle at last swelled to a flood, there was a gap of several months through which Britain had to live and to continue to draw vital supplies from the United States. Ways and means whereby this gap might be closed quickly became entangled in the Congressional processing of the lend-lease legislation, and the story of Anglo-American financial relations throughout 1941 is therefore an integral part of the lend-lease story. The revolution of American policy at the end of 1940 unfortunately did not set a term to the United Kingdom's financial difficulties, but at least Britain's poverty was never again so absolute. It became instead the poverty of the poor relation; this was already brought home to British negotiators before the Bill was through Congress and, for all the generosity of that 'most unsordid act in history', the British never escaped from this position.

---

[1] *The Economist* leading article, 4th January 1941. cf. a personal letter from Sir Frederick Phillips (in Washington) to a colleague in London: 'Without the brilliant handling of the situation by the President (though I well realise how it must have irked you) I do not believe anything would get through'.

CHAPTER XIII

THE LEND-LEASE TANGLE

(i)

'The Most Unsordid Act'

FROM THE BEGINNING OF 1941 until late in 1944 Anglo-American financial relations were ruled by the Americans' lend-lease policy; this essential unity forbids any further chronological break until the 'Stage II' discussions in the autumn of 1944. It might be supposed that the entry of the United States into the war in December 1941 fundamentally altered the position and that thenceforward the ruling concept would have been the pooling of resources. In some fields—in the allocation of material resources—substantial progress was made in this direction, but in the financial field it made no headway. The concept of financial pooling in fact never emerged from its initial haziness, and perhaps the British had only themselves to thank for this. The concept is inherently difficult, and London did not produce a clear plan for overcoming the difficulties in a manner acceptable to the United States. The hints at a retrospective plan which would have involved a large cash payment in respect of the past were not at all to American liking. Any hopes that rose on this score in the United Kingdom Treasury were soon acknowledged to be idle; Britain's position remained what it had been through 1941, that of the dependent partner receiving aid that became gigantic but remained in principle marginal to her own utmost effort. The story of 1941–44 is one story, unbroken by the noise of Pearl Harbour.

It is a story, above all else, of unexampled generosity on the part of the American nation. Unless this all-important fact is remembered throughout, these chapters are bound to convey a false impression, an impression insulting alike to the Americans who gave and to the British who strove to justify acceptance of the colossal stream of munitions, of food, of aircraft and of materials to sustain both direct war production and civilian life in these islands. Between March 1941 and September 1945 this flow cost the United States Government some 30 thousand million dollars, which had to be collected in taxes or by the issue of bonds pledging future taxpayers. This flow was started by people who knew that their fathers had been dragged into the previous war partly by financial entanglement; it was started by people who knew that it must lead to their own participation in the present war. It was started by people for whom the second war crowned the disillusionment that had followed the first—a war their fathers had fought 'to make the world safe for democracy'. It is true that the stated American objective in lend-lease was 'the defense of the United States', but it was not easy for a people with such geographical advantages to convince themselves that these enormous supplies were really necessary for this purpose. In retrospect the historian may emphasise that American participation was sooner or later inevitable, that the decision represented no choice but the acceptance of the inexorable implications of the American love of freedom; but a nation of millions of people is not brought readily to decisions of this kind. No Englishman who lived through 1938 has any right to stint his admiration for the initiation of lend-lease. It was 'the most unsordid act'.

It is necessary to emphasise all this, however briefly, because the story to be told in this chapter is the story not of the flow of lend-lease goods but of certain difficulties that arose in connection with it. The scope of this book allows space only for these troubles, and not for their noble counterpart which was—and remains— always the more important. That there were troubles—interminable arguments, misunderstandings, irritations—was due at bottom to circumstances that may be obvious enough in the leisurely re- flections of a later generation but could not be remembered—and so serve as healthy correctives—in the hurly-burly of war.

First, and perhaps most fundamental of all, it was a new thing for Britain not to be the leading Power, and it was an equally new thing—and equally disturbing—for the Americans to have the lead. The British authorities just did not realise how much they were taking for granted: they knew what they had achieved (above all in 1940) and it scarcely entered their heads that the Americans were not equally aware of the achievement. The United Kingdom authorities were not used to explaining everything at length: they had led the world's struggle for freedom and felt entitled to the necessary help in their struggle. The Americans equally unconsciously based their habits on the immense resources and productivity of their country: the decision to aid Britain was their decision, they felt generous, and they resented British pretensions.

The political distance between the two nations—a distance that had to be bridged before partnership could be approached—is easily underestimated. Although so much of the American stock went from these islands—sometimes because of it—Britain was not really popular with Americans at large. Britain was regarded as imperialist, used to ordering much of the world about—and the

American Union was not prepared to be ordered about. An Englishman thinks of George III either as Farmer George or (in a scholar's phrase) 'the spiritual ancestor of Colonel Blimp'[1]; to an American he is one of the villains of history. To use this contrast as a symbol of Anglo-American differences will strike most Englishmen as silly, but it will be understood in the United States, and this difference itself underlines the moral.

The political difficulties encountered by the Roosevelt Administration in its lend-lease policy began with the isolationist principles—the reluctance to be dragged into the war. But that was only the beginning, a beginning to which the events of December 1941 put an end. After that the two nations had identity of immediate aims, but there was trouble as soon as both looked ahead. British authorities, sensing (inadequately enough, as the event showed) the impoverishment that lay ahead, were perforce concerned to preserve what little they could in the way of financial and commercial prestige and technical freedom. This made the Americans feel that we were dragging our feet in the war effort, in favour of post-war reserves, the Sterling Area, Imperial Preference and all that. Meanwhile they themselves had become attached to new aims for a post-war trading world, aims to which British reservations (tiny as they were) seemed diametrically opposed. And besides these apparent (though largely unreal) clashes of principle, President Roosevelt and his men had to cope with the pressures of particular interests, which the American political machine always tends to magnify. President Roosevelt had, in short, to guard against attacks both from the guardians of principle and from the guardians of interests; his habit was to seek 150 per cent. cover for both. In London it was impossible to avoid the feeling that the United States Administration was over-fearful of Congressional reactions; always there was the temptation to tell American officials how to explain things to their own people.

There were important differences, too, in the machinery and methods of government in the two countries, differences that were not appreciated until they had been experienced at close contact. Unfortunately the British took a long time to grasp the difference between the responsibility of a British Minister or civil servant, on the one hand, and a member of the United States Administration on the other. The clear line of responsibility running down a British Department can leave a foreign body in no doubt about whether the United Kingdom Government as such has or has not agreed upon something; this was the system which United Kingdom representatives, whether Ministers or permanent or temporary civil servants, accepted so deeply that they were apt to assume

---

[1] Richard Pares, *King George III and the Politicians*. (Oxford, 1953), p. 69.

that it had a precise parallel in Washington. They learned, the hard way, that Washington knew no such clear line of responsibility, and that agreement reached with one official did not bind his Department, that agreement with a Departmental head did not bind the Administration, and that what the President said might be one thing but what Congress allowed him to do, quite another. This different American constitution had another effect the British were slow to understand and which therefore acted as a constant irritant. The comparative lack of responsibility of the individual in the American Government allowed individuals to speak in public without embarrassment of the Administration. 'Thinking aloud', in very free terms, was permissible and views thoroughly frightening to United Kingdom representatives were often uttered without any serious thought of the implications. In time, the British learned to thicken their skins and not be unduly depressed by these utterances. But while they were learning this lesson, the differences between the ways of the two countries made for trouble.

If there were directions in which British slowness to understand American ways made for trouble, it was equally true that the Americans' acceptance of Britain's needs was hindered by their lack of understanding of London's financial position. The literature about the Sterling Area is virtually a post-war literature, even in Britain itself. Few people really understood how the Sterling Area system worked, and those few took it all so completely for granted that it rarely occurred to them that it might be important to uncover its mysteries to a wide audience. In the early days of the war it was not in fact of much direct relevance to the size of Britain's need for help. Later—as United Kingdom indebtedness to other parts of the Sterling Area piled up and as the Americans began to spend large sums in the Area—the existence of the Sterling Area did become of outstanding relevance to the estimation of Britain's needs both during the war and in the post-war transition. Yet when Americans did begin to learn that the Sterling Area existed, they all too often believed it to be a nefarious arrangement whereby the United Kingdom might restrict the post-war markets for American exports. When Lord Keynes went to Washington in the autumn of 1944, he found it urgently necessary to dispel misconceptions on this subject. During the previous three or four years they had been an irritant of rapidly mounting importance.

These misunderstandings, on both sides, were the more persistent because war-time circumstances had magnified the distance between London and Washington. It was not merely that all private and business travel was virtually suspended; the increased official representation was gravely handicapped by the slowness of communication between London and Washington.

Cable facilities were badly overstrained, the journey by sea was long, even in summer, and air communication was at first almost as slow except in good spells of summer weather. In the critical winters of 1940–41 and 1941–42 six weeks could elapse before a reply by letter could come to hand. This was bad enough in itself, but it inevitably had the effect of making the United Kingdom representatives in Washington more self-reliant—and therefore more out of touch with London. At the other end of the line, the men in London—all of them carrying a fantastically heavy load—omitted to pass to Washington critical information or, more often, just did not stop to think how useful the information might be to their colleagues across the Atlantic. In the later stages there was great improvement in this matter—transport improvements facilitated more rapid communication and more frequent movement of personnel, and in both Washington and London United Kingdom officials came to realise the value, when negotiating with the United States Administration, of having full and up-to-date information on the tips of their tongues.

British shortcoming in providing information had very deep roots and it is no wonder that representatives in Washington remained, to the very end, substantially handicapped in this respect. Partly it was due to the failure of the administrative machine to meet new needs; partly it was due to deep-rooted distrust—perhaps one may say a national distrust—of statistical evidence lacking 100 per cent. reliability; partly it was due to security-mindedness in the face of American leakages. Whitehall had rarely had to face inquisitions on matters of financial policy; apart from the budget, the man-in-the-street knew 'high finance' was above his head, and the Treasury had grown up without the habit of having to explain its actions. Nor had its business called traditionally for a large battery of statistics—the Inland Revenue could guess the yield of taxes reasonably closely, and that was almost all that mattered. There is a sense in which the Treasury official was traditionally the very shrewd amateur, and this was not the animal to deal with the Americans in 1941. But the defects—from the point of view of Anglo-American relations—were by no means confined to the Treasury. Neither inside nor outside Whitehall were there either statistics or the minds to produce statistics on the American scale. Some of the statistical requirements were entirely novel—authorities in London had not, until 1939, had to tackle the problem of splitting the prospective balance of payments regionally—and progress was necessarily slow. In some fields progress was slower than it need have been, owing to an initial failure of Whitehall to realise the scale of the trained manpower that would be required not only in the Treasury but also (and perhaps more) in the other Departments on which the Treasury depended for framing its estimates. Traditional attitudes mattered too. The Englishman thinks statistical inquiries a nuisance, and often he thinks them a waste of time if they cannot be meticulously accurate. When he does not know the figures, he is most unwilling to guess, although his guess may be more than good enough for the purpose in hand. He therefore distrusted American statistics which he knew must include a large element of guesswork, while his American counterpart interpreted British unwillingness as secretiveness designed to conceal facts disadvantageous to the British case. Moreover, the British official sometimes believed it his duty to conceal the facts: the Bank of England was the repository of many of those most relevant, and the Bank for good or ill maintains the traditions of confidence between banker and customer, traditions built in the days before the Bank of England was the purely public institution of our own century. There were sometimes incidents to remind the British to be careful about telling the Americans all their secrets. The Americans were not then, as they later became, more 'security-minded' than the British, and information handed in strict confidence on one day could leak into the American Press the next day. All these circumstances were against a ready flow of statistical and other information in the east-west direction; and because it was Britain that was asking for money, this was the direction that mattered.

There were difficulties also of a more personal kind. Reference has already been made to the traditional British Treasury official as a very shrewd amateur. By the Americans, usually unsophisticated and suspicious about finance, the amateurishness passed unnoticed but the shrewdness heightened their suspicions. Of the British officials who engaged in war-time negotiations with American Government Departments, almost all will remember their pained realisation that their opposite numbers regarded them as smart fellows whose subtle arguments concealed some design of commercial imperialism. The distrust of Keynes's brilliance was only the extreme case. Yet there was the other side to the Americans' relations with Keynes: in fact, in their attitude to him one sees as through a magnifying glass both sides of the personal relationships that grew between men from the two sides of the Atlantic. One of Lord Keynes's own phrases best epitomises this: 'friendship and exasperation advancing hand in hand'.[1] To supplement the underlying unity of war-time purpose, there was this growth of personal friendship—albeit coupled with exasperation—between the men who had to face the problems marginal to the lend-lease

---

[1] The phrase occurs in his report on the Stage II negotiations.

flow. For there were problems, problems of great difficulty inherent in the American view of the nature of lend-lease. When discussions opened, the United States was still a neutral country and Britain, fighting almost alone, had exhausted all her most liquid international reserves. She had therefore to accept whatever conditions the United States Government attached to material assistance; the British might make representations, but before pressing representations on any point they had to assess the risk they would run of alienating the United States Administration. Sometimes they did not have even the chance to make representations, but were abruptly faced with a unilateral decision. This was a position to which the British authorities never completely reconciled themselves, but it was natural enough, having regard to the legal and political basis of lend-lease in the United States itself. Material provided on lend-lease was material on which American money was being spent 'for the defense of the United States', and members of the United States Administration considered themselves answerable in detail for the strictness with which supplies were confined to what was necessary for the defense of the United States. They were under no obligation to agree with representatives of other nations. Morally the position was changed by the entry of the United States into the war, but it remained substantially unchanged in terms of United States politics, and completely unchanged in terms of United States law and United States administrative arrangements.

Foremost among the conditions the Americans imposed was that Britain should help herself to the utmost, and draw to the utmost on her Allies both inside and outside the Commonwealth, before resorting to American aid. At the very outset, the United States Administration publicly committed itself to the view that the United Kingdom's remaining assets could be used to pay the bills falling due under pre-lend-lease contracts; but the liquid assets had gone, and lend-lease provided no way of turning unmarketable assets into dollars. So there arose the problem of 'interim finance', which the United Kingdom sought to solve by persuading the United States Administration to squeeze 'the old commitments' into the framework of lend-lease. Beyond the initial period when this principle was manifest in 'the problem of the old commitments', it persisted as an underlying desire on the American side to adjust the amount—and therefore the scope—of lend-lease in such a way as to leave London's reserves at the barest minimum. As the war went on, Britain's efforts to get the old commitments taken over, and then to get as much as possible of current supplies squeezed into lend-lease, gave way to British efforts to persuade the Americans that London must hold an international reserve proportioned to her liabilities—but at bottom the arguments were the same from beginning to end.

A second problem, which raised its head almost as soon as the President's signature on the Lend-Lease Act was dry and which trailed on for years, was that of the conditions attached to goods supplied under the Act. Two sets of conditions were rapidly accepted by the United Kingdom. One condition, that no private profits should arise in the handling of the goods, was quickly settled, though it at first gave rise to some strange talk. The second, whereby the embodiment of lend-lease goods in British exports was restricted, proved much more troublesome and remained so for a long time.

The Act called for negotiation of some 'consideration', other than current money payment, whereby the recipient nation was to discharge the implicit debt. There was general anxiety to avoid post-war monetary debts, but this did not mean that Britain was to get something for nothing. Congress left it to the President to negotiate the 'consideration'. In part the requirement was met, after the United States entered the war, by reciprocal aid. For the rest, some non-monetary consideration had to be negotiated, and so began the long foreshadowing of America's post-war aims and their war-time clash with the defensive attitudes of an impoverished Britain. The long-run aims of both could run together, but during the war there were continual fears that Britain's difficulties would for a time stand in the way.

Reciprocal aid, arising logically enough as part of the consideration for lend-lease, was soon entangled with the problem of lend-lease 'take-outs'[1] and with the American nagging at Britain's reserves. The extension of reciprocal aid to raw materials, partly for reasons of this kind, in turn became entangled with discussions on the export restrictions.

In the succeeding sections of this chapter these major problems— the old commitments and the scraping of the barrel, the conditions of lend-lease, the consideration for lend-lease, and the development of reciprocal aid—will be discussed in turn; but it is essential to remember that this unravelling of the strands is a simplification and that all were being handled, to a considerable extent simultaneously, by very much the same groups of men on both sides of the Atlantic. The tone set early in 1941, on the one side by the strange mixture of Rooseveltian largeness and Congressional politics, on the other side by the exhaustion of British reserves, entered into every aspect of Anglo-American negotiation. At the end of the year, British hopes that all would be changed by America's emergence as an active Ally similarly affected the approach to

[1] The 'take-outs' were items at some time covered by lend-lease but for one reason or another excluded at some date before the general termination of lend-lease.

every problem; so too did the realisation that those hopes were vain, and that London's claim to a reasonable reserve had to be justified not by any pooling principle but as a prerequisite of tolerable international trading conditions after the war. And it was from this angle that Anglo-American discussions approached the knotty problems of 'Stage II', when the German war would be over but Japan remained to be beaten.

(ii)
Interim Finance and 'The Old Commitments'

If there had been no gap between President Roosevelt's announcement of his plan and the commencement of United States finance for supplies to Britain,—if, that is to say, 'the old commitments' had been automatically absorbed in lend-lease— there would have been no problem of interim finance. As it was, an interim appeared before the lend-lease flow took care of the gap in London's balance of payments. More fundamentally, the gap for which dollars had to be found was the gap between the assets Britain could quickly turn into cash (and did liquidate before 1941) and that larger total of which America said Britain must strip herself before she would be eligible for aid. Unmarketable assets could not, whatever Mr. Morgenthau and his colleagues thought, be transformed into dollars overnight—and so the United Kingdom was faced with the tremendous task of finding dollars for the old commitments. Fortunately there seemed to be some hope that goodwill in the United States Administration would be directed towards helping the United Kingdom to a tolerable solution of this problem. Even before the lend-lease plan had been announced, this willingness to help in the problem of interim finance had been evident. Indeed, President Roosevelt jumped in with an eagerness that proved embarrassing.

The incident occurred in the course of London's efforts to scrape the Empire's gold barrel. American officials had, some weeks previously, indicated that they expected London to mobilise every ounce of gold that was under the control of the United Kingdom and Commonwealth Governments and the refugee Governments allied with the United Kingdom. As is explained in an earlier chapter,[1] there was some hesitation about collaring the substantial French reserves of gold and dollars without parallel action by Canada. On 12th December Sir Frederick Phillips reported definite pressure from Mr. Morgenthau; Phillips recommended that the

---

[1] pp. 335-6 above.

questions 'should now be forced to immediate conclusion both with Canada and Allied Governments. It is,' he significantly added, 'the U.S. suspicion that we are not seriously trying to realise what assets we can that is causing the whole difficulty.' The Treasury in London instructed Sir Frederick Phillips to explain the difficulties in obtaining both the French gold and that of the refugee Governments, and to seek some indication—for passing on to the owners of the gold—that the United States would after the war enable Britain to repay the gold. The matter thereupon went to the President who, accepting the difficulty of taking the French gold at the moment, startled the British authorities by arranging for a United States warship to call at Capetown for all the gold that could be mustered there.[1] This was not an offer; it was a statement of the President's decision and of action taken.[2] Every hair in the Treasury stood on end. Here was Britain having to scrape together every conceivable ounce of gold to see her through while the American political machine ground on, and almost all the gold we could reasonably call our own was to be entrusted to the chances of a single ship, the winter seas, unlit ships, submarines—and the inevitable leakage of information that Britain's last reserves were afloat in a single ship.

On the 31st a message went from Prime Minister to President. It was a *cri de coeur*: how long was Congress going to debate lend-lease while the British were fighting for their lives, and what was going to be done about the heavy commitments of existing orders? 'They burned a large part of the City of London last night . . . . . but . . . . the spirit of the Londoners was as high . . . .'. But this was preceded by a paragraph looking the President's Christmas gift horse directly in the mouth: 'First, sending the warship to Cape Town to take up the gold lying there may produce embarrassing effects. It is almost certain to become known. This will disturb public opinion here and throughout the Dominions and encourage the enemy, who will proclaim that you are sending for our last reserves. If you feel this is the only way, directions will be given for the available Cape Town gold to be loaded on the ship. But we should avoid it if we can. Could we, for instance, by a technical operation, exchange gold in South Africa for gold held for others in Ottawa and make the latter available for movement to New York? We must know soon because the ship is on its way.'[3] The reference to gold in

---

[1] The point of the operation was that immediately upon shipment equivalent dollars would be placed at the disposal of the United Kingdom authorities in New York. Britain's pipe-line was, in effect, concertinaed. As the United States Treasury does not hold gold abroad, 'earmarking' of the gold, without physical removal, was ruled out.

[2] 'This is', added Sir Frederick Phillips, 'very much the President's way of handling business. Decision is taken and acted upon before we are informed'.

[3] W. S. Churchill, *op. cit.*, Vol. II, pp. 507-8.

Ottawa was to French gold, some of which had already been switched against gold held in Durban; the suggestion now put to the President was that French gold might also be switched against the £30 millions of gold in Cape Town, in preference to entrusting this precious cargo to a single ship.

Some good came out of the Prime Minister's protest: the point about secrecy was taken and the United States cruiser (the *Louisville*) was diverted to Simonstown for the sake of secrecy. After playing with the idea of loading only a small amount, the British decided to make the most of the Americans' co-operation and all the £42 millions[1] available was loaded on 10th January. The story ends with a Washington telegram of 26th January reporting safe arrival. Each side drew its own moral: the Treasury had learned something of President Roosevelt's ways, and a new lease of life had been given to Mr. Morgenthau's suspicion that the British sometimes asked for things they did not really need.

The mobilisation of gold stocks inevitably loomed large in Anglo-American discussions during those weeks when Britain's cupboard was bare and the Capitol Hill was still in the talking stage. But the help these gold stocks afforded could only be fleeting, and thoughts were already reaching out on the British side towards meeting 'the old commitments', and on the American side towards shaping the lend-lease legislation and administrative framework. The Prime Minister, in his letter to the President at the end of December, raised the question of how these immensely heavy payments were to be met. In their anxiety to avoid any delay in the placing of vital British contracts, President Roosevelt and his advisers did indeed give some encouragement to the hope that the Americans would legislate for the inclusion of some at least of the old contracts in lend-lease. Developments in Congress, however, quickly put all such notions out of court, and Anglo-American discussions began to run into the channels that were to shape financial relations through a very long period. The United States Government was never committed to paying all Britain's dollar defence bills from a certain date; the principle that emerged was rather that Britain must meet her old commitments as far as possible by stripping herself of her remaining assets, and that the United States would take care of new commitments in so far as these were beyond Britain's capacity. This implied quite extraordinary efforts to liquidate overseas assets and demonstrations to that effect. Since this was not merely an exceedingly difficult process, but also one of limited and uncertain value, it was at the same time necessary for the United States

---

[1] Since the £30 million had been mentioned, there had been further arrivals from the mines.

2B

Administration to find ways and means of squeezing some of the old commitments on to its own pay-roll.

One suggestion was that United States Departments, which were trying to cover the United Kingdom's new contractual requirements by placing the contracts themselves, should take over the existing contracts. But this would raise the question of recoupment of the large sums already paid by the United Kingdom under these contracts, and in any case the smallness of the sums immediately available to United States Departments made it improbable that any substantial relief could be obtained in this way during the interim period.[1] Discouragement in this direction was not, however, due to any reluctance in the United States Administration. Sir Frederick Phillips was by this time in constant touch with Mr. Morgenthau and other 'very friendly elements' in the Administration, and was able to report that these people were trying hard to find ways and means of getting the United Kingdom round the corner. Mr. Morgenthau proposed that a group of United States investment trusts should buy a large block of direct investments, that all the United States securities remaining in United Kingdom hands should be sold forthwith, and that the Reconstruction Finance Corporation should buy, and pay in advance for, supplies from the Sterling Area of strategic materials such as rubber, tin, wool, and jute. Although these suggestions were not presented in any practicable form, and indeed appeared to London to hold out little promise of quick dollars on the requisite scale, Sir Frederick Phillips urged London to take care how they were received; it had become urgent to remove the impression in the United States Administration that London was holding back valuable assets.[2] The imminent struggle in Congress—it was expected to be long and bitter—made it imperative that the facts as to Britain's resources and commitments should be fully known to Mr. Morgenthau and that he should have full discretion to disclose them.

The Treasury was at this stage just managing to keep its head above water in terms of dollars. Partly by using the Belgian gold,[3] partly by using French gold against earmarking of newly-mined gold in South Africa,[4] and partly because dollar receipts were

---

[1] The United Kingdom had paid $550 millions against deliveries not yet made.

[2] Belief that the United Kingdom still had vast, mobilisable resources was not confined to the United States; a Treasury official visiting Ottawa found just the same view there. Considering how important Canadian dollars had already become, the United Kingdom Treasury had been very casual in its treatment of Ottawa, and had only itself to thank when Ottawa's ignorance was embarassing. (cf. p. 336 above).

[3] cf. pp. 370-1 above.

[4] i.e. 'switching'. On the difficulty of using the French gold, see pp. 335-6 above.

mysteriously but so happily always a little above estimates,[1] default was just avoided. But little arithmetic was needed to show that lend-lease must make an extraordinarily wide sweep if the United Kingdom was to have any elbow room at all during the first year. The United States Administration advised that, subject to centralisation of purchase through the British Purchasing Mission, all orders after the passing of the Bill, including food, oil, tobacco and cotton as well as the more obvious 'defense articles', could be financed by the United States Government; neither the President nor Mr. Morgenthau was frightened when told that this might mean commitments of $10,000 millions by mid-1942. But London's net dollar needs under old 'defense' contracts would be about £300 millions in the year 1st March 1941 to 28th February 1942; marketable securities might yield £125 millions and 'direct investments' at a guess £50 to £75 millions. London would be at least £100 millions ($400 millions) short, without making any allowance for (a) time-lags in centralising (and therefore bringing under lend-lease) purchases of food, tobacco, cotton etc., (b) delays in arranging lend-lease supplies of arms for Dominions and Allies, or (c) dollars for purchasing any essential articles whose eligibility was disputed by the lend-lease authorities.[2] The United Kingdom representatives in Washington therefore asked that the President should obtain an appropriation[3] enabling him to take over the £338 millions ($1,350 millions) of old commitments and to refund the £195 millions ($780 millions) already advanced on these defence contracts. The reply to this request would be 'the keystone to our financial position over the next year'. If such an appropriation were forthcoming, the United Kingdom could meet all needs remaining outside lend-lease, and would have a little elbow-room which might materialise in a reserve of £150 millions in gold and dollars at the end of the year. Without the appropriation, not even a hand-to-mouth existence was assured.

Mr. Morgenthau was fully informed of this position and, though obviously worried by it, he nevertheless encouraged the British authorities to continue placing new contracts which Sir Frederick Phillips certified were essential to the development of Britain's military effort. The immense importance of preserving this goodwill was by this time thoroughly appreciated by the United Kingdom

---

[1] This small but persistent excess of dollar receipts above expectations remained for years an unsolved problem in balance of payment statistics. Though in a direct way a comfort to the British authorities, it was an embarrassment when the statistics had to be discussed with United States officials.

[2] In calculating the £300 millions of net dollar needs, allowance had been made for minimum gold payment to Canada and for the anticipated extension of lend-lease to the arms requirements of the other Dominions.

[3] i.e. Congressional authority to spend. cf. footnote on p. 411.

authorities, and the length to which they were prepared to go in order to help President Roosevelt and Mr. Morgenthau in their political battles was shown by 'the Courtauld sale.'

Ever since the preliminary conversations with Mr. Morgenthau in the summer of 1940, the British authorities had known that they must attack the problem of mobilising the direct investments, but they had been slow in getting to grips with it. Their motives were a mixture of reluctance to sell and a hope that other means could be found to tide over a long period through which the complexities of the problem might be unravelled. The difficulties even of marshalling information were considerable, while the prospective difficulties of turning these largely intangible assets into reasonable amounts of hard cash appalled everyone who looked at the problem. It seemed unbelievable that, when all these difficulties were explained to our good friend the President, he could possibly expect the business to be accomplished overnight. By Christmas 1940, however, Sir Frederick Phillips and Mr. Purvis[1] in Washington began to sense the urgency with which the United States Administration was looking for results, results that would demonstrate to Congress and to the public that Britain was really stripping herself before taking aid from the United States Government. Experts were therefore sent from London to tackle the practical details of realisation. As weeks continued to go by without any spectacular sales, American suspicion increased. 'From every reliable source', reported Mr. Purvis in mid-February, 'I hear that general feeling in business and Congress circles is that we are not playing straight.' After a War Cabinet dicussion, the Prime Minister instructed the Ambassador in Washington to offer a joint Anglo-American agency, with final decision resting with the Americans, for disposal of the direct investments. This offer, though not accepted, did much to dispel suspicion in the Administration, but Mr. Morgenthau still demanded immediate results. He was due to appear before the Senate Committee on the Lend-Lease Appropriation Bill (under which the Administration would be authorised to place contracts up to 7 billion dollars),[2] and he transmitted as from the President what was 'practically an ultimatum—that some important company must be sold within a week'.

The Viscose Corporation of America, owned as to 97 per cent. by Messrs. Courtaulds, was the only one possible. Its position had been most closely investigated by the British experts, who had found sufficient interest expressed by the American market: a

---

[1] Mr. A. Purvis was Chairman of the British Supply Council in North America.

[2] 'Billion' is used here and throughout this book in the American sense of one thousand millions.

syndicate of banks was actually in preliminary negotiation for it. But to clinch the bargain within a week meant substantial sacrifice— and an indefinite sacrifice, since a firm price would not be settled in that time. Though the easiest—or rather least difficult—of the 'direct investments' to sell quickly, the Viscose investment exemplified all too clearly the broad disadvantages attached to liquidation: the connection between Courtaulds and the American rayon industry would be irrevocably cut, and nothing could be got for the goodwill transferred or destroyed. The current value of the tangible assets was stated by Courtaulds to be $120 millions, and the 1940 earnings, before taxation, had been about $11 millions.[1] For 90 per cent. of these assets the Treasury was assured, under the contract signed in that week of the ultimatum, a mere $40 millions; there was provision for the Treasury to share in any additional sum realised as the bankers' syndicate resold, and eventually the total received was about $54 millions. The Treasury had taken away from Courtaulds far more than it was able to sell in New York. When in 1942 the Courtauld claim was settled, the firm received the sterling equivalent of $109 millions.[2] The differences between these various figures provoked a number of Parliamentary Questions, especially when it was realised that over $4 millions had gone to New York bankers as commission on a riskless transaction.[3] In general, however, the necessity of the sacrifice was accepted. At worst it was the price of Britain's reluctance to acknowledge the seriousness and urgency of America's political demands.

This price having been paid in order to preserve the goodwill of the United States Administration and, in particular, to ease Mr. Morgenthau's conscience when he faced Congress, the British authorities may be excused for having hoped that a new spirit would henceforth prevail. It was not unreasonable to suppose that, once the Lend-Lease Bill was through Congress, the Administration would use its legal powers fully in order to satisfy the United Kingdom requirements, not only under the approved defence programme (covered by the proposed seven billion dollars' appropriation) but also to give the marginal requirements and even elbow-room. The event was far otherwise. The Lend-Lease

---

[1] The British experts dealing with the matter in New York were advised by United States bankers that $75 millions was about 'the real value of the business in present circumstances'.

[2] Courtaulds had bowed to the inevitable and submitted to the invidious distinction thrust upon them without special legislation. There was no ready way of fixing fair compensation, and it was not settled until July 1942.

[3] For Parliamentary Questions, see H. of C. Deb., Vol. 372, Cols. 820-1 (19th June), 1915-16 (1st July), 1496-99 (3rd July); Vol. 373, Cols. 311-13 (10th July), 723-4 (17th July), 751 (17th July), 790-3 (22nd July). For London Press comment, see daily newspapers of 17th, 18th and 19th March, 1941.

Act contained no obstacle to the transfer of the old commitments or even to the refund of advance payments, but in the Congressional struggle Mr. Morgenthau and the United States Director of the Budget bound the Administration far more narrowly than the terms of the Act. In the very days when the Courtauld sale was being forced through, the position had become dominated by Mr. Morgenthau's statements to Congress. The Administration was forging new fetters for itself—and for the United Kingdom Government. To Mr. Morgenthau's previous promises, first that the United Kingdom's existing dollar resources were sufficient to meet its dollar commitments, and secondly that the whole of the new South African gold would be used to make purchases in the United States, the Director of the Budget on 15th March added assurance to the Congressional Appropriations Committee (i) that none of the 7 billion dollars would be used to pay for materials delivered under old United Kingdom contracts, (ii) that the United Kingdom had sufficient dollars in sight to meet these liabilities, and (iii) that any British assets in the United States, beyond those so used, would be given as security for defence articles supplied under lend-lease.

Bleak as Britain's outlook now seemed, it was not quite as desperate as it looked from London. Mr. Keynes went over in May 1941—the first of a succession of tremendously important official visits[1]—and found that Mr. Morgenthau was not merely still fundamentally Britain's friend in this matter, but also that he was still determined somehow or other to take over a small part of the old commitments.[2] Contrary to British assumptions, the Director of the Budget was not a United States Treasury official, and Mr. Morgenthau evidently did not feel himself a hundred per cent. bound by the former's statements. Secondly, the figures presented to Congress had been somewhat trimmed, with the result that Mr. Morgenthau believed that he could arrange for some $300–400 millions of contracts to be taken over. He had on his own responsibility encouraged the United Kingdom to enter into new contracts in January and February and he was, it appeared to Mr. Keynes, ready to accept the implication. Accepting this as an indication of the fundamental willingness of the most important members of the Administration, Mr. Keynes put to them the case for much more substantial relief from the old commitments. There

---

[1] On this first occasion some American newspapers gave Mr. Keynes a cool reception. There were particularly references to his 'instigation' of the New Deal and 'the national disaster' of pump-priming.

[2] A note from Mr. Keynes on this visit includes the story that there had been a State Department draft and a Treasury draft of the Lend-Lease Bill, and that Mr. Morgenthau took his political life in his hands to get the President to sponsor the Treasury draft, which was in terms far more generous to the United Kingdom.

were certain supplies which could be switched to lend-lease only with great difficulty, either because of administrative complexity, or because of political or legal difficulties arising from the Lend-Lease Act. The United States Administration would be saved a great deal of trouble if all such goods could be kept out of lend-lease, and if the United Kingdom could always be ready to pay cash for any item over which political difficulty arose. Similarly non-warlike supplies for the rest of the Sterling Area could be left outside. All this could be envisaged if only the United Kingdom had a clear assurance of a reasonable margin of dollars. To provide this margin for two years ahead, Mr. Keynes proposed that the United States should take over existing defence contracts and refund advances made under them. On 1st May 1941 this would mean a refund of about $700 millions and future payments of $1,300 millions.

No amount of pleading would tempt the Americans to a clean-cut settlement of this kind. United States Treasury officials instead searched for reasons whereby they might justify taking over contracts as from as early a date as possible: 1st January 1941 would have gone a long way to help, but 11th March seemed the more likely date. Under these circumstances, the best that could be hoped for was fulfilment, and perhaps a slight stretching, of Mr. Morgenthau's personal engagement to find $300–400 millions. This was far from sufficient to meet the 1941 requirements, let alone provide any elbow-room for 1942. By the end of May, therefore, the British authorities abandoned hope of a solution in this direction, and looked round urgently for other ways and means.[1] One suggestion was that the United Kingdom should sell to the United States, for future delivery but against immediate payment, stocks of certain commodities that war developments had rendered surplus—wool and Egyptian cotton were the obvious candidates. This scheme did not get far, partly because there was not a hope that it would quickly run to the big figures required, partly because the British authorities felt that such sales would be crippling to the post-war export drive now seen to be imperative. The Bank of England produced a plan—they thought of it very much as a *pis aller*—for a Monetary Agreement under which the United States Treasury would sell dollars against sterling. This had certain political awkwardness. It appeared inconsistent with the President's idea of getting rid of the money sign and it was thought unlikely that the Americans could indefinitely run the two principles—lend-lease and holding sterling—side by side;

---

[1] On 14th June Mr. Keynes telegraphed that the United States Treasury officials had finally declared their inability to get round the commitment made to Congress by the Director of the Budget.

above all it did not look the kind of proposal that would be agreed and brought into operation quickly. While the notion was being rather academically debated in London, Mr. Keynes in Washington was in fact raising just enough dollars by other means. The Bank's plan was accordingly never put to the United States Administration, though it remained in men's minds for some little time: 'if in fact our cash balance had ever actually run out', Sir Frederick Phillips wrote afterwards,[1] 'they would have been, I think, driven back on this method of helping us.'

The cash did not actually run out at this stage: at mid-June 1941 the British authorities could muster about $150 millions. But even if Mr. Morgenthau were successful in raising the $300–400 millions—which at this time seemed doubtful—the strain of the 'old commitments' would still be great. The strain was in the following months overcome by Mr. Keynes's negotiation of a loan from the Reconstruction Finance Corporation—'the Jesse Jones loan'.[2] Unlike all other schemes for raising dollars, this had great political attraction in Washington, in that it disposed of the complaints that Britain was holding back valuable investments in the United States and elsewhere. The idea was mentioned between Mr. Jesse Jones and Sir Edward Peacock in New York in February, and it was developed by Mr. Keynes in May 1941 as a way— alternative to the ruinous and difficult Courtauld way—of fulfilling Mr. Morgenthau's promise that Britain's pre-lend-lease contracts should be covered by the use of her remaining dollar resources. The remaining dollar resources were mostly the 'direct investments', including the insurance assets which called for special treatment, and outstanding payments on the contracts required some $900 millions more than the United Kingdom had yet been able to provide. Speedy realisation of anything like this sum was beyond possibility—it was difficult enough to find items that could bring in $100 millions quickly.[3] Then, suggested Mr. Keynes, let the Reconstruction Finance Corporation or other suitable body lend say $900 millions against a lien on all the direct investments, these remaining the property of their present owners, any sale proceeds and income being turned over to the Reconstruction Finance Corporation. Even with a much smaller figure, there would be great attraction in any scheme which, while contributing sub- stantially towards the 1941 dollar gap, would put an end to American agitation about Britain's remaining American assets.

---

[1] 19th September 1941.

[2] Mr. Jesse Jones was head of the Reconstruction Finance Corporation, a United States Government Agency originally established for salvaging banks and other firms in difficulties in the Great Depression of the early 'thirties.

[3] Such a list was asked for and prepared in January; it included the Courtauld assets.

Opinion in the United States was swinging rapidly in favour of some such plan. *The New York Times*,[1] reporting the Courtauld sale, said that the operation 'should convince the most determined sceptic of the dire financial straits in which Great Britain stands and of her determination to strip herself of every available asset. . . . '; and it went on to question whether it was in the long-run interest of the United States that Britain should be finally stripped. In this atmosphere United Kingdom representatives in Washington and New York found that the seed quickly germinated, not least in the Reconstruction Finance Corporation itself. The Corporation did actually make an indirect loan to the British authorities through an American subsidiary of the British American Tobacco Company,[2] but exploration of further transactions of this kind—particularly covering the valuable insurance assets—underlined the desirability of some simpler and more comprehensive procedure. For this purpose, and incidentally to clarify the legitimacy of lending to Britain despite the Neutrality Act, legislation was necessary. The Congressional Bill increased the resources of the Reconstruction Finance Corporation, and permitted loans to foreign Governments on American securities as collateral 'for the purpose of achieving the maximum dollar exchange value' for the securities; Mr. Jesse Jones told Congress outright that the new powers were to forestall liquidation of British assets at distress prices.[3] The Bill became law on 10th June, by which date Mr. Keynes and Sir Frederick Phillips were ready with a broad outline on which they sought instructions from London. Thereafter rapid progress was made.

The amount discussed was 'about $400 millions'; this was arrived at by estimating net dollar requirements to the end of 1941, after allowing for Mr. Morgenthau's 'take-over', the sale of Viscose, market sales of securities to date and various oddments.[4] As collateral security Mr. Jesse Jones was to be asked to select what assets he thought best for the sum under discussion, and the British hoped that the United States Administration would acknowledge all other assets as unsuitable for any further use 'and so removed from the political arena'. Interest and sinking fund on the loan would be the responsibility of the United Kingdom

---

[1] 18th March 1941.

[2] The loan, in April 1941, was to the American management of the Brown Williamson Tobacco Corporation to allow them to buy out the interest of the British Corporation. There was a suggestion that the Viscose transaction might be transformed into a similar arrangement with Courtaulds, but the matter had gone too far—and had too much publicity.

[3] Statement to the House of Representatives Committee on 7th May 1941.

[4] The $900 millions for which Mr. Keynes was looking was designed to allow some 'elbow-room' and to avoid reliance on further Morgenthau take-overs or market sales of securities. Another minor factor bridging the gap between $900 and $400 millions was the usual small excess of dollar accruals over estimates (cf. p. 387).

Government and not that of the individual companies (who, however, would have to pledge the assets and the income therefrom). The period of the loan would be moderately long—25 years was mentioned—with United Kingdom option to accelerate redemption. Mr. Jesse Jones demanded 3 per cent. interest, Mr. Keynes trying in vain to get this down to 2½. The assets to be pledged were shares (other than directors' qualifying shares) of American subsidiaries of British insurance companies, listed securities of American corporations already vested in the United Kingdom Treasury, and both listed and unlisted securities not yet vested, in American corporations in which the percentage of British ownership was substantial. In addition, there would be assigned to the Reconstruction Finance Corporation the earnings of United States branches of 41 British insurance companies not incorporated in the United States. As these would not be represented by any pledged securities, the Reconstruction Finance Corporation sought a particular assurance against withdrawal of the assets during the currency of the loan.

In subsequent discussion, the amount of the loan was settled at $425 millions. This was amply covered by the British assets: on the American reckoning, these totalled at least $700 millions. The income from these assets would, it was estimated, allow amortisation of the loan in fifteen years, and this was settled as the life of the loan—subject to United Kingdom option to extend for five years provided two-thirds of the principal had been repaid within the fifteen years. The arrangements for pledging and the rights accorded to the Reconstruction Finance Corporation in the event of default made it necessary for the United Kingdom Government to assume further powers by legislation.

Although the scheme had been initiated in an unusually favourable atmosphere, the United Kingdom representatives were shocked, after the broad basis had been easily settled, to meet an attitude of 'ungenerous bargaining'. The negotiations were in the hands of American men of business who, when lending American money, very naturally considered themselves entitled to name their terms and stick to them. The details were therefore argued as though the Reconstruction Finance Corporation was obliged to apply the conditions insisted upon in their ordinary loans. But the only real stumbling block was not of this order. The Americans proposed a clause, which became known as the 'War Disaster Clause', which originally ran thus: 'That upon notice from the President of the United States that the international policy of the U.S. Government requires such action, the Corporation, by the direction of the President, shall have all rights with respect to the collateral to the same extent as if a default under the terms of the

Note had occurred and had not been cured within the time, if any, permitted by the terms of the Note.' The contingency in mind was of course defeat of the United Kingdom by Germany. The Treasury at once recoiled from a public document containing the implication that Britain might be defeated: the American journalists would, of course, be told by Mr. Jesse Jones that this was what it meant. In any case, the Reconstruction Finance Corporation had no need of such a clause, for in the contingency the United States authorities would freeze the pledged assets. These objections were reiterated, but Mr. Jesse Jones was adamant: he wanted to be able to show Congress that this was a business loan with business-like safeguards, and he spoke to the British Ambassador of the alternative of raising money by selling the assets. The question was eventually referred to the President, whom the British representatives hoped to find sympathetic. The President supported Mr. Jesse Jones on the main issue, but suggested a slightly less objectionable wording. His new draft provided that the collateral should pass to the United States upon notice from the President that impairment of the collateral required such action. The phrase 'impairment of the collateral' was wider than the displaced phrase 'international policy of the United States'; it could be explained in London as covering impairment for any reason whatever, and this would not be inconsistent with American reference to its covering the case of enemy occupation.

If the loan was to be obtained—and its essential features had great attractions—the President's view had to be accepted. The Chancellor of the Exchequer reluctantly swallowed the disaster clause in its new dress, and the agreement was signed in Washington on 21st July 1941. The terms were published in a White Paper[1] the next day, when the Chancellor announced the settlement. The necessary powers to take sufficient title to the assets were assumed by the Financial Powers (U.S.A. Securities) Act (which received the Royal Assent on 29th July) and by Statutory Order signed on 5th August.[2]

This 'satisfactory arrangement', as the Chancellor of the Exchequer described it,[3] was entirely successful in putting an end to American complaints that the British were clinging to realisable assets. The $425 millions did in a sense fill the 1941 dollar gap, but only on the assumption that a substantial part of the old commitments would be taken over in fulfilment of Mr. Morgenthau's personal undertaking. By itself it went no way at all towards reconstituting an adequate reserve or allowing that elbow-room

---

[1] Cmd. 6295.

[2] S.R. & O. (1941) No. 1139.

[3] H. of C. Deb., Vol. 373, Cols. 799-801.

which would have opened escape from agitations over the precise scope of lend-lease.[1] The British authorities were therefore compelled to keep alive the promised assumption of some $400 millions of the old commitments, and to watch for opportunity to press bigger figures. At first, far from such opportunity offering, the prospect became gloomier. In mid-August Sir Frederick Phillips reported that Congress was being difficult about detailed appropriations and that $300 rather than $400 millions now appeared as the highest likely figure. When the United States entered the war, however, the British authorities thought they saw their chance. To meet the new urgency of their requirements, the United States Service Departments were stepping in to take over deliveries of planes and munitions produced under British contracts; the logic of the situation was that all such contracts should be pooled forthwith—and that there should be a financial pooling to match. Neither at this nor at any later stage did the United States Administration or public opinion follow this through to the logical conclusion, but at least the United States Treasury was prepared to listen to suggestions that some pooled contracts should be brought under lend-lease.

The weeks went by without any real progress on this new front. The United States Departments talked sympathetically but apparently felt unable to take so momentous a step without a Presidential directive, and were awaiting an opportune moment for raising the question in that quarter. This delay was unfortunate for the United Kingdom authorities, whose cash-box was once again emptying, (partly because Mr. Morgenthau had been able to make little progress towards implementing his undertaking that $300–$400 millions of the old commitments should be taken over[2]) while sources of replenishment were likely to fall as reciprocal aid was extended.[3] The British were therefore obliged to add to arguments of justice and logic the argument that their cash was running out. They very properly coupled this with the claim to hold a reasonable reserve, a claim that was becoming more urgent now that the sterling balances were running up fast.[4] Americans had much to learn on this subject, and it was unfortunate that Britain's plight forced a premature crystallisation of policy: the United States Administration at this time began thinking in figures

---

[1] The need for that elbow-room was to be underlined again and again during the late months of 1941, when the United States Appropriations system, so different from the British, was constantly cramping the flow of new contracts.

[2] In May 1942 Mr. Morgenthau still acknowledged his personal obligation in this matter.

[3] See below, p. 432.

[4] cf. Chapter IX.

altogether inadequate to London's international position.[1] The immediate need to concentrate attention on London's reserves may also have tended—not quite logically—to divert attention from a development of the pooling principle. Certainly discussion of London's critical reserve position at this juncture helped to shape Anglo-American relations for the rest of the war, and to do this before the Americans had learned much about London's obligations.

The short-term results of stressing Britain's precarious position were more welcome. On 5th May 1942 British representatives in Washington were at last able to report substantial progress in 'take-overs'. The United States War Department had withdrawn its objection to the transfer of certain pre-lend-lease contracts, and agreement had been reached on the sale to the United States Government of certain capital works the United Kingdom had financed and was financing in connection with the expansion of United States armament industries. These and a few miscellaneous concessions made up $290 millions, partly in cash and partly in relief from contractual payments falling due. With this, it was calculated that the United Kingdom could pay its way to March 1943 and was likely to be in a stronger position thereafter. There was some possibility that the United States would also take over all the remaining aircraft contracts. This would have meant a further $450 millions, but it did not materialise.[2] Even without it, the present and prospective improvements seemed almost unbelievable after the nightmare months of bare cupboards. The United Kingdom authorities had given up all hope of immediate elbow-room, but in their optimistic moments they thought they saw it not so very far ahead. Reviewing the position on 9th June 1942, Keynes wrote '. . . . we are in no serious risk of running short of dollars . . . . . it is now quite out-of-date to regard our dollar problem as the essence of our financial difficulties. That is a hangover from the pre-lend-lease and early lend-lease days . . . . .' That the concessions gained by Sir Frederick Phillips in May 1942, so small in comparison with those sought by Mr. Keynes a year earlier, should have effected this transformation is perhaps surprising. In fact the transformation had already been partly effected by months of penury during which many of the old commitments were worked off. Lend-lease was at last in spate, so that a comparatively small easement—a Micawber's sixpence—made a world of difference to how London felt.

---

[1] See Section (vi) of this chapter.

[2] In view of the recent improvement in the prospect, the United Kingdom thought it wise not to press the matter to the necessary Presidential level.

(iii)
The Conditions attached to Lend-Lease:
the Export White Paper

It is now necessary to return from the transformation upon which Mr. Keynes remarked in mid-1942 to that earlier transformation of March 1941. The initiation of lend-lease, by the Lend-Lease Act of 11th March 1941, followed by the first appropriation (27th March), foreshadowed a flow of goods of which the American people were depriving themselves and which they were putting at the disposal of the British. Although some 'consideration' was to be negotiated, there was no question of immediate payment. Americans, not yet themselves at war and not easily appreciating how far the British economy was already mobilised, were quick to claim that private interests in Britain should not be allowed to pick up benefits forgone by American citizens. Where the United States had not charged the cost, it was not for British commercial interests to pick profits. And most emphatically, materials given by the American people should not be used to enable British exporters to cut the throats of their American competitors. In relation to both these aspects, British policy was designed to forestall by self-imposed regulations any restrictive action by the United States Government; but in pursuing this policy there was the closest consultation with the United States Administration, and the White Paper, in which British policy was formulated in some detail, was in substance an international agreement although in form a unilateral declaration.

The easier of the two problems related to the handling of lend-lease goods. Section 4 of the Lend-Lease Act prohibited the transfer of goods to others than the United Kingdom Government without the President's consent, and the British Supply Council had to ensure that the President's consent was obtained in appropriate cases. Many of the goods would of course pass directly into Service use, but others—much of the food, raw materials and semi-manufactured goods—would have to pass through private hands for distribution either to consumers or to processors. The United Kingdom Government had undertaken that wherever possible distribution would be effected on a 'pure' agency basis; there would be no profit on resale, and the agents would receive only remuneration fixed in strict relation to the services rendered. The application of this rule would be exceedingly awkward in many cases; 1941 was not the time to create new agencies solely to handle lend-lease supplies, nor could Britain find armies of officials to check the activities of private firms handling lend-lease goods.

But the United States Administration, on realising the extent to which the United Kingdom proposed to put lend-lease goods through private channels, took fright. They feared a political eruption if their opponents heard of any remuneration that could be represented as private profit derived from handling goods so generously provided by the American taxpayer. When the British pointed out that the elimination even of controlled profits would mean a change in the entire system of distribution, Mr. Morgenthau replied 'Well, you may have to'.

Fortunately, the American view was not pressed to that length. Discussion went forward on the basis that the United Kingdom Government should give a public undertaking that no 'profiteering' would be permitted in the handling of lend-lease goods and that full details of the controls exercised would be furnished to the United States authorities. As a beginning, the British welcomed the visit to London of a United States Treasury representative who would see for himself how the United Kingdom's Government-controlled system of distribution was working. The Departments concerned were able to show him how elaborately the profits of food wholesalers and retailers were ascertained and controlled, and how exceedingly difficult it would be to formulate an entirely new distributive system. It soon became clear that there would be no trouble over food, tobacco and cotton, for which the United States Department of Agriculture was responsible and on which a favourable opinion had been obtained from the President. Other materials—for some of which new distributing agencies had to be organised in the United Kingdom—were carefully watched. With goodwill on both sides the whole question was soon substantially settled,[1] although, as the agreed statement relating to it was to be part of the White Paper whose main concern was export policy, final disposal had to wait upon the much more difficult negotiations on export policy. There was in July an outbreak of Ministerial interest, and later, when the White Paper was about to be published, there was a last-minute flurry over the passage on food distribution, but no difficulty of principle arose at any stage. The White Paper[2] eventually contained three paragraphs that stated the general principle of controlling agents' remuneration, and referred to the special arrangements for foodstuffs and for the milk products distributed under welfare schemes.

The other problem, export policy, was an altogether harder nut to crack. Owing to the diversion of productive capacity to

---

[1] It seems likely that all the agitations on this question had arisen through a misunderstanding on the part of Mr. Morgenthau, and that there was never inside the United States Administration any substantial questioning of the British arrangements.

[2] Cmd. 6311 of 19th September 1941.

direct war purposes, Britain's export trade was already a long way below its peace-time level. But owing to the great need for dollars for war purposes—a need not ended by lend-lease—special effort had been made to maintain substantial exports to the American continent. These exports competed sharply, as they had done for generations, with the exports of United States firms—and that was where the trouble began. Should British exporters use lend-lease materials in the production of goods to be sold in competition with United States exporters, whose supplies of those very materials were restricted in order that Britain might have them under lend-lease?

Whatever else may be said about the handling of this question, the British authorities were exceedingly quick off the mark. The President's ink on the Lend-Lease Act was scarcely dry before the Board of Trade and the Treasury were in consultation on its implications for export policy. Accusations of unfair competition and wasteful use of materials were to be expected, and there would be advantage in some understanding with the United States Administration before such accusations began to fly around. Quick as they were, however, the British officials were already too late. Weeks before the first lend-lease supplies reached British ports, American commercial interests were complaining that British machinery manufacturers were damaging United States exporters in South America, that Britain was still sending large quantities of tinplate to the Argentine, and that Sheffield cutlery and razor-blades were still to be seen in the local drug-stores. The outcry reached the floor of Congress and a general enquiry into British trade with Latin America was mooted.[1] Every effort was made, not only by British representatives but also by the United States Administration, to answer individual criticisms in detail. On 10th July 1941 Mr. Keynes gave a Press Conference at the Embassy in Washington, answering the accusations both in general terms and in detail. He pointed to the contraction there had already been in Britain's export trade, explained the need for such trade as was still going on (it was, for example, Britain's only means of paying for essential food from the Argentine), and stated that Britain had gone so far as to cancel several major contracts in South America because these required materials similar to those being provided under lend-lease. President Roosevelt made some helpful remarks on the same lines at his own Press Conference shortly afterwards.[2] This was all to the good, but it was not enough; the United States Administration considered the problem as

---

[1] See Representative O'Connor's resolution No. 266 of 9th July 1941.

[2] He returned to the charge with some forthright condemnation of allegations of British misuse of lend-lease funds. (*The New York Times*, 27th August 1941).

political dynamite and was anxious for further action before the next round of lend-lease appropriations had to be sought in Congress.

American and British officials therefore continued consultation on the terms that could be set out in an agreed published statement. In July the plan was to have an exchange of letters between General Burns, then Lend-Lease Executive Officer, and Mr. Purvis; and substantial progress was made in the drafting of these letters. An important point quickly accepted by the Americans was 'the principle of substitution'. This covered the many awkward cases—particularly where cotton and steel were concerned—in which it was impossible to identify in the final products the precise source—lend-lease or other—of the raw materials. It was agreed that where supplies from the United States formed a much smaller proportion of total supplies than the proportion going into war production, the supply from the United States should be deemed to have been imported for war purposes, no matter what the use to which particular consignments were put.[1] The Americans were also ready to recognise, and to note in the proposed documents, Britain's need for foreign exchange. The British, for their part, were ready to announce their restriction of exports of materials similar to lend-lease materials to the irreducible minimum necessary for the prosecution of the war.

These negotiations on the official level in Washington resulted in the production of a draft statement which was telegraphed to London on 1st August. It was not subjected to critical examination at this stage, largely because of a precipitate intervention by Mr. Winant, the United States Ambassador, who took the matter up personally with Ministers in London. He handed a memorandum to the Prime Minister and the Lord President and then appears to have hinted to the Chancellor over the 'phone that the President foresaw political trouble on the matter in general. The Chancellor therefore arranged to see Mr. Winant on 28th July. The President of the Board of Trade was unfortunately out of London, and the other Ministers went to the critical meeting without any adequate briefing on the problems of the export trade—without, indeed, knowing until the meeting began that Mr. Winant wished to discuss these as well as the relatively simple distribution problems. The outcome of the meeting was a draft which conceded all the substantial points for which the Americans were asking. British officials supposed that this Ministerial draft would now supersede the official draft prepared in Washington. In the extreme confusion

---

[1] Mr. Keynes reported that 'everyone regards the principle of substitution as logical when you put to them the opposite. That is to say, if they question substitution, you say—"Do you mean then that so long as any steel articles are being imported into the United Kingdom, the United Kingdom shall have no steel exports whatever, however large their output?" This *reductio ad absurdum* is always successful.'

which followed—confusion probably inevitable when negotiations
had been simultaneously proceeding in both capitals and on quite
different levels of authority—London officials suddenly realised
that the 'Burns letters', as the Washington version was called, were
still very much alive. After ignoring it for several weeks, they
hastily gave this draft fresh attention, and were horrified to
find that it virtually prohibited Britain's staple export trades.
After admitting the need for some exports, the draft called
upon the United Kingdom 'to make every effort to concentrate her
exports in the field of traditional articles, such as Scotch Whisky,
fine textiles etc., and other similar articles and cut down the
exportation of articles similar to those being provided through
lend-lease funds to the irreducible minimum necessary to supply
or obtain materials essential to the war effort'. On a broad
interpretation of the 'irreducible minimum' this might have been
tolerable, but British officials had enough experience of the methods
of the United States Administration to know that no dependence
could be placed on this slender life-line. What was worse was the
fantastic impression given by the phrase about Britain's traditional
exports.[1] The impression conveyed was, wrote Professor Robertson,
that 'of a picturesque little nation whose trading reputation depends
on a few specialities popular in fashionable circles in Boston and
New York, but which had presumptuously, under the temptation
of lend-lease, gone outside its "traditional" field to try its hand at
real industry like metallurgy and the staple textile trades, and has
now humbly promised to draw in its horns again. "Traditional
articles" indeed! Shades of the great textile inventors, ironmasters,
railway contractors etc., of the 19th century! . . . . . . what chance
have our Board of Trade negotiators of Trade Treaties and the
like if we once accept this caricature of British trade?'

In the hectic days that followed, with lines crossing and recrossing
to make confusion worse confounded, the British negotiators
concentrated their efforts on obtaining a document that would
not spell complete disaster for the exports that were truly the
traditional staples. The export of goods produced from lend-lease
materials must of course be renounced in principle, but it was
important to make quite explicit its qualification by the principle of
substitution.[2] The Americans sought a rather more sweeping
renunciation, referring to competition with American exporters;
the British thought this tolerable only where the products embodied
goods in short supply in the United States. Finally, the United

---

[1] As originally handed to United Kingdom representatives in Washington, the phrase
had been even more insulting; but the Americans agreed to substitute 'fine textiles'
for their original 'Harris tweeds'.

[2] Other minor qualifications were accepted by the Americans: as, for example, to
cover the export of repair parts for British machinery in operation abroad.

Kingdom agreed to abjure any opportunity to apply 'materials similar to those supplied under lend-lease in such a way as to enable their exporters to enter new markets or to extend their export trade at the expense of the United States exporters'; and the 'short-supply' restriction was accepted for all materials obtained from the United States whether under lend-lease or by payment.

Almost to the last, negotiations continued in both capitals, and no summary can do justice to the welter of confusion in which drafting and re-drafting continued.[1] However, on 10th September 1941 the Foreign Secretary was able to write to the United States Ambassador enclosing 'a memorandum on the policy of His Majesty's Government in the United Kingdom with regard to exports from this country and with regard to the distribution here of lend-lease material'.[2] The paragraphs about distribution were satisfactory. On export policy there was much heart-burning in London. The statement was in form unilateral, but officials knew from the start that it was in fact an international agreement. It was an agreement whereby Britain's export trade was at best likely to be subject to finicking control and at worst to crippling restrictions. Taken literally its provisions would have constituted an outrageously rigid control of British exports. On the day following publication of the White Paper, a meeting was held in London to decide what it meant, and a division of opinion started. On the same day, in Washington, the British asked for lists of what the United States considered to be in short supply—and another dynasty of arguments was started. And Congress, for whose benefit the agreement was originally mooted, took very little notice of it. Whether the United Kingdom export trade immediately suffered substantial hurt is open to doubt: by this stage of the war the pressure on resources in British industry and the shipping difficulties had become so extreme that exports were bound to suffer, with or without the White Paper. What is certain is that any hurt the export trades did receive was very serious in its rupture of long-standing connections, especially in South America, and in the difficulties imposed on the days when British traders would have to pick up the strands. That United Kingdom Ministers, already becoming aware of the immensity of post-war tasks, thought fit to accept this position, can be explained only by acknowledging the extremity with which they felt dependent upon American aid and upon the United States Congress which was voting the money for lend-lease.

---

[1] A private account of the negotiations has the sub-title, 'International Agreements as they should not be negotiated'.

[2] Cmd. 6311. The most important provisions relating to British exports were as stated in the previous paragraph. For a fuller account see *Civil Industry and Trade, op. cit.*, pp. 145-51.

Less than three months after publication of the White Paper the United States entered the war; this, in the British view at least, made the White Paper completely out-of-date. It must be superseded, they considered, 'by something better: the joint planning of essential exports on a basis of equality and maximum efficiency.' There were encouraging signs of a similar turn of thought in the United States: the establishment of the Combined Raw Materials Board seemed to provide a precedent for some joint machinery through which United Kingdom and United States export policies could be framed and translated into raw material requirements to be passed to the Combined Raw Materials Board. The State Department and other branches of the United States Administration were believed to sympathise with United Kingdom views. Mere reports of sympathy were, however, small compensation for the practice of the Office of Lend-Lease Administration (OLLA); this had set itself up as a policeman of British export policy and showed no sign of adjusting its attitude to the fact of the new belligerent alliance. In April 1942, however, London learned that OLLA, while still wishing to retain the White Paper, was disposed to take a broader view of its application. This change of tone opened the way for advance, and through several weeks in the summer of 1942 it seemed possible that agreement might be reached. But it was just another false dawn: it became all too clear that, while they cared little about British exports to other parts of the world, the Americans wanted South American markets to be their own preserve and for this purpose continuance of the unilateral British declaration, policed by a United States Department, suited their book. British hopes for an openly bilateral statement, followed by freedom from the American policeman, were doomed to disappointment, and by the end of 1942 agreement was further away than it had looked six months earlier.[1]

The year 1943 almost repeated the experience of 1942. Through the first half of the year there was virtually no inter-Governmental discussion of the subject, while the legalistic spirit with which OLLA sought to police United Kingdom exports was a renewed source of irritation. In London, thoughts were turning to problems of post-war reconstruction and from this viewpoint a fresh effort to salvage economic relations with Latin America was high on the priority list. In the summer there was accordingly a new high-level approach to the United States Administration, stressing the anachronism of the White Paper. Once again the initial reception was sympathetic, only to be followed by months of deterioration

---

[1] There was an attempt at joint programming of exports, but it failed dismally. (See *Civil Industry and Trade*, op. cit., pp. 165-73).

in the detailed negotiations. When reciprocal aid was extended to raw materials supplied to the United States by the United Kingdom and Colonies, one more reason was added to the case for revision of the White Paper.[1] The United Kingdom found it intolerable to submit to unilateral restrictions when materials were included in mutual aid. Yet even this change brought no real response from the American side and London began to think seriously of unilateral repudiation of the White Paper. Ministers did in fact decide that some public pronouncement was necessary, and in November 1943 the President of the Board of Trade informed the Commons that, in view of the changed circumstances, the Government considered that 'the unilateral undertaking contained in this White Paper should be replaced by a new statement. His Majesty's Government and the United States Government are now engaged in negotiations as to the form which a new joint and reciprocal declaration should take'.[2] These negotiations never came to a conclusion; as in 1942 so in 1943, the position at Christmas looked more hopeless than at midsummer and the British authorities, despairing of any reasonable settlement, turned to the possibility of paying hard cash for all important materials used in exports. In the spring of 1944 there was yet one more attempt to agree a joint declaration replacing the White Paper; the basis was that mutual aid should be confined to essential war purposes, and that there should be mutual payment for materials used in exports. Almost on the eve of publication, this too was abandoned: discussions on Stage II and Stage III were about to begin; and the United Kingdom Government thought the export question had better be merged into these wider talks. In short, the White Paper was never revised; instead, the British bought their freedom to earn, if not bread and butter, at least bread.

(iv)

The 'Consideration' for Lend-Lease: the Emergence of Article VII

Section 3(b) of the Lend-Lease Act provided: 'The terms and conditions upon which any such foreign Government receives any aid authorized under Subsection (a) shall be those which the President deems satisfactory and the benefit to the United States may be payment or repayment in kind or property or any other direct or indirect benefit which the President deems satisfactory'.

[1] cf. pp. 421 *et seq.*
[2] H. of C. Deb., Vol. 393, Col. 1312.

On 13th June 1941, in his first quarterly report to Congress under the Act, President Roosevelt was able to announce that work had started 'on the agreements to fix the terms and conditions, under Section 3(b)'. Work certainly had started, in the sense that Mr. Keynes had had conversations with Mr. Harry Hopkins and Mr. Dean Acheson, and there had been one discussion between the President, the British Ambassador and Mr. Keynes. The President entrusted the negotiations not to the Treasury but to the State Department, on the ground that political rather than financial issues were at stake. This was, as United Kingdom negotiators were quick to remark, all to the good: it was also the State Department's opportunity to advance the free trade doctrines with which it had become imbued under Mr. Cordell Hull.

The first indications of American ideas were that a distinction might be drawn between 'strictly warlike' supplies, which would be regarded as finally sunk in the common military effort, and such other supplies as food and tobacco for which some return, beyond participation in the common effort, would be expected; ships and 'warlike raw materials' would perhaps be pushed into the first category. Suggestions that the specific consideration for the second category might include rubber and tin for strategic reserves and ships built over a period of years, quickly encountered arguments that any substantial supplies of this kind would impair the United Kingdom's post-war trading position, which was by now not only a worry to British authorities but also causing some concern to far-sighted Americans who feared its implications for international economic policy. British haste to hedge such commitments around with crippling reservations was matched by the speed with which the Americans dropped the idea. Similar difficulties helped to push out of court a proposal that the United Kingdom should bear the cost of equipping United States defence bases in British territory (e.g. the West Indies). As notions of this kind—they did not reach the stage of becoming 'proposals'— failed to find support, the point of struggling with the awkward distinction between 'warlike' and 'non-warlike' supplies disappeared and the whole matter moved away from an attempt to find material 'consideration' and began to emerge as an essay in post-war political aspirations. This was very much to President Roosevelt's taste. 'He believes', the British Ambassador reported after their conversation on July 8th, 'it will be better to limit ourselves to a preliminary agreement in very general terms . . . . . . He mentioned the International Police Force, Economic Union in the West Indies, Economic Union in the Pacific, including Dutch possessions, as examples of ideas he might want to explore later but also as examples of matters which it would be inadvisable to offer for

public discussion now. . . . . . He did not want us to offer reciprocal
lend and lease arrangements for some hypothetical future occasion'.

Following this interview, the President instructed the State
Department to prepare, in collaboration with Mr. Keynes, a
draft for his consideration. It was now possible to crystallise the
view that 'a purely economic and pecuniary consideration' should
be excluded; on the other hand, the State Department was able
to insert a non-discrimination clause of the kind hinted by Mr.
Dean Acheson in preliminary conversation with Mr. Keynes.
These two points were the heart of the draft; they were both in
Article VII, and from this date onwards 'Article VII' was at the
centre of Anglo-American economic relations.

The preamble expressed, in language echoing the American
Declaration of Independence, a declaration of common purpose.
Articles I, III and IV recapitulated in substance some relevant
passages from the Lend-Lease Act. Article II provided for reciprocal
aid, over a wide field, from the United Kingdom and Article VI
provided that this should be taken into account in the final
settlement. Article V provided that the President might ask for
the return, after the war, of defence articles not destroyed, lost or
consumed. All these six Articles, with the preamble, were
acceptable to the British, both in substance and in detail.[1] Article
VII, on the other hand, was to prove a headache for seven months
before agreement was reached. As handed to Keynes on 28th July
1941, it ran:

> The terms and conditions upon which the United Kingdom
> receives defense aid from the United States of America and
> the benefits to be received by the United States of America in
> return therefor, as finally determined, shall be such as not to
> burden commerce between the two countries but to promote
> mutually advantageous economic relations between them and
> the betterment of world-wide economic relations; they shall
> provide against discrimination in either the United States of
> America or the United Kingdom against the importation of any
> produce originating in the other country; and they shall provide
> for the formulation of measures for the achievement of these
> ends.

This draft was brought to London by Mr. Keynes at the end of
July 1941, and his recent close contact with Mr. Acheson and
others in the State Department enabled him to advise the authorities

---

[1] Mr. Acheson had been asked whether Article II was intended to cover strategic
material such as tin, and the hope was expressed that it did not mean that any current
supplies then being paid for in cash would cease to be paid for. The reply was that
there was no intention to disturb in any way existing arrangements; but that if, at some
future time, the United States were to have difficulty in making payment, they would
then be free to ask for reciprocal concessions.

in London just how far American thought had developed. 'The substantial issues', he wrote, are reserved for Article VII. The first part of this is not quite so clear nor so satisfactory to us as the form of words I had drafted. But it is meant to say, and it does in fact say, that there will be no war debts. That is to say, no deliveries of cash or goods having merely economic significance. It is of enormous importance for us to get this settled now and not leave us to the mercies of different conditions and very possibly a different President. But the second part with the undertaking against "discrimination", whatever that may mean, is of an awkward character and is not made less awkward by the elucidations of the meaning of this which I obtained from Mr. Acheson in conversation. My opinion is, and Mr. Acheson as good as admitted it, that the State Department have taken the opportunity to introduce their pet idea in language which they mean to be technical; whereas the President himself had nothing so definite in view and meant only to require that we should agree to co-operate and to do so in a certain spirit and with a certain general purpose'.

In view of the importance of the non-discrimination issue, it is also worth noting a paragraph in Mr. Keynes's accompanying record of his conversation with Mr. Acheson on 28th July 1941:

> Under Article VII I pointed out the word 'discrimination' was ambiguous. I asked whether our acceptance of this Article would preclude a system of imperial preferences. Mr. Acheson replied he thought it would. I then asked whether it would preclude import and exchange control. Mr. Acheson replied it might be interpreted in that way. Some people might so interpret it, but he doubted whether anything so cut and dried or technical was in the President's mind. The President had in view the general approach to the economics of the post-war world, which should be one excluding special privileges on nationalistic or imperialistic lines. . . . .

The British Ambassador's advice was that while it was obviously of the first importance not to quarrel with the Americans on this issue if it could be avoided, any commitment in terms as definite as those suggested should be avoided. London should, he recommended, offer broader talks 'not with the State Department but with persons nominated by the President and representing the Treasury, commercial and other Departments as well as the State Department'. No doubt the Ambassador's intention was to get the 'pet idea' of the State Department qualified by exposition of the British case to other American Departments where keener appreciation of unpleasant economic realities might be expected. But in London discussion turned immediately not to tactics but to policy; it was felt that a mere undertaking to discuss would not satisfy the Americans, and that some immediate progress must be made on the major issues of policy.

There were substantially two obstacles in the way of acceptance of the American formula. First, Imperial Preference was not merely a policy dear to the heart of several Ministers; it was a system established in agreement with the Dominions and was the basis of important trading relationships. Second, as a senior official of the Treasury put it: 'The immediate post-war period will certainly be one of vast difficulty for ourselves in external monetary and commercial relations . . . . it seems to most of us quite inevitable for a long time to come, and, at any rate to some of us, a desirable thing in itself[1] in the strangely altered conditions of the future, that there should be a form of orderly regulation through the medium of exchange control, trade and payments agreements, output arrangements and the like, worked so far as may be possible in an imperfect world in a spirit of international neighbourliness'. In their rather different ways, these two aspects of British hesitation were so serious that a start had to be made at once in emphasising them to the American authorities. In seeking an alternative form for Article VII, London therefore strove to emphasise, first that Imperial Preference could only be modified gradually, in full agreement with the Dominions, and above all in return for real concessions in American tariff policy; and second that in any case the United Kingdom's post-war trading policy would be cramped by her prospective dollar problem.

At this stage (August–September 1941) the more extreme imperialists in United Kingdom Government circles were encouraged in their fight for Imperial Preference by a minor victory in the phrasing of the Atlantic Charter. The story of the meeting of the President and the Prime Minister on *The Prince of Wales* off Newfoundland in August 1941, and their issue to the world of a statement of war aims, is well known.[2] The fourth point in the British draft ran: 'Fourth, they will strive to bring about a fair and equitable distribution of essential produce, not only within their territorial boundaries, but between the nations of the world'. To this the President wished to add 'without discrimination and on equal terms'. As so amended, this paragraph, the United States Secretary of State emphasised, 'embodied the ideal for which the State Department had striven for the past nine years'.[3] The Prime

---

[1] It was this current of opinion in favour of bilateralism of which Americans were particularly suspicious and against which they sought explicit safeguards.

[2] For Sir Winston Churchill's own account, see Volume III of *The Second World War*, pp 385–388.

[3] Wording as in Churchill, *loc. cit.*

Minister at once referred to the Ottawa Agreements and to the necessity of consulting the Dominions if this formula were pressed, and he indicated the likelihood that in the end he would still have to reject the critical words, 'without discrimination'. The President did not press the matter further, and the Atlantic Charter was published to the world without this phrase.

Successful persuasion on that occasion did not, however, mean that the State Department had surrendered one jot or tittle of its doctrine. Negotiation of the Atlantic Charter had been, at the final stage, very much a personal matter between the two leaders, and President Roosevelt's willingness to concede the point may have indicated that he had no such definite views as the State Department. More probably the Americans dropped the phrase in the interest of speedy settlement of the major document, knowing full well that their real chance to insist upon it was in the consideration for lend-lease. At any rate, those in London who thought that the Americans had dropped their doctrine were disabused in the course of the autumn. It became clear that while the Americans were prepared to face exchange control and import control, they insisted that Britain should regard the abolition of Imperial Preference as a cardinal objective.

It might be supposed that the entry of the United States of America into the war, which occured at this juncture, would have caused an upheaval in these negotiations, or indeed have put an end to them. The basis had hitherto been that a country, non-belligerent if not neutral, was providing material to the belligerent country, and the issue at stake was the return the belligerent might make in consideration of this aid. The two countries now became Allies in a common struggle, and it might have been supposed, and was in fact privately argued in London, that both nations should contribute to their utmost without any further mutual obligation.

Two kinds of circumstance in fact ruled otherwise. The first was that the Lend-Lease Act had only recently emerged from the complex American legislative machine, and under this Act the British had already accepted aid and thereby accepted the obligation to make return in whatever way might be prescribed under that Act. To drop 'consideration' now would necessitate putting something in place of the Lend-Lease Act, and in this process isolationists would argue that Britain had dragged the United States into the war in order to wriggle out of obligations previously assumed. It may be that, in the revulsion against Pearl Harbour, isolationist arguments would have been drowned; at any rate, the risk might have been faced. But the other aspect could not be thus easily dismissed; the entry of the United States into the war at once sharpened the whole subject of 'war aims', and by the Atlantic Charter the Allies had already proclaimed that equal access to trade and materials would be among these aims. For the sake of cementing the alliance, it was now more than ever necessary that definition should be given to the common purpose in which the Allies were joined. Negotiations already in train, on an item to which the American Administration attached importance, could not be dropped in mid-air.

Some measure of agreement on 'consideration', therefore, remained just as important as before. At the same time, the new relationship between the two countries meant that there was still great danger in too easy acceptance of American views. The Americans were a long way from clear on exactly what they wanted, but they did want quickly some form of acknowledgment from Britain, whose representatives were therefore tempted to agree easily to some vague form of words. But even more important than any agreement on war aims was the maintenance of American trust in Britain's good faith. Keynes, who perhaps worked more consistently, more patiently and more successfully in this than in any other matter, was horrified at easy acceptance as a means towards 'getting our own way in the long run'. 'What will draw suspicion', he wrote, 'will be our agreeing to unreasonable demands against our better judgment, and then inevitably having to find some way of slipping out of our ill-advised words'. A genuine agreement, in which the substantial requirements of both sides were recognised, remained at least as important as before Pearl Harbour.

There was, however, consequentially upon Pearl Harbour some slight relaxation of the timetable. It had appeared that the Administration would need to tell Congress in January, when presenting a new lend-lease appropriation, that agreement had been reached.[1] Now the relation between supplies for the United States Defense Departments and supplies for Britain had changed and the bill was being presented to Congress neither as early nor in as stark nakedness as had been intended. Also, although entry into the war had involved no lasting diversion from such topics as this, urgent military matters had proved a temporary distraction, and the Prime Minister, when he met the President at Christmas, found the atmosphere propitious for some deferment. But at the end of January, the 'consideration' question had to be

---

[1] The Lend-Lease Act had to be renewed from year to year, and this gave Congress an annual opportunity for general discussion. But the Act did not itself provide the funds: Congress had from time to time to vote ('appropriate') funds for the purposes of the Act, and as each appropriation approached exhaustion the Administration had ot go back to Congress to justify the voting of further funds.

faced once more: information came that the President felt strongly that an agreement ought to be concluded without further delay. There followed a fortnight of hectic cabling and War Cabinet discussions. Some members of the War Cabinet held very strong views on Imperial Preference and would have liked to have seen it openly preserved as a permanent policy. It was, however, crystal clear that the Americans would stomach no extremity of this kind. They intended that Britain should commit herself at least to modify Imperial Preference as circumstances permitted; or more simply, to its abolition. Even those members of the United Kingdom Government most in sympathy with the basic principles underlying the American drafts felt that economic circumstances compelled some hedging of the early post-war position, and the United Kingdom negotiators therefore fully explored the possibility of coupling the Agreement (essentially a statement of intentions) with an exchange of interpretative notes. These attempts inevitably tripped over the real stumbling block—it was impossible to draft anything that added a safeguard for Britain without making the Americans believe that Britain had no intention of ever modifying Imperial Preference. In the end, the President appealed to the Prime Minister to make the Agreement without any accompanying exchange of notes. The President gave his personal view that the Agreement simply committed the United Kingdom and the United States of America to 'a bold, forthright, and comprehensive discussion looking forward to the construction of what you [the Prime Minister] so aptly call "a free, fertile economic policy for the post war world"'. Of Imperial Preference, he said that Article VII contained no commitment to abolish Imperial Preference. 'I realise that that would be a commitment which your Government could not give now if it wanted to'. The United Kingdom War Cabinet accepted this personal assurance from the President, though it could not then be published, as substantially as valuable as an interchange of interpretative notes.[1] The Dominion Governments, who had been kept in close touch with the negotiations, were informed of this communication, and of the War Cabinet's conclusion that the Agreement should be signed without more ado.

The Mutual Aid Agreement was therefore signed on 23rd February 1942. It was, in the words of the preamble, 'a preliminary agreement' between nations 'engaged in a co-operative undertaking.' The broad terms were announced by Mr. Attlee in the House of

---

[1] The assurance was subsequently made public by Mr. Churchill in the House of Commons, 13th December 1945. (H. of C. Deb., Vol. 417, Col. 723).

Commons the next day.[1] The critical Article VII had finally emerged in these words:[2]

> In the final determination of the benefits to be provided to the United States of America by the Government of the United Kingdom in return for aid furnished under the Act of Congress of the 11th March 1941, the terms and conditions thereof shall be such as not to burden commerce between the two countries, but to promote mutually advantageous economic relations between them and the betterment of world-wide economic relations. To that end, they shall include provision for agreed action by the United States of America and the United Kingdom, open to participation by all other countries of like mind, directed to the expansion, by appropriate international and domestic measures, of production, employment and the exchange and consumption of goods, which are the material foundations of the liberty and welfare of all peoples; to the elimination of all forms of discriminatory treatment in international commerce, and to the reduction of tariffs and other trade barriers; and, in general, to the attainment of all the economic objectives set forth in the Joint Declaration made on the 14th August 1941 by the President of the United States of America and the Prime Minister of the United Kingdom.
>
> At an early convenient date conversations shall be begun between the two Governments with a view to determining, in the light of governing economic conditions, the best means of attaining the above-stated objectives by their own agreed action and of seeking the agreed action of other like-minded Governments.

Mr. Attlee was asked what precisely was meant by the elimination of discriminatory treatment. He replied that as far as the reduction of tariffs and preferences was concerned 'no commitments were undertaken by either party in advance of discussions'. The 'conversations' envisaged in the concluding sentence of the Article did not in fact begin for some time—but the problem remained a continual preoccupation of those engaged in all Anglo-American discussions.

(v)

Reciprocal Aid

Almost before the United States Congress had made lend-lease a fact, reciprocal aid by Britain to the United States began quietly and in a small way as a perfectly natural response to American

---

[1] H. of C. Deb., Vol. 378, Cols. 25-27.
[2] Cmd. 6391 (1942).

generosity. The British financial system, tortuous as it sometimes appears to the spending sections of the spending Departments, had in war-time sufficient elasticity to allow this novelty to come to birth without any heaving of the legislative machine. The terms of the Vote of Credit were wide enough to cover any form of defence expenditure, and reciprocal aid was very reasonably counted as defence. Consequently, no legislative problem arose when, shortly before Congress passed the Lend-Lease Act, the Minister of Aircraft Production decided to send to the United States some Royal Air Force equipment which the United States authorities wanted for use in the training of their own personnel. Anticipating that the Americans would expect to receive this equipment without payment, the Minister gave instructions that, while a note of the cost should be kept, no bill should be sent at the time of delivery. Further transactions being envisaged, Treasury views were sought on the general principle. No-one questioned the correctness of the Minister's decision: even if the amounts had been much larger, they would still have been trifling in comparison with what Britain was to receive. There was not even to be a statement of account to be set against liabilities accruing under lend-lease: the Treasury wanted to avoid use of 'the money-sign'. The United Kingdom Government accountants could easily take care of the innovation.

So reciprocal aid began, without any inter-Governmental discussion and without any request from the United States authorities. It began simply because United Kingdom Ministers and officials on every level felt that they could not look stingy in the face of that 'most unsordid act'. It was a pity that circumstances made it impossible to let matters stay on this informal and untrumpeted basis. But relations between the supply Departments of the two Governments had even at this stage become so close that there was no logical stopping point. Once begun, the principle of not sending in the bill was bound to spread—and it was bound to be inspected more closely, by both parties. To each item that was, in the interest of good relations, slipped into the reciprocal aid bag, there was some close parallel which had to be included as soon as a question arose about it. From military supplies and facilities in the United Kingdom it was easy to pass to other materials sent to the United States for Governmental purposes. Raw materials were being supplied to United States Governmental or quasi-Governmental agencies, such as the Metal Reserve Corporation, for strategic reserves. Should these also be included? And if they were included, would it not be logical to include all exports to the United States including such valuable items as rubber and tin? 'One supposes', a Treasury official wrote in April 1941, 'that we may come to something like that position, but we ought clearly to leave the U.S. authorities to raise the matter with us.'

For, much as it was tempted by logic to reach the simple conclusion, the United Kingdom Government was not in a position to forego cash payments for all supplies to the United States. The Lend-Lease Act was to provide 'for the defense of the United States' and it was perfectly clear that the Administration could not, even on the most generous interpretation, bring under its wing every dollar requirement of the United Kingdom. Moreover, as we have seen in discussing the problem of 'the old commitments', the Administration had committed itself to the exclusion not only of those items that had no direct bearing on defence needs but also of vital military supplies coming forward under old contracts. Britain's need to earn dollars was therefore still extremely urgent. The position of other parts of the Sterling Area—particularly the Dominions—under lend-lease had not yet been clarified, and their needs also had to be considered. In short, London could not afford to extend reciprocal aid as rapidly and widely as everyone would have liked. The United Kingdom had perforce to restrict reciprocal aid to military stores and incidental services that did not, at that date, add up to much.

It was necessary also to avoid the use of any phrases—such as 'reverse lend-lease'—that might imply the existence of a formal understanding with the United States Government. There was no such understanding, and the United Kingdom authorities felt that they could not afford to take any initiative. They would simply desist from presenting such bills as would probably irritate.

As long as the United States were not in the war, reciprocal aid could be left thus undefined; and as long as the United Kingdom remained burdened with 'the old commitments', the United Kingdom authorities could not afford generous gestures. But at the end of 1941 the relevant conditions were changing every aspect of the problem. Military alliance implied a bigger flow of British defence supplies into American hands as well as a bigger flow of American defence supplies into British hands; the tempo of interchange of supplies, services and of technical knowledge increased beyond all recognition. Secondly, the prospect that large American Forces would have to operate in Sterling Area countries made it impossible further to delay questions whose awkwardness was all too well known in Treasury Chambers. Should the burden be left where it fell—whether on India, or Australia, or Egypt? Or should it be borne by Britain? Or should the Americans pay their own bills in some or all of these countries? In the context of these questions the Americans were entitled to have their own views on the sharing of

burdens within the British Commonwealth; and these views affected
their attitude on reciprocal aid from India and the Dominions.
Nor were these the only 'frontier questions' on reciprocal aid.
What was to be done about shipping, now to be shared here, there
and everywhere? And, if raw materials were still to be generally
excluded, what about raw materials supplied either to United
States Forces abroad or for processing into lend-lease goods destined
for Britain or other Allies?

Many of these questions were not altogether new and at least
they had been foreseen; but the sums involved were now no longer
small—the Treasury could not just pay up and smile, nor could
it shut its own eyes and hope the Americans would not notice.
The whole matter had to be brought into the open. In many
quarters it was supposed that all the reciprocal aid questions would
automatically be swept up in some great financial pooling plan
that would replace lend-lease; this was, as we have already seen,[1]
an illusion. But from another source there was pressure of a different
kind: the negotiations on 'consideration', culminating in the Mutual
Aid Agreement of February 1942,[2] were demanding some definition
of reciprocal aid as part of the consideration called for under the
Lend-Lease Act. The agreement mentioned the subject only in
very general terms, but in the discussions leading to it United States
representatives stressed their desire for regular arrangements
covering aid both from the United Kingdom and Colonies and
from the Dominions. Efforts were therefore made both to codify
the practice that had grown up as regards supplies and services
from the United Kingdom and to persuade the Dominions to follow
suit.

British practice had by this time more or less settled on these
lines:

(a) Munitions, military stores and analogous services provided
for the United States Government were included in reciprocal
aid. The margin stretched out to include machine tools, but
not any supplies to United States contractors as distinct
from Governmental 'agencies'.

(b) Where it was convenient and more economical for the
British authorities to provide supplies or services to United
States Forces, they were provided under reciprocal aid.

(c) Where United States Forces were supplied with goods that
had originated as lend-lease supplies from the United States,
no payment was asked.

---

[1] p. 375 above.
See pp. 405-13 above.

On the other hand,

(d) Where it was more convenient for the United States Forces to make local purchases, they did so with cash which was not refunded.

(e) The United States provided all pay and allowances for their Forces.

(f) Raw materials and commercial supplies generally were excluded from reciprocal aid.

Reciprocal aid, as developed on these lines, differed in three important ways from lend-lease. First, there was the exclusion of raw materials which was due primarily to the British need for dollars. Secondly, whereas Britain's requirements under lend-lease were all centralised in London, vetted by the United States Office of Lend-Lease Administration (OLLA), and procured by United States Government contracts placed in Washington, reciprocal aid supplies and services to the United States were procured here, there and everywhere with only the minimum guidance from the Treasury in London. The limits of reciprocal aid were in fact set by the convenience of United States Army Commanders in procuring supplies. Thirdly, whereas OLLA had to get specific appropriations from Congress and was under constant fire, reciprocal aid was covered under broad statutory powers— even the general principle had not been the subject of Parliamentary authority—and no element in Parliament would ever criticise a wide and generous extension of reciprocal aid.

These differences had important implications which came to the forefront in the 1942–43 discussions. First, the different constitutional position had allowed reciprocal aid to begin and to grow to large proportions without public discussion of principles or indeed public realisation of what was happening, whereas lend-lease details were from the first under close discussion in the United States. Secondly, the decentralisation which was the essence of reciprocal aid inevitably meant variety of practice; this was responsible for misunderstandings and bad feeling which the British had to dispel by continual extension of the frontiers of aid. Thirdly, whereas OLLA kept exact accounts, it was impossible to value many reciprocal aid services, and any attempt to keep accounts would have involved extravagant diversion of manpower. The United Kingdom authorities in 1942 had good reasons for preserving all these differences. They could not afford to make reciprocal aid 100 per cent. reciprocal to lend-lease, and any public parade of the subject would create pressure to make it so. They believed decentralised procurement was the only efficient way of providing for American Forces in Allied territories—a condition not parallelled

2D

by United Kingdom requirements on American soil. Finally, they could not afford the manpower for meticulous accounting, nor was there any way of putting figures on such aid as the knowledge British physicists were contributing to the development of atomic weapons.

The reluctance of the United Kingdom authorities to formulate reciprocal aid principles and to make them the subject of formal agreement with the United States Government was parallelled by the difficulties that faced the Dominion Governments when they were asked to join in reciprocal aid. Australia, coming into the front line of the Pacific War, was faced by a potentially huge bill. New Zealand foresaw American troops eating up her 'cash crops'. South Africa, receiving very little under lend-lease, thought the cost of reciprocal aid might far outweigh the benefits she was receiving. These problems were under constant discussion between Britain and the Dominions in 1942 and became entangled in the financial relations between them;[1] thereby Australia and New Zealand were persuaded to come into the reciprocal aid system. South Africa preferred to remain outside any formal system, though for a time actually providing some reciprocal aid supplies.[2] The differing circumstances of Australia, New Zealand and the United Kingdom added to the reluctance of the United Kingdom authorities to enter into any agreement whereby reciprocal aid might be pushed into a formal framework reflecting the United States system of lend-lease. Accordingly, when at last (on 3rd September 1942) it was possible to publish a formal exchange of letters publicising reciprocal aid,[3] the opening phrases disclaimed any principle of uniformity: 'While each Government retains the right of final decision, in the light of its own potentialities and responsibilities, decisions as to the most effective use of resources shall, so far as possible, be made in common, pursuant to common plans for winning the war'.

The exchange of letters between Lord Halifax and Mr. Cordell Hull covered only the United Kingdom and Colonies; closely parallel letters passed between the United States Government on the one hand and the Governments of Australia and New Zealand on the other. In all of them the scope of reciprocal aid was defined on the broad lines of United Kingdom practice as outlined above.[4]

---

[1] cf. Chapter X.

[2] When requested in July 1943 to supply raw materials on reciprocal aid, South Africa replied by saying that she would rather have all her United States supplies on a cash basis. The final agreement for cash payment on both sides was not signed until April 1945.

[3] Cmd. 6389.

[4] Australia formally limited reciprocal aid to provision of supplies to United States Forces in Australia; but the Australian authorities did not in fact keep strictly within this limit. The United Kingdom and New Zealand did not include, in their agreements, any parallel to this Australian clause.

On the face of it, the United Kingdom Treasury could not have felt dissatisfied with the document of September 1942, reluctant though it had been to come to it. Raw materials and the pay of United States personnel remained outside, and the effect was therefore to allow the Sterling Area to continue earning a substantial dollar income by selling raw materials and to hold out the prospect of a much bigger dollar income when the American Armies streamed across the seas. This dollar income was of course still vital to London, but one of the original reasons for clinging to it was ebbing as the pre-lend-lease contracts ran off. The 1942 agreement, for such reasons as this, could be no more than an interim arrangement; the ground under it was already changing when it was signed.

Besides the more fundamental questions affecting reciprocal aid, a long-standing American dissatisfaction over statistics was, in the Spring of 1943, coming to a head. In June the United States Administration told British representatives that figures on the value of reciprocal aid must be produced. This was natural enough, considering that the United Kingdom had stressed the importance of reciprocal aid, and that the United States Administration was using it as a political argument for generosity in the administration of lend-lease. The quantitative figures for particular recognisable items had their own impressiveness, but people (in both countries) wanted to know how the totals looked. Congress and the American Press evidently found it difficult to understand why value estimates could not be provided, and the Administration feared that continued failure would breed an atmosphere of mystery and suspicion. The United States Army authorities had also a private reason for demanding figures: Congressmen were arguing that Army appropriations should be reduced now that the Army was receiving substantial quantities of reciprocal aid, and Army representatives were being pressed to account in terms of money.

Although this American pressure was reasonable enough—after all, the taxpayers' money was being poured out for lend-lease and Congressmen had a duty as the taxpayers' watchdogs—the British authorities had good reasons for their continued reluctance to produce figures. If they were to be anything like comprehensive, a huge increase in records, in the theatres of war as well as at home, would be necessary, and at this stage of mobilisation the Government was unwilling to direct the labours of thousands of clerks into a task adding nothing to the common war effort. Secondly, any figure produced would raise questions in Congress as to how it had been compiled, and the British would have to reveal the answer they had given to the awkward question of the rate of conversion of sterling values into dollar values. United States Army instructions stipulated that prices should be converted at $4 to the £; but this presented no fair picture. Goods made in Britain at the British level of costs were worth to the Americans what they would cost in terms of America's more highly paid labour. At this stage of war mobilisation man-hours were the limiting factor, and conversion of British costs at $4 to the £ would therefore understate the relief afforded to American production by British supplies. There was not merely the difficulty of choosing a multiplier in substitution for the official rate of exchange—there was the infinitely greater difficulty of explaining and defending the choice.

Thirdly—and most fundamentally—the comparison of global figures of reciprocal aid and lend-lease seemed to the British inconsistent with the principle of pooling, a harking back to the money sign, and potentially a revival of the War Debt issue which mutual aid had been intended to kill. In his Report to Congress in June 1942, President Roosevelt had stated 'the lend-lease principle' in terms which perfectly expressed the British conception, but there was, among British negotiators, little faith that this had penetrated to public opinion in the United States. Publication of global figures in terms of pounds or dollars was all too likely to give a handle to those who were still thinking that the United States was lending a huge net sum to the United Kingdom, a transaction that would by implication leave the United Kingdom under a financial obligation to the United States.

Nevertheless, there had for some time been agitations on the British side for some more precise and more resounding publicity about the scale of reciprocal aid. As early as April 1942 the British Broadcasting Corporation represented to the Treasury that lend-lease was receiving much publicity in Europe while the United Kingdom's reciprocal aid went virtually unsung. At that date any possible figures would have been relatively too small to be impressive, but this was an argument that lost force as reciprocal aid grew, and in the course of 1943 there was increasing feeling that we were letting a good case go by default. It was a case that the United Kingdom Government had to make not only to Europe but also to the British public itself and above all to public opinion in the United States.

Accordingly, when pressure from Washington suddenly came to a head in June–July 1943, British reluctance was not altogether unmixed, and the inevitability of compliance was quickly accepted. Figures were hastily—at the expense of much midnight oil—compiled and included in a draft White Paper to be laid before Parliament immediately before the Recess early in August 1943. In the hectic days that followed there was in Washington an astonishing *volte face* that must have tried the British representatives as sorely as any other war-time episode in Anglo-American financial relations. The upshot was that the White Paper was shelved.

To understand the extraordinary events of those August days, it is necessary to realise that this question of reciprocal aid figures was linked—one could only guess how closely—with three other issues simultaneously under discussion through the spring and summer. First, American interest in the growth of London's reserves of gold and dollars had become explicit and there was some inclination to prune lend-lease in order to restrict this growth. Secondly, the extension of reciprocal aid to cover raw materials was now under discussion; the completion of pre-lend-lease contracts had greatly eased the dollar position, and the time was therefore ripe for this long foreseen change. It had the advantage in British eyes of underlining the pooling principle. Thirdly, there was an attempt to revise the Export White Paper; the British had found this not only tiresome but also inconsistent with the pooling principle, and they hoped that the United States would modify its attitude rather than submit to corresponding restrictions on the use of raw materials to be supplied on reciprocal aid. These three issues were all linked with each other, and they were linked with the publication of reciprocal aid figures because that publication was obviously—as the grand exposition of reciprocal aid—the moment for announcing extension to raw materials.

Clearance of all these matters would have been much easier if the British had known the relative importance attached to each by the Americans. In fact they did not know, and, what was even more confusing, different United States Government Departments and individuals held widely differing views. Through July London had proceeded on the assumptions that the Americans wanted raw materials on reciprocal aid as quickly as possible, and that they wanted both reciprocal aid publicity and the announcement about raw materials in order to make the continuance of massive lend-lease more acceptable to their political machine. The sudden increase in American pressure in June and July, and particularly Washington's anxiety to be able to report progress when the President would send his Lend-Lease Report to Congress in August, lent support to this interpretation of American policy. On this basis London had decided to supply as reciprocal aid raw materials from the United Kingdom and Colonies, and had made representations to India and the Dominions in support of the request made directly to them by the United States Government; and London had prepared the troublesome factual material on the value of reciprocal aid already provided.

India and the Dominions naturally wanted a few weeks to look into the question. Methods of procurement had to be considered without the help of any clear statement of American views, and more fundamentally the Commonwealth countries were by this time thinking ahead to their post-war dollar requirements. As regards raw materials from the United Kingdom itself and the Colonies, there were also procurement problems, particularly in relation to running private contracts. While, therefore, Britain accepted the principle, the Americans had to be told that arrangements would take a little time, and the 1st October was suggested as the commencing date. The Americans also had to be made to understand, on this occasion as on many others throughout the war, that London could not answer for the Dominions.

These points were more or less accepted by the State Department and by Mr. Stettinius and his immediate associates in the Office of Lend-Lease Administration, and in the first days of August the terms of the British announcement were being discussed informally with them in anticipation of publication on the afternoon of Wednesday 5th August. At 9.30 a.m. that morning the Treasury received a bombshell from Washington: by the time the Chancellor had spoken to Mr. Winant and to the Foreign Secretary, only two hours were left in which to make the arrangements *not* to publish the White Paper. The postponement was due to objections raised by Mr. Morgenthau. In London there had been the closest contact with the United States Embassy, and in Washington with Mr. Stettinius and officials in the State Department; in neither place had the United Kingdom representatives been given any warning that Mr. Morgenthau or anyone else might be a stumbling block.

Just what was at the bottom of it all must be, in British sources, a matter for surmise. It appears that Mr. Stettinius was expecting some objection, and therefore delayed until the last minute clearance of the matter with Mr. Morgenthau, fully confident that he could overcome the latter's doubts. Personal jealousies between Mr. Morgenthau and Mr. Stettinius may have made the position more delicate; at any rate, when Mr. Morgenthau was at last consulted, he was completely intransigent and the whole effect of any British publicity would have been ruined. His objections were alleged to relate to the disappointingly low figures for reciprocal aid and to the limitations of the United Kingdom offer on raw materials.[1] The United Kingdom Government's offer was necessarily limited to supplies from the United Kingdom and Colonies, and at that date no corresponding decisions had been taken by other members of the Commonwealth; the starting date of 1st October 1943 was thought unduly late; and objection was raised to the British intention

---

[1] One of Mr. Morgenthau's objections was due to a misunderstanding: Mr. Stettinius had given the British representatives a list of commodities to be covered, and the British had taken this list more literally than apparently the Americans had intended.

to restrict reciprocal aid raw materials to supplies to the United States Government to the exclusion of private firms in the United States. To each of these objections the United Kingdom had an answer: in relation to the date of the original American request (June) the starting date was remarkably early; the Americans had been slow to ask the Dominions and the latter were, with prompting from London, not being unreasonably dilatory; and the United Kingdom proposal to supply only to the United States Government was merely an imitation of the mechanics whereby lend-lease materials came to Britain. Nevertheless, Mr. Morgenthau declared himself not satisfied and made it clear that he would publicly disclose his dissatisfaction if London proceeded with its announcement on 5th August.

While they speculated on what really lay behind this episode, the British now had to make up their minds afresh about the date of the White Paper and the announcement about raw materials. For there was no question of dropping either: alike in Washington and in London postponement, not cancellation, was the view. The tendency on the American side, once the August moment was passed, was to begin arguments all over again and to delay— for reasons of internal politics—British publicity. In London, on the other hand, opinion was swinging much more heavily in favour of early pronouncements. Although Mr. Morgenthau and others had said that the British figures would be disappointing to a Congress that had got the figure of $1½ billions into its head, the United Kingdom Treasury now felt that Britain had a good story to tell the public—British as well as American. In Britain neither Parliament nor public had been told the full range of reciprocal aid. In the United States the case was going by default. No answer had been given to misinformed attacks in the American Press, and it seemed likely that in a forthcoming Congressional enquiry more mud would be thrown at the British. Whatever the United States Administration thought, the time had come for an appeal above its heads, and above the heads of Congress, to public opinion in the United States and indeed in the world at large.

The Congressional enquiry, whose imminence served to underline the need for a statement of the British case, was differently viewed by the United States Administration. The enquiry arose out of a much-publicised Report by the 'Five Senators' who had been touring the theatres of war. The critical nature of their comments on the administration of lend-lease had been greatly exaggerated, and the Administration therefore expected a tough time with Congress. For some weeks the Administration begged British representatives to defer publication of the White Paper until the Congressional discussions were out of the way. And there were other circumstances making the Americans anxious that Britain's move should be delayed. Most important, perhaps, was the increasing hesitation inside the United States Administration over Britain's offer of raw materials. The British plan was, it will be recalled, for supply to the United States Government; the Americans had always been afraid that this would militate against efficiency, for which they preferred to trust the channels of private trade. Reluctance on this ground was reinforced by fears for the livelihood of the private traders, and a reorganisation of the relevant United States Departments[1] unfortunately strengthened just those circles where these interests were strongest. At the end of October there was therefore still complete deadlock on this question. For closely similar reasons the Americans were adamant on the United Kingdom proposal that reciprocal aid raw materials should be subject to restrictions parallel to those imposed under the Export White Paper, though there seemed a likelihood that they would accept the alternative of relaxation of restrictions on British use of lend-lease materials. Yet a further reason for delay in any publicity was the inability of Australia and India to come to any final decision about supply of their raw materials under reciprocal aid.

But while on the American side there seemed to be all sorts of reasons for delaying Britain's announcements, the United Kingdom Government felt every day more strongly that something must be said. The very Congressional enquiry that made the Americans reluctant was to the British just one more reason for putting the British viewpoint in the shop-window. And while American hesitation over the procurement of raw materials might be a reason for delaying the implementation of new plans, it was not a sufficient reason for keeping silent about Britain's offer. On these among other grounds the War Cabinet decided late in October

---

[1] On 26th October 1943 Mr. Leo T. Crowley was appointed Foreign Economic Administrator 'to bring under a single umbrella', the overseas economic organisations of the United States Administration, viz., the Office of Lend-Lease Administration (OLLA), the Office of Economic Warfare (OEW), the Office of Foreign Relief and Rehabilitation (OFRRO), the Office of Foreign Economic Co-operation, formerly part of the State Department, and the Commodity Credit Corporation. The new organisation was known as the Foreign Economic Administration (FEA) and was divided into two Departments, (i) the Bureau of Supplies, responsible for all export and import control, including lend-lease shipments, foreign procurement and requirements, (ii) the Bureau of Areas, responsible for all overseas areas which were classified as liberated areas, necessitous areas and general areas.

Many of the personnel of the old Agencies with whom the British Missions had built up long and friendly associations found, after reading of the new set-up in the news-papers, that they had been assigned no specific duties in the new organisation and consequently resigned within a few weeks.

From the British point of view the reorganisation created much confusion and uncertainty on future policy, and Anglo-American relations suffered noticeably when there disappeared the friendly, intimate atmosphere in which discussions at official level on all sorts of high and low matters had been conducted in the days before the Foreign Economic Administration existed.

that a revised White Paper, with text toughened and simplified[1] and figures brought down to the end of June, ought to go forward without further delay. The War Cabinet further agreed that the Prime Minister should send a personal message to the President explaining the case and seeking his support. Before, however, the Prime Minister's message went off, Lord Keynes, hot-foot from Washington, brought news that the Administration was now in favour of immediate publication. The Congressional enquiry had gone off at half-cock, the effect upon it of the White Paper was no longer feared, and the more sympathetic views of the State Department and other particularly helpful quarters had prevailed.

British plans to publish the White Paper on 11th November therefore went ahead more happily, and the only immediate question between London and Washington became whether simultaneous publicity in the United States might be prefaced by a Presidential blessing. American officials thought it could be done; the British for their part knew that the President's word could help, but refrained from counting their chickens. As lately as 7th September President Roosevelt had taken an ominous step in repudiating an official who had been too bold in enunciating 'the pooling principle',[2] and by this time Whitehall had become all too familiar with President Roosevelt's 'famous political instinct' for deciding that action was 'politically dangerous'.[3] But this time happily the President agreed to send a message to Congress, on the same day as the Chancellor's statement in the House of Commons, repeating with his own blessing the substance of the White Paper.

So at long last it was with full American support that the White Paper appeared. On 11th November 1943 the Chancellor of the Exchequer told the House of Commons that he had 'laid a Report on Mutual Aid in the Vote Office'.[4] He added some brief comments thrusting home the case the Government was making to the world. After referring to the origin of lend-lease, the Chancellor mentioned the subsequent entry of the United States into the war and the United Kingdom's determination 'to develop the pooling of resources

---

[1] Lord Beaverbrook and Lord Keynes each had a hand in this process; they agreed in unusual measure.

[2] The President had not himself propounded the pooling principle since the summer of 1942. When the President's quarterly report on lend-lease went to Congress in August 1943, it included an official's sentences: 'The Congress in passing and extending the Lend-Lease Act made it plain that the United States wants no new war debts to jeopardise the coming peace. Victory and a secure peace are the only coin in which we can be repaid.' The President went out of his way to repudiate these sentences: 'He would not have worded the second sentence the way it had been . . . . There were all kinds of coin, whether or not they jingled.'

[3] The phrase comes from Lord Keynes.

[4] H. of C. Deb., Vol. 393, Cols. 1296-99.

among the Allies. Lend-lease, therefore, has ceased to flow in one direction only. It has become a system of mutual aid.' He went on to announce the offer of raw materials, foodstuffs and shipping services from the United Kingdom and Colonies, as a duty 'consistent with the conception of the pooling of resources'; the offer was 'to mark our wholehearted acceptance of the principle of a general pooling of resources'. Finally he referred to 'another aspect of our external financial burden, the vast scale of which is liable to be overlooked'. This was the sterling expenditure in the Middle East and India, which 'we have to borrow and carry forward as a heavy burden into the times of peace'—a liability that 'must be taken into account in considering the scale of our external financial effort as a whole, and our ability to shoulder additional burdens'.

In President Roosevelt's parallel Message to Congress[1] the decision about raw materials was announced in terms closely similar to the United Kingdom announcement. For reciprocal aid up to 30th June 1943, the United Kingdom and Commonwealth figures were translated from pounds sterling to dollars at the official rate of exchange, but warning was given that 'this may be misleading because the rate of exchange used cannot, especially under war conditions, always reflect comparable values in terms of purchasing power, man-hours of work or materials . . .' There was also repeated emphasis on the 'incomplete accounting' and on the limitation of this report to only a part of the Commonwealth's expenditure on reverse lend-lease. There was, too, a prefatory passage referring to the pooling of resources as 'the overwhelming benefit which the United States has received from its lend-lease programme'; the Message also concluded on this note so agreeable to London ears. What was by contrast totally absent from the President's Message was any parallel to the Chancellor's reference to the prospective burden incurred by Britain's colossal sterling expenditure in India and the Middle East. This omission was no accident: it was all too symptomatic of the American failure to appreciate just how burdensome was this expenditure. Treasury representatives had already been trying to impress upon the Americans the relevance of these mounting sterling liabilities to the question of London's reserves. The continued nagging at this question through the rest of the war was to show how little impression they had yet made, and how restricted was the Americans' notion of 'the pooling of resources' to which lip-service had been paid in the Presidential Message.

---

[1] *Twelfth Report to Congress on Lend-Lease Operations*, 78th Congress, 1st Session. House Document No. 353.

(vi)

The Struggle for an Adequate Reserve

Although at the beginning of the war the British authorities were prepared to regard as expendable over a period London's entire reserves of gold and dollars, and although those reserves were in fact exhausted early in 1941, the high importance first of clinging to and then of rebuilding a minimum reserve was always in mind. In addition to the convenience of a working balance—a reason at least as important in war as in peace—there were two considerations to which the authorities attached great importance. First, the supply of war material and essential foodstuffs from overseas was greatly increased by the willingness of the supplying countries to hold sterling, and their readiness to hold sterling depended partly on the knowledge that it was adequately backed by gold. Secondly, the United Kingdom needed to have a reserve at the end of the war, both to finance an import surplus in the reconstruction period and to allow the elbow-room essential if foreign trade was to be freed from the shackles of bilateralism. Both these reasons gathered force as the war progressed. As the sterling balances accumulated, both inside and outside the Commonwealth, maintenance of confidence in sterling became ever more important. Similarly, as the Americans and Canadians showed themselves more and more keen that the post-war world should be one of unhampered multilateral trade, and as they sought to commit the debtor Britain to the same course, it became ever more important that London should emerge from the war with reserves that would give her manœuvrability in her trading relations with the outside world.

The United States Administration at first overlooked these considerations. We have seen how it promised Congress that Britain should exhaust all realisable assets in paying for pre-lend-lease supplies. Afterwards the Administration did reluctantly accept, in some measure, Britain's claim to a reserve, but the figures it would contemplate were always lower than those London claimed as necessary. So this conflict on reserves was always underlying arguments about lend-lease and reciprocal aid. The British occasionally sought, even at early stages, to bring the conflict to the surface; finally they decided that in the Stage II discussions the question must be brought right into the centre. What emerged at that closing stage is the subject of Chapter XV; before that is reached, it is appropriate to look back at this struggle for London's reserves, running like a restless shuttle through the threads of the lend-lease story.

The preparation of Britain's brief on this subject began as early as October 1940, when Sir Frederick Phillips was about to leave for Washington. Emphasis was to be placed on 'how impossible our position would be after the war if we were denuded of all our assets in the course of it', and on the need for a minimum reserve of £120–£150 millions. Without this, either our post-war trade policy must be totalitarian or the pound would be exposed to uncontrollable depreciation. The lower figure was quickly dropped and when in January 1941 Lord Halifax, on taking up his appointment as Ambassador at Washington, was briefed on the need for American aid, he was told that 'we have always fixed in our minds the sum of £150 millions as the absolute minimum of gold reserve with which we ought to start under the new dispensation . . .' Just how officials arrived at the figure of £150 millions is not clear; probably they saw no reason to depart from the figure generally assumed right since the First Report of the Cunliffe Committee in 1918.[1] A few weeks later, when London held practically no reserve at all, the reconstitution of a reserve was high enough on the priorities list to secure a place in the distress message handed to Mr. Morgenthau for the President.[2] Unfortunately, the Secretary of the United States Treasury and the Director of the Budget, in their statements to Congress about British requirements, made no reference to the need for reserves—indeed by implication they denied the need.[3]

Mr. Keynes had therefore, when he visited Washington in May 1941, to begin at the beginning. He thought it best to desist from putting the claim on the more general grounds. Instead, he urged that a reserve would ease the burdens of administering and defending the Lend-Lease Act. 'If the British Treasury', he wrote to Mr. Morgenthau,[4] 'had a reasonable reserve against contingencies, both they and the American Administration of the Lend-Lease Act would be subject to much less embarrassment whenever items came forward which the latter felt to be for any reason open to criticism, since the British Treasury would have no difficulty in accepting those criticisms immediately. It would also mean that the British Treasury could take the responsibility of itself financing an entirely unforeseen requirement which might develop and might be difficult for legislative reasons to bring within the ambit of the lend-lease

---

[1] The supporting arguments adduced by the Cunliffe Committee (paragraph 41, reprinted in T. E. Gregory, *British Banking Statutes and Reports;* Vol. 2, pp. 357-58) were defective, but the order of magnitude was supported by the Macmillan Committee, which however advocated more elasticity above a bare minimum of £100 millions. (p. 151 of *Report of the Committee on Finance and Industry*, Cmd. 3897 of 1931).

[2] 27th February 1941.

[3] For these statements, see p. 390 above.

[4] 16th May 1941.

procedure except after an inevitable delay.' Mr. Keynes failed in his main purpose, but the Jesse Jones loan and the minor administrative adjustments he secured[1] enabled him in July 1941 to make less depressing calculations. Though London's reserves were then only about £40 millions and would remain below £150 millions through the first half of 1942, there was a prospect of their reaching £250 millions by the end of 1943. He told Mr. Morgenthau that we should in due course reach £150 millions, 'not too much to provide for contingencies but enough to afford relief from anxiety'. The United States Administration's tacit acceptance of this was at any rate a great advance from the attitude of early 1941. The United Kingdom Treasury gained further confidence when in October 1941 the President, disliking the big figures proposed for the second lend-lease appropriation, ordered a general reshuffling of the proposals but did not re-open the attack on the United Kingdom's reserves. The squeezing of aid for Russia into an appropriation originally intended for the United Kingdom alone was a serious threat, but when they made their calculations the British officials expected to scrape through and to accumulate a reserve of £150 millions by the end of 1943.

An immediate effect of the entry of the United States into the war was to excite hopes that this, like other problems, would vanish overnight through acceptance by the United States of the principle of pooling. The possibility—on past experience, the probability— that the Americans would prove difficult on the reserves question was just one more reason for urging immediate extension of the general principle of pooling of resources, which had lately been blazoned abroad by the President and Prime Minister after the latter's journey to Washington. Britain must, officials urged, make a determined stand now, or resign herself to having to go hat-in-hand to the United States for the remainder of the war. The officials very quickly realised that the latter was to be Britain's fate, and they had therefore to face the problem of explaining to the Americans the need not merely for the £150 millions but for a reserve increasing as Britain's external liabilities increased.

The claim for a rising reserve was certainly going to come as a shock to Washington. Now that Britain's pre-lend-lease liabilities were running off and lend-lease was taking care of a large part of Britain's dollar requirements, could not London get along quite comfortably with a smaller reserve than that hitherto thought the proper minimum? This was a pertinent question, but London had also to consider how its sterling liabilities to India, the Middle East, and the Argentine had increased and, especially as the war

---

[1] See p. 391 *et seq.*

spread in the Far East, were likely to go on increasing. Unfortunately, the United States Administration—let alone Congress—did not readily grasp the economics of the Sterling Area; sterling liabilities—especially those to India—were surely 'all inside the family' and why need London hold a gold reserve against them? The prospect of having to educate not only the Administration but a far wider circle was not relished, and there was even less relish in giving some point to the lecture by disclosing the figures. The size of the sterling balances and their rapid growth had not been published. They could not be given to Congress without Parliamentary disclosure; even official communication to the United States Administration without disclosure to Parliament would be objectionable. Yet it was considered vital to London's credit, on which continued supplies against payment of sterling depended, 'that these figures should be kept in the highest degree secret.' Keynes argued from this that, if the Americans could be told only of part of London's liabilities, they should be told only of part of London's assets. Otherwise American opinion would believe that the United Kingdom was getting richer and richer the longer the war lasted, whereas of course the United Kingdom was getting poorer and poorer. Being hat-in-hand, the dilemma could not be ignored: British representatives had to say something, for there was already pressure for more reciprocal aid and for 'take-outs' from lend-lease in order to keep London's reserves down.

The immediate decision was to disclose the position 'in general terms', and this was done in a formal memorandum presented in Washington on 18th April 1942: 'The annual increase in the liabilities now being incurred by the United Kingdom to countries other than the United States of America and Canada, is not less than four times the total amount of the present output of gold by the Sterling Area, and His Majesty's Government are anxious that the gold output should be retained as a partial reserve against these liabilities.' Gold could be retained only if the remaining pre-lend-lease contracts were absorbed into lend-lease. If a settlement on these lines could be reached, His Majesty's Government would be prepared to meet both the United States desire for increased reciprocal aid and the Administration's difficulties over marginal lend-lease items. This attempt to bring about a major revision of financial relations failed. Nevertheless, through most of 1942 the United Kingdom authorities continued their struggle to secure acceptance of one of the points introduced in the message just quoted: the distinction between the dollar reserve, on which a ceiling would be agreed, and the gold reserve which the United Kingdom should be free to accumulate without

limit against the mounting liabilities in sterling.[1] In October 1942
the United States Treasury made it clear that it would have none of
this 'fiction': to it gold and dollars were interchangeable, and it
was London's total reserves—or perhaps the Sterling Area's total
reserves—that it felt itself bound to limit.

Although some comfort was drawn from Mr. Harry White's
view that the Administration was unlikely to press any immediate
decision, this was not quite satisfactory. The British representatives
wanted positive acceptance of their case, and this they failed to
secure. The Americans continued to think in terms of absolute
figures while London was thinking in proportional terms—London
needed a reserve growing as the sterling balances owned by other
countries grew. In desperation, the Treasury and the Bank of
England began to play with various ideas for 'spreading the gold
around'—paying some to the various countries holding large
sterling balances. Although these ideas were to be developed in
1943 when the decision to sell gold in India and the Middle East
was substantially influenced by them, they led to no immediate
action in 1942. Instead, the British authorities decided yet again
to try a frank and open approach to the United States
Administration. The approach was made by the Chancellor of the
Exchequer in a personal message to Mr. Morgenthau on 19th
January 1943. The United Kingdom's external reserves must be
related to the growing liabilities; the Chancellor appreciated Mr.
Morgenthau's immediate troubles—'Mine', he added' 'will not
be less'.

This approach, like so many others on this problem, brought
no clear statement of policy from the United States authorities.
The difficulty at bottom was that there was on the American side
no real understanding of the nature of the Sterling Area or of
London's obligations as banker to that area. Consequently, while
individuals such as Mr. Morgenthau or Mr. White might, after
receiving careful explanations, concede that Britain had a case, it
was quite impossible—until the end of 1944—to secure any helpful
crystallisation of policy in the Administration. On this occasion
the only reply the Chancellor received was to the effect that the
United States Treasury was always ready to consult with British
representatives; but ground was at this very moment being lost.
The Administration was being attacked both on details of lend-lease
and on the growth of British balances at the expense of the United
States taxpayer. The matter was referred to the President, who

[1] The Bank of England, always specially mindful of the need to maintain confidence
in sterling, was particularly anxious to press this distinction on the United States
authorities.

ruled that United Kingdom reserves should be held in range $600–1000 millions.[1] Not until August 1943 did the British authorities know firmly that there had been any such judgment, but they quickly sensed that there had been something of the kind. OLLA began to object more freely to marginal applications for lend-lease supplies, and tobacco for civilian consumption—a matter of $48 millions in the new Appropriation Bill—was taken right out of lend-lease. The pressure continued, and in the early summer came the request—forecast in private conversations back in October 1942—for extension of reciprocal aid to cover raw materials from the Sterling Area. All these moves by the United States Administration were at bottom designed to check the growth in London's reserves, and this fact was eventually grasped by the British authorities who sometimes had their own and rather different motives for gracefully accepting the changes. When, for example, there was the question of extending reciprocal aid to raw materials, reckoned to cost $130 millions a year, the British thought not only of the relief in 'warding off further molestations of our gold and dollar balances', but also that 'on the whole this seems a small price to pay if it helps the President to further the general concept of financial pooling . . .' Similarly, when in the winter of 1943–44 London's reserves rose to $1200 millions and OLLA's attack on machine tools and various other lend-lease items opened, the United Kingdom authorities thought that they would at least get relief from arguments over many Export White Paper cases.[2]

That the Americans were thinking primarily of the growth of London's reserves was particularly apparent in the suggestion that 1st July 1943 should retrospectively be the commencing date for raw materials on reciprocal aid and that the United Kingdom should actually repay dollars received in the interim. A financial adjustment of this kind had no proper place in any scheme for the mutual free exchange of raw materials, as the Chancellor wrote to Mr. Morgenthau on 3rd September 1943. The time had come, he thought, to try to shake Mr. Morgenthau on the reserves question; and in his letter—to which a full statistical memorandum was attached—he explained how Britain's effort was causing rapid accumulation of external debt against which increasing reserves ought to be held.

---

[1] This ruling emerged from a ministerial committee which did not include Mr. Morgenthau. After receiving the President's approval it was regarded as a Presidential 'directive': it made Mr. White's personal assurance of October 1942 completely worthless.

[2] cf. above pp. 404-5. The list also included tobacco for the Armed Forces, which had been spared when tobacco for civilians was taken out in January 1943.

To this letter no reply was received. Private conversations indicated no change in the American position, but United Kingdom representatives took every opportunity to ensure that the United States Treasury at least acknowledged the existence of the British arguments, and of Britain's inability to agree to any outright limitation imposed by the United States Administration. Nevertheless, further cuts were made in lend-lease allocations to the United Kingdom, and, although some of these were inspired by new motives, it was all too clear that the growth of London's reserves was still regarded as invalidating the case for the current scale of aid. Further informal approaches elicited confirmation that, although Mr. Morgenthau and Mr. White were at least beginning to understand the existence of the United Kingdom's case, the official line of the Administration was still governed by the President's earlier ruling. Feelings were by this time running high. The price paid, a few weeks back, to push the President further along the road towards a proper pooling of resources appeared to have been wasted. There were invidious comparisons with Russia, which was receiving lend-lease without question, although it had reserves twice those of London[1] and no liabilities on the other side of the sheet. Representations on the highest level were imperative, and the Chancellor took the problem to the Prime Minister in anticipation of a projected meeting with the President. The question was in fact raised at their Cairo meeting; exactly what was said went unrecorded, but the Prime Minister appears to have wrung sympathetic words out of the President.

It was disappointing, to say the least, to find that this sympathy was not going to protect the United Kingdom from further massive cuts in the lend-lease programme. As a New Year's card, the British representatives in Washington were greeted with a new list of 'take-outs', presented in the first place as a unilateral decision by the United States Foreign Economic Administration. After protest at the 'intolerable' manner in which this was flung at the heads of the United Kingdom authorities, its finality was qualified and discussion was allowed to proceed. The discussion revealed that the items in the new list had been selected as open to political attack which might endanger the continuance of lend-lease, and Mr. Morgenthau, though he would not commit himself to paper, clearly implied that there was no present intention of reducing the United Kingdom's dollar balance in any other way. Mr. Morgenthau's implicit undertaking was repeated explicitly by a Foreign Economic Administration official a fortnight later. It seemed that these latest cuts were to be the end of the attack.

---

[1] This was what the United States Treasury believed at the time. It is still not possible to say what the figure actually was.

2E

They were not. Out of the blue, on 23rd February, came a telegram from the President to the Prime Minister. The sting was in the second paragraph.

> Quite apart from these lend-lease negotiations, I have been wondering whether it would be feasible for you to consider so ordering your financial affairs as to reduce your gold and dollar holdings available in this country to the neighbourhood of about $1 billion. What do you think should and can be done?

The indignant surprise with which this was received in London[1] naturally produced a variety of drafts for a stiff reply. On 9th March the Prime Minister replied by reiterating in forceful terms the broad case that had been put so repeatedly during 1943. A second telegram offered the suggestion that a portion of London's reserve might be put less conspicuously in the limelight. In reply, the President signalled no change: the matter should be discussed with the United States Treasury in Washington—a process that had already gone on so long and so fruitlessly.

There were thoughts during the next few months of returning to the charge, but in the absence of a renewed major assault from the American side, the United Kingdom Government eventually decided to defer further high-level discussion until it could be taken in conjunction with other broad issues in the Stage II negotiations in the autumn of 1944. Meanwhile reserves rose,[2] and the United States authorities politely averted their gaze. Various other excuses were found—particularly on low levels—for taking out small items from lend-lease, and the United Kingdom's desire to purchase its freedom in export policy[3] also helped to avert open conflict on the reserves issue.

The references to United States-Russian relations made in the President-Prime Minister exchanges in the winter of 1943–44, and the raising of temperatures in these discussions more generally, were in some measure an expression of a feeling of frustration and disappointment that had on the British side been boiling up for years. On the level of general principle, there was the disappointment at the absence of any move towards a pooling of financial resources, or towards any true reciprocity[4]. The Americans, being the paymasters, naturally felt themselves entitled to impose conditions which, according to their understanding, appeared reasonable

---

[1] 'Indignant surprise' was the Chancellor's expression when he minuted the Prime Minister on 24th February 1944.

[2] To $1,614 millions at mid-1944.

[3] cf. pp. 404-5 above.

[4] The President obviously lost interest in the pooling principle; this change may have been due to a desire to have a free hand for the United States in post-war arrangements.

enough. They continued, for example, to cut lend-lease and to look for increased reciprocal aid when London's reserves tended to increase. They did not offer more generous lend-lease, or offer to forego reciprocal aid, on the ground that United States gold reserves were unnecessarily high. Similarly, the Administration insisted on 'policing United Kingdom exports', although the Export White Paper was a unilateral statement, but they would not submit their own export trade to similar restrictions when raw materials were provided under reciprocal aid. And this attitude on fundamental principles was rubbed in all the time by the over-zealous scrutinizing and punctiliousness of certain branches of the United States Administration. The continuous inquisitions and criticisms to which British representatives were subjected by their American opposite numbers caused much private irritation and sense of frustration. It was just as well that the closeness and friendliness of personal contacts both in Washington and in London allowed a little private relief from time to time. On one such occasion a British representative ventilated a question of major interest. Why, he asked, were we subjected to these inquisitions from which the Russians were entirely free? The Americans admitted that the Russian attitude would be to refuse to answer questions and to say that they intended to go on with the war with American help if hey could get it, or without American help if they could not. Treasury officials sometimes, in their more frustrated moments, must have wondered whether they were doing right in devoting so much energy to the answering of American questions. Some of the most able men in the country were largely preoccupied with these Anglo-American financial relations, and the collection of information often involved a real drain on clerical man-power. Should the British have saved their energies by following Russia's taciturnity?

In reply to this question four important points may be made. First, an unco-operative taciturnity would have ruled out, or at least gravely impeded, the joint administration of resources. With all their limitations, the Combined Boards and the wider informal co-operation associated with them did succeed in a more economical distribution of pooled resources. If Britain had merely demanded supplies and taken only what the Americans would give without inquisition, Britain's war production would certainly have been less without any corresponding addition to America's efforts. Nor was it merely a matter of distribution of resources: the two countries had much to learn from each other in how to make the most of the available supplies, and this pooling of technical knowledge meant a real addition to the Allies' success in waging war. In short, the disposition to meet America's point of view made directly for efficiency in the immediate end of prosecution of the war.

Secondly, there were fellow-members of the Commonwealth to be considered. In a Grand Alliance, Russia might be able to play a lone hand, but Britain never could. With Britain there went into and out of the war a whole family of nations. The attitude of their Governments towards the United States Government, and even more the American attitude to the Commonwealth countries, would have been vitally different if Britain had not taken the lead in willingness to talk things over with the Americans. Closely linked with this was the position of sterling. Earlier in this chapter stress has been laid upon the difficulty encountered by London in securing American understanding of the peculiar position of sterling and of the importance of London's reserves, but at least there was some understanding, and under lend-lease Britain was allowed to accumulate and hold some reserves. Without this support—inadequate as it may have seemed—there could have been no continued confidence in sterling in India and other parts of the Commonwealth, in the Middle East or indeed anywhere in the world. Shaky and reluctant as it sometimes seemed, America's support of sterling was critical for the maintenance of war supplies both inside and outside the Commonwealth.

Thirdly, the long years of argument between American and British officials, in spite of all the irritations and misunderstandings, did in the end yield a net balance of understanding, of mutual respect and of personal friendship. This was a fund upon which Britain was able to draw, to the great advantage of all, when post-war problems had to be tackled. The process of educating responsible Americans in the mysteries of the Sterling Area and the British economic position has been difficult enough in all conscience; without the background of war-time discussions and contacts it would have been a hopeless task.

Thus for both war-time and post-war reasons British policy had to contrast with Russia's aloof taciturnity. But there is a fourth reason which in the longest run is perhaps the most important of all. In an important sense Britain was not fighting the war against 'one man', nor against any nation; rather we (and the Americans too) were fighting for a principle, the principle that when differences arise they must be argued out between reasonable people. The strength of Anglo-American friendship, not only for waging war but also in the years ahead, depended upon the application of this principle in every sphere of Anglo-American relations. The British financial authorities were therefore surely right to aim always at bringing differences to the conference table where they could be candidly faced and thrashed out between reasonable men. Washington habits did not, it is true, readily lend themselves to this ideal: the Administration would take unilateral decisions affecting Britain's vital interests, and coherent discussion was all too often impossible in Washington meetings. Nevertheless, it was right that British representatives should stomach—as they did— these administrative peculiarities, and just continue the struggle to persuade.

There could, then, be no imitation of Russia's attitude. British representatives had to curb their impatience and bear with the American procedures. But how far and how fast should they give way to American demands, demands that seemed ever more threatening to Britain's economic viability? Were the Treasury representatives right to show caution and hesitation at every turn? Or should they have been more compliant, casting Britain's bread upon the waters in the confidence that American generosity, uninhibited by suspicions of London's cleverness, would always make all well on the night? There were sometimes important differences within the Treasury on this question, and it is notable that the bread-casting theory was most strongly held by officials in close contact with American officials of high but not quite the highest rank. At that level frankness and understanding were perhaps at their maximum, uncluttered by the more professional political instincts found at the very top.

Just what middle course should have been held between the two extremes, of Russian taciturnity on the one hand and unprotesting compliance on the other, is impossible to judge in a general way. A course did however have to be chosen day by day by the British authorities. Naturally enough, it varied from time to time. There were times when United Kingdom Ministers and their advisers were inclined to think their opposite numbers too slow to say 'Boo' to Congressmen playing a professional politician's game, and that a bid directly to United States public opinion would be profitable.[1] But on the whole, and despite accumulating frustrations, lengthening and deepening knowledge of American personalities and American ways strengthened readiness to put all cards on the table. Certainly as they collected their thoughts in the summer of 1944, preparing to negotiate the reorientation demanded by Stage II, it was this attitude of extreme frankness that prevailed among the Chancellor's advisers.

---

[1] There were episodes in 1944-45 in which the expected Congressional difficulties did not materialise: the most important related to London's reserves (see p.471, footnote 1) and the easing of the Export White Paper restrictions (see pp. 473-4). Lord Keynes, writing after the Stage II negotiations, said that his experiences in Washington had taught him 'the value of our excellent system of professional scapegoats, known as Ministers, with skins thickened by experience or natural endowment, whose duty it is to suffer vicariously for the sins of all the administrative tribe. American officials are open to Press abuse and Congressional criticism. Yet they are without any real responsibility or adequate opportunity to reply and it saps their nerve.'

CHAPTER XIV

THE SHADOW OF DEBT, 1944–45

I: THE DEFENCE OF STERLING

(i)

Indebtedness to Other Parts of the World

FROM THE EARLIEST days of the war we have tried to
avoid incurring debts in foreign currencies or in gold. In
this we have been successful beyond any expectation which
would have been reasonable before the event. There is
the Jesse Jones loan in United States dollars which we can
liquidate at any time by selling the marketable securities
hypothecated against it. There is the no-interest loan in
Canadian dollars, corresponding to Canadian securities we
ourselves hold. There is the gold set aside against our debt to
Portugal. . . . . Apart from these we owe the outside world
nothing but sterling. . . . . We have persuaded the outside
world to lend us upwards of the prodigious total of £3,000
millions.

So WROTE LORD KEYNES at the beginning of the review of the
external debt with which he prefaced his paper on 'Overseas
Financial Policy in Stage III' in the spring of 1945. He was
characteristically quick to claim a paradoxical comfort: 'The very
size', he continued, 'of these sterling debts is itself a protection.
The old saying holds. Owe your banker £1,000 and you are at
his mercy; owe him £1,000,000 and the position is reversed'.
Unfortunately the old saying was not perfectly apt, for Britain
owed this sum not to one 'banker' but to many—to a number of
creditors who were widely diverse in political attitude toward
Britain, in their own economic problems and in the urgency of
their post-war needs. Nevertheless, it was necessary to look at the
picture as a whole if, in the final stages, Britain's approach to the
United States for a financial settlement was to have an
appropriately broad basis. The Anglo-American negotiations from
the autumn of 1944 until the end of the war were coloured, and
rightly coloured, by the existence of Britain's indebtedness to many
other countries. It is therefore appropriate before reviewing (in the
next chapter) those Anglo-American negotiations, to glance back at
the accumulation of Britain's liabilities in other directions.

438

At the end of 1944, the external liabilities of the United Kingdom had grown to £3,073 millions, and by mid-1945 they had grown further to £3,355 millions. The corresponding figure at the end of 1939 had been about £550 millions[1].

These liabilities were distributed as follows:

	£ millions	
	end-1944	mid-1945
STERLING AREA		
Australia, New Zealand, South Africa, Eire	342	384
India, Burma, Iraq, Palestine and other Middle East	1537	1732
Colonies and other Sterling Area countries	555	607
Total Sterling Area . . .	2434	2723
NORTH AND SOUTH AMERICA . .	280	303
EUROPE AND OVERSEAS DEPENDENCIES .	299	267
REST OF WORLD	60	62
Total . .	3073	3355

Within the Sterling Area, the total balances held included working balances in the hands of private banks and funds held by the Currency Boards and Crown Agents for the Colonies as well as the accumulations in the hands of Central Banks. About 40 per cent. of the whole was in respect of India, over 20 per cent. represented the Colonial Empire, and 15 per cent. represented Egypt and the Sudan—the remaining one-quarter representing the Southern Dominions, the Irish Republic, and a number of other territories. These Sterling Area balances had been rising at the rate of about £600 millions a year from the end of 1942 onwards, and the rise continued until the end of the war.

Liabilities to countries outside the Sterling Area were more or less stable during the latter years of the war. Apart from the United States and Canada, the biggest elements in these balances were for Argentine and Brazil in South America, and a number of European countries of which Portugal, Norway and Holland (with their dependencies) were the most important.

At the end of 1944 the total had already passed £3,000 millions and the rate of growth was causing anxiety. When Keynes was writing early in the spring of 1945, it seemed reasonable to assume that, if the war ended early in 1946, Britain's debt to the other

---

[1] These are the figures quoted, according to the definitions then current, in the Anglo-American Loan negotiations in autumn 1945 (Cmd. 6707, tables 6 and 7). A more complete analysis, more consistent with the definitions used in post-war Balance-of-Payments White Papers, appears in Cmd. 8354 of September, 1951. (For these figures see Appendix I, Table 8). The area definitions in particular differ considerably from those current in 1945.

Sterling Area countries would total total £3,000 millions and her debt to the rest of the world (including the Jesse Jones loan from the United States and the Canadian interest-free loan) another £1,000 millions. And it was perfectly clear that through a transition period after the war Britain's current earning capacity in the outside world would fall a long way short—by hundreds of millions a quarter—of her subsistence needs.

Of the total indebtedness, the large items relating to the United States, Canada, India, the Middle East and the Southern Dominions have been discussed in earlier chapters.[1] Brief reference, looking back to the early days and forward to the end of the war, must now be made to financial relations with certain other areas—the Colonial Empire, South American neutrals, European neutrals and certain Allies in Europe.

(ii)

Financial Relations with the Colonies

The story of financial relations with the Colonial territories is essentially one of the extension to those territories of the policies ruling at home, with the important qualification that an eye was kept all the time on the development and welfare aims which were receiving special attention immediate before the war. The general peace-time principle had been that the Colonies should finance their own defence forces and indeed should be generally self-supporting. In the immediately pre-war years this general principle of self-support had begun to be seriously questioned, and the outbreak of war caught British Colonial policy on the threshold of a new phase, enlarging the United Kingdom taxpayer's responsibility for some expenditure on Colonial development and welfare. The particular principle of the financing by the Colonies of their own defence forces remained unchanged, although the United Kingdom Treasury expected to find the money where defence expenditure was related to the wider purposes of Imperial defence.

On the outbreak of war the Colonial Governments were given general guidance bringing them into line with developments at home: they were to have their own exchange restrictions, conforming as far as possible with those applicable in the United Kingdom;[2] they were in particular to have regard to the need for economising in dollars; they were to step up their defence expenditures at the

---

[1] For the Jesse Jones loan, see Chapter XII; Canada, Chapter XI; India and the Middle East, Chapter IX; Southern Dominions, Chapter X.

[2] cf. p. 235 above.

expense of increased taxation, and they were to encourage voluntary savings to check inflation and to help the Empire's war effort generally. Their defence Services were developed in consultation with the Service Departments at home, and London accepted new responsibilities for the additional equipment and stores. Responsibility for the financing of this additional defence effort was settled for each Colony separately. For some of the Colonies the formula adopted was that the United Kingdom Treasury found everything above 125 per cent. of the Colony's pre-war defence expenditure, though the wind was tempered to other Colonies whose financial position was weaker; these agreements continued in force throughout the war and for some time after. Colonial Governments were asked to mobilise savings by their own issues of bonds, and these conformed with the United Kingdom policy of holding interest rates at low and stable levels throughout the war.[1] In all these arrangements the Colonial territories were conforming with those made in other parts of the Commonwealth; their willingness to support the war was further demonstrated by gifts from internal revenues, gifts which in effect supplemented the agreed contributions to the cost of the armed forces. Meanwhile expenditure by the Imperial Government under the new Colonial development and welfare policy was, like expenditure on social welfare at home, held back though never completely suppressed.

The calamities of 1940 had the effect in the Colonies, as elsewhere, of whipping up enthusiasm for the war, so increasing expenditure on the armed forces; this increase, in accordance with the 1939 arrangements, fell mainly on the home exchequer. There were other important effects. The fall of France upset the strategic situation of the Colonial Empire—in particular the defection of French territories in Africa exposed the British African Colonies to unforeseen dangers.[2] The new conditions also tended to accentuate the divergent economic experience of the various Territories. While Malaya, Ceylon, Northern Rhodesia, Trinidad and British Guiana were enjoying unprecedented demands for their staple exports, others—West Africa, Jamaica and Palestine among them— were falling into deep depression.[3] These economic developments and reassessment of the Colonial political situation in a prolonged war led to a review of economic policy in 1941. The effort to raise Colonial standards of living could not be postponed indefinitely, and when Lord Moyne went to the Colonial Office, the Prime Minister enjoined him to make all possible progress under the Colonial Development and Welfare Act. Unnecessary consumption

---

[1] H. of C. Deb., Vol. 376, Cols. 494-6 (20th November 1941).

[2] *The Economist*, 30th November 1940.

[3] *The Economist*, 22nd February 1941 (article, 'Colonial Black Spots').

had of course to be restricted even more rigorously than before, both by import restrictions and by taxation. To the extent that the enforced economies of war-time could not, during the war, be matched by expenditure on new development schemes, the Colonies would have spare financial resources. In the light of long-term policies, it was inappropriate that these should be gifts to the cause of Imperial defence; instead, they might be used as interest-free loans until after the war, when their repayment would come in useful to finance the larger schemes that would then be possible.[1]

Meanwhile shipping stringency, the general shift in the import programmes of a world at war, and the upheaval of world prices were demanding other action. Some Colonies, finding their markets collapsing, were supported by bulk purchase, even where the products had to be destroyed. Others, meeting enlarged demands at rising prices, were experiencing inflation. For the latter territories London's policy was to avert the Colonial inflation and moderate the burden on the United Kingdom Treasury by making long-term contracts at prices below world prices. This method was reasonable only if the rise in the cost of living in the Colonies could be restrained, and here again the United Kingdom's policy at home set a precedent for the subsidisation of certain items for stabilisation purposes. The authorities were aware that there might be awkward problems ahead, if world prices did not come down after the war to meet the artificially low levels at which certain Colonial products were thus held. But while the war lasted the Colonies benefited by the moderation of inflationary disturbance of their economies without losing the substance which was in any case unobtainable; and the Mother Country benefited by moderation of the sterling claims which these more prosperous Colonies were accumulating.

Nevertheless, the war went on long enough to allow these accumulations to become, for the more fortunate Colonies, substantial. When the war ended the balances of East and Central Africa totalled £133 millions, that of West Africa £93 millions and that of Malaya £87 millions; the total for all Colonies was £670 millions.[2] This was part of the debt the United Kingdom had to shoulder and—not foreseeing quite how things would work out in the post-war world—the United Kingdom authorities had to envisage the probability that the Colonies would want to spend the sterling after the war, and to spend it elsewhere if the United Kingdom itself could not provide the goods. The policy of 'Development and Welfare', which the United Kingdom was

---

[1] The Colonial Secretary likened such loans to the post-war credits system recently embodied in the income tax and excess profits tax at home.

[2] These figures include 'normal' balances, which might be reckoned an appreciable proportion of this total.

determined to implement fully after the war,[1] would argue in favour
of allowing the Colonies to spend the claims they had accumulated.
The policy indicated, moreover, a determination to spend on these
objects the proceeds of United Kingdom taxation. Clearly the
finance of Colonial development was likely to be a source of strain
on the United Kingdom balance of payments after the war.

(iii)

South American Sterling

Among the debts to neutrals, there were two important items in
South America: the Argentine's sterling balance, running close to
£100 millions at the end of the war, and Brazil's running up towards
£40 millions. Each one of the South American countries has its
own tangled story of financial relations with war-time Britain, and
the burden on the highly-skilled manpower of the Bank of England
and the Treasury was quite disproportionate to the attention that
can be given in a review of this kind. Each country had its own
peculiarities, its interest for Britain as a source of supply, its political
atmosphere and attitude to Britain, its arrangement of monetary
affairs, its dependence on British capital and its long-run interests
in the outside world. But in spite of this diversity, it is possible to
see a certain uniformity in the approach by British experts to the
problems of financial relations with all these countries. First, there
was the vital necessity to establish and maintain payment
arrangements that would facilitate the flow of essential supplies,
and to ensure that these arrangements involved the minimum burden
on Britain's available gold and hard currency reserves. Secondly,
there was the desire, as explained in Chapter VIII, to establish
'official rates of exchange' for sterling as the sole basis for war-time
trade, and to starve out of existence the free market for sterling.
Thirdly, there was some concern for established British financial
interests in these countries—not out of any tenderness for individual
investors, but purely to maximise over a period their contribution
to Britain's invisible income from abroad. Lastly, there was concern
for Britain's general commercial stake in these countries. Traditional
trade connections in South America were known to be of great value
to Britain as an exporting country. As the war went on, British
representatives had to stand by and see one by one the old
connections broken—broken, it seemed irremediably, just when
the immense task of a post-war export drive was looming ahead.

---

[1] This was already apparent in the House of Commons debate on Colonial policy,
20th November 1941 (H. of C. Deb., Vol. 376, Col. 516). The determination infused
all subsequent discussions of Colonial policy, both inside and outside official circles.

For the most part, the British authorities had to swallow these losses and to watch American interests stepping into their shoes, but there were times when these issues were taken into account—at least they were never forgotten.

The biggest South American problem, in terms of what was at stake, was the Argentine. This country was an extremely important source of supplies—food, feedingstuffs for the agricultural programme, and hides for keeping armies and people adequately shod. There were substantial British investments in the railways, public utilities and elsewhere in the country; these were able to provide means of payment for Britain, and they helped to provide a market for British export industries. On the other side, the Argentine habitually depended upon British coal and tinplate. With these mutual interests, strong banking connections between the two countries, and a centralised control of exchange transactions in Buenos Aires, it was not difficult for the Bank of England to secure, in October 1939, a payments arrangement which the Bank preferred to call not an 'Agreement' but a *'Modus Vivendi'*.[1] This provided, in effect, that all transactions between the Argentine and the Sterling Area should be settled in Special Account sterling, canalised through the Argentine Central Bank.[2] It envisaged the use by the Argentine of any surplus accruals of sterling for the purchase of Argentine securities held in Great Britain; pending such purchases, any surplus above a working balance should be protected against depreciation of sterling, by the setting aside of gold at the Bank of England for the account of the Argentine Central Bank, such gold to be available only for resale to the Bank of England. This 'gold-set-aside clause' was used in other payments agreements concluded by the Bank of England at this period;[3] the 15 per cent. depreciation of sterling in 1939 was still fresh in the memory, and it was therefore necessary to concede this protection to suppliers who, when so protected, were willing to hold sterling.[4]

This *Modus Vivendi* was renewed for three months from 25th January 1940, and for six months from 25th April 1940. Before the expiry of the latter period the complexion of the war, of the Argentine economic situation and of the United Kingdom's external finances had all changed so radically that, although the arrangements had

---

[1] It was characteristic of the division of labour—and knowledge—between the Treasury and the Bank of England in Latin American questions at this time that the precise terms of the agreement between the central banks were not known to the Treasury until the autumn of 1940.

[2] For some transactions pesos remained unavoidable; to allow for these the Argentine Central Bank undertook to supply the Bank of England with pesos at $16 \cdot 9575 = \pounds 1$.

[3] e.g. with Brazil, Uruguay and the Nitrate Corporation of Chile.

[4] As actual gold was set aside, the Argentine Central Bank was not allowed any interest on its sterling balance.

proved technically satisfactory, both Governments were disposed
to look for some change. The intensified blockade, now covering
a much larger part of Europe, and Britain's increasing shipping
difficulties had greatly aggravated the problem of South American
'surpluses'—surpluses of commodities normally exported—and the
Argentine Government therefore pressed for United Kingdom
commitments to certain minimum purchases irrespective of shipping
availabilities. At the same time Argentina was desperately short of
coal; in fact a little later the problems of coal shortage and maize
surplus became so acute that the Argentines married the two
problems by burning maize as fuel. The British, for their part, were
concerned that the Argentine authorities had not used their surplus
sterling for repatriation of securities, and therefore had gold set
aside already to the amount of £6¼ millions, with much more in
prospect. The inclination to leave alone a technical arrangement
that was working well was therefore suppressed, and from the
summer of 1940 onwards various drafts of an agreement between
the two Governments were sporadically under discussion. Although
British officials sometimes thought that the draft was almost ready
for signature, no new agreement was in fact made during the war
period. The *Modus Vivendi* of 1939 continued to govern transactions,
subject only to a revision, agreed in October 1940, of the gold
clause. From that date additions to the Argentine sterling balances
were no longer covered by the actual setting aside of gold; instead
the Argentine Central Bank accepted a revaluation guarantee. The
effect of this change was that, while the Argentine retained its
protection against depreciation of sterling, the United Kingdom
ceased to provide actual gold and the Argentine Central Bank
received interest on its surplus sterling. The failure for so long to
clinch a new agreement was due partly to the weakness of the
British bargaining position, and partly to political uncertainties
in the Argentine. The British, though needing a minimum of
Argentine supplies so desperately that they were compelled to run
up a large debt guaranteed in gold, could give the Argentine
satisfaction neither in adequate purchases of her surplus products
nor in maintaining an adequate flow of coal and other supplies.
Argentine willingness nevertheless to hold an increasing amount of
sterling, and likewise British willingness to run up such a debt
unprotected by any firm agreement about its disposal, depended
upon the knowledge that the sterling could and would be used for
the purchase of British investments in the Argentine. At first, when
the sums involved looked reasonably small, the idea was that
Argentine securities should be repatriated piecemeal. But by the
spring of 1941, when the Argentine's sterling balance had risen
to £8 millions and its further growth was obviously going to be

substantial, an Argentine Government project to nationalise the British-owned railways was revived. For some considerable time the project had, for reasons of internal Argentine politics, to remain in the background. There was also some reluctance on the British side, due to appreciation of the importance of this British railway organisation as a backbone of the British commercial community in the Argentine.

During late 1942 and 1943, however, circumstances made agreement more likely on terms the British could accept. Washington was taking an interest and was disinclined to see any weakness towards the Argentine, and, partly on account of the growth of debt within the Sterling Area, views against any gold concessions to the Argentine hardened. Then a political revolution in the Argentine in mid-1943 made the nationalisation of the railways a feasible proposition. From then until the end of the war this subject was under continual discussion between the two Governments; once it was clear that this would be the solvent of the Argentine sterling balances, the British were inclined to play long in order to get a fair price. Meanwhile, they no longer sought any repatriation of Argentine Government and other bonds, as the piecemeal approach would have left the balance too small to cover the single major operation of railway nationalisation. Not until the Eady Mission went to the Argentine after the war was the business settled—by the Anglo-Argentine Agreement of 17th September 1946. The knowledge that a debt of over £100 millions (to which the Argentine balance rose late in 1945) could and would be disposed of in this way was, however, a great consolation to the United Kingdom Treasury long before the consummation.

With Brazil the problems were, for the British, altogether easier and smaller. In the early stages Brazil was chronically short of sterling, and Anglo-Brazilian trade did not seem to the United Kingdom authorities to make a payments agreement essential. In the spring of 1940, however, the anxiety to kill the free market in sterling led to negotiation and an Agreement was signed on 7th August 1940. In this a 'gold-set-aside' clause of the kind then common was easily conceded by Britain, Brazil's prospective continuing shortage of sterling making it a matter of little importance. Both before and after the agreement the really important problem was how to keep Brazil supplied with sufficient sterling to enable her to conform to the agreement consistently with servicing her foreign debt. Again and again the United Kingdom Treasury advanced sterling to Brazil to enable her to maintain these payments, on the ground that a debt service once in default too easily remains in default. In 1940–41, in preference to continuing or enlarging these advances, the Treasury asked the

Ministry of Supply to make special purchases of Brazilian cotton, though Brazilian requests for a British commitment to a purchasing programme were resisted. Instead, Brazil's sterling shortage was eased by allowing the transfer to her, in payment for her exports, of sterling held by Canada and other countries.[1] No sooner was this done than Brazil began to accumulate sterling—not at the Argentine rate, but at a rate embarrassing enough. This was due in part to the fall in United Kingdom exports, but more to the intensification of British demands for Brazilian products, especially rubber to replace the lost supplies from the Far East. There was always, however, the sponge of Brazil's old debts ready to absorb any heavy accumulation of sterling, so that although Brazil finished the war with some £40 millions of sterling, this did not cause many sleepless nights for the guardians of Britain's finances.

Elsewhere in South America sterling balances were not uncomfortably large. The Peruvian story had much similarity with the Brazilian: in the earlier years, the United Kingdom made special purchases in order to provide Peru with sufficient sterling to avoid default on her old-standing financial obligations to Britain, but the swing in the trade balance in mid-war left Peru long of sterling at the end. Chile, thanks to her important fertiliser exports, was well in hand with sterling at quite an early date; Bolivia and Uruguay, as sources of metals and cattle products respectively, also tended to accumulate balances after the early lean years. All of them had their problems for the United Kingdom Treasury, which had to keep them, as holders of sterling, happy enough to maintain sterling's longer-term chances as an international currency. But there was not with any of them a major problem of staving off a gigantic creditor.

(iv)

Financial Relations with the European Neutrals

Among the European neutrals, the problems varied from the Spaniards' chronic shortage of sterling to the embarrassingly large accumulation in Portuguese hands, with the Swiss and Swedish problems in between. The Civil War had left Spain almost destitute,

---

[1] These 'third-country' transfers of sterling had important attractions for the United Kingdom: they moderated the embarrassing increases in the sterling holdings of some countries, and they helped to maintain the reputation of sterling as an international currency. But it was important to avoid generalisation of the process, which could easily have allowed a market, at depreciated rates, to spring up in 'transferable sterling'. The balance of advantage lay clearly in the general policy of bilateralisation of payments and persuading countries to hold the sterling they themselves accumulated, and in the final stages the United Kingdom authorities rarely agreed to any deviation from this general line.

and only by a special clearing arrangement was it possible to maintain any flow of trade in 1939. Though she did have some valuable war-time products (iron ore, pyrites and mercury among them), Spain had little chance in the conditions of 1939–45 to shake her economy free from a hand-to-mouth basis. The practical question was always how much support must be afforded to her in order to buttress her neutrality against German seduction. The experts on strategy attached high importance to continuing Spanish neutrality, and United Kingdom Treasury policy vis-à-vis Madrid was dominated by this thought. This policy, integrating Spain with the war-time sterling system, was both important and successful, but it never threatened to place Spain among Britain's post-war creditors.

Switzerland's financial strength contrasted sharply with Spain's penury. Here the bargaining conditions did not allow Britain to draw resources against the neutral's need for sterling or willingness to accumulate a sterling balance. The practical problems, while the war lasted, were to ensure exclusive use of the official rate of exchange and to avoid indebtedness in terms of Swiss currency. But the United Kingdom authorities did at first try for a payments agreement, under which the United Kingdom would be able to cover the anticipated heavily adverse balance of payments by payment of sterling which the Swiss National Bank would hold. The Swiss, on their side, wanted the United Kingdom to maintain some import of luxury goods from Switzerland which Britain could not afford. Also the Swiss disliked both the mechanism necessary for enforcing a payments agreement, and the precedent such an agreement might afford to the Germans from whom pressure was to be expected; and they wanted $3\frac{1}{2}$ per cent. interest for a bankers' credit in Swiss francs. There being no basis here for an agreement, the United Kingdom carried on without. While Swiss importers were able to use cheap sterling bought on the free market, the Anglo-Swiss position threatened embarrassment with other countries whose transactions were all at the official rate,[1] but this difficulty disappeared when the more effective exchange regulations were made in June 1940.[2]

Relations were at this juncture substantially changed by the fall of France. The adverse balance which had hitherto been running looked as though it might disappear. It also became necessary for measures of economic warfare to be toughened, and from this time onwards Swiss anxiety for relief from these measures afforded a useful bargaining weapon in British hands; use of it was qualified

---

[1] This became important when the free sterling rate fell sharply in the spring of 1940.

[2] For the United Kingdom exchange control developments, see Chapter VIII above.

only by appreciation of Switzerland's value as Protecting Power. The Swiss continued to offer bankers' credits—in Swiss francs—at rates of interest the British would not stomach, and payments continued to be on a hand-to-mouth basis, the British buying as little as they could and paying gold deposited in Canada. Late in 1942 negotiations reached the point of a draft agreement. This provided for the Swiss to hold a small amount of sterling, on which they were to have an exchange guarantee; beyond this Britain was to pay gold in London or Ottawa. The agreement was never signed; the Swiss continued to accept gold in Ottawa (for which they had little war-time use) without any formal agreement. Late in 1943, feeling the pressure of the blockade, the Swiss showed renewed interest in the 1942 draft. At this time the United Kingdom was not interested in the accumulation of sterling in Swiss hands; British officials anticipated an adverse balance of some £10 millions in 1944, and were quite ready to see this amount of gold go. This suited the Swiss, especially when they found that the British (and the Americans) were now willing to let gold go actually to Europe.[1] The British, for their part, were willing enough to get away from the hand-to-mouth basis, and sensed the general value—especially for the next stage—of better economic relations with Switzerland. An agreement was therefore initialled at the end of 1943, whereby the United Kingdom was to be provided with Swiss francs against gold in London, the Swiss having the right to take the gold to the Continent. The agreement was to run for a minimum of one year, thereafter being subject to three months' notice on either side.

As the European war came to an end, some alteration became urgent. The United Kingdom needed all the credit it could get on tolerable terms; even more it had to avoid special terms with any one country which might be ground of complaint from some other country. The Swiss fought hard to lend Swiss francs, rather than to hold sterling. When they saw that the British would not play on this basis, they pressed for an exchange guarantee to protect them against depreciation of any sterling they should hold. The British authorities would have none of this: they were now conceding an exchange guarantee to no-one in Europe. A Swiss negotiator was asked 'to discover good reasons for depreciating sterling, which he said he was quite unable to do'. In the end, the United Kingdom quite ruthlessly exercised the threat of excluding Switzerland from sharing in the benefit of the revival of United Kingdom tourist expenditure in Western Europe, and the Swiss fell into line. The Agreement[2] provided that the Swiss would in three years

---

[1] Hitherto the Anglo-American view had been that gold in Europe might come in useful for the Germans; this view was now dropped.

[2] Signed on 12th March 1946, Cmd. 6756.

2F

accumulate up to £15 millions sterling, of which £10 millions could be in the first year. Thus, having been forced by the Swiss attitude to pay their way through the war, the British authorities at the end exercised their new bargaining power to borrow from Switzerland during the transition period.

Relations with Sweden were not unlike those with Switzerland: through most of the war the British bargaining position was relatively weak and it was not until post-war prospects became dominant that British negotiators were able to wring substantial credit facilities from the Swedish authorities. In the first winter of the war the United Kingdom had to make heavy purchases of timber, woodpulp and special steels; after the German occupation of Norway and Denmark, imports were limited to such small supplies of vital metal products as were worth running through the blockade, and the shipping services became the only important item in the balance of payments. Sweden, for her part, was able to get from Britain few of the supplies she needed and perforce turned to Germany. This economic dependence on Germany had serious repercussions on her relations with Britain; it was, for example, only in 1943 that Sweden was persuaded to put an end to certain unneutral arrangements such as the facilities for the transit of German troops. The bargaining position led, when a payments agreement was negotiated in December 1939, to concession of gold settlement for almost the whole balance accruing to Sweden.[1] Gold due to Sweden was to be delivered in London or South Africa at Sweden's option, and it was to be freely disposable.

This agreement was renewed from time to time, the only important modification being that in February 1941, when the United Kingdom was desperately short of gold. The liability to pay gold was limited to £650,000 a month, any amount above this being held as sterling by Sweden until the end of the war, when it was to be convertible into gold at the price fixed in the original agreement. Even this concession to British needs was terminated in the renewal at March 1943, the position then becoming that all balances over £3·6 millions were convertible into gold immediately. As the end of the war came into prospect, the bargaining position swung in Britain's favour, and the United Kingdom authorities decided to exploit their relative strength to extract some credit from Sweden in the transition period, and to get it on terms that would not reflect adversely on the standing of sterling. The United Kingdom Departments were interested in placing long-term contracts in Sweden (timber and shipping were the big items) but

---

[1] An odd feature of the first agreement was that it covered only United Kingdom, and not all Sterling Area payments to Sweden. This administratively awkward limitation was removed when the agreement was renewed.

they were persuaded to hold off pending re-negotiation of the payments agreement. Sweden saw that her own need for British goods was going to be extreme: Britain might have difficulty in supplying them, but a disorganised and devastated Germany was going to have even greater difficulty. Also, Swedish producers were extremely keen to re-establish their markets in Britain: their anxiety showed itself in the offer of private banking credits secretly made in London in the autumn of 1944.[1] Lastly, Sweden's wider international interests were so important to her that her Government was willing to pay a price in order to help in the re-establishment of international monetary relations on a sound footing; the United Kingdom negotiators had merely to persuade the Swedes that the 'sterling club' was the one to join for this purpose.

The United Kingdom approach was on the basis that Britain required about £50 millions[2] credit to cover the adverse balance during the transition period (in effect, to enable her to buy goods and services Sweden desperately wanted to sell), that Sweden should, like the South American neutrals, be prepared to hold large amounts of sterling without any corresponding United Kingdom liability to hold kronor, and that the United Kingdom was going to hold the foreign exchange value of sterling fixed but was not going to give exchange guarantees to anybody. The Swedes resisted on three points. The figure of £50 millions looked uncomfortably large, and might be quoted as a precedent by another powerful neighbour wanting goods on credit. Secondly, if the credit was not to be in kronor, the value of their sterling must be protected by an exchange guarantee. Thirdly, they wanted firm undertakings about supplies from Britain—above all, they wanted to be sure of coal. After a winter of tough negotiations, and confirmation by the War Cabinet of the central principles the United Kingdom negotiators were seeking to enforce, agreement was at last reached on 6th March 1945. The first and third Swedish objections were overcome by the replacement of a figure by a mutual undertaking to hold each other's currency without limit, and an exchange of information as to probable British requirements and probable British supplies. The Swedes thus knew what order of credit they were granting, without openly committing themselves to a figure that might prove an awkward precedent, while the

---

[1] The offer was rejected because the United Kingdom authorities preferred to keep all such arrangements outside ordinary commercial channels. By dealing with all countries on an inter-governmental or inter-central bank basis, it was easier to apply common principles, to employ non-commercial arguments, and to prepare for subsequent internationalisation of sterling.

[2] This estimate (sometimes stated as £52 millions) gained some mystical significance from the fact that it coincided with the amount of gold actually paid by the United Kingdom to Sweden during the war.

British gave some indication of what might be available without formal guarantee of specific supplies.

The Swedish request for an exchange guarantee had, in particular, been the subject of prolonged argument, but on this the British stood absolutely firm. A Bank of England official told Riksbank representatives on 9th November 1944 that he 'knew the Chancellor's mind on this and was absolutely certain that the Chancellor would not budge an inch on a proposal which struck at the very roots of his plans for rehabilitating sterling. Before the war such a proposal would never have been considered and although we had had to concede a few guarantees during the early part of the war when things were going badly for us we were all determined to get rid of them at the earliest possible opportunity, which so far as Sweden was concerned meant *now*'. The real point was that the United Kingdom was determined to establish confidence in sterling by showing that all the other countries who were going to hold sterling had agreed to hold it without guarantee. A sterling in which there was such demonstrable confidence had a reasonable chance of becoming once more a freely transferable currency—in fact, a genuinely international currency.

The best known Portuguese exports to Britain are probably her wine and sardines, and it might be supposed that expenditure in that direction could easily be cut to a negligible figure in total war. But there are other items, such as cork and rosin, that did not lend themselves readily to control in the early part of the war and were anyway partly needed for war production; also there were important pre-emptive purchases to be paid for, and the sardines had a special value in maintaining the vestigial variety that made war-time feeding tolerable. The general political and economic position of the country had also to be considered: although the Portuguese Government was particularly friendly towards Britain, German propaganda was always active, and it would have been impolitic to ignore Portugal's dependence—and that of her colonies—on a substantial flow of international trade.

These considerations were perhaps not thought out very coherently in United Kingdom financial circles in the early part of the war, when attention was fully engrossed in other directions. Portugal was brought into the circle of bilateral sterling countries simply as part of the broad operation of killing the market in free sterling, and it was certainly not by original design that she became the holder of a substantial sterling balance. When the United Kingdom authorities recognised Lisbon as an important potential market in free sterling,[1] they decided that there must be an agreement of

---

[1] There was no exchange control in Lisbon, and the market there in all the principal currencies was both free and flexible.

the 'special accounts' type, and a Ministry of Economic Warfare representative was instructed to open negotiations in Lisbon. After various interim arrangements, an agreement between the two central banks was signed on 20th November 1940; it was accompanied by an exchange of letters between the two Governments fixing the rate of exchange at 100 escudos to the £. All transactions between the two monetary areas were to be conducted in sterling and channelled through a system of special accounts. Apart from a working margin, Portugal's sterling balance was to earn interest in London, and was guaranteed in terms of gold. At the termination of the agreement there were to be discussions on the terms of delivery of gold for this balance: this delivery was to be within five years after termination of the agreement, and until precise terms were settled the sterling balance could be used only for payments to the Sterling Area.

Early in 1941 the United Kingdom authorities became concerned at the rate at which Portugal was accumulating sterling under this agreement, having regard to the United Kingdom's reserve position and the fact that the balance would become convertible into gold within five years of termination. It was suggested that Portugal might be allowed to use some of her sterling for settlements with third countries—a proposal that always had the attraction that it constituted a reminder of sterling's tradition as an international currency. But there were dangers in setting the fashion, particularly the danger that a run of transfers of sterling among the special account countries might well end with Portugal holding even more sterling than at the beginning. So no initiative of this kind was taken. The balances continued to climb: £18 millions at the end of 1941, £37 millions at the end of 1942, and prospectively going above £50 millions in 1943. During 1943, therefore, when the United Kingdom authorities for a time were paradoxically embarrassed by their accumulation of gold,[1] there was some suggestion that part of Portugal's balance should be paid off in gold. When difficulties were being encountered with the Swiss, expenditure on Swiss francs in Lisbon, where there was a market in them, had special attractions, and this added to the case for offering gold to Lisbon. But there were doubts about the timeliness of talking afresh to the Portuguese—they might have awkward requests to make about commodities—and the question dragged on until London's revised attitude on its gold reserves silenced it in 1944. Meanwhile Portugal's balance had passed £55 millions at the end of 1943.

In the autumn of 1944 Anglo-Portuguese financial relations began to assume their post-war look. Far from being willing to pay

---

[1] See p. 431 *et seq.*

gold immediately to reduce the debt, the British now tried to persuade Portugal to drop her right to gold within five years and to agree to future transactions being conducted on the basis that London was seeking to enforce for Western Europe generally. All that Britain had to offer was membership of a club whose common interest should be in rebuilding the position of sterling, and a readiness to purchase a moderate quantity of certain luxury goods. An essential preliminary was to get a partial freezing of the Portuguese sterling balance. On this the Portuguese appeared surprisingly forthcoming, but it was only after prolonged hesitation that a gold guarantee was foregone. Agreement was not finally reached until August 1945, covering the war-time balances, and April 1946, when faced with the alternative of a cut in United Kingdom purchases from Portugal, the latter accepted a monetary agreement of the type that had become standard between the United Kingdom and Western European nations. The 1945 agreement provided that of the war-time balance (now £76 millions), £15 millions should be available for the purchase of capital goods in the Sterling Area, and that the remaining £61 millions should be blocked for ten years and thereafter repaid in gold over a period of twenty years. The expendable £15 millions were subsequently increased by £5 millions, this being the accrual of sterling in Portugal's favour between the August 1945 agreement and April 1946 agreement. The gold value of all these sums was guaranteed by the United Kingdom: it was considered impossible to withdraw the guarantee from the sum that Portugal could, under the war-time agreement, have withdrawn in gold in the first five years after the war, and which she was now consenting to block for long periods. In the monetary agreement of April 1946, however, the British did not feel able to agree to a gold guarantee for the sterling accruals, estimated at £10 millions a year at first. They did, however, (with the provisions of the unratified United States Loan Agreement in mind) agree to consider within twelve months the convertibility of the new sterling accruing to Portugal.

(v)

The European Allies and 'The Sterling Club'

With the European Allies, whose countries had all been occupied by the Germans since 1940, financial relations had naturally followed a different course, but the problems as they appeared in the closing stages of the war were closely parallel to those confronting the United Kingdom authorities in other directions. Nearly £60 millions of French balances in the United Kingdom had been blocked in 1940 under Trading-with-the-Enemy regulations;[1] and France had substantial gold reserves in America. The inter-governmental claims—as between the United Kingdom Government and both the Vichy Government and the Free French Committee in London—were complicated and by no means negligible; any arrangement designed to establish monetary stability would have to take them into account. The total sterling balances (including those blocked by the Custodian) of the Belgian monetary area[2] were nearly £30 millions in mid-1944; this included several millions earned by Congo producers under the operation of the war-time agreements whereby the Congo virtually formed part of the Sterling Area. Dutch war-time net earnings had been very large, especially from shipping and from exports of the Dutch colonies before the Japanese onslaught of 1942. At mid-1944 they amounted to some £75 millions, in addition to some £90 millions owned by two great Dutch companies temporarily operating from the United Kingdom. Norway held about £70 millions in London, principally the accumulation of her net shipping earnings during the war.[3]

It was important, in establishing post-war monetary arrangements, to ensure that these accumulations of claims on London should not be spent at a rate that would constitute an undue burden on the Sterling Area's balance of payments. As it was anticipated that the Sterling Area was likely to have favourable balances with Western Europe as a whole, the important point was to secure that sterling should not be thrown freely on to markets outside the Sterling Area. In seeking protection against the spending of sterling outside the Sterling Area, the United Kingdom negotiators were helped by the fact that these countries did possess substantial reserves of gold. Part of Belgium's gold had been lent to the United Kingdom in the pre-lend-lease gap of 1940–41, but this had been repaid in March 1943 and her £175 millions were again intact.[4] France had in the United States and Canada £285 millions in gold and dollars;[5] and Norway about £13 millions. These reserves

---

1 United Kingdom balances blocked in France were £13·7 millions.

2 Belgium, Luxemburg and the Congo.

3 The only substantial change after mid-1944 was a spectacular increase in Belgium's sterling resulting from the expenditure of British and Commonwealth forces in Belgium in the autumn and winter of 1944-45; Belgium cancelled one-quarter of these as a contribution to the Allied cause.

4 £87 millions in United Kingdom custody, £42 millions in the United States and £46 millions at Dakar.

5 This included £65 millions in dollars paid by the United Kingdom in 1940 on the taking-over of French contracts in the United States and Canada (see footnote on p. 335 and also p. 367). Under an agreement of March 1945 France repaid these dollars in instalments to the United Kingdom (Cmd. 6613).

would enable these countries to make urgent purchases in the dollar area, and reconstitute some central bank reserves of the old-fashioned kind, all without any support from the United Kingdom.[1] The sterling balances could therefore, without hardship to anyone, be restricted to expenditure in the Sterling Area; it was of course of the first importance that the countries should undertake so to restrict their use. The existence of these reserves, most of which the Allies had retained throughout Britain's most difficult period, also constituted an unanswerable reason against giving sterling credit to any of these countries that tended to over-spend sterling: the United Kingdom should not supply further sterling on credit, but only in return for the gold or dollars with which the Allies were relatively well provided.

The Allied Governments, on their side, had something to gain by coming to terms with London before they re-established authority in their own countries. A monetary agreement with London would be a specific achievement to which the refugee Governments could point in justification of their existence, and the Dutch and Belgians as early as May 1944 were anxious to enhance their prestige in this way. The importance of this was partly due to the memory of the currency disorders of 1918–26; Belgium had then suffered a heavy depreciation of her currency, and the Dutch might this time be in similar danger. Their representatives in London were therefore anxious not merely to return with their gold reserves intact, but also with working arrangements for exchange stability firmly established. Their anxiety was London's opportunity.

This anxiety to re-establish their currencies on a secure foundation was, however, responsible for one stumbling-block in the negotiations. If the Allies were to refrain from rapidly unloading their sterling balances, they wanted the gold value of the balances guaranteed. Willing as they were to participate in a rehabilitation of sterling, they could remember 1931, when Dutch bankers particularly had suffered by the depreciation of sterling. The United Kingdom authorities, mindful of their huge sterling obligations in the Sterling Area where a gold guarantee would be entirely inappropriate, felt that they could not afford to make any concession either as regards pre-existing balances or working balances. In September 1944 the Chancellor of the Exchequer explained to the Belgian and Dutch representatives that his refusal to give a gold guarantee was final: we should, he said, 'have to work very hard to maintain the position of sterling in the post-war period, but nevertheless, it was his intention and that of his colleagues, to take no action which could in any way be considered

---

[1] The prospective International Monetary Fund would also, it was anticipated, provide some relief for any dollar difficulties of these countries.

as reflecting on our faith in the full stability of our currency. To concede the Revaluation Clause asked by the Dutch and the Belgians would be to open the door wide to similar demands elsewhere . . . . . .' He was prepared to concede a clause whereby the United Kingdom undertook not to alter the official rate of exchange except after 'mutual consultation'.[1]

The Belgian and Dutch Governments in London did not press this point further, and an agreement with the Belgians was signed on 5th October 1944.[2] A similar agreement with the Dutch was almost settled, but owing to difficulties over the substantial balances of the Royal Dutch Oil Company, actual signature was delayed until 7th September 1945.[3] With Denmark and with Norway, which were not liberated until the spring of 1945, agreements were signed on 16th August[4] and 8th November 1945[5] respectively. In the Danish and Norwegian agreements the exchange-rate clause did not provide for mutual consultation but for 'as much notice as may be practicable'. The other main provisions of these four agreements ran on parallel lines. All transactions between the two monetary areas concerned were to be at the official rate of exchange, and the central banks undertook to supply their respective currencies, at the official rate, for these transactions. The Bank of England undertook to hold only working balances of the other currencies; beyond these sums, the other countries could obtain net sterling requirements only by selling gold to the Bank of England, and the British authorities expected that this clause would in fact operate to provide some gold for London. The other parties' obligations to hold sterling were not restricted to working balances— they undertook also to hold sterling up to amounts agreed in each case as representing 'pre-agreement sterling' balances of their residents.[6] Sterling was to be available for all purposes within the Sterling Area, and an important provision allowed what came to be known as 'administrative transferability'—the use of sterling for transfer to other countries by specific arrangement. All parties attached high value to this clause; the United Kingdom authorities

---

[1] The United Kingdom Treasury was well aware of the difficulties that might arise in interpreting the word 'consultation', but it did not attach great practical importance thereto because the alteration of exchange rates was going to be the particular concern of the International Monetary Fund. A clause in the European monetary agreements provided for review if either party should join an international currency organisation.

[2] Cmd. 6557.

[3] Cmd. 6681.

[4] Cmd. 6671.

[5] Cmd. 6697.

[6] The 'military balances'—i.e. sterling balances arising from the purchase of local currency for the use of British forces in Belgium in 1944-45—were dealt with outside the agreement. Belgium in the event made a contribution by cancelling a substantial fraction of this claim on London.

hoped to be able gradually to extend the transferability of sterling, and thereby to make sterling a fully international currency which other countries would be increasingly willing to hold.

All these agreements were regarded as purely transitional arrangements; they were subject to review after mutual consultation and were terminable after three years unless otherwise determined. Broadly they established stable exchanges in Western Europe with sterling as a key currency, and went some way towards the rehabilitation of sterling as an international currency consistently with limiting the threat to sterling constituted by the existence of Western Europe's war-time sterling balances.

With France financial relations were altogether more complex, and despite France's huge gold reserves, the United Kingdom authorities were not able to achieve such a satisfactory result. The Simon-Reynaud Agreement of 1939 had worked just long enough, before the fall of France, to leave a trail of claims and counter-claims behind it. Then there had been the taking over of French contracts in North America, and the requisition of ships and cargoes in 1940. For a short time claims and counter-claims were also running up between the United Kingdom and the Free French (the Committee of National Liberation), but these had by two agreements of 19th March 1941 been brought under the Mutual Aid umbrella. The prospective entry of Allied troops into France in 1944 necessitated a further agreement; this was signed on 8th February 1944.[1] This fixed a rate of exchange between the pound and the franc (200 francs=£1) and provided for unlimited credit on either side. Neither party could claim gold in exchange for any part of its holding of the other's currency, but any net balance was to be adjusted to compensate for depreciation of either currency against the other (not against gold). This agreement of 1944 was simply a stop-gap to enable the Allied troops to obtain francs, and the British authorities intended to seek different terms to cover the resumption of trade. London had particularly in mind the fact that France had a total gold reserve of some £570 millions, and another £140 millions or so in dollars. In these circumstances there could be no question of continuing the unlimited credit allowed to France under the stop-gap arrangements of 1944; indeed it was difficult to see why France needed any credit at all. But France was represented by a hard bargainer in M. Pleven, and London was ready to concede much in order to get hold of some of the French gold before the mutual obligations of war-time alliance were forgotten. Both sides were anxious to get monetary arrangements established that would allow a resumption of normal trading

---

[1] H. of C. Deb., Vol. 396, Cols. 1627-1629.

relationships as rapidly as possible with the minimum risk of a bout of international currency disorder.

The upshot of the tough bargaining, which occupied February and March 1945, was the financial agreement of 27th March 1945;[1] this cleared all the war-time transactions out of the way and provided the necessary framework for resumption of trading relations, though it was to terminate as early as 28th February 1946. The French paid, by instalments, $158 millions representing repayment of dollars paid by the United Kingdom to French account when French contracts in the United States were taken over in 1940. The United Kingdom undertook to supply to France materials, equipment and installations surplus to United Kingdom requirements to the value of £45 millions. Apart from these two items,[2] all claims and counter-claims arising from the prosecution of the war were waived, though private assets blocked by Custodians were of course to be released on both sides. In order to develop trade, the United Kingdom agreed to allow credit to France up to £100 millions, the French correspondingly allowing credit up to 20 milliards of francs. At the end of a year the balance was to be struck and it was anticipated that it would stand in favour of the United Kingdom: it would then be discharged in gold to the amount of one-third of the *gross* French payments and the remainder in sterling.[3] The official rate of exchange—still 200 francs = £1— was not to be altered without prior consultation between the two Governments.[4]

The agreement did not work out quite as expected, largely because the rate of 200 francs to the £ grossly over-valued the franc, so that French goods could not be imported on reasonable terms into the Sterling Area. The French on the other hand could pay British prices and were in dire need of supplies. The credit allowed to France was therefore exhausted in about half the year and it was raised by steps to £150 millions. The relative price position was greatly improved by the franc devaluation of December 1945, but the French were still unwilling to commit themselves to anything but temporary arrangements. Nevertheless, the British authorities were able to feel that their successive agreements with

---

[1] Cmd. 6613.

[2] The effect of the two together was that the United Kingdom received dollars for war materials no longer needed.

[3] It was conceivable that French sterling balances would not suffice—in this event there were to be consultations. The point of relating the gold to *gross* French payments was that discouragement of British purchases in France was avoided. The British wanted freedom to purchase essential goods at reasonable prices in France, and the French were anxious to get entry into the Sterling Area markets.

[4] It was in fact altered to 480 francs = £1 in December 1945; the Chancellor sent a message to M. Pleven recognising the appropriateness of the step.

the French had contributed to the protection of sterling, and that the pressure exercised by French purchases upon the real resources of the Sterling Area in 1944–46 had been rewarded by appreciable accessions to London's reserves of gold and dollars.

Thus by the autumn of 1945 the United Kingdom financial authorities were able to look round large parts of the world and feel that they had staved off any immediate threat implicit in the existence of the war-time accumulations of sterling. In South America the important items in the account were for Argentine and Brazil, where the existence of British assets (for some of which the local Governments had an appetite) encouraged firm holding of the sterling balances. Among the European neutrals, the only big debt was to Portugal, whose authorities had come to a reasonable accommodation with us; the others had been persuaded that it was in their interest to help the United Kingdom through the transition period. Allies in Western Europe had been interested in the maintenance of international monetary stability; they were relatively well-off in gold, but British trade was going to be important to them, and they had been willing to concede London's essential conditions for the sake of membership of a 'sound sterling club'. Arrangements with France were not so satisfactory, but at least had the merit that they enabled London to tap the massive French hoards of gold and dollars. Within the war-time Sterling Area, on the other hand, a huge structure of unconditional debt cast its shadow. The large sums for the account of the British Colonies were nominally subject to administrative edict issuing from London, but politically they looked like being the white man's burden. Even larger, and demanding more immediate treatment, were the balances due to India and the Middle East. And beyond all this there was the tremendous problem of finding dollars to see the Sterling Area through the post-lend-lease period.

(vi)

The Rate of Exchange

In all negotiations with neutrals and Allies in Europe there was an assumption, or rather an affirmation, that the pound sterling was to be held stable in terms of gold. Of all major questions of financial policy during the war, that on which least was said and written was probably the dollar-sterling exchange rate. Although settled in a somewhat haphazard way at the beginning of the war, it had acquired a certain inertia at an early stage and drifted from that into a fixity almost comparable with the laws of the Medes and Persians. In the last weeks before the outbreak of war, the dollar value of the pound had been allowed to fall, in the face of heavy withdrawals of foreign funds from London, from about $4·68 to about $4. No doubt this was mentioned in top-level discussions between the Treasury and the Bank of England, but no trace whatever is to be found in the Treasury files. In the final stages of sterling's fall, the Exchange Equalisation Account stood aside and the pace and ultimate extent of the fall were therefore the phenomena of a free market—the rate fell until enough sellers of sterling were deterred and enough buyers attracted for sales to be matched with purchases. Exchange control, with its concomitant supersession of a free market by a purely official market, was clamped down at the moment when sterling stood just above $4. No longer needing to drop the rate as a check upon sales of sterling, the authorities' preference for a stable rate reasserted itself and they thought that a rate of $4 looked about right. The prestige of sterling was important from the start, and in the absence of clear cause the rate had to stick where it had happened to be on the critical date. It was thought best to fix something just wide of the round figure because it would look less committal and be less difficult to adjust if experience showed that adjustment was necessary. So $4·03 it was.

When the helter-skelter of August-September 1939 was over, there was time—and need—for some thoughts about the balance of trade, especially in relation to the development of export policy. In this context there was, as has been mentioned earlier[1], some review, on the Treasury's most academic level, of the rate of exchange. While opinion leaned slightly towards some upward movement of the pound—principally on the ground of inelasticities of supply and demand for British exports in war conditions—no strong conclusions emerged, at any rate no conclusions strong enough to attract serious interest in more effective corners of Whitehall and Threadneedle Street. The question just drifted, and as it drifted 'the official rate' (as it had now become necessary to describe the $4·03 rate) gained in authority from successive payments agreements in which the derivative rates for other currencies were embodied. Then, as the growth of sterling balances became a matter of inter-governmental concern, insistence on the stability of sterling in terms of gold and dollars became of the first importance. This was most obviously the case within the Sterling Area, where the balances were covered by no guarantees or other protective clauses, but it was also pertinent where there

---

[1] pp. 238-9 above.

was a gold guarantee. For devaluation in the latter case would mean either gold payment or increase in the sterling debt, either of them most unwelcome. Much the most satisfactory course was, in fact, for the United Kingdom to persuade other countries that there was no point in such guarantees because sterling's stability was a certainty, and this was the course taken in the latter part of the war.

Many of the disadvantages of changing the rate would not have attached to a *rise* in the dollar value of sterling. But this was not envisaged by other countries as a practical possibility: Britain was obviously undergoing, and would continue to experience, great strain in her balance of payments, and all experience pointed to a falling pound as the practical risk. And though a theoretical case could have been made out for a higher valuation of sterling in the transition period, for a country that had to develop a tremendous growth of exports a rise in the pound would not have been reasonable as a long-term policy, nor would it have looked a tenable one. The choice was between stability and devaluation. It was the policy of the United Kingdom authorities to persuade other countries that the choice in favour of stability had been made and would be held.

The Bretton Woods arrangements, to which Britain was substantially committed, pointed in the same direction. Again, it was theoretically possible to change the exchange rate when the International Monetary Fund fixed initial par values; but a devaluation of the pound then would, quite apart from other repercussions, have given a bad start to an institution in which substantial stability of the leading currencies was more or less implicit; and 'revaluation' as a transition-period possibility, to be followed eventually by a drop in sterling, would also have been contrary to the spirit of the Bretton Woods' times. The assumption all round was that sterling should be stable, and the United Kingdom authorities did everything they could to encourage this view.

The only private doubts to reach the official papers were expressed in connection with suggestions that the dollar rate might be moved from 4·03 to the simpler 4·00. This question—at first glance a minor technical question—arose in the latter part of 1943 as a by-product of relations between Allied forces in North Africa and other occupied territories. For the sake of convenience, the simple cross-rate of 4 dollars to the £ was inevitably used by people in the theatres of war. The simultaneous existence of the 4·03 rate for all other official purposes—including the War Departments at the metropolitan ends of the supply lines—was a nuisance to the civil servants, and suggestions emanated from Washington that the simpler of the two rates should be universally adopted; it would imply a simple price for gold—175s. per ounce.[1] In relation to this proposal, the broader question was first looked at by a circle of Bank of England and Treasury experts. It was recognised that, having regard to the United Kingdom's very complex structure of international financial commitments, even this minor change could not be made in a hole-and-corner way. One argument—and it was a powerful argument considering the guarantees attaching to American Registered Accounts[2] and the need to encourage rather than discourage the holding of sterling balances—was that it would be noted as depreciation and partial repudiation, and would be taken as indicating Britain's attitude to her creditors and the likelihood of further depreciation. Against this it was argued that a minor alteration of this kind, obviously and avowedly designed to remove administrative inconvenience, would be interpreted as indicating acceptance by the United Kingdom of the $4 rate for the early post-war years, and would therefore encourage the firm holding of sterling. And this assumption of a $4 rate was, it was urged, one that London could safely encourage: '. . . . throughout the various discussions over the past year or two it has been tacitly assumed by all of us that $4 would be the rate, and we have plenty of evidence that this rate is accepted and in fact desired by U.S. Treasury. It is obviously impossible to see far into the future and we do not feel that any useful purpose would be served by trying to make calculations and estimates of comparative price and cost levels. As a general proposition, however, so far as can at present be foreseen it does not seem likely that a $4 rate would over the next few years be against the interests of the Sterling Area.' The double negative of the last sentence was typical: few economists would criticize the lack of confidence, in these circumstances, in the usefulness of purchasing power parity calculations, and the attachment to the $4 rate was akin to trust in innocence until guilt is proved, rather than a sure faith in its appropriateness to Britain's post-war trading position. There was little dissent to this general argument in favour of $4 or thereabouts, and what dissent there was died away in the first half of 1944.

Thereafter the only question debated at all was that of the minor adjustment, from $4·03 to $4·00. The arguments against any early action prevailed, though the question was revived from time to time. In mid-1945 the United Kingdom authorities felt strong enough to remove one hurdle, by terminating the guarantee attaching to registered sterling. This move was made more palatable to world opinion by being combined with a move which had the air

---

[1] 175s. corresponded to $35 an ounce and $4 = £1.

[2] Holders of registered sterling were entitled to convert their sterling into dollars at $4·025 to the £ at any time. (See pp. 248-9 above).

(though scarcely the substance) of an advance towards multilateralism, and holders of registered sterling were allowed three months in which to convert into dollars at the guaranteed rate.[1] Actual change in the rate was deferred until the United Kingdom notified the newly-established International Monetary Fund of its proposed par of exchange, in 1946. The middle rate was then settled not at the tidy $4 but at $4·03.

From about March 1944 onwards 'the question of the dollar/sterling cross-rate' had thus become the question of $4·03 *versus* $4·00 or thereabouts. The more substantial issue had been left behind; with the progress of the war—entailing progressive growth of London's sterling balances and the urgency of establishing new monetary agreements for the transition period— adherence to virtual stability of the rate had become a fundamental tenet of British financial policy. Its importance was not limited to the maintenance of confidence by the war-time accumulators of sterling; it had become of the first importance in relation to efforts to re-establish a stable currency system for Western Europe, and to rehabilitate sterling as an international currency. It had also some significance in Anglo-American relations for, as will be seen in the next chapter, the United States were about to turn away from war-time needs or a faithful Ally's deserts as their basis for aid to Britain, and were about to insist upon linking aid with the design of restoring to Britain the capacity to take her place in a multilateral trading world of stable currencies and open doors.

---

[1] Press Notice of 30th June 1945. The 'United States Registered Accounts' and 'Central American Accounts' were now merged into a single category, 'American Accounts', but as the old accounts had carried a gold convertibility guarantee, the advance towards multilateralism was only nominal.

CHAPTER XV

THE SHADOW OF DEBT 1944-45
II: THE LAST PHASE OF LEND-LEASE

(i)
The Need for a New Approach

FROM THE EARLY MONTHS of 1944 the United Kingdom authorities were acutely aware of the need for high level discussions on what was to happen after the defeat of Germany—in Stage II, as the interval between that event and the defeat of Japan came to be called. The applicability of the fundamental principles of lend-lease—its purpose was 'the defense of the United States'—was evidently going to be restricted. Recently all had been discouragement; the wholesale elimination of capital goods in November 1943 had been followed by 'the Crowley take-outs' costing the Sterling Area $200 millions,[1] and there was a continuing tendency for allocations to be squeezed down. Without a new direction from the top, supplies for 1945 (assumed identical with the first part of Stage II) were obviously going to be quite inadequate in relation to Britain's continuing military needs, her minimum reconstruction requirements and her sterling liabilities. Preliminary soundings[2] indicated that the Americans were not thinking of Stage II as calling for different treatment from that appropriate in Stage III. On this basis the principle of lend-lease might be withdrawn immediately after V-E Day; Britain would then perhaps be provided by some more orthodox kind of loan. The United Kingdom authorities recoiled from any such thought. From the earliest days of the war they had wished to avoid carrying war debts into the peace; now, knowing how crippled Britain would emerge, they felt they must not at any price add, before the end of the war, a dollar debt to the United States to the sterling debt piling up in the Middle East. At best, it had become known that the United States Government was thinking of restricting lend-lease to military supplies needed solely for the war against Japan and, in the non-munitions field, foodstuffs. Restriction of this order had its logical basis in the 'marginal

---

[1] cf. above, pp. 433-4.

[2] e.g. in informal conversions with Mr. Stettinius in April and May 1944.

principle', which had previously governed the scale of lend-lease, and in the legal basis of lend-lease—the defence of the United States[1]. To secure some tolerable scheme of aid during Stage II, it was essential to insist upon a distinction between Stage II and Stage III and upon the unwisdom of reviving the dollar sign before the completion of Stage II. On 9th June 1944 the Chancellor instructed the Ambassador in Washington to press this view at once, and the earlier uncertainty as to the proper level of negotiation gave way to a growing realisation that an approach must be made on a very high level.[2] A new Presidential directive, clearly supplanting the marginal principle and giving a wider interpretation of United States defence needs, was absolutely essential if Britain was to be kept in a fit condition to continue the struggle.

The mounting sterling debt provided another reason for seeking a new basis in Anglo-American financial relations. The sterling balances of India were, despite the substantial contributions made by India herself, growing by hundreds of millions a year even under the strategic plans of 1943 and 1944. In Stage II, with Germany defeated, the weight of the Allied effort would swing to the East. This would mean bigger expenditure both for Commonwealth forces and, under current arrangements, for reciprocal aid to United States forces. The British Treasury regarded this prospective acceleration of expenditure in India as 'intolerable'; the United States must be asked to make some approach to a genuine pooling of the burden. To persuade the United States Administration, let alone Congress, that the burden of expenditure within the Commonwealth was 'intolerable' was not going to be easy.[3] In the event persuasion failed and Britain somehow tolerated the intolerable, but in 1944 this was emphatically a question to raise with the United States Administration.

There was also the Export White Paper. Persuasion on the official level was getting nowhere, and administration continued to be—on the most favourable interpretation—legalistic. There was little hope that enough resources could be spared to enable Britain's export trade to leap up in Stage II itself. But if the United Kingdom was

---

[1] The Administration's intentions, as described above, were explained to Lord Keynes and his Treasury colleagues when they visited Washington in August 1944, on the way home from Bretton Woods.

[2] The uncertainty had been common to officials on both sides. As soon as he realised the kind of aid for which Britain would look, Mr. Stettinius urged that the Chancellor of the Exchequer should visit Washington. For several weeks this seemed the likeliest approach and it was only at the last minute that it gave way to the idea that the broad principles should be raised at the Octagon meeting between the President and the Prime Minister.

[3] Even those most ready to learn about Britain's difficulties stumbled at the lesson that debts 'within the family' could be crippling.

ever to become viable again, there must at least be a beginning of a drive to multiply the volume of 1943–44 exports by five.[1] Explanation of these intentions helped American officials to appreciate the distinction drawn between Stage II and Stage III, but they were not ready to accept the implication and in July 1944 it became clear that the whole matter would have to be discussed in an altogether broader context.

Finally, as every off-the-record conversation with American opposite-numbers seemed to underline, it was urgently necessary to intensify the education of American opinion on the nature of Britain's economic problems. There was far too little understanding in the United States of America of the privations being suffered by the civil population, of the inadequacy of London's reserves, of the implications of debt within the Sterling Area, and of the distance the export drive must go.[2] If anything like a satisfactory revision of financial relations was to emerge—indeed if revision in the wrong direction was to be escaped—the process of education in these matters had to be carried to the highest levels in the Administration, to begin as soon as possible, and to be spread as widely as possible.

There was an awkward dilemma here. All experience had tended to show that understanding on the part of the Administration was not enough, and that efforts to meet the British case might be effectively hamstrung by less well-informed movements in Congress and outside. This factor was of particular importance in 1944, for the Presidential election and the biennial election of Congress were due in November. Yet to broadcast Britain's vulnerability to the world was to excite distrust of sterling, and at this stage it was more important than ever before that overseas holders of sterling should be willing to accept further sterling payments. The dilemma had to be accepted, but its existence was one more reason for high secrecy in the preparation of the United Kingdom brief until the United Kingdom Government could get, in the highest quarter, commitments covering the broadest issues.

In inter-departmental discussions preceding the preparation of the United Kingdom brief, there was some difference of opinion on whether the United Kingdom should offer outright to pay for raw materials and non-munition manufactured goods. To do so would obviously reduce both work and friction, but would cost

---

[1] i.e. to 150 per cent. of pre-war volume, the level indicated by first guesses at the post-war balance of payments.

[2] It must not be supposed that nothing at all had been done to educate the American public in these matters. President Roosevelt, in his 16th Report to Congress on lend-lease, drew attention to the contrasting changes in United Kingdom and United States exports, and he explicitly pointed the moral that Britain should be allowed to begin reconversion as soon as war requirements tailed off. (Note in *The Economist*, 9th September 1944).

dollars. The net amount in dollars might not be substantial, after allowing for items for which cash would certainly have to be paid, and after allowing for simultaneous termination of reciprocal aid for raw materials; but any readiness to pay dollars would look inconsistent with the United Kingdom plea of dollar destitution. The United Kingdom was also going to emphasise maintenance of 'the pooling principle'—inoperative though it had been in the realm of finance—and it would be a pity to retrace the steps taken avowedly in that interest. But the Board of Trade and the Ministry of Supply were extremely anxious for freedom in the export drive, and the Ministry of Supply was hoping to relax a number of its raw material controls in Stage II. In the following weeks the difficult attitude of the United States Administration in relation to Export White Paper questions strengthened the view that freedom to export must be the paramount consideration, and eventually the United Kingdom representatives went into the Stage II negotiations with the intention that raw materials should be paid for after the end of 1944, even if Stage II did not follow immediately.

(ii)

The Stage II Negotiations

On 18th July 1944 the War Cabinet reviewed the whole situation, both immediate and prospective, of Britain's external receipts and expenditure. Looking ahead, the War Cabinet authorised both immediate steps to initiate the export drive and early negotiations with the United States Government about the extent of United States aid to Britain in Stage II. These negotiations were to be based on a full statement of Britain's needs, with full explanation and justification. Then there were seven weeks of discussions of tactics. In this awkward interval the United States authorities were beginning to demand figures showing Britain's programmes and requirements of American supplies, and the United Kingdom Treasury had to choose between premature disclosure[1] and leaving the Americans to think out figures for themselves—figures that might be almost as difficult to dislodge as would preliminary United Kingdom figures that later required revision. But some delay had to be accepted, because the broadest issues could be settled only at the very top. Even when Mr. Morgenthau came to London in August, nothing could be settled, though the Chancellor

---

[1] The final munition programmes were extremely difficult to calculate, and firm figures were not available until the last minute.

of the Exchequer made full use of his opportunity to 'put all the cards on the table, face upwards'.[1]

The case the Chancellor made on this occasion rested on the historical fact that 'we had waged the war on a basis of unlimited liability, quite regardless of financial consequences' and upon the determination that, despite those dire consequences, '(i) we should not emerge from the war as applicants for Poor Relief, and (ii) there would be no repudiation of our liabilities'. To meet the future the United Kingdom must set about quintupling the current level of exports, and must receive sufficient lend-lease assistance in Stage II.

This was, in the broadest terms, the case presented by Britain when the President and the Prime Minister met at Quebec between the 13th and 16th of September. This, the Second Quebec or Octagon Conference, was primarily concerned with military strategy. Inevitably therefore it was with some difficulty that the central economic issues were pushed on the table. Moreover the Chancellor of the Exchequer was not a member of the British delegation. On the American side, Mr. Harry Hopkins was absent; those who took the lead on economic affairs therefore were Mr. Morgenthau and the United Kingdom Paymaster-General, Lord Cherwell. The Prime Minister found Mr. Morgenthau more interested in 'the Morgenthau Plan' for the pastoralisation of Germany than in anything else; apparently Mr. Morgenthau's idea was that the suppression of German industry would open opportunities for Britain which would go far in solving Britain's longer-range economic problems. The British did however manage to focus attention on the more immediate issues, and the President accepted the central part of the British case, i.e. first, the United Kingdom's military effort in the first year of Stage II should in terms of supplies be about 75 per cent. of its current effort, falling to 60 per cent. in the second year. Second, lend-lease supplies should be roughly proportioned to this effort so as to leave some margin for easement of the plight of the British civilian; the President did not accept the precise United Kingdom proposal for the reckoning of lend-lease requirements, but he did agree that the supplies judged implicit in the broad programme of action should be provided under lend-lease. Third, the need to liberate the United Kingdom's export trade was in some measure agreed. Fourth, a joint Anglo-American committee was established to negotiate details.[2] After some hesitation it was agreed that Lord

---

[1] Lord Keynes, looking back from December 1944, believed that this conversation was the turning point in the attitude of the United States Treasury on the reserves question.

[2] It will be noticed that these four points included no reference to the reserves question. According to Lord Keynes, this had not entered into the Quebec conversations 'and the force of our case, and probably even its existence, never reached the President'.

Keynes should lead the British team in this Committee; Mr. Morgenthau took the lead on the American side.

By the time Lord Keynes arrived in Washington at the end of September, some important figures in the United Kingdom brief were already requiring revision in the light of events, and before presenting this weighty document to Mr. Morgenthau[1], Lord Keynes and his colleagues had to alter its balance. Keynes was 'pretty shattered' by London's new forecast of the decline in the reserves,[2] and decided to put altogether new emphasis on the claim for adequate reserves. This claim was, he thought, the kernel of the matter: 'We can get all the rest and still be in a very bad way indeed'. The struggle ahead was to persuade the Americans that acceptance of the claim was a mutual and not only a British interest.[3]

There followed two months of difficult work in this Committee (the American team was, as usual, constantly changing), but it did bear fruit.[4] The principal achievements were four. The programmes for military supplies were agreed, substantially on the scale requested by British representatives, although they failed to obtain, as a safeguard against subsequent political or administrative changes, a formal document detailing agreed quantities.[5] Secondly, the Americans recognised that the United Kingdom reserve

---

[1] This document was of great importance in getting the negotiations off on the right footing. Lord Keynes's own first intention had been to depend on oral exposition, but he accepted the advice of Sir Robert Sinclair (the Chief Executive of the Ministry of Production, who had, until recently, been representative of his Minister on the Combined Production and Resources Board in Washington), in favour of a full statement in writing. There was in fact never 'opportunity for continuous or coherent oral exposition to the right audience', but ample documentation was greatly appreciated. The 'cohort of researchers, economists and statisticians' could, if they were given full material and explanations, 'become your best friends and advocates. In the long run their influence is considerable; most certainly their criticism is dangerous . . . . I am convinced that in the past we have made a great mistake and handicapped our representatives in Washington by an economy of information'.

[2] Most of the 1943-44 growth in London's reserves had been due to the United States cash payments to their Forces in the United Kingdom and elsewhere in the Sterling Area. As these Forces went elsewhere—and eventually back to the United States—the rise in London's reserves dwindled and was eventually reversed.

[3] In the pithy introduction to the document handed to Mr. Morgenthau, the fourth 'conclusion of policy' ran: 'It is in the mutual interest that the British reserve of gold and dollars, which is already dangerously inadequate, should not suffer by the end of 1945 any significant deterioration below its present level'.

[4] Its success was largely due to fine team-work on the British side, inspired by the leadership of Lord Keynes at his best. One of his colleagues reported home: 'I doubt whether he has ever written or spoken with more lucidity or charm'. Keynes's own comment was: 'We have never had a more brilliant and effective team. . . . . There was not a weak spot'.

[5] The United Kingdom Delegation made some attempt to have their final understandings with the United States Administration set out in a formal document. But Keynes, after making some soundings, decided against pressing for this. Their word, he thought, 'is as good as, if not better than their bond. . . . Any document we could have got would have been stuffed with jokers so that if they had a mind to escape at a later date nothing would have prevented them from doing so'. The United States Administration publicly committed itself to the main principles in an announcement issued at the end of November 1944.

position was serious, and that they might have to do something to protect it.[1] Thirdly, agreement was reached on the advance towards freedom for the United Kingdom's export trade. Fourthly, the United Kingdom representatives believed that in the intermediate ranks of the United States Administration there was a new realisation of the desperate economic straits to which Britain was reduced. In the long run this was perhaps the most valuable result of all, but the events of the next nine months were to abound in disappointments on this score. In part this was due to the upset of the United States Administration upon President Roosevelt's death, but probably the advance had anyway been over-rated by Keynes's team at the end of 1944.

The scale of lend-lease assistance required to fit the proposed scale of Britain's continued military effort had been exceedingly difficult to work out; at first thought to be of the order of $4,000 millions, it was estimated at $3,400 millions just before the Octagon Conference, and was actually stated there as about $3,000 millions. The Joint Committee—'with remarkable ease and celerity'—agreed on $2,838 millions. The scale of non-munitions supplies sought under lend-lease depended upon what was settled about raw materials and manufactured goods. On the basis that these should be paid for from 1st January 1945, an estimate of $3 billions was originally put forward. In the course of negotiations this was reduced to $2,596 millions, but in thus squeezing it the American negotiators recognised that this would leave the British perilously short and they promised to find $250 or 300 millions on miscellaneous items to help the United Kingdom. There were many British claims outstanding, some of them having been left in polite suspense when lend-lease began; these became known as 'the half-dead cats' and British negotiators, feeling that the claims had been reiterated to the point of tiresomeness, would have preferred to replace them by 'a new live dog'. A share of the burden shouldered by the United Kingdom in the Middle East and India would have served as the 'new live dog', but it became evident that circumstances were against American agreement.[2] The 'half-dead cats' had therefore to be kept alive and, by admitting a few of these claims and by making new rulings of lend-lease eligibility, the Americans duly eased the United Kingdom position to the extent of the promised $250–300 millions.[3]

---

[1] The increase in London's reserves had failed to develop into the 'political bombshell' the United States Administration had feared and this no doubt made United States negotiators more open to persuasion on this problem.

[2] Hardly any United States Forces were to be based in India or the Middle East.

[3] Mr. Morgenthau and Mr. Stettinius were both, according to Lord Keynes, fully convinced of the need for a larger measure of relief, but partial defeat had in the end to be accepted.

The amounts of non-munition supplies on lend-lease for Australia, New Zealand and India were agreed to the satisfaction of their Governments; for munitions no separate arrangements were made, as it was intended that the Dominions should get their supplies mainly through the United Kingdom. By contrast, the reciprocal aid arrangements for Stage II were vigorously debated. The United States War Department attempted to get Australia and New Zealand to remove the limitations they had felt obliged to put upon their aid in the form of food supplies for United States forces in the East, and there was also an attempt to make lend-lease munitions for the United Kingdom and Dominions depend upon the United Kingdom's underwriting of all Commonwealth reciprocal aid. Both these attempts—either of which would in the end have meant heavier burdens for the United Kingdom as well as worse feelings within the Commonwealth—were strongly resisted by the Dominions and United Kingdom alike. Allies were found in other United States Departments, the underwriting proposal was dropped and only minor extensions of reciprocal aid were made.

On the Export White Paper, the agreement was at any rate better than had seemed likely during the abortive negotiations in the spring and summer. In many ways this proved the most difficult subject tackled by the Committee, thanks to the keen interest politicians on both sides of the Atlantic were taking in it. The United Kingdom Government had not merely to get a new agreement at the earliest possible moment in order to prepare the export drive; it had also to get a new agreement quickly if it was to avoid sharp Parliamentary criticism at the end of November.[1] The United States Administration's task, by contrast, was to accord to United Kingdom exporters a wide measure of freedom, whilst leaving President Roosevelt free to declare that no new formal agreement had been made.[2] His Administration had publicised V-E Day as the date for reconversion in the United States to begin; any appearance of an earlier date for the United Kingdom was likely to raise a storm in American politics. The contortions of the President's advisers in the face of this dilemma were, to the

---

[1] Export policy was to be debated in the House of Commons on the days 14th–17th November. On strong representations from Lord Keynes, the subject was postponed until the opening of the new Session (on the 29th); it was also to be raised in the House of Lords on 5th December. The price paid for securing postponement of the Commons debate was, the Treasury telegraphed to Keynes, 'an increased expectation of a satisfactory Government announcement on export freedom as soon as the new session of Parliament opens on 29th November'.

[2] Keynes wrote of his interview with the President: 'The President declared to me without qualification that we must have our export freedom. He made no objection to a public announcement . . . . but he also made it clear that it must all be so expressed that he would be free to confirm that there would be no change whatever in the general conditions of lend-lease before V-E Day'.

United Kingdom negotiators, exasperating in the extreme. Well-disposed officials—and there were more of these than appeared at first sight—would give assurances which others, equally well disposed, would find incompatible with the President's intentions. Keynes sometimes had great difficulty in getting all the relevant people into a room together or, having got them there, to hear them speak with one voice.

However, after Herculean exertions and many disappointments, a *modus vivendi* was reached in time to allow United Kingdom Ministers to make their statements at the appointed time, and to avoid in these statements anything gravely embarrassing to President Roosevelt.[1] The basis was that, although there would be no formal withdrawal of the White Paper, after the defeat of Germany the United Kingdom would have complete freedom to export, subject always to requirements for the war against Japan and to a liability to reimburse the United States for any lend-lease goods identical with goods exported from the United Kingdom. The United Kingdom negotiators had failed to get this arrangement—a substantial modification of the White Paper—applied as from 1st January 1945; a partial remedy was for the United Kingdom to pay for raw materials and manufactured goods, so removing most of the contentious cases. For the rest, the United States Departmental head chiefly concerned (Mr. Crowley of the Foreign Economic Administration) undertook to give the United Kingdom the maximum freedom practicable by administrative measures under the Export White Paper of 1941—incidentally a final reminder that this document was regarded as a binding international agreement. The United Kingdom authorities in fact made up their minds that the teeth of the restrictions must be drawn by paying for any materials in question, and just hoped that the American undertaking would serve to minimise the dollar cost of this resolution.

All this meant, as the Prime Minister emphasised when reporting on 30th November 1944 to the House of Commons,[2] that without any reduction in the United Kingdom's proportional contribution to the waging of war, some improvement in the civilian diet would be possible, rather more temporary and emergency houses could be built, and efforts to increase the export trade could begin at once. This was what the Government meant in terms of help on

---

[1] H. of C. Deb., Vol. 406, Cols. 69-74.

[2] *Ibid.* The announcement had its difficulties: in the words of *The Economist* (9th December 1944, p. 767) 'It was necessary to convince the British public that most of the restrictions that have accompanied lend-lease are to disappear, and also to convince the American public that none of the principles of lend-lease has been altered'. The Prime Minister said that his statement had been agreed 'almost sentence by sentence with our American colleagues'.

the home front. The agreements were significant—and this the Prime Minister diplomatically did not explain—as a departure from a ruling principle of the lend-lease administration ever since its commencement. Hitherto lend-lease had been available only for marginal supplies required for the maximisation of the war effort but impossible to squeeze out of our own fully-mobilised resources; in place of this 'marginal principle', Quebec decided that in Stage II the United Kingdom should receive from the United States sufficient supplies to allow some measure of reconversion. The supplies needed were related to the 'order of battle' decided upon in the Quebec discussions on strategy, and the United Kingdom authorities therefore regarded their claim to lend-lease supplies as conditional upon these military plans. The change in the basis of lend-lease was accepted by the United States as consistent with the lend-lease criterion of 'the defense of the United States'. Their excuse for this reconciliation was the British plea that after five years of war the British effort could be maintained only by more repairs of bombed houses and more variety in the diet; but there was some ground for interpreting the change as indicating deeper appreciation of Britain's impoverishment and its implications for the post-war world.

(iii)

January to July 1945

Any development of this kind was of the first importance from the aspect of Stage III negotiations. In May 1945, when Stage II at last arrived, Stage III (the reconstruction period after the defeat of Japan) still looked a long way away. The first expectation of a two-years' Stage II had generally given way to an 18-months basis, and a few optimists were thinking that it might only last one year.[1] This was dreadfully long to war-weary peoples, but it was not so very long when compared with the time experience had shown to be necessary for evolving and agreeing new financial arrangements with the United States Government. The Stage III arrangements would have to be fundamentally new; lend-lease supplies were for 'the defense of the United States' and must therefore come to an end with Stage II. Forward-looking American administrators, newly aware of the depth of Britain's difficulties, began turning their minds towards the problems of

---

[1] At the Terminal Conference at Potsdam between the two Governments in July 1945, 18 months remained the planning basis for Stage II.

the next stage[1] and British representatives in Washington and elsewhere had to be ready to talk.

Fresh from 'seeking large scale financial aid on the basis of a hard luck story of how Britain had held the fort alone . . . . regardless of financial considerations', as he described his Stage II negotiations, Lord Keynes had reflected on the underlying attitude to be adopted in the inescapable next round. He was not sure how far the story of past efforts would carry United Kingdom negotiators if it were not coupled with the very strong conviction 'that our future strength is an objective of major concern to the U.S.A. and Canada'. He believed that financial assistance to get the United Kingdom through Stage III would be forthcoming but 'our chief trouble will be to prevent the attachment of inconvenient strings'. If the strings were meekly accepted, they would multiply and toughen. They must as far as possible be resisted. Above all, 'financial independence of the United States at the earliest possible opportunity should be a major aim of British policy'.

Such soundings as were made in the early months of 1945 showed that the United States Administration was by now thinking in terms of loans for Stage III. These loans would probably be tied to expenditure in the United States. British needs, however, were for covering the adverse balance of payments of the Sterling Area with the rest of the world, and tied loans might force Britian into undesirable dependence on expensive American goods. Moreover, the principle that international loans should *not* be tied had been conceded by United States representatives at the Bretton Woods discussions on post-war monetary reconstruction, and British experts were naturally quick to point to inconsistency between the tied loans now mooted for Stage III and the general principles of multilateralism which had made real progress at Bretton Woods. The American response was a revival of complaints about the Sterling Area as a device for excluding American exporters and—more positively—a reminder that the United Kingdom had undertaken to embark on discussions of international economic policy in accordance with Article VII of the Mutual Aid Agreement.[2] Nothing emerging in these talks encouraged the United Kingdom Treasury to press for early talks on Stage III, and the general line taken, even when the United States was opening the door for loans to other nations, was to defer the uncomfortable act of asking the United States for a Stage III loan.

---

[1] Mr. Richard Law, Minister of State at the Foreign Office, had as far back as April 1944 an important conversation with Mr. Stettinius about aid to Britain in Stage III (not yet so called). The conversation proved to be premature and foreshadowed little of the hurdles that were yet to be overcome.

[2] cf. above, Chapter XIII, Section (iv).

From a comfortable belief that the autumn's discussions had brought financial relations on to a tolerable basis for 1945 and from speculations about relations, which might not be so tolerable, in a more remote future, the British financial authorities were abruptly shaken in the spring of 1945. Three events closely following one another brought the British authorities up against the problems they would have to face on the termination of lend-lease. In March the Lend-Lease Act was renewed for war purposes only. In April President Roosevelt died suddenly. In May the German war ended. A fourth event—the Lend-Lease Continuation Act in June—served merely to emphasise the limits that Congress had drawn in March.

The Lend-Lease Act had been renewed by Congress every March without difficulty, although the onset of the Congressional review had always been a reason for pruning by the Administration. In March 1945, when the collapse of Germany was imminent, it was only natural that special attention should be given to the implications of the end of the war. The Act was an Act for the defence of the United States, it involved heavy expenditure of United States resources, and it was alleged by interested parties to threaten a handicap in the post-war race for markets. Congress therefore inserted a proviso that no lend-lease funds should be used for post-war relief, rehabilitation and reconstruction,[1] and insisted that the system should be terminated with the war, and Administration officials, notably Mr. Crowley of the Foreign Economic Administration, gave categorical assurances to this effect. It would be ungrateful to say that they leaned over themselves backwards to do so, since President Roosevelt had already interested himself in the establishment of new agencies—particularly U.N.R.R.A.—which were designed to take care of the needs of the post-war transition. Lend-lease was to be cut off, but other sources of American aid were to be turned on. But this was cool comfort for the British, who saw little prospect that relief pouring into devastated Europe would fill the breach in the Sterling Area's balance of payments before reconversion could bear fruit in the multiplication of exports. The assurances given in Congress, inevitable as they were, abruptly reminded the British that there was unlikely to be a sufficient interval for settlement of outstanding problems.

Hitherto, difficult as negotiations had been, the British had always felt that in the last resort President Roosevelt would step in and capitalise the goodwill of the American people towards Britain. On 12th April came the shock of Roosevelt's death. Though there was no reason to suppose that his successor would be less friendly, it was damaging enough that there should be a *new* President, however well-disposed he might be. The change had

---

[1] Report in *The New York Times*, 15th March 1945.

two such aspects: in the new President himself, and in the personnel of his Administration. President Truman inevitably lacked at first the tremendous prestige and authority that President Roosevelt had latterly enjoyed, in the Administration, in Congress, and in the nation. President Truman's own previous position had not brought him at all closely in contact with Britain's problems—only their manifestations in Congressional debate were familiar to him; it was therefore only to be expected that United Kingdom representatives should find him ill-informed. The change in President brought with it some other changes in the personnel of the Administration; discontinuities in personnel meant difficulty for British negotiators, for reasons not peculiar to Anglo-American financial relations. More than this, those who remained in office were inevitably unsure of their standing in the new Administration; they were therefore unwilling to venture new commitments, and tended to stand upon the letter of the law. All this made it extremely difficult to make any advance in the new problems now pressing upon the British representatives. 'Since the death of Roosevelt', they reported in mid-May 'there is lamentable lack of someone in authority on the United States side who is able and willing to put the case forcefully to Congress'. And this applied not only to new problems but also to the defence of principles that had been agreed the previous autumn. Far from making any progress, the British found it impossible to consolidate the ground so hardly won in that round.

The catastrophe of April was followed in May by the end of the German war. It would be ridiculous to use the same noun for this event, nor, of course, did it come with the suddenness of President Roosevelt's death. But in its effect of precipitating the curtailment of lend-lease before there was anything to put in its place, V-E Day was responsible for grave deterioration in financial relations. Owing to the pressure to release resources immediately for reconversion, 'a wave of economy' swept through the Administration and through Congress. It seems probable that this was really responsible for President Truman's directive that military supplies under lend-lease should be confined to those required for operations against Japan[1]; that is to say, supplies had to be cut somewhere, and the Japanese war had priority to the exclusion of lend-lease supplies for Occupation Forces in Europe. A rule of this kind struck at the Keynes-Morgenthau agreement of the previous autumn and at the broad principles agreed at Quebec. In some Administration quarters there was a disposition to stand by Quebec but Mr. Morgenthau, it was reported to London, wrote denying that there had been any overall agreement and asserting that the programmes approved by him were for budgetary and production purposes of

---

[1] On this incident, see Harry S. Truman, *Year of Decisions, 1945*, pp. 145 *et seq.*

the United States Government only, and that they were not technically binding. When Mr. Brand, the United Kingdom Treasury representative, took this up with Mr. Morgenthau, the latter said he had given no thought to the matter since the conclusion of the negotiations, and that he was 'quite rusty'. Mr. Brand gave him an aide mémoire. Failing satisfaction on a lower level, the Prime Minister cabled on 28th May 1945 to President Truman, with scarcely more result. Consequent upon the end of the German war, lend-lease required further legislative action, and the Continuation Act passed in June definitely restricted lend-lease supplies to those required for direct use against Japan. On 5th July the President issued a directive in accordance with this, although foodstuffs were in fact continued under lend-lease.

The Prime Minister took the matter up with the President at the Potsdam Conference held from 16th–26th July. Mr. Churchill (who ceased to be Prime Minister while the Conference was in progress) reported that the President's attitude was most warm and comforting in these matters; the only relevant general principle conceded then and there was a definition of 'basic undertakings considered fundamental to the prosecution of the war' and of certain additional tasks 'to assist the execution of the overall strategic concept'. These undertakings and tasks were believed to cover the occupation of Germany and Austria. It remained to be seen whether administrative action in the United States would take this as a basis for allocating lend-lease supplies. The President also at this Conference intimated his willingness to open negotiations for post-war finance.

(iv)

The End of Lend-Lease

The vague commitments of the Potsdam Conference left practical day-to-day questions in a very unsatisfactory position at the beginning of August 1945. British supply officers were being harried at every turn by lend-lease eligibility questions, and nothing had been settled about finance after V-J Day, except what the United States legislative position implied—that lend-lease would definitely end.[1] United Kingdom Departments realised by this time that they might have to accommodate themselves to an abrupt change, and had been realising that reversion to more normal methods of

---

[1] The United Kingdom Treasury also had to remember that lend-lease shipments to Russia were stopped six days after V-E. Day but the United Kingdom Government had always in its financial dealings with the United States Government behaved very differently from the Russians, and felt entitled to different treatment.

procurement could not be achieved overnight. There were therefore proposals that some items still on lend-lease—timber was an important example—might be taken simultaneously out of lend-lease and reciprocal aid, on a date agreed ahead without waiting for the end of the war. Nothing of this kind had made much progress when the fear of an abrupt end to lend-lease was all too fully justified. The Japanese surrendered on 15th August. On the 11th a British representative in Washington was warned by a Foreign Economic Administration official that lend-lease shipments were likely to terminate very quickly indeed, and suggested that the United Kingdom should arrange for shipments to be covered by a loan, under Clause 3(c) of the Lend-Lease Act. Even before the Japanese surrender, administrative action to stop lend-lease was being taken by the Americans on a Departmental level, but a week of further ominous rumblings went by before the final blow fell. It came by telegram on the 19th, saying that a Sunday newspaper reported that the White House decided on the 17th that all Allied nations receiving lend-lease would have notice on Monday (20th) or Tuesday that 'the programme has been terminated'. The United Kingdom Food Mission telegraphed the same day (Sunday the 19th) to say that they had been informed that loading of lend-lease foodstuffs had been stopped and that no high-level State Department or Foreign Economic Administration officials were available for consultation. The actual formal letter notifying the United Kingdom was handed over in Washington in time for telephoning to a meeting in London at 6.30 p.m. on the 20th.[1]

This formal letter showed that the United States Administration was redeeming its promise to Congress very thoroughly.[2] Its main points were:

(i) there were to be no new contracts on lend-lease,
(ii) supplies in the process of manufacture or awaiting shipment could be received only against payment or on appropriate conditions,
(iii) all existing supplies which had already been transferred could be retained against payment,
(iv) requisitions on terms of cash reimbursement could still be made during the next 60 days, after which they would cease,
(v) the United Kingdom was asked to make an inventory of lend-lease supplies still under United Kingdom control, including all items which had not been lost, destroyed or consumed.

---

[1] Those present were the Chancellor of the Exchequer, the Foreign Secretary and their principal advisers.

[2] cf. R. F. Harrod, *The Life of John Maynard Keynes*, p. 595.

Given the avowed purpose of lend-lease, given the legislative
position and the Administration's categorical assurances to Congress,
given the headlong pace at which the American nation was plunging
into demobilisation and reconversion, no other course was open
to President Truman. Nor had British representatives in Washington
any right to expect any different issue. But there had been hope,
if not expectation, that some tapering-off might be conceded,
and this hope had received encouragement from Americans away
from Washington.

The shock in London was not altogether due to this misleading
encouragement. That the United States Government, after years of
closer co-operation with the United Kingdom than had ever before
been known between Great Powers, should have taken such drastic
measures unilaterally, without any prior negotiation, left British
Ministers and officials gasping for breath. In retrospect, it is easy
to say that they should not have been surprised; but they were
not alone in their reaction. Press exclamations were not confined
to this side of the Atlantic: a leading article in *The New York Times*
on 22nd August showed keen understanding of the seriousness of
the step. Mr. Morgenthau, now out of office, wrote[1]: 'On August
21st, the U.S. Government, without warning, brutally terminated
the operating of the Lend-Lease Act, cutting our allies adrift at a
time when they were still maimed and crippled by the war'.

The Prime Minister (now Mr. Attlee) told the House of Commons
on the 24th August.[2] After explaining that termination meant
that stocks of food and other supplies in the United Kingdom
or in transit would have to be paid for in cash or under credit
arrangements to be negotiated, he commented:

> 'We have not anticipated that operations under the Lend-Lease
> Act would continue for any length of time after the defeat of
> Japan but we had hoped that the sudden cessation of this
> great mutual effort, which has contributed so much to victory,
> would not have been effected without consultation and prior
> discussion of the difficult problems involved in the disappearance
> of a system of so great a range and complication. We can, of
> course, only demobilise and reconvert gradually, and the sudden
> cessation of a support on which our war organisation has so
> largely depended puts us in a very serious financial position.
> Excluding altogether the munitions which we have been
> receiving under lend-lease and Canadian Mutual Aid and will

---

[1] The sentence appeared in the extracts published in *Collier's Magazine* in the autumn
of 1947, from Mr. Morgenthau's voluminous diaries. He had resigned on 6th July
1945 and had been succeeded by Judge Vinson. The latter was present at the critical
White House meeting, but left before the end.

[2] H. of C. Deb., Vol. 413, Cols. 753-5.

no longer require, our overseas outgoings on the eve of the defeat of Japan were equivalent to expenditure at the rate of about £2,000 millions a year, including the essential food and other non-munition supplies which we have received hitherto under lend-lease but must now pay for. Towards this total in the present year, 1945, our exports are contributing £350 millions and certain sources of income, mainly temporary, such as receipts from the United States Forces in this country and reimbursements from the Dominions for war expenditure which we have incurred on their behalf, £450 millions. Thus the initial deficit with which we start the task of re-establishing our economy and of contracting our overseas commitments is immense.' There was still hope, he said, 'of a possible continuance of a limited range of lend-lease for military purposes'.[1] Reciprocal aid would 'conform to the same dates of partial or complete termination as lend-lease'.

Mr. Churchill, as Leader of the Opposition, supported the Prime Minister's wish that there should be no immediate debate, but he was no doubt expressing the feelings of many members on both sides of the House in his own brief comment: 'I cannot believe that it is the last word of the United States; I cannot believe that so great a nation whose lend-lease policy was characterised by me as "the most unsordid act in the history of the world", would proceed in a rough and harsh manner to hamper a faithful ally, the ally who held the fort while their own American armaments were being prepared. . . . . .'

The time-table of events in those August and September days shows that, if the Americans were in a hurry to take this decisive action, the British could be just as quick in grappling with the problems thrown at their heads. The problems were both short-term and long-term—or, more exactly, immediate and short-term. The immediate problem was to get vital food and other supplies moving again from the United States to Britain. The short-term problem was to negotiate financial support to replace lend-lease in the post-war transition period.

Supplies already in the pipeline (i.e. on the way to the United Kingdom) would actually continue to arrive without further action by the United Kingdom authorities; but they would not be disposable for consumption or other use unless the United Kingdom Government in some way acknowledged liability to pay for them. The sum in question was large—it was later agreed at $296 millions, against which could be set $125 millions for reciprocal aid in the

---

[1] There had been a hint of this in Mr. Crowley's Press Conference, reported to London by telegram of 21st August 1945.

2H

pipeline running in the opposite direction.[1] The Government agreed to take the goods under a 'lend-lease credit agreement' to be negotiated, reserving the right to reject any supplies no longer required in view of the end of hostilities. The terms of this lend-lease credit (a '3(c)' credit) had already been indicated to United Kingdom representatives in Washington—a 30 years' loan at $2\frac{3}{8}$ per cent. These were the terms being offered to all recipients of lend-lease; the United Kingdom authorities thought that these terms were more appropriate to a commercial transaction and that, whatever was done about other lend-lease recipients, the United Kingdom deserved better treatment. They asked for the release of supplies against a credit the terms of which should be for discussion. They were given reason to believe that this was acceptable, only to meet a few days later American reiteration of 30 years and $2\frac{3}{8}$ per cent.[2] Not until 6th September did the President, in response to the Prime Minister, confirm that pipeline supplies could continue against credit terms to be negotiated.

Even more serious was the question of getting new supplies into the pipeline at the other end. On the basis of the American decision, action had already been taken to stop procurement of foodstuffs and materials, with the result that the pipeline was 'sucking wind'. If this continued for more than a week or so, the subsequent gap in arrivals in the United Kingdom would be very serious indeed, *and would occur whatever was arranged for later procurement.* To avert a very serious gap in food supplies for the autumn, the United Kingdom Government was compelled to accept, without any delay for negotiation, the United States terms of cash reimbursement. The Treasury Delegation in Washington, in authorising Departmental representatives to proceed on this basis, emphasised that such procurement must be limited to urgent requirements not obtainable elsewhere. Not a single article was to be so procured unless it was absolutely unavoidable, even if severe new restrictions of civilian consumption resulted. Procurement through the United States official channels, even on this reimbursement basis, was permitted only for sixty days. Commercial channels for procurement, disrupted by American insistence under lend-lease, could not be restored overnight. For foodstuffs, it was at first impossible to see what could be done; for other goods, Departments were instructed to restore commercial channels as rapidly as possible.

There were also complicated questions arising on the termination of lend-lease shipping services. Here the United Kingdom was not so completely dependent on American views, as reciprocal aid

---

[1] The $296 millions included $284 millions for civilian Departments, and only $12 millions for Service Departments.

[2] Mr. Crowley's Press Conference on 24th August 1945.

in shipping services was relatively much weightier. On 7th September the United Kingdom representatives in Washington were informed of a 30-days' extension of lend-lease for shipping services. The extension of military lend-lease, the possibility of which had been mentioned in the Prime Minister's announcement, dwindled to very little: it ended on 2nd September except for assistance to Allied forces engaged against Japanese forces which had not surrendered.[1]

The longer-range problems were only less urgent than these frantic efforts to protect the immediate supply line. In addition to the urgency of reinforcing Britain's reserves against the tremendous strain already falling upon them, there was the bargaining point that the United Kingdom ought not to go far in using 'termination credit' before it knew the terms for this credit. The Foreign Economic Administrator (Mr. Crowley) had, when notifying the termination of lend-lease, invited the United Kingdom authorities to enter into immediate conversations, and the Prime Minister, when he made his announcement, told the House of Commons that he was inviting Lord Halifax to return to Washington with Lord Keynes and Departmental officials to open the conversations. Private talks with Mr. Clayton (Assistant Secretary of State), who spent that August in London largely in attempts at long-range to ease the strains of lend-lease termination, confirmed British expectations that the coming negotiations would have to range over a wide field. Besides the clearing up of lend-lease, and the urgent question of financing the Sterling Area's deficit in the transition period, there was the 'Article VII' problem of commercial policy to be tackled, and there were problems of exchange convertibility and related questions left over from the monetary discussions at Bretton Woods.

What line should Britain take in these tremendously important negotiations? To Lord Keynes this question was part—a critical part—of the wider problem of Britain's financial relations with the entire outside world, and he had been thinking hard all through the spring and summer. The resulting memoranda are among the most brilliant pieces he ever wrote. Unfortunately he had to say some very disagreeable things in them and their circulation was therefore extremely restricted, but the chief papers were circulated to the successive Cabinets, and eventually carried conviction and so formed the basis of the instructions he received from Mr. Attlee's Government at the start of his mission. After reviewing the probable state of the balance of payments and the structure and origins of London's external debt, Keynes characterised the three courses

---

[1] This exception was trivial, but United Kingdom representatives, sore though they were, thought it would be 'rather churlish to refuse'.

open—or which might be opened—to Britain as Starvation Corner, Temptation, and Justice.[1]

'Starvation Corner' was the position to which Britain would drift by doing nothing about the external debt. It would involve intensified rationing, planning and direction of foreign trade 'somewhat on the Russian model', and a policy of economic and political isolation in the world generally. The arguments against it were the retaliation it would provoke, the fact that Britain's interest in foreign trade was best served by the multilateral trading principles the Americans and Canadians now wanted, and the dependence of London's position in the Sterling Area upon a freely convertible currency.

The 'Temptation' was to accept an American loan of the requisite size—'$5 billions without doubt and perhaps the full $8 billions spread over a period'—*on their own terms*. This would involve using some of the borrowed dollars to pay off part of the sterling debt to Commonwealth and other countries; it would involve putting ourselves at the mercy of the United States of America and weakening our influence in international economic policy. But the main objection, Keynes argued, was 'not in these details, but in the whole proposed set-up being an outrageous crown and conclusion of all that has happened. The war would end by placing on Germany an external burden of $20 billions or less; it would end by placing on us a burden of $20 billions or more. . . . . She would plead to Russia from time to time for mercy and deferment; and so should we to the United States. . . . . The fundamental reasons for rejection are incommensurable in terms of cash'.

And so he turned to the third course, which he labelled 'Justice'. Its approach was 'a general reconsideration of the proper burden of the costs of the war'.

> For a hundred good reasons we have had to accept during the war a post-war burden entirely disproportionate to what is fair . . . . we did it in the interests of getting on with the war without waste of time or loss of war-like efficiency. As a result, we, and we only, end up owing vast sums, not to neutrals and bystanders, but to our own Allies, Dominions and Associates, who ought to figure in the eyes of history as our mercenaries, unless the balance is redressed. This does not apply particularly to the United States; indeed, to them (and to Canada) proportionately least of all. It applies all round. Nevertheless, it is only through appropriate action by the United States and Canada that there is a prospect of an agreed general resettlement. . . .

---

[1] The following paragraphs give only the most summary indication of the case Keynes took to Washington. For the reason given in the concluding sentences of this book, the more extended treatment which alone could do justice to this theme would be inappropriate here.

He therefore proposed that the United States should first be approached, and asked

(i) for $3 billions 'as a sort of retrospective lend-lease to replace the equal sum spent on purchases in the United States before lend-lease came into full operation, for what afterwards became a common war, and

(ii) up to a further $5 billions at call over a period, 'at a token rate of interest and on easy terms of repayment'.

If these sums were forthcoming, the United Kingdom could enter into certain commitments as to progress towards a multilateral trading system. The United Kingdom would also proceed to approach the various members of the Sterling Area with proposals for dealing with the sterling balances in ways that would acknowledge the special nature of their origin, and would enable Britain to shoulder her burdens consistently with movement towards the kind of trading world the Americans and Canadians, and indeed the British too, wanted.

The settlement envisaged was thus one that would enable the nations to move forward into a tolerable sort of world, and in that sense it was a forward-looking plan. But the basis of the settlement would be essentially backward-looking. It would, in particular, redress the balance that was turned against Britain by her willingness, in the earlier part of the war, to shoulder the burden alone. This approach was authorised by the Prime Minister and his principal colleagues,[1] and it was on this basis that Lord Keynes opened the negotiations in Washington in September 1945. He began with a great exposition of Britain's state and of Britain's claim to justice, to a backward-looking settlement that would enable her to move forward in the direction all desired. But impressive as the exposition was,[2] it misfired completely. The Americans were not interested in looking backward. They were not interested in adding, to the $30 billions they had already paid, further billions in consideration of services rendered by Britain in 1939, 1940 or any other year; Britain had, after all, taken her own decision to fight for her own purposes. Though willing to say that lend-lease left no debt behind, the Americans were in every other

---

[1] There was no Cabinet Minute on the question. Keynes put his case to a Meeting of Ministers on 23rd August 1945 over which the Prime Minister presided. He expressed the view that 'he should not be authorised to agree to anything [in the way of United States proposals] except an out and out grant.' Not all present at the Meeting were as optimistic as Keynes that the United States would come round to the United Kingdom way of thinking. The Americans were insisting that talks on commercial policy should take place simultaneously with those on finance, but Keynes was advised to defer the former until the arrival of Sir Percival Liesching (Second Secretary to the Board of Trade) at the end of September.

[2] R. F. Harrod, *op. cit.*, pp. 602-3.

respect interested only in a forward-looking arrangement, an arrangement whereby they would lend to the United Kingdom, on terms that should be as nearly commercial as Britain could bear, the minimum sum necessary to put Britain on her feet. The difficult negotiations of the ensuing three months and the Loan Agreement which followed are therefore the beginning of the post-war story and not, as Lord Keynes had hoped, the closing chapter of the war-time story. For this reason they can have no place in this book. The Americans had in effect rung down the curtain when they ended lend-lease almost on the morrow of V-J Day, leaving Britain the greatest debtor in the history of the world. That they had second thoughts was to be shown a few years later, when the generosity of the Marshall Plan outshone even that of lend-lease; meanwhile, Britain had to face the transition from war to peace in financial conditions likely to cramp reconstruction at every turn.

Appendices

APPENDIX I

Statistics of National Income and Expenditure, Central Government Finance and the Balance of Payments

The tables in this appendix are based on material that has already been published elsewhere.

Tables 1—6 and Table 14 are taken from *The Statistical Digest of the War*, H.M.S.O. and Longmans, 1951 (in this series).

Tables 7—13 are based on figures published in the White Paper on *Reserves and Liabilities 1931 to 1945* (Cmd. 8354), and in *North American Supply* by H. Duncan Hall, H.M.S.O. and Longmans, 1955 (in this series).

Tables 1 to 5 show summary statistics of national income and expenditure and of Central Government finance from 1938 to 1945. These statistics were compiled in 1950. Since then, some of the definitions and estimates have been substantially revised and the figures shown here, especially in Tables 1, 2 and 3, are not comparable with the figures for 1938 and for years after 1945 contained in the current official estimates of national income and expenditure.

In Tables 7—13 are assembled the basic facts about the development of the United Kingdom (and Sterling Area) external financial position in the Second World War, which for this purpose is taken as running from September 1939 to December 1945. This material was prepared by the Treasury in 1951. No such accurate information was available during the war itself.

Complete accounts of this kind were not collected during the Second World War. There are good records of dollar incomings and outgoings, and good records of our relations with Canada. There are good records, likewise, of relations with some individual non-sterling countries. All this steadily improved from 1940 onwards, although it never reached the clarity of definition and comprehensiveness that has been developed since. The data about relationships with other Sterling Area countries are more fragmentary. Material on Lend-Lease and Reciprocal Aid is very complex and much more research would be needed before it could be broken down in detail with any certainty.

In these tables an attempt has been made to express the balance of payments in a manner which includes free deliveries under Lend-Lease and Reciprocal Aid alongside cash transactions; in other words, this seeks to cover the whole of the international transfers to and from the United Kingdom, and not simply those that were paid for in cash. In the summary, Table 7, a division is made between 'War' transactions— munitions transfers and inter-governmental payments for war supplies and services—and 'Civil' transactions. It is impossible to draw a hard-and-fast line between the two, and some items have no doubt been included in one which, on a precise definition, should be in the other. Nevertheless, the distinction is of some significance.

It would no doubt be possible to improve these figures if substantially more research work were done. Additional research might establish details more firmly. But it must be recognised that in any event there are huge gaps in the records, especially in the early years of the war, and it would be impossible by any expenditure of effort to provide estimates that could be regarded as being even as reliable as our returns for post-war years. On the other hand, there is no reason to suppose that research would lead to significant alterations of the general picture as presented in these tables.

Table 1 : National Income, Depreciation and Expenditure

£ million

	1938	1939	1940	1941	1942	1943	1944	1945
National income								
Wages	1,735	1,835	2,100	2,400	2,655	2,800	2,815	2,810
Salaries	1,110	1,150	1,220	1,350	1,390	1,450	1,515	1,580
Pay and allowances of the armed forces . . .	78	124	386	621	805	999	1,175	1,223
Professional earnings . .	84	82	78	80	86	94	98	105
Income from farming . .	60	80	143	191	217	231	208	194
Profits of other sole traders and partnerships . . .	440	460	490	545	580	585	610	690
Trading profits of companies .	543	715	965	1,105	1,260	1,290	1,280	1,225
Operating profits of public enterprises . . .	25	22	22	33	77	91	72	22
Rent of land and buildings .	395	404	408	404	400	400	401	403
Income arising in the United Kingdom . . .	4,470	4,872	5,812	6,729	7,470	7,940	8,174	8,252
Net income from abroad .	168	140	140	110	70	60	50	50
National income . . .	4,638	5,012	5,952	6,839	7,540	8,000	8,224	8,302
Provision for depreciation . .	450	470	490	490	505	510	515	535
National income and provision for depreciation . . .	5,088	5,482	6,442	7,329	8,045	8,510	8,739	8,837
National expenditure Consumption:								
Personal expenditure on consumers' goods and services .	4,304	4,422	4,661	4,933	5,210	5,291	5,562	6,027
Public authorities' current expenditure on goods and services	724	1,198	3,100	4,239	4,715	5,054	5,076	4,217
Additions to assets : Gross domestic capital formation (1) . . .	770	(808)	(345)	(87)	(8)	(137)	(44)	(693)
Net lending abroad and purchase of assets and financial claims from overseas . .	−70	−250	−804	−816	−663	−680	−659	−875
Gross national expenditure at market prices . . .	5,728	6,178	7,302	8,443	9,270	9,802	10,023	10,062
Subsidies . . .	37	47	102	176	209	241	258	302
less Indirect taxes . .	−677	−743	−962	−1,290	−1,434	−1,533	−1,542	−1,527
Gross national expenditure . .	5,088	5,482	6,442	7,329	8,045	8,510	8,739	8,837

Source: Central Statistical Office

(1) The figures given for this item are residuals, not direct estimates.

Table 2: Revenue Account of Persons

£ million

	1938	1939	1940	1941	1942	1943	1944	1945
Receipts								
Wages	1,735	1,835	2,100	2,400	2,655	2,800	2,815	2,810
Salaries	1,110	1,150	1,220	1,350	1,390	1,450	1,515	1,580
Pay and allowances of the armed forces	78	124	386	621	805	999	1,175	1,223
Mixed incomes	584	622	711	816	883	910	916	989
Rent, dividends and interest .	1,111	1,139	1,167	1,153	1,205	1,234	1,291	1,335
Transfer incomes . . .	272	263	266	280	300	325	356	503
Personal income	4,890	5,133	5,850	6,620	7,238	7,718	8,068	8,440
Payments								
Expenditure on consumers' goods and services	4,304	4,422	4,661	4,933	5,210	5,291	5,562	6,027
Direct taxes:								
On income	364	382	565	730	875	1,108	1,254	1,301
On capital	78	77	79	163	160	151	156	158
Additions to tax reserves . .	5	30	63	192	146	71	21	34
Net saving	139	222	482	602	847	1,097	1,075	920
Personal outlay and saving . .	4,890	5,133	5,850	6,620	7,238	7,718	8,068	8,440

Source: Central Statistical Office

Table 3: Combined Capital Account

£ million

	1938	1939	1940	1941	1942	1943	1944	1945
Receipts								
Net saving by:								
Persons	139	222	482	602	847	1,097	1,075	920
Companies	170	175	175	175	215	235	235	245
Public authorities . . .	−81	−455	−2,056	−2,733	−2,797	−2,708	−2,565	−2,027
Additions to tax reserves by:								
Persons	5	30	63	192	146	71	21	34
Companies	10	104	335	282	208	62	−13	−59
Provision for depreciation by:								
Enterprises	360	385	410	415	425	430	435	450
Public authorities . . .	90	85	80	75	80	80	80	85
Transfers from public authorities .	7	12	52	263	221	190	117	170
Total sums set aside . . .	700	558	−459	−729	−655	−543	−615	−182
Payments								
Gross capital formation at home(1)	770	(808)	(345)	(87)	(8)	(137)	(44)	(693)
Net lending abroad and purchase of assets and financial claims from overseas . . .	−70	−250	−804	−816	−663	−680	−659	−875
Gross capital formation at home and abroad	700	558	−459	−729	−655	−543	−615	−182

Source: Central Statistical Office

(1) The figures given for this item are residuals, not direct estimates.

Table 4: Central Government Revenue

£ million

	1938	1939	1940	1941	1942	1943	1944	1945
Direct taxes								
Income tax and surtax . .	371	410	551	741	921	1,184	1,353	1,426
National defence contribution .	15	28	24	23	27	33	35	34
Excess profits tax . . .	—	—	44	211	318	453	482	440
Death duties . . .	78	77	79	88	94	97	107	119
War damage premiums . .	—	—	—	75	66	54	49	39
Miscellaneous	—	—	8	5	—	-2	-3	-4
Total . .	464	515	706	1,143	1,426	1,819	2,023	2,054
Indirect taxes								
Customs and excise duties . .	337	382	474	676	851	992	1,088	1,092
Motor vehicle duties . . .	35	34	37	38	32	27	28	35
Stamp duties. . . .	21	19	14	14	16	17	17	23
Post Office surplus . . .	11	8	19	25	31	36	39	37
War risks insurance premiums .	—	14	124	239	199	152	58	14
Miscellaneous	8	8	8	8	8	9	9	10
Total . .	412	465	676	1,000	1,137	1,233	1,239	1,211
Total tax revenue . . .	876	980	1,382	2,143	2,563	3,052	3,262	3,265
Income from property								
Miscellaneous	20	22	18	33	79	93	80	33
less National debt interest . .	-223	-231	-242	-271	-328	-386	-445	-492
Total revenue	673	771	1,158	1,905	2,314	2,759	2,897	2,806

Source: Central Statistical Office

Table 5 : The Finance of the Central Government Deficit on Current Account

£ million

	1938	1939	1940	1941	1942	1943	1944	1945
Public borrowing at home								
Small savings	4	62	466	602	600	719	702	668
Other public issues (net) . .	73	10	567	1,031	1,047	1,059	896	1,176
Floating debt	−179	280	517	903	476	1,017	1,081	557
Tax reserve certificates . .	—	—	—	17	453	177	113	41
Total . .	−102	352	1,550	2,553	2,576	2,972	2,792	2,442
Finance through Government agencies								
Extra-budgetary receipts, etc. .	254	185	598	217	210	−100	−60	−298
less Sinking funds . . .	−11	−14	−12	−17	−13	−15	−16	−16
Total . .	243	171	586	200	197	−115	−76	−314
Gifts and loans from abroad								
Canadian Government interest-free loan	—	—	—	—	157	−4	−13	−14
Reconstruction Finance Corporation loan	—	—	—	87	4	−7	−11	−10
Credit granted by the United States Government as part of the Lend-Lease settlement .	—	—	—	—	—	—	—	161
Total . .	—	—	—	87	161	−11	−24	137
less Lending and net capital formation	−33	−33	−21	−18	−25	−20	−20	−134
Total deficit on current account .	108	490	2,115	2,822	2,909	2,826	2,672	2,131

Source : Central Statistical Office

Table 6: Value and Volume of the External Trade of the United Kingdom (1)

	1938	1939	1940	1941	1942	1943	1944	1945
Value (£ million)								
Imports:								
Total imports . . .	920	886	1,152	1,145	997	1,234	1,309	1,104
Retained imports . . .	858	840	1,126	1,132	992	1,228	1,294	1,053
Exports:								
Exports of United Kingdom produce and manufactures . .	471	440	411	365	271	234	266	399
Re-exports	62	46	26	13	5	6	15	51
Volume index(2): (*1938* = *100*)								
Retained imports:								
Total	100	97	94	82	70	77	80	62
Food, drink and tobacco .	100	94	78	72	73	78	74	60
Raw materials and articles mainly unmanufactured . .	100	98	105	62	63	59	61	60
Articles wholly or mainly manufactured	100	100	112	121	72	94	102	62
Exports:								
Total	100	94	72	56	36	29	31	46
Articles wholly or mainly manufactured:								
Total	100	94	76	62	40	31	35	45
Textiles	100	101	80	69	55	36	36	41
Metals	100	87	65	47	29	23	29	42
Other	100	100	91	83	46	41	42	55

Source: Board of Trade

(1) The figures for 1942 to 1945 exclude imports, exports and re-exports of munitions.

(2) Quantities revalued at 1938 prices and expressed as a percentage of the value of imports or exports in 1938.

Table 7: Gold and Dollar Reserves

On last day of	E.E.A. holdings of gold, U.S. and Canadian $ £ million	Change £ million
September 1939—December 1940		− 395
August 1939 . . .	503	
September 1939 . . .	519	+ 16
December 1939 . . .	545	+ 26
March 1940 . . .	491	− 54
June 1940 . . .	390	− 101
September 1940 . . .	223	− 167
December 1940 . . .	108	− 115
1941		+ 33
March	70	− 38
June	65	− 5
September	69	+ 4
December	141	+ 72
1942		+ 113
March	163	+ 22
June	205	+ 42
September	238	+ 33
December	254	+ 16
1943		+ 203
March	296	+ 42
June	352	+ 56
September	401	+ 49
December	457	+ 56
1944		+ 144
March	504	+ 47
June	571	+ 67
September	589	+ 18
December	601	+ 12
1945		+ 9
March	603	+ 2
June	624	+ 21
September	603	− 21
December	610	+ 7

NOTES

Gold valued at 168s. per ounce fine until March 1945 and 172s. 3d. thereafter. U.S. dollars valued at $4·03 = £1 and Canadian dollars at $4·45 = £1, the rates operative throughout the period.

Holdings of non-dollar currencies by the Exchange Equalisation Account were comparatively small during the period 1939–45. The end year totals (in £ million, valued at rates operative at each date given) were: 1939, 3; 1940, 12; 1941, 13; 1942, 13; 1943, 21; 1944, 22; 1945, 8.

Figures of change in reserves correspond (when rounded) to those in Tables 9 and 10.

Table 8: External liabilities

I. PRE-WAR BASIS

£ million

On last day of	British Empire	Europe	Rest of World	Total
1939—June	328	197	17	542
December	362	134	21	517
1940—June	434	78	31	543
December	544	98	38	680
1941—June	676	152	53	881
December	924	180	66	1,170

II. POST-WAR BASIS

On last day of	Dollar Area	Other Western Hemisphere	O.E.E.C. Countries	Other non-£ Countries	Total non-£ Area Countries	U.K. Dependent Overseas Territories	Other £ Area Countries	Total £ Area	All Countries
1941—December	208	8	208	183	607	205	460	665	1,272
1942—June	36	19	236	235	526	224	535	759	1,285
December	41	33	280	301	655	258	729	987	1,642
1943—June	51	51	323	371	796	284	887	1,171	1,967
December	38	84	345	450	917	326	1,107	1,433	2,350
1944—June	62	101	367	495	1,025	348	1,307	1,655	2,680
December	52	125	376	548	1,101	368	1,546	1,914	3,015
1945—June	50	144	417	611	1,222	391	1,741	2,132	3,354
December	36	164	421	613	1,234	447	2,007	2,454	3,688

NOTES

The figures in Part I show the net liabilities, whether expressed in sterling or in foreign currencies, of banks (including accepting houses and discount houses) in the United Kingdom to their overseas offices and to other account-holders abroad; British Government securities held by banks in bearer form or on nominee accounts for overseas account generally; funds held by the Currency Boards and the Crown Agents for the Colonies; and overseas loans to His Majesty's Government expressed in sterling or Sterling Area currencies. The figures in Part II show the net liabilities in sterling of banks (including accepting houses and discount houses) in the United Kingdom to their overseas offices and to other account-holders abroad, including any British Government securities held for account of banks; funds held by the Currency Boards and the Crown Agents for the Colonies; overseas loans to His Majesty's Government expressed in sterling or Sterling Area currencies; and, so far as known, United Kingdom sterling securities held by official bodies but not those held by private individuals or firms. Both series include funds of enemy and enemy-occupied countries, including those of Allied Governments resident in the United Kingdom during the war.

In Part I the Mandated Territories and Egypt are included under British Empire. In Part II area definitions are those current at the 31st December 1950 for exchange control purposes. In particular, Canada and the 'American Account' countries of Central and South America are included under Dollar Area, and Southern Rhodesia, Irish Republic, Burma, Iraq and Iceland under Other Sterling Area.

Table 9: *United Kingdom Balance of Payments 1939–1945*
Summary—September *1939 to December 1945*

£000 *million*

	Total	U.S.A.	Canada	R.S.A. (1) (excl. Egypt and Palestine)	Other
CURRENT DEFICIT					
'War' transactions					
Munitions	5·4	4·1	1·3	0·0	0·0
Other Government payments	3·6	0·0	0·0	2·3	1·3
Total war expenditure .	9·0	4·1	1·3	2·3	1·3
Reciprocal aid . . .	2·1	1·3	—	—	0·8
Government receipts . .	1·8	0·0	0·7	0·7	0·4
Deficit	5·1	2·8	0·6	1·6	0·1
'Civil' transactions					
Food imports . . .	2·8	0·8	0·6	1·0	0·4
Raw materials . . .	2·1	0·6	0·3	0·7	0·5
Other imports (incl. ships and oil)	1·9	1·8	0·0	0·1	—
Shipping (net) . . .	0·6	0·7	0·1	−0·2	0·0
Other invisibles (net) .	−0·5	−0·2	−0·2	−0·2	0·1
United Kingdom exports .	−2·0	−0·2	−0·2	−1·1	−0·5
Deficit	4·9	3·5	0·6	0·3	0·5
Deficit 'War' and 'Civil' .	10·0	6·3	1·2	1·9	0·6
MEANS OF FINANCING . .					
Inter-area transfers (including errors and omissions) .	—	0·5	−0·1	−0·9	0·5
Grants, etc.					
To U.K.	7·5	6·7	0·8	—	—
By (−) U.K. . . .	−2·1	−1·3	—	—	−0·8
Total	5·4	5·4	0·8	—	−0·8
Disinvestment, etc.					
Sale of investments . .	1·1	0·2	0·3	0·6	0·0
Requisitioning of balances of gold and dollars . . .	0·1	0·1	—	—	—
Accumulation of liabilities (sterling and dollar) . .	3·5	0·2	0·2	2·2	0·9
Total	4·7	0·5	0·5	2·8	0·9
Drawings on or additions to (−) *gold and dollar reserves* .	−0·1	−0·1	—	—	—
TOTAL .	10·0	6·3	1·2	1·9	0·6

(1) R.S.A.=Rest of the Sterling Area, i.e. the Sterling Area except for the United Kingdom.

Table 10: United Kingdom General Balance of Payments

£000 *million*

	Sept.-Dec. 1939	1940	1941	1942	1943	1944	1945	Total
Current account debits								
Imports (including *all* supplies of munitions)								
Munitions	0·1	0·2	0·5	0·8	1·4	1·7	0·7	5·4
Food, drink and tobacco	0·1	0·4	0·4	0·4	0·4	0·6	0·5	2·8
Raw materials and semi-manufactures	0·1	0·3	0·3	0·3	0·4	0·4	0·3	2·1
Other (including ships)	0·0	0·1	0·1	0·3	0·5	0·5	0·4	1·9
Total	0·3	1·0	1·3	1·8	2·7	3·2	1·9	12·2
Shipping (cash + lend-lease)	0·0	0·1	0·2	0·2	0·2	0·3	0·1	1·1
Government overseas expenditure (excl. munitions)	0·0	0·4	0·4	0·6	0·7	0·7	0·8	3·6
Total debits	0·3	1·5	1·9	2·6	3·6	4·2	2·8	16·9
Credits								
Exports (cash)	0·1	0·4	0·4	0·3	0·2	0·2	0·4	2·0
Reciprocal aid (incl. services)	—	—	—	0·1	0·7	0·8	0·5	2·1
Other Governments' expenditure in United Kingdom	0·0	0·1	0·1	0·2	0·4	0·6	0·4	1·8
Shipping (cash)	0·0	0·1	0·1	0·1	0·1	0·1	0·0	0·5
Other (net) and errors and omissions	0·0	0·1	0·2	0·2	0·1	0·0	-0·1	0·5
Total credits	0·1	0·7	0·8	0·9	1·5	1·7	1·2	6·9
Deficit on current account + errors and omissions (= disinvestment and financing)	0·2	0·8	1·1	1·7	2·1	2·5	1·6	10·0
MEANS OF FINANCING								
Grants, etc.								
From U.S.	—	—	0·3	1·0	2·0	2·4	1·0	6·7
Canada	—	—	—	0·2	0·1	0·2	0·3	0·8
To (–) U.S.A.	—	—	—	-0·1	-0·4	-0·5	-0·3	-1·3
Other	—	—	—	—	-0·3	-0·3	-0·2	-0·8
Total	—	—	0·3	1·1	1·4	1·8	0·8	5·4
Disinvestment, etc.								
Sales of Investments	0·0	0·2	0·3	0·2	0·2	0·1	0·1	1·1
Requisitioning of balances of gold and dollars	0·1	0·0	—	—	—	—	—	0·1
Accumulation of liabilities (sterling and dollar)	0·1	0·2	0·6	0·5	0·7	0·7	0·7	3·5
Total	0·2	0·4	0·9	0·7	0·9	0·8	0·8	4·7
Drawings on or additions to (–) gold and dollar reserves	0·0	0·4	-0·1	-0·1	-0·2	-0·1	0·0	-0·1
TOTAL	0·2	0·8	1·1	1·7	2·1	2·5	1·6	10·0

NOTE

To some extent the pricing of lend-lease goods was too high for purposes of comparing economic efforts—though not for the construction of a hypothetical war-time balance of payments. This applied mainly to munitions, where the figure of 5·4, above, might be reduced to 3·9 if a more 'appropriate' exchange rate was used; and to shipbuilding reducing 'other imports' from 1·9 to 1·8. See Appendix III, Table 11, p. 539.

Table 11 : United Kingdom Balance of Payments with Rest of Sterling Area
(excluding Egypt, Sudan, Palestine and Transjordan)

£ *million*

	Sept. 1939-Dec. 1940	1941	1942	1943	1944	1945	Total
Debits							
Imports: Food, drink and tobacco . .	210	150	150	130	150	160	950
Raw materials . . .	160	110	100	100	120	90	680
Other	30	20	20	20	20	20	130
Total . . .	400	280	270	250	290	270	1,760
Overseas war expenditure . . .	100	200	360	470	500	650	2,280
Total payments .	500	480	630	720	790	920	4,040
Credits							
Exports	280	200	170	120	150	190	1,110
Other Governments' expenditure in U.K.	50	80	120	140	150	130	670
Other (net)	120	80	50	40	40	60	390
	450	360	340	300	340	380	2,170
Deficit on current account	50	120	290	420	450	540	1,870
Errors and omissions, non-dollar inter-area transfers, private capital movements, etc.	—	20	−90	40	90	50	110
Total (equivalent to identified financing) .	50	100	380	380	360	490	1,760
IDENTIFIED FINANCING							
Inter-area Transfers (gold and dollar)							
Purchases of gold (−) . . .	−190	−140	− 90	−110	− 90	− 90	−710
Net U.S. $ surplus of R.S.A. (−) .	− 50	− 30	− 50	−120	−120	− 30	−400
Net Canadian $ deficit of R.S.A. .	10	20	50	30	20	30	160
Total	−230	−150	− 90	−200	−190	− 90	−950
Disinvestment, etc.							
Sales of investments	50	120	130	140	60	60	560
Increase in liabilities . . .	230	130	340	440	490	520	2,150
Total	280	250	470	580	550	580	2,710
TOTAL IDENTIFIED FINANCING .	50	100	380	380	360	490	1,760

Table 12: Sterling Area Balance in United States Dollars (gross)

$000 million

	Sept. 1939-Dec. 1940	1941	1942	1943	1944	1945	Total
Debits							
U.K. Imports: (1)							
Cash: Munitions	0·6	1·2	0·6	0·1	0·1	0·0	2·6
Food, drink and tobacco	0·2	0·0	0·0	0·1	0·1	0·2	0·6
Raw materials	0·4	0·1	0·0	0·0	0·0	0·0	0·5
Other	0·9	0·2	0·1	0·0	0·1	0·5	1·8
Lend-Lease							
Munitions	—	0·2	1·8	4·4	5·6	1·8	13·8
Food	—	0·3	0·5	0·6	0·8	0·3	2·5
Raw materials	—	0·1	0·4	0·6	0·6	0·3	2·0
Other	—	0·2	0·7	1·8	1·7	1·2	5·6
Total Imports	2·1	2·3	4·1	7·6	9·0	4·3	29·4
Other debits	0·7	0·6	1·1	1·2	1·4	1·1	6·1
Total U.K.	2·8	2·9	5·2	8·8	10·4	5·4	35·5
R.S.A. payments and lend-lease supplies	0·5	0·7	1·0	1·3	1·3	1·2	6·0
Total debits	3·3	3·6	6·2	10·1	11·7	6·6	41·5
Credits							
U.K. Exports	0·2	0·1	0·1	0·1	0·1	0·1	0·7
Reciprocal aid	—	—	0·3	1·5	1·9	1·3	5·0
Expenditure of U.S. Forces	—	0·0	0·1	0·2	0·5	0·2	1·0
Other credits (incl. errors and omissions)	0·6	0·6	0·6	0·6	0·4	0·7	3·5
Total U.K.	0·8	0·7	1·1	2·4	2·9	2·3	10·2
R.S.A. receipts and reciprocal aid	0·7	0·8	0·7	1·1	1·4	1·3	6·0
Total credits	1·5	1·5	1·8	3·5	4·3	3·6	16·2
Deficit							
Sterling Area deficit on current account with U.S.A.	1·8	2·1	4·4	6·6	7·4	3·0	25·3
Capital items entering gold and dollar deficit	0·8	0·0	0·0	−0·1	0·0	0·2	0·9
Total deficit with U.S.A.	2·6	2·1	4·4	6·5	7·4	3·2	26·2
Gold and dollar payments to Canada	0·2	—	0·0	0·2	0·1	0·1	0·6
Other Countries	0·5	0·2	0·1	0·2	0·5	0·3	1·8
New gold, and gold and dollar dishoarding (−)	−1·4(4)	−0·6	−0·4	−0·4	−0·3	−0·4	−3·5
Total net gold and dollar deficit (2)	1·9	1·7	4·1	6·5	7·7	3·2	25·1
FINANCING OF DEFICIT							
Grants, etc. (2)							
Reciprocal aid							
(a) U.K.	—	—	−0·3	−1·5	−1·9	−1·3	−5·0
(b) R.S.A.	—	—	−0·3	−0·6	−0·6	−1·5
Lend-Lease							
(a) U.K. (and colonies)	—	1·1	4·2	8·1	9·8	3·8	27·0
(b) R.S.A.	—	0·0	0·6	0·9	1·0	0·6	3·1
Total	—	1·1	4·5	7·2	8·3	2·5	23·6
Disinvestment, etc.							
Sales of investments, etc.	0·3	0·3	0·0	0·1	0·0	0·1	0·8
Loans (3): R.F.C.	—	0·4	0·0	—	—	—	0·4
Lend-Lease settlement	—	—	—	—	—	0·6	0·6
Total	0·3	0·7	0·0	0·1	0·0	0·7	1·8
Drawings on reserves of gold and U.S. dollars (3)	1·6	−0·1	−0·4	−0·8	−0·6	0·0	−0·3
TOTAL FINANCING OF DEFICIT	1·9	1·7	4·1	6·5	7·7	3·2	25·1

(1) Including *all* lend-lease supplies attributable to U.K. (not only imports).

(2) Note that sales of investments, etc.—apart from collateral—are regarded as *financing* items.

(3) Belgian 1941–43 gold loan excluded in this table.

(4) Includes −0·2 for change in private dollar balances, and −0·4 (possibly too low) for gold windfalls.

Table 13: Sterling Area Balance with Canada

	Sept. 1939–Dec. 1940	1941	1942	1943	1944	1945	Total	Total
				£ million				$000 million
Debits								
U.K. Imports, etc.:								
Munitions (1) . . .	70	130	210	260	330	290	1,290	5·2
Food, etc. . . .	70	70	70	90	110	130	540	2·2
Raw materials . . .	50	60	40	40	40	40	270	1·1
Other	—	10	10	10	0	0	30	0·1
Total	190	270	330	400	480	460	2,130	8·6
Other payments . . .	30	40	50	60	50	50	280	1·1
Total U.K.	220	310	380	460	530	510	2,410	9·7
R.S.A. payments . .	30	50	70	50	60	80	340	1·4
Total debits	250	360	450	510	590	590	2,750	11·1
Credits								
U.K. Exports	40	30	30	20	20	20	160	0·7
Canadian expenditure in U.K. etc.	—	20	40	210	250	160	680	2·6
Other receipts (incl. errors and omissions) . . .	50	50	70	70	70	60	370	1·5
Total U.K.	90	100	140	300	340	240	1,210	4·8
R.S.A. Receipts . .	20	30	20	20	20	30	140	0·6
Total credits	110	130	160	320	360	270	1,350	5·4
Sterling Area deficit on current account	140	230	290	190	230	320	1,400	5·7
MEANS OF FINANCING .								
Inter-area Transfers								
Gold and U.S. $ payments .	60	—	10	40	20	20	150	0·6
Grants, etc.								
Canadian Contribution . .	—	—	220	—	—	—	220	1·0
Mutual aid and refunds and advances to								
(a) U.K.	—	—	—	120	200	260	580	2·2
(b) R.S.A.	—	—	—	0	20	20	40	0·2
Total .	—	—	220	120	220	280	840	3·4
Disinvestment, etc.								
Sales of investments . .	60	60	80	20	20	20	260	1·1
Loans . . .	—	—	160	0	−10	−10	140	0·5
Increase in U.K. sterling liabilities . . .	20	170	−180	10	0	0	20	0·1
Total .	80	230	60	30	10	10	420	1·7
Drawings on Canadian dollar holdings	0	0	0	0	−20	10	−10	0·0
TOTAL .	140	230	290	190	230	320	1,400	5·7

(1) Including (1940–42) factory construction.

Table 14: External Disinvestment by the United Kingdom

£ million

	Total	1939 September to December	1940	1941	1942	1943	1944	1945 January to June
Total	4,198	212	811	820	674	689	663	329
Realisation of external capital assets	1,118	58	164	274	227	189	143	63
Increase in external liabilities (1) (2)	2,879	80	179	564	519	647	608	282
Decrease or increase (–) in gold and U.S. dollar reserves (2) (3)	152	57	474	–23	–75	–150	–99	–32
Unallocated	49	17	–6	5	3	3	11	16

Source: Treasury

(1) Comprising banking liabilities, less assets, and funds held in the United Kingdom as cover for overseas currencies, etc.

(2) After deduction of outstanding liabilities to provide gold against sterling liabilities and of liabilities to convert U.S.A. holdings of sterling into dollars on demand.

(3) Gold valued at 172s. 3d. per ounce fine and dollars at £1 = $4·03.

APPENDIX II

War-time Budgets

SUMMARY

1939: 27th September

	£ millions
Total estimated expenditure in 1939–40 (revised) .	1,933*
Total estimated revenue in 1939–40 at existing rates (revised)	888
Yield of taxation changes in full year . . . +	227

	Estimated gain or loss in full year
PRINCIPAL CHANGES IN TAXATION	
DIRECT TAXATION	*£ millions*

Increased standard rate of income tax from 5s. 6d. to 7s. in ⎫
1939–40 and 7s. 6d. in 1940–41   .   .   . ⎪

Reduced rate raised from 1s. 8d. to 2s. 4d. on first £135 in ⎬ + 146
1939–40 and to 3s. 9d. on first £165 in 1940–41   .   ⎪

Personal allowances to be reduced in 1940–41   .   .⎭

Surtax rates increased by amounts varying up to 1s. 3·6d.   +   8

Estate duty on estates between £10,000 and £50,000 increased by 10 per cent. The increase of 10 per cent. on estates over £50,000 imposed in April 1939 was increased to 20 per cent.   .   .   .   .   . +   6

Excess Profits Tax of 60 per cent. substituted for Armaments Profits Duty   .   .   .   .   .   .   †

INDIRECT TAXATION

Beer:

24s. per bulk barrel (of 36 gallons); equivalent to 1d. a pint on all beer, increasing the duty on beer of average gravity from 2d. to 3d. a pint   .   .   .   . + 27·0

Spirits:

10s. per proof gallon; equivalent to 1s. 2d. a bottle for most spirits, increasing the duty from 8s. 5½d. to 9s. 7½d. a bottle for standard brands of whisky   .   .   . + 3·5

---

* Including £502 million authorised to be met from borrowing under the Defence Loans Acts.

† No estimate available when Budget was presented.

	£ millions

Wine: Light:
2s. per gallon, equivalent to 4d. a bottle, increasing the duty
on Continental table wine from 8d. to 1s. a bottle and on
Commonwealth table wine from 4d. to 8d. a bottle   .

Wine: Heavy: } + 1·5
4s. per gallon, equivalent to 8d. a bottle, increasing the duty
on port, sherry, etc. from 1s. 4d. to 2s. a bottle and on
fortified Commonwealth wine from 8d. to 1s. 4d. a bottle

British Wine:
2s. per gallon, increasing the duty from 3d. to 7d. a bottle   +   0·6

Tobacco:
2s. per lb., i.e. from about 6¾d. to 7¾d. per packet of 20
full-sized cigarettes of the popular brands   .   .   +   16·0

Sugar:
9s. 4d. per cwt. of refined sugar, with corresponding increases for glucose, molasses and saccharin; equivalent to
an increase in the duty on sugar from 1d. to 2d. a lb.   .   +   18·0

1940: 23rd April

Total estimated expenditure in 1940–41 . . .	2,667
Total estimated revenue in 1940–41 at rates in force in 1939–40	1,133
Yield of taxation changes in full year . . . +	128

PRINCIPAL CHANGES IN TAXATION

Estimated gain or loss in full year

DIRECT TAXATION §   £ millions

Increased standard rate of income tax from 7s. to 7s. 6d. .   +   32

Reduced rate raised from ⅓ to ½ of standard rate but zone in
which reduced rate applicable extended from first £135 } + 14
to first £165 of taxable income   .   .   .
Exemption limit reduced from £125 to £120   .   .

Earned income allowance reduced from ⅕ to ⅙ with max.
£250   .   .   .   .   +   7

Married personal allowance reduced from £180 to £170 .
Children's allowance reduced from £60 to £50 for each } + 7
child   .   .   .   .

Surtax to be chargeable on incomes in excess of £1,500
(instead of £2,000)*   .   .   .   .   .   †

Excess Profits Tax increased to 100 per cent. during passage
of Finance Bill   .   .   .   .   .   †

---

§ The changes in income tax were originally made in the September 1939 Budget and confirmed in the April 1940 Budget.

* Cancelled when surtax rates above £2,000 were increased in second budget of 1940.

† No estimate available.

POST OFFICE CHARGES   *£ millions*
Letter rate increased to 2½d.   .   .   .   ⎫
Postcard rate increased to 2d.   .   .   .   ⎬ +   14·5
Dearer postal orders, telephone services and telegrams   .   ⎭

INDIRECT TAXATION

Beer:

17s. per barrel (of 36 gallons) at a gravity of 1027 degrees or
less, with larger increases at higher gravities; equivalent
to nearly 1d. a pint on beer of average gravity, the duty
on which was thus increased to 3·9d. a pint   .   .   +   18·0

Spirits:

15s. a proof gallon; equivalent to 1s. 9d. a bottle for most
spirits, increasing the duty to 11s. 4½d. a bottle for
standard brands of whisky   .   .   .   .   +   7·0

Tobacco:

4s. per lb., increasing the duty on a packet of 20 full-sized
cigarettes to about 10d.   .   .   .   .   +   23·0

Matches: ⎫
4s. 3d. per 144 containers of 31/50 matches made in the   ⎪
United Kingdom, with corresponding increases for   ⎪
containers of other sizes and for imported matches, i.e.   ⎪
from about ½d. to 1d. per box of 50 matches   .   .   ⎬+   4·0

Mechanical Lighters: Imported: ⎪
2s. each; from 1s. 6d. to 3s. 6d.   .   .   .   ⎪

Mechanical Lighters: Made in U.K.:   ⎪
1s. 6d. each; from 1s. to 2s. 6d.   .   .   .   ⎭

Purchase Tax:

The intention was announced to introduce a new tax on
purchases by retailers from wholesalers   .   .   *

1940: 23rd July

Total estimated expenditure in 1940–41   .   .   .   3,467†
Total estimated revenue in 1940–41 at existing rates   .   1,234
Yield of taxation changes in full year   .   .   .   + 239

                                                            Estimated gain or
PRINCIPAL CHANGES IN TAXATION   *loss in full year*

DIRECT TAXATION   *£ millions*

Increased standard rate of income tax from 7s. 6d. to 8s. 6d. +   68
Reduced rate on first £165 of taxable income raised from
3s. 9d. to 5s. .   .   .   .   .   .   +   16
Surtax raised by 9d. in the £ between £2,000 and £15,000
and by 6d. between £15,000 and £30,000   .   .   +   11

---

* No estimate available.

† Of the figure of £3,467 millions, £800 millions represented increased expenditure
to be met by Votes of Credit over the estimate provided for at the time of the first Budget.

£ *millions*

Estate Duty increased to 20 per cent. above the pre-war
rates for estates between £10,000 and £50,000 and to 30
per cent. above pre-war for estates of £50,000 and over   +   6

INDIRECT TAXATION

Beer:
16s. per barrel of 36 gallons at a gravity of 1027 degrees or
less, with larger increases at higher gravities; equivalent
to nearly 1d. a pint on beer of average gravity, the duty
on which was thus increased to 4.8d. a pint .   .   +   13.0

Wine: Light:
2s. per gallon, equivalent to 4d. a bottle, increasing the duty ⎫
on Continental table wine to 1s. 4d. a bottle and on   ⎪
Commonwealth table wine to 1s. a bottle   .   .   ⎪

Wine: Heavy: ⎬ +   1.5
4s. per gallon, equivalent to 8d. a bottle, increasing the duty ⎪
on port, sherry, etc. to 2s. 8d. a bottle and on fortified   ⎪
Commonwealth wine to 2s. a bottle   .   .   . ⎭

British Wine:
2s. per gallon, increasing the duty from 7d. to 11d. a bottle   +   .65

Tobacco:
2s. per lb., increasing the duty on a packet of 20 full-sized
cigarettes to 11¼d.   .   .   .   .   .   +   9.0

Entertainments: Living Theatre:
New scales imposing ½d. on duty-exclusive prices from 3½d. ⎫
to 6d. and raising the duty by ½d. or 1d. on most prices ⎪
above 11½d.   .   .   .   .   .   ⎪

Cinemas, sports and other entertainments: ⎬ +   4.0
New scales imposing ½d. on duty-exclusive prices from 3½d. ⎪
to 5d. and increases on most higher prices, rising from   ⎪
1d. at 10d. to 4d. at 2s. 11d. and so on   .   ⎭

Purchase Tax:
A schedule of 23 classes of goods covering a wide range of
consumer goods but excluding food, liable to Purchase
Tax at a full rate of 33⅓ per cent. and a reduced rate of
16⅔ per cent. was published with the Finance Bill which
provided that it was to come into force by Treasury Order.
The Order, with a slightly revised Schedule, came into
effect on 21st October 1940   .   .   .   +   110.0

1941: 7th April

Total estimated expenditure in 1941–42 .   .   .   4,207
Total estimated revenue in 1941–42 at existing rates   .   1,636
Yield of taxation changes in full year   .   .   .   +   252

DIRECT TAXATION

£ *millions*

Increased standard rate of income tax from 8s. 6d. to 10s. + 88

Reduced rate on first £165 of taxable income raised from
5s. to 6s. 6d. . . . . . + 37

Earned income allowance reduced from ⅙ to ¹⁄₁₀ . . + 50

Personal allowance for married taxpayers reduced from ⎫
£170 to £140; and for unmarried taxpayers from ⎪
£100 to £80 ⎬ + 75
⎪
Exemption limit reduced from £120 to £110. ⎭

Farming profits to be chargeable under Schedule D instead
of Schedule B in certain cases . . . . + 3

Additional tax payable in respect of reduced earned income
and personal allowances to be refunded after the war in
a manner to be determined by Parliament . . ..

20 per cent. of net amount of excess profits tax paid at the
rate of 100 per cent., after deducting any repayments on
account of deficiencies, to be refunded after the war in a
manner to be determined by Parliament . . ..

INDIRECT TAXATION

Patent Medicines:

The intention was announced to repeal the Medicine Stamp
Duty and Vendors' Licence Duty, as most patent
medicines had become liable to Purchase Tax. The
repeal was effected as from 2nd September 1941 by the
Pharmacy and Medicines Act, 1941 . . . — ·84

1942: 14th April

Total estimated expenditure in 1942–43 . . . 5,286

Total estimated revenue in 1942–43 at existing rates . 2,469

Yield of taxation changes in full year . . . + 146

DIRECT TAXATION

£ *millions*

Wife's maximum earned income allowance increased from
£45 to £80 . . . . . . — 25

£ *millions*

Farming profits to be chargeable under Schedule D instead
of Schedule B where annual value of land exceeded £100;
where less than £100 tax under Schedule B to be three
times annual value instead of single annual value　　.　+　7

INDIRECT TAXATION

Beer:
37s. 1½d. per barrel of 36 gallons, at a gravity of 1027
degrees or less, with proportionate increases at higher
gravities; equivalent to 2d. a pint on beer of average
gravity, duty on which was thus increased to 6·3d. a
pint *　.　.　.　.　.　.　+　48·0

Spirits:
40s. 0d. a proof gallon; equivalent to 4s. 8d. a bottle for
most spirits, increasing the duty to 16s. 0½d. a bottle for
standard brands of whisky　.　.　.　.　+　15·0

Wine: Light:
6s. 0d. a gallon on still wine; equivalent to 1s. 0d. a bottle,
increasing the duty on Continental table wine to 2s. 4d.
a bottle and on Commonwealth table wine to 2s. 0d.
a bottle　.　.　.　.　.　.

Wine: Sparkling:
12s. 3d. a gallon on sparkling wine, increasing the duty on
champagne from 3s. 5d. to 5s. 5½d. a bottle　.　.

Wine: Heavy:
12s. 0d. a gallon; equivalent to 2s. 0d. a bottle, increasing
the duty on port, sherry, etc. to 4s. 8d. a bottle, and on
fortified Commonwealth wine to 4s. 0d. a bottle　.

$\left. \right\}$ + 1·7

British Wine:
6s. 0d. a gallon on still wine, increasing the duty from 11d.
to 1s. 11d. a bottle; 12s. 3d. a gallon on sparkling wine,
increasing the duty from 1s. 11d. to 3s. 11½d. a bottle　.　+　0·47

Tobacco:
10s. 0d. a lb., increasing the duty on a packet of 20 full-
sized cigarettes to 1s. 5d.　.　.　.　.　+　90·0

Entertainments: Living Theatre:
Doubling of most rates on duty-inclusive prices above 7d.

Cinemas, sports and other entertainments:
Doubling of most rates on duty-inclusive prices above 7d.

$\left. \right\}$ + 14·0

---

* In order to conserve materials, the average gravity of beer was reduced by four
degrees between July 1940 and April 1942. At the rates of duty then in force this was
equivalent to a reduction in duty of ½d. a pint, and it was for this reason that the duty
on beer of average strength, which was 4·8d. per pint after the Budget of July 1940,
was raised only to 6·3d. per pint by the Budget of 1942.

Purchase Tax:　　　　　　　　　　　　　　　　　　　*£ millions*

The rate of tax was increased to 66⅔ per cent. on certain ⎫
goods formerly charged at 33⅓ per cent. These included ⎪
apparel and footwear if made of fur or silk; silk fabric, ⎪
pile fabrics and woven-figure fabrics and domestic ⎪
textile articles made from them; mirrors and cut glass- ⎪
ware; leather trunks, bags, purses and wallets; cameras ⎪
and photographic goods; musical instruments, gramo- ⎬ + 　10.0
phones and records; jewellery and imitation jewellery ⎪
and clocks and watches of precious metals; pictures, ⎪
prints, vases, fancy goods, etc.; perfumery, cosmetics and ⎪
and some other toilet requisites　.　　.　　. ⎪
Account books and plain writing books formerly exempt ⎪
were made chargeable at 33⅓ per cent .　　.　　. ⎭

The intention was announced to exempt Utility cloth,
clothing and footwear from tax, by Treasury Order.
Treasury Orders to this effect came into force on 1st June
and 3rd August 1942 .　　.　　.　　.　　. — 　15

(A further exemption for Utility furniture came into force
by Treasury Order on 1st January 1943).

1943: 12th April

Total estimated expenditure in 1943–44　.　　.　　. 5,756
Total estimated revenue in 1943–44 at existing rates　. 2,805
Yield of taxation changes in full year　.　　.　　. + 103

| | *Estimated gain or* |
| PRINCIPAL CHANGES IN TAXATION | *loss in full year* |

DIRECT TAXATION　　　　　　　　　　　　　　　　　　　*£ millions*

Dependent relative allowance increased from £25 to £50
in certain cases　.　　.　　.　　.　　.　　. — 　7
Entitlement to housekeeper allowance extended　.　　. — 　2
Estate duty rate of interest reduced from 3 to 2 per cent. .　— 　·3

POST OFFICE CHARGES

Increase in telegraph and trunk telephone rates　.　　. + 　2·4

INDIRECT TAXATION

Beer:

20s. 3d. per barrel of 36 gallons at a gravity of 1027 degrees
or less, with proportionate increases at higher gravities;
equivalent to just over 1d. a pint on beer of average
gravity, the duty on which was increased to 7·4d. a pint + 　33·0

Spirits: £ *millions*

20s. 0d. a proof gallon; equivalent to 2s. 4d. a bottle for
   most spirits, increasing the duty to 18s. 4½d. a bottle for
   standard brands of whisky .   .   .   .   +   8.8

Wine: Light:

3s. 0d. a gallon on still wine equivalent to 6d. a bottle,
   increasing the duty on Continental table wine to 2s. 10d.
   a bottle, and on Commonwealth table wine to 2s. 6d.
   a bottle .   .   .   .   .

Wine: Sparkling:

   6s. 3d. a gallon on sparkling wine, increasing the duty on
   champagne from 5s. 5½d. to 6s. 6d. a bottle .   .   +   ·46

Wine: Heavy:

6s. 0d. a gallon; equivalent to 1s. 0d. a bottle, increasing
   the duty on port, sherry, etc. to 5s. 8d. a bottle, and on
   fortified Commonwealth wine to 5s. 0d. a bottle .

British Wine:

3s. 0d. a gallon on still wine, increasing the duty from
   1s. 11d. to 2s. 5d. a bottle; 6s. 3d. a gallon on sparkling
   wine, increasing the duty from 3s. 11½d. to 5s. 0d. a
   bottle .   .   .   .   .   .   +   ·44

Tobacco:

6s. 0d. a lb., increasing the duty on a packet of 20 full-sized
   cigarettes to 1s. 9d. .   .   .   .   .   +   58·0

Entertainments: Living Theatre:

Progressive increases in the rates of most duty-inclusive
   prices above 1s. 0d. .   .   .   .   .

Cinemas, sports and other entertainments:

Progressive increases, higher at each point than for the
   living theatre, on duty-inclusive prices above 1s. 0d. .   +   9·4

Purchase Tax:

The rate of tax was increased to 100 per cent. on those goods
   which had been made chargeable at 66⅔ per cent. in the
   previous Budget .   .   .   .   .   +   6
By Treasury Order exemption from tax was extended to
   Utility household textile articles, haberdashery, soft
   furnishings and bedding, with effect from 3rd May 1943 —   6

1944: 25th April

	£ millions
Total estimated expenditure in 1944–45 . . .	5,937
Total estimated revenue in 1944–45 at existing rates .	3,098
Yield of taxation changes in full year . . .	— 8

PRINCIPAL CHANGES IN TAXATION

Estimated gain or loss in full year

DIRECT TAXATION

£ millions

Excess profits tax minimum standard increased from £1,000 to £2,000 and other standards raised by £1,000, both with effect from 1st April 1944 . . . — 12.5

INDIRECT TAXATION

Beer:

2s. 3d. per barrel of 36 gallons at a gravity of 1027 degrees or less, with proportionate increases at higher gravities; fractionally increasing the duty to 7.5d. per pint, on beer of average gravity. (This increase offset reductions in the controlled price of barley and was not passed on to the consumer) . . . . . + 4.3

1945: 24th April

	£ millions
Total estimated expenditure in 1945–46 . . .	5,565
Total estimated revenue in 1945–46 at existing rates .	3,265
Yield of taxation changes in full year . . .	— 11

PRINCIPAL CHANGES IN TAXATION

Estimated gain or loss in full year

DIRECT TAXATION

£ millions

Excess profits tax standards increased by $\frac{1}{10}$ of amount by which they fell short of £12,000, with effect from 1st April 1945 . . . . . — 12

INDIRECT TAXATION

Hydrocarbon oil:

It was proposed to relieve from duty oil used in chemical synthesis . . . . . . — .4

Spirits:

It was proposed to repeal the allowances paid on industrial alcohol and on certain other spirits, as a corollary to the simplification of the system of Excise control . + 1

Both these proposals were dropped from the Finance Bill under the Caretaker Government, but were subsequently implemented after being reintroduced in the Budget of 23rd October 1945.

Table 1 : Income Tax : Rates and Allowances

	1937–38	1938–39	1939–40	1940–41	1941–42	1942–43	1943–44 to 1945–46	1946–47
Standard rate of tax in the £	5s. 0d.	5s. 6d.	7s. 0d.	8s. 6d.	10s. 0d.	10s. 0d.	10s. 0d.	9s. 0d.
Allowances, deductions and reliefs granted to individuals :—								
Exemption limit	£125	£125	£125	£120	£110	£110	£110	£120
Earned income allowance—Proportion of earned income and maximum allowance	$\frac{1}{5}$th (£300)	$\frac{1}{5}$th (£300)	$\frac{1}{5}$th (£300)	$\frac{1}{6}$th (£250)	$\frac{1}{10}$th (£150)	$\frac{1}{10}$th (£150)	$\frac{1}{10}$th (£150)	$\frac{1}{9}$th (£150)
Age allowance to individuals aged 65 or over whose total income does not exceed £500—proportion of total income	$\frac{1}{5}$th	$\frac{1}{5}$th	$\frac{1}{5}$th	$\frac{1}{8}$th	$\frac{1}{10}$th	$\frac{1}{10}$th	$\frac{1}{10}$th	$\frac{1}{4}$th
Personal allowance—Married persons	£180	£180	£180	£170	£140	£140	£140	£180
Other persons	£100	£100	£100	£100	£80	£80	£80	£110
Increased personal allowance where wife has earned income up to	£45	£45	£45	£45	£45	£80	£80	£110
Housekeeper	£50	£50	£50	£50	£50	£50	£50	£50
Unmarried person's female relative taking care of children	£50	£50	£50	£50	£50	£50	£50	£50
Children under 16 years of age or over 16 if continuing full-time education } each child	£60	£60	£60	£50	£50	£50	£50	£50
Certain dependent relatives incapacitated by old age or infirmity—For each relative	£25	£25	£25	£25	£25	£25	£50	£50
Reduced rate of tax in the £ chargeable on the first portion of the taxable income.	1s. 8d. on £135	1s. 8d. on £135	2s. 4d. on £135	5s. 0d. on £165	6s. 6d. on £165	6s. 6d. on £165	6s. 6d. on £165	3s. 0d. on £50; 6s. 0d. on £75

NOTE: Relief is also given for Life Insurance Premiums and in certain cases for Dominion tax.

2K

Table 2: Surtax Rates (Excess of Income Tax over Standard Rate)

Slice of Income	Rate of Surtax per £ of Income							
	1937–38		1938–39		1939–40 to 1945–46		1946–47	
	s.	d.	s.	d.	s.	d.	s.	d.
Under £2,000	Nil		Nil		Nil		Nil	
£ £								
2,000 — 2,500	1	$1\frac{1}{5}$	1	3	2	0	2	0
2,500 — 3,000	1	$4\frac{1}{2}$	1	6	2	3	2	6
3,000 — 4,000	2	$2\frac{2}{5}$	2	6	3	3	3	6
4,000 — 5,000	3	$3\frac{3}{5}$	3	6	4	3	4	6
5,000 — 6,000	3	$10\frac{1}{5}$	4	3	5	0	5	6
6,000 — 8,000	4	$4\frac{4}{5}$	5	0	5	9	6	6
8,000 — 10,000	5	6	6	3	7	0	7	6
10,000 — 12,000	6	$0\frac{3}{5}$	7	6	8	3	8	6
12,000 — 15,000	6	$0\frac{3}{5}$	7	6	8	3	9	6
15,000 — 20,000	6	$7\frac{1}{5}$	8	6	9	0	10	0
20,000 — 30,000	7	$1\frac{4}{5}$	9	0	9	6	10	6
30,000 — 50,000	7	$8\frac{2}{5}$	9	6	9	6	10	6
Over 50,000	8	3	9	6	9	6	10	6

Excess Profits Tax

The excess profits tax came into force as from 1st April 1939, and was repealed as from 31st December 1946. The rates chargeable were:

Per cent.

Accounting period (or portion thereof) falling between
    1st April, 1939 and 31st March, 1940   60
    1st April, 1940 and 31st December, 1945   .   .   .   100*
    1st January, 1946 and 31st December, 1946   .   .   60

During its currency excess profits tax was an alternative tax to the profits tax, only the higher of the two taxes being chargeable.

* Including 20 per cent. refundable post-war.

Profits tax

The Finance Act, 1946, provided that the National Defence Contribution should, as from the beginning of 1947, be known as the 'Profits Tax'.

Rates up to 31st December, 1946, were :
       Companies and other bodies corporate   5 per cent.
       Individuals and firms   .   .   .   4 per cent.

In the case of a building society the rate was subject to an overriding maximum of $1\frac{1}{2}$ per cent. of the total profits before deduction of interest on loans from members or depositors.

No Profits Tax was, however, payable where the profits for a Chargeable Accounting Period of twelve months did not exceed £2,000, and in cases where such profits exceeded £2,000 but did not exceed £12,000 an abatement of one-fifth of the amount by which the profits fall short £12,000 was allowable.

Table 3: Profits Tax and Excess Profits Tax: Budget Estimate, Exchequer Receipt and Net Receipt

Year		Budget Estimate	Exchequer Receipt	Net Receipt			
				England and Wales	Scotland	Northern Ireland	United Kingdom
		£	£	£	£	£	£
1937–38	P.T.	2,000,000	1,420,000	1,386,835	120,547	3,089	1,510,471
1938–39	P.T.	20,000,000	21,890,000	19,893,451	1,996,682	126,494	22,016,627
1939–40	{ P.T.	25,000,000	26,940,000	24,412,192	2,163,752	170,881	26,746,825
	E.P.T.		40,000	60,589	—	1,044	61,633
1940–41	{ P.T.	70,000,000	24,085,000	21,697,542	2,512,945	150,012	24,360,499
	E.P.T.		72,103,000	64,551,287	8,452,178	776,696	73,780,161
1941–42	{ P.T.	210,000,000	21,883,000	19,774,871	2,023,839	80,436	21,879,146
	E.P.T.		247,160,000	222,266,523	22,780,346	2,756,309	247,803,178
1942–43	{ P.T.	425,000,000	30,635,000	27,583,770	2,691,544	204,542	30,479,856
	E.P.T.		346,887,000	311,063,974	31,773,121	5,136,969	347,974,064
1943–44	{ P.T.	500,000,000	33,446,000	30,712,033	2,555,392	274,600	33,542,025
	E.P.T.		466,668,000	425,286,875	35,514,078	6,911,264	467,712,217
1944–45	{ P.T.	500,000,000	33,304,000	30,795,160	2,538,743	242,729	33,576,632
	E.P.T.		477,134,000	432,750,027	34,938,907	7,009,999	474,698,933
1945–46	{ P.T.	500,000,000	35,485,000	32,079,929	2,705,424	357,553	35,142,906
	E.P.T.		430,877,000	393,287,486	30,811,752	6,477,324	430,576,562
1946–47	{ P.T.	325,000,000	32,107,000	29,853,576	2,281,348	226,438	32,361,362
	E.P.T.		325,391,000	294,653,200	26,294,873	4,301,159	325,249,232

Table 4: Rates of Estate Duty

Range of net capital value of estate		Rate of duty per cent. when the death occurred—				
Exceeding	Not exceeding	After 31st July, 1930, and before 26th Apr., 1939	After 25th Apr., 1939, and before 28th Sept., 1939	After 27th Sept., 1939, and before 24th July, 1940	After 23rd July, 1940, and before 10th Apr., 1946	After 9th April, 1946
£	£					
100	500	1	1	1	1	—
500	1,000	2	2	2	2	—
1,000	2,000	3	3	3	3	—
2,000	3,000	3	3	3	3	1
3,000	5,000	3	3	3	3	2
5,000	7,500	4	4	4	4	3
7,500	10,000	4	4	4	4	4
10,000	12,500	5	5	5·5	6	6
12,500	15,000	6	6	6·6	7·2	8
15,000	18,000	7	7	7·7	8·4	10
18,000	20,000	8	8	8·8	9·6	10
20,000	21,000	8	8	8·8	9·6	12
21,000	25,000	9	9	9·9	10·8	12
25,000	30,000	10	10	11·0	12·0	14
30,000	35,000	11	11	12·1	13·2	16
35,000	40,000	12	12	13·2	14·4	18
40,000	45,000	13	13	14·3	15·6	20
45,000	50,000	14	14	15·4	16·8	22
50,000	55,000	15	16·5	18·0	19·5	24
55,000	60,000	16	17·6	19·2	20·8	24
60,000	65,000	16	17·6	19·2	20·8	27
65,000	70,000	17	18·7	20·4	22·1	27
70,000	75,000	17	18·7	20·4	22·1	27
75,000	80,000	18	19·8	21·6	23·4	30
80,000	85,000	18	19·8	21·6	23·4	30
85,000	90,000	19	20·9	22·8	24·7	30
90,000	100,000	19	20·9	22·8	24·7	30
100,000	110,000	20	22·0	24·0	26·0	35
110,000	120,000	20	22·0	24·0	26·0	35
120,000	130,000	22	24·2	26·4	28·6	35
130,000	140,000	22	24·2	26·4	28·6	35
140,000	150,000	22	24·2	26·4	28·6	35
150,000	170,000	24	26·4	28·8	31·2	40
170,000	175,000	24	26·4	28·8	31·2	40
175,000	200,000	24	26·4	28·8	31·2	40
200,000	225,000	26	28·6	31·2	33·8	45
225,000	250,000	26	28·6	31·2	33·8	45
250,000	300,000	28	30·8	33·6	36·4	50
300,000	325,000	30	33·0	36·0	39·0	55
325,000	350,000	30	33·0	36·0	39·0	55
350,000	400,000	30	33·0	36·0	39·0	55
400,000	450,000	32	35·2	38·4	41·6	55
450,000	500,000	32	35·2	38·4	41·6	55
500,000	600,000	34	37·4	40·8	44·2	60
600,000	750,000	36	39·6	43·2	46·8	60
750,000	800,000	36	39·6	43·2	46·8	65
800,000	1,000,000	38	41·8	45·6	49·4	65
1,000,000	1,250,000	40	44·0	48·0	52·0	70
1,250,000	1,500,000	42	46·2	50·4	54·6	70
1,500,000	2,000,000	45	49·5	54·0	58·5	70
2,000,000	—	50	55·0	60·0	65·0	75

NOTE : When the death occurred before 10th April, 1946, the following provisions apply :

Small estates—where the gross value does not exceed £300—a fixed duty of 30s. may be paid.

Small estates—where the gross value exceeds £300 and does not exceed £500—a fixed duty of 50s. may be paid.

Estates not exceeding £100 net are exempt.

When the death occurred after 9th April, 1946, estates not exceeding £2,000 net are exempt.

APPENDIX III

Mutual Aid between the U.S. and the British Empire, 1941-45[1]

By R. G. D. Allen

The author is greatly indebted to Professor Allen and to the Council of the Royal Statistical Society for permission to reprint the following article from the Journal of the Royal Statistical Society, Vol. CIX, Part III, 1946. In the Journal the article was followed by a report of the discussion on the paper held at the Royal Statistical Society.

CONTENTS

The mutual aid settlement

Mutual aid and combined planning

U.S. lend-lease aid

British reciprocal aid

Comparisons of lend-lease and reciprocal aid

The composition of mutual aid

British Empire supplies of munitions

Conclusion

---

[1] The Allies developed during the war a multilateral system under which goods were supplied and services rendered to each other without commercial payment. This is mutual aid in the widest sense. In this paper, however, the term is restricted to comprise only the dual system of lend-lease aid from the U.S. to the British Empire and of reciprocal aid to the U.S. from the various governments within the British Commonwealth. Only incidental reference is made to aid to and from third countries (Russia, China, France, etc.) and to aid between the governments of the Empire. The position of Canada in the mutual-aid system needs to be noted. Canada did not receive lend-lease aid from the U.S., nor did she provide reciprocal aid to the U.S.; purely U.S.-Canadian transactions remained throughout on a cash basis. The large contributions of Canada to the Empire's war potential—in men, munitions and materials—were made in part in the form of 'mutual aid' similar to lend-lease from the U.S. This Canadian form of mutual aid was also extended to Russia and other countries. The fact that Canada receives only passing reference in this paper is not to be interpreted as a lack of recognition of the important part she played in mutual aid in the wider sense.

The data used in this paper are obtained in the main from published sources. Material prepared by the Treasury for publication in the White Papers on Mutual Aid (Cmd. 6483, 1943 and Cmd. 6570, 1944) and certain data subsequently made available from the same source are the basis for the tabulations of reciprocal aid from the U.K. Data on lend-lease aid, and also on reciprocal aid from Empire countries other than the U.K., are taken from the records of the U.S. agencies responsible for lend-lease—now the State Department (Office of the Foreign Liquidation Commissioner), previously the Foreign Economic Administration. The main source is the Report to Congress on Lend-lease Operations made quarterly by the President, and additional analyses of the same basic material are taken from Congressional Hearings on the Lend-lease Act and Appropriations, from the reports of the Senate Committee investigating the National Defense Programme and from other Congressional documents. The adjustments and manipulations of the basic data, and all comparisons and conclusions derived from the data, are made on my own responsibility. These draw on my experience as a British official concerned with the operation of mutual aid from 1941 to 1945, during which period I became familiar with the detailed statistical material available internally to British and U.S. agencies. Since this responsibility is mine, I wish to make it clear that neither the Treasury nor the U.S. State Department is in any way committed by my handling of their data.

The Mutual Aid Settlement. Lend-lease aid began in March 1941, nine months before the U.S. entered the war, as the result of an Act passed by the U.S. Congress 'to promote the defense of the U.S.' Aid was furnished to countries 'whose defense the President deems vital to the defense of the U.S.' Lend-lease operations were developed and extended after Pearl Harbor, and the system of reciprocal aid from the British and other Allies was introduced, as essential pieces of the machinery for the combined planning of the war. However, the terms of the Lend-lease Act were never changed to adjust them to the new conditions of full U.S. participation in the war. In particular, the terms remained under which the U.S. was to receive, in return for Lend-lease aid, 'payment or repayment in kind or property, or any other direct or indirect benefit which the President deems satisfactory.' The phrasing of the original Act makes it clear that the U.S. intention from the beginning was that lend-lease should be a purely war-time operation. At subsequent hearings in Congress on Lend-lease Appropriations and on extensions of the Lend-lease Act—including hearings as late as March-April 1945—it was repeatedly stated by the U.S. Administration that lend-lease would cease at the close of hostilities. Apart from minor exceptions, straight lend-lease and reciprocal aid did in fact terminate on the official V-J Day—*i.e.*, from 12.01 a.m. on September 2, 1945—though the machinery itself continued to operate for several months thereafter to clear the 'pipeline' against a later cash settlement. The bitter feeling engendered at the time, now happily forgotten, was mainly a reaction to the abrupt manner in which the end was announced in Washington.

The mutual-aid account between the U.S. and the U.K. is not only closed; it is also settled finally and completely. The settlement was arranged so harmoniously as to pass almost unnoticed amidst the turmoil of the Loan Agreement. The mutual aid settlement and an understanding on commercial policy were two joint statements by the U.S. and the U.K. agreed and issued at the same time as the Financial Agreement of December 6, 1945 (Cmd. 6708–09). Though the settlement was closely associated with the Loan, it was an independent arrangement not subject to implementation by Congress of the Financial Agreement itself. As we have seen, the President had sufficient powers under the Lend-lease Act itself to agree the terms of the final 'benefit' to the U.S. in the winding up of the mutual aid account.[1]

The settlement of the U.S.-U.K. mutual aid account is expressed in terms of hard cash. The details of the specific agreements making up the settlement are set out in a joint memorandum (Cmd. 6778) signed in Washington on March 26, 1946, following the more general statement of December 6, 1945. An exposition of the agreements and further details of the dollar sums involved are given in a letter dated March 7, 1946, from the U.S. Secretary of State to Senator Mead (Senate Document, 79th Congress, 2nd Session, Report No. 110, Part 5, Appendix XVIII).

---

[1] Similar settlements between the U.S. and the Dominions and India can be made within the framework of the Lend-lease Act, and these are now under discussion.

A total sum of $650 millions is given as due from the U.K. to the U.S. to be paid on the same terms as the proposed loan. Of the total, $118 millions is a first estimate, to be adjusted by closer accounting later, of the net amount due to the U.S. in the off-setting arrangements under mutual aid after V-J Day. The clearing of the lend-lease 'pipeline' gives the U.S. an estimated credit of $301 millions, against which are set $130 millions for clearing the reciprocal aid 'pipe-line' and $53 millions for the net amount due to the U.K. on other claims in connection with mutual aid.

The U.S.-U.K. agreements (Cmd. 6778) do not specify further dollar figures, but the U.S. Administration has released additional details (in the Senate Document quoted), presumably without committing the U.K. to agreement on every figure. According to these U.S. estimates, some $60 millions represents a payment by the U.K. for the acquisition of surplus property owned by the U.S. and of the U.S. interest in installations in the U.K. For this sum, the U.K. takes over tangible assets previously the property of the U.S. and valued at about $350 millions at original cost to the U.S.

There remains a sum of $472 millions due to the U.S. in final settlement of the mutual aid account proper in the whole period of operation from March 11, 1941, to V-J Day. The method of calculation of this figure is complex, but the broad principles are clear. First, there are no financial obligations whatever for mutual aid goods destroyed or consumed during the war. Such goods 'were used to defeat our enemies, thus achieving the primary purpose of lend-lease and reciprocal aid. Neither country profits financially at the expense of the other as a result of such mutual action, since both were devoting maximum shares of their national output to war production' (Senate Document, p. 87). Secondly, all naval vessels and all merchant ships of 100 gross tons and over provided under mutual aid and existing at V-J Day are returnable to the supplying government (Cmd. 6778, Memorandum, para. 3). Similarly, installations constructed under reciprocal aid for U.S. forces in the U.K. and colonies are transferred back to the U.K., and lend-lease installations in the U.S. are acquired by the U.S. (Cmd. 6778, Agreement VII, para. 5). Thirdly, the title to lend-lease munitions and other supplies held by U.K. forces at V-J Day remains with the U.S., and is not transferred to the U.K. The U.S. retains the right to recapture such equipment, though the right is not generally to be exercised. The value of the equipment 'did not enter the financial settlement and should not be considered in appraising the financial results' (Senate Document, p. 88). The right of the U.K. to recapture reciprocal-aid stores in the hands of U.S. forces at V-J Day is equally protected. Fourthly, mutual aid stocks of petroleum held by military and civilian agencies throughout the world at V-J Day are subject to a re-distribution between the two countries as described in a specific agreement on petroleum (Cmd. 6778, Agreement VI, particularly Annex IX). In round figures, the re-distribution is as follows:

	Million tons	$ millions*
Lend-lease petroleum held by U.K. . .	4·1	145
Reciprocal-aid petroleum held by U.S. . .	0·8	25
Total mutual-aid petroleum . .	4·9	170
Acquired by: U.K.	3·3	115
U.S.	1·6	55

* Cost plus full ocean freight.

On balance, therefore, the U.K. acquires and the U.S. provides a net amount of $2\frac{1}{2}$ millions tons of petroleum at an original cost of $90 millions, including ocean freights. The figure of $472 millions includes a payment for this net acquisition of petroleum stocks by the U.K.

Finally, the remainder of the $472 millions is intended to cover stocks of lend-lease goods held at V-J Day for civilian use in the U.K. and colonies with a deduction for reciprocal-aid stocks of civilian types held by the U.S. (Cmd. 6778, Agreement III). These goods include agricultural, mining and other machinery and a great range of foodstuffs, raw materials and manufactures. Machine tools, however, are not included, since they were subject to separate arrangements for acquisition by the U.K. after they were made ineligible for lend-lease in 1944. In addition, the sum is extended to cover certain non-combat aircraft of lend-lease origin transferred to the U.K. for civil or military use,[1] a few small ships of under 100 gross tons and the lend-lease constituent of installations in the U.K. and colonies (Cmd. 6778, Agreements V and VII).

Hence, as a result of the mutual aid settlement, considerable stocks of lend-lease goods of civilian types, held by the U.K. on V-J Day, are acquired outright by the U.K. The U.S. Administration estimates these stocks at $690 millions at original cost (Senate Document, pp. 88–90):

		$ millions
Undistributed civilian stocks of mutual-aid origin:		
Held by U.K.: Food	240	
Raw materials . . .	180	
Manufactures . . .	20	
Less held by U.S. (raw materials) . . .	—40	400*
Lend-lease machinery held by U.K. . . .		85*
Net acquisition of petroleum by U.K. . .		90
Non-combat aircraft and small ships . . .		80
Lend-lease interest in installations		35
Net total		690

* At f.a.s. cost plus 10 per cent. for mutual-aid share of ocean freights.

[1] The aircraft transferred comprise 72 Dakota (DC-3 type) aircraft for civil air lines, 600 Dakotas and 43 other types for military transport use. All other non-combat aircraft of lend-lease origin held by the U.K. at V-J Day are returnable to the U.S., but 671 Dakotas are to be leased for a limited period and certain Liberator transports and Harvard trainers are to continue for a time in military use.

The payment of $472 millions by the U.K. is for these stocks and for nothing else.[1] The U.S. therefore obtains a return of nearly 70 cents on the dollar for the goods which are sold to the U.K. in the mutual aid settlement.

The calculations summarised in Table 11 below show that, in round figures, total lend-lease aid from the U.S. to the U.K. amounted to $27,000 millions—$2,000 millions for ships, nearly $14,000 millions for munitions, nearly $2,000 millions for petroleum, over $6,000 millions for other goods and $3,000 millions for services. At roughly comparable prices, the U.K. provided reciprocal aid to the U.S. to the value of nearly $6,000 millions—$900 millions for construction, $2,250 millions for military stores, $1,200 millions for petroleum, $400 millions for other goods and $1,200 millions for services. The item for services on each side of the account is very largely composed of shipping freights and other charges concerned with transportation and maintenance of mutual aid goods. It can be treated best as an addition to the recorded value of transfers under mutual aid to convert the valuation from ex-works to delivered. With services distributed in this way, the balance in favour of the U.S. in the mutual aid books can be analysed in very round figures :

	$ millions
Ships and construction*	1,000
Military stores	13,000
Petroleum	500
Other goods	6,500
Total	21,000

* Including maintenance of buildings.

The closing of the mutual aid account can be freely interpreted in the following terms. Naval and merchant ships provided under lend-lease and construction under reciprocal aid can be ignored in the settlement. The ships not lost are returnable to the U.S. The installations constructed under reciprocal aid are handed back to the U.K., including the U.S. contribution to their cost. The use of the ships and installations during the war was obtained without payment in the settlement. The account for military stores is wiped out in the settlement without payment both as to munitions consumed and as to those remaining at V-J Day, estimated at over $5,000 millions in U.K. hands. The U.S. retains title to, and the right to recapture, military stocks of lend-lease equipment, and limits are imposed on the power of the U.K. to dispose of such equipment. An exception is made of non-combat aircraft (and some small ships), which are either transferred to the U.K. against a payment

---

[1] It would appear that the payment 'is deemed to include an adequate compensation for the value of such (lend-lease supplies held by U.K. forces) as may be released for civilian use in the U.K. and British Colonial Dependencies.' These releases, however, will be made in practice only 'to a very limited extent' (Cmd. 6778, Agreement IV, para. 7).

or returnable to the U.S. Petroleum supplies were largely pooled between the U.S. and the U.K. in the interests of saving shipping space. This mutual aid account is not far out of balance in dollar terms and a redistribution of closing stocks is made against a small payment from the U.K. The remaining account in goods other than munitions and petroleum shows a balance of $6,500 millions on the U.S. side. Food and other supplies for British civilians and materials for British war industry dominate this group, but it also includes food and other material directly or indirectly for the use of the forces. Undistributed civilian stocks and machinery held by the U.K. from this account are valued by the U.S. at around $500 millions, and the major part of the sum of $472 millions due to the U.S., perhaps $300–350 millions, can be regarded as in payment for the acquisition of these stocks at V-J Day.

A very large dollar sum standing to the credit of the U.S. on the mutual aid books, therefore, is wiped out in one sweep, and a possible source of post-war disharmony removed. The cancellation of more than $20,000 millions of lend-lease credit is a recognition of the combined effort in the defeat of Germany and Japan. The U.S. also acknowledges the contributions made by the British outside the mutual aid account in dollars and pounds. These contributions, though not measurable, are sufficiently obvious. There was the extra mobilization of British men and women for war service and war production, greater and longer sustained than in the U.S. There was the invaluable contribution to the build-up of U.S. armament production in the form of British cash contracts for munitions awarded to private U.S. firms before lend-lease, contracts on which deliveries and payments were made until 1943, and which were never taken over into lend-lease. There was the exchange of military and technical information and the pooling of research experience, all important to the U.S., particularly in the early days after Pearl Harbor.

The mutual aid settlement was expected to have, and in fact does have, strings attached. It was no accident that the Loan Agreement of December 6, 1945, the joint statement on the mutual aid settlement and the second joint statement on commercial policy were all agreed and issued together. Between them, they define the 'general obligations' assumed by the U.S. and the U.K. on commercial policy, and in particular on the development of multilateral trade in the post-war world. These obligations were first expressed explicitly in Article VII of the Mutual Aid Agreement of February 23, 1942 (Cmd. 6341), and reaffirmed in the joint statement on commercial policy of December 6, 1945. The mutual aid settlement states that the two governments take 'full cognizance' of these obligations. They are more specifically defined, particularly as to exchange arrangements, in the Financial Agreement; indeed, one of the essential purposes of the loan is to assist the U.K. in assuming the obligations on the promotion of multilateral trade.

With all such imponderables in mind, we can reasonably conclude that a fair balance has been struck between accounting in terms of dollars and pounds and benefits not assessable in value terms. So what has been described by Mr. Churchill as 'the most unsordid act in history' passes into history through a quiet but equally unsordid agreement. The main purposes of this paper are to offer a partial and preliminary estimate of the importance of mutual aid in the conduct of the war, to indicate what has been achieved by this, one of the many examples of combined planning under the stress of war, and to hold out the hope that the experience will bear fruit in the development of peace-time co-operation.

Mutual Aid and Combined Planning. After Pearl Harbor, the war could have been fought with independent contributions from each of the Allies. To be equitable, each contribution would need to be in proportion to the capacity of the country—*e.g.*, armed forces furnished in proportion to the male population of fighting age and munitioned to the extent permitted by industrial capacity. This was clearly not a practicable proposition in 1941–2, when the Russians were in dire straits, and when U.S. strength was potential rather than actual. In any case, even if feasible, the method would not have been the best way of mobilizing the strength of the Allies and of maximizing the impact against the enemy.

In fact, the conduct of the war was planned very differently. Though always imperfect and sometimes halting, the governing idea was to plan on a combined basis to take advantage of the potentialities of each of the Allies. Many limitations were never overcome, such as those imposed by the different types and calibres of weapons used by the various national forces. Even so, the conduct of the war provided a striking example of the 'division of labour' between countries. We can see, in broad outline, the division between the U.S., the U.K. and Canada from facts recently made available (*The Impact of the War on Civilian Consumption in the U.K., the U.S. and Canada*, H.M.S.O., 1945).

The U.K. maintained a larger proportion of her man-power in the armed forces than the U.S. Though the differential diminished as the war progressed, it was never quite eliminated. Canada's position was

Table 1: Strength of the Armed Forces

At June	U.K.			U.S.		
	Total labour force, millions	Armed forces		Total labour force, millions	Armed forces	
		Strength, millions	% of labour force		Strength, millions	% of labour force
1939 . .	21·0	0·56	3	51·8	0·36	0·7
1941 . .	22·7	3·76	16½	54·0	1·75	3
1943 . .	23·8	5·08	21	60·8	9·17	15
1944 . .	23·5	5·24	22	62·2	11·53	18½

NOTES

From *The Impact of the War on Civilian Consumption* (H.M.S.O., 1945), Table 3. Total labour force includes unemployed but (in the U.S.) excludes domestic servants. U.K. armed forces include full-time civil defence. All figures relate to June except U.S. armed forces and U.S. agricultural employment which are yearly averages.

broadly similar to that of the U.S., while other sections of the Empire, and particularly the two southern Dominions, followed the U.K. pattern. The mobilization in the armed forces in the U.K.—and in Australia, New Zealand and India—was far in excess of what could be supplied from domestic capacity for production of munitions. The gap was bridged by the receipt of munitions supplies from the U.S. and Canada, since 1942 almost entirely under lend-lease and mutual aid. As part of the combined plan, the U.S. (and Canada) put smaller armed forces in the field, but provided more munitions.

However, even with this large and relatively assured supply of military stores from North America, the U.K. mobilized a greater proportion of civilians for war work than did the U.S. One reason was that the U.K. was in the front line of the war and needed to devote some of her resources for purposes (*e.g.* A.R.P. and repair of bomb damage) which the U.S. was spared. Another factor was the lower productivity in munitions production, as in manufacturing as a whole, in the U.K., requiring a large labour force to supply armed forces on the same scale.

Table 2: War Mobilization of the Labour Force at June 1944

	U.K.		U.S.	
	Millions	*Per cent.*	*Millions*	*Per cent.*
Armed forces . . .	5·2	22	11·5	18½
War employment . .	7·8	33	13·4	21½
Other employment · .	10·4	45	36·3	58
Unemployed . . .	0·1	*	1·0	2
Total labour force	23·5	100	62·2	100

* Less than 0·5 per cent.

NOTES

From *The Impact of the War on Civilian Consumption*, Table 4 and Appendix XIII. Total civilian employment is allocated between direct and indirect war work and other work. Other notes as in Table 1.

Even this does not tell the whole story. By D Day in mid-1944, the U.K. had 55 per cent. of her labour force on war duties, while the U.S. had 40 per cent. To achieve this the U.K. had far less resources of man-power to draw upon than had the U.S., and hence the diversion from employment for the civilian home market (and non-war export) was correspondingly higher in the U.K. The war-induced increase in the occupied population was of comparable size in the two countries. The U.S., however, had a much larger pre-war pool of unemployed to draw upon, and could count upon a natural increase in the labour force due to population growth which was not available to the U.K. Consequently, as Table 3 shows, the U.S. mobilization was achieved by diverting only 6¼ millions from civilian employment (including non-war exports) to the war sector. Over 7 millions were so diverted in the U.K. between

1939 and 1944, in addition to about 1½ millions already switched from peace to war production in 1939.

Table 3: Sources of Man-power Mobilized for War

Millions

	U.K.	U.S.
Peace-time defence employment	0·5	0·5
1939: Diversion from home civilian and export employment	1·5	—
1939–44: War-induced increase in labour force · ·	2·5	7·0
Natural increase in labour force · · .	—	3·4
Decrease in unemployed . . .	1·3	7·75
Diversion from home civilian and export employment*	7·2	6·25
Total on war work at June 1944 · ·	13·0	24·9

* Residual item.

NOTES

From *The Impact of the War on Civilian Consumption*, p. 9 and Appendix XIII. Peace-time defence employment is a round figure. Total war employment in the U.K. at mid-1939 is estimated at 2 millions, 0·56 million in the armed forces and civil defence and the balance on production of military supplies. See also Saunders, 'Manpower Distribution, 1939–45: Some International Comparisons,' *Manchester Statistical Society*, February 1946.

The high degree of British mobilization for war was made possible only by the importation into the U.K. of food and other consumption goods, and of raw materials for the industrial machine, on as large a scale as shipping would permit. This is the second way in which the U.S. and Canada helped, very largely after 1941 under lend-lease and mutual aid. Other parts of the Empire added their contributions of food and raw materials, but the extra supplies under lend-lease and mutual aid were the marginal and perhaps decisive factor without which the degree of mobilization could not have been maintained.

The 'division of labour' was not all in one direction. The U.K. and other Empire countries have supplied the U.S. with all kinds of goods and services under reciprocal aid. The supplies were mainly for U.S. troops in the European and Pacific theatres, supplies more economically furnished locally than by shipment from the U.S. Other goods were sent under reciprocal aid to the U.S. as a contribution to the American war effort at home.

All that can be entered in a mutual-aid account, expressed in value terms, is the transfer of goods and of ordinary services such as shipping. This is the account which will be considered in the following analysis, and which inevitably shows a large balance in favour of the U.S. To complete the account, we have to set the extra munitions and other supplies provided by the U.S. against the services of British fighters and war workers maintained by the extra supplies—and to take into consideration the balance of other mutual services in the conduct of the war. As we have indicated, all this has been assessed, not unfairly, in the lend-lease settlement.

U.S. Lend-lease Aid. Between March 11, 1941, and August 31, 1945, total lend-lease aid furnished by the U.S. to all countries amounted to $43,600 millions. This total comprises the value of all goods transferred and of all services rendered which could be accounted for in the period. It excludes $700 millions for production facilities constructed in the U.S. with lend-lease funds and $1,300 millions for other expenditures out of lend-lease moneys not charged to foreign governments. The estimate is on a revised basis of reporting by the U.S. State Department (Office of the Foreign Liquidation Commissioner), successor to the Foreign Economic Administration. The changed basis is described in the *21st Report to Congress on Lend-lease Operations* (January 1946), which, together with the earlier reports in this quarterly series, is the main source of the data used in the following account.

The total of $43,600 millions approximates quite closely to the value of all lend-lease aid during the complete period of operation, excluding only what was currently or subsequently paid for in cash. On the one hand, a small part of the total, amounting to around $1,000 millions, consisted of goods and services provided on a cash reimbursible basis to Canada, France, the Netherlands and other countries. This should properly be subtracted from the figure of $43,600 millions. On the other hand, certain additions should be made to the total. Lend-lease aid was continued to V-J Day, so that the period used here falls one day short of the full length of lend-lease operations. All goods transferred, though not necessarily exported, and all services rendered by V-J Day are counted as 'straight' lend-lease. Goods in process of production out of lend-lease funds at V-J Day, or awaiting transfer on that day, constitute the lend-lease 'pipeline,' and subsequent transfers of such goods are against cash payment from the foreign government concerned, usually under an off-setting arrangement with reciprocal aid to the U.S. Certain exceptions have been made to this rule, straight lend-lease being continued to China and Belgium and for some shipping charges for a limited time after V-J Day. All this amounts to a small addition to the figure of $43,600 millions, an addition which may be taken as counterbalancing approximately the deduction for cash reimbursement of lend-lease.

An analysis of the total is given in Table 4 which shows that lend-lease aid to the British Empire amounted to a little over $30,000 millions as compared with less than $11,000 millions to Russia and less than $3,000 millions to all other countries together. A very small part of the British Empire total represents munitions and other goods paid for in cash by Canada. However, a significant proportion, perhaps more than one-quarter, of the figure recorded for countries other than the British Empire and Russia is lend-lease aid on a cash reimbursible basis. As a round figure for lend-lease proper during the whole period of operation, 70 per cent. of all lend-lease aid from the U.S. was rendered to the British Empire.

Of the total of $30,000 millions of lend-lease aid to the British Empire, $2,100 millions represents naval and merchant ships transferred to the British flag and not properly allocable to individual countries within the Empire. Some of these vessels were lost during the course of the war. The others are, generally speaking, returnable to the U.S., under the conditions of the original transfer, now that the war is over. The figure recorded for all the ships in the lend-lease account is the full cost of construction (if new) or the current value at transfer (if used); it is neither a valuation of the services rendered by the ships during their war service under the British flag, nor the original cost less depreciated value on return. To attempt to estimate 'value received' more closely is not worth while for present purposes, and the recorded figure can be left as it is for what it is—namely, the original cost or value to the U.S. of all vessels transferred under lend-lease terms to the British flag for war service.

A total of $24,600 millions of munitions, raw materials, food and manufactured goods was transferred to the British Empire. Most of these goods will appear in the records of U.S. lend-lease exports as shipped from the U.S. to the U.K. and other British countries or as taken direct to war theatres overseas. There remain, however, some transfers under lend-lease which do not get recorded as U.S. exports. Munitions and other stores sent from the U.S. on government vessels—*e.g.*, lend-lease aircraft taken aboard R.N. carriers in U.S. ports—are not shown as exports. Other lend-lease goods are used or otherwise retained in the U.S. and lend-lease transfers include some material of foreign origin handed over without passing through the U.S. at all.

The official records of lend-lease transfers, unlike those of lend-lease exports, do not differentiate between countries within the Empire, and it is quite impossible to unscramble them because of the complications of transfer and re-transfer between one Empire country and another. An approximate, and necessarily rather rough, method is therefore adopted in Table 4 to distribute transfers according to country of destination or intended destination. The method is explained in the notes to the Table, but consists essentially of using the proportionate distribution of exports each year to give the distribution of transfers, thus sweeping in *pro rata* those transfers which do not appear as U.S. exports, and also allowing for changing amounts held in the U.S. awaiting export.

Distribution by country of destination, however, does not necessarily imply that the goods should be accounted to the corresponding Empire government. The three Dominions can be charged, as a first approximation, with the amounts shown as destined for export to them. This ignores such lend-lease supplies on their account as went direct to their forces serving abroad. Against this, lend-lease goods retained in the U.S. or shipped on government vessels are probably largely on U.K. account, but are here allotted *pro rata* to all Empire countries. The approximation may represent a slight understatement of the indebtedness of the Dominions under lend-lease, but the error must be so small as to be safely ignored in the present rough allocation. India raises more troublesome problems which cannot be gone into here in any detail; indeed, the accounting between the U.K. and Indian governments for war stores, including lend-lease, is a complicated process not yet completed. As a rough shot, simply to round off the picture, we have taken here one-third of munitions and of industrial products (including petroleum) and two-thirds of agricultural produce sent to India under lend-lease as on Indian Government account with the remainder charged to the U.K.

Table 4: U.S. Lend-lease Aid to August 31, 1945

$ millions

	1941, March-Dec.	1942	1943	1944	1945 Jan.-June	1945 July-Aug.	Total
Aid to British Empire:							
Ships (sail-away) . . .	65	195	1,078	540	160	69	2,107
Munitions destined for:							
U.K.	86	987	2,797	3,807	822	149	8,648
Australia	8	152	280	225	180	54	899
New Zealand . . .	—	52	58	21	8	5	144
South Africa . . .	—	40	88	55	10	1	194
India	8	230	371	555	227	31	1,422
Colonies	8	74	129	89	23	2	325
Other war theatres . .	76	610	1,205	1,349	493	169	3,902
Other goods destined for:							
U.K.	576	1,404	1,782	2,405	1,094	181	7,442
Australia	6	83	165	167	52	10	483
New Zealand . . .	1	17	35	28	11	3	95
South Africa . . .	—	20	29	18	—	—	67
India	1	87	175	295	157	51	766
Colonies	2	20	32	75	97	9	235
Services	245	786	807	1,137	270	99	3,344
Total aid to British Empire	1,082	4,757	9,031	10,766	3,604	833	30,073
Aid to Russia	20	1,376	2,436	4,074	2,169	595	10,670
Aid to other countries . .	..	..	..	..	..	..	2,872
Total lend-lease aid . .	..	..	..	..	..	..	43,615

NOTES

Data relate to goods transferred and services rendered under lend-lease, as recorded by F.E.A. and published in the Reports to Congress on Lend-lease Operations made quarterly by the President. Certain major revisions were made in the cumulative returns after June, 1945. Aid to the British Empire shown in this table agrees with the revised F.E.A. figures cumulatively to June 30, 1945, and to August 31, 1945. The analysis by periods to mid-1945 is obtained from differences in F.E.A. cumulative figures on the unrevised basis, except for adjustments in services and in industrial products (metals and machinery) arising from the revision. All the F.E.A. revisions in the cumulative figure for aid to Russia (the net effect being not larger than $50 millions) are carried in the July–August 1945 entry in this table. The analysis by periods must therefore be accepted with caution. No attempt is made to allocate aid to other countries by periods since the F.E.A. revisions are mainly in this category.

The classification adopted is as follows:

Munitions: aircraft, ordnance, combat and motor vehicles, and related equipment; small water-craft and naval equipment; signal, engineer. quartermaster, medical, chemical warfare and other military stores.

Ships (sail-away): naval and merchant vessels delivered under their own power.

Other goods: agricultural products, raw materials, petroleum and manufactures.

Services: ship repair, freights, ships' stores and other shipping services; ferrying of aircraft; training of personnel; storage and transportation; materials and charges for construction of bases; miscellaneous expenses.

This follows the F.E.A. classification, except that miscellaneous military stores (signal, engineer, etc.), are estimated and transferred from 'other goods' to 'munitions.'

Ships (sail-away) are separated from other items in the F.E.A. category of 'watercraft' by the use of export records.

Allocation of transfers of munitions and other goods by country of actual or intended destination is based on export records (U.S. Department of Commerce for F.E.A. as published in the President's quarterly Reports to Congress on Lend-lease Operations). Transfers of munitions, except for the category of miscellaneous military stores (signal, engineer, etc.) are allocated to Empire countries and to Egypt and Sudan according to exports each year with allowance for the amounts held in the U.S. awaiting export (assumed to be one month's supply). The balance of the transfers is thrown, with those allocated to Egypt and Sudan, into the category of 'other war theatres.' This includes munitions on British account for direct export to N. Africa, Italy, N.W. Europe and other theatres, and also munitions exported on government vessels such as aircraft put aboard R.N. carriers in U.S. ports. Total transfers of miscellaneous military stores are distributed by countries in proportion to other munitions. Transfers of other goods are allocated by countries in proportion to exports, agricultural produce and industrial products being handed separately. The first allocation of industrial products includes miscellaneous military stores, which are then switched (distributed as indicated) from this category to munitions.

Lend-lease exports to Canada are included with the U.K. throughout. Since Canada did not receive lend-lease aid, these exports are of four kinds :

(*a*) goods exported from the U.S. for shipment through Canada to other destinations, mainly the U.K.;

(*b*) supplies for use by the U.K. in Canada;

(*c*) components sent for incorporation in Canadian production on U.K. account, or material in substitution for such components;

(*d*) stores purchased by Canada through lend-lease channels on a cash reimbursement basis.

The last category, which is small, should properly be excluded from lend-lease transfers; it is here swept in with the other categories in transfers to the U.K.

There remains a sum of rather more than \$3,500 millions charged to the British Empire for services rendered under lend-lease. Almost \$3,000 millions of this total consists of shipping services of one kind or another, mainly freight charges, but also including ship repairs and ships' stores. The balance is divided not unevenly among four other categories of services: the ferrying of aircraft, other transportation and storage charges, the training of personnel and charges in connection with the construction of bases. Practically the whole of the total for services, therefore, can be regarded as an addition to the value of goods transferred to cover the cost of transportation from the point of origin within the U.S. to various parts of the world. As a first approximation we can take a flat percentage addition, which comes to about $13\frac{1}{2}$ per cent., to the value of goods destined for each area. There is, indeed, a longer haul to Australia, New Zealand or India, and more exports to these areas were carried in U.S. bottoms than to the U.K. Against this, some services, such as the ferrying of aircraft, should be much more largely attributed to the U.K.

The results of these allocations of lend-lease aid to various Empire countries are assembled in Table 5. The Indian figures are rough estimates but the others are sufficiently reliable for present purposes. The U.K. is charged with \$27,000 millions,[1] or about 90 per cent., of the total lend-lease aid to the British Empire. The U.K. figure comprises the value of all ships, at original cost to the U.S., transferred to the British flag, the value of all goods destined for the U.K., the colonies and war

---

[1] An estimate of \$26,000 millions has been given for lend-lease aid to the U.K. in a U.S. Senate report (Senate Document, 79th Congress, 2nd Session, Report No. 110, Part 5, p. 33). No indication is given of how this rather lower figure is derived.

theatres overseas, a part of the value of goods destined for India and the appropriate proportion of services rendered under lend-lease.

Table 5: U.S. Lend-lease Aid to the British Empire to August 31, 1945

$ millions

Government account	Ships (sail-away)	Munitions	Other goods	Services	Total
U.K. . . .	2,107	13,823	8,113	2,980	27,023
Australia . .	—	899	483	188	1,570
New Zealand .	—	144	95	32	271
South Africa . .	—	194	67	35	296
India . . .	—	474	330	109	913
Total . .	2,107	15,534	9,088	3,344	30,073

NOTES

From Table 4, with allocations by countries as described in the text. Services are allocated in proportion to the total of goods (munitions and other goods) attributed to the countries. In particular, the figure of $913 millions for India is derived on the rough basis indicated in the text from an overall figure of $2,486 millions of goods destined for India (including $298 millions for shipping services). What portion of this should ultimately be taken on Indian or U.K. government account is an issue which this paper does not attempt to prejudge.

The total of lend-lease aid to the British Empire and its allocation by countries, as given in Table 5, are very close approximations to the amounts of aid received during the whole period of lend-lease. A small amount should be deducted from the U.K. figures for munitions and other stores purchased by Canada but procured out of lend-lease funds (see notes to Table 4). On the other hand, small amounts should be added throughout for transfers on September 1, 1945, to complete the period to V-J Day, and for shipping freights continuing for a short time after V-J Day.

Table 4 also shows lend-lease aid by years. As estimates of actual transfers made year by year, these figures are less accurate than the totals for the whole period. They are obtained as differences of cumulative totals reported at various dates, and so represent transfers reported in the year, together with the net adjustments made in the year on the value of transfers previously reported. The revised form of the cumulative totals after June 30, 1945, has also necessitated some small adjustments in the previous figures for aid to the British Empire; these revisions are confined to the figures for industrial products and for services. The corresponding revisions in the data for aid to Russia are quite small, and are carried in the entry for July–August 1945. The main effect of the changed basis of reporting is in aid to other countries, and no attempt is made in Table 4 to allocate this lend-lease figure by years. The yearly data of Table 4, therefore, can be relied on for a broad picture, but should not be subject to very fine analysis.

The timing of lend-lease aid to the British Empire clearly corresponds to the development of war production in the U.S. and to the general course of the war. After small beginnings in 1941, when the U.S. indeed had little to send even to embattled Britain, the flow of lend-lease goods and services mounted rapidly to $9,000 millions in 1943 and to a peak rate of a little over $12,000 millions a year just before D Day in June 1944. A year later the flow had decreased to scarcely more than half the peak rate. The supply of munitions and other forms of lend-lease aid were well timed to bring maximum force to bear against Germany in the months following the invasion of Europe. The three Dominions received only a small proportion, a little over 7 per cent., of total lend-lease aid to the British Empire. It is significant, however, that the greatest flow of munitions to Australia occurred during the last months of lend-lease, when Australia was a base from which operations against Japan were conducted.

In contrast, lend-lease aid from the U.S. to Russia was built up more slowly in 1942 and 1943 when a good deal of the burden of supplying Russian forces fell on Britain. U.S. assistance, however, was longer sustained. Lend-lease supplies to Russia were at the rate of $4,000 millions per year by mid-1944 and did not fall below this level until V-E Day in May, 1945. A peak rate of nearly $5,000 millions a year was reached early in 1945 to lend force to the final Russian blows against Germany. Altogether, lend-lease aid to Russia amounted to more than one-third of aid to the British Empire.

Lend-lease was never intended to sweep in all British dollar transactions. In the first place, it did not take over contracts for munitions placed by the British government in the U.S. before March, 1941, payments and deliveries on which were not completed until the end of 1943. In round figures, deliveries actually taken by the British on these contracts came to $1,400 millions in 1940–1 and to $700 millions in 1942–3.[1] Secondly, there were numerous items not eligible for lend-lease or too small and troublesome to be obtained through the machinery of lend-lease procurement. The extent to which dollar payments for U.S. goods were reduced to a 'hard core' of items ineligible or unsuitable for lend-lease is seen in Table 6. This shows 'cash' exports from the U.S. to the British Empire, excluding Canada and Newfoundland, provisionally obtained as the difference between two sets of figures, only approximately comparable, for total and lend-lease exports. The bulk of the deliveries from British munitions contracts in the U.S. is included in these figures, but not all, since some deliveries were retained in the U.S., sent to Canada or to non-Empire destinations. A rough calculation indicates that the following (in $ millions):

1939—750; 1940—1,050; 1941—1,050; 1942—250;
1943—150; 1944—350

can be taken for cash exports exclusive of munitions from British government contracts.

---

[1] Including capital payments ($100 millions) but excluding deliveries diverted to the U.S. ($400 millions). These are munitions contracts only; there were additional government contracts for steel, machine-tools, etc. The rough estimates given here are based on the records of the British Supply Missions in U.S.

Table 6: U.S. 'Cash' Exports to the British Empire, 1939–45

(excluding Canada and Newfoundland)

$ millions

Exports to:	1939	1940	1941	1942	1943	1944	First half of 1945 (annual rate)
U.K. . .	505·4	1,010·8	1,064·7	*	*	143·7	263·8
Australia . .	61·6	75·5	78·0	73·1	27·4	25·3	35·6
New Zealand .	16·5	18·2	29·2	12·8	11·4	13·4	13·6
South Africa .	70·1	105·4	188·4	49·7	48·8	68·9	119·0
India . .	42·8	68·4	89·6	90·6	29·5	47·9	69·2
Colonies . .	75·2	82·6	156·6	71·5	49·4	78·0	87·0
Total . .	771·6	1,360·9	1,606·5	*	*	377·2	588·2

* In 1942–43, total exports data do not incorporate corrections made in lend-lease returns—*e.g.*, charges on British copper refined in the U.S. The corrections are significant only for exports to the U.K. The recorded difference between total and lend-lease exports to the U.K., about $450 millions in the two years, cannot be taken as an accurate measure of cash exports in these years.

NOTES

Provisional estimates obtained by difference from U.S. Department of Commerce returns of total exports and of lend-lease exports, which are approximately but not exactly comparable. Australia includes New Guinea, South Africa includes Southern Rhodesia and Colonies comprise Burma, colonies, protectorates and mandates.

It is clear that British purchases in the U.S. increased in 1940–1 over 1939. Excluding munitions, and allowing for increased prices, we can estimate the rise at around one-quarter. The largest increases were in exports to South Africa, West Africa, Burma and Malaya. After 1941 the switch to lend-lease was rapid in its effect on cash exports to the U.K., but slower for other exports, particularly to Australia, India and the colonies. (The fall in cash exports to the colonies is the result of the Japanese conquest of Hong-Kong, Malaya and Burma.) The hard core was reached in 1943, and then, as the end of the war approached, more items were made ineligible for lend-lease, and cash exports rose steadily throughout 1944 and 1945. Even so, in the first half of 1945 U.S. exports to the U.K. paid for in dollars were only one-half the 1939 rate in value, and perhaps nearly 40 per cent. in volume. The two southern Dominions were also taking, for cash, less from the U.S. than before the war. By V-E Day, U.S. cash exports to other British countries were well above the 1939 rates in value, and somewhat above in volume. The normal sources of imports into these areas had been greatly cut down and, outside the U.K. and the southern Dominions, shipping was less of a limiting factor.

Table 7 summarizes the position in round figures. The two years 1940–1, between the end of the Neutrality Act limitations and the entry of the U.S. into the war, represent the period of British cash purchasing in the U.S. and the beginnings of lend-lease. The following three and a half years, from the beginning of 1942 to mid-1945, saw the U.S. at war and lend-lease operating at full blast. In this period all but 5 per cent. of munitions supplies and all but 11 per cent. of other goods obtained by the British from the U.S. were under lend-lease.

Table 7 : U.S. Supplies of Munitions and Other Goods to the British Empire, 1940–45

(excluding Canada and Newfoundland)

$ *millions*

	1940–41	1942–44 *and first half* 1945
Munitions: for cash	1,400	700
under lend-lease	200	14,900
Other goods: for cash	2,100	1,000
under lend-lease	600	8,200

NOTES

Munitions for cash are deliveries on British cash contracts in the U.S. Other goods for cash are exports. Munitions and other goods under lend-lease are transfers, as recorded by F.E.A. The figures for munitions are those of Table 17, excluding Canadian purchases and ship construction and repair under lend-lease.

British Reciprocal Aid. Public imagination has been caught by the original idea of U.S. lend-lease and by the sweeping nature of its operations. Reciprocal aid from the British Empire came later, and has been largely overlooked by the public, particularly in the U.S. Reciprocal aid accounts, by the very nature of the constituents, are more difficult to maintain, and there are gaps and some overlapping in the records of the various British countries furnishing aid.

Reciprocal aid was provided by the U.K. Government to the U.S. following the Mutual Aid Agreement of February 23, 1942 (Cmd. 6341). This agreement provides that, in contributing to the defence of the U.S., the U.K. government 'will provide such articles, services, facilities or information as it may be in a position to supply.' The flow of reciprocal aid had begun by the middle of 1942. It consisted of supplies and services of all kinds to U.S. forces stationed in the U.K. and in overseas theatres, and of the construction of military installations for use by these forces. At first, apart from small shipments (*e.g.*, of benzol) to the U.S., reciprocal aid was confined to the local servicing of U.S. troops. Later on, before the end of 1943, reciprocal aid was extended to the furnishing of raw materials and foodstuffs, mainly from colonial territories, for shipment to the U.S. An analysis of U.K. reciprocal aid provided to the U.S. up to V-J Day is given in Table 8, based on data assembled and issued by H.M. Treasury.

A total of around £1,200 millions was supplied to the U.S. under reciprocal aid, both from the resources of the U.K. and from abroad, but all at the expense of the U.K. government. As with U.S. lend-lease, the analysis of total reciprocal aid into various periods (Table 8) depends on differences of cumulative totals, and so represents aid reported in each period together with adjustments in amounts previously reported. However, several major adjustments have been made in the figures for various periods. The more important additions, deductions and revisions to the reported cumulative totals of aid to the U.S. have been carried back to the periods to which they properly relate. For example, the figure of £100·9 millions for construction in the U.K. in the year ending mid-1944 includes £27·5 millions for the Mulberry Harbour transferred to the U.S., though this item was not reported until later.

Table 8: U.K. Reciprocal Aid to September 1, 1945

£ millions

	To June 30, 1943	Year ending June 30, 1944	Year ending June 30, 1945	July 1– Sept. 1, 1945	Total
Aid to U.S.:					
In U.K.:					
Military stores . . .	46·3	61·6	74·1	7·6	189·6
Petroleum . . .	5·4	58·9	135·1	14·2	213·6
Food	0·1	8·1	8·9	2·0	19·1
Services . . .	41·9	108·3	128·8	18·5	297·5
Construction . . .	92·0	100·9	19·6	6·4	218·9
In U.S.:					
Military stores . .	17·6	5·6	1·5	0·5	25·2
Food and materials .	2·3	19·4	37·1	6·4	65·2
Miscellaneous and Services	4·5	2·5	0·2	0·1	7·3
In Overseas Theatres:					
Military stores . .	16·7	29·2	24·5	2·5*	72·9
Petroleum, India . .	2·4	12·0	38·3	8·0*	60·7
Petroleum, Other . .	—	6·5	13·2	2·8	22·5
Construction . . .	0·5	7·9	0·3	—	8·7
Total aid to U.S. . .	229·7	420·9	481·6	69·0	1,201·2
Aid to Russia . .	187·7	93·3	27·0	4·0	312·0
Aid to other countries . .	..	..	..	..	382·8†
Total reciprocal aid .	..	..	..	..	1,896·0

* Estimated in the absence of full returns.

† Incomplete, obtained by summing returns given cumulatively for different countries to various dates from March 31 to September 1, 1945.

NOTES

From White Papers on Mutual Aid (Cmd. 6483, 1943 and Cmd. 6570, 1944) and cumulative data subsequently made available by H.M. Treasury. Figures of petroleum provided in India are from U.S. Army records supplied to F.E.A., not from Treasury returns; two-thirds of the U.S. Army's valuations are taken as landed cost of petroleum met on U.K. Government account, the remaining one-third representing handling charges on Indian government account. Additions, deductions and revisions were made in the Treasury cumulative returns from time to time. The most important of these are here carried back or spread over the periods to which they properly relate. For example, £27·5 millions for the Mulberry Harbour transferred to the U.S. was first reported in the cumulative returns to September 1, 1945, but is here included under construction in the year ending June 30, 1944. Other major additions carried back include construction and building maintenance by the War Office and military stores transferred in the U.S. Deductions for previous incorrect reporting, here carried back, include aircraft reported transferred in the U.K. but actually transferred in N. Africa, clothing and other stores for combined operations first classed as reciprocal aid and an over-valuation of petroleum transfers in the U.K. Less important revisions are carried in the periods in which they were reported.

The classification follows closely that for U.S. lend-lease (Table 4). Military stores include all munitions and other stores for direct use by foreign forces, with the exception of petroleum and food. Services are mainly transportation, but also include building maintenance. The construction figure represents the cost to the Service Departments of the construction of military installations, and includes the whole cost of the Mulberry Harbour.

Aid to the U.S. in the U.K. comprises all transfers of goods and services to U.S. forces in the U.K., but shipping services and petroleum bunkers are on a world-wide basis. Aid in the U.S. includes both goods transferred in the U.S. (*e.g.*, from British cash contracts) and food and materials exported from U.K. and the colonies to U.S. Aid in overseas theatres includes transfers and construction in the colonies, as well as in N. Africa, Egypt, Italy, N.W. Europe and other war theatres.

It is clear that reciprocal aid was timed to meet the needs of U.S. forces and to maximize the combined impact against the German enemy in Europe. Goods and services rendered to the U.S. were built up to a rate of about £500 millions a year by the middle of 1944, and sustained at this rate until early in 1945 before falling off slowly. The nature of reciprocal aid gradually shifted, construction work declining and being replaced increasingly by current military stores, petroleum and shipping services as the military campaigns developed.

Reciprocal aid was also extended by the U.K. to Russia, China, European Allies, Portugal and Turkey. The formal agreements and arrangements with these countries were made later than that with the U.S., but they were retroactive to include credits granted earlier, in some instances before the Lend-lease Act itself. Supplies to Russia, dating back to the autumn of 1941, amounted to £310 millions by V-J Day in 1945. The equipment and maintenance of the forces of Allied countries over-run by the enemy were undertaken from the summer of 1940 onwards, at British expense where the governments concerned (*e.g.*, Czechoslovakia, Poland, Greece) were not able to finance themselves. Credits were advanced at first for this purpose, but these were later taken over and extended under mutual aid arrangements. A total of more than £380 millions was provided by V-J Day as reciprocal aid to governments other than the U.S. and Russia. Altogether, reciprocal aid from the U.K. to countries other than the U.S. was at least as large a part of total reciprocal aid as lend-lease from the U.S. to non-British countries was to total lend-lease. In round figures, U.S. lend-lease aid was divided 70 per cent. to the British and 30 per cent. to other countries, while U.K. reciprocal aid was split 65 per cent. to the U.S. and 35 per cent. to other countries.

The U.S. has also received reciprocal aid from the governments of Australia, New Zealand and India. Estimates of the amounts involved converted to £ sterling at official rates of exchange, are shown in Table 9. The returns on which the figures for the Dominions are based were furnished by the respective governments to F.E.A. for incorporation in the President's quarterly reports to Congress. The government of India has not released data on Indian reciprocal aid and the figures shown in Table 9 are assembled from other sources. Estimates of the value of exports from India to the U.S. under reciprocal aid are made from the records of British Supply Missions in Washington and the valuations of reciprocal aid in India are taken from U.S. Army returns to F.E.A., as published in the President's quarterly reports. Since they are not derived from Indian government records, the estimates for India in Table 9 must be accepted with some caution.

As for the U.K., the assistance consisted primarily of supplies, services and construction for U.S. forces serving locally—here, in the Pacific and India-Burma-China theatres. In 1944, however, India began to ship raw materials and foodstuffs direct to the U.S. under reciprocal aid and continued shipments until the middle of 1945. In three years, from mid-1942 to mid-1945, the three governments supplied aid to the U.S. to a total amount of approximately £380 millions sterling.

Reciprocal aid from the British Empire to the U.S. in the whole period up to V-J Day is summarized in Table 10. In addition to the data shown in Tables 8 and 9, the totals of Table 10 include estimates for reciprocal aid from Empire countries other than the U.K. in the last two months before V-J Day. Total reciprocal aid to the U.S. amounted to £1,600 millions in the whole period. The U.K. financed £1,200 millions of this total, or about three-quarters. As we have seen (Table 5), the U.K. can be appropriately charged with a larger proportion, about 90 per cent., of total lend-lease aid from the U.S. to the British Empire.

Table 9: Other Empire Reciprocal Aid to the U.S. to June 30, 1945

£ millions sterling

		Year ending June 30,			Total
		1943	1944	1945	
Australia:	Military stores	15·1	22·7	19·2	57·0
	Food	9·7	19·8	26·1	55·6
	Services	7·4	30·0	24·4	61·8
	Construction	16·3	14·0	2·3	32·6
	Total	48·5	86·5	72·0	207·0
New Zealand:	Military stores	1·3	4·1	4·0	9·4
	Food	3·1	9·9	14·8	27·8
	Services	3·0	2·5	1·5	7·0
	Construction	5·2	1·1	0·3	6·6
	Total	12·6	17·6	20·6	50·8
South Africa:	Total	—	0·1	0·1	0·2
India:	Military stores	1·0	4·6	14·8	20·4
	Petroleum	1·2	6·0	19·2	26·4
	Food	1·0	4·4	5·0	10·4
	Services	0·7	5·0	10·5	16·2
	Exports to U.S.	—	3·0	12·4	15·4
	Construction	7·8	11·6	13·1	32·5
	Total	11·7	34·6	75·0	121·3

NOTES

Australia, New Zealand and South Africa—from Dominion records supplied to F.E.A. and reported in the President's Reports to Congress on Lend-lease Operations. India—exports to U.S. (raw materials and food) estimated from records of British Supply Missions in the U.S.; other estimates from U.S. Army records supplied to F.E.A. Transfers of petroleum in India were on U.K. government account as to landed cost and on Indian government account as to handling charges in India. The figures given here represent the latter only, taken as one-third of the total valuation of petroleum transfers recorded by the U.S. Army. Conversions from local currencies to £ sterling at official exchange rates.

Table 10: British Reciprocal Aid to the U.S. to September 1, 1945

£ millions sterling

Government account	Construction	Military stores	Petroleum	Other goods	Services	Total
U.K. . . .	227	288	297	90	299	1,201
Australia . .	33	59	*	60	64	216
New Zealand	7	10	*	30	7	54
South Africa . .	*	*	*	*	*	*
India . . .	34	24	30	27	19	134
Total . .	301	381	327	207	389	1,605

* Less than £0·5 millions.

NOTES

From Tables 8 and 9 with the addition of estimates for reciprocal aid from Australia, New Zealand and India in the period July 1 to September 1, 1945.

Comparisons of Lend-lease and Reciprocal Aid. Lend-lease aid has been shown as valued by the U.S. in dollars, and reciprocal aid as valued by Empire countries (except in the case of India) and converted to £ sterling at official rates of exchange. Any direct comparison raises the awkward, almost insoluble, question of the appropriate relation between the dollar and the £ sterling. The official rate of exchange has no relevance to this problem. What is required is *either* an estimate of what lend-lease aid to the British Empire would have cost if the goods had been produced and the services rendered in British countries, *or* an evaluation of what reciprocal aid to the U.S. would have cost at the U S. prices used in the accounting of U.S. lend-lease aid.

For munitions and military stores (excluding food), an item-by-item comparison of unit costs in the U.S. and the U.K. indicates that an appropriate average rate of conversion is around $7 to £1. The rate is high because, quite apart from differences in the real costs of munitions production, the method of valuing output of munitions is very different in the two countries. In general, strict cost-accounting methods in the U.K. kept down the prices paid for munitions and other stores on government contract. In the U.S., the Service Departments used 'standard' dollar costs, changed from time to time, in the evaluation of their military procurement, and hence in their estimates of lend-lease aid. These costs are not the same as, and generally are slightly in excess of, actual expenditures. More important, U.S. munitions costs and expenditures are inflated in comparison with those in the U.K. because of the high level of profits in the munitions trades and of the 'cost plus' methods of contracting often adopted in the U.S. Throughout most of the war the main job in the U.S. was to get munitions quickly without regard to expense. It was only relatively late in the war that re-negotiation of contracts had any significant effect on U.S. munitions costs.

The rate of $7 to £1 for munitions and other military stores is an average of a very wide range of individual rates obtained from the relation of U.S. to British unit costs for comparable items. The individual rates range from some as low as $3 to £1—for example, for many important types of military motor vehicles—to others as high as $10 or more to £1, as in the case of certain ship construction costs. An average of around $7 to £1 is obtained by weighting with the distribution of total production of munitions in the U.S. or with the distribution of supplies made available under lend-lease, the latter being a very fair representative selection from the whole of U.S. production. The same round average is obtained if the weighting is done with U.K. production of munitions. However, military stores provided by the U.K. under reciprocal aid differ in composition from total production in the U.K., being lightly weighted with combat types and more heavily with other forms of equipment. But there appears to be little correlation between the individual conversion rates and the types of stores most frequently provided under reciprocal aid and, at least as a first approximation, the average rate of $7 to £1 is appropriate to military stores in the reciprocal-aid account. We shall therefore take this rate for our conversion of mutual aid valuations of munitions and other military items from dollars to £ sterling, and conversely.

For other goods and for services only a fragmentary comparison of the U.S. and U.K. prices used in mutual-aid valuations is possible. The appropriate conversion rate, however, would seem to be not far from the official rate of exchange. We shall take here a round average rate of $4 to £1 for converting mutual aid values for goods other than military stores and for services. It will then be seen (Table 11) that the

Table 11: Comparison of Lend-lease Aid to the British Empire and Reciprocal Aid to the U.S. to V-J Day

Government account	In $ millions		In £ millions sterling	
	Lend-lease aid from U.S.	Reciprocal aid to U.S.	Lend-lease aid from U.S.	Reciprocal aid to U.S.
U.K.: Ships and construction	2,107	910	301	227
Military stores . .	13,823	2,014	1,975	288
Petroleum . .	1,850 *	1,187	462 *	297
Other goods . .	6,263 *	361	1,566 *	90
Services . . .	2,980	1,195	745	299
Total . .	27,023	5,667	5,049	1,201
Australia . . .	1,570	1,041	296	216
New Zealand . .	271	248	52	54
South Africa . .	296	1	53	†
India . . .	913	610	178	134
Total . .	30,073	7,567	5,628	1,605

* Approximate division between petroleum and other goods.

† Less than £0·5 million.

NOTES

From Tables 5 and 10. Conversion from dollars to £ sterling and conversely at $7 to £1 for Military Stores (including Ships) and at $4 to £1 for all other goods and services average conversion rate works out at a little over \$5.3 to £1 for all lend-lease aid and at about \$4.7 to £1 for all reciprocal aid. The latter figure is the lower because the proportion of munitions—relatively highly priced in U.S. lend-lease—is higher in lend-lease than in reciprocal aid. The first White Paper on Mutual Aid (Cmd. 6483, para. 30) assessed U.S.-U.K. costs at around \$6 to £1 on the average, but this would appear to be an over-estimate of the rate. It must be stressed that, in using the conversion rates we have suggested, we are not rejecting the official exchange rate as a false rate, for example, in any comparison of present U.S.-U.K. costs of consumers' goods, but simply as an inappropriate rate for the particular valuations adopted in lend-lease and reciprocal aid.

Table 11 shows comparisons of lend-lease and reciprocal aid obtained both by translating lend-lease aid into comparable British prices and by evaluating reciprocal aid in comparable U.S. prices. It must be remembered that this table gives only an approximate allocation of U.S. lend-lease aid among British countries. Though there may be a slight under-statement of aid properly attributed to the Dominions, the greatest uncertainty is in the division between the U.K. and Indian governments. This does not greatly affect the total for the U.K., but it does make the amount attributed to India subject to a large percentage range of error. It must also be remembered that the figures for reciprocal aid from India are not obtained from or with the agreement of the supplying government.

The comparisons of Table 11, however, suffice for the broad conclusion that the British Empire provided reciprocal aid to the U.S. to the value of between 25 and 30 per cent. of lend-lease aid received from the U.S. The rate for the U.K. alone, however, was lower—between 20 and 25 per cent. In the two other main areas of mutual aid, the proportion of reciprocal aid was higher—about 70 per cent. in Australia and a very uncertain figure for India, which appears here as nearly 75 per cent. and may be greater. South Africa received relatively little lend-lease aid, but provided practically no reciprocal aid. Mutual aid between the U.S. and New Zealand was also on a small scale—New Zealand being a small country—but here there was an almost exact balance between the two sides of the account.

Apart from the U.K., therefore, lend-lease aid to the Empire was not very much larger than the reciprocal aid provided to the U.S. in return. An important factor, after Pearl Harbor, was the difficulty of shipping to and from India, Australia and New Zealand. It was never easy to get large shipments of lend-lease or other cargoes through to these areas or to move their normal exports. For the same reasons, it was reasonable and practical for these countries to supply U.S. forces on the spot, saving valuable shipping space from the U.S.

The balance in favour of the U.S. in the mutual aid account is primarily in the account with the U.K., and some further analysis of this is needed. Total lend-lease aid to the U.K. in nearly four and a half years of operation was around \$27,000 millions, of which \$2,100 millions was for ships, \$13,800 millions for munitions, \$8,100 millions for other goods (including nearly $2,000 millions for petroleum) and $3,000 millions for services. Against this, the U.K. provided about $5,700 millions worth of reciprocal aid in three and a quarter years—$900 millions for construction, $2,000 millions for munitions (in the broad sense of military stores), $1,200 millions for petroleum, $400 millions for other goods and $1,200 millions for services. In this comparison, however, we should make allowance on one side or the other for the value of certain aircraft originally paid for in dollars by the U.K. and later diverted to the U.S. An amount of around $250 millions was claimed by the U.K. on this score in the mutual aid settlement. The claim was rejected and the amount was 'regarded as taken into account in the general settlement' (Cmd. 6778, Agreement 11, para. 3). For our present purpose, the amount can be appropriately added to reciprocal aid, making the munitions figure $2,250 millions and the total almost $6,000 millions.

Reciprocal aid was furnished in a shorter period—roughly $3\frac{1}{4}$ instead of $4\frac{1}{2}$ years—and by a country very much smaller in population and resources than the U.S. The relative strengths of the two countries is $2\frac{3}{4}$ to 1 by population and 3 or 4 to 1 in terms of industrial power. Reciprocal aid of about $6,000 millions is equivalent to perhaps $20,000 millions for a country the size of the U.S., and this comes within hailing distance of the $27,000 millions of lend-lease aid.

We can refine such measures of reciprocal aid in relation to lend-lease aid, allowing for the differing resources of the two countries without a conversion of dollars into pounds sterling or conversely.

U.S. lend-lease aid to the British Empire can be related to each of a number of more comprehensive U.S. figures, of which total war expenditures, national income and gross national product are three of the more readily available totals. Against a relation of this kind, we should set British reciprocal aid to the U.S. similarly related to the corresponding war expenditures, national income or gross national product of the whole of the British Empire (excluding Canada and Newfoundland). This is not a practical proposition, since it is scarcely possible to define, still less to measure, such concepts as the national income for the colonies or India. It is better to concentrate on the U.K. alone, and relate reciprocal aid from the U.K. to the U.S. to war expenditures, national income or gross national product of the U.K. It should be noticed that it is not then appropriate to reduce the U.S. relation by taking lend-lease aid to the U.K. alone. The U.K. relation we aim at is, in fact, an indication of the relation for the Empire as a whole. Broadening the scope would increase both the numerator (reciprocal aid) and the denominator (*e.g.*, national income), and one such extension, to include Australia and New Zealand, is perfectly possible. It may be argued, however, that all lend-lease aid—to Russia and other countries as well as to the British—and similarly all reciprocal aid, should be taken into relations of the kind we have in mind. There is point to this, but it is in fact of little consequence. We have seen that the proportions of lend-lease and of reciprocal aid to third countries are roughly the same. If we establish a rough equivalence in mutual aid between the U.S. and the British Empire, then we have also established a similar equation for all lend-lease and reciprocal aid, at least within the margins of error with which we are inevitably confronted.

The data for the comparisons are set out in Table 12 for the period of 3½ years between the entry of the U.S. into the war and the middle of 1945, ignoring only the small amounts of mutual aid provided in 1941 and in the last two months before V-J Day. It must be stressed that the relations we seek are not cut and dried. There is a large number of possible relations, all more or less appropriate; indeed, there are almost as many different definitions of (*e.g.*) national income as there are statisticians willing and able to provide estimates.

Table 12: Mutual Aid in Relation to War Expenditure and National Income

United States ($ millions)	1942	1943	1944	First half 1945	Total (3½ years)
War expenditure	47,600	81,100	86,400	43,300	258,400
National income	137,400	173,500	184,500	95,000	590,400
Plus depreciation, etc. . . .	11,800	12,000	12,300	6,200	42,300
Minus net income from abroad .	200	100	100	100	500
Gross national product (home produced)	149,000	185,400	196,700	101,100	632,200
Lend-lease aid to British Empire:					
Total	4,760	9,030	10,770	3,600	28,160
Home produced	4,400	8,500	9,890	3,010	25,800
Lend-lease aid in per cent. of:					
War expenditure	10·0	11·1	12·5	8·3	10·9
National income	3·5	5·2	5·8	3·8	4·8
Gross national product . . .	3·0	4·6	5·0	3·0	4·1

United Kingdom (£ millions)	Year ending June 30,			Total (3 years)
	1943	1944	1945	
War expenditure	4,275	4,480	4,495	13,250
National income	7,935	8,315	8,425	24,675
Plus depreciation, etc. . . .	475	475	475	1,425
Minus net income from abroad .	130	120	105	355
Gross national product (home produced)	8,280	8,670	8,795	25,745
Reciprocal aid to U.S.: Total . .	230	421	482	1,133
Home produced	212	311	257	780
Reciprocal aid in per cent. of:				
War expenditure	5·4	9·6	10·7	8·6
National income	2·9	5·1	5·7	4·6
Gross national product . . .	2·6	3·6	2·9	3·0

NOTES

Lend-lease aid from Table 4. Home produced lend-lease aid is total *less* all petroleum transferred and estimated foreign purchases transferred under lend-lease (*e.g.*, munitions from Canada and sugar from Cuba).

Reciprocal aid from Table 8, assuming (with only a small error) that aid to the U.S. began on July 1, 1942. Home produced reciprocal aid is total *less* all petroleum transferred, colonial produce exported to U.S., overseas construction and the overseas-produced part (estimated at one-quarter) of stores transferred by the War Office and Air Ministry in the U.S. and overseas war theatres.

War expenditure, national income and gross national product from *The Impact of the War on Civilian Consumption*, Appendix XII, where these concepts are adjusted to a broadly comparable basis for the U.S. and U.K. Estimates are added for the first half of 1945, and U.K. estimates for years ending June 30 are obtained by interpolation.

War expenditure is total government expenditure for war purposes *less* indirect taxes; changes in privately-held inventories on goverment contracts are not included.

National income and gross national product are at factor cost, excluding indirect taxes, and exclude national debt interest. U.S. national income differs from the U.S. Department of Commerce series by the addition of corporate income taxes, net income from owner-occupied houses and subsistence of armed forces. U.K. national income differs from the official series (Cmd. 6623, 1945) only in minor respects—*e.g.*, by the addition of employers' social security contributions.

Gross national product is national income, as defined here, *plus* depreciation and similar allowances, *minus* net income from abroad. U.K. net income from abroad in 1945 is taken from *Statistical Material Presented During the Washington Negotiations* (Cmd. 6707, 1945), and estimated for other years on the basis of available data on overseas disinvestment and debt increase.

In the percentage figures, home-produced lend-lease and reciprocal aid are related to gross national product, while total lend-lease and reciprocal aid are used for the other relations.

First, mutual aid can be related to total war expenditures, the latter being taken net of indirect taxes and the former being almost exclusive (by its method of estimation) of such taxes. For the whole period under review, U.S. lend-lease aid to the British Empire represented 11 per cent. of U.S. war expenditures, and the corresponding proportion was nearly 9 per cent. for the U.K. At the peak rate of flow of mutual aid, the U.S. was devoting not far short of 15 per cent. of all her war expenditures to lend-lease aid to the British Empire (first half of 1944), while the U.K. spent about 12 per cent. of the total cost of the war on reciprocal aid to the U.S. (late in 1944).

The second relation is between total mutual aid and national income, the latter being defined on a comparable basis for the two countries and at factor cost, excluding indirect taxes and interest on the national debt. The notes appended to Table 12 explain in more detail the national income concept involved. In the whole period of mutual aid, almost identical proportions of national income, about $4\frac{3}{4}$ per cent., were devoted to lend-lease in the U.S. and to reciprocal aid in the U.K. At peak, late in 1944, the proportions were nearly 7 per cent. in each country.

These two relations are, in a sense, financial concepts, and are based on all types of mutual aid financed by the respective governments. In each country some mutual aid was provided in the form of goods produced, or services rendered, abroad by other than the country's own nationals. Similarly, some part of the national income is derived from abroad. A different type of relation can be devised to set the home-produced part of mutual aid against domestic national output or product. The latter can now be measured conveniently in gross terms, including depreciation and similar charges, but net income from abroad must be excluded. Table 9 shows the derivation of this gross national product concept from the national income figures already used. Comparability between the two countries is preserved. The only difficulty is in the series for net income from abroad for the U.K., no official estimates being yet available for the war years. An estimate for the year 1945 has been published in one of the White Papers on the Loan Agreement (*Statistical Material presented during the Washington Negotiations*, Cmd. 6707). This values net income from abroad at £97 millions, apparently excluding insurance transactions, but including the net foreign income of British oil companies :

	£ millions
Gross U.K. receipts from abroad (excluding insurance and oil) . .	136
Plus net receipts of oil companies	+ 34
Minus gross U.K. payments abroad (excluding insurance and oil) .	− 73
Net income from abroad (excluding insurance) . . .	97

From what is known of overseas disinvestment and of the increase in overseas liabilities, we can offer the following figures as indicative of net income from abroad in earlier years :

	1942	1943	1944	1945
£ millions . .	135	125	115	97

The estimates in Table 12 are then interpolations for years ending at June 30th.

It is rather difficult to estimate the home-produced content of mutual aid. First, much of the petroleum supplied under both lend-lease and reciprocal aid comes from non-domestic sources. Further, as we have already said, petroleum supplies during the war were largely pooled and derived from the most convenient sources for all the various uses. For example, a good proportion of the petroleum originally lend-leased by the U.S. found its way back under reciprocal-aid disguises to U.S. forces in the U.K., India and elsewhere. For these reasons, it is better to leave petroleum out altogether in estimating home-produced mutual aid. Secondly, estimates can be made (as described in the notes to Table 12) for the value of stores in lend-lease and reciprocal aid which were produced outside the U.S. and the U.K. respectively. These values are deducted from the totals of mutual aid less petroleum. There remains the question of how to handle that part of mutual-aid stores produced domestically which consists of imported goods. We have ignored this element on the assumption that, to the extent that it cannot be offset by exports, it can be roughly cancelled by the home-produced element in mutual-aid stores produced abroad and in net petroleum transfers. This calculation of home-produced mutual aid may work out slightly in favour of the U.S.

The results of the comparison of home-produced mutual aid with home-produced gross output are given in the last lines of the two parts of Table 12. About 4 per cent. of total domestic output in the U.S. was directed to the British Empire under lend-lease in the whole period of operation, and at peak the proportion was nearly 6 per cent. The corresponding proportion for the U.K. was about 3 per cent. in the three years from mid-1942 to mid-1945, with a peak of about 4 per cent. in the spring of 1944 before D Day.

The conclusion, therefore, is that all measures point to the same general result. Relative to her resources, the U.K. contribution in the form of reciprocal aid to the U.S. may have been rather less, but certainly it was not much less, than the U.S. contribution in the form of lend-lease aid to the British Empire.

Table 13: Reciprocal Aid from Australia and New Zealand in Relation to National Income

	Year ending June 30,			Total (3 years)
	1943	1944	1945	
Australia (£ millions Aus.):				
Net national income . . .	1,180	1,300	1,350	3,830
Reciprocal aid to U.S. . .	60·8	108·4	90·3	259·5
Per cent. of net national income	5·2	8·3	6·7	6·8
New Zealand (£ millions N.Z.):				
Private income . . .	230	240	246	716
Net national income (estimated) .	214	223	228	665
Reciprocal aid to U.S. . . .	15·7	21·9	25·7	63·3
Per cent. of net national income	7·3	9·8	11·3	9·5

NOTES

Net national income of Australia and private income of New Zealand from semi-official sources. Reciprocal aid as in Table 9, but in local currency.

We have already seen that reciprocal aid from Australia and New Zealand to the U.S. was large relative to lend-lease from the U.S. to these countries. Reciprocal aid was also a larger proportion of the national income of Australia and New Zealand than lend-lease was of the U.S. national income. As the data of Table 13 indicate, Australia contributed about 7 per cent. and New Zealand not far short of 10 per cent. of national income in the form of reciprocal aid to the U.S. It has been stated, moreover, that Australian reciprocal aid to the U.S. represented approximately 18 per cent. of her total war expenditures (*21st Report to Congress on Lend-lease Operations*, January 1946, p. 33). A comparable figure for the U.K. would be 9 per cent. for reciprocal aid to the U.S. and about 14 per cent. for all reciprocal aid in the three years ending mid-1945. Further, in relation to U.S. war expenditures in the three and a half years from Pearl Harbor to the middle of 1945, the proportion was 11 per cent. for lend-lease to the British Empire and about 16 per cent. for lend-lease to all countries. Reciprocal aid from the two southern Dominions to U.S. forces in the Pacific was, in a sense, the practical substitute for the assistance which could no longer be provided to the U.K. But, whichever way it is regarded, there can be no doubt of the size of the contributions of these two Dominions to the combined war effort.

The Composition of Mutual Aid. The following tables are designed to show the broad composition of the items making up lend-lease and reciprocal aid and the variation in the composition in the course of the war. Petroleum transferred under mutual aid is omitted altogether from the calculations for the reasons already adduced—namely, that dealings in petroleum products were so multilateral as to amount to an almost complete pooling of resources.

2M

Of all lend-lease aid to the British Empire between March 11, 1941, and V-J Day, excluding petroleum, munitions in the broad sense accounted for 65 per cent. and war services, mainly in connection with shipping, represented a further 10 per cent. Of the remaining 25 per cent., half was food and the other half was distributed over a wide range of goods—cotton, tobacco, lumber, metals, machinery, and all kinds of manufactures. Details are shown in Table 14.

Table 14: Composition of U.S. Lend-lease Aid to the British Empire

	March-Dec. 1941	1942	1943	1944	Jan.-Aug. 1945	Total
$ millions:						
Total lend-lease aid	1,082	4,757	9,031	10,766	4,437	30,073
Less petroleum	83	232	372	799	656	2,142
Total, excluding petroleum	999	4,525	8,659	9,967	3,781	27,931
Per cent.:						
Aircraft and equipment	2·0	17·8	18·8	23·6	27·7	21·0
Ships, equipment and repairs	14·1	8·5	17·9	9·3	9·2	12·0
Ordnance and ammunition	7·8	15·4	12·1	9·0	7·8	10·8
Vehicles and equipment	6·7	9·5	17·0	14·6	9·4	13·5
Other munitions	1·1	2·3	4·5	11·0	10·2	7·1
Total munitions	31·7	53·6	70·3	67·5	64·3	64·4
Foodstuffs	29·1	14·3	9·5	11·7	12·7	12·2
Other agricultural produce	8·0	3·2	2·4	2·4	3·7	2·9
Metals	9·3	6·4	4·9	3·5	5·4	4·8
Machinery	2·4	4·2	3·4	2·7	2·6	3·1
Other manufactures	1·5	2·7	1·1	1·8	2·4	1·8
Services, excluding ship repairs	17·9	15·5	8·4	10·6	9·0	10·8

NOTES

Goods transferred and services rendered under lend-lease classified as in Table 4, but with ship construction and ship repairs included under munitions.

Other munitions comprise signal, engineer, quartermaster, chemical warfare and medical stores; radio, radar and other electrical equipment included here and not with the equipment of aircraft, ships and vehicles. Other agricultural produce includes cotton, tobacco, lumber and many less important items. Other manufactures is a residual group of which the main items are chemicals, rubber, textiles, civilian clothing and medical supplies.

We have seen, from the data of Table 12, that the U.S. provided lend-lease aid to the British Empire to the extent of between 4 and 5 per cent. of her total production. It is instructive to follow the variation of such a percentage from one category of lend-lease aid to another. The available data are summarized in Table 15.

The dominant position of munitions in lend-lease aid—to supply the relatively larger strength of the British armed forces—is clear from these two tables. Until the beginning of 1944, the supply of lend-lease munitions to the British Empire was built up, not only in total dollar terms, but also in proportion to all lend-lease. At the peak rate of flow over 70 per cent. of lend-lease aid, exclusive of petroleum, consisted of munitions, and the British Empire was then receiving no less than 12 per cent.

of all U.S. munitions production under lend-lease. In fact, over a two-year period from the beginning of 1943 to the end of 1944 the U.S. sent to the British under lend-lease terms about 11½ per cent. of all the munitions she produced. In terms of value, aircraft and related equipment were the most important of all lend-lease munitions; allocations to the British kept pace with the rapidly expanding production in the U.S., and ran consistently around 12½ per cent. of total output after Pearl Harbor. But, relative to U.S. production, tanks and motor vehicles

Table 15: U.S. Lend-lease Aid to the British Empire in Relation to Total U.S. Production

	1942	1943	1944	First half 1945
Lend-lease as per cent. of total production:				
Aircraft and equipment	12·4	11·9	13·5	11·8
Ships, equipment and repairs	5·5	11·8	6·7	5·4
Ordnance and ammunition	10·4	10·0	8·8	4·6
Vehicles and equipment	9·8	26·7	29·4	12·1
Other munitions	1·4	3·4	9·9	5·5
Total munitions	7·6	11·2	11·7	7·6
Foodstuffs	4·3	4·4	5·4	3·9
Other agricultural produce	4·3	5·6	4·4	5·0
Metals	3·9	4·2	3·4	3·5
Machinery	2·6	5·7	7·1	4·2
Other manufactures	0·7	0·6	1·1	0·7

NOTES

Goods transferred under lend-lease classified as in Table 14. Total U.S. production from unpublished valuations by the War Production Board. Total munitions production is valued at 'standard' costs at different dates and the values used here are approximations to current costs as follows:

Year 1942—standard costs of August 1942.
Year 1943—standard costs of August 1943.
Year 1944—average of standard costs of August 1943 and of 1945.
First half 1945—standard costs of 1945.

Other munitions in total production comprise, as in lend-lease, signal, engineer, quartermaster, chemical warfare and medical stores; petroleum, raw materials, industrial equipment, food and subsistence are all omitted. Total production other than munitions is as estimated by W.P.B. at August 1945.

were easily the largest category of munitions, with some 28 per cent. of all vehicles made in the U.S. allotted to the British Empire under lend-lease in the two years 1943–44. Ordnance and ammunition were more important lend-lease items in the early months than they were later, when the U.S. had large forces in the field. Later on, radio and other signal stores, engineer equipment, clothing and other quartermaster supplies became an increasingly important part of lend-lease munitions—*e.g.*, for the re-equipment of British forces for operation against the Japanese.

Food and manufactures for civilians, raw materials and equipment for industry, were supplied under lend-lease, and were important, and even decisive, in maintaining the high mobilization of the British labour force for war purposes. The supply of lend-lease food, beginning in 1941 at the same time as rationing on the points system, certainly added variety to the British diet. The contribution of the U.S. should, however, be kept in proper perspective. Not only were the lend-lease supplies from the U.S. marginal to Britain, they were also marginal from the point of view of U.S. agriculture and industry. They represented well under 5 per cent. of total U.S. production of such supplies, even in the peak years of 1943–44. The largest contribution was in machinery, over 6 per cent. of total U.S. output being sent to the British Empire under lend-lease in 1943–44, before most of the items were made ineligible for lend-lease in the last few months of the war. In the same two years, foodstuffs, cotton, tobacco, lumber and other agricultural produce supplied to the British represented about 5 per cent. of U.S. agricultural output. The proportion for iron, steel and other metals was under 4 per cent., and much lower figures were recorded for other manufactures.

A broad picture of the composition of reciprocal aid from the British Empire to the U.S. is given in Table 10. Further details are only available for reciprocal aid from the U.K., and even here estimates are needed to fill out some gaps in the data, as explained in the notes to Table 16. Very broadly, U.K. reciprocal aid consisted of 30 per cent. in each of

Table 16: Composition of U.K. Reciprocal Aid to the U.S.

	Year ending June 30,			July 1–Sept. 1, 1945	Total
	1943	1944	1945		
£ millions:					
Total reciprocal aid . . .	230	421	482	69	1,201
Less petroleum . . .	8	77	187	25	297
Total, excluding petroleum .	222	344	295	44	904
Per cent.:					
Aircraft and equipment . .	7·0	6·5	3·1	1·8	5·3
Ordnance and ammunition .	8·4	4·0	4·1	2·5	5·0
Vehicles and equipment . .	3·0	1·1	1·6	2·0	1·8
Other military stores . . .	18·0	16·4	25·1	17·7	19·7
Total military stores . .	36·3	28·1	33·9	24·0	31·8
Foodstuffs	—	4·1	7·7	11·1	4·6
Raw materials	2·8	4·5	7·9	8·4	5·4
Construction	41·7	31·7	6·7	14·5	25·2
Building maintenance . . .	1·2	6·2	5·9	3·9	4·8
Other services . . .	18·0	25·5	37·8	38·1	28·3

NOTES

Goods transferred and services rendered under reciprocal aid as in Table 8. Classification by type of stores as shown in the Treasury returns. Aircraft and equipment includes radio, radar and electrical equipment. Other military stores include engineer stores, scientific instruments, transportation stores, clothing, camp and barrack equipment, medical supplies, together with materials of all kinds for use by U.S. forces. Foodstuffs comprise both food for U.S. forces and bulk exports from the colonies. Raw materials include only bulk exports and materials transferred in the U.S.; materials such as timber, chemicals and permanent way supplies for U.S. forces are included under military stores. Other services comprise shipping, inland transport, postal, broadcasting, printing, laundries and many others.

Some categories of reciprocal aid are not given in detail in the Treasury returns, and estimated distributions are used here. Transfers of 'ordnance and R.E. stores' by the War Office in the U.K. before July 1943 are divided by categories according to the proportions found in the two years ending June 30, 1945, and the same method is used in allocating War Office transfers in overseas theatres in the whole period. Air Ministry transfers in overseas theatres are classified in proportion to the transfers by this Ministry in the U.K. in the whole period. Other transfers of stores in overseas theatres are lumped together under 'other military stores.'

the three main categories—construction including building maintenance, military stores, shipping and other services. The remaining 10 per cent. consisted of bulk exports of foodstuffs and raw materials to the U.S., together with food provided to U.S. forces in the U.K. This is for the whole of the period, but the composition of reciprocal aid shifted greatly as the war progressed. The construction of military installations and their maintenance dominated reciprocal aid in the early days. At one time nearly one-third of the total building labour force in the U.K. was employed on the construction and maintenance of airfields, barracks, hospitals and other projects for U.S. troops. Later on current military stores in great variety were a large proportion of reciprocal aid, particularly in the months after D Day, and the provision of shipping and other services and the export of bulk food and materials to the U.S. continued to increase up to V-J Day.

Military stores, or munitions in the broadest sense, formed about 30 per cent. of all reciprocal aid furnished to the U.S. by the British Empire. This is a much lower proportion than found in lend-lease aid, of which 65 per cent. was munitions if the construction, equipment and repair of ships are included—or over 50 per cent. if these are excluded as more analogous to construction and maintenance on the reciprocal aid side.[1] Further, whereas combat munitions are the bulk of the military stores provided under lend-lease, the reciprocal aid items are a much more miscellaneous group.

Important contributions to the combat equipment of U.S. forces were indeed made under reciprocal aid. Amongst aircraft transferred to the U.S. air forces were 125 photographic-reconnaissance Mosquitos, over 400 Spitfires in the U.K. and 250 more in North Africa, and about 550 Horsa gliders for airborne operations. American aircraft were fitted with radar equipment of British manufacture and design, equipment for blind bombing, for identification and for other purposes. Ten corvettes were handed over to the U.S. Navy and about 4,500 barrage balloons were sent to the U.S. for the defence of her cities in the early days after Pearl Harbor. Transfers of ordnance included 25-pounders and ammunition, a variety of bombs, including some 12,000-pounders, and many types of small arms ammunition. Altogether, however, little more than one-third of the value of military stores provided under reciprocal aid was combat material—ordnance, ammunition, aircraft, tanks and related equipment.

---

[1] The gap between the proportions of munitions in lend-lease and reciprocal aid is wider in these value terms than in volume since munitions are relatively dearer in the U.S.

The main contribution of reciprocal aid in the direct military sense was probably the saving of shipping space through the local provision of a great range of expendable stores for the use of U.S. forces in all parts of the world. In the U.K. alone in the two years to mid-1944 it has been estimated that the military supplies provided under reciprocal aid would have required the use of 1,000 ships if they had been brought in from the U.S. (*17th Report to Congress on Lend-lease Operations*, November 1944). In the same two-year period the estimated proportion of current U.S. Army requirements in the European theatre met by the U.K. under reciprocal aid was as follows in terms of shipping tons :

Quartermaster Corps	.	.	63	per cent.
Engineer Corps	.	.	58	
Medical Corps	.	.	49	
Chemical Warfare	.	.	25	
Signal Corps	.	.	22	
Air Forces	.	.	21	

U.S. forces in this theatre were supplied under reciprocal aid with practically all their requirements of such varied stores as Bailey bridges, auxiliary gas-tanks, jerricans for the distribution of motor spirit and spark-plugs for aircraft engines. Tyres, both new and recapped, were provided to meet a large proportion of U.S. service requirements in the U.K. and in Australia. Army clothing of all types was a large proportion of reciprocal aid in Australia, New Zealand and India.

Equally important was the local provision of food for U.S. forces, since this not only saved shipping space, but also gave U.S. troops a diet of fresh fruit, vegetables and other foods. Reciprocal aid in the U.K. included nearly £20 millions worth of food, much of it bulky—for example, 70,000 tons of flour, nearly 100,000 tons of vegetables and 20,000 tons of corned beef. The contribution was greater, however, in the Pacific and South-East Asia theatres. Australia supplied food to the value of about £60 millions sterling, New Zealand £30 millions sterling and India over £10 millions sterling. Together these three countries provided almost 2 million tons of food under reciprocal aid, meeting a large proportion of the total needs of U.S. forces in these combat areas.

Towards the end of 1943 certain exports of bulk foodstuffs and raw materials to the U.S. were brought under reciprocal aid. These came from the U.K. and the colonial Empire on U.K. account and, later on, from India at the expense of the Indian Government. Such exports grew in volume in 1944–45, and the shipments amounted to £80 millions in less than two years, £65 millions on U.K. account and £15 millions from the Government of India. The major items provided by the U.K. included nearly 150,000 tons of copra and cocoanut oil from Ceylon and the Pacific islands, over 250,000 tons of cocoa and 50,000 tons of palm oil and kernels from West Africa, £5 millions worth of tea from India and Ceylon, well over 100,000 tons of rubber from Ceylon and the African colonies, and nearly 350,000 tons of benzol from the U.K. There were numerous other exports, such as steel plates from the U.K., sisal from East Africa, copper from Cyprus, hides and goatskins from East Africa and other sources and raw sugar from Fiji and Queensland. In the same way, from the spring of 1944, India made available and shipped to the U.S. large quantities of materials on which the U.S. was heavily dependent. Jute and jute products comprised more than half the total value, and other large exports included mica, shellac, rubber and tea.

Services under reciprocal aid, around 30 per cent. of all aid to the U.S. from the Empire, also increased in importance as the U.S. forces were deployed against Germany and Japan. As in lend-lease aid, the main services were charges in connection with the movement of freight and troops, for shipping, rail and road transport of all kinds. Building maintenance, including the provision of fuel and light, was a major service item, particularly in the U.K. But services of many other types were rendered to U.S. forces in various parts of the world—postal and telegraph, broadcasting, printing, laundries, dry cleaning, boot repair and others in great variety. In addition, the U.K. devised and carried out numerous projects in the joint war effort for British and American forces alike. The Pluto oil pipeline to the Continent and the Fido fog dispersal system were two of the more publicized examples.

British Empire Supplies of Munitions. Munitions production in the U.S. was quite small even at the time of the entry of the U.S. into the

Table 17: British Empire Supplies of Munitions from the U.S.

	Empire supplies ($ millions)			U.S. production	
	Purchases	Lend-lease	Total	$ millions	% to Empire
All munitions:					
1940 (second half) . . .	400	—	400	2,000	19·1
1941	1,200	300	1,500	8,600	17·3
1942	900	2,400	3,300	32,000	10·5
1943	600	6,100	6,700	54,400	12·3
1944	400	6,700	7,100	57,700	12·3
1945 (first half) . . .	100	2,000	2,100	25,500	8·1
Total (five years) . .	3,600	17,500	21,100	180,200	11·7
Of which:					
Aircraft and equipment .	2,100	5,600	7,700	47,300	16·3
Ships, equipment and repairs	200	3,300	3,500	41,100	8·5
Ordnance and ammunition .	700	3,000	3,700	34,200	10·8
Vehicles and equipment .	400	3,700	4,100	19,300	21·2
Other munitions . .	200	1,900	2,100	38,300	5·5

NOTES

Empire purchases comprise deliveries on cash contracts, from the records of the British Supply Missions in the U.S., and Canadian purchases of finished munitions and of munitions components in the U.S., from estimates prepared by the Department of Munitions and Supply, Ottawa. Lend-lease to the Empire as in Table 14, including ship construction and repairs.

U.S. production from unpublished valuations by W.P.B. as in Table 15, with the addition of Canadian purchases of munitions components in the U.S. The latter, almost entirely by private contractors in Canada, are excluded from the W.P.B. valuations, though munitions components provided under lend-lease are included.

war. What expansion had been realized was in part the legacy of cash orders placed by the U.K. and other Empire governments with individual U.S. firms and with the encouragement of the U.S. Administration. From the middle of 1940 to the end of 1941 deliveries on these contracts were coming forward in growing volume, and the British were receiving between 17 and 20 per cent. of all munitions turned out in the U.S. In the first year of U.S. participation in the war lend-lease deliveries gradually replaced those on cash orders, a lend-lease contract often being introduced as a follow-up of a cash order for the same item. In this year the proportion of U.S. output of munitions coming to the British declined to a little over 10 per cent. The proportion rose again to 12 per cent. in 1943–44, when the machinery of lend-lease and of the assignment of munitions was working smoothly and well (Table 17).

Over the period of five years from the middle of 1940 to the middle of 1945, during which U.S. armament production was first built up and then began to taper off, the British Empire obtained nearly 12 per cent. of all munitions produced in the U.S.—almost 10 per cent. under lend-lease and 2 per cent. for cash. The proportion was 21 per cent. for tanks and motor vehicles, 16 per cent. for aircraft and related equipment, 11 per cent. for ordnance and ammunition and smaller figures for other munitions. British cash contracts placed before the introduction of lend-lease were very largely for aircraft, engines and other air equipment. Deliveries on these orders in the eighteen months up to the end of 1941 were 40 per cent. of all aircraft production in the U.S., and even then the contracts were by no means fully delivered. This is a good indication of the contribution made by British contracts towards the development of the American aircraft industry for war. It was British ordering which established U.S. production of such important types as the Mustang fighter (developed from the Spitfire design), the Hudson and Ventura bombers and the Harvard trainer. Cash contracts from the British for ordnance and ammunition were also substantial, and deliveries in the eighteen months from the middle of 1940 were over one-quarter of all U.S. output of these items. The U.S. remained a large producer of weapons and ammunition of British design until quite late in the war, but her contribution might have been larger had there been a greater standardization of types and calibres.

We can now complete the picture by looking at deliveries of munitions from the U.S. from the other angle, that of British Empire supplies from all sources. Table 18 is designed for this purpose, and shows all munitions becoming available to the Empire, including what was later transferred to the U.S., Russia and other Allies. To obtain the total and distribution of Table 18 we value all munitions produced or delivered as far as possible at comparable U.S. costs. Further, to avoid duplication in components such as aircraft engines or empty shells made in one country for incorporation in end-products in another, we allot components to the country of their production, with corresponding deductions from the value of the end-products made in other countries. No allowance is made, or can be made, for trade in raw materials and semi-fabricated goods between countries. This means, for example, that the Canadian contribution to Empire supplies of munitions shows up as a relatively low figure, since Canada is heavily dependent on the U.S. for components. Table 18 is a distribution of supplies of munitions proper; it is not designed to show the proportionate shares of the various countries in the over-all war effort. In a more comprehensive story we should need to include the very large contributions from Canada in the form of foodstuffs, aluminium, copper, nickel, lumber and other materials.

Table 18: British Empire Supplies of Munitions from all Sources

	Sept.-Dec. 1939 and 1940	1941	1942	1943	1944	First half 1945	Total
Total supplies ($ millions)	9,200	13,000	19,900	24,800	24,700	9,300	100,900
Per cent. from:							
U.K.	90·7	81·8	72·6	62·4	61·2	66·1	69·5
Canada	2·6	5·2	8·6	8·8	8·9	10·0	7·9
Eastern Group	1·1	1·5	1·9	1·9	1·2	1·7	1·6
Purchases in U.S.	5·6	9·1	4·7	2·4	1·5	1·2	3·7
U.S. lend-lease	—	2·4	12·2	24·5	27·2	21·0	17·3

NOTES

Total supplies of munitions becoming available to Empire countries from domestic production and from the U.S., including munitions later transferred to Allies. The coverage of munitions is as in Tables 14, 15 and 17. Components are included in country of production, not in that of incorporation in end-products. Valuations are as far as possible at comparable U.S. costs.

U.K. production from estimates by Ministry of Production of home expenditures on munitions 1939–43, extended to 1944–45 by index-numbers of munitions production (*The Impact of the War on Civilian Consumption*, pp. 11 and 145). Conversion to dollars by rates appropriate to different categories of munitions as obtained from comparisons of unit costs of comparable stores. The average rate of conversion is nearly $7 to £1. The conversion has been checked by a more detailed comparison for 1943 on the lines described in *The Impact of the War on Civilian Comsumption*, pp. 11 and 143.

Canadian production based on estimates, substantially at constant 1944 costs, by the Department of Munitions and Supply, Ottawa (*The Impact of the War on Civilian Consumption*, p. 153). These figures are here adjusted to a current cost basis, reduced by the exclusion of freight and inspection costs and of components purchased from abroad by contractors, and increased by the addition of war plant expansion amortised over five years.

Eastern Group production is almost entirely in Australia, New Zealand and India. Estimates of expenditures on munitions compiled by Ministry of Production are converted to dollars as for the U.K. U.S. purchases and lend-lease are as in Table 17 with the addition of purchases before July 1940.

At the U.S. costs used here, just over $100,000 millions of munitions became available to the British Empire from the beginning of the war to the middle of 1945. Of this total, 69½ per cent. came from domestic production in the U.K. and another 9½ per cent. from Canada and other parts of the Empire. The remaining 21 per cent. was drawn from the U.S., both for cash (over one-sixth) and under lend-lease (nearly five-sixths). These are approximately the same proportions as quoted for a rather shorter period in *Statistics Relating to the War Effort of the U.K.* (Cmd. 6564, para. 34). The main change during the war was the gradual shift from dependence on production in the U.K. to supplies drawn from North America. The U.S. and Canada together provided under

10 per cent. of all Empire supplies of munitions in 1940, but the proportion then rose to 36 per cent. in 1943 and to nearly 38 per cent. in 1944. By D Day in 1944, the U.S. alone was supplying 30 per cent. of all the Empire's munitions, practically all on lend-lease terms. Towards the end of 1944, however, assignments of munitions from U.S. production began to fall off, and the decline continued until V-J Day.

Conclusion. Lend-lease aid from the U.S. to the British Empire is valued at $30,000 millions. Reciprocal aid from the whole of the Empire to the U.S. amounts to £1,600 millions. There is therefore a large sum standing to the credit of the U.S. in the mutual-aid account, however the translation between pounds sterling and dollars is made. The credit arises very largely in the account between the U.S. and the U.K., in which about $27,000 millions of lend-lease aid stands against £1,200 of reciprocal aid. At comparable U.S. dollar costs, the latter amount certainly cannot be put at more than $6,000 millions. The whole of this mutual-aid account between the U.S. and the U.K. has been cancelled in a final settlement negotiated in December 1945 at the same time as the Loan Agreement. The U.K. is to pay, on the same terms as the proposed loan, a relatively small sum stated by the U.S. Administration as $472 millions. In return, the U.K. acquires stocks of lend-lease goods on hand at V-J Day—all undistributed civilian stocks of foodstuffs, raw materials and manufactures, together with machinery and installations and certain transport aircraft, small ships and petroleum supplies— estimated at nearly $700 millions at original cost to the U.S. In the official phrasing (Cmd. 6708, para. 2 of the Joint Statement):

> 'In arriving at this settlement both governments have taken full cognizance of the benefits already received by them in the defeat of their common enemies. They have also taken full cognizance of the general obligations assumed by them in Article VII of the Mutual Aid Agreement of 23rd February, 1942, and the understandings agreed upon this day with regard to commercial policy.'

In relation to the resources of the respective countries, however, reciprocal aid may be a little less, but certainly not much less, than lend-lease aid. Between 4 and 5 per cent. of total U.S. national income or output (according to the method of calculation) was diverted to the British Empire in the form of lend-lease goods and services. Reciprocal aid from the U.K. to the U.S. was about the same proportion of national income if all aid financed by the U.K. is included, but the percentage is rather lower if only those goods and services domestically produced are counted. Higher proportions are found for Australia and New Zealand; nearly 7 per cent. and 10 per cent. respectively of the national incomes of these countries was given to the U.S. as reciprocal aid.

The contribution of reciprocal aid to the combined war effort is less fully appreciated than that of lend-lease. When troops invade enemy territory, it is quite usual for them to 'live off' the country—but the situation is not quite as simple when forces are operating in or from friendly countries. The U.S. was fortunate in the war in that her forces for the invasion of German and Japanese territories were based, not on the U.S., but on Allied countries and, in particular, on the U.K., Australia, New Zealand and India. The problem was how to 'live off' these countries without arousing ill-feeling. The solution was found in the system of reciprocal aid. Under reciprocal-aid arrangements, the U.S. obtained without cash payment the military installations and the host of services which, in any case and for the most part, would have been provided locally. In addition, the U.S. received, from local resources under reciprocal aid, large quantities of military and other stores which could have been brought from the U.S. if shipping had been available for use on an extravagant scale. The contribution of reciprocal aid, in brief, was the better and quicker equipping and servicing of U.S. troops in overseas theatres and the saving of valuable shipping space.

The composition and contribution of lend-lease aid were quite different. Food and other supplies for British civilians, materials and equipment for British industry and services of various kinds played their part in lend-lease aid and helped to maintain the British war effort at a high level for so long. But the main purpose of the lend-lease system, at the outset and throughout the war, was to provide munitions, and particularly combat equipment, directly to the armed forces of the Allies of the U.S. This purpose was undoubtedly realized. By sending 65 per cent. of all lend-lease aid in the form of munitions, mainly of combat types, the U.S. enabled the Empire to maintain a very large proportion of her man-power in the armed forces. There are two facts which demonstrate the importance of U.S. munitions, whether bought for cash or received under lend-lease, to the British war effort. One is that the Empire obtained nearly 12 per cent. of all the munitions produced in the U.S. from mid-1940 to the end of the war. The other is that these munitions from the U.S. represented over 20 per cent. of British supplies from all sources. There can be no doubt that the course of the war was greatly influenced, and its length shortened, by the inclusion of mutual aid in the wider arrangements for the combined conduct of the war.

Indeed, mutual aid—lend-lease from the U.S. and reciprocal aid from the British—can only be assessed adequately in the context of the whole combined planning of the war. The content and direction of mutual aid were constantly changed to fit in with the demands of military operations and to help break open the bottlenecks which developed in the production and distribution of war supplies. One of the most important of the parts played by mutual aid was in the attack on the most persistent bottleneck of all, the losses and shortages of shipping. One example suffices to illustrate. Under lend-lease arrangements, foodstuffs in concentrated form—dried eggs, dried milk, cheese, canned meat and others—were produced in specially built plants in the U.S. for quick shipment to the people of Britain. At the same time, the food supplies of the southern Dominions and India which would have been exported to the U.K. but for shipping difficulties were used to maintain U.S. forces in the nearby areas of the Pacific and S.E. Asia. How obvious and easy are such arrangements under the system of mutual aid, and how difficult it might otherwise have been to achieve the same results in the economy of shipping.

Mutual aid was a military operation always integrated with the wider military plans of the Allies. In the winter of 1941–42 the Russians needed immediate supplies of munitions, and as much as could be spared and delivered was sent under mutual aid, largely from the U.K. as the nearest source of supply. Meanwhile, lend-lease and reciprocal-aid money was expended on building up supply routes to Russia, together with the related assembly, repair and storage facilities so that later on an augmented flow of mutual aid goods could reach Russia by the sea lanes, through Persia and by the airways across Africa and over the top of the world. Mutual aid supplies to Russia were then built up steadily to a peak rate of $5,000 millions a year early in 1945, as the Russian armies swept from Stalingrad to the gates of Berlin.

The bulk of lend-lease supplies from the U.S., despite all the assistance to Russia, continued to go to the British Empire, and practically all reciprocal aid received by the U.S. was from British countries. In 1941 British troops were already in the field, and British war workers were at their machines, standing practically alone against German domination. It was the deliberate and combined policy to maintain and to increase British war mobilization, which was never quite equalled by the U.S. even in the last year of war. Lend-lease aid to the British, rising to a peak flow of over $12,000 millions a year just before D Day in 1944, was one of the means whereby this policy was implemented. At the same time, reciprocal aid prepared the way for fighting forces of the U.S., first by the construction of base installations, and then through the provision of an increasingly wide range of stores and services. It was the enemy who dictated that the opportunity for this return service should fall to the U.K., and not to France, Belgium or Holland, and to Australia, New Zealand and India rather than to China. But it was through mutual aid that the opportunity was exploited to the full.

The mutual aid account in value terms is incomplete. We must look at reciprocal aid, not only as so many pounds, shillings and pence, but as the means of servicing U.S. troops most economically and of releasing ships better employed on carrying munitions to the battle-fronts. We must look at lend-lease aid, not only as so many millions of dollars, but as one of the means of maintaining the fighting strength of the Allies of the U.S., and hence to be considered in relation to the sacrifices particularly of the British and Russian peoples. We can value lend-lease supplies of food, materials and munitions but not the services of British soldiers and war workers maintained by these supplies. There is no rate of exchange between dollars and the currency of 'blood, sweat and tears.' The mutual aid settlement between the U.S. and the U.K., and the others still to be negotiated, take this wide view of war-time achievements, and look ahead to continued co-operation in the critical years of peace to come.

APPENDIX IV

Quotations from unpublished documents of Sir Winston Churchill

1. *The quotation from Mr. Churchill on p. 78 is taken from the following minute, dated 19th February, 1941 to the Chancellor of the Exchequer, Sir Kingsley Wood.*

Chancellor of the Exchequer,

I have been much disturbed by what you told me yesterday of your intentions. I cannot believe that an Income Tax of that rate would be compatible with National thrift or enterprise. Taken with the Super-tax it amounts to almost complete confiscation of the higher rates of income. If such a proceeding were capable of finding the money for the war, there would be justification. As in fact however it can only find a trifle and is avowedly adopted in order to placate other elements in public opinion, this cannot be pleaded. If you suppose you can collect at these high rates without waste or great diminution of effort, without striking a deadly blow at good housekeeping and good management in every form, you are greatly mistaken. People will be indifferent to whether they earn an income or not, and will live on their capital, as many are doing now, with the result that death duties will suffer.

The same spirit of deference not to sound financial canons but to harping and insatiable left-wing propaganda has led to the folly of 100% excess profits tax, with all the waste and carelessness that arises therefrom. The fact that the Income Tax was raised to the enormous figure of 8/6 at such an early stage is a complete justification for not making a further increase now. It is now the turn of those whose incomes have been increased and even doubled by the war to pay a larger share.

Kindly let me have the result of the application of what you propose for the different scales of income, showing the income and sur-tax.

(Intld.) W.S.C.

2. *The quotation from Mr. Churchill on p. 336 is taken from the following telegram, dated 25th August, 1940.*

I and my colleagues have recently considered how we should deal with the gold worth £70 millions entrusted by the Bank of France to the Bank of England for custody. We have taken a different view from that which I understand you were disposed to take when Sir F. Phillips on our instructions mentioned to you the analogous question of the gold entrusted to the Bank of Canada and the U.S. dollars which we have to pay to the Bank of Canada for the credit of the State of France under the arrangements made for the assignment to us of French contracts in the U.S.A. I should therefore like to explain our reasons fully.

557

The Bank of France, whose headquarters are in Paris, is in territory occupied by the enemy. Our Trading with the Enemy legislation (and I understand yours also) regards territory declared to be occupied by the enemy on the same footing as enemy territory. We therefore decided that the gold must be vested in the Custodian of Enemy Property and this has been done.

The Custodian's duty is to protect the interests of the Bank of France in regard to this asset in any settlement after the war, but not to maintain it in the form of physical gold for the benefit of the Bank of France so long as it remains in occupied territory and under German domination. The Custodian's duty, in our view, does not make it improper for him to sell the gold to us for sterling, subject to a full obligation on our part to account for this asset at its full gold value in our settlement with France after it has been freed from German domination. This therefore is the course which we think it right to adopt.

It is true that we are not at war with France, but France is temporarily in enemy occupation and under enemy domination. The gold must therefore in any event remain blocked until France is free again. To allow gold to remain blocked instead of purchasing it for sterling would confer no benefit on the Bank of France but would seriously prejudice the war effort of the Empire. There is no future hope for the French nation except through the victory for which we are all fighting and our trusteeship for the future existence of a free France cannot be rated as less important than our trusteeship for the post-war financial interests of the Bank of France.

We have considered whether to buy this gold from our Custodian of Enemy Property now or to postpone this till later. We think it should be bought at once. That is the normal and natural procedure under our Trading with the Enemy legislation, and if it is not followed some action at present unforeseen—whether technical or political—might be initiated by the Bank of France under German direction and render the purchase difficult or cause it to appear overbearing.

Moreover, we cannot long postpone the purchase without serious detriment to our own essential interests.

As you know, on the capitulation of France we decided to make every effort to increase our imports of munitions and war supplies from the United States. We met with a helpful response in many directions and in addition we were enabled to take over the whole of the French contracts. The result has been that our resources in gold and United States dollars have in recent weeks been drawn upon at a much faster rate than hitherto, and it has become clear that they will be exhausted much sooner than had previously been expected. The magnificent help which we have received from Canada has also, of course, involved some additional drain on our resources, though much reduced by the generous way in which you are making dollars available for us.

The total of dollar securities owned by residents here, which we have requisitioned or shall requisition, though substantial, is small in relation to our total present and future commitments; moreover, owing in particular to the state and character of the American market, realisation is at present a difficult and tardy process and affords only a modest alleviation of our immediate difficulties.

We are relying, therefore, on financial help from the United States in due course, and I am confident that we shall not look for this assistance in vain. We cannot, however, expect that this aid will take practical shape until perhaps some time after the election in November. On no account can we suffer our stock of gold and dollars to be reduced below the essential minimum working balance before this new fortification of our position can be solidly arranged.

It is for these reasons that I have come to the conclusion that our purchase of the gold should not be delayed. I have explained our views at length as I want them to be in your mind when you are considering what course of action to adopt in regard to the French gold entrusted to the Bank of Canada. It is, I understand, worth some £90 millions and lies in your jurisdiction. Should it seem right to you, in the light of the explanation I have given, to adopt the same course as we have adopted, it would be of great value to the cause for which we are both fighting. Our resources for obtaining supplies from the United States of America otherwise than as gifts are rapidly disappearing. No one can foresee what course events may take in the United States of America, and though I have good reason for feeling confident of their intention to give us all possible help, I am reluctant to leave anything undone by which our position may be made more secure. If you feel able to give your assent, I am anxious that this gold should be vested in your Custodian, that except to the extent that you may wish the Canadian Exchange Control to purchase any part of it for your war effort, it should be sold by him for sterling and added to the War Chest here. There would of course remain an obligation to reach an appropriate settlement of this and many other matters when a free State of France will be restored after the war. That obligation will be ours.

I must refer also to the more complicated question which I understand Sir Frederick Phillips discussed with you at greater length and which arises from the arrangement that we should pay United States dollars to the Bank of Canada in New York for the credit of the French State in respect of French payments made for goods which will, under the assignment of contracts, be delivered to us. These payments will be made gradually, and I am not suggesting that immediate action is called for in regard to them, but I would earnestly hope, for the reasons I have given, and notwithstanding the doubts which you have expressed and which I quite appreciate would be decisive in any but the extraordinary conditions in which we find ourselves, to receive your agreement in principle with the view that at the appropriate time these dollars should be sold for sterling and added to the War Chest by a procedure corresponding to that applicable to the gold.

I know you will do your utmost to help us, as you always have done in this great battle for our very existence. Nothing at this moment could do so much to strengthen our position as to enable us with due regard to French interests and to her ultimate security to use these financial resources for the common cause.

APPENDIX V

CHART SHOWING THE SEQUENCE OF MAIN EVENTS IN FINANCIAL POLICY

Chapters II–IV **War-time Budgets**	Chapters V–VII **Capital**	Chapters VIII & XIV **Foreign Exchange**
1939 JUNE	22 Cttee. set up to decide war savings policy. p. 189	
JULY	Cttee. on Economic Information recommended rationing of investment expenditure. p. 163 20 Stamp Cttee. reported on defence expenditure and economical and financial problems. p. 153	
AUGUST	Phillips Cttee. advocated control of investments. p. 164 24 Bank Rate raised from 2 to 4%. p. 157	
SEPTEMBER 27 Budget day. Supplementary war budget pp. 26-31	3 Def. Reg. No. 6 imposed control of investments. p. 164 12 Capital Issues Cttee. set up. p. 164	3 Exchange Control introduced. pp. 233-4 Currency Restrictions Exemption Order made creating Stg. Area. p. 235
OCTOBER	Correspondence with banks on restriction of bank advances. p. 185 26 Chancellor and P.M. decided rate of interest should not go above 3%. p. 161	*Modus Vivendi* between B. of E. and Argentine Central Bank. p. 444
NOVEMBER 14 Keynes' articles in *The* –28 *Times* on 'How to Pay for the War' pp. 33-4 Central Statistical Branch of War Cabinet set up. p. 71	War Savings Campaign launched. p. 189	Documentary proof required for form E.1 p. 243
DECEMBER Ministerial Cttee. on Economic Policy agreed to food prices being subsidised. p. 63		12 Simon-Reynaud Financial Agreement with France. p. 458 31 Payments agreement with Sweden. p. 450

CHAPTER IX **India & Middle East** 30 JAN. Chatfield Report p. 252	CHAPTER X **South. Dominions**	CHAPTER XI **Canada**	CHAPTERS **XII, XIII & XV U.S.A.**
	20 B. of E. short-term loan to New Zealand Govt. p. 300 25 H.M.G. announced £5 m. defence credit and £4 m. export credit to New Zealand Govt. p. 300		
			26 Registration of Securities Order p. 363
	6 Wool Purchase Agreement with Australia, New Zealand and S. Africa. pp. 291, 301, 309		
19 H.M.G. decided to assist Egyptian Govt. with disposal of cotton crop. p. 275		17 Agreement on Stg. Area's purchase of Can. $ through B. of E. and Bank of Canada. p. 327	
		H.M.G. agreed to buy wheat and farm produce. p. 328	4 U.S. amended Neutrality Laws and passed Cash & Carry Legislation p. 363
	H.M.G. undertook to protect New Zealand's Stg. balance. p. 301	Agreement on method of financing stg. overdraft for first year of war. p. 332 17 Empire Air Training Scheme Agreement. p. 330	

CHAPTERS II–IV **War-time Budgets**	CHAPTERS V–VII **Capital**	CHAPTERS VIII & XIV **Foreign Exchange**
1940 JANUARY		
	13 Try. Circular to local authorities prohibiting issue of new securities. p. 165	8 List of bankers authorised to approve Form E.1 published. p. 243
	17 Conversion of 4½% Conversion Loan into 2% 1943-45 Stock. p. 198	
31 H. of C. informed of general policy of stabilisation of certain food prices. p. 64	30 Means Test question deferred by Cttee. on Economic Policy. p. 192	
FEBRUARY		
MARCH		7 Dollar Invoicing Order issued. p. 241
	12 3% War Loan 1955-59 issued. p. 198	25 Dollar Invoicing Order came into effect. p. 241
	18 Chancellor announced policy on rate of interest. p. 162	Free rate for £ fell to $3.44. p. 244
APRIL		9 Chancellor's statement in H. of C. on free rate for £. p. 244
23 Budget day. pp. 35-44 (i) Introduction of purchase tax. pp. 36-9 (ii) Proposal to limit dividends. pp. 39-41 (iii) Chancellor on voluntary saving. p. 42	23 Chancellor in Budget Speech announced (i) plan to limit all dividends. p. 176 (ii) withdrawing savings up to £375 from Means Test calculations. p. 192	
MAY 10 Sir K. Wood, Chancellor of the Exchequer. p. 45 Ernest Bevin, Minister of Labour. p. 46	Chancellor appealed to all Companies to limit dividends voluntarily. p. 176	12 Sale of stg. securities by non-residents prohibited. p. 247
23 Second reading of Bill limiting dividends (later dropped). p. 41 29 E.P.T. raised to 100%. pp. 41, 46-8		
JUNE Keynes began work at Treasury. p. 45	National Savings Week p. 193	7 Exchange Control regulations tightened. p. 247
25 Catto appointed Financial Adviser to Chancellor. p. 45	25 Tap issue of War Bonds 1945-7, 2½%. p. 203	

CHAPTER IX **India & Middle East**	CHAPTER X **South. Dominions**	CHAPTER XI **Canada**	CHAPTERS XII, XIII & XV **U.S.A.**
	18 H.M.G. agreed to lend up to £12 m. of Australia's external war expenditure. p. 294		
14 Indian Defence Expenditure Plan agreed. p. 253			17 First Vesting Order for U.S. securities. p. 365
			13 Second Vesting Order for U.S. securities. p. 365
Indian Govt. told India to be arsenal for Near & Middle East Commands. p. 254			Decision taken to enter into dollar commitments regardless of U.K. shortage of dollars. p. 367
			16 French contracts in U.S. & Canada taken over by H.M.G. p. 367

Chapters II–IV **War-time Budgets**	Chapters V–VII **Capital**	Chapters VIII & XIV **Foreign Exchange**

1940 (*continued*)
JULY
    Chancellor advised of need to spread collection of income tax throughout year. p. 100
23 Supplementary budget day. pp. 48-57
    (i) Details of purchase tax announced. pp. 50-3
    (ii) Compulsory deduction of income tax by employers announced. p. 100
	4 Chancellor announced first issue of T.D.Rs. p. 220	17 Exchange Control regulations clarified and simplified. p. 249

AUGUST War Cabinet decided to subsidise food. p. 64		7 Payments agreements with Brazil with gold-set-aside clause. p. 446

SEPTEMBER
    Keynes' estimate of dimensions of budget problem about £400 m. p. 71
    Lord Stamp examined proposals for excess earnings tax. p. 76		

OCTOBER		Revaluation guarantee substituted for gold-set-aside provision in *Modus Vivendi* with Argentine Central Bank. p. 445
NOVEMBER	Chancellor announced there would be no ceiling to issue of T.D.Rs. p. 205	Payments agreement with Portugal. p. 453
DECEMBER	27 2½% National War Bond, 1946-48 and 3% Savings Bonds 1955-65 issued. p. 205	

Chapter IX India & Middle East	Chapter X South. Dominions	Chapter XI Canada	Chapters XII, XIII & XV U.S.A.
			3 Warning to U.S. that H.M.G's. dollars would soon run out. p. 367 Sir F. Phillips' first war-time visit to U.S. p. 367
7 H.M.G. undertook to set up Cotton Buying Commission in Egypt. p. 276	1 Wool Agreement with S. Africa brought into line with that of Australia and New Zealand. p. 311	Agreement on method of financing stg. overdraft for second year of war. p. 334	
			Try. in briefing Sir F. Phillips for U.S. visit stated U.K. needed minimum gold reserve of £120-150 m. p. 428
		11 H.M.G. forced to ask Canadian Gvt. to purchase more stg. or make temporary loan to solve stg. overdraft problem. p. 335	16 Third Vesting Order for U.S. securities. p. 366 Sir F. Phillips' second war-time visit to U.S. p. 369
	New Zealand began using 'terms of trade' arguments to justify higher prices for dairy produce. p. 302	13 Canadian Govt. agreed to sell H.M.G. $50m. against stg. p. 336	8 P.M's. letter to President stating 'the minimum action necessary'. p. 373 17 Presid't announced lend-lease proposals to Press Conference. p. 373 29 Presid't's 'Fireside Chat' on lend-lease. p. 373 31 P.M. raised with President problem of interim finance. p. 385

Chapters II–IV **War-time Budgets**	Chapters V–VII **Capital**	Chapters VIII & XIV **Foreign Exchange**
1941 JANUARY 7 Dimensions of budget problem revised to £350–450 m. p. 72 14 War Cabinet considered amendment of E.P.T. p. 88 Madge Survey on effect of compulsory savings on wage-earners. p. 82	Tap issue of Savings Bonds opened. p. 206	
FEBRUARY Chancellor decided he would have to raise income tax. p. 77 19 P.M. objected to Chancellor's proposal to increase income tax. p. 78	12 H.M.G. accepted amendment to Consolidated Fund (No. 1) Bill prohibiting borrowing above 3% p. 162	25 Payments agreement with Sweden modified to limit H.M.G. gold liability to £650,000 per month. p. 450
MARCH Chancellor presented proposals on Post-War Credits to War Cabinet. p. 83 Dimensions of budget problem revised to £500 m. p. 72		19 Financial agreement with Free French Govt. p. 458
APRIL 7 Budget day. (i) Price stabilisation. pp. 64-7 (ii) New tax proposals–direct taxation. pp. 74-80 (iii) Post-War Credits pp. 80-5 (iv) E.P.T. pp. 85-90 (v) Certain concessions to manual wage-earners re travelling expenses due to war conditions. p. 114 (vi) Farmers' basis of tax assessment altered. p. 116 (vii) Conditions upon which E.P.T. would be refunded mentioned p. 119 7 Publication of first National Income White Paper. p. 71		
MAY	1 Conversion stock issued to cover local govt. maturities and also Australian Govt. maturity. p. 171	
JUNE		Review of colonial economic policy. p. 441

Chapter IX India & Middle East	Chapter X South. Dominions	Chapter XI Canada	Chapters XII, XIII & XV U.S.A.
		16 Canadian Govt. agreed to sell H.M.G. further $25 m. against stg. p. 336	10 *Louisville* sent to S. Africa to fetch U.K. gold. p. 385 11 Fourth Vesting Order for U.S. securities. p. 366, fn. 2
7 First Vesting Order for Indian Securities. p. 257			21 H.M.G. offered U.S. joint Anglo-U.S. Agency for disposal of Br. direct investments p. 388
		27 Canadian Govt. agreed to sell H.M.G. dollars against stg. without limit but asked for exchange guarantee. p. 339	4 Agreement with Belgian Govt. about using Belgian gold. p.371 Morgenthau's ultimatum that some important company must be sold within week. p.388 15 U.S. Director of Budget's assurances to Congress about 'Old Commitments.' p. 390 16 Courtauld's Viscose Co. sold p. 389
Middle East Supply Centre established. p. 280 Cotton Commission transformed into Joint Anglo-Egyptian Commission. p. 276		20 Canadian Govt. signed Hyde Park Agreement with U.S. p. 340	19 Fifth Vesting Order for U.S. Securities. p. 366, fn. 2
			Keynes' first wartime visit to U.S. p. 390 Keynes urged on U.S. Admin. need for H.M.G. to have minimum reserve. p. 428

Chapters II–IV **War-time Budgets**	Chapters V–VII **Capital**	Chapters VIII & XIV **Foreign Exchange**
1941 (*continued*) JULY		
AUGUST		
SEPTEMBER	1 Second issue of 3% Defence Bonds. p. 196 War Weapons Weeks (Sept.-Oct.) p. 193	
OCTOBER	Ministers agreed interest on Tax Reserve Certs. should be tax free. p. 215	
NOVEMBER Keynes formulating sug- gestions for 1942 budget to be a social policy budget. p. 97		20 Debate on Colonial policy in H. of C. p. 443
DECEMBER	16 Chancellor announced issue of Tax Reserve Certs. p. 216	

Chapter IX **India & Middle East**	Chapter X **South. Dominions**	Chapter XI **Canada**	Chapters XII, XIII & XV **U.S.A.**
			8 President's conversation with Br. Ambassador on 'Consideration' for lend-lease. p. 406 10 Keynes' Press Conference on export policy. p. 400 21 Jesse Jones Loan Agreement. p. 395 28 U.S. draft of Article VII handed to Keynes. p. 407
			14 Atlantic Charter p. 409
	1 Restriction of imports by S. African Govt. p. 312	5 H.M.G. agreed to Canadian prices for farm produce p. 342	10 Export White Paper agreed p. 403
	10 1st Vesting Order for S. African securities. p. 315		
	Australian import restrictions tightened. p. 293		
			7 U.S. entered war. p. 410
23 Second Vesting Order for Indian securities. p. 258			

Chapters II–IV **War-time Budgets**	Chapters V–VII **Capital**	Chapters VIII & XIV **Foreign Exchange**
1942 JANUARY		
FEBRUARY		
MARCH		
APRIL White Paper 'The Taxation of weekly wage-earners' published. p. 101 14 Budget day. (i) Chancellor defended existing basis of tax assessment. p. 101 (ii) Increase in married women's earned income allowance. p. 113 (iii) Further concessions re travelling expenses. p. 114. (iv) E.P.T. post-war credits to accrue by 'statutory right'. p. 119 (v) Increased taxes on beer, spirits, wine and tobacco. pp. 132-3 (vi) Entertainments tax doubled. pp. 134-5		
MAY	Correspondence between Try. & Stock Exchange on 'Placing'. p. 178	
JUNE		

Chapter IX India & Middle East	Chapter X South. Dominions	Chapter XI Canada	Chapters XII, XIII & XV U.S.A.
		27 Canadian P.M. announced $1 billion gift and $700 m. interest-free loan to H.M.G. p. 345	
			23 Mutual Aid Agreement. p. 412
	H.M.G. agreed Australia's stg. balance should not be less than £40 m. p. 295 fn. 15% increase in prices paid by H.M.G. under Wool Agreement. pp. 295, 311		U.S. agreed to certain 'take-overs'. p. 397
			9 Keynes' view that dollar shortage no longer H.M.G's. main problem. p. 397

Chapters II–IV **War-time Budgets**	Chapters V–VII **Capital**	Chapters VIII & XIV **Foreign Exchange**
1942 (*continued*) JULY		
AUGUST		
SEPTEMBER	1 Third issue of 3% Defence Bonds. p. 196	
OCTOBER		
NOVEMBER		
DECEMBER		

Chapter IX India & Middle East	Chapter X South. Dominions	Chapter XI Canada	Chapters XII, XIII & XV U.S.A.
	15 H.M.G. reached agreement with New Zealand on defence expenditure: renewed assurances about stg. balances and postwar maturities. p. 305		
23 Anti-Inflation Conference, Cairo. p. 281			3 Exchange of Letters on reciprocal aid. p. 418
			Harry White's assurances about growth of U.K. reserves. p. 431
	9 Gen. Smuts asked for one more vesting in return for U.K. option on £90 m. S. African gold: promised to look into S. African contribution to overseas forces. p. 316 18 Australia agreed to 9s. per day capitation rate: H.M.G agreed to maintain Australia's stg. balance and waive interest on £12 m. loan. pp. 294-5		
Decision taken to sell gold as commodity in Persia. p. 282	18 Second Vesting Order for S. African securities. p. 316	H.M.G. agreed to pay Canadian Govt. U.S.$150 m. while awaiting Canadian plans for further financial assistance. p. 350	

Chapters II–IV **War-time Budgets**	Chapters V–VII **Capital**	Chapters VIII & XIV **Foreign Exchange**
1943 JANUARY	1 One pound issue of Savings Certificates. p. 195	
FEBRUARY		
MARCH	Wings for Victory Weeks (March to July). p. 193	H.M.G. repaid Belgian gold. p. 455 Payments agreement with Sweden revised. Limit on H.M.G's gold liability removed. p. 450
APRIL 12 Budget day. (i) Chancellor promised to consider current earnings basis for tax assessment. p. 102 (ii) Housekeeper and dependent relative allow- ances raised. pp. 114-5 (iii) Further exemptions from purchase tax on certain utility cloths, etc. p. 129 (iv) Further increases in taxes on beer, spirits, wine and tobacco. p. 136		
MAY		
JUNE		

Chapter IX India & Middle East	Chapter X South. Dominions	Chapter XI Canada	Chapters XII, XIII & XV U.S.A.
		24 Canadian Govt. agreed to take over cost of R.C.A.F. squadrons. p. 351 Canadian Govt. informed H.M.G. of their plan for Mutual Aid. p 351	19 Chancellor's personal message to Morgenthau on H.M.G's. reserve. p. 431 President privately stipulated that U.K's. reserves should not rise above $1,000 m. p. 432
	New Zealand began repaying advances H.M.G. had previously made. p. 305		
		21 Canadian Mutual Aid Act passed providing $1,000 m. p. 351 27 Canadian Govt. agreed to purchase U.K. munition factories in Canada. p. 351	
11 Decision taken to sell gold as commodity in India and Middle East. pp. 268, 282			U.S. pressure on H.M.G. to publish reciprocal aid figures and give raw materials as reciprocal aid. pp. 420-2

Chapters II–IV **War-time Budgets**	Chapters V–VII **Capital**	Chapters VIII & XIV **Foreign Exchange**
1943 (*continued*) JULY 29 War Cabinet took note of P.A.Y.E. proposals which T.U.C. supported. p. 102		
AUGUST		
SEPTEMBER 21 Death of Sir K. Wood. p. 99 22 Fin. Sec. announced introduction of P.A.Y.E. p. 107 24 Sir J. Anderson appointed Chancellor of the Exchequer. p. 99		
OCTOBER		
NOVEMBER		
DECEMBER		20 Financial agreement with Switzerland. p. 449

CHAPTER IX India & Middle East	CHAPTER X South. Dominions	CHAPTER XI Canada	CHAPTERS XII, XIII & XV U.S.A.
			5 U.S. requested H.M.G. *not* to publish reciprocal aid figures. p. 422
18 Gold sales in India began. p. 268		Agreement on mechanics of Mutual Aid. p. 353	
			3 Chancellor's letter to Morgenthau on U.K. reserves and reciprocal aid. p. 432
			26 F.E.A. set up. p. 424
	2 Australia repaid to H.M.G. £12 m. previously borrowed. p. 296 9 Gen. Smuts and Chancellor agreed on— (i) S. Africa's expenditure on overseas forces. p. 309 (ii) S. African supplies of gold for H.M.G. p. 318 (iii) S. Africa's selling gold in India to cover rupee requirements for goods. p. 317		11 Reciprocal Aid White paper published. p. 425 Capital goods cut from lend-lease. p. 433
H.M.G. agreed Indian Govt. should have dollar Reconstruction Fund. p. 264			P.M. raised question of reserve with President at Cairo Meeting. p. 433

Chapters II–IV **War-time Budgets**	Chapters V–VII **Capital**	Chapters VIII & XIV **Foreign Exchange**
1944 JANUARY		
FEBRUARY		8 Temporary financial agreement with Free French Govt. p. 458
MARCH	Salute the Soldier Weeks (March to July). p. 193	
APRIL 6 P.A.Y.E. scheme came into operation. p. 104 25 Budget day. (i) E.P.T. standards raised. p. 120 (ii) Tax evasion regulations tightened. p. 122 (iii) Chancellor announced new basis for taxation of motor cars, special wear and tear allowances for new plant and industrial buildings, etc. p. 140		
MAY		
JUNE	Agreement signed between Try. and Stock Exchange on permission to deal ('Grey Market Agreement'). p. 179	

CHAPTER IX India & Middle East	CHAPTER X South. Dominions	CHAPTER XI Canada	CHAPTERS XII, XIII & XV U.S.A.
	H.M.G. agreed to lump sum adjustments of long-term food contracts with Australia. p. 296		7 U.S. presented H.M.G. with further list of 'take-outs' (Crowley take-outs). p. 433
		11 Mutual Aid Master Agreement p. 354	President's telegram to P.M. on limiting H.M.G's reserves. p. 434
			President agreed that reserves question should be discussed later in Washington. p. 434
	5 H.M.G. agreed Australia should have £10 m. in gold. p. 297		
		14 New Mutual Aid Appropriation for $800 m. passed by Canadian Parlt. p. 355 Canadian Govt. terminated Hyde Park Agreement with U.S. p. 356 Canadian Govt. agreed to take over $200 m. expenditure on overseas forces and asked for $250 m. in dollars from H.M.G. p. 356	H.M.G. asked U.S. for new approach on aid for Stage II. p. 466

Chapters II–IV **War-time Budgets**	Chapters V–VII **Capital**	Chapters VIII & XIV **Foreign Exchange**
1944 (*continued*) JULY		
AUGUST		
SEPTEMBER		
OCTOBER		5 Monetary agreement with Belgium. p. 457
NOVEMBER	6 Five year 1¾% Exchequer Bonds issued on tap. p. 209	
DECEMBER		

Chapter IX India & Middle East	Chapter X South. Dominions	Chapter XI Canada	Chapters XII, XIII & XV U.S.A.
H.M.G. decided to discontinue gold sales to India and Middle East. pp. 270, 283. 19 Report of Official Cttee. on Indian financial questions. pp. 254-5	H.M.G., while refusing to accept terms of trade argument, conceded £12 m. for past and £4 m. a year increase for future long-term dairy contracts with New Zealand. p. 303		18 War Cabinet decision on export drive and need for Stage II negotiations with U.S. p. 468
		28 Canadian Govt. agreed to measures providing H.M.G. with $655 m. U.K. sold Canada U.S. $80 m. p. 358	Morgenthau's visit to London. Chancellor stated H.M.G's case for aid in Stage II. pp. 468-9
			13-16 2nd Quebec (Octagon) Conference. p. 469 Keynes left for U.S. for Stage II discussions. p. 470
		Further visit by Keynes to Ottawa on Stage II requirements. p. 359	30 Statement in H. of C. on Export White Paper Policy. p. 473

Chapters II–IV **War-time Budgets**	Chapters V–VII **Capital**	Chapters VIII & XIV **Foreign Exchange**
1945 JANUARY		
FEBRUARY		
MARCH		6 Monetary agreement with Sweden. p. 451 27 Financial agreement with France. p. 459
APRIL 24 Budget day. (i) Further E.P.T. concessions to small businesses. p. 126 (ii) Double taxation agreement with U.S. p. 141		
MAY	7 Fourth issue of 3% Defence Bonds. p. 197	
JUNE	13 Tap Issue of $2\frac{1}{2}$% War Bond, in place of $1\frac{3}{4}$% Exchequer Bonds. pp. 206, 210	

Chapter IX India & Middle East	Chapter X South. Dominions	Chapter XI Canada	Chapters XII, XIII & XV U.S.A.
		23 Canadian Govt. announced Mutual Aid would continue for 1945. p. 359	
			13 Lend-Lease Act renewed. p. 476
U.S. gold sales in India suspended p. 270	S. Africa agreement with U.S. to pay cash for lend-lease goods. p. 318		12 Death of President Roosevelt. p. 476
3 Report of Select Cttee. on National Expenditure on Indian financial questions. p. 255		19 Financial discussions in U.K. led to agreement on non-discrimination on essentials in return for further Mutual Aid for Stage II. p. 361	8 V.E. Day. p. 477 28 P.M. cabled President on lend-lease. p. 478

Chapters II–IV **War-time Budgets**	Chapters V–VII **Capital**	Chapters VIII & XIV **Foreign Exchange**
1945 (*continued*) JULY		
AUGUST		8 Agreement with Portugal on wartime stg. balances. p. 454 16 Monetary agreement with Denmark. p. 457
SEPTEMBER		7 Monetary agreement with Netherlands. p. 457

CHAPTER IX India & Middle East	CHAPTER X South. Dominions	CHAPTER XI Canada	CHAPTERS XII, XIII & XV U.S.A.
			5 President's directive limiting lend-lease to goods required in Japanese war. p. 478 16-27 Potsdam (Terminal) Conference. p. 478
			11 H.M.G's Washington representatives warned that lend-lease might terminate suddenly. p. 479 19 Press reports that lend-lease was to end 20th or 21st Aug. p. 479 24 P.M.'s statement in H. of C. on lend-lease. p. 480 Keynes left for financial talks in U.S. p. 483
		1 Canadian Mutual Aid ceased. p. 361	2 Military lend-lease terminated. p. 483 7 Lend-Lease shipping services extended for 30 days. p. 483

Index

INDEX.